A Ravel Reader

A RAVEL
READER

Correspondence : Articles : Interviews

COMPILED AND EDITED BY

ARBIE ORENSTEIN

NEW YORK : COLUMBIA UNIVERSITY PRESS

The publisher gratefully acknowledges the generous support of
publication costs given by the National Endowment for the Humanities
and by Alice Tully.

Library of Congress Cataloging-in-Publication Data
Ravel, Maurice, 1875–1937.

    A Ravel reader: correspondence, articles, interviews / compiled and
edited by Arbie Orenstein.

      p. cm.

    Includes bibliographical references and index.

    ISBN 0-231-04962-5

    1. Ravel, Maurice, 1875–1937—Correspondence. 2. Ravel,
Maurice, 1875–1937—Interviews. I. Orenstein, Arbie. II. Title.

ML410.R23A4   1989

780'.92—dc20

[B]   89-25228

       CIP

Columbia University Press
New York   Oxford

Casebound editions of Columbia University Press books are Smyth-
sewn and printed on permanent and durable acid-free paper ∞

Design by Richard Hendel

Printed in the United States of America

c 10 9 8 7 6 5 4 3 2 1

For my wife Mina

and my children Michelle and Adam

Contents

Illustrations appear as a group following page 366.

Illustrations

Preface

This book is a natural outgrowth of my first study, *Ravel: Man and Musician,* published by Columbia University Press in 1975. In preparing that study, one point became increasingly clear: among the most perceptive comments about Ravel's life and art were those made by the composer himself. The focus of this book, therefore, is on Ravel in his own words, both written and spoken. The most important writings to come from Ravel's pen are of course his music manuscripts, which constitute his ultimate legacy. The documents in this book will shed much light on that legacy, and on a host of related matters. The composer's written words have been divided into two parts, letters and articles, the latter including replies to several inquiries; the spoken words consist of press interviews. Three documents have been selected which offer a survey of Ravel's career and musical thought: an autobiographical sketch drawn up by his colleague and biographer Roland-Manuel, a brief statement on aesthetics entitled "Some Reflections on Music," and Ravel's formal lecture, "Contemporary Music," delivered in Houston, Texas, on April 7, 1928. Finally, a number of appendixes are included whose titles are self-explanatory; of particular importance are Ravel's analyses of his own music, and Jean Touzelet's "Historical Interpretations (1911–1988)," a fresh approach to discography which future authors may wish to imitate.

The largest part of this book is devoted to Ravel's correspondence. It appears that he wrote about 1500 letters in the course of his lifetime, and these documents, like those of other creative artists, form an inner diary of his career. One may observe Ravel's personal interests and train of thought, his joys and sorrows, frustrations and quirks, his battles with critics, travels and concert tours, his period of military service during World War I, advice to young musicians, and a wealth of observations about the vibrant Parisian musical scene. His earliest known letter was written at the age of twenty-three, while a student at the Conservatoire, and the last one was signed in October 1937, some eight weeks before his death at the age of sixty-two. With the exception of one letter copied out in English, which he did not understand, all of his letters are in French, the only language in which he was fluent. He knew some Basque, and would occasionally use a Basque phrase, but no complete letter in this language has yet come to light. Ravel was proud of the French language and wrote with care and skill. His letters are almost always dated, often with a printed return address, and, in the postwar years, his monogram. If the formal letters bespeak a personal blend of simplicity and sophistication, politeness, modesty, clarity, and polish, the colorful notes written to friends reveal a joie de vivre, tender warmth, playfulness, and ironic humor. There are also touching letters of condolence, and moments of despair, particularly during the upheaval of World War I. The vocabulary includes some esoteric terms, colloquialisms, slang, and on rare occasion, vulgarity. As one might expect, the largest number of letters were sent to close friends. There were about 250 letters to the Godebski family, and some 150 to Roland-Manuel and Maurice Delage. But there was practically no correspondence with colleagues such as pianist Ricardo Viñes and mezzo-soprano Jane Bathori. In an interview with this writer, Madame Bathori explained why this was so: "There was no need to write. We saw each other all the time."

Like many in his generation, Ravel held a writing instrument between the second and third fingers of his right hand, pulling it toward himself as he wrote, and the result in this case was an angular and sharply chiseled handwriting. Over the years, there were two noticeable changes in his penmanship: at age twenty he began to form the letter *a* as " ϑ " (rather than " *a*"), and during the last few years of his life, owing to a debilitating disease, his handwriting became smaller and withered. A number of letters were typewritten in the postwar years, and in 1926 Ravel had a telephone installed in his home. Despite these ultramodern conveniences, old habits prevailed, and the volume of his handwritten letters continued unabated.

The only book until now dealing with Ravel's correspondence, Chalupt and Gerar's *Ravel au miroir des ses lettres* (Paris, 1956), presented some 190 letters. Unfortunately, a study of the holographs indicates that many letters were printed with omissions, perhaps in order to "protect" Ravel or other individuals. This is certainly unnecessary today, more than half a century after the composer's death. Of the 350 letters in this book, some 200 have remained unpublished until now, 80 have been partially printed in French, and 70 have previously appeared in French in their entirety. (Only a handful have ever appeared in an English translation.) These letters are addressed to some 100 correspondents, who can be identified in almost every case. Also included are some letters sent to Ravel, and several letters written about him. One may thus observe the composer as a son, brother, nephew, friend, and colleague.

Letters are fragile documents, and some letters and even entire collections have already been lost or destroyed. Thus, a "complete" edition, although a desirable goal for the future, will in fact prove to be an impossibility.

If the choice of letters is highly selective, all of Ravel's articles that could be traced have been included. The total comes to nineteen articles (and three replies to inquiries), which appeared between 1909 and 1933. Ten articles are concert reviews that Ravel wrote as a professional critic for *La Revue musicale de la S.I.M.* (three reviews from February to April, 1912), and *Comœdia illustré* (seven reviews from January 1913 to June 1914). His critical observations reflect a strong desire for impartiality, clear aesthetic priorities, and keen artistic intuition. Moreover, when he reviews works by Falla, Fauré, or Stravinsky, among others, Ravel speaks not only as a critic, but as a close friend of the artist in question. A few remarks will undoubtedly raise some eyebrows: Beethoven's *Missa Solemnis* is curtly dismissed as an "inferior" work, and there is some harsh criticism of Brahms' Second Symphony. One need not agree with all of Ravel's views in order to appreciate his brilliant insights, razor-sharp clarity, probity coupled with gentle irony, and some vivid descriptions of theatrical productions, which make the reader feel that he is also sitting in the audience. Other articles are scattered singly in various publications, and their topics range from Debussy's *Images* and Fauré's songs to Nijinsky's choreography and the importance of jazz. Ravel's last article, published in November 1933, deals sympathetically with the plight of the young generation of composers.

The choice of press interviews is once again selective: the thirty which have been chosen are presented in their entirety, and originally appeared between 1911 and 1933 in American, Argentinian, Austrian, British, Danish, Dutch, French, Spanish, Swedish, and Swiss publications. Other important interviews, no doubt, have yet to be traced. (A detailed list of articles and interviews is found in the bibliography.) In a letter to Cipa Godebski (see letter no. 82), Ravel admitted that he once wrote back "nothing but fibs" in reply to an interviewer's questions, and on another occasion he complained to a Dutch journalist about being misquoted. Despite these problems, the interviews are usually frank and revealing. They not only complement the letters and articles, but often deal with important issues that are not raised elsewhere.

In 1975, the centenary celebrations of Ravel's birth included many special concerts, recordings, and exhibitions on both sides of the Atlantic, and in 1985 the first issue of a new journal, *Cahiers Maurice Ravel*, provided further evidence that Ravel has entered the pantheon of twentieth-century composers. In a brief necrology, "Homage to Ravel, 1875–1937," which appeared in *Modern Music* (January–February 1938), a young American composer, Elliott Carter, perceptively summarized the importance of Ravel's art as follows:

> Maurice Ravel was an exponent of that careful, precise workmanship, elegance, and grace he so admired in the music of Mozart, of whom he was not an unworthy descendant. The type seems to grow rarer as this troubled century progresses. His work, however, was a monument to the dignity and precision that even now all worthy musicians should strive for

and that French music has at its best always captured. Combined with an extraordinary sense of style and infallible ear was a refinement of taste and a unique inspiration that made every work he wrote right and final in its own category. All his life he shunned cheapness and facility, yet his style and manner of orchestration have already left their mark on all music, from the simplest jazz to the most elaborate works of Stravinsky. His music will always be a great glory to the art he practiced so long and so well.

We should idolize neither the man nor his extraordinary epoch, in which French music, literature, and painting stood at the forefront of European cultural life. Rather, let us recall Kierkegaard's dictum: "Life can only be understood backwards; but it must be lived forwards." Ravel's life and thought have already receded into history; we may perhaps best understand them as they unfold in the composer's own words.

Acknowledgments

I t is a pleasure to acknowledge the assistance of institutions and many individuals in preparing this book. Many others were previously acknowledged in *Ravel: Man and Musician.* Six months of full-time research in Paris were made possible by a grant from the Fondation Singer-Polignac, Dr. Etienne Wolff, president, to whom I express my deep gratitude. I am also pleased to acknowledge a City University of New York PSC-BHE Research Award. This book could not have been published without the kind cooperation of Madame Alexandre Taverne, the present inheritor of the estate of Maurice Ravel. The insights of the late Roland-Manuel and Manuel Rosenthal, two of Ravel's distinguished disciples, will be found in these pages, along with those of some fifty other colleagues of the composer whom I have interviewed over the past two decades. To all of them I owe a special debt of gratitude. In addition, I wish to thank Jean-Michel Nectoux for his devoted reading of the manuscript and his many helpful suggestions; Jean Touzelet, for his excellent discography found in Appendix F, and for his many kindnesses over the years; Bruno Sébald, who catalogued Ravel's personal record collection (Appendix G); François Lesure and the music staff of the Bibliothèque Nationale for their generous assistance; J. Rigbie Turner (the Pierpont Morgan Library) and Wayne Shirley (Music Division of the Library of Congress) for their prompt replies to my inquiries. In addition to the individuals who are cited in the text, I am also grateful to all of the private collectors and public institutions who kindly provided me with photocopies of Ravel's autograph letters in their collections. Their names appear in appendixes H and I.

I am indebted to the following individuals who translated parts of this book: the interviews in Dutch, Ludi P. Kerman; those in Danish and Swedish, Åsa Hornfeldt; passages in Basque, Pierre Courteault. My English translation of the French texts was reviewed with Micheline Weisbroat, to whom I am particularly grateful.

For assistance of various sorts, I wish to thank Felix Aprahamian, Caroline Bent, Lionel Carley, Phyllis Golding, Roy Howat, Dietrich Klose, Jean-Jacques Lemoine, Roger Nichols, Mathilda Orenstein, Vivian Perlis, William Rosar, Alain Schindler, Susan A. Spectorsky, Catalina Vásquez, and Piero Weiss. I am grateful to the editors of *La Revue musicale* for permission to quote from back issues, Rice University for permission to reproduce Ravel's speech entitled

"Contemporary Music," which first appeared in the Rice Institute Pamphlet of April 1928, and Columbia University Press for permission to quote from my book, *Ravel: Man and Musician*. Finally, to those individuals who preferred to remain anonymous, and to all who assisted in many different ways, I express my esteem and gratitude.

A Ravel Reader

Introduction

"Beauty is truth, truth beauty"—that is all
Ye know on earth, and all ye need to know.
—JOHN KEATS, Ode on a Grecian Urn

All of life's pleasure consists of getting a little closer to perfection, and
expressing life's mysterious thrill a little better.
—MAURICE RAVEL

Joseph Maurice Ravel was born in Ciboure, France, a Basque
fishing village near the Spanish border, on March 7, 1875. At
his birth, his mother, Marie Delouart, of Basque descent, was
thirty-five years old, and his father, Pierre Joseph, a Swiss civil engineer, was
forty-three. Born of Catholic parents, the infant was baptized at the local parish
church of Saint Vincent. The Ravels had been married in Paris on April 3,
1873, and a few months after their son's birth they settled there. Three years
later, a second son, Edouard, was born. He would follow in his father's
footsteps as an engineer.

The origins of the Ravel family have been traced back to the Collonges-
sous-Salève, a village in France's Haute-Savoie. During the latter part of the
eighteenth century, one François Ravex or Ravet (the name was apparently
written both ways) lived in this village, and it appears that the name Ravel came
about from a subsequent misreading of the final *t* in Ravet. His son, Aimé
Ravel, was born in Collonges-sous-Salève in 1800, but moved to Versoix, in the
canton of Geneva, and later became a Swiss citizen. Pierre Joseph Ravel, one of
five children, was born in Versoix in 1832, and although he was to pursue a
career as an engineer, the father of Maurice Ravel was keenly interested in
music. He possessed an inventive, inquisitive mind, and played a pioneering
role in the developing automobile industry. Pierre Joseph frequently took his
sons to visit factories of all sorts, and both boys were fascinated with the
machines they saw and the sounds they heard. Thus, from his father, Maurice
appears to have inherited a healthy, open-minded curiosity about all aspects of
life, and a particular interest in precision craftsmanship.

Maurice Ravel's attachment to his mother was undoubtedly the deepest
emotional tie of his entire life. In a remarkably candid letter to Ida Godebska
written on December 27, 1919, he reminisced: "I'm thinking that it will soon
be 3 years since she has departed, and my despair increases daily. I'm thinking

I

about it even more, since I have resumed work, that I no longer have this dear silent presence enveloping me with her infinite tenderness, which was, I see it now more than ever, my only reason for living." Among the composer's earliest memories were the Spanish folk melodies sung to him by his mother, and through her he inherited a love of the Basque country, its people, and its folklore, as well as a deep sympathy for the music of Spain. Madame Ravel's only known letter (no. 129) suggests that she spoke French quite well, but never learned to write it. She possessed a keen sense of humor and was somewhat of a freethinker, two traits among many transmitted to her elder son.

The Ravels were a liberal, sensitive, and devoted couple, and if Maurice was his mother's favorite, Pierre Joseph held a special affection for his younger son Edouard. The family's means appear to have been modest but adequate, and when it became clear that the elder child would pursue a career in music, he received unqualified encouragement and support. Thus, Maurice Ravel was fortunate enough to have a happy childhood, and there would be no crisis over a choice of career: it was to be music from the very beginning, and the only problem was whether he would pursue a career as a concert pianist or as a composer.

It appears that Ravel's formal education was limited to his early piano lessons, and, later on, his music studies at the Conservatoire, which took place intermittently between the ages of fourteen and twenty-eight. Thus, whatever he knew about French literature, history, science, and so on, he learned almost entirely through his own efforts. While indicating some natural talent as a composer, he was often reluctant to practice the piano, and an occasional parental bribe was required to keep him at the keyboard when it would have been more inviting to play in the streets of Montmartre. Nevertheless, on November 4, 1889, the young musician managed to pass the Conservatoire's piano entrance examination. As it turned out, his long apprenticeship was largely marked by one academic failure after another. On the other hand, his career as a student was one of immense growth, and it was against the backdrop of the Conservatoire that Ravel would pass from adolescence to maturity. Here he would meet a host of musicians, and would cement many lifelong friendships, from among both students and professors. At the Conservatoire, he methodically analyzed the standard masterworks of the Baroque, Classical, and Romantic periods, and performed a wide variety of nineteenth-century piano music. It may be added that if Ravel's knowledge of European music from Gregorian chant through seventeenth century appears to have been relatively limited, he would become acquainted with an enormous amount of music written during his lifetime, much of which is now forgotten.

Ravel's private activities during his student days are best described in the extraordinary journal of Ricardo Viñes. Both youngsters were blessed with an insatiable curiosity, and while their mothers conversed in Spanish, they played through an imposing variety of piano four-hand music, both original works and transcriptions, ranging from Mozart, Mendelssohn, and Franck, through Rimsky-Korsakov, Balakirev, Borodin, Glazunov, Chabrier, and Satie. After classes, the boys would take long walks, or play games of all sorts, copy out poetry, make drawings, attend concerts, or visit art galleries. On August 15, 1892, the young pianists spent virtually the entire day at the keyboard, "experimenting with new chords." The results of these and other discoveries were revealed in the "Habanera" for two pianos, completed in 1895, in which Ravel boldly affirmed his predilections for sophisticated harmony, sensuality, and Hispanic dance rhythms. It was about this time that he made the crucial decision to devote himself to composition. In addition to his hard-won maturity as a composer, any hopes he might have entertained for a career as a concert pianist were thoroughly dashed, not only by Ricardo Viñes, but by other exceptionally gifted pianists at the Conservatoire.

About 1900, the nucleus was formed of a group of enthusiastic devotees of the arts who were to call themselves the *Apaches*. The name was coined by Ricardo Viñes, and rather curiously it refers to underworld hooligans. To some extent the young men considered themselves "artistic outcasts"—constantly defending what they considered important, whether or not the public agreed. The *Apaches* were ardent supporters of Debussy's *Pelléas et Mélisande* during its stormy infancy, and faithfully attended innumerable recitals of contemporary music. With the distaff element strictly excluded, the group met far into the night, discussing painting, declaiming poetry, and performing new music. The coterie met fairly regularly until the outbreak of World War I, and it was an extremely important influence on Ravel. Not only were his own intellectual horizons broadened, but it was at the *Apaches* meetings that he met many of his future collaborators and lifelong friends. Among the members of the group were the poets Tristan Klingsor and Léon-Paul Fargue, the painter Paul Sordes, Abbé Léonce Petit, the conductor Désiré-Emile Inghelbrecht, the decorator Georges Mouveau, pianists Marcel Chadeigne and Ricardo Viñes, and composers André Caplet, Maurice Delage, Manuel de Falla, Paul Ladmirault, Florent Schmitt, and Déodat de Séverac. Other members of the group included the critics Michel D. Calvocoressi and Emile Vuillermoz, and Ravel's close friends Pierre Haour and Lucien Garban. The group usually met on Saturday evenings, either at the studio of Paul Sordes on rue Dulong, at the home of Tristan Klingsor on avenue du Parc Montsouris, or at the apartment of Maurice Delage on rue de Civry. The *Apaches* had their own secret theme song (the opening of Borodin's Second Symphony), their own nicknames (Ravel was called "Rara"), and even their own phantom member "Gomez de Riquet," a character invented by Ravel as a pretext for leaving a tedious rendezvous or a dull evening party. It would be difficult to recapture the great excitement and unbounded enthusiasm of the *Apaches* meetings. Léon-Paul Fargue wrote that "Ravel shared our predilections, our weaknesses, our manias for Chinese art, Mallarmé and Verlaine, Rimbaud and Corbière, Cézanne and Van Gogh, Rameau and Chopin, Whistler and Valéry, the Russians and Debussy." Amid this warm atmosphere of mutual encouragement, Ravel first performed his *Jeux d'eau*, "Oiseaux tristes," and the Sonatine. Fargue's matinal arrivals at the meetings, generally about 1:00 A.M., signaled the closing of the piano lid, but the discussions would continue with renewed vigor.

In addition to the *Apaches* meetings, Ravel occasionally attended the Tuesday receptions of the *Mercure de France,* and through his friendship with Misia Godebska, he became associated with the literary milieu of *La Revue blanche.* In these circles, he would meet Henri de Régnier, Thadée and Alexandre Natanson, Jules Renard, Paul Valéry, Léon Blum, Claude Terrasse and Franc-Nohain. There were also musicales in middle- and upper-class salons, and Ravel faithfully attended those of Madame René de Saint-Marceaux and Princess Edmond de Polignac, who commissioned the *Pavane pour une Infante défunte.* At the home of Madame de Saint-Marceaux, amid a congenial atmosphere of musicians, writers, and artists who caricatured the musicians as they performed, Fauré often presided at the keyboard, and among the guests one might encounter Pierre de Bréville, Colette, Debussy, Vincent d'Indy, or André Messager. Ravel participated in the informal performances of contemporary music, and on one occasion he improvised at the piano as the young American Isadora Duncan performed interpretive dances.

The richness of French musical life at the turn of the twentieth century may be seen in the fact that two distinct schools of composition were vying with each other for musical leadership. The older school consisted of César Franck's followers headed by Vincent d'Indy, whereas the leader of the newer, progressive element was Claude Debussy. Nor should one overlook the subtle elegance of Gabriel Fauré, the neoclassical art of his teacher Camille Saint-Saëns, and the pathbreaking experimentation of Erik Satie. It is perhaps not surprising that Ravel, who was some thirteen years younger than Debussy, was immediately classified as one of his followers. In addition to the heated battles of the critics, French audiences did not hesitate to jeer or applaud during the performances of contemporary music, and a combative spirit filled the concert halls. While the Société Nationale de Musique, founded in 1871, presented a wide variety of contemporary French music, the Société des Concerts du Conservatoire, founded in 1828, generally performed works from Bach through Wagner. Owing to important advances in musicology, the vast treasures of Gregorian chant, and of Renaissance and Baroque music were becoming accessible, and were featured at the important concerts of the Schola

Cantorum, directed by Vincent d'Indy. In the opera house and the concert hall Wagner reigned supreme, and virtually every aspect of French cultural life felt the striking impact of the Bayreuth master. In addition to the ever popular French operetta, the operas of Massenet, Meyerbeer, Mozart, Puccini, and the nineteenth-century Italian school were frequently heard, and in 1904 the 1000th performance of *Carmen* was given at the Opéra. The Colonne, Lamoureux, and Pasdeloup orchestras frequently programmed works by Beethoven and Wagner, and generally emphasized the music of the Viennese Classical school and the Romantic era. Among the many outstanding younger recitalists one could hear Pablo Casals, Alfred Cortot, Arthur Rubinstein, and Jacques Thibaud.

Only a handful of letters have come down to us from Ravel's student days. In addition to his piano lessons and instruction in harmony, composition, and orchestration, he was writing his early compositions, which proved to be highly controversial, competing unsuccessfully for the Prix de Rome, and teaching privately in order to support himself. Indeed, works such as *Jeux d'eau* (1901), the String Quartet (1903), and the song cycle *Shéhérazade* (1903) were considered "dangerous" by the more conservative faculty members, and this undoubtedly played a role in his repeated failure to win the Grand Prix. The trickle of letters turns into a steady stream following the 1905 Prix de Rome competition, from which Ravel was eliminated in the preliminary round, touching off a scandal. At this stormy juncture, he accepted a timely invitation from Alfred and Misia Edwards to join them aboard their luxurious yacht *Aimée* for an extended vacation in Belgium, Holland, and Germany, and in the summer of 1905 he wrote to Madame René de Saint-Marceaux: "During all of this time, I didn't compose two measures, but I was storing up a host of impressions, and I expect this winter to be extraordinarily productive. I have never been so happy to be alive, and I firmly believe that joy is far more fertile than suffering." This last statement tells us a good deal about Ravel's personal and artistic make-up. Furthermore, not only was the winter of 1905 rich in achievement, but the years preceding World War I proved to be the most intensely productive in his entire career.

The 1905 Prix de Rome fiasco marked an important turning point in Ravel's life. Gone forever were academic fugues, dull cantatas, and sterile battles with conservative and reactionary juries. Looking back on his career, Ravel might well have been amused at its paradoxical aspects. At the Conservatoire, he had received a first prize as a pianist (with second prize in the July 1891 competition going to Alfred Cortot!), but never as a composer. Moreover, some of his most avowed opponents on the Prix de Rome jury had in fact catapulted him to fame and had also caused the collapse of the conservative-reactionary element at the Conservatoire. In the fall of 1905, Gabriel Fauré assumed the directorship of the Conservatoire, and owing to a program of bold reforms, a renewed sense of dedication and enthusiasm filled the classrooms. At this time, Ravel accepted an exclusive contract from the publisher Durand, which included an annuity, and this close association would last throughout his lifetime. He now completed the Sonatine and *Miroirs* (1905), the *Histoires naturelles* (1906), *L'Heure espagnole* and the *Rapsodie espagnole* (1907), *Gaspard de la nuit* (1908), *Ma Mère l'Oye* (1908–1910), *Valses nobles et sentimentales* (1911), *Daphnis et Chloé* (1909–1912), *Trois Poèmes de Stéphane Mallarmé* (1913), and the Trio (1914). In addition, he composed a handful of minor works, completed several acts of an unfinished opera, *La Cloche engloutie,* and carried out several transcriptions. During this period, Ravel's music began to extend far beyond the confines of the Société Nationale de Musique, as the Sonatine was heard in Lyon, the *Rapsodie espagnole* was introduced at the Concerts Colonne, and various works were performed throughout western Europe, the United States, and North Africa. With a performance of the *Rapsodie espagnole* at an important festival of French music held in Munich (1910), the première of *L'Heure espagnole* at the Opéra-Comique (1911), and the creation of *Daphnis et Chloé* by Diaghilev's Ballet Russe (1912), Ravel's reputation as one of France's leading composers was firmly established.

During this period, in the company of Nelly and Maurice Delage, many short trips were taken within France, from the Riviera to Mont-Saint-Michel, and from Alsace-Lorraine to the Basque territory. Ravel also visited Spain, Italy, and Switzerland, and concertized on three occasions in England (1909, 1911, and 1913). Although the major works listed above are now considered landmarks in the annals of twentieth-century music, two contemporary views of the Mallarmé poems may be taken as representative of the wide spectrum of critical opinion with which Ravel's new works were greeted. The critic of London's *Daily Mail* (March 18, 1915) observed that the compositions "are among the most recent and interesting examples of modern song. The tiny orchestra is handled with utmost delicacy and intimacy of expression. . . . Mr. Thomas Beecham conducted and Mme. Jane Bathori-Engel sang the very difficult vocal part with great insight and expressiveness." On the other hand, the critic of the *Westminster Gazette,* writing on the same day, called attention to the bewildered but attentive audience, and thus one notes the politeness of English audiences as opposed to French audiences of the day. "An attentive audience listened in absolute bewilderment to some of the strangest exercises in ultramodern cacophony which it would be possible to imagine. . . . Now and then the divergence between the voice part and the accompaniment seemed so pronounced as almost to suggest that Mdme. Bathori-Engel was singing one number while the instrumentalists were playing another."

As he had often done before, Ravel spent the summer months of 1914 in the Basque country, taking long walks, swimming, boating, and visiting with friends. He was working on a trio when the guns of August announced the end of an epoch. At age twenty, Ravel had been exempted from military service because of a hernia and general weakness, but now, at thirty-nine, he was determined to serve his country. One important reason was that his brother Edouard and many friends had enlisted. Another significant factor was mentioned in a letter (no. 119) to Cipa Godebski: "And now, if you wish: Vive la France! but, above all, down with Germany and Austria! or at least what those two nations represent at the present time. And with all my heart: long live the Internationale and Peace!" Ravel was torn between patriotism and curiosity for adventure, and the terrible thought of leaving his aged mother. "If you only knew how I am suffering!" he wrote to Maurice Delage on August 4 (letter no. 117). "If I leave my poor old mama, it would surely kill her. . . . Yes, I'm working; and with an insane certainty and lucidity. But, during this time, the blues are at work too, and suddenly I find myself sobbing over my sharps and flats!. . . . This has been going on for 4 days, since the tocsin."

Following several abortive attempts to enlist, Ravel finally joined the Thirteenth Artillery Regiment as a truck driver in March 1915. Some duties were extremely hazardous, involving the transportation of war materiel at night under heavy enemy bombardment, and on several occasions near the front at Verdun, Ravel literally came within inches of losing his life. Above all, he was obsessed by his mother's failing health, and the frequent lack of news from friends. His own health had deteriorated sharply: in addition to frequent insomnia and poor appetite, he finally underwent an operation for dysentery in September 1916. Following a satisfactory convalescence, which was largely spent devouring book after book, Ravel suffered the deepest grief of his entire life: on January 5, 1917, Marie Delouart Ravel died at the age of seventy-six. The immediate effect of this tragedy was some three years of virtual silence with regard to composition, and from 1920 until his swan song, *Don Quichotte à Dulcinée* (1932–33), an average of only one composition a year would be completed.

Following a difficult period of postwar adjustment, Parisian musical life gradually returned to its former vigor and diversity. While the Colonne, Pasdeloup, and Lamoureux orchestras emphasized the works of Wagner, Beethoven, Saint-Saëns, Franck, Rimsky-Korsakov, Mozart, Berlioz, Mendelssohn, and Debussy, the Société Musicale Indépendante, founded in 1910, played an active role in presenting contemporary music. In addition to its festivals of English and American music, Arthur Honegger, Albert Roussel, and Arnold Schoenberg participated in special recitals devoted to their works. Under Ravel's leadership as vice president and later as president, the Société Musicale Indépendante introduced the works of many younger composers, among them Louis Durey, Paul Hindemith, Jacques Ibert, Marcel Mihalovici, Darius Milhaud, Roland-Manuel, Manuel Rosenthal, Alexandre Tansman, and Joaquín Turina. In addition to the Concerts du Conservatoire and those of the Société Nationale, subscription concerts were conducted by Vladimir Golschmann, Serge Koussevitzky, Robert Siohan, and Walther Straram, while the French musicologist Henry Prunières organized recitals devoted to contemporary chamber music. Among the leading ballet companies were the troupe of Ida Rubinstein, the Ballet Russe, and the Swedish Ballet. At the Opéra, the works of Wagner and Meyerbeer continued to enjoy popularity, and in 1925 the 1500th performance of Gounod's *Faust* was given.

In the 1920s and 1930s, Ravel divided his time between Paris, the Basque country, his increasingly frequent concert tours, and his new villa in Montfort l'Amaury, a sleepy village some thirty miles west of the capital. Le Belvédère (literally "the beautiful view") provided a quiet, country atmosphere conducive for work, with Paris easily accessible by bus and train. Now located at 5 rue Maurice Ravel, the villa is a national museum open to the public. The home has been preserved exactly as Ravel left it, and it offers some important insights into the composer's unique personality: a Japanese garden, many Japanese prints, an Arabic coffee set—showing his penchant for the exotic—and finely wrought bibelots, mechanical birds, music boxes, and carved statuettes—showing his predilection for perfectly crafted miniatures of all sorts. In the study, adjacent to the Erard piano and the composer's desk, there is a fine portrait of Madame Ravel painted by her brother-in-law Edouard, and a portrait of Pierre Joseph Ravel by Marcellin Desboutin (see plate 1). To these small, immaculately polished rooms, which were tended by his faithful housekeeper Madame Reveleau, who had served the Ravel family for many years, the composer added his Siamese cats, upon whom he lavished loving attention. Ravel's mischievous humor often came to the fore when guiding his friends through the villa, for when his guests gazed in admiration at a "rare" Monticelli, he would enjoy informing them that it was an imitation. Indeed, throughout the villa, there is a curious juxtaposition of rare authenticity and flagrant pastiche, together with an aura of make-believe enchantment, not unrelated to the exoticism of *Shéhérazade* or the childlike humor of *L'Enfant et les sortilèges*. The library contains about 1,000 volumes and reflects the composer's demanding taste as a bibliophile. There are many rare, beautifully bound editions, among them the complete works of Balzac, Hugo, La Fontaine, Molière, Proust, Racine, and Voltaire. A large part of the library is devoted to memoirs of individuals such as Alexandre Dumas, Casanova, or La Comtesse de Boigne, and many books reflect Ravel's interests in gardening, travel, general history, interior decorating, animals, and personal grooming. There are also many books with dedications from colleagues and admirers, among them Joseph Conrad, Franc-

Nohain, Paul Painlevé, and Jules Supervielle. Despite a large collection of scores from Bach to Schoenberg, there are relatively few books about music. Of particular interest are collections of Basque music, Spanish dances, folk melodies from around the world, Negro spirituals, and French operettas, together with many personally dedicated scores from colleagues, among them Louis Durey, Francis Poulenc, and Alexandre Tansman.

From the balcony of Le Belvédère—hence its name—one gazes upon a breathtaking view of the flowing countryside of the Île-de-France. Friends and colleagues occasionally gathered at the villa for a Sunday afternoon luncheon in the garden, and the day would often end with a long walk in the nearby Rambouillet Forest, where Ravel was intimately acquainted with every bird-call and every byway. The guests included many of the composer's favorite interpreters: pianists Robert Casadesus, Jacques Février, and Henri Gil-Marchex, singers Jane Bathori, Marcelle Gerar, and Madeleine Grey, violinists Hélène Jourdan-Morhange and Jacques Thibaud. There were old friends such as Maurice and Nelly Delage, Cipa and Ida Godebski, Monsieur and Madame Roland-Manuel, and younger musicians Vladimir Golschmann, Arthur Honegger, Jacques Ibert, Manuel Rosenthal, Germaine Tailleferre, and Alexandre Tansman. Other guests included the sculptor Léon Leyritz, whose fine bust of Ravel is found in the Paris Opéra, and the painter Luc-Albert Moreau, who drew many sketches of the composer.

The isolation of Le Belvédère and the tranquility of the Basque country were offset by innumerable social and professional engagements in Paris. In the postwar years Ravel was forced to adjust to a new, uncomfortable situation, in which he was no longer a member of the avant-garde, but rather a follower of the trends set by Schoenberg, *Les Six,* Prokofiev, and others. Some of the new sounds in the air were those of jazz, polytonality, and atonality, as the lush velvet of impressionism gave way to the hard steel which had been prophesied in *Le Sacre du printemps.* In addition, many composers were turning to a spare texture, in reaction to the mammoth orchestrations of Wagner, Mahler, and Strauss. The postwar years thus presented many fresh challenges. Ravel listened a great deal, absorbed, and composed with difficulty, as the following chronology indicates: Sonata for Violin and Cello (1920–22); *L'Enfant et les sortilèges* (1920–25); *Chansons madécasses* (1925–26); Sonata for Violin and Piano (1923–27); the two piano concerti (1929–1931). (The *Boléro* was composed between July and October, 1928, but Ravel acknowledged that it was "an experiment in a very special and limited direction.")

Although not an outstanding pianist or conductor, Ravel was increasingly in demand as an interpreter of his music. He concertized on several occasions in Austria, Belgium, Holland, Italy, Spain, and Switzerland, and appeared in Germany, central and eastern Europe, Scandinavia, Scotland, and North

America. Outside of Paris, he performed most often in London, where his music was particularly well received by the public and press.

Ravel's international reputation reached its zenith in 1928 as a result of his four-month concert tour in North America. The critics were lavish in their approbation, and the audiences enthusiastic. At an all-Ravel program given by Koussevitzky and the Boston Symphony Orchestra in Carnegie Hall, the entire audience stood up and applauded as the composer took his seat. Deeply touched by this spontaneous gesture, Ravel turned to Alexandre Tansman and observed, "You know, this doesn't happen to me in Paris." Although the itinerary was exhausting, he managed to rest on the long train rides which brought him to some twenty-five cities from New York to California and from Canada to Texas. Among the many highlights of the trip were a visit to the Bronx home of Edgar Allan Poe, an excursion to Niagara Falls, and a visit to the Grand Canyon, whose majesty and beauty Ravel found overwhelming. He was fascinated by the dynamism of American life, its huge cities, skyscrapers, and its advanced technology, and was impressed by its jazz, Negro spirituals, and the excellence of American orchestras. American cuisine was apparently another matter: "I am seeing magnificent cities and enchanting regions," he wrote to Hélène Jourdan-Morhange, "but the triumphs are exhausting. In Los Angeles, I slipped away from the people; besides, I was dying of hunger" (letter no. 295).

Upon arrival at Le Havre on April 27, Ravel was greeted by Edouard, the Delages, Marcelle Gerar, Hélène Jourdan-Morhange, and several other close friends. In June, the Société Musicale Indépendante presented a special Ravel festival with the participation of the composer and several younger colleagues, mezzo-soprano Madeleine Grey, violinist Claude Lévy, cellist Maurice Maréchal, and the American pianist Beveridge Webster. Soon after, with the efficient planning of Marcelle Gerar, some forty friends gathered at Le Belvédère for a Sunday afternoon luncheon in honor of the composer's triumphant tour, and the festivities finally ended in a cabaret about 4 A.M. By this point, invitations of all sorts were pouring in: a concert tour in Spain, a request from Oxford University to accept an honorary doctoral degree, a series of concerts in Holland, a recital of chamber music in Bordeaux. In addition, before leaving for North America, Ravel had promised to compose a ballet for Ida Rubinstein. During a brief vacation in Saint-Jean-de-Luz, just before going for a morning swim, he poked out a melody on the piano with one finger. "Don't you think this theme has an insistent quality?" he asked Gustave Samazeuilh. "I'm going to try and repeat it a number of times without any development, gradually increasing the orchestra as best I can." The ballet soon became incredibly popular, much to the surprise of its composer, and to this day the *Boléro* remains an international best-seller. Shortly after completing the *Boléro*, Ravel appeared in academic garb at Oxford University, which conferred upon him the degree of Doctor of Music, *honoris causa.* A concert tour in Spain with Madeleine Grey and Claude Lévy, and brief visits to Geneva and Bordeaux rounded out a year of extraordinary activity.

In the early months of 1929, Ravel participated in several festivals of his music given in England, Switzerland, and Austria, and following all of these exhausting travels, he looked forward to a long vacation. Following many years of periodic insomnia and occasional bouts of neurasthenia, he found it more difficult than ever to undertake fresh projects. Since 1928, a piano concerto in G major had been contemplated, as well as an opera, *Jeanne d'Arc,* based on the novel by Joseph Delteil. Work on the concerto was interrupted by a commission from the Austrian pianist Paul Wittgenstein, who had lost his right arm in World War I. Intrigued by the challenge of writing a concerto for the left hand, Ravel completed the work in about a year. The Piano Concerto in G Major was finally introduced in Paris on January 14, 1932, with Marguerite Long as soloist and Ravel conducting. A few days later, disobeying doctor's orders, the composer undertook a taxing three-month tour with Madame Long, performing the Concerto in some twenty European cities from London to Bucharest. In London, Ravel shared the podium with Malcolm Sargent, in Berlin with Wilhelm Furtwängler, and in Bucharest he was received in private audience by the royal family and decorated by King Carol II.

Following this triumphant tour, Ravel returned to the Basque country for an extended rest. Two recent commissions were being contemplated, a ballet for Ida Rubinstein, *Morgiane,* based on the tale of Ali Baba and the Forty Thieves, and music for a film, *Don Quixote,* with Feodor Chaliapin in the title role. While only fragmentary sketches of *Morgiane* were committed to paper, the music for *Don Quixote* proved to be the composer's swan song. The final song, based on the rhythm of the Spanish *jota,* ends with the words "Je bois à la joie" (I drink to joy). Ravel thus bade farewell to his art with an homage to the Spain of his fantasy, concluding with an exuberant toast to the joy of living.

If his art terminated in a mood of carefree joy, Ravel's final years proved to be poignant and tragic in the extreme. While vacationing at Saint-Jean-de-Luz in the summer of 1933, he found it impossible to coordinate his motions while swimming, and encountered unusual difficulty in writing. His physicians spoke of cerebral anemia, mental fatigue, apraxia, the inability to perform purposeful movements, and aphasia, involving difficulty in speech and a partial loss of memory. Ravel appeared overworked, exhausted, and, of course, fearful of this ominous development. Following several months of complete rest his condition improved, and in November 1933 he led the Pasdeloup Orchestra in the *Boléro* and the Concerto in G Major with Marguerite Long as soloist. This engagement appears to have marked his final public performance.

One of the last letters that Ravel was able to write was sent to Marie Gaudin on March 12, 1934. Its conclusion is heartrending: "Write me sometimes. I will try to answer you although it costs me entire days of torture to do so; I began this letter over a week ago" (no. 335). One can only admire Ravel's indomitable courage as he undertook the Herculean task of relearning the letters of the alphabet. His efforts were ultimately unsuccessful, and the few letters written during the last three years of his life were all dictated.

Although Ravel spoke with great difficulty, and at times appeared oblivious to his surroundings, at other times he was painfully aware of his helpless condition. "I can still see him at Montfort l'Amaury," Hélène Jourdan-Morhange recalled, "seated in an armchair on the famous balcony whose view he loved so much, with a distant, forlorn gaze . . . I became uneasy and asked: 'What are you doing there, dear Ravel?' He replied simply, 'I am waiting.'" Ravel was indeed waiting for nothing less than a miracle, which tragically would never come to pass.

One pleasure which Ravel continued to enjoy was travel, and in February 1935, accompanied by Léon Leyritz, he set out for Spain and North Africa. During the trip, several colorful festivities were given in his honor, and every opportunity was taken to hear Moorish and Arabic music. In Morocco, amid the exotic scales, quarter tones, and the wail of the muezzin calling the faithful to prayer, Ravel was pleasantly surprised one day to hear a young man whistling the *Boléro.* Following this wonderful voyage, which seemed to spring out of a page from the Arabian Nights, the return trip was made through Seville and Cordova. In August, the two companions set out from Saint-Jean-de-Luz for Spain, this time visiting the Cantabrian coast. This trip marked the composer's farewell to Spain, a country he had often called his second musical homeland. Although diverted by these travels, Ravel's condition continued to worsen. His friends watched over him, taking him to concerts and doing their best to keep him occupied. He often stayed with Edouard at Levallois Perret, or with the Delages, and at Le Belvédère Madame Reveleau catered to his every wish.

Despite the inexorable process of a debilitating aphasia, Ravel continued to serve his art well into the last year of his life. He coached Jacques Février on the Concerto for the Left Hand, and in June 1937 he offered counsel to Madeleine Grey and Francis Poulenc, who were soon to perform *Don Quichotte à Dulcinée.* One of the last concerts Ravel attended was led by Désiré-Emile Inghelbrecht, conducting the Orchestre National. Following a performance of *Daphnis et Chloé,* he began to sob: "I still have so much music in my head," he told Hélène Jourdan-Morhange, "I have said nothing. I have so much more to say."

During the autumn of 1937, Ravel's health deteriorated sharply, and on December 17 he was admitted to the clinic on rue Boileau in Paris. After much agonizing deliberation, Edouard Ravel and the composer's closest friends decided to risk a delicate brain operation, which was performed by the celebrated surgeon Dr. Clovis Vincent. No tumor was found, and Dr. Vincent succeeded in equalizing the level of the cerebral hemispheres, one of which had become depressed. Two days after the operation, Ravel was asked if he would like to see his brother. He promptly replied "Ah! Yes indeed!" These were apparently his last words before lapsing into a coma. His cruel four-year agony finally came to an end during the early morning hours of December 28, 1937.

The death of Maurice Ravel engendered innumerable expressions of grief, particularly in Europe and North America. Among many others, Milhaud, Prokofiev, and Stravinsky acknowledged the passing of a master musician. A simple burial service took place on December 30 in the presence of a large gathering of friends and colleagues. Led by Edouard Ravel, the mourners included Georges Auric, Jane Bathori, Robert Casadesus, Arthur Honegger, Darius Milhaud, Francis Poulenc, Igor Stravinsky, and Ricardo Viñes. During the brief civil ceremony, a eulogy was delivered by the Minister of National Education, Jean Zay, who spoke on behalf of the French government, and following the service, burial took place at the cemetery in Levallois Perret.

During Ravel's lifetime, his music was performed throughout Europe, North and South America, and from North Africa to the Orient. His career intersected with those of many outstanding personalities of the day—Ansermet, Bartók, Casals, Debussy, Heifetz, Monteux, Nijinsky, Prokofiev, Stravinsky, Vaughan Williams—the list could easily be extended. Granted honorary awards and citations by universities, ministers, and kings, Ravel's career was brilliant and rich in achievement. Behind it all lies the subtle complexity of the man. His physical appearance was striking. To Roland-Manuel, Ravel resembled a jockey, to Colette, a squirrel. His short height (about 5 feet, 3 inches), and light frame (about 108 pounds), were notable, as were his taut, bony features, and his gentle, mischievous brown eyes. After experimenting with a mustache, side whiskers, and a full beard, he became clean-shaven from about the age of thirty-five, and his dark brown hair slowly changed to silvery white. At the time of *Daphnis et Chloé,* Madame Nijinsky described the composer as "a charming young man, always a little extravagantly dressed, but full of gaiety." Indeed, Ravel's dandyism included being up-to-date with the latest fashions in clothing. He was among the first to wear pastel-colored shirts in France, and on one occasion, a young composer who came for advice was surprised to find him dressed in a white sweater, white pants, white stockings, and white shoes. Beveridge Webster, who met the composer in the 1920s, recalled "a tiny man with an enormous head, a huge nose and an enormous intellect." A French journalist, Nino Frank, writing in *Candide* in 1932, perceptively captured the inner spirit of the man:

Those who expect to meet the legendary Ravel, abrupt and distant, find instead a tiny man, elegant and smiling, his eyes sparkling with mirth and perspicacity, who speaks in a rather deep voice. Photographs have popularized the chiseled lines of his face, with its silvery hair and black eyebrows, a face that seems designed by a geometer, portraying strong determination; in reality, his face radiates an inexpressible affectionate bonhomie, an extraordinary youthfulness, and a brilliant intelligence, which humanize these features. Slim and small like a Spaniard, Ravel expresses himself without any petulance, with a mixture of modesty and timidity which is disconcerting.

The essential features of Ravel's colorful and somewhat elusive personality were set during his student days. Alfred Cortot recalled his twenty-year-old colleague as a "bantering, intellectual, and somewhat distant young man, who read Mallarmé and visited Erik Satie." Ravel was indeed "somewhat distant," for outside of a few close schoolmates, he generally maintained an air of cool detachment. A certain bantering humor and a deliberate attempt at mystification helped him to keep others at a distance, and this aspect of his personality appears to indicate the influence of Satie. Rather than to Satie's bohemianism, however, he was attracted to Baudelaire's description of the dandy, who was supposed to exhibit simplicity and elegance in grooming and to carry out a dignified quest for beauty. Thus, Ravel gave careful attention to his grooming and wardrobe, and discussed the colors of his ties and shirts with the utmost seriousness. Behind this mask, he was attracted to things which were complex and even contradictory, and was oriented toward all that was "poetry, fantasy, precious and rare, paradoxical and refined." This description, by Ricardo Viñes, offers an important clue to the elegance, refinement, and preciosity underlying many of Ravel's early compositions. Other revealing observations are found in Viñes' journal entry dated November 1, 1896. On this Sunday morning, the young musicians went to the Saint Gervais church to hear a mass by the Italian composer Francesco Soriano (1549–1621). In the afternoon they attended a concert of the Lamoureux Orchestra, which included a performance of the Prelude to *Tristan and Isolde.* Viñes describes how, "seemingly so cool and cynical, Ravel, the supereccentric decadent, trembled convulsively and cried like a child" at the performance. Although considered a failure by most, Viñes continued, he is in fact a superior artist. "He is, moreover, very complicated, there being in him a mixture of Middle Ages Catholicism and satanic impiety, but also a love of Art and Beauty which guide him and which make him react candidly." The "mixture of Middle Ages Catholicism and satanic impiety" is not a reference to religion, but rather to Ravel's strong acceptance of artistic tradition coupled with a thirst for individual exploration and innovation. Above all, he was sensitive, indeed hypersensitive, to artistic beauty, and this ideal was to remain his continual guide. Thus, by his early twenties, Ravel's personality was rather firmly set in its own paradoxical way. Correct and cool with strangers, he was fun-loving and amusing with friends, optimistic, independent, headstrong, and idealistic. As he matured, these qualities were essentially unaltered. Other youthful traits, however, such as tendencies toward sarcasm, deliberate mystification, and certain affectations were shed in later years. Sir Lennox Berkeley has recalled the many contradictions in Ravel's personality. He was

> very reserved and yet gregarious in that he loved to be surrounded by friends, a man of passionate loyalties but of seeming indifference to the larger issues in life, having in some ways a childlike simplicity yet seeking to appear a sophisticated man of the world. He was of very small stature with a head that seemed too big for his body. In everything he was out of the ordinary. . . . Unlike many great men, the more successful and famous he became, the less he would allow any trace of self-importance to show itself. I used to meet him sometimes after concerts when he would take me, generally with another student or young composer, to one of the big cafés in the St. Lazare district where he would talk with us about the music we'd heard. It strikes me now, though it didn't then, that he could so easily have spent the evening in better company both socially and intellectually, but I think he was bored by the world he had already conquered, and preferred to be with young musicians however humble. He was apt to prolong the evening by inviting us to accompany him to a night club. It was in these establishments that one first heard the real virtuoso playing that has characterised good jazz ever since. Ravel loved it, and would remain until the early hours when he would at last walk back to his hotel at a leisurely pace. He suffered from insomnia, and these nocturnal ramblings were I think an excuse not to go to bed. . . .
>
> There certainly was with him a barrier that one knew must not be crossed; though he clearly had an affectionate nature, he hated anything too demonstrative and always remained slightly aloof.

Ravel's personal habits have frequently been described by those who knew him. Although a confirmed hermit when composing, he enjoyed Parisian nightlife, the conversations, the lights, the jazz, and the crowds. "I can see him now," Léon-Paul Fargue recalled, "a sort of debonair wizard, buried in his corner at the Grand Ecart or Le Bœuf sur le toit, telling me endless stories which had the same elegance, richness, and clarity as his compositions. He could tell an anecdote as well as he could compose a waltz or an adagio." A heavy smoker of cigarettes, Ravel also enjoyed sharp condiments, exotic dishes, cocktails, and fine wines. He excelled in swimming and was an indefatigable walker. Even during his terminal illness, there was a youthful agility in his step, and the Forest of Rambouillet, the streets of Paris, and large areas of the Basque territory held few secrets for him. Ravel's meticulous grooming was counterbalanced by a curious disorder in his personal affairs. He was somewhat absent-minded and often lost track of time, particularly in antique shops, when buying gifts, or when examining rare editions for his library. When Léon Leyritz was finishing his bust of the composer, he wanted to verify some details. "I'll come tomorrow between 10 P.M. and 3 A.M.," was the sensible reply. Indeed, deadlines and schedules were anathema to Ravel. In the postwar years, when plagued by some creative impasses, his solution was to travel. If the new location proved to be helpful, he stayed; if not, he left. This strong sense of independence, both as an artist and as an individual, lies at the heart of Ravel's personality. "I love to work freely and without prejudice," he told a Danish journalist. "I have always done that. Therefore I do not belong to any school, or to any particular party. I have always been free." And in a letter to Florent Schmitt, written in 1921, he referred to his refusal to accept the Legion of Honor, which had created an uproar: "My logic? There's nothing surprising about it: it's to do only what I want, according to what appeals to me. People tell you off, but who gives a damn, right?"

Relatively little can be said about the great issues of life, owing to Ravel's extreme reserve. "People are always talking about my having no heart," he told Jacques de Zogheb, a neighbor at Montfort l'Amaury. "It's not true, and you know it. But I am Basque. The Basques feel deeply but seldom show it, and then only to a very few." Despite his Basque-Swiss heritage, Ravel was above all a Frenchman. He pointed out some interesting generalities about his countrymen (and to some extent himself) in an interview with a Viennese journalist in February 1932:

> Like the Austrian, he is communicative, but never wears his heart upon his sleeve. He never lets a stranger approach him too closely, he doesn't want to be understood at any cost, and he never bites off more than he can chew. Perhaps that makes him insular and shortsighted. Still, surely he is always clear and precise, like the clear landscape of "gentle France," with its perpetually clear blue sky.

Ravel never married, and this has given rise to much speculation. No love letters have come to light, probably because they were never written. Although not insensitive to feminine charm and beauty, it is clear that the dominant woman in his life was his mother, and, in a rare comment about marriage, he wrote in January 1919 to Madame Alfredo Casella: "Morality . . . this is what I practice, and what I am determined to continue. Artists are not made for marriage. We are rarely normal, and our lives are even less so." And to Manuel Rosenthal he explained as follows:

> You see, an artist must be very careful when he wishes to marry someone, because an artist never knows to what extent he may render his companion unhappy. He is obsessed by his creative work and by the problems which it poses. He lives a little like an awakened dreamer, and that's not amusing for a woman who lives with him. One must always consider that when one wishes to marry.

Had circumstances been different, Ravel might have married Hélène Jourdan-Morhange. But they met in 1917 (she was twenty-nine, Ravel forty-two), shortly after her first husband, the painter Jacques Jourdan, had been killed in the war. Friends of Ravel have told me that he wanted to marry her but she refused, and others have claimed that she wanted to marry Ravel but he refused. Although she lived with Luc-Albert Moreau for several decades, it is suggestive that she married him only after Ravel's death. Whatever the exact truth may be, their relationship was one of particular affection and understanding. Ravel often stated that his only mistress was music. Although there were discreet encounters with prostitutes (according to D.-E. Inghelbrecht's testimony as recorded in Stuckenschmidt's biography), they were ultimately inconsequential. If never destined for fatherhood, Ravel had an extraordinary rapport with the children of his friends. He told the Godebski children enchanting fairy tales and apparently enjoyed playing with their toys as much as they did. His extreme sophistication was curiously combined with a childlike enthusiasm and wonder. In a touching letter to Maurice and Nelly Delage, Mimie Godebska wrote that when she heard the news of Ravel's death, it was like losing her own father for the second time.

Although born of Catholic parents and baptized as an infant, Ravel was not a practicing Catholic and did not accept the last rites of the Church. He apparently was an agnostic, relying upon his inner conscience and moral sensitivity. The library at Montfort l'Amaury contains a French translation of the Old and New Testaments, as well as a translation of *I Fioretti* (The Little Flowers) of Saint Francis, a work which he particularly admired. Ravel participated in several concerts whose proceeds were donated to various charities. On August 23, 1925, one such recital was given in the parish hall of the church in Montfort l'Amaury, which is just around the corner from Le Belvédère. The parish priest occasionally visited with his illustrious neighbor, and told him on one occasion, "Monsieur Ravel, you are the most Christian of my parishioners." In the 1930s, a number of musicians, refugees from Nazi Germany, found their way to Le Belvédère, where they received both encouragement and financial assistance. This action is characteristic of Ravel, who gave generously to charity and abhorred all racism. An admirer of Léon Blum and Paul Painlevé, his political views were socialistic. The one newspaper he subscribed to, *Le Populaire de Paris*, now defunct, was a well-known socialist organ. In economic terms, Ravel gradually moved from the lower middle class to the upper middle class, and by the end of his career he was wealthy. In addition to Durand's fixed annuity and special sums for his manuscripts, there were generous fees from patrons who commissioned works. Furthermore, in 1928, Ravel earned over $11,000 for his North American tour, at a time when a luxury seven-passenger automobile cost just over $2,000 and a first-class airmail letter from the United States to France was five cents (it is now about nine times that amount).

Like any other human being, Ravel had his moods and quirks. He was very sensitive about his short height, and his limited abilities as a pianist and conductor. If he had a compliment to pay, it was often communicated to a third party. Thus, when Marcelle Gerar went to Le Belvédère for an audition, she was received properly but coolly. Only later, through a mutual friend, did she learn that Ravel was impressed with her ability, and soon after she was asked to concertize with the composer. Criticism, on the other hand, was usually given directly to the person involved. "Your ballet is very bad," he told a young composer; and then with a gentle smile, "I tell you this because I know you can do much better." A revealing, paradoxical touch is found in Le Belvédère, where the panels in the living room and bedroom were designed and painted by the master of the house. In the privacy of his bedroom, Ravel drew a series of columns—all of them upside down! This paradoxical aspect has been noted in both of his operas: in *L'Heure espagnole,* the characters almost become automatons, but the automatons chime with the tender warmth of life; in *L'Enfant et les sortilèges,* the child is cruel, but the animals are humane. As a young man, Ravel was attracted to paradoxes of all sorts, and in later years he enjoyed exploring the paradoxical aspect of art with colleagues. Although he stated that art was "false" and "a marvelous imposture," this notion must be seen in its proper perspective—namely, that he believed art to be a quest for beauty, rather than truth, an idea he derived from the writings of Poe.

Behind all the quirks, surprises, and paradoxes of the man lie his unshakable artistic probity and integrity. Ravel believed in his art and fought for it, not in the grand manner of a Berlioz, which he considered grotesque, but in a modest, dignified way. He brought his music before the public and took keen interest in performances of his works both in France and abroad. He stood up to Diaghilev, Toscanini, and anyone else he thought to be misinterpreting his art, and defended the music of Debussy, Stravinsky, and others from the attacks of critics. No doubt Ravel would have wished to compose more, particularly during the postwar years, but he endured extended periods of silence rather than compromise with his ideals. If the "meaning of life" may be interpreted as how one spends one's time between two eternities, then its ultimate meaning for Maurice Ravel was to create music which was as perfect, as polished, and as beautiful as he could make it. This was his passion; indeed, his obsession.

Ravel's views of the nature and meaning of art were primarily based upon his formative studies at the Conservatoire, his reading of Baudelaire and Poe, and, of course, his personal amalgam of these and other elements. He stated that his objective as a composer was to seek "technical perfection. I can strive unceasingly to this end, since I am certain of never being able to attain it. The important thing is to get nearer to it all the time." How was one to approach the objective of technical perfection? According to Ravel, one submitted to a thorough and rigorous academic training. In addition to analyzing scores and studying the traditional precepts of harmony, counterpoint, and orchestration, together with his colleagues at the Conservatoire, he wrote four-part fugues in open score, using the soprano, alto, tenor, and bass clefs. Ravel believed this type of training to be crucial, as it developed the technical skills which were needed to solve compositional problems. Indeed, the initial sketches of *Morgiane,* which were the very last notes to come from his pen, consisted of nothing more than a melody and figured bass—the identical procedure that he had used as a student in order to analyze compositions. In later years, the following advice was given to young composers: "If you have nothing to say, you cannot do better, until you decide to give up composing for good, than say again what has already been well said. If you have something to say, that something will never emerge more distinctly than when you are being unwittingly unfaithful to your model." Ravel was convinced that composers should learn their craft like painters—by imitating good models. Yet, as Jean Cocteau pointed out in *Le Coq et l'Arlequin,* "an original artist *cannot* copy. Thus, he has only to copy in order to be original." This observation is particularly apt with regard to Ravel's music, in which there is often a model which is ultimately eclipsed.

In explaining what he looked for in a composition, Ravel stressed the importance of "musical sensitivity," and that "a composer must have something to say." Calvocoressi pointed out that he was particularly attracted to

points of originality in idiom and texture. When calling attention to some beautiful thing, he would often wind up with: 'Et puis, vous savez, on n'avait jamais fait ça!' [And then, you know, that hasn't been done before!] Questions of form seemed to preoccupy him far less. The one and only test of good form, he used to say, is continuity of interest. I do not remember his ever praising a work on account of its form. But, on the other hand, he was very sensitive to what he considered to be defective form. (*Musicians Gallery,* 1933.)

In addition to the axioms of imitation as the gateway to mastering one's craft and the objective of technical perfection, Ravel was convinced that a work of art is the product of a composer's individual consciousness, which is inextricably bound to his national heritage: "The manifestation of these two types of consciousness in music may break or satisfy all the academic rules, but such circumstance is of insignificant importance compared with the real aim, namely, fullness and sincerity of expression." It is apparent that Ravel's "fullness and sincerity of expression" are solidly within French tradition. Calvocoressi noted that his preference for writing shorter compositions was due to a "deliberate, carefully thought-out aesthetic choice," and this terseness of logic is characteristic of French art. One also observes emotional reserve rather than expansiveness, elegance and preciosity, humor and tenderness, all of which is underpinned by a marked sensuousness. There is also a less common but distinct thread of drama extending from *Un Grand Sommeil noir, Si morne!*, and *Gaspard de la nuit*, through *La Valse*, the *Chansons madécasses*, and the Concerto for the Left Hand.

Ravel's critical opinions, which will be examined in detail later on, offer important insight into his aesthetic values. Although some contemporaries appear to have been overrated, he immediately recognized the importance of Debussy and Milhaud, Bartók and Kodály, Richard Strauss, Falla, Vaughan Williams, Stravinsky, and Schoenberg, at a time when many of these composers were subjected to the crudest diatribes. However, he had serious reservations regarding Beethoven, Berlioz, Brahms, Wagner, Franck, and d'Indy, whose expansive architecture or metaphysical aspirations were far removed from his own artistic priorities. If the thread from Beethoven to d'Indy was problematic, the line from Mozart through Schubert, Mendelssohn, Chopin, Bizet, Massenet, Gounod, Chabrier, Saint-Saëns, Satie, and Fauré was closer to Ravel's aesthetic orientation. It would be difficult to exaggerate his admiration for the Russian school, particularly for Borodin, Mussorgsky, and Rimsky-Korsakov; while fully aware of the deficiencies found in some of their music, their straightforward spontaneity, orchestral color, exoticism, and modality were seen as a fresh direction worthy of imitation, particularly as it offered a strong antidote to Wagnerian influence. Despite Schoenberg's influence, Ravel believed that the main stream of French music would not follow his path, nor would it rally to the amalgam of French and Germanic elements found in the teaching of d'Indy.

Posterity has seen fit to link the names of Debussy and Ravel, and a comparison of their achievements may perhaps best highlight Ravel's individual aesthetic path. Both composers were pianists who were trained at the Conservatoire, and whose national inheritance encompassed a millennium of music. Their approbation of Mozart, Chopin, Chabrier, and Mussorgsky, and their reservations with regard to Beethoven, Wagner, and d'Indy, were rather similar. They shared common friendships with Satie, Falla, and Stravinsky, and were strongly attracted to Baudelaire, Mallarmé, and Poe. Despite their common heritage and many points of contact, Ravel claimed that he had followed a direction "opposite to that of Debussy's symbolism," and, influenced by Poe, had decided "to abandon the vagueness and formlessness of the early French impressionists in favor of a return to classic standards." Whereas Debussy's melody is often elliptical, purity and omnipresence of melody characterize Ravel's art. Both composers boldly extended harmonic practice within the framework of tonality, and, although Debussy was generally more adventurous in this area, the unique conclusion of Ravel's "Surgi de la croupe et du bond" is perhaps the closest example in the work of either composer of a complete suspension of tonality. The strikingly open structure found in the art of Debussy is offset by his younger colleague's preference for masking the essentially classical outlines of his works. Despite Ravel's unequivocal comment that Debussy was "the most phenomenal genius in the history of French music," he criticized his colleague's "lack of architectonic power" in larger forms, and told Henri Sauguet that *La Mer* was poorly orchestrated. Details of craftsmanship were of vital concern to Ravel, and he generally found Debussy's treatment of the percussion section weak. Moreover, he criticized *L'Île joyeuse* as poorly written for the keyboard, calling it an orchestral reduction for the piano.

From our vantage point, it is evident that each composer influenced the other to some extent, keeping in mind that once an artist achieves his own personality, external influences are of secondary importance. If *Shéhérazade* and the *Miroirs* indicate the spirit of Debussy, the *Estampes* bespeak the achievements of Ravel. It is possible that the clearer outlines and structures found in Debussy's late works came about through Ravel's influence, and Debussy's call for a thinner, less congested art was taken up by Ravel, *Les Six,* and much of the postwar generation. Ernest Ansermet has recalled a meeting with Debussy in which the composer gave him a score of the *Nocturnes* covered with corrections of all sorts. When asked which ones were valid, Debussy replied, "I am no longer sure. They are all possibilities. Take this score and use those which seem good to you." One could scarcely imagine Ravel making such a statement. For him, there was but one final product—the one which was as perfect as he could make it. In the last analysis, the creative personalities of Debussy and Ravel were widely divergent. Debussy's productivity was effusive, uninhibited, and opened up fresh paths, whereas Ravel's small output, emotional reticence, and innovation within tradition were coupled with an unrivaled technical mastery of his craft.

No discussion of Ravel's art would be complete without commenting on the decisive importance of Edgar Allan Poe's writings. Poe's marked influence upon modern French literature has frequently been observed, and, among others, Baudelaire and Mallarmé translated his works, which proved to be a revelation for Ravel. In August 1892, Maurice showed Ricardo Viñes two very dark and somber drawings that he had made, based on Poe's short stories "A Descent into the Maelstrom" and "MS. Found in a Bottle." Soon after, he composed the *Ballade de la Reine morte d'aimer* (Ballad of the Queen who died of love; for voice and piano) and "Entre cloches" (Among bells; for two pianos), in which the tintinnabulation of bells reflects Poe's spiritual influence. Ravel's fascination with bells, clocks, and chimes would extend throughout his career, and the obsessive tolling pedal point found in "Le Gibet" hauntingly conjures up the tension and terror found in Poe's writings. Above all, it is in *The Poetic Principle* that one finds the closest approximation to Ravel's aesthetic:

> *That* pleasure which is at once the most pure, the most elevating, and the most intense, is derived, I maintain, from the contemplation of the Beautiful. In the contemplation of Beauty we alone find it possible to attain that pleasurable elevation, or excitement, *of the soul*, which we recognize as the Poetic Sentiment, and which is so easily distinguished from Truth, which is the satisfaction of the Reason, or from Passion, which is the excitement of the Heart.

Ravel's art strove neither for passion nor for truth, but rather for "the contemplation of the Beautiful," through the satisfaction of the mind, by means of the ear's pleasure. Thus, a final paradox was perfectly stated by Keats, who already knew that by creating his own beauty, Ravel would thereby create his own truth. In addition, with his striving for clarity, balance, and good taste, the composer of *Daphnis et Chloé* created an art which embodies the timeless values of the French nation.

A survey of Ravel's art indicates a small body of music written over a creative period of four decades, from the early 1890s to the early 1930s. There are approximately sixty compositions, of which slightly more than half are instrumental: fifteen pieces and suites for the piano, eight chamber works, six orchestral works, several ballets, and two piano concerti. The vocal music consists of eighteen songs and song cycles with accompaniment for piano, chamber ensemble, or orchestra, several settings of folk melodies, one work for unaccompanied mixed chorus, and two operas. It would be misleading to divide this music into periods of apprenticeship and maturity, for Ravel's earliest compositions were on the whole remarkably characteristic. The "Habanera" and the *Menuet antique* were written by a twenty-year-old student, and with the completion of *Jeux d'eau* at the age of twenty-six, the composer's style was firmly set. These early works indicate many of the trends he would pursue: a predilection for dance rhythms, the music of Spain, archaic pastiche and contemporary impressionistic techniques. Thus, from the outset, Ravel's approach to composition might be called metamorphic—that is, in each new undertaking he would cover fresh ground, placing his personal stamp upon widely differing techniques and idioms. Ravel's observation that as a child he was sensitive "to every kind of music" offers an important clue to the striking diversity found in his art. This innovative approach to musical style was explained to a French journalist as follows:

> The true personality for a composer . . . is not to seek to have one which is immediately recognizable and stylized in unchanging formulas. That is the weak side of Richard Strauss, who is otherwise a musician of genius, whereas the example of a Stravinsky, constantly seeking to renew himself and ceaselessly exploring extremely varied domains, seems infinitely preferable to me. (Pierre Leroi, *Excelsior*, 1931.)

An important aspect of Ravel's artistic creed was his predilection for remodeling his music. It appears that once a composition was perfected, the attempt was made to draw out all of its inherent possibilities. Indeed, almost half of his works were reshaped in one manner or another: a considerable number of piano pieces and vocal accompaniments were orchestrated, and several keyboard works were transcribed and then mounted as ballets. Thus, rather curiously, the composer's only orchestral compositions, properly speaking, are the overture to *Shéhérazade*, the *Rapsodie espagnole, Daphnis et Chloé, La Valse*, a "Fanfare" for the ballet *L'Eventail de Jeanne, Boléro*, and the piano concerti. The key influences on his orchestral technique were the scores of Rimsky-Korsakov (particularly *Scheherazade, Mlada*, and the *Capriccio espagnol*), and Richard Strauss (largely *Don Juan* and *Till Eulenspiegel*). The treatises of Berlioz and Rimsky-Korsakov were thoroughly assimilated, and Widor's *Technique de l'orchestre moderne* was frequently consulted for its useful technical data. Ravel's orchestral technique was the fruit of long years of study, incessant questioning of performers, much experimentation, and innumerable rehearsals. He was intrigued by the seemingly limitless resources of the modern orchestra, and his scores indicate a natural extension of each instrument's technical resources and range, careful attention to the linearity of each part, and the seeking out of fresh combinations of timbre. He was particularly sensitive to rhythmic and coloristic subtleties in the percussion section and wrote for the harp with marked skill. The brass family, on the other hand, is generally treated in a relatively traditional fashion. It would appear that within the limit of human capability and efficacy of writing, any instrument may assume any role, and here the Ravelian elements of surprise and even paradox came to the fore. The E♭ saxophone will somehow conjure up an old castle in Ravel's orchestration of Mussorgsky's *Pictures at an Exhibition*, while in *Ma Mère l'Oye*, a melodic passage is given to the weak bass register of the celesta. In the daybreak episode from *Daphnis et Chloé*, the woodwinds and strings perform extended and agile harplike passages, while in the *Chansons madécasses*, the flute will evoke a trumpet, and the piano a gong.

The diversity of Ravel's instrumental music is matched by the striking variety of his vocal works. From the preciosity of Pierre de Ronsard to the complex symbolism of Mallarmé, from the exoticism of Evariste de Parny to Colette's sensitive portrayal of childhood, Ravel rarely repeated himself, setting Alexandrines and poems in prose from the Renaissance through the twentieth century. Most often, he turned to free verse and poems in prose. Unlike the more adventurous instrumental style, the vocal writing indicates traditional tessitura with relatively little interest in virtuosity. Behind this diversity lies the composer's desire for textual clarity, correct prosody, and his individualistic and sophisticated literary taste.

As a creative artist, Ravel was keenly aware of his strengths and weaknesses. "It is true," he told Manuel Rosenthal," that I possess genius. But what does that mean? If everyone knew how to work like I do, then everyone would write music which exhibits as much genius as mine. But everyone does not know how to work like I do, and therein lies the essence of genius—knowing how to work intelligently, and how to organize one's ideas." A different view was expressed in a concert critique: "The principle of *genius*, that is of artistic creation, can be established only by instinct, or sensibility." This problematic duality of craftsmanship and inspiration was perceptively summed up by Ravel when he observed that he knew exactly how he composed the *Boléro*, but did not know how he composed *Daphnis et Chloé*. If the childlike side of his personality demanded that a visitor see no pencil, eraser, or music paper on his piano, the fact is that the smallest creative act required an immense amount of labor, and this largely accounts for his small oeuvre as well as his many incomplete projects. In this one area of creativity, Ravel was closer to Beethoven than to Mozart. For many years he attempted to write a symphony, but finally gave it up. He never turned to the theme and variations, and composed neither for the organ nor for the church. A complete accounting of the elements in Ravel's art would run the gamut from Gregorian chant to Gershwin, passing through the Renaissance, Baroque, Classical and Romantic eras. He managed to keep his personal touch in a style which varied from the classical simplicity of *Ma Mère l'Oye* to the transcendental romantic virtuosity of *Gaspard de la nuit*, from the luxuriant, caressing sonority of *Daphnis et Chloé* to the austere violence of the *Chansons madécasses*, and from Renaissance pastiche to adaptations of jazz. His achievement is neither eclectic, nor can it be summed up in one all-encompassing label. It is thoroughly French in orientation, and is solidly based upon traditional practice. In the last analysis, like any other significant artist, Ravel fashioned his own laws and created his own universe: his Swiss-Basque heritage and Parisian sophistication, his subtle humor, his fascination with travel and exoticism, his interest in animals and children, and his keen observations of nature are mirrored in his art, as are the disorientation and tragedy of World War I. Behind all of these multifarious threads lies the composer's sovereign conscience, and, in the words of Tristan Klingsor, "the ironic and tender heart which beats under the velvet vest of Maurice Ravel."

I

Ravel's Career and
Musical Thought

I : : :

An Autobiographical Sketch by Maurice Ravel[1]

Roland-Manuel[2] has explained the genesis of the Autobiographical Sketch as follows. In 1928, the Aeolian company, a firm specializing in player pianos, inaugurated a series of recordings on specially perforated rolls, which would also contain autobiographical comments drawn up by the composer. Monsieur Henri Dubois, the artistic director of the company, asked Ravel to participate in the project. Rather than write his own commentary, the composer in turn asked Roland-Manuel to act as his secretary in an interview. Although M. Dubois rejected the interview format, it was agreed that Ravel would dictate an autobiographical statement which he would later retouch. For whatever reason, he never corrected his colleague's notes and withdrew from the project. Thus, the following article is based on Roland-Manuel's uncorrected draft.[3]

I was born in Ciboure, a township in the Lower Pyrenees next to Saint-Jean-de-Luz, on March 7, 1875.[4]

My father, originally from Versoix, on the shore of Lake Geneva, was a civil engineer. My mother belonged to an old Basque family.

At the age of three months, I left Ciboure for Paris, where I have lived ever since.

Even as a child, I was sensitive to music—to every kind of music. My father, who was much better versed in this art than most amateurs, knew how to develop my taste and stimulate my zeal.

Instead of solfeggio, the theory of which I never learned, I began to study the piano about the age of six. My teachers were Henri Ghys,[5] followed by M. Charles-René,[6] from whom I took my first lessons in harmony, counterpoint, and composition.

In 1889 I was admitted to the Paris Conservatoire in the preparatory piano class of M. Anthiôme,[7] and two years later I was in the class of Charles de Bériot.[8]

: : :

First Compositions

My first compositions, which have remained unpublished, date from about 1893.[9] I was then in M. Pessard's[10] harmony class. Emmanuel

Chabrier's[11] influence was apparent in the *Sérénade grotesque* for piano, and that of Satie[12] in the *Ballade de la Reine morte d'aimer.*

In 1895, I wrote my first published works: the *Menuet antique* and the "Habanera" for piano. I believe that the "Habanera" contains the germ of several elements which were to predominate in my later compositions.[13]

: : :

In 1897, while studying counterpoint and fugue with André Gédalge,[14] I entered Gabriel Fauré's[15] composition class. I am pleased to acknowledge that I owe the most valuable elements of my technique to André Gédalge. As for Fauré, his advice as an artist gave me encouragement of no less value.

My unfinished, unpublished opera *Shéhérazade* dates from this period; it was rather strongly influenced by Russian music. I competed for the Prix de Rome in 1901 (when I received third prize), in 1902, and in 1903.[16] In 1905, the jury excluded me from the final round of the competition.

Jeux d'eau, which appeared in 1901, marks the beginning of all the pianistic innovations which have been noted in my works. This piece, inspired by the sound of water and the musical sounds made by fountains, cascades, and streams, is based on two themes, like the first movement of a sonata, without however submitting to the classical tonal scheme.

: : :

My String Quartet in F (1902–03) reflects a preoccupation with musical structure, imperfectly realized, no doubt, but which appears much clearer than in my previous compositions. *Shéhérazade,* in which Debussy's influence, at least spiritual, is rather evident, dates from 1903. Once again, I succumbed to the profound fascination which the Orient has exerted upon me since childhood.

The *Miroirs* (1905) form a collection of piano pieces which mark a rather considerable change in my harmonic evolution; this disconcerted musicians who until then had been thoroughly accustomed to my style.[17] The earliest of these pieces—and, it seems to me, the most characteristic—is "Oiseaux tristes," the second composition. In this work, I evoke birds lost in the torpor of a very somber forest, during the hottest hours of summertime.

: : :

After the *Miroirs,* I composed a Sonatine for piano and the *Histoires naturelles.* The direct, clear language and the profound, hidden poetry of Jules

Renard's works tempted me for a long time. The text itself demanded a particular kind of musical declamation from me, closely related to the inflections of the French language. The first performance of the *Histoires naturelles* at the Société Nationale de Musique in Paris provoked a genuine scandal, followed by lively polemics in the musical press of the time.[18]

The *Histoires naturelles* prepared me to compose *L'Heure espagnole*, a comic opera with a libretto by M. Franc-Nohain,[19] which is itself a sort of conversation in music. It affirms my intention of renewing the tradition of opera buffa.

Ma Mère l'Oye, children's pieces for piano, four hands, dates from 1908.[20] My intention in these pieces was to evoke the poetry of childhood, and this naturally led me to simplify my style and restrain my writing. I extracted a ballet from this work which was produced at the Théâtre des Arts; the work was written at Valvins for my young friends Mimie and Jean Godebski.

Gaspard de la nuit, piano pieces after Aloysius Bertrand,[21] are three romantic poems of transcendental virtuosity.

: : :

The title *Valses nobles et sentimentales* sufficiently indicates my intention of composing a series of waltzes in imitation of Schubert. The virtuosity which forms the basis of *Gaspard de la nuit* gives way to a markedly clearer kind of writing, which crystallizes the harmony and sharpens the profile of the music. The *Valses nobles et sentimentales* were first performed amid protestations and boos at a concert of the Société Musicale Indépendante, in which the names of the composers were not revealed. The audience voted on the probable authorship of each piece. The authorship of my piece was recognized—by a slight majority. The seventh waltz seems to me the most characteristic.

: : :

Daphnis et Chloé, a choreographic symphony in three parts, was commissioned by the director of the Ballet Russe, Serge Diaghilev. The argument is by Michel Fokine, then choreographer of the celebrated company. My intention in writing it was to compose a vast musical fresco, less concerned with archaism than with faithfulness to the Greece of my dreams, which is similar to that imagined and depicted by French artists at the end of the eighteenth century. The work is constructed symphonically according to a very strict tonal scheme by means of a few motifs; their development assures the work's symphonic homogeneity.

Sketched in 1907,[22] *Daphnis* was reworked several times, particularly the finale. First performed by the Ballet Russe, it is now in the repertoire of the Opéra.

Trois Poèmes de Mallarmé: I wished to transpose Mallarmé's poetry into music, especially that preciosity so full of meaning and so characteristic of him. "Surgi de la croupe et du bond" is the strangest, if not the most hermetic of his sonnets. In this work, I used approximately the same instrumental ensemble that is found in Schoenberg's *Pierrot lunaire*.

The Trio, whose first theme has a Basque flavor, was composed entirely in 1914, at Saint-Jean-de-Luz.

At the beginning of 1915 I enlisted in the army, and because of this my musical activities were interrupted until the autumn of 1917, when I was discharged. I then finished *Le Tombeau de Couperin*. The homage is directed less in fact to Couperin himself than to French music of the eighteenth century.[23]

After *Le Tombeau de Couperin*, poor health prevented me from composing for some time. I resumed composing with *La Valse*, a choreographic poem, which I had first thought of even before the *Rapsodie espagnole*. I conceived of this work as a sort of apotheosis of the Viennese waltz, mingled with, in my mind, the impression of a fantastic, fatal whirling. I situated *La Valse* in an imperial palace, about 1855. Although essentially intended to be danced, it has only been staged until now in the Antwerp theater and at Madame Rubinstein's[24] ballet performances.

The Sonata for Violin and Cello dates from 1920, when I settled in Montfort l'Amaury. I believe that this Sonata marks a turning point in the evolution of my career. In it, thinness of texture is pushed to the extreme. Harmonic charm is renounced, coupled with an increasingly conspicuous reaction in favor of melody.

On a different level, *L'Enfant et les sortilèges*, a lyric fantasy in two acts, also conforms to analogous preoccupations. The predominant concern with melody derives naturally from the story, which I took the liberty of treating in the spirit of an American operetta. Madame Colette's[25] fairy tale libretto justifies this liberty. The vocal line must dominate. The orchestra, though not renouncing virtuosity, is nevertheless of secondary importance.

Tzigane is a virtuoso piece in the style of a Hungarian rhapsody.

The *Chansons madécasses* seem to me to bring a new element, dramatic—indeed erotic, resulting from the subject matter of Parny's poems.[26] The songs form a sort of quartet in which the voice plays the role of the principal instrument. Simplicity is all-important. The independence of the part writing is pronounced, and it will be even more conspicuous in the Sonata for Violin and Piano.

I asserted this independence in writing a sonata for violin and piano, instruments which are in my opinion essentially incompatible. Far from balancing their contrasts, the Sonata reveals their incompatibility.

In 1928, I composed a *Boléro* for orchestra at the request of Madame Rubinstein. It is a dance in a very moderate tempo and absolutely uniform with regard to the melody, harmony, and the rhythm, which is marked unceasingly by the snare drum. The only element of variety is provided by the orchestral crescendo.

This is my essential work until now; in a future which I cannot foresee, I plan to write a concerto for piano and orchestra[27] and a large vocal work based on Joseph Delteil's *Jeanne d'Arc*.[28]

NOTES

1. Roland-Manuel, "Une Esquisse autobiographique de Maurice Ravel," *La Revue musicale* (December 1938), pp. 17–23.

2. The pseudonym of Alexis Manuel Lévy (1891–1966), French musicologist, composer, and critic. Introduced to Ravel by Erik Satie in 1911, he studied composition with Ravel and soon became one of his closest associates (see plate 2).

3. Following the publication of the Autobiographical Sketch, Roland-Manuel made two additions to the text, which are inserted in the copy of *La Revue musicale* in the Music Division of the Bibliothèque Nationale. These revisions (on the "Habanera" and *Miroirs*) will be found in notes 13 and 17 below.

4. A copy of the birth certificate is reproduced in Orenstein, *Ravel: Man and Musician*, plate 1, following page 218. It states that on March 8, 1875, at noon, Gracieuse Billac, aged 50, an illiterate fishmonger, appeared at the Town Hall of Ciboure. She declared that Marie Delouart, the wife of Pierre Joseph Ravel, presently living in Ciboure at 12 rue du Quai, gave birth to a male infant at 10:00 P.M. the previous evening, and wished to name him Joseph Maurice.

5. In May 1882, shortly after his seventh birthday, Maurice took his first piano lesson with Henry Ghys (1839–1908), who observed that his young pupil appeared to be "intelligent." Emile Decombes, a professor at the Conservatoire, was the young musician's second piano teacher. On June 2, 1889, twenty-four of his pupils, among them Reynaldo Hahn and Alfred Cortot, performed excerpts from various piano concerti in a recital at Salle Erard. Maurice played an excerpt from Moscheles' Third Concerto, thus marking his earliest known public performance.

6. In a letter to Roland-Manuel, Charles-René, a pupil of Léo Delibes, wrote about the coherence and melodic originality found in Ravel's earliest compositions: "There was a genuine unity in his artistic development; his conception of music was natural for him, and not, as with so many others, the result of effort" (Roland-Manuel, *A la gloire de Ravel*, Paris: Editions de la Nouvelle Revue Critique, 1938, p. 27).

7. Professor Eugène Anthiôme observed that his pupil was "rather gifted" and would progress well with serious effort. In July 1890, Maurice received second prize in the final competition of the academic year, and in July 1891 he was awarded first prize, thus enabling him to advance to the class of Charles de Bériot. Ravel's first prize—the

second prize went to none other than Alfred Cortot—turned out to be the only one he would ever receive at the Conservatoire.

8. In the fall of 1891, Maurice entered the piano class of Charles de Bériot (1833–1914) and the harmony class of Emile Pessard (1843–1917). Because of his repeated failures to win a prize, as required by the bylaws of the Conservatoire, he was dismissed from both classes in July 1895. On the basis of Professor Bériot's reports, it appears that Ravel played a wide variety of nineteenth-century music in a spirited, highly emotional manner. He was capable of performing well when he practiced, but when he did not, which was often the case, his playing appears to have exasperated his teacher.

9. Most of Ravel's early works written in the 1890s, which were long considered lost, were recovered by this writer and published by Salabert in 1975. In addition to the *Sérénade grotesque* (piano, c. 1893), and the *Ballade de la Reine morte d'aimer* (voice and piano, poem by Roland de Marès, c. 1893), other compositions include *Sites auriculaires* (two pianos, 1895–97, consisting of "Habanera" and "Entre cloches"), a Sonata for Violin and Piano (in one movement, 1897), *Chanson du rouet* (voice and piano, poem by Leconte de Lisle, 1898), *Si morne!* (voice and piano, poem by Emile Verhaeren, 1898), and the Overture to *Shéhérazade* (orchestra, 1898). *Sites auriculaires* and the Overture to *Shéhérazade* were performed but once in Ravel's lifetime and promptly retracted. All of the other works were given their world première at Charles S. Colden Auditorium in Queens College, Flushing, New York, on February 23, 1975, in a concert which was recorded live by the Musical Heritage Society (MHS 3581).

10. At first, Professor Pessard found his student to be "a rather good harmonist," who had some "natural ability." Soon after, however, it appears that Maurice arrived late to class, and although "very gifted," he was also "somewhat heedless" with regard to his work. Reading between the lines of Professor Pessard's reports, one gets the impression that Ravel quickly assimilated everything the good professor had to teach and was captivated by harmonies which were far in advance of those taught in class. Nevertheless, he thoroughly assimilated Henri Reber's *Traité d'harmonie* (which was approved by the Conservatoire in 1862) and its supplement by Théodore Dubois (1889).

11. In February 1893 Ravel and Ricardo Viñes performed the *Trois Valses romantiques* for Chabrier (1841–1894). The meeting made a lasting impression on Ravel, who maintained a lifelong interest in Chabrier's music.

12. In the early 1890s, Joseph Ravel introduced his son to Erik Satie (1866–1925), who was leading a Bohemian life in Montmartre and playing the piano at the Café de la Nouvelle Athènes. Satie's colorful personality and unorthodox music made a strong impression on the young musician, who would later take pleasure in furthering his colleague's career. In the postwar years, Satie aligned himself with the younger generation and turned against his former benefactor. Despite this, Ravel continued to treat him with deference.

13. Additional statement by Roland-Manuel: "I believe that the 'Habanera,' with its ostinato pedal point and its chords with multiple appoggiaturas, contains the germ of several elements which were to predominate in my later compositions." Among these elements, one may note the influence of Spain and of dance rhythms. Furthermore, a

similar type of harmonic language is found in "Noctuelles" (*Miroirs*) and "Le Gibet" (*Gaspard de la nuit*).

14. Gédalge (1856–1926) joined the faculty of the Conservatoire in 1905, and his *Traité de la fugue* was used as the standard text for the study of counterpoint. A distinguished pedagogue, he taught many composers, among them Arthur Honegger, Darius Milhaud, and Florent Schmitt. Upon learning of Gédalge's death, Ravel wrote the following brief homage:

> I heard the news in Oslo; it was a severe blow. You may not understand everything that Gédalge meant to me: he taught me to realize the possibilities and structural attempts which may be seen in my earliest works. His teaching was of unusual clarity: with him, one understood immediately that *technique* is not simply a scholastic abstraction. Friendship was not the only reason that I dedicated the Trio to him: the homage goes directly to the teacher. (*La Revue musicale*, March 1, 1926, p. 255.)

15. The cordial, liberal atmosphere of Fauré's class has been compared to that of Mallarmé's salon. Fauré (1845–1924) followed Ravel's career with keen interest, and Ravel reciprocated this affection, dedicating *Jeux d'eau* and the String Quartet to his "dear teacher" (see plate 3). Fauré's final class report, written in June 1900, offers a perspicacious description of his twenty-five-year-old student: "Very good student, hardworking and punctual. Musical nature very taken with innovation, with a disarming sincerity!" Despite this encouragement, Ravel was expelled from his composition class in July 1900, as he failed to win a prize in two consecutive fugue competitions. (One fugue was given a zero by the director of the Conservatoire, Théodore Dubois, with the following comment: "Impossible, owing to terrible inaccuracies in writing.") Nevertheless, Ravel continued to participate in Fauré's class as an auditor. Listed in the Conservatoire's registry as a "former student," he remained an auditor until 1903, when he left the Conservatoire for the last time.

16. Actually, Ravel entered the Prix de Rome competition for the first time in May 1900. After submitting a fugue and a choral piece, *Les Bayadères*, he was eliminated in the preliminary round. (The autographs of all his Prix de Rome essays are found in the Music Division of the Bibliothèque Nationale.)

17. Additional statement by Roland-Manuel:

> The title *Miroirs* (Mirrors), five piano pieces composed in 1905, has authorized my critics to consider this collection among those works which belong to the impressionist movement. I do not contradict this at all, if one understands the term by analogy. A rather fleeting analogy, moreover, since impressionism does not seem to have any precise meaning outside the domain of painting. In any case, the word Mirror should not lead one to assume that I wish to affirm a subjectivistic theory of art. A sentence by Shakespeare helped me to formulate a completely opposite position: . . . 'the eye sees not itself But by reflection, by some other things.' (*Julius Caesar*, act 1, scene 2.)

18. The *Journal* of Jules Renard (1864–1910) contains the following entry for January 12, 1907:

M. Ravel, the composer of the *Histoires naturelles*, dark, rich, and elegant, urges me to go and hear his songs tonight. I told him I knew nothing about music, and asked him what he had been able to add to the *Histoires naturelles*. He replied: I did not intend to add anything, only to interpret them.

But in what way?

I have tried to say in music what you say with words, when you are in front of a tree, for example. I think and feel in music, and should like to think and feel the same things as you. There is instinctive, sentimental music, like mine—naturally you must learn your craft first—and intellectual music, like [Vincent] d'Indy's. The audience this evening will consist mainly of d'Indys; they don't recognize feeling and don't wish to explain it. I take the opposite view, but they must find my work interesting since they are willing to program it. This test tonight is very important for me. In any case I can rely on my interpreter [Jane Bathori]: she is excellent. (Jules Renard, *Journal*, edited by Léon Guichard and Gilbert Sigaux, Paris: Librairie Gallimard, 1960, pp. 1100–01.)

19. The pen name of Maurice-Etienne Legrand (1873–1934). Nohain is the name of a river near Corbigny, the author's birthplace. His work often contains curious rhymes, humorous situations, and charming buffoonery, all of which abound in the libretto of *L'Heure espagnole*. This one-act comedy was first performed in 1904 at the Odéon theater with marked success. Ravel wrote to Franc-Nohain, requesting permission to adapt the play. The author, like Jules Renard, was amazed that anyone would consider setting his work to music, but willingly gave his permission.

20. Inadvertently dated 1918 in the text.

21. The reputation of Aloysius Bertrand (1807–1841) rests entirely upon *Gaspard de la nuit*, which was written about 1830 and published posthumously in 1842. The complete texts of "Ondine," "Le Gibet," and "Scarbo" appear in the Durand edition, and the hauntingly evocative Romanticism of Bertrand's visions are remarkably interpreted in these descriptive tone poems.

22. Much ink has been spilled over this date. Roland-Manuel wrote in a footnote: "Ravel is mistaken by two years. The inaccuracy is indisputable as the Ballet Russe appeared for the first time in 1909." Indeed, Ravel's letter to Madame René de Saint-Marceaux indicates that initial work on the ballet libretto began in June, 1909 (see letter no. 64). However, Serge Lifar claimed that Diaghilev and Ravel met in 1906, and it was thus possible that some work on *Daphnis*—perhaps not as yet conceived of as a ballet— might have been carried out before 1909. (Serge Lifar, "Maurice Ravel et le Ballet," *La Revue musicale*, December 1938, p. 75.)

23. Nevertheless, in 1914, while working on *Le Tombeau de Couperin*, Ravel returned to the world of eighteenth-century French music by writing a piano transcription of a forlane by François Couperin (1668–1733), taken from the chamber music entitled *Concerts royaux*. (The transcription has been printed in my article "Some Unpublished Music," pp. 330–31.)

24. The Russian dancer Ida Rubinstein (1885–1960) began her career in Diaghilev's Ballet Russe and later formed her own company. She was also a generous patroness of the arts. Among the ballets she introduced were Debussy's *Le Martyre de Saint Sébastien* (1911), Schmitt's *La Tragédie de Salomé* (1919), d'Indy's *Istar* (1924), Honegger's *L'Impératrice aux rochers* (1927), and Stravinsky's *Le Baiser de la fée* (1928).

25. The celebrated author Sidonie-Gabrielle Colette (1873–1954) frequently wrote about life as she had experienced it, from her childhood in Burgundy to her career as a mime dancer in the music halls of Paris. The enchanting world of animals, particularly cats, is another important motif in her work, and herein lies an important link between the librettist and the composer of *L'Enfant et les sortilèges*. The work was introduced at the Monte Carlo Opera in March, 1925, some twenty-five years after Colette and Ravel first met.

26. The *Chansons madécasses*, twelve poems in prose by Evariste-Désiré de Parny (1753–1814), appeared in 1787. Although Parny claimed to have collected and translated several songs of the Madagascan natives, the fact is that he never set foot in Madagascar and did not speak Malagasy. Ravel considered his cycle of three songs to be one of his most important postwar compositions, as it achieved a maximum of expression while utilizing a marked economy of means.

27. Following the *Boléro*, Ravel completed three works: two piano concerti, one for the left hand and the other in G Major, and the song cycle *Don Quichotte à Dulcinée*, based on the poems by Paul Morand.

28. Although *Jeanne d'Arc* was not even partially sketched, Ravel discussed it at length in an interview printed in *Excelsior* on September 24, 1933 (see p. 499). Ravel and Delteil (1894–1977) were on cordial terms, and the composer's library contains several personally dedicated books by the author, including two copies of *Jeanne d'Arc* (Paris: Bernard Grasset, 1925 and 1926).

Some Reflections on Music[1]

I have never felt the need to formulate, either for the benefit of others or for myself, the principles of my aesthetic. If I were called upon to do so, I would ask to be allowed to identify myself with the simple pronouncements made by Mozart on this subject. He confined himself to saying that there is nothing that music can not undertake to do, or dare, or portray, provided it continues to charm and always remains music.[2]

I am sometimes credited with opinions which appear very paradoxical concerning the falsity of art and the dangers of sincerity. The fact is I refuse simply and absolutely to confound the *conscience* of an artist, which is one thing, with his *sincerity*, which is another. Sincerity is of no value unless one's conscience helps to make it apparent. This conscience compels us to turn ourselves into good craftsmen. My objective, therefore, is technical perfection. I can strive unceasingly to this end, since I am certain of never being able to attain it. The important thing is to get nearer to it all the time.

Art, no doubt, has other *effects*, but the artist, in my opinion, should have no other aim.

NOTES

1. Roland-Manuel, "Lettres de Maurice Ravel," p. 53. According to Roland-Manuel, this statement concluded the interview which resulted in the Autobiographical Sketch.

2. It is fitting that Ravel turned to Mozart for aesthetic counsel, as he revered the Austrian master above all other composers. Indeed, throughout his career, Ravel emulated Mozart's clarity of expression, perfection of workmanship, and his unique ability to balance classical symmetry with the element of surprise. Ravel once observed that his own music was "quite simple, nothing but Mozart," a statement which contains a goodly element of truth. In a letter to his father dated September 26, 1781, in which he discussed *The Abduction from the Seraglio*, Mozart wrote about Osmin's aria in act 1 as follows:

For just as a man in such a towering rage oversteps all the bounds of order, moderation, and propriety, and completely forgets himself, so must the music too forget itself. But as passions, whether violent or not, must never be expressed in such a way as to excite disgust, and as music, even in the most terrible situations, must never offend the ear, but must please the hearer, or in other words must never cease to be music, I have gone from F (the key in which the aria is written), not into a remote key, but into a related one, not, however, into its nearest relative D minor, but into the more remote A minor. (Alfred Einstein, *Mozart, His Character, His Work*, New York: Oxford University Press, 1962, pp. 384–85.)

3 : : :

Contemporary Music[1]

On April 6 and 7, 1928, at the invitation of the Rice Institute (now Rice University) in Houston, Texas, Ravel participated in two recitals devoted to his music.[2] As he had previously done during his four-month tour in North America, the composer played several of his piano pieces (among them the Sonatine, "La Vallée des cloches" from Miroirs, and the "Rigaudon" from Le Tombeau de Couperin), and assisted in performing various vocal and chamber works (Shéhérazade, and the recently completed Sonata for Violin and Piano). The recital on April 7 was preceded by a lecture entitled Contemporary Music. *It is paradoxical but true that this lecture—apparently the only one Ravel ever gave—has come down to us in an English translation.[3] The translator is still unknown and the French text has yet to be recovered.[4] All of this notwithstanding, the lecture itself is of extraordinary interest. Stressing the importance of national and individual consciousness in the creation of a work of art, Ravel discusses the contemporary European musical scene, evaluating the achievements of a number of his colleagues, among them Debussy, Satie, and* Les Six, *interspersed with revealing observations about his own compositions and creative process. He touches upon the musical relationship of Liszt and Wagner, the work of Bartók and Kodály, the influence of Schoenberg, the poetry of Mallarmé, and concludes by urging his hosts to return to their roots—jazz, blues, Negro spirituals, and so on—in order to create a genuinely American school of music.*

Ravel presents an optimistic survey of the contemporary scene in concise, dignified language. A personal blend of impartiality, candor, and modesty is evident throughout this remarkable lecture.

It is of course impossible to offer any adequate survey of contemporary music or even of one of its phases within the space of a single lecture; moreover, I hasten to admit that there is only one thing which I should find still more difficult, and that would be to explain my own music or comment upon it; indeed, were I in position fully to explain my music, I should then be inclined to doubt its worth and value. The reasons which lead me to this conclusion are, perhaps, different from those generally cited by lecturers on art. For instance, it is often said that music defies analysis, whereas other fine arts, such as painting, sculpture, and architecture, have not a medium of manifestation so intangible, elusive, and evanescent as the vibration of sound. On this point I differ somewhat, because I am under the impression that current progress in acoustical science makes possible dimensional measurements of sound as many and as varied as are those of other means of artistic expression, employed, for example, in architecture. I would even say that since the young Russian scientist, Theremin, has perfected his original instruments, and can now transform ethereal vibrations into tonal vibrations of any pitch, intensity, or quality that he may desire, the sound part of music would seem to have come quite within the reach of analysis. So it is not because of the elusiveness of sound vibrations that I consider it impossible to explain or judge a work of musical art; indeed, I have the same feeling about other works of art whether in painting, sculpture, or architecture. Would it be, then, that I do not accept the so-called classical laws of harmony, counterpoint, and so on? Whether I recognize their validity or not is of little importance to me in judging contemporary compositions, for these classical laws originated in works of the past; they have been formulated and adopted by teachers in their efforts to find a permanent basis, solid and suitable, for their courses of instruction; and this body of doctrine has undergone change after change in accommodating itself to new laws peculiar to new compositions appearing from time to time. No academic attempt to establish permanent laws, however, ever helped or hindered the advancement of work in art. The matter might be summed up by saying that in musical treatises there are no such laws as would be of any avail in judging a contemporary musical work of art. Apparently the uselessness of all such arguments must come from the fact that such would-be laws are dealing only with the obvious and superficial part of the work of art without ever reaching those infinitely minute roots of the artist's sensitiveness and personal reaction. The elusive roots, or sources, are often sensed as two in character: one might be called the national consciousness, its territory being rather extensive; while the other, the individual consciousness, seems to be the product of an egocentric process. Both defy classification and analysis as well, yet every sensitive artist perceives the value of their influence in the creation of a real work of art. The manifestation of these two types of consciousness in music may break or satisfy all the academic rules, but such circumstance is of insignificant importance compared with the real aim, namely, fullness and sincerity of expression. We have here to do, perhaps, with that inner motion which purposely sets our intelligence and perception to seek its own development in its own atmosphere and tradition—not its historical tradition, but the tradition which heredity makes one feel to be true to one's nature. Such search may be intensively selective, and then becomes a clearing process applied to our natural gifts and supervised by our individual consciousness. Here, again, I insist that no stated laws can be given whereby to judge the degree of perfection attained in this process on the part of the individual, inasmuch as what we are attempting to discover is only sensed and as yet unknown. So were I able to explain and demonstrate the value of my own works, it would then prove, at least from my personal point of view, that they are constructed altogether of obvious, superficial, tangible elements within easy reach of formal analysis, and, therefore, that these works of mine are not perfect works of art. The difficulty remains when one attempts either to classify or to state definitely relative estimates of one's contemporaries in music, not excepting those among one's own countrymen. Indeed, from this point of view, any attempt to arrive at a definite judgment with respect to a work of art seems to me to be folly.

On the initial performance of a new musical composition, the first impression of the public is generally one of reaction to the more superficial elements of its music, that is to say, to its external manifestations rather than to its inner content. The listener is impressed by some unimportant peculiarity in the medium of expression, and yet the idiom of expression, even if considered in its completeness, is only the means and not the end in itself, and often it is not until years after, when the means of expression have finally surrendered all their secrets, that the real inner emotion of the music becomes apparent to the listener. Thus, for example, if we consider present-day reviews of the compositions of Arnold Schoenberg and Darius Milhaud, it often seems as though chromatism and atonality on the one hand, and diatonism versus polytonality on the other, were the only significant traits of these two artists; nevertheless, in either case, it often seems as though such a judgment would reveal but the garb concealing or adorning their emotional sensitiveness, and we should always remember that sensitiveness and emotion constitute the real content of a work of art. Furthermore, the acute and subtle perception guiding the artist in his creative work is itself in continuous evolution, for, just as any of the ordinary senses may be trained and made to perceive better to-day than yesterday, so this perception within the individual and national heritage of atmosphere and tradition may become keener and keener year after year, leaving no place for standardized and permanent classification.

I may be able to express my thought more perfectly if we consider briefly these ideas of nationalism and individualism in their relations to music. And what I hazard to express in this connection is my individual understanding of the more striking characteristics of contemporary music as exhibited in the works of some of my friends. At all events, I hope in this way to illustrate my thought more adequately.

For example, in the works of Darius Milhaud, probably the most important of our younger French composers, one is frequently impressed by the vastness of the composer's conceptions. This quality of Milhaud's music is far more individual than his use, so frequently commented upon, and often criticised, of polytonality (a conception of the simultaneous use of several tonalities, of which we may find embryonic examples as early as the chorals of J. S. Bach, in certain passages of Beethoven, and in the definite use thereof by Richard Strauss). If we consider broadly one of his larger works, the "Choéphores," we soon discover that on attaining the climax of a series of utterances tragic in character, in the course of which the most sweeping use is made of all the resources of musical composition, including polytonal writing, Milhaud nevertheless reaches still profounder depths of his own artistic consciousness in a scene where a strong pathetic psalmody is accompanied only by percussion. Here it is no longer polytonality which expresses Milhaud, and yet this is one of the pages where Milhaud most profoundly reveals himself. Of similar significance is the fact that in one of his latest works, *Les Malheurs d'Orphée*, in its recent American première at one of the New York concerts of Pro Musica, Milhaud's occasional use of polytonality is so intricately interwoven with lyric and poetic elements as to be scarcely distinguishable, while his acknowledged artistic personality reappears clothed with a certain clarity of melodic design altogether Gallic in character. Again, we might note the singularly dramatic qualities of Delannoy, the facile and popular musical content of works of Poulenc, the accuracy of form and elegance of orchestration in Roland-Manuel, and the peculiar tendency on the part of G. Auric to etch his music sharply, often to the point of an acute and satiric vein. Such inherent and widely divergent traits appertain to different individuals rather than to a single school; and this could also be said of the genial music of Germaine Tailleferre. In Arthur Honegger, still another member of what a French critic has labeled the *Groupe des Six*, we find, not only individual traits, but hereditary and racial characteristics altogether different from those of the four composers just mentioned, and this racial consciousness of Honegger he expresses without reserve. From his musical education, received at the hands of French teachers on French soil, Honegger seems to have conserved a facility in writing which he uses for self-expression along the lines of German expansiveness, and his music remains true to his racial consciousness—that is to say, the German consciousness, for he was born of German-Swiss parentage. The latter statement is meant neither in a derogatory sense, nor in one of praise; it simply says that, while we can reconcile the various tendencies expressed by Milhaud, Poulenc, and Auric, as being all equally rooted in French national consciousness, it is from the German national consciousness that the art of Honegger springs. If we should consider still other young French musicians, we should find this phase of racial consciousness again in evidence; for we should not find the German character in the curiously dramatic qualities of M. Delannoy's music, or in the refined and intimate music of Roland-Manuel.

This national consciousness of musicians distinctively German is expansive, while our French consciousness is one of reserve. In virtue of the indissoluble ties binding each to his respective national consciousness, it is, of course, inconceivable that either one should be able to express himself adequately in the language of the other. Nationalism does not deprive the composer either of his personal soul or of its individual expression, for each creative artist has within him laws peculiar to his own being. These laws, peculiar to the artist himself, are, perhaps, the most momentous elements at play in the whole process of musical creation; they seem to be determined through an interplay of national and individual consciousness; and they can be imparted to the artist by no teacher, for they spring from his own heritage, and are first perceived only by himself. Such laws in the course of years may become those of a school, of pupils, or imitators, or of followers, but whenever a real artist appears, he evolves from his own consciousness new laws peculiar to himself. Incidentally, I should like to remark that musicians who are true alike to their national consciousness and to their own individuality often appreciate compositions altogether different from their own, but a Germanized French musician or a Gallicized musician of Germany will have a tendency to fail in understanding the musical works of others—the hybrid failing to recognize other personalities because of the loss of its own individuality. If we should now consider our lawful portion of inheritance from other musicians, the evident value of such a heritage, and the eventual danger of plagiarism, I should place on the legitimate side exchanges in emotional expression, the influence of experimental or incomplete compositions, which may be absorbed or assimilated without loss either of individual or of national consciousness; while, on the opposite side, I would put all efforts, either through imitation or plagiarism, to conceal absence or weakness of personality. It may sometimes be extremely difficult to decide these questions with respect to a particular work, but here again, the keen perception of the artist is the only dependable guide. Perhaps one of the most curious cases of exchanges of influence is that of Hérold, Weber, and Rossini; these three composers were strongly influenced in turn by a common characteristic of their respective works—namely, their romanticism; but each of the three held these interchanges of influence subservient to his own respective national consciousness. It was French romantic music that Hérold wrote, Rossini's romanticism was obviously Italian, while Weber remained to the end a German romanticist. Such influences enlarge the horizon of the aspiring artist without contracting either his personality or his heritage. Relations of this sort in works of some of my predecessors or contemporaries I shall be pointing out later on in this lecture. It is very important to estimate these influences carefully, inasmuch as they may be of good or ill effect, depending upon the quality of the influence and even more upon the strength of the personality subjected to them. For example, the influence of Liszt on Wagner was altogether considerable, and yet the personality of the latter was in no way impaired, despite the generous way in which he used the artistic heritage of his father-in-law. The thematic influence of Liszt on Wagner is certainly more than obvious, but the æsthetic of Wagner, however extensive, is essentially individual. Another significant influence, somewhat unique, and deriving at least partially from Chabrier, is that of Erik Satie, which has had appreciable effect upon Debussy, myself, and indeed most of the modern French composers. Satie was possessed of an extremely keen intelligence. His was the inventor's mind par excellence. He was a great experimenter. His experiments may never have reached the degree of development or realization attained by Liszt; but, alike in multiplicity and importance, these experiments have been of inestimable value. Simply and ingeniously Satie pointed the way, but as soon as another musician took to the trail he had indicated, Satie would immediately change his own orientation and without hesitation open up still another path to new fields of experimentation. He thus became the inspiration of countless progressive tendencies; and while he himself may, perhaps, never have wrought out of his own discoveries a single complete work of art, nevertheless we have to-day many such works which might not have come into existence if Satie had never lived. This influence of his was not in the least dogmatic, and, for this reason, of all the greater value to other musicians. Debussy held him in the highest esteem. Influences such as his are as fertile soil, propitious to the growth of rare flowers, wherein the individual consciousness, the indispensable seed, nourished in better surroundings thus provided, may still unfold according to its own essential nature, national, racial, or individual.

As often as not, the national consciousness is the creative artist's original source of inspiration. For example, the objectivity and clarity of design exhibited by our earliest composers furnished a rich heritage to our incomparable C. A. Debussy, the most phenomenal genius in the history of French music. Does this mean to say that Debussy was only an imitator? Certainly not! Again, is the symbolism of Debussy, his so-called impressionism, at variance with the Gallic spirit? Quite the contrary, because beneath the fine and delicate lacework of atmospheric surface, one may easily discover a refined precision of design, characteristically French. His genius was obviously one of great individuality, creating its own laws, constantly in evolution, expressing itself freely, yet always faithful to French tradition. For Debussy, the musician and the man, I have had profound admiration, but by nature I am different from Debussy, and while I consider that Debussy may not have been altogether alien to my personal inheritance, I should identify also with the earlier phase of my evolution Gabriel Fauré, Emmanuel Chabrier, and Erik Satie. The æsthetic of Edgar Allan Poe, your great American, has been of singular importance to me, and also the immaterial poetry of Mallarmé—unbounded visions, yet precise in design, enclosed in a mystery of sombre abstractions—an art where all the elements are so intimately bound up together that one cannot analyze, but only sense, its effect. Nevertheless I believe that I myself have always followed a direction opposite to that of Debussy's symbolism.

Let us now turn to another aspect of my own work which may be of more immediate interest to you. To my mind, the "blues" is one of your greatest musical assets, truly American despite earlier contributory influences from Africa and Spain. Musicians have asked me how I came to write "blues" as the second movement of my recently completed sonata for violin and piano. Here again the same process, to which I have already alluded, is in evidence, for, while I adopted this popular form of your music, I venture to say that nevertheless it is French music, Ravel's music, that I have written. Indeed, these popular forms are but the materials of construction, and the work of art appears only on mature conception where no detail has been left to chance. Moreover, minute stylization in the manipulation of these materials is altogether essential. To understand more fully what I mean by the process to which I refer, it would be sufficient to have these same "blues" treated by some of your own musicians and by musicians of European countries other than France, when you would certainly find the resulting compositions to be widely divergent, most of them bearing the national characteristics of their respective composers, despite the unique nationality of their initial material, the American "blues". Think of the striking and essential differences to be noted in the "jazz" and "rags" of Milhaud, Stravinsky, Casella, Hindemith, and so on. The individualities of these composers are stronger than the materials appropriated. They mould popular forms to meet the requirements of their own individual art. Again— nothing left to chance; again—minute stylization of the materials employed, while the styles become as numerous as the composers themselves.

In my own work of composition I find a long period of conscious gestation, in general, necessary. During this interval, I come gradually to see, and with growing precision, the form and evolution which the subsequent work should have as a whole. I may thus be occupied for years without writing a single note of the work—after which the writing goes relatively rapidly; but there is still much time to be spent in eliminating everything that might be regarded as superfluous, in order to realize as completely as possible the longed-for final clarity. Then comes the time when new conceptions have to be formulated for further composition, but these cannot be forced artificially, for they come only of their own free will, and often originate in some very remote perception, without manifesting themselves until long years after.

For the last fifteen or twenty years musicians and critics alike have taken great interest in the two divergent tendencies I have already mentioned: atonality and polytonality. And in the impassioned discussions of partisans we have often heard or read that atonality is a blind alley leading nowhere, but I do not accept the validity of this opinion; because, while as a system it may be so, it certainly cannot be as an influence. In fact, the influence of Schoenberg may be overwhelming on his followers, but the significance of his art is to be identified with influences of a more subtle kind—not the system, but the æsthetic, of his art. I am quite conscious of the fact that my *Chansons madécasses* are in no way Schoenbergian, but I do not know whether I ever should have been able to write them had Schoenberg never written. On the other hand, it has often been said that my music has influenced many of my contemporaries. In particular it has been claimed with some insistence that the earlier appearance of my *Jeux d'eau* possibly influenced Debussy in the writing of his *Jardins sous la pluie,* while a coincidence, even more striking, has been suggested in the case of my *Habanera*; but comments of this sort I must leave to others. It could very well be, however, that conceptions, apparently similar in character, should mature in the consciousness of two different composers at almost the same time without implying direct influence of either one upon the other. In such case, the compositions may have numerous external analogies, but we can feel the difference in individuality of the two composers, just as no two human beings are ever altogether identical—considering of course at the moment only those composers who have actually sought and discovered their own personality. Again, if under apparently similar outward expression we fail to find dissimilar inner manifestations, it is likely that one of the two composers is a plagiarist of the other.

But we have been wandering somewhat from the subject of our lecture, and, perhaps, for no better reason than that I am unable to say much more about my own compositions and the methods by which they have been brought into being. When the first stroke of a work has been written, and the process of elimination begun, the severe effort toward perfection proceeds by means almost intangible, seemingly directed by currents of inner forces, so intimate and intricate in character as to defy all analysis. Real art, I repeat, is not to be recognized by definitions, or revealed by analysis: we sense its manifestations and we feel its presence: it is apprehended in no other way.

Before closing this short address I wish to say again how very happy I am in visiting your country, and all the more so because my journey is enabling me to become still more conversant with those elements which are contributing to the gradual formation of a veritable school of American music. That this school will become notable in its final evolution I have not the slightest doubt, and I am also convinced that it will realize a national expression quite as different from the music of Europeans as you yourselves are different from them. Here again, for the nurture of the most sensitive and imaginative of our young composers we should consider national heritage in all its entirety. There are always self-appointed promoters of nationalism in plenty, who profess their creed with a vengeance, but rarely do they agree as to the means to be employed. Among these nationalists in music we can always distinguish two distinct clans constantly waging their warfare of criticism. Now criticism is easy, but art is difficult. Most of these nationalists are painstaking enough in criticism, but few of them are sufficiently so in self-examination. One group believes that folk-lore is the only requisite to national music; the other predicts the birth of national music in the individual of to-day. Meanwhile, within the first clan itself dissension goes on: "Folk-lore? But what in particular is our folk-lore? Indian tunes? But are they American? . . . Negro spirituals? Blues? But are these American?" and so on, until nothing is left of national background. And the field is at last wide open for those musicians whose greatest fear is to find themselves confronted by mysterious urges to break academic rules rather than belie individual consciousness. Thereupon these musicians, good bourgeois as they are, compose their music according to the classical rules of the European epoch, while the folk-lorists, apostles of popular airs, shout in their purism: "Can this be American music if inspired by Europe?" We are thus caught up in a vicious and unproductive circle, unless we turn once more to the past and consider how certain works, held to be essentially national in character, were produced. Wagner is generally regarded as purely Germanic and yet, as we have already remarked, a great deal of his thematic material was derived from the highly imaginative Franz Liszt, a Hungarian whose own works often and indubitably exhibit a rich flavor of Hungarian folk-lore. It is quite certain that Wagner's remarkable achievement depended upon his success in formulating his own style of manifestation, yet one may doubt that he would ever have written as he did if the abundant wealth of material accumulated by Liszt had not been more or less at his disposal. For example, to the completion of such a work as *Tristan und Isolde,* Wagner's extraordinary skill in construction, Liszt's unusual thematic genius, and folk-lore as well—all made contribution. Folk-lore and individual consciousness are alike necessary; and, in nations that are still young from a musical point of view, persistent fidelity of search in these two directions seems to be the greatest lack on the part of composers. With respect to individual consciousness let us not deceive ourselves: its discovery and development is more often than not a lifelong process. Nor should individuality ever be confused with eccentricity. Now, as to collecting the popular songs of which the national folk-lore is made up, I could do no better than cite the remarkable record of two distinguished Hungarian musicians, Béla Bartók and Zoltán Kodály, in personality altogether unlike, but mutually interested in folk-lore. These gentlemen, from 1905 to 1918, collected more than twelve thousand such songs of Hungary and adjacent countries. Of this number at least six thousand are Hungarian, and Bartók says that he could easily collect an additional thousand every year. Moreover, while assembling in tangible form this incomparable national heritage of Hungarian musicians, Messrs. Bartók and Kodály have with equally painstaking care preserved the quality of its material in accurate documentary form by recording the songs on gramophone disks, which are capable of catching and holding permanently the most elusive of folk-lore characteristics, including small variations in pitch, intensity, and quality of sound, for which the cruder medium of our ordinary written musical notation is utterly inadequate.

In conclusion I would say that even if negro music is not of purely American origin, nevertheless I believe it will prove to be an effective factor in the founding of an American school of music. At all events, may this national American music of yours embody a great deal of the rich and diverting rhythm of your jazz, a great deal of the emotional expression in your blues, and a great deal of the sentiment and spirit characteristic of your popular melodies and songs, worthily deriving from, and in turn contributing to, a noble national heritage in music.

NOTES

1. Lecture delivered under the auspices of the Rice Institute Lectureship in Music by Maurice Ravel in the Scottish Rite Cathedral, Houston, Texas, April 7, 1928.

2. The programs are reprinted in Orenstein, *Ravel: Man and Musician*, plates 13 and 14.

3. First printed in *The Rice Institute Pamphlet*, 15 (April 1928), pp. 131–45, the speech was reprinted together with an introduction by Bohdan Pilarski, "Une Conférence de Maurice Ravel à Houston (1928)," in the *Revue de musicologie*, 50 (December 1964), pp. 208–21. Although it is true that Ravel could have delivered his lecture only in French, it is clear that he had an English translation with him. The archives of the Cleveland Museum of Art (where Ravel and soprano Lisa Roma gave a lecture-recital on Sunday afternoon January 22, 1928) contain a condensed version of his speech (in English), which was read on several occasions during the North American tour.

4. Roland-Manuel undoubtedly assisted in preparing the French text (see Ravel's postcard to him—no. 289).

II

Correspondence

1. Pierre Joseph Ravel to his mother[1]

Pensionnat Saint François   December 12, 1845
Onex, Canton de Genève[2]
Dear Mama

I forgot to ask you when you came to see me if you would agree to allow me to study music because M. Angelin told us that the music teacher will be coming next week and I would indeed be happy if you would kindly allow me to learn because it would give me much pleasure, my dear Mama. I had said that I would like to play the flute but was told that this would give me a stomach ache so I would prefer to play the trumpet if you would be so kind. Next week we will also begin drawing which will give me much pleasure. In your reply, write to me about yourself and about my dear papa and my sisters. Embrace my papa and my sisters, also give my greetings to our parish priest, to M. and Mme Dubouches and to my aunt. Adieu my dear mama, I embrace you with all my heart. Adieu

Your respectful son
Joseph Ravel

1. This letter, written by Maurice Ravel's father at the age of thirteen, is the earliest known letter written by a member of the Ravel family. It is addressed to Madame Ravel, grocer in Versoix, Canton of Geneva, Switzerland (see plate 4).
2. Saint Francis Private Boarding School, Onex, Canton of Geneva.

2. to Madame René de Saint-Marceaux[1]

Hôtel du Nord   Saturday the 20th [August 1898]
Granville
Madame,

The little symbolist, very happy that you deign to occupy yourself a bit with his music, deeply regrets to have perpetrated no new vocal work in recent days. Some may believe that remorse overwhelms him. Not he, unfortunately, for he is incorrigible and quite ready to do nothing about it. While waiting, he is doing a bit of fugue and a lot of bicycling. He will take the liberty of addressing to you his latest composition, which dates from at least two months ago, and which by chance is singable.[2]

As for the bizarre contexture of certain phrases, I strongly suspect that the musical Alcibiades wished them to be so.[3]

Pardon him, Madame, and kindly accept his most respectful homage.
Maurice Ravel

1. In the late 1890s, Gabriel Fauré began to take his composition class to the home of the Parisian hostess Madame René de Saint-Marceaux, who frequently performed their

vocal works. In an unpublished diary, she recalled Ravel's reaction to her performance of the two *Epigrammes de Clément Marot*: "Is he pleased to hear his music? One can't tell. What a strange chap. Talented, with so much mischievousness" (diary in the private collection of B. de Saint-Marceaux). This "mischievous" quality, coupled with Ravel's ironic, cool humor, is evident in this extraordinary letter, written during the summer of 1898, when the twenty-three-year-old student was engaged as a pianist in the casino at Granville, a popular seaside resort in Normandy.

2. The composition in question is the *Chanson du rouet* (Song of the Spinning Wheel), for voice and piano, based on a poem by Leconte de Lisle. Completed on June 2, 1898, it was first published by Salabert in 1975.

3. If the "musical Alcibiades" bears any reference to the Athenian statesman, Ravel may have compared himself, as it were, to a musical lawgiver, in order to justify certain "bizarre" liberties. Indeed, one passage in the *Chanson du rouet* contains a quotation from the Gregorian sequence *Dies Irae,* which is harmonized with Chopinesque chromaticism! (The autograph of this letter is reproduced in Orenstein, *Ravel: Man and Musician,* plate 5.)

3. Gabriel Fauré to Ernest Chausson[1]

[c. May 20, 1899][2]

My dear friend,

It is I who encouraged Ravel to propose his work to our committee. Had I not urged him to do so, he would have postponed it forever. With regard to his membership in the Société Nationale, he affirmed to me that he asked Bréville[3] about it. Perhaps the matter was forgotten. The promise that his piece would be performed has filled him with joy. Wouldn't it be a very cruel reversal to remove his name from the program, when he is presently copying out his work from morning till night? Shouldn't the Société Nationale encourage young musicians? Didn't it encourage us when we were <u>just starting out</u>?

I am therefore imploring you to help Ravel. I do so particularly as it was I who caused him to take this step, which would now be construed as a blunder! The members of the committee, fellow professors and colleagues, most of whom are my friends, will agree that I have rarely asked them for any favors. I would find it extremely painful to have this recommendation rejected.[4]

Very cordially yours,

Gabriel Fauré[5]

1. Chausson (1855–1899), a distinguished composer, studied with César Franck and Jules Massenet. He served for ten years as the secretary of the Société Nationale de Musique.

2. This undated letter was written shortly before a concert of the Société Nationale on May 27, 1899, which was to include Ravel's overture to *Shéhérazade.*

3. The French composer Pierre de Bréville (1861–1949) was an active member of the Société Nationale, serving as its secretary and later as president of its governing board.

4. Fauré's plea was heeded, and as a result, Ravel made his debut as a conductor, leading the overture to *Shéhérazade*. His reactions to the concert are found in the following letter to Florent Schmitt.

5. Letter printed in Jean-Michel Nectoux, "Ravel/Fauré et les débuts de la Société Musicale Indépendante," p. 301.

4. to Florent Schmitt[1]

[Paris]   Friday the 9th [June 1899]

You must think me completely indifferent, dear friend, and with good reason, but I have a few excuses all prepared. First of all, I wasn't at the Conservatoire this past week, and therefore I didn't receive your letter until last Monday. My second excuse is that I am struggling with some <u>divertissements</u> which I can't seem to get rid of. How I envy you, immersed in the pleasure of your cantata![2]

Let's talk a bit about the National Evening:[3] Koechlin's piece was very successful as we expected; its effect is truly charming, and it was the part of the concert which seemed to me to be the most <u>felicitous</u>.[4] That's no doubt why G.-V.[5] devoted only three lines to him.

As this . . . (choose the epithet) stated very accurately, *Shéhérazade* was strongly booed. They applauded also, and in all honesty I must admit that the applauders were more numerous than the protestors, because I was called back twice. Moreover, d'Indy,[6] whose behavior toward me was first-rate, was over-joyed that "people could still become impassioned about something."

As far as I could judge from the podium, I was satisfied with the orchestra-tion. It was generally found to be picturesque: the *Ménestrel* even called it "curious."[7]

I couldn't remind Koechlin about the visit he owes you, as I haven't seen him since receiving your letter.

Best of luck, dear friend, for your final days of detention.[8] Kind regards to our friends.

A cordial handshake,

Maurice Ravel

7 rue Fromentin

1. Fellow students in Fauré's composition class, Ravel and Florent Schmitt (1870–1958) remained lifelong friends.

2. Following four unsuccessful attempts, Schmitt finally won the Grand Prix de Rome in 1900 with his cantata *Sémiramis*. Ravel's "divertissements" refer in an ironic way to the writing of academic fugues, or the setting of dull texts for mixed chorus and orchestra.

3. A humorous reference to the Société Nationale concert, as Ravel suggests an

interrelation between this "National Evening" and France's "National Evening" (July 14).

4. On Saturday evening, May 27, 1899, the Société Nationale de Musique presented its 278th concert. Among the pieces performed were Charles Koechlin's choral arrangement of the Russian folk melody *Song of the Volga Boatmen*, and Ravel's first work for orchestra, the overture to *Shéhérazade*. Classmates at the Conservatoire, Ravel and Koechlin (1867–1950) remained lifelong friends. Koechlin was a distinguished theorist and teacher, as well as a prolific composer (see my article, "Ravel's Letters to Charles Koechlin").

5. The critic and novelist Henri Gauthier-Villars (1859–1931), who used the pseudonym Willy, is chiefly remembered as Colette's first husband. He criticized the overture to *Shéhérazade* as follows:

A jolting debut: a clumsy plagiarism of the Russian school (of Rimsky faked by a Debussyian who is anxious to equal Erik Satie) disaffects the audience, which, irritated besides by the aggressive bravos of a bunch of young claques, protests and boos. Why this cruelty? I regret it with regard to young Ravel, a mediocrely gifted debutante, it is true, but who will perhaps become something if not someone in about ten years, if he works hard. (Gauthier-Villars, *Garçon l'audition!*, Paris, 1901, p. 125).

6. During the first two decades of the twentieth century, Vincent d'Indy (1851–1931) was perhaps the most influential musician in France. One of the founders of the Schola Cantorum, he became director of the school in 1904, and through his many pupils, his doctrines were taught throughout France, and as far away as South America. His theories, which were based upon the music of Beethoven, Franck, and Wagner, combined solid classical development, cyclical structures, and an aesthetic based on Christian faith, love, and mysticism. Although Ravel's personal rapport with d'Indy was cordial, he repudiated his aesthetics and did not care for his music. D'Indy, in turn, had little sympathy for Ravel's music, which he found to be overly refined, pithy, and lacking in genuine emotion and structural coherence.

7. Actually, the reviewer of the *Ménestrel* was somewhat more critical, observing that the "curious" orchestration did not conceal the overture's imperfections (review signed "O. Bn." in *Le Ménestrel*, vol. 65, no. 23, June 4, 1899, p. 184).

8. The finalists for the Prix de Rome competition were isolated in their studios at the Compiègne Palace for an entire month, and were required to set an extended cantata text for several solo voices and orchestra.

5. to Dumitru Kiriac[1]

March 21, 1900

Dear friend,

It was really right of me to criticize you for your indifference, wasn't it? And, if you think of me sometimes, you must say to yourself that I was somewhat impertinent to be teaching you a lesson. But you would never be able to treat me as harshly as I am treating myself, almost daily.

I have no excuses regarding my conduct, except, first of all, my incoercible epistolary laziness, and then, the work in which I have been immersed during the past few months.

I am indeed preparing for the Prix de Rome,[2] and have seriously begun work. The fugue is beginning to come rather easily, but I am rather worried about the cantata. For the January examinations, I had patiently elaborated a scene from *Callirhoé*,[3] and was strongly counting on its effect: the music was rather dull, prudently passionate, and its degree of boldness was accessible to those gentlemen of the Institute.[4] As for the orchestration, Gédalge found it skillful and elegant. All of this ended up in a miserable failure. Fauré tried to cheer me up, but Monsieur Dubois[5] assured him that he was deceiving himself about my musical talent.

What is disturbing is that the criticisms were not addressed to my cantata, but indirectly to *Shéhérazade*, at whose performance, you may recall, the director was present. Will it be necessary to struggle for 5 years against this influence? I'm very sure that I will never have the courage to maintain the same attitude until the end.

But I think that I've talked enough about myself and my work. It appears that you didn't obtain the position you were hoping for. Demets[6] told me that you were raising rabbits. Was that the reason you left us? How you must miss the vicissitudes of city life, and the air, the nice, unwholesome air of Paris!

It is true that you can meditate, work as you wish, and write to your friends. Take advantage of it, especially with regard to your friends. I hope that Madame Kiriac continues to enjoy Bucharest, and that the climate, no doubt different from ours, still suits her. Remember me to her, along with my respectful compliments.

No hard feelings, right, my dear Kiriac? and a cordial handshake from yours truly,

Maurice Ravel

1. The Romanian ethnomusicologist and composer Dumitru Kiriac (1866–1928) was a fellow student in Fauré's composition class (see the letter from Kiriac and Brailoiu to Ravel, no. 213).

2. The Prix de Rome competition was conducted in two stages. The preliminary round consisted of writing a four-part fugue based on a given subject, and setting a short text for mixed chorus and orchestra. These two assignments had to be completed within a week. Some twenty candidates generally entered the preliminary round, and usually five or six were allowed to go on and compete for the first prize, which entailed setting an extended cantata text for several solo voices and orchestra. The winner of the Grand Prix was assured a modest stipend for four years. The first two years were to be spent at

the Medici Villa in Rome, the third year in Germany or Austria, and the fourth year in Rome or Paris. Following this period, the composer could be supported for several more years by a private foundation. Thus, winning the Grand Prix could mean a minimum of four and a maximum of seven years of untroubled artistic growth, coupled with special opportunities for the performance of one's compositions.

3. This cantata text by Eugène Adénis-Colombeau (1854–1923) had previously been used for the 1899 Prix de Rome competition. Ravel's music has not been recovered.

4. The French Institute, whose five divisions include the Académie des Beaux-Arts, was the official body under whose aegis the Prix de Rome competition took place. Other divisions within the French Institute include the Académie Française and the Académie des Sciences.

5. The French composer, author, and teacher Théodore Dubois (1837–1924) was the director of the Conservatoire from 1896 until 1905.

6. Eugène Demets published some of Ravel's earliest works, among them the *Pavane pour une Infante défunte* and *Jeux d'eau.* In 1923, his catalogue was sold to Max Eschig.

6. to Florent Schmitt

Monday, April 8, 1901

My dear Schmitt,

How can I describe my behavior towards you? I prefer to let you do it, as my indulgence discovers excellent reasons every day for suppressing my remorse. The most important reason, which is still rather feeble, is (or is it one at all?) my incoercible epistolary laziness. Other reasons may be added—choral pieces and fugues in preparation for the competition—together with the transcription of Debussy's wonderful *Nocturnes,* in collaboration with Bardac.[1] Having indicated some ability for this kind of work, I was assigned the task of transcribing the third piece, "Sirènes," all alone. It is perhaps the most perfectly beautiful of the *Nocturnes* and certainly the most perilous to transcribe, particularly as it hasn't been heard.[2]

How I pity you, my dear friend, for being too far from Paris to hear such things! This and Liszt's *Faust,* that astonishing symphony in which the most conspicuous themes of the *Ring* cycle file past (but written earlier, and, more-over, orchestrated so much better).

However, despite the profound pity that I feel for you, I would perhaps, who knows? rather be in your place. Does Rome inspire you with delectable inspirations? Is "La Peau de chagrin" progressing well,[3] and will it be your *Damoiselle élue,*[4] or, Phoebus forbid! your *Impressions d'Italie?* I hope you will reply soon to all of these questions.

It is unlikely that you will ever receive a letter from Mlle Toutain, as a young lady should not correspond with a young man. This argument, furnished by the mother of the young lady, seemed specious to me, as I have always considered a woman who writes fugues as something of a hermaphrodite.[5]

My epistolary effusions must come to an end, or I'll be guilty of arriving late for Mme David's dinner, where I expect to provide some new slander about you.

Looking forward to a prompt and complete reply, a cordial handshake from yours truly,

Maurice Ravel

1. Raoul Bardac (1881–1950) studied at the Conservatoire and later took private lessons with his stepfather, Claude Debussy (see Ravel's comments about him in letter no. 179). Despite the collaboration of the young composers, the two-piano score of Debussy's complete *Nocturnes,* published by E. Fromont in 1909, indicates that the transcriptions were done by Ravel alone.

2. Although "Nuages" and "Fêtes" were introduced on December 9, 1900, the first complete performance of the *Nocturnes* did not take place until October of 1901.

3. Schmitt's piece, apparently based on the novel by Balzac, has remained unpublished.

4. Winners of the Prix de Rome were required to send at least one composition each year to the Academy of Fine Arts in Paris. Debussy's cantata *La Damoiselle élue* (1887–89) falls into this category, as does Gustave Charpentier's *Les Impressions d'Italie* (1887–89), a symphonic suite in five movements. Charpentier (1860–1956) won the Prix de Rome in 1887, and is largely remembered for his *verismo* opera *Louise.*

5. Some two years younger than Ravel, Marie Juliette Toutain received a premier prix in piano and harmony at the Conservatoire. Thus, her academic career was more successful than Ravel's.

7. to Lucien Garban[1]

19 Boulevard Pereire[2]   July 26, 1901
[Paris 17]
Dear friend,

It is only since yesterday that I decided to reply to the many congratulatory messages which arrived on the occasion of the happy event.[3] Some correspondents, I'm sure, will hold it against me, but I hope that you won't be among them. You can't imagine the exhaustion engendered by such a competition!

On top of that, we moved, and I needed several days to resume my customary activities in a new atmosphere. Moreover, the atmosphere is charming, and I am writing to you lulled by the whistling of locomotives.[4] I already perceive a forthcoming *Sites auriculaires*![5]

Let's chat a bit about the competition: Caplet's Grand Prix surprised everyone.[6] His cantata was certainly one of the most mediocre, as a composition, I mean, but its orchestration was quite remarkable. Almost everyone here would have given me the first prize. (Massenet[7] himself voted for me every time). A rather curious thing was disclosed to me: I possess a melodic tap at a place which you will not permit me to designate more clearly, and music flows from it effortlessly. This gracious metaphor comes from your dear teacher X. Leroux,[8] who together with Vidal[9] was very enthusiastic on my behalf. I was even assured—I shudder as I relate—that Lenepveu[10] praised my cantata very much, but not to the point of preferring it to that of his own pupil.

You will say to me, "Why didn't you obtain the Grand Prix?" Who would have believed it? My orchestration played this nasty trick on me. Although my composition was among the first to be finished, it happened that my orchestration was begun late, and there remained very little time for it. It turned out to have been done somewhat too hastily.

I'll have to begin all over again, that's all. Well now, the next competition promises to be tough! There will be 3 second-prize winners to contend with, plus Bertelin, as well as the age limit, and the required honorable mention.[11] I wouldn't advise you to submit your candidacy this year; you would have very little chance of being accepted.

And the counterpoint? You should undoubtedly be writing various works in 4 parts. It's great to be young! ‹ (point of irony)[12]

With regard to Debussy, I believe that his address is 48 rue Cardinet but I'm not positive.[13] If you have any doubts, mail your letter to me and I will forward it to him. His songs have been published.[14] I am acquainted with two of them, which, although written some time ago, are none the less fine works. If you wish to write to him, hurry up; he is supposed to be leaving town at the end of the month.

Bardac is in Italy. He took along some cantata texts with the vague intention of adorning them with outmoded but adequate music.

Do you expect to be passing through Paris in the course of your peregrinations? If so, I hope to have the pleasure of seeing you. I will remain here until at least mid-August.

Please present my respects and my thanks to H[is] R[oyal] H[ighness],[15] and thank those gentlemen as well.

A cordial handshake from your

Maurice Ravel

Best regards from my parents and my brother.

1. Lucien Garban (1877–1959) studied at the Conservatoire and later became a proofreader for Durand and Company. He meticulously studied Ravel's autographs and remained a close lifelong friend of the composer (see plate 5).

2. Just below this line in the autograph, Ravel wrote his former address, 40 bis, rue de Douai, Paris, and crossed it out.

3. Ravel had just received third prize in the 1901 Prix de Rome, which turned out to be his only award in five years of competing. Camille Saint-Saëns was particularly impressed with his cantata, and in a letter to Charles Lecocq, dated July 4, 1901, he observed that "the third prize winner, whose name is Ravel, appears to me to be destined for an important career." In awarding the prize, the jury observed that the cantata was distinguished by its "melodic charm" and its "sincerity of dramatic sentiment."

4. The two sides of Boulevard Pereire are separated by railroad tracks.

5. An early work for two pianos, *Sites auriculaires* (1895–97) consists of two pieces, "Habanera" and "Entre cloches" (Among Bells), which respectively indicate the influence of Spain and of Edgar Allen Poe. The titles suggest an interest in synesthesia: sites that are to be comprehended, as it were, by means of the ear. Honegger's *Pacific 231* would later brilliantly realize a musical vision of a locomotive.

6. The gifted composer and conductor André Caplet (1878–1925) was a close associate of Debussy.

7. Jules Massenet (1842–1912) won the Prix de Rome at the age of twenty-one and went on to become one of the leading French operatic composers of his day. He was also an influential teacher at the Conservatoire.

8. Xavier Leroux (1863–1919) studied with Massenet at the Conservatoire and is best remembered for his *verismo* operas. He was a professor of harmony at the Conservatoire from 1896 until his death.

9. Paul Vidal (1863–1931), the French conductor, composer, and teacher.

10. Charles Lenepveu (1840–1910), whose compositions and teaching reflected a highly conservative outlook. He came under sharp attack during the 1905 Prix de Rome competition when it was disclosed that all of the six finalists were his pupils.

11. The age limit for entering the Prix de Rome was thirty, and the leading contenders for the 1902 competition would essentially be the finalists from 1901: Gabriel Dupont, Ravel, Albert Bertelin, and Aymé Kunc. The winner of the Grand Prix in 1902 turned out to be Aymé Kunc, a notably obscure composer.

12. This grammatical mark was introduced by Jean-Jacques Rousseau, who unsuccessfully urged its adoption.

13. Debussy was in fact living at 58 rue Cardinet.

14. A reference to Debussy's three songs set to poems by Paul Verlaine ("La Mer est plus belle," "Le Son du cor s'afflige," and "L'Echelonnement des haies"). Completed in 1891, they were first published by Hamelle in 1901.

15. At this time, Garban was acting as secretary to a German nobleman.

8. to Jane Courteault[1]

40 bis, rue de Douai   August 2, 1901
Paris

Thank you so much, my dear Jane, for your good wishes, and I'm so upset that it has taken me such a long time to reply! The reason for it is the exhaustion which sets in from overworking for close to two months.

The competition is very hard, but its fatigue is considerably alleviated when one receives some recognition. And a third prize is very satisfactory for a first attempt.

Perhaps we will soon have the opportunity to talk about all of this in person. We hope to be able to go to Saint-Jean-de-Luz towards the end of August, but this is only in the planning stage, and I don't dare count on it too much. It would be so delightful for all of us to be together once again! Those lovely bike and auto excursions! We are thinking of driving down to see you, and have already taken several trips in my father's car, which is completely satisfactory. That's a good sign!

Please convey my respects and my thanks to your aunt, my dear Jane, and believe me your very affectionately devoted

Maurice Ravel

Warmest regards from all of us.

1. Jane Courteault (1880–1979) and her sister Marie Gaudin (1879–1976) were close friends of the Ravel family. Their brothers, Pierre and Pascal Gaudin, were both killed by the same shell in World War I, and the "Rigaudon" from *Le Tombeau de Couperin* was dedicated to their memory.

9. to Eugène Demets

Monday, March 31, 1902

Dear Monsieur Demets,

I believe that Viñes[1] is supposed to play my two pieces at the [Société] Nationale next Saturday.[2] I would be grateful, if of course there is still time, to have the epigraph of the second piece (*Jeux d'eau*) included in the programs: Dieu fluvial riant de l'eau qui le chatouille (H. de Régnier).[3]

If possible, send me a lot of tickets.

Thanks in advance, and believe me, dear Sir, very truly yours,

Maurice Ravel

1. Born in Lerida, Spain, Ricardo Viñes (1876–1943) studied in Barcelona and then continued his musical education at the Conservatoire (see plate 6). In November 1888 he met Maurice Ravel, "the boy with the long hair," and they became best friends. Viñes went on to enjoy a brilliant career, in which he introduced virtually all the keyboard works of Debussy and Ravel, as well as a remarkable variety of contemporary music (see Nina Gubisch, "Le Journal inédit de Ricardo Viñes").

2. Viñes introduced the *Pavane pour une Infante défunte* and *Jeux d'eau*. The critics generally agreed that the *Pavane* was elegant and charming, but *Jeux d'eau* was thought to be cacophonic and overly complicated. It now appears that the *Pavane* is a minor work, as the composer himself acknowledged, while *Jeux d'eau* is firmly established as an important landmark in the literature of the piano.

3. This verse appears in "Fête d'eau," from the collection *La Cité des eaux* (1902): "A river god laughing at the water which titillates him." Henri de Régnier (1864–1936) inscribed this epigraph in Ravel's manuscript of *Jeux d'eau*, which is in the Music Division of the Bibliothèque Nationale.

10. to Frederick Delius[1]

St.-Jean-de-Luz   Wednesday the 10th [September 1902]
My dear Delius,

I received your letter with some delay, owing to my own carelessness: I had neglected to leave my address at Angoulême, where your postcard has remained until now. I hope you will excuse me.

The transcription is progressing well, but I must ask you to give me till the end of the month to finish it: however, I hope to be able to send it to you before then.

In your reply, please let me know if it is absolutely necessary to transcribe the prelude for two hands. A four-hand transcription would be considerably more effective.[2]

Very cordially yours,
Maurice Ravel
41 rue Gambetta
St.-Jean-de-Luz
(Lower Pyrenees)

1. In 1902, Frederick Delius (1862–1934) entered a one-act opera *Margot la rouge* in a competition sponsored by the Italian publisher Sonzogno. Ravel accepted a flat fee for arranging a piano-vocal score from the original orchestral version, and this turned out to be the sole artistic encounter between the composers. Delius' orchestration, considered lost for many years, was recently recovered and first performed by the Opera Theater of St. Louis in June, 1983 (see the *New York Times*, June 10, 1983).

2. In the piano-vocal score (Paris: Lévy-Lulx, c. 1905), the prelude is transcribed entirely for two hands (the first page of Ravel's autograph is reproduced in Orenstein, *Ravel: Man and Musician*, plate 6).

11. to Frederick Delius

St.-Jean-de-Luz   Friday, October 3 [1902]
My dear Delius,

By the same mail you will receive the transcription of *Margot*. I am keeping the orchestral score for a few more days in order to make the changes we agreed upon. It was wrong of me not to speak to you about this matter earlier;

my transcription was almost finished when I received your postcard, but I think that everything can be worked out. From now on, you may proceed with the translation. The modifications shouldn't be very important, and besides, the translator will certainly have to make others.

As regards the music, I have corrected obvious mistakes (omitted accidentals, etc.). I have transcribed literally certain doubtful passages, and will discuss these with you later, except for several measures (scene five—"Pourquoi me confier ces choses-là"),[1] which seemed obscure, and which I have left blank. I would also like to point out a verse in the orchestral score which has no music (scene two, The Landlady: "Il te pince donc bien, ton nouveau béguin.")[2]

Please write to me at the same address, 41 rue Gambetta, as soon as you have received the score.

See you soon, my dear friend. If you see Schmitt, give him my best regards.[3] Cordially yours,

Maurice Ravel

1. "Why confide those things in me."

2. "So your new lover has really smitten you."

3. Florent Schmitt had already carried out four operatic transcriptions for Delius. Although Ravel never acknowledged any musical debt to Delius, the following observation has been made regarding "Asie," from the song cycle *Shéhérazade*:

> At times the effects he achieves with a soaring soprano line set against a glowing, many-stranded orchestral background are startlingly reminiscent of Delius's technique, itself demonstrated in a number of passages in *Margot* where the soprano is dominant or is joined briefly by the baritone.
>
> It may, then, be said that while Ravel later acknowledged Debussy's "spiritual influence" on the cycle, he seems to have remained unaware of the technical avenues subconsciously opened to him through his absorption, for a time, of some of the music of Delius's maturity. (Lionel Carley, *Delius: A Life in Letters, I, 1862–1908*, Cambridge: Harvard University Press, 1983, p. 206.)

12. to Jane Courteault

[Paris]   Friday, September 11, 1903

My dear Jane,

No, I can't believe that you are angry with me, and I trust that you only gave me that look in order to scare me. You can see that the result is immediate. Besides, I wasn't totally without an excuse. When we received Madame Gaudin's kind invitation, Edouard had already been in London for a short while, and I awaited his return in order to answer you. He came back only four days ago, and it is likely that he will have to return to London soon, this time, probably, with my father. You can see that in these circumstances it will be impossible for me to visit the Basque country (and God only knows how much I find this heartbreaking!), and to relive the wonderful moments that we all shared last year.

I'm back to the grind, and now think of the Prix de Rome as a bad dream which I absolutely forbid to happen again. Despite his victory, Laparra[1] won't have pleasant memories of the competition either, and I don't think he would like to relive the moment when Fauré, his professor and mine, declared before the entire Institute that the jury's decision was scandalous and obviously prepared in advance. Moreover, that was certainly everyone's opinion. Nevertheless, Fauré's conduct was very courageous, first of all because Laparra was his student, and secondly, by doing that, he permanently excluded himself from the Institute, whose first vacancy was supposed to go to him. As for the fortunate winner, owing to the unexpected position of his teacher, he was seized by a fit of hysteria.

You say that the weather in Saint-Jean-de-Luz is magnificent? You're lucky! Here, after a summer in which it rained ceaselessly, we enjoyed 4 or 5 tropical days. And now it's raining again and freezing.

Warmest regards from all of us to all of you. You'll write soon, my dear Jane, won't you? A cordial handshake from yours truly,

Maurice Ravel

Do you remember the piece of rope you gave me for good luck?[2] On the day of the competition, after the decision, I wanted to divide it among my interpreters as a token of my gratitude . . . Oh well! Nobody wanted a piece of it!!!

ПᴿЯ

Laparra wrote to me in very elegant Basque, but forgot to give me his address. If you see him, please ask him if he received the postcard I am sending him by the same mail.

1. Raoul Laparra (1876–1943) was a gifted composer who is largely remembered for his operas, among them *La Habanera* (1908) and *L'Illustre Fregona* (1931).

2. Literally "the rope of the man who hanged himself." A piece of this rope was traditionally kept, like a rabbit's foot, for good luck.

13. to Eugène Demets

19 Boulevard Pereire   [c. 1904][1]
[Paris 17]

Dear Monsieur Demets,

In reply to your letter, please convey the following information to the person who asked: my terms are 20 francs a lesson (once a week).

Very truly yours,
Maurice Ravel

1. This date is approximate, as the Ravel family lived at 19 Boulevard Pereire from July 1901 until 1905.

14. to Maurice Delage[1]

[Compiègne]   [May 8, 1905][2]
I'm setting M. Guinand's poetry (sic) to music.[3]
I simply had to tell you!
   Maurice Ravel

1. The French composer Charles Maurice Delage (1879–1961) met Ravel in the early 1900s and soon became a close associate. The initial stage of their lifelong friendship was summed up by their mutual friend, the critic Michel D. Calvocoressi. Delage "was a truly remarkable case. He had reached the age of twenty-three without even giving a thought to music, and he suddenly developed a passion for it after hearing Debussy's *Pelléas et Mélisande*. . . . Ravel—who, so far as I know, had never done any teaching before—was interested in him from the first, and handled him with infinite skill, tact, and patience" (*Musicians Gallery*, p. 61). In addition to his own output—a small but distinguished catalogue of works—Delage carried out several transcriptions of Ravel's music (see plate 2).

2. This postmark appears on Ravel's undated postcard. A picture of the grounds surrounding the Château de Compiègne, the site of the Prix de Rome competition, is on the face of the card. Compiègne is just north of Paris.

3. Ravel set Edouard Guinand's text, *L'Aurore*, for tenor soloist, mixed chorus, and orchestra. (In 1884, Debussy had set his cantata text *L'Enfant prodigue*.) The authors of the Prix de Rome texts were usually amateurs, whose texts were frequently banal.

15. Romain Rolland to Paul Léon[1]

162 Boulevard Montparnasse   Friday, May 26, 1905
Paris
Dear Sir,
   I read in the papers that there is no *affaire Ravel*. I believe it my duty to tell you (in a friendly way and just between ourselves) that this question exists, and cannot be evaded. I am completely disinterested in this *affaire*. I am not a friend of Ravel. I may even say that I have no personal sympathy for his subtle and refined art. But justice compels me to say that Ravel is not only a student of promise—he is already one of the most highly regarded of the young masters in our school, which does not have many. I do not doubt for an instant the good faith of the judges. I do not challenge it. But this is rather a condemnation for all time of these juries; I can not comprehend why one should persist in keeping

a school in Rome if it is to close its doors to those rare artists who have some originality—to a man like Ravel, who has established himself at the concerts of the Société Nationale through works far more important than those required for an examination. Such a musician did honor to the competition; and even if by some unhappy chance, which I would find difficult to explain, his compositions were or seemed to have been inferior to those of the other contestants, he should nevertheless have been rewarded outside of the competition. It is a case rather analogous to that of Berlioz. Ravel comes to the competition for the Prix de Rome not as a pupil, but as a composer who has already proved himself. I admire the composers who dared to judge him. Who shall judge them in their turn?

Forgive me for mixing into an affair that does not concern me. It is everyone's duty to protest against a decision which, even though technically just, harms real justice and art, and since I have the pleasure of knowing you, I feel I should give you—I repeat, entirely between ourselves—the opinion of an impartial musician.

Very truly yours,

Romain Rolland

N.B. Isn't there any way for the State (without going against its decision) at least to prove its interest in Ravel?

R.R.

1. The noted author and humanitarian Romain Rolland (1866–1944) wrote this eloquent letter to the art historian Paul Léon (1874–1962), then an under-secretary of the Académie des Beaux-Arts. Ravel's elimination in the preliminary round of the 1905 Prix de Rome led to one of the most spectacular scandals in the annals of the Conservatoire. The *affaire Ravel* was not only hotly debated by music critics, but turned out to be front-page news in the French dailies (Rolland's letter was published in *La Revue musicale*, December 1938, pp. 173–74). Although Ravel's elimination has been explained as a personal expression of the jury's hostility, an impartial study of his fugue and choral piece shows considerable justification for his disqualification. In addition to numerous minor errors in the choral piece, *L'Aurore* (The Dawn), one passage contains seven consecutive measures of parallel octaves between the soprano and bass parts—a blatant infraction of traditional four-part writing which any first-year student at the Conservatoire would have eschewed. (The passage is printed in *The Music Forum*, 3, 1973, pp. 306–07). Moreover, in what appears to be a gesture of defiance, the fugue, like *Jeux d'eau*, ends on a chord of the major seventh (which was corrected by a member of the jury). When viewing these obvious academic blunders, the jury must have assumed that Ravel was either not taking his work seriously or was disdainful of them. Both assumptions appear to have been correct. Thus, the long, simmering feud between the headstrong revolutionary and the highly conservative jury members finally came to a dramatic denouement.

16. to Jean Marnold[1]

towards Liège   June 11, 1905

Dear Monsieur Marnold,

I was terribly busy during the few days which preceded my departure, because of a piece for the harp commissioned by the Erard Company.[2] A week of frantic work and 3 sleepless nights enabled me to finish it, for better or worse. Right now, I am relaxing on a marvelous trip, and I'm tempted each day to thank those gentlemen of the Institute.[3] Your article in the *Mercure* was read with delight on board.[4]

I wasn't able to reply to the person whose card you had sent to me; I didn't take the card with me, and consequently have neither the name nor the address, which, moreover, you hadn't given me. What should I do? If there is still time, would it be too much of an imposition to ask you to send me the information? If you would be willing to do it, please write to Levallois[5] and your letter will be forwarded. I'm hurrying to go up to the bridge again; I've caught sight of an unusual and magnificent factory. We are coming into Liège.

My sincere apologies for the bother, and many thanks for your article. Give my kind regards to Mme and Mlle Marnold, and believe me, dear Monsieur Marnold,

Very sincerely yours,
Maurice Ravel

1. Cofounder of the *Mercure musical* and critic for the *Mercure de France,* Jean Marnold (1859–1935) was an ardent supporter of Ravel and soon became a trusted friend.

2. The *Introduction and Allegro,* for harp, accompanied by string quartet, flute, and clarinet, was dedicated to Albert Blondel, the director of the Erard Company, which supplied the Conservatoire with its harps and pianos.

3. During the stormy events surrounding the Prix de Rome competition, Ravel accepted an invitation from his friends Alfred and Misia Edwards to join them aboard their luxurious yacht *Aimée* for an extended vacation in Belgium, Holland, and Germany. (The monogram of Misia Edwards, seen above, is similar to Ravel's ⌐⊓R, which is often found on his personal stationery and printed scores.)

4. In an article entitled "Le Scandale du Prix de Rome" (*Mercure de France,* June 1, 1905, pp. 466–69), Marnold attacked the Prix de Rome jury's decision to eliminate Ravel in the preliminary round of the competition. Is it possible, he asked, that the composer of *Jeux d'eau* and the String Quartet was incapable of writing an academic fugue and a choral piece, after having been a finalist in three previous competitions?

Furthermore, he explained, all of the six finalists were pupils of the same professor of composition, Charles Lenepveu, who was concomitantly a member of the Prix de Rome jury! Marnold wrote: "We must know, if, for now and all time, awards are to be extorted by intrigue or conferred by imbeciles. . . . For the future of our music, it is high time to sweep away this clique of pedants, equivocators, and spiteful cads." As a result of this scandal, Ravel was catapulted to fame, Théodore Dubois resigned as director of the Conservatoire and was replaced by Gabriel Fauré, and the curriculum of the Conservatoire underwent considerable revision.

5. In 1905, the Ravel family moved to the Parisian suburb of Levallois Perret.

17. to Maurice Delage

Maastricht   June 15, 1905
First impression of Holland. Cathedrals and carillons in the night. A small, sleepy town.

ПR [1]

1. This message is written on the face of a picture postcard of Maastricht, which depicts two rows of houses separated by a dike and a canal.

18. to Maurice Delage

Amsterdam   June 24, 1905

YACHT
AIMÉE

We're in dry dock in the port. The bridge is being caulked and something—I don't know what—is being prepared in anticipation of the next few crossings. We have been here 3 days and I still haven't been to the museums. There are so many things to see. Amsterdam is completely different than I imagined it: a mass of multicolored houses with figured gables; palaces and modern monuments which are peculiar in color and architecture. There are canals everywhere. The entire city is built on piles, which give it terrific character, but in fact make a horrible stench. Upon arriving, I hurried to the zoo and the aquarium. I feel that I will return there several times.

Yesterday, an excursion to Alkmaar: a cheese market with carillons ringing ceaselessly. En route, a most magnificent sight: a lake bordered by windmills, and in the fields, windmills as far as the horizon. No matter where you looked, you saw nothing but revolving vanes. Viewing this mechanical landscape, you could end up believing yourself to be an automaton.

With all that, I don't need to tell you that I'm not doing a thing. But I am storing things up, and I believe that a lot will come out of this trip. In any case, I am perfectly happy for the moment, and it was very wrong of me to alarm you in a moment of despair. You know how capable I am of taking the most tragic things, and, good heavens, there are worse things than that![1]

Write to Amsterdam. We're supposed to remain here one more week.

I shake your paw affectionately.

Maurice Ravel

1. Referring to the Prix de Rome fiasco.

19. to Maurice Delage

On the Rhine, towards Düsseldorf   July 5, 1905

YACHT
AIMÉE   My dear friend,

Since yesterday we have been in Germany, on the German Rhine. It isn't the tragic and legendary Rhine I imagined at all: lacking are water nymphs, gnomes, and Valkyries, with castles[1] on steep cliffs amidst pine trees, Hugo,[2] Wagner, and Gustave Doré.[3] It's rather like that a bit farther down, towards Cologne, it seems. For the moment, it is as interesting, perhaps even more so. What I saw yesterday will remain embedded in my memory, as will the harbor in Antwerp. After a lazy day on a very wide river between hopelessly flat banks devoid of character, we came upon a city of chimneys and domes spewing forth flames as well as reddish and blue fumes. It was Ahaus, a gigantic foundry in which 24,000 men work night and day. As Ruhrort was too far, we went ashore here. So much the better, or else we would have missed an extraordinary sight. We went down to the mills at nightfall. How can I tell you about these smelting castles, these incandescent cathedrals, and the wonderful symphony of traveling belts, whistles, and terrific hammerblows which envelop you? And everywhere the sky is a scorching, deep red. Then, a storm broke out. We returned horribly drenched, in different moods. Ida[4] was terrified and wanted to cry. So did I, but for joy. How much music there is in all of this!—and I certainly intend to use it.[5]

We left this morning in rainy weather. The sun was very pale and high up. Blue masses continually broke through the yellow fog. Then, we perceived something like huge, enchanted palaces, which turned out to be the monumental factories which dot the region.

The landscape is now becoming more peaceful, with river banks flat once again, and small forests appearing from time to time. We expect to sleep at Düsseldorf tonight.

Write to me in Frankfurt, it will be safer. We should be there in 5 or 6 days. I shake your paw affectionately.

Maurice Ravel

We are in sight of Düsseldorf.

1. Ravel used the German word "Burg," which means a castle.

2. Victor Hugo wrote about a trip through the Rhineland in his work *Le Rhin* (1842).

3. The gifted nineteenth-century French painter and sculptor Gustave Doré was a prolific illustrator of books.

4. Ida Godebska. See letter no. 22, note 1.

5. Ravel's unfinished opera, *La Cloche engloutie* (The Sunken Bell), based on the play by Gerhardt Hauptmann, was described by its translator and librettist André Ferdinand Hérold as follows:

> The scenes which occur in the factory of Henry the founder were to have been of striking power. Ravel did not envision a small artisan's workshop; he imagined a huge factory, equipped like the most grandiose one sees today, and he would have utilized the innumerable sounds of hammers, saws, files, and sirens. (A. Ferdinand Hérold, "Souvenirs," *La Revue musicale*, December 1938, p. 198.)

20. to Maurice Delage

Frankfurt   July 12 [1905]

We arrived last night. I've already seen the museum, which contains a wonderful Rembrandt, some Cranachs, and above all, a Velázquez! As for the old city, it's incredible. It's so well preserved that it seems faked. A host of memories: the birth houses of Goethe, Rothschild, and Luther; the house in which the 1870 peace was signed. I had lunch in a magnificent garden. In brief, a day which could have been exceptionally splendid, but for my preoccupation with letters from you and Sordes.[1]

Come now, old chap, both of you, and you especially, who know the slightly ridiculous aspect of my personality—my sensibility—how could you have thought of playing such a cruel joke on me about the mission?[2] Couldn't you sense the palpitation which would jolt me upon reading the news? Yes, in spite of everything, I'm accepting, I'm even accepting it terribly. The insane desire which I have for such a thing makes me believe in its reality. For after all, there is nothing impossible about it. The appointment of my teacher to an important official post,[3] and above all, the customary worthiness of the people to whom these missions are confided, give me some hope. No, old chap, one doesn't joke about these things, and besides, I'm sure—I would stake my life on it—that you aren't the instigator of this hoax.

Write quickly. I'm in such a state that I no longer savor anything about me. I will only be completely reassured in Cologne, where I will receive your reply if you send it immediately. We won't stay more than 2 days in Frankfurt. *If it were true* (I'm an idiot, I know), but if it is so, send me a telegram here. I know that you won't be angry with me for my reproaches, right?

Kind regards,

Maurice Ravel

1. The painter Paul Sordes, a member of the *Apaches.*
2. Details of this proposed mission to the Orient are found in letter no. 22.
3. Gabriel Fauré's directorship of the Conservatoire.

21. to Maurice Delage

Middleburg   July 20, 1905

YACHT
AIMÉE

This is the last city in Holland in which we spend the night, old chap. Tomorrow, we stop at Vlissingen and pick up a pilot for the crossing. Tomorrow night Ostend, where we will stay one or two days (perhaps a visit to Bruges), and we will arrive at Le Havre by sea. Thus, I will be in Paris in a few days. We'll be together in less than a week, speaking of everything we wrote about, and then everything we didn't write but thought about, and then, damn! I can't conceal my joy at returning. That's my greatest joy, despite the nostalgia of a dazzling voyage whose marvelous memories will remain with me a long time. For our farewell to Holland, the weather turned fair once again. The crossing from Dordrecht to Veere was splendid, and we again saw schools of seals in the North Sea. We took a rapid trip to Veere, formerly a majestic town, today a village with opulent remains. Middleburg concludes this series of Dutch towns, which are so curious. It is one of the most typical, with a sumptuous town hall and, above all, an unforgettable abbey. I don't need to tell you how happy I will be to see you when I arrive. Write back immediately to Le Havre and let me know where you are. I'll send you a telegram just as soon as I arrive.

See you soon, my dear friend.

Kind regards,

Maurice Ravel

22. to Ida Godebska[1]

August 9, 1905

My dear friend,
I found your card upon returning to Paris for the second time. In fact, as soon as I returned, I left again in order to spend several days in Mary-sur-Marne.[2] For a change, this visit was devoted to numerous outings in canoes, rowboats, sailboats, and sculls. Oh, the nostalgia for water! I'm now back on land, alas!, and almost all alone. All of our friends, except for the Benedictuses, are on vacation. The Edwardses are in Trouville, and I've seen them only once since my return. I'm really bored! So, I got back to the grind. Moreover, I'll have to move at top speed, as I will be going to Brittany for the third time next month.

The mission? Oh yes! it still torments me. I'll try to expose my "state of mind" to you without rambling too much. You recall what I said following the memorable and ridiculous scene with the telegram: a moment like this, so profound, so perfect, would almost suffice for me, and would console me by itself, even if nothing were to come of it. Well, it wasn't as Platonic as it seemed. I thought of the many separations—from family, friends, perhaps, who knows? definitive. So, I was tempted to rejoice when Calvocoressi informed me of the Minister's intentions concerning me, if I may venture to put it that way. The plan was as follows: the first opportunity would be taken to entrust me with the pretense of a mission, which would allow me to remain in Paris, or at least not too far away. Through that simple pretext, I would be put on the payroll. Thereupon, I went to see Gaveau, who, as you know, had urged me to come back from Amsterdam to see him. At that point, I learned that the above-mentioned Gaveau, an attaché in the Ministry of Fine Arts, was the one who had this brilliant idea, and had communicated it to the Minister. Needless to say, when I found that out, I couldn't resist telling him of my desire to go to the Orient, which he took note of. Naturally, on the way home, I began to regret having spoken so thoughtlessly. But everything seems to be ganging up against me. Last night, I visited Madame Benedictus, whose brother was recently appointed a counselor to the court of appeals of . . . Pondicherry!! That set off ecstatic epistolary impressions: an exotic atmosphere, motley crowds, palaces, elephants, monkeys, gazelles, Ceylon, Jakarta, darn it! The effect was soon felt: this morning I emerged from the train station in Constantinople, on to a terrace overlooking the Bosporus, and as I was leaning over to gaze upon a marvelous site, I was awakened. I uttered some inhuman grunts, and wanted to go back to sleep, but that proved impossible. Well, that's where things stand.[3] What I would like is a formal order enjoining me to leave right now. Long live autocracy! There, 8 pages in which I have bored you with my tergiversations. Don't be angry with me. Being so talkative makes the distance between us seem shorter. I'm beginning to be sentimental, and that won't do at all. It's time to stop. Tell Jean that I'm preparing some extraordinary folded paper hens for him, and kiss the delicate fingers of my fiancée.[4] Affectionate regards to Cipa, and, dear friend, believe in the sincere friendship of yours truly,

Maurice Ravel

1. In June 1904 Ravel was introduced to Xavier Cyprien (Cipa) Godebski (1864–1937) and his wife Ida (1872–1935), who soon became two of the composer's closest friends (see plate 5). A frequent guest at their modest Paris apartment on rue St. Florentin, and later on rue d'Athènes, Ravel also enjoyed staying at their country home "La Grangette" (The Little Barn) at Valvins, near Fontainebleau. Here, he composed *Ma Mère l'Oye* for the Godebski children Mimie and Jean. The Sonatine was dedicated to Ida and Cipa Godebski, and "Le Cygne" from the *Histoires naturelles* as well as *La Valse* were dedicated to Cipa's half sister Misia. Married three times, her salons continually attracted the most talked-about personalities of the day. Her first husband was Thadée Natanson, cofounder of *La Revue blanche*; her second husband was Alfred Edwards, the wealthy and influential publisher of *Le Matin*; finally, she married the Spanish painter José Maria Sert. Some 250 letters to various members of the Godebski family have been preserved.

2. The Delages had a summer home there.

3. Ravel's mission never did materialize.

4. A gentle reference to Jean's sister Mimie, then five years old. On occasion, Ravel was their baby-sitter.

23. to Madame René de Saint-Marceaux

Hôtel de la Plage   August 23, 1905
Morgat[1]
Dear Madame,

Your kind letter arrived with some delay. I had already left Ostend when it arrived there. A change of itinerary was the reason it remained at the general delivery in Trouville. It was then sent to Paris, and finally to Morgat, where I have been for some time already, in this splendid region which almost makes me forget the marvelous trip that I took over a period of two months.

I see from your questions that the letter I wrote to you from Dordrecht shared the fate of many others. In it, I told you about the beginning of a magnificent voyage through Belgium, Holland, and the banks of the Rhine up to Frankfurt, through rivers, canals, and seas, in the yacht of my friends the Edwardses. I saw unforgettable things in this marvelous situation. During all of this time, I didn't compose two measures, but I was storing up a host of impressions, and I expect this winter to be extraordinarily productive. I have never been so happy to be alive, and I firmly believe that joy is far more fertile than suffering. It's an opinion as valid as any other. We'll see this winter if I was mistaken. While awaiting the pleasure of bringing you the fruit of these considerable labors, I would be very happy to hear from you.

Please remember me to M. de Saint-Marceaux, and, dear Madame, believe in the respectful friendship of yours truly,

Maurice Ravel

1. A seaside resort in Brittany (see plate 7).

24. to Madame Jean Cruppi[1]

Hôtel des Bains de Mer   August 27, 1905
Roscoff[2]

Dear Madame,

It has been a long time since I've given you any sign of life—since Dordrecht, I believe, where I replied to your kind letter with a few ecstatic words. It was, however, only the beginning of this unforgettable voyage. I had only begun my visit to Holland, that charming, childlike, and somewhat baroque country. I knew absolutely nothing about the banks of the Rhine, which are so diverse, with their wooded hills, their old-fashioned castles,[3] their gigantic and magnificent factories. I don't have to tell you that I didn't attempt to compose anything during this time, but I was storing up so much! I have a host of projects, more or less grandiose, with which to occupy my winter. I spent only a few days in Paris, during which I finished the Sonatine, and finally began the symphony which I have been thinking about for two years.[4] Then, in order to rest from this labor, I set out again for Brittany, which I will explore until mid-September. It is delightful to come back to unusual regions, pleasurably revisiting those districts which are so varied, with desolate landscapes of such subtle coloration, dramatic boulders, and, above all, the sea!

For the first time in my life, I don't want to return to Paris, that city of snares, hate, and slander, all of which await you when you have been away for several months. Yet, I have lived in this deceitful atmosphere for a long time, and I am still naive enough to be disillusioned about friends and even about indifferent acquaintances.

Please forgive me for pestering you with my idiotic mood. It comes over me sometimes—fortunately it doesn't last very long. The weather is turning fair again, and I'm going to go boating. I don't have to tell you how happy I would be to hear from you. Please send my kind regards to Monsieur Cruppi, your daughter, and your young friends. Dear Madame, believe in the respectful friendship of yours truly,

Maurice Ravel

If you would be kind enough to write, address your letter to 11 rue Chevallier, Levallois Perret, and it will be forwarded.

1. Ravel dedicated *Noël des jouets* and *L'Heure espagnole* to Mme Jean Cruppi, whose husband would become an influential minister in the French government. Her personal intervention was largely responsible for securing the first performance of *L'Heure espagnole* (see letter no. 46, note 7).

2. This seaside resort in Brittany is near Morgat.

3. Ravel used the German word "Schloss," which means a castle.

4. Ravel's comments about this little known symphony are found on p. 497.

25. to Ida Godebska

Thingvellir   September 2, 1905
Iceland

For heaven's sake, yes! I took a short trip to Iceland. But I will soon be returning to Brittany, from where I'll write again.

Kind regards,

Maurice Ravel

26. Hubert Pernot[1] to Michel Dimitri Calvocoressi[2]

Fontenay-sous-Bois (Seine)   December 28, 1905
7 rue de Clos d'Orléans
Dear Sir,

While looking over the program of your lecture, I almost regretted having moved; I personally hope that you will give it again, as it has been a very long time since I have heard Greek folk melodies—I almost should say pure Greek folk melodies—even though I still spend a good part of my time with the dialects of Chios.

I am pleased that you find certain parts of my collection worthy of being harmonized, and I am very happy to grant you the authorization that you desire. If you wish to publish them for voice and piano, don't you think (in case you include the Greek words) that it would be a good idea for us to talk a bit about it? I don't wish to interfere with your publication, but I might be able to give you some useful information, either by explaining the words in my collection more precisely, or by pointing out more suitable words which might be adapted equally well. But you will decide for yourself. If by chance you need me, I am at your disposition. Although Fontenay is outside the fortifications of Paris, it can be reached easily and quickly, and is only 15 minutes from the Bastille train station. Just drop me a note to be sure to find me at home.

Very cordially yours,

H. Pernot

Please give my best regards to Skiadoressi.

1. Pernot spent the summers of 1898 and 1899 collecting folk melodies on the island of Chios, off the western coast of Asia Minor. Three of Ravel's *Five Greek Folk Songs* were taken from his collection. The entire song cycle was first performed by soprano Marguerite Babaïan at a lecture-recital presented by Calvocoressi during the 1905–06 season. (See Hubert Pernot, *Mélodies populaires grecques de l'île de Chio,* Paris: Imprimerie Nationale, 1903. Pernot recorded the folk melodies, which were later transcribed by Paul Le Flem.)

2. Ravel and Calvocoressi (1877–1944) met in 1898 and became lifelong friends. A gifted critic and translator, Calvocoressi wrote articles and books in English and French; his fluent knowledge of Greek led to the creation of the *Five Greek Folk Songs,* and his expertise in Russian assisted Ravel in dealing with the Ballet Russe. His book of recollections, *Musicians Gallery,* contains much important insight into Ravel's career.

27. to Déodat de Séverac[1]

L'Ermitage   January 31, 1906
[Draveil (S. & O.)][2]

My dear Séverac,

I thought I would see you yesterday at the Cruppis, and tell you of my keen regret at not being able to go to the home of Mme de Saint-Marceaux. I didn't know that *Le Coeur du moulin* would be performed there, but I console myself in thinking that I will hear it in a better situation, that is, on stage.[3]

I would also have wanted to excuse myself for plagiarizing you (as Lalo would say). But that's really not my fault. Besides, how could I have suspected that there would be such a close relationship between a boat on the ocean and a festive southern country house?!![4]

I trust that you won't be too angry with me.

Till next Saturday, an affectionate handshake.

Maurice Ravel

1. Although Déodat de Séverac (1873–1921) studied in Paris at the Schola Cantorum, most of his life was spent in southern France, his birthplace. His music frequently reflects his native region, and has been called "Mediterranean."

2. A suburb south of Paris. (S. & O. refers to the Seine and Oise rivers.)

3. Séverac's opera in two acts, *Le Coeur du moulin* (The Heart of the Mill), with libretto by Maurice Magre, was introduced at the Opéra-Comique on December 8, 1909.

4. Ravel was playfully exaggerating. Writing in *Le Temps* on January 30, 1906, Pierre Lalo observed that two pieces from the *Miroirs*, "Une Barque sur l'océan" and "La Vallée des cloches," exhibited in a "completely different manner, a very distant and transposed echo of the feeling which inspires *En Languedoc*, M. de Séverac's most important work." The piano suites *Miroirs* and *En Languedoc* each contain five pieces. Composed about one year apart, they were introduced by Ricardo Viñes. Despite their many differences, "Une Barque sur l'océan" and "Vers le Mas en fête" (At the festive southern country house) share the elements of water imagery, and even a glissando on the black keys.

28. to Mademoiselle ?[1]

February 4, 1906

Mademoiselle,

Upon receiving your first letter, I confess to having been slightly offended by conduct which is usually reserved for a valet, rather than a professor, whatever his artistic merit may be. But, when you informed me that my students had made their decision unanimously, I was astounded. So this is how my efforts are rewarded, for trying nearly two years, and in a rather disinterested manner, to awaken musical ideas in people who didn't care very much about them. At times, I arrived late to class, but, not once did I find all of my students present, which might have occurred simply out of common courtesy. The day of the lesson, arranged beforehand by mutual agreement for Sunday morning, was repeatedly changed for various pretexts: high masses, courses at the Sorbonne, or waking up late. With too much indulgence, I admit, I would tolerate students coming and going at their own convenience, rather often without doing any work. I would have hoped that the dryness of the initial principles would have been the only reason for this, and that the study of composition, properly speaking, would restore diligence.

And now, at this very moment, because I had forgotten the last change of date for my class, I am the object of an insolent measure!

The financial rewards which I derived from this course will not, thank God!, make me regret being rid of such . . . ungrateful students. The presence of women in the class prevents my using a harsher term.

Please accept, Mademoiselle, my most respectful regards.

Maurice Ravel

I would be grateful if you would communicate the present letter to those ladies and gentlemen. It is intended only for them.

As you are not involved in this impropriety, I would not want you to take the least part in all of this.

ᒥ

1. When Ravel taught music, he customarily gave private lessons to professional musicians. The little known episode revealed in this letter sheds some light on his tribulations in dealing with a class of mediocre students. This letter was addressed to a friend of someone in the class. A reproduction of the autograph is found in Georges Léon, *Maurice Ravel* (Paris: Seghers, 1964), plates 2 and 3 following p. 64.

29. to Pierre Lalo[1]

February 5, 1906

Dear Sir,

First of all, I wish to thank you sincerely for the long discussion you devoted to my latest pieces in your article, which, although not always laudatory, was serious and sincere. You would find it ridiculous, as indeed I would, for me to defend my conception of music against yours. I will leave that task to my future works, which is more logical.

I would however like to draw your impartial attention to the following point. You dwell upon the fact that Debussy invented a rather special kind of pianistic writing. Now, *Jeux d'eau* was published at the beginning of 1902, when nothing more than Debussy's three pieces, *Pour le piano*, were extant. I don't have to tell you of my deep admiration for these pieces, but from a purely pianistic point of view, they contained nothing new. As a point of information, I would like to mention the *Menuet antique* (composed in 1895, published in 1898), in which you will already find some attempts at this writing.[2]

I hope you will excuse this legitimate claim, and, dear Sir, believe me, very truly yours,

Maurice Ravel

1. Pierre Lalo (1866–1943) was the son of the distinguished 19th-century French composer Edouard Lalo. An influential music critic, he wrote for *Le Temps*, the *Courrier musical*, and *Comœdia*. Ravel's letter was in reply to his review of the *Miroirs*, which appeared in *Le Temps* on January 30, 1906. The composer and the critic would remain at swords' points for some three decades. Lalo wrote:

> The principal new work of the evening was a suite of five piano pieces by M. Maurice Ravel, which do not at all resemble students' exercises. I have often spoken about this young musician, one of the most finely gifted of his generation, despite several very apparent and rather annoying faults. The most striking one is the strange resemblance of his music to that of M. Claude Debussy. It is a resemblance so extreme and so striking that often, when listening to a piece by M. Ravel, one thinks one is hearing a fragment of *Pelléas et Mélisande*. . . . At first, one might think

that this extraordinary similarity is the result of assiduous imitation. Not at all. It appears to come from a natural affinity and an inner analogy. . . . But he is still very young; perhaps his art, which is so elegant, refined, so naturally musical, so singular and harmonious at one and the same time, will in the future become less exterior, more intimate, and more human. The first sign of an evolution of this sort was found in the five piano pieces recently performed at the Société Nationale. . . .

Following Chopin, Schumann, and Liszt, M. Debussy has created a new manner of writing for the piano, a special style of particular virtuosity. . . . Today, one hardly hears any pieces which do not contain the arabesques, passage work, and the arpeggios discovered by M. Debussy.

2. Ravel's claim with regard to *Jeux d'eau* is certainly correct. However, the *Menuet antique*, which was his first published work, does not appear to contain any noteworthy pianistic innovations.

30. to Jean Marnold

L'Ermitage   February 7, 1906
[Draveil (S. & O.)]
My dear Marnold,

I should have thanked you several days ago, and was counting on doing it in person. And I must hasten to tell you how much your article consoled me after the one in *Le Temps*.[1]

It isn't because of your praise (well yes, a little bit), but above all because you have better understood what I'm trying to do. Delicate, refined, quintessential, damn it! I didn't think I had deceived myself that much. You have seen other things in my latest pieces, and I am grateful to you for it.

What I'm undertaking at the moment is not subtle: a grand waltz (sic), a sort of homage to the memory of the great Strauss—not Richard, the other one, Johann.[2] You know of my deep sympathy for these wonderful rhythms, and that I value the joie de vivre expressed by the dance far more deeply than the Franckist puritanism. Indeed, I know very well what awaits me from those morose followers of this neo-Christianity, but I don't care.[3]

I will try to see you on Sunday in the late afternoon. Kind regards to your family, and thank you once again.

Very cordially yours,
Maurice Ravel

1. Referring to Lalo's review of the *Miroirs* (letter no. 29, note 1). Writing in *Le Mercure musical* of February 1, 1906, Marnold was enthusiastic:

With his infallible fingers, Ricardo Viñes delightfully revealed the sonorous arabesques of "Alborada del gracioso," and had to repeat it, amid the applause which was addressed both to him and to the music. Soon, when these pieces are published by Demets, it will be possible to judge the exceptional value of their musical content even better. (Vol. 2, no. 3, pp. 121–22.)

Marnold went on to call the entire suite "exquisite," and singled out "Oiseaux tristes" and "Une Barque sur l'océan" as "absolute masterpieces."

2. Ravel completed *La Valse* in 1920, some fourteen years after his initial conception of the piece.

3. See letter no. 4, note 6.

31. to Léon Vallas[1]

[Levallois Perret]   April 8, 1906

Dear Sir,

I am very happy that my Sonatine pleased the public of *La Revue musicale*,[2] but on the other hand a bit startled by their objections with regard to its difficulty. What will they say about the *Miroirs*, which I myself cannot manage to play correctly! It is true that I have not practiced the piano for a good number of years. Moreover, for the time being, I'm not writing piano pieces, and, apart from a concerto,[3] I'm hardly planning anything but symphonic or lyric works.

When you visit Paris, I would be very happy to meet you. I don't dare make an appointment with you in my home, which is far too eccentric, and would ask you to select the place where we should meet.

In any case, I hope you will be able to attend the concert of the Société Nationale, which has been set for the 26th of this month at Salle Erard, in which a short piece of mine for voice and orchestra will be performed.[4] I think that your position as a critic will obviate the need for an invitation. If not, please let me know.

See you soon, dear Sir. With best wishes,

Maurice Ravel

1. The French musicologist and critic Léon Vallas (1879–1956) wrote important studies on Debussy, Franck, and on musical life in Lyon. Active in the musical life of that city, he organized lecture-recitals there, and in 1903 he founded the *Revue musicale de Lyon*.

2. Madame Paule de Lestang, the wife of Léon Vallas, gave the first performance of the Sonatine in Lyon on March 10, 1906.

3. A reference to *Zazpiak-Bat*, a piano concerto based on Basque themes, which was abandoned during World War I. The Basque title means "The Seven are One," referring to the unity of the seven Basque provinces. (A discussion of this work is found in Orenstein, "Some Unpublished Music," pp. 327–28.)

4. *Noël des jouets* was sung by Jane Bathori with Ravel conducting.

32. to Maurice Delage

June 12, 1906

Yes, old chap, I know that my behavior is shameful, but I also know that you won't be angry with me when you understand the reasons. For 2 weeks I've been working nonstop. I have never worked with such frenzy. Well, yes, at Compiègne—but that was less amusing. It is thrilling to write a work for the theater.[1] I won't say that it comes all by itself, but that's precisely the most wonderful part of it. By Jove! in a few days I'll be sure of what I'm doing. Laziness, pessimism, bitter reproaches from my parents for not answering letters and not eating—that's of no importance. In this jolly business there are some wonderful moments.

How are things at Pouldu?[2] Here, after some rain, the weather is tolerable. Indeed, for the past few days, we have been spoiled. The bosom of the Naiads, where I go each morning to imbibe some conceptual forces for the day, has been unable to refresh me: understand by that image, whose elegance surpasses its simplicity, that I often visit the Grande Jatte baths, which are not far from my home.

The *Apaches* are quiet, for the moment. It's none too soon (in this regard, there will still be a lot of things to tell you when you return).

A gallant adventure by our congenial heartbreaker L. P. F.[3] with a young lady from Hannover. If I may say so, I was informed of this through the indiscretions of both parties. My father's condition remains the same. We're leaving on Friday for Switzerland. Write to me between now and then.

Kind regards,

Maurice Ravel

1. Ravel was beginning to work on *La Cloche engloutie.*
2. A tiny spa in Brittany.
3. Probably referring to the French poet Léon-Paul Fargue, who was a member of the *Apaches.*

33. to Misia Edwards

July 19, 1906

My dear friend,

I'm writing from Weber's,[1] between the celebration of the Cruppi wedding and the reception. I received your letter with some delay, as I spent several days visiting with friends at Maisons Laffitte.[2] Nevertheless, I hope that you will receive this in Cologne, without wishing you any further mishaps,[3] if I may venture to put it that way.

The heat has turned very tropical once again, and were I not to heed the call of duty, which is dictated by *La Cloche engloutie,* I would obey my father's wish; every day, he implores us to depart for Switzerland—the trip was promised to him.

Here is some news: first of all, my reconciliation with Gauthier-Villars, who made so many overtures that I could no longer decently refuse him. The results were almost immediate: two days later, I was praised in the *Echo de Paris.* Moreover, Viñes received a letter in which the illustrious critic declared that he was "charmed by my gracious pardon and my intelligence."

2: A letter from Camille Mauclair[4], to whom I had sent a thank-you note, assuring me of his admiration.

3: A missive from Judas Köln, more generally known under the pseudonym of Edouard Colonne,[5] asking me for something for this winter. Perhaps I'll make up my mind to undertake "Vienna," which is intended for you, as you know.[6] A thousand affectionate regards to all, and particularly to you from yours truly,

Maurice Ravel

Mme Benedictus gave me a corsage, an Arabic veil, and a rose which belong to you. I'm going to drop them off at your concierge. If you're returning to Paris at a decent hour, let me know beforehand.

1. A well-known Parisian café, where writers and artists frequently met.

2. Just northwest of Paris.

3. The Edwardses were vacationing on the yacht *Aimée.*

4. The pen name of Camille Faust (1872–1945), the French critic, poet, novelist, and art historian.

5. A charming reversal (Köln is the German name of Cologne, which in French is a homonym of Colonne). His first name was in fact Judas, which he changed to Jules and then to Edouard (see letter no. 48, note 2).

6. "Vienna" would ultimately become *La Valse.*

34. to Jane Courteault

July 28, 1906

My dear Jane,

You mustn't be angry with me this time. I have been very preoccupied since we had the pleasure of seeing Madame Gaudin. And I wasn't able to work as much as I would have liked. The reason for it is my father's condition. Your mother saw him in a state of great depression. The terrible anxieties which he has had all his life, and particularly in recent years, have weakened him. Edouard's absence, which fortunately didn't last very long, contributed toward aggravating the situation. Edouard returned home some time after Madame Gaudin's departure. Papa, believing himself to be completely cured, resumed work and tired himself out far too much. The result of that became evident soon enough: almost 2 months ago, he was stricken by a cerebral hemorrhage. Fortunately, it was not very serious. It occurred while he was asleep. He didn't suspect a hemorrhage. He is slowly beginning to recover. With great difficulty we manage to avoid further accidents, but that in itself is a terrible warning. We are trying to hide the situation from him, which he doesn't seem to suspect, still believing that it's the result of his neurasthenia. He preserves all of his lucidity, however, which doesn't always occur in these circumstances, is eating not badly and sleeps well. He walks very little and occasionally rides in an automobile. Our plan to spend the summer vacation with you is ruined: papa is strictly forbidden to be by the sea. He was advised to go to Switzerland, and will be leaving towards the 15th of August. I will accompany him alone; a stay like that would be far too expensive for 4 people. My poor mamma is not very well either. Arthritis set in quickly in her wounded leg, and she drags her foot pitifully.

That's the news from here: you can see that it's not very pleasant. However, I am continuing to work. I am encouraged by the reviews of the critics, and from time to time I receive the most flattering articles. Some even come from America. I'm happy about it, particularly for my parents, who experience new joy each time.

Write to me soon with better news from your family. Don't stress my father's condition in your letters. Write only about neurasthenia, so I can show your letters to him.

Warmest regards from all of us to all of you, and a cordial handshake from yours truly,

Maurice Ravel

35. to Maurice Delage

Hermance   August 20, 1906

Here I am in Switzerland, old chap, and really, I no longer miss the sea so much. Things aren't entirely the same here, but they're still quite nice. On occasion, the lake[1] amazingly conjures up the Mediterranean; the shores, however, aren't so gray. Their coloration is vivid and paradoxical, with tinsel shadings. And then, those boats, with their bright sails and antiquated shapes. Above all, there is a mild climate of extraordinary purity. My father is in fine spirits, and his headaches seem to have almost disappeared.

The inhabitants are also very curious. I had a cousin in the watch business, whom I found playing first violin in the Geneva theater.

I'm awaiting a piano in order to return to *La Cloche engloutie,* temporarily interrupted. I hope that a miserable, whitish sore on my finger—I don't know where it got caught—which made me suffer horribly, isn't going to prevent me from working. That wouldn't do. . . . Just think—in addition to what existed in the first act, there is already a large part of the second. (You want an opera in 5 acts? You'll have it in 1 week!)

Interrupted by a gentleman who died last year. Will write you the details shortly.

Kind regards,
Maurice Ravel

1. Lake Geneva.

36. to Ida Godebska

11 rue Chevallier   October 18, 1906
Levallois (Seine)

Hurry back![1] If the Autumn Salon closes, you'll miss the Gaugins! I'm finishing the orchestration of "Une Barque sur l'océan,"[2] working on the *Histoires naturelles,* and will return to *La Cloche engloutie.* Send more detailed news. Your card was superb! Garban, here for a short visit, gave me the names of all the ladies, who are English actresses. A handshake to Cipa, and see you soon.

Affectionately,
Maurice Ravel

1. The Godebskis were at Saint-Georges de Didonne, near Royan, in southwestern France.

2. The orchestration was performed on February 3, 1907, with Gabriel Pierné conducting the Colonne orchestra. Ravel promptly retracted it, and the score was first published in 1950 by Eschig.

37. Jules Renard to Auguste Durand[1]

44 rue du Rocher   January 18, 1907
Paris VIIIᵉ

Sir,

I authorize you to reproduce the *Histoires naturelles* (The Peacock, The Cricket, The Swan, The Kingfisher, and The Guinea-Fowl) for a collection of songs by M. Ravel.

Very truly yours,
Jules Renard

1. Auguste Durand (1830–1909) founded the publishing company bearing his name in 1869. His son Jacques (1865–1928) continued in his father's footsteps. Following the publication of the Sonatine, in 1905, Durand published virtually every composition by Ravel, and paid him an annuity throughout his lifetime.

38. to Madame ?

February 16, 1907

Madame,

It is with deep emotion that a <u>young</u> person receives such a rare testimonial of artistic sympathy. We need similar encouragement. Despite the sincerity of one's impressions, and the hidden but tenacious will to attain the goal of one's pursuits, it is somewhat distressing at times to observe the public's hostile incomprehension. With each new endeavor, the critics recall your former virtues, so that, each time, one goes through some very painful moments of doubt. That is why I am happy to ascertain that at least someone in the audience reacted with the same emotion: hence, I have not deceived myself. And it is a great joy for a passionate materialist to learn that he accurately evoked those scenes which he himself found so moving.

I thank you profoundly, Madame, for the great satisfaction that your letter brought me.

I am taking the liberty of sending you an invitation for an afternoon recital which will be devoted almost entirely to my works.[1] Above all, there will be a performance of the *Histoires naturelles* by J. Renard, my most recent work, which I am particularly fond of. I hope to have the pleasure of seeing you there, and beg you, Madame, to believe in my respectful gratitude.

Maurice Ravel

1. On February 22, 1907, the Cercle Musical, an organization devoted to chamber music, presented a recital which included a work by Beethoven, Ravel's String Quartet, the *Histoires naturelles*, and the first performance of the *Introduction et Allegro.*

39. Claude Debussy to Louis Laloy[1]

Friday, March 8, 1907

Dear friend,

Nervous people are unbearable, and that's why you must forgive me! We sincerely regret that your wife is indisposed, and hope that she will accompany you next Tuesday evening. You will be coming for dinner, won't you?

With regard to Ravel, I recognize your customary ingenuity. If, as it seems to me, he hasn't exactly found "his path," he can thank you for having shown him one.[2]

But, entre nous, do you sincerely believe in "humorous" music?[3] First of all, it doesn't exist by itself; it always requires an occasion, either a text or a situation. Two chords, with their feet in the air, or in any other preposterous position, are not necessarily "humorous," and can only become so when placed in proper context.

I agree with you in acknowledging that Ravel is exceptionally gifted, but what irritates me is his posture as a "trickster," or better yet, as an enchanting fakir, who can make flowers spring up around a chair. Unfortunately, a trick is always prepared, and it can astonish only once!

Now there's nothing wrong with having fun. An art only concerned with making her smile would even be a very polite apology to Music, who so many people torment and bore!

I hope to see both of you on Tuesday evening. Kind regards,
Claude Debussy[4]

1. The distinguished French musicologist and critic Louis Laloy (1874–1944) was a close friend of Debussy and on cordial terms with Ravel. He founded the *Mercure musical* with Jean Marnold, and his articles also appeared in *La Grande Revue* and the *Gazette des beaux-arts*. In an important book of memoirs (*La Musique retrouvée*, p. 167), Laloy summed up his view of the Debussy-Ravel imbroglio:

I did everything possible to prevent a misunderstanding between them, but too many thoughtless meddlers seemed to take pleasure in making it inevitable, sacrificing for example Debussy's Quartet to that of Ravel, or raising absurd questions of priority between Ravel's "Habanera" and the second piece of Debussy's *Estampes*. The two musicians then stopped visiting each other. As their esteem was mutual, I can bear witness to the fact that they both regretted this rupture.

2. Laloy had suggested that Ravel listen to the voice of the "mocking goblin," thus correctly pointing out that humor and irony were innate elements in Ravel's art.

3. Debussy's comments in this paragraph and the next relate to the *Histoires naturelles*. In fact, his letter was largely a reply to Laloy's enthusiastic review of Ravel's song cycle. However, as François Lesure has aptly noted (in "'L'Affaire' Debussy-Ravel"), Debussy's opinions occasionally vary from one correspondent to another. Thus, he wrote to Jacques Durand on February 25, 1907: "Dear friend, thank you for the *Histoires naturelles*. . . . It's excessively curious! artificial and chimerical, somewhat like a sorcerer's house. Nevertheless, 'The Swan' contains some very lovely music."

4. This letter is printed in the article by François Lesure, "Correspondance de Claude Debussy et de Louis Laloy (1902–1914)," *Revue de musicologie*, 48 (July–December 1962), p. 25.

40. to Georges Jean-Aubry[1]

March 23, 1907

Sir,

The songs cited by Calvocoressi are of purely documentary interest. And that is truly all they deserve. Only one of them, *Sainte* by Mallarmé (composed in 1896), will be published soon by Durand. The other pieces, particularly those set to poems by Verlaine, are far too juvenile.[2]

At the moment I have several songs in rough draft, of which two are set to Verlaine's poetry. If one of them is finished on time, I will send you a copy before submitting it for publication.[3] But I don't dare count on that too much: the sun seems to be sulking, and I am unable to write 2 measures in this depressing weather.

I want to tell you how much I am touched by your interest in my music. People strive so much, particularly most recently, to prove that I am deceiving myself, or better, that I am attempting to deceive others! At times I cannot help but feel a certain annoyance at this.

That is why I wish to thank you most sincerely for your letter, and beg you, Sir, to believe in my artistic sympathy.

Maurice Ravel

1. The French author and critic Georges Jean-Aubry (1882–1949) actively promoted contemporary French music throughout his career, and was on close terms with many of the leading composers of the day (see plate 2). He was introduced to Ravel by Ricardo Viñes in January of 1906, following Viñes' first performance of the *Miroirs*. During the 1920s he lived in London, where he edited the music journal *The Chesterian* (see p. 439).

2. Ravel was apparently referring to *Un Grand Sommeil noir* (which was first published posthumously in 1953), and "Le Ciel est, par-dessus le toit," both of which are from the collection *Sagesse*. (Sketches of the latter song are reproduced in Orenstein, "Some Unpublished Music," pp. 292–95.)

3. A reference to *Sur l'herbe* (from Verlaine's *Fêtes galantes*), the manuscript of which is dated June 6, 1907.

41. to the Editor of *Le Temps*[1]

[c. late March 1907]

Sir,

I have received an article published in *Le Temps* on March 19, in which my name appears very often. M. Pierre Lalo, with his consummate skill which is well known, attempts once again to prove that I have no personality. That is all very well and good. What is more serious, is that he attributes to "certain musicians" some rather strange remarks regarding an artist of genius, Claude Debussy.[2]

In keeping with current practice, M. Lalo does not name the "young musicians" whom he accuses so lightly. But as my name is cited rather often in the article, a regrettable confusion might occur, and some uninformed readers might believe that I am one of the musicians in question. A little more clarity was called for. I would like to issue a formal denial to M. Lalo, and challenge him to produce one single witness who has heard me utter such absurdities.

It doesn't matter to me if I am considered an impudent plagiarist by those who know my works only through reviews. I do not wish to pass for an imbecile, however, even in their opinion.

I am appealing solely to your civility, Sir, in requesting that you insert the present letter in *Le Temps,* in the same place and in the same type as M. Pierre Lalo's column.[3]

Thanking you in advance, I am,

Very truly yours,

Maurice Ravel

1. This letter was printed in *Le Temps* on April 9, 1907.

2. In his article on March 19, 1907, Lalo stated the views of young musicians with regard to Debussy as follows:

> Young French musicians owe him nothing; between them and him there is neither influence nor imitation, but rather natural coincidence and similarity, engendered by a common sensibility. It is completely erroneous and unjust to claim that they resemble M. Debussy; one could just as well say that M. Debussy resembles them.

Lalo then proceeded to attack this point of view.

3. In his reply to Ravel's letter (both printed in *Le Temps* on April 9, 1907), Lalo observed that "M. Ravel defends himself without having been accused." It was clear from my article, Lalo continued, that M. Ravel was not one of the musicians who had made some "strange remarks" about Debussy. Lalo then quoted part of Ravel's letter to him written in February 1906 (see letter no. 29), dealing with the pianistic innovations found in *Jeux d'eau.* Here was proof, Lalo intimated, that Ravel did in fact think that he owed little to Debussy.

42. to Ida Godebska

[Hôtel du Raz-de-Sein]   August 3, 1907

[Pointe-du-Raz]

Will the Grangette inn be too crowded towards the 20th? Upon returning from Brittany, I'm going to move in there. My parents are in Switzerland, I suppose; I haven't heard anything from them. Write to me at Morgat par Crozon (Finistère), Hotel Téréné. Your father-in-law's statue is adorned by a superb votive offering: a crutch! What a gaffe![1]

Affectionate regards to all,

 MR

1. Cyprien Godebski, Ida's father-in-law, sculpted a statue, "Our Lady of Shipwrecked Persons," which is at Pointe-du-Raz in Brittany, overlooking the Atlantic ocean. A yearly pilgrimage is made there on August 15.

43. to Jane Courteault

Grand Hôtel de la Plage   August 16, 1907
Morgat (par Crozon)
Finistère

This time, my dear Jane, I think that I fully deserve your harsh criticism. And yet, I still hope that you will forgive me once more. As usual, it's only when traveling that I find the time to write. Yet, it is rather difficult to do it during a trip like this one. I left Paris by car more than a month ago, traveling across Brittany and following a most capricious itinerary. This is how I'm relaxing from the fatigue brought about by an insane amount of work: in less than 3 months, I wrote a comic opera in one act, *L'Heure espagnole,* based on a libretto by Franc-Nohain. This work will probably be performed at the Opéra-Comique this winter, the director having declared that we won't have to wait a long time.[1] These then are some excuses which perhaps will grant me your pardon.

My parents are in Switzerland. I was told that they decided to go abruptly, as my father's condition permitted it. My poor papa continues to weaken, and has hardly been able to walk for 2 months. It seems that his stay in Switzerland has done him a lot of good, as much as one can hope for, which, unfortunately, is not very much. You should write to them. Their address is Pension Chenevard, Bellevue (Canton of Geneva). They are supposed to remain there at least until the 20th of this month. About that time, I will be leaving Morgat. I won't be returning to Paris directly, and will only pass through there. I'm going to stay at the home of some friends, near Fontainebleau, in order to finish my work. Between now and then, I'll send you some postcards so that you'll always have my address. I do hope you won't be angry with me, and that you'll want to send me a long letter, telling me all the latest news.

See you soon, my dear Jane. Warmest regards to all, and a cordial handshake from yours truly,

Maurice Ravel

1. After innumerable delays, *L'Heure espagnole* was finally presented at the Opéra-Comique on May 19, 1911.

44. to Jean Marnold

La Grangette   September 12, 1907
Valvins
Par Avon (S. & M.)
Dear friend,

It has already been some time since I arrived in Valvins, but things have only recently calmed down. There were a few more jolting automobile rides during the past few days, and then I resumed work, interrupted by swimming, boating, and diabolo.[1] If I find a free moment during my brief stay in Paris next Monday, I will come by to see you.

Kind regards to your family.

Very cordially yours,

Maurice Ravel

1. A game played with a wooden spool which is whirled and tossed on a string tied to two sticks, held one in each hand.

45. to Georges Jean-Aubry

[11 rue Chevallier]   October 26, 1907

[Levallois (Seine)]

Dear friend,

In haste; first, please excuse my silence: work.

Here are the names and addresses of my cousins:[1]

<u>on the one hand</u>, M. and Mme Edouard Ravel,[2] 15 Quai de l'Ile.

on the other: send 3 tickets to Mme Perrin,[3] 58 rue de Berne.

Be careful! don't seat these 2 groups together, because they don't get along.

Here is the variant which will restore Verlaine's text:

Ce vieux vin de Chypre   est ex[quis][4]

You can expect a less succinct letter shortly.

Very cordially yours,

Maurice Ravel

My respectful and kind regards to Mlle H. Luquiens.[5]

1. That is, Ravel's Swiss cousins.

2. See Mme Ravel's letter (no. 68).

3. Literally, Mme Perrin, widow.

4. "This old wine from Cyprus is ex[quisite]," from Verlaine's poem *Sur l'herbe* (measure 6 of Ravel's song). In the manuscript, Ravel omitted the word "vieux," writing instead an eighth note for "Ce"; he later reconsidered, and the printed score is as above.

5. The French soprano Hélène Luquiens had sung the première of Ravel's *Les Grands Vents venus d'outremer* (poem by Henri de Régnier) in June 1907, accompanied by the composer.

46. to Ida Godebska

[11 rue Chevallier]   January 20, 1908
[Levallois]
Dear friend,

I must seem guilty, no doubt, but if you could imagine my insane existence during these past few days, you would forgive me. To make up for it, I will tell you in detail about my adventures with *L'Heure espagnole*. Last Tuesday, I display my best Toledo voice,[1] and go to see Carré[2] with Bathori[3] alone (Engel[4] was prevented from coming at the last minute). I hum more off key than ever, begin by snapping 3 strings on a dance hall piano, let Bathori attack the bravura arias, and then we await the supreme decision: Refused. . . . It is impossible to impose such a subject on the innocent ears of the Opéra-Comique subscribers. Imagine: those lovers are concealed in clocks which are carried up to the bedroom! We know very well what they are going to do there!! (sic) I must admit that it is the most improper situation presented on stage since Jean Schopfer.[5] Perverted no doubt by unwholesome reading, when I see lovers involved "in the shade," I always assume dishonorable intentions. Thanks to that severe moralist, the director of the Opéra-Comique, I now see that my interpretation was shameful, and that the most serious faux pas of Carmen, Manon, Chrysis, and Queen Fiamette[6] was putting their finger in their nose too often. And besides, isn't it unbelievable: a woman who admires the biceps of a man! (sic) I find this deacon-like mentality rather surprising in Carré. Isn't he still very young to be thinking of becoming a hermit?

But listen to this: the next day I broke the news to Mme C. (the wife of the new Minister).[7] She was shocked, and her first impulse was to write to Carré. After mature consideration, she decided nevertheless to follow her impulse, and the result was a most pungent correspondence. I'll tell you all about it on Friday. For the moment, I'm holding back my fury, as I need all of my composure to keep the critics in low gear: I'm afraid of things skidding out of control.

I'm going just now to see Misia, with Delage. See you on Friday. Affectionate regards to all from yours truly,

Maurice Ravel

1. The action of *L'Heure espagnole* is set in Toledo, Spain, in the 18th century.

2. Albert Carré was the director of the Opéra-Comique from 1898 to 1913, and he shared the directorship with Emile and Vincent Isola from 1919 to 1925.

3. The mezzo-soprano Jane Bathori (the stage name of Jeanne-Marie Berthier, 1877–1970) was not only a faithful performer of Ravel's vocal works, but in her brilliant career which spanned some four decades, she interpreted the vocal works of virtually every important French composer from the late 1890s until the outbreak of World War

11. Georges Jean-Aubry succinctly summarized Madame Bathori's vital contribution by calling her "modern French song incarnate" (see plate 5).

4. Emile Engel, Madame Bathori's husband, was a singer and voice teacher.

5. The pseudonym of Claude Anet, author of such sensational plays as *Notes sur l'amour* (1708) and *La Fille perdue* (The Fallen Maiden).

6. Bizet's *Carmen* and Massenet's *Manon* are famous operatic heroines. Lesser known are Chrysis, the heroine of Camille Erlanger's *Aphrodite* (1906), based on the novel by Pierre Louÿs, and Xavier Leroux's *La Reine Fiamette* (1903), based on a libretto by Catulle Mendès.

7. Jean Cruppi (1855–1933) served as a member of the French parliament for some 25 years. On January 4, 1908, he was appointed Minister of Commerce and Industry, and for several months in 1911 he was Minister of Foreign Affairs.

47. to Ralph Vaughan Williams[1]

La Grangette   March 3, 1908
Valvins par Avon (S. & M.)
Dear Sir,

First of all, forgive me for not having written sooner. I've had an enormous amount of work lately. My *Rapsodie espagnole* is supposed to be performed at a Colonne concert on March 15, and only the 4th movement is orchestrated!

Let's talk now about your work. Upon receiving this letter, send your score and the transcription to M. Marcel Labey,[2] c/o Maison Pleyel, on rue Roche-chouart. If the Société Nationale can give 2 orchestral concerts, your *Fantasia*[3] will be performed. If not, it will be more difficult, as French composers would naturally have priority in a Society which calls itself *National.* In any case, I don't have to tell you that I will do my utmost to assure the performance of a work by a pupil of whom I have every reason to be proud.

Please give my kind regards to Mrs. Williams, and believe in my keen sympathy.

Maurice Ravel

PS: Should the *Fantasia* arrive at my home, I have left instructions that it be delivered to its destination.

1. In the winter of 1907, with Calvocoressi acting as intermediary, Ravel was introduced to Ralph Vaughan Williams (1872–1958), to whom he gave some lessons in composition and orchestration. The lessons extended over a period of some three months, and consisted mainly of orchestration, either of Ravel's piano music, or of works by Rimsky-Korsakov and Borodin. Vaughan Williams recalled his lessons with Ravel as follows:

He was much puzzled at our first interview. When I had shown him some of my work he said that for my first lessons I had better "write a little minuet in the style of

Mozart". I saw at once that it was time to act promptly, so I said in my best French, "Look here, I have given up my time, my work, my friends, and my career to come here and learn from you, and I am not going to write a 'little minuet in the style of Mozart' ". After that we became great friends and I learned much from him. For example, that the heavy contrapuntal Teutonic manner was not necessary. "Complex but not complicated" was his motto. He showed me how to orchestrate in points of color rather than in lines. It was an invigorating experience to find all artistic problems looked at from what was to me an entirely new angle. Brahms and Tchaikovsky he lumped together as "both a bit heavy." Elgar was "entirely Mendelssohn", his own music was "quite simple, nothing but Mozart". He was against development for its own sake—one should only develop for the sake of arriving at something better. He used to say there was an implied melodic outline in all vital music, and instanced the opening of the C minor symphony [by Beethoven] as an example of a tune which was not stated but was implicit. He was horrified that I had no pianoforte in the little hotel where I worked. "Without the piano one cannot invent new harmonies". (Ursula Vaughan Williams, *R.V.W.*, p. 79.)

2. A minor composer of the day, Marcel Labey (1875–1955) was the secretary of the Société Nationale for nearly 50 years.

3. Probably a reference to the symphonic impressions for orchestra, *In the Fen Country*, written in 1903–04 and subsequently revised. As it turned out, the piece was not performed.

48. to Ida Godebska

Monday [March 9, 1908][1]

Exhausted. No time to sleep. Saw Colonne[2] last night. Worked till 12:30 A.M. He is skipping the *Scherzo* by Lalo[3] in order to give me more time. (Don't say anything to the son of the lamented master.)

At the same concert, songs by Rimsky-Korsakov sung by Mme Adam de Wieniavsky.

Affectionate regards to all,

Maurice Ravel

1. This postmark appears on Ravel's undated postcard. A photograph of Levallois Perret is found on the face of the card.

2. The French conductor Edouard Colonne (1838–1910) founded the Concerts Colonne in 1873. He conducted the first performance of the *Rapsodie espagnole* at a Sunday afternoon concert on March 15, 1908. The program began with the overture to Edouard Lalo's *Le Roi d'Ys*, followed by Schubert's *Unfinished Symphony*, excerpts from Rimsky-Korsakov's opera *Christmas Eve*, Fauré's Ballade for Piano and Orchestra, with Alfred Cortot as soloist, the *Rapsodie espagnole*, excerpts from Rimsky-Korsakov's opera *Snow Maiden*, César Franck's *Symphonic Variations*, with Alfred Cortot, and finally, the march from act 2 of *Tannhäuser*.

3. Edouard Lalo's *Scherzo* was published by Durand in 1884. It is his orchestral transcription of the second movement from his Third Trio for piano, violin, and cello (opus 26).

49. to Cipa Godebski

11 rue Chevallier   March 26, 1908
Levallois (Seine)
Dear friend,

Here is the article by Lalo that you asked for: he's consistent.[1] I swear to you that I didn't enclose 25 louis inside a score sent to his address, and yet he slipped me a compliment: my music doesn't resemble that of Paul Dukas.[2] I certainly know, by Jove, that my qualities aren't those of a Jew![3] He could also have mentioned that my music is dissimilar to that of M. de Camondo,[4] but that's a different price.

I'll come to see you soon. Right now, there are soirées and dinners to attend: next Sunday it's Mme Schnerb, and I'm supposed to be invited this Sunday by Carle Dauriac.

I still have some proofs and scores to correct, and then I'll resume work. On what? *La Cloche engloutie,* the Trio,[5] Symphony, *Saint Francis of Assisi*?[6] Still don't know. Saw Mme Droz yesterday, to whom Carré confided that *L'Heure espagnole* wouldn't be understood. I realize that it's a bit abstruse.

See you soon, and affectionate regards to all.

Maurice Ravel

Here's an excerpt from Willy.[7] That way you'll have a second opinion[8] (but with a cedilla, right?)

1. Pierre Lalo discussed Paul Dukas' opera *Ariane et Barbe-Bleue* and the *Rapsodie espagnole* in *Le Temps* on March 24, 1908: the opera was warmly praised but the orchestral suite was soundly thrashed.

2. Dukas (1865–1935) studied at the Conservatoire and taught there. A brilliant essayist and scholar, he also bequeathed some 15 highly regarded compositions.

3. Despite this momentary outburst, Ravel was in fact philo-Semitic, and strongly opposed to racism in any form. He set several Hebraic melodies, and many of his close friends were Jewish.

4. The Count Nissim de Camondo, who was Jewish, was a celebrated art collector and amateur composer.

5. An early reference to the Trio, which was completed in 1914.

6. Nothing appears to have survived of this work, which was to have been based on *I Fioretti de San Francesco* in an adaptation by Ricciotto Canudo. (Ravel owned a copy of *I Fioretti* in a French translation by Arnold Goffin.) Manuel de Falla conjectured that the sketches of Saint Francis preaching to the birds were used in *Ma Mère l'Oye* (see "Notes sur Ravel," p. 85).

7. Using another nom de plume, "L'Oeuvreuse" (the Usherette), Willy praised the *Rapsodie espagnole*, comparing Ravel's orchestral technique favorably with that of Richard Strauss. His article appeared in *Comœdia* on March 23, 1908. (Ravel enclosed the articles by Pierre Lalo and Henri Gauthier-Villars with his letter.)

8. An untranslatable pun; literally, "Like that, you will not hear only one voice." "Son" means "voice," but without the cedilla it becomes "con," an obscene term for an idiot, referring to Lalo.

50. to Ida Godebska

[Mary sur Marne]   April 20, 1908

The nerve! Who didn't answer Ravel? I'm waiting before I write.

ITR

Compliments of the season.[1]
M. Calvocoressi
No room. Sorry.
M.D.[2]

1. Written in English.
2. Maurice Delage, who was acting as host to his friends during the Easter holiday.

51. to Ida Godebska

Friday [May 22 or June 5, 1908]

Dear friend,

I will come to see you on Monday. Heaven grant that the friends of La Grangette be few! I intend to stay there for several days in order to correct the orchestral proofs of the *Rapsodie*.[1]

Last night you missed the introduction of Cipa and Canudo.[2] There were proper and reciprocal salutations, and a drink at the Opéra bistro: "So, we'll see you at La Grangette on Saturday?—Of course, old boy." All of this took place during an intermission. Before you know it they'll be sitting on the Mallarmé bench, which is just the place for emotional breakups![3]

Debussy said last night to a person who was going to a performance of *Boris Godunov*:[4] "Go see it, all of *Pelléas* is found in it!" If every upsurge of snobbism is going to affect him to that extent, he's got more disillusionment coming.[5]

See you Monday, and warmest regards to all.

Maurice Ravel

Canudo will be coming for lunch on Monday, so I'll show him the way.

1. The *Rapsodie espagnole*.
2. The Italian novelist and poet Ricciotto Canudo (1877–1923) was active in the Parisian literary scene. The library at Montfort l'Amaury contains several of the author's

works with personal dedications, and in 1918 Ravel composed a short two-piano piece entitled *Frontispice*, which served as an introduction to Canudo's collection of poetry *S.P. 503; Le Poème du Vardar* (Postal Sector 503; The Poem of the Vardar).

3. The next-door neighbors at La Grangette were Dr. and Mme Edmond Bonniot, the son-in-law and daughter of Stéphane Mallarmé (the poet spent much time at his house in Valvins, and died there). The "Mallarmé bench" was apparently the scene of a disagreement between Ravel and Ida Godebska. (Ravel seems to imply that Cipa and Canudo were not on good terms.)

4. The Thursday evening performance of *Boris Godunov* which Ravel refers to was presented by Diaghilev at the Opéra, with Chaliapin in the title role, on May 21 or June 4, 1908. Ravel's letter was thus written on a Friday, either May 22 or June 5.

5. It must be kept in mind that Debussy and Ravel deeply admired Mussorgsky's music, and both copied out his scores for the purpose of study. Thus, Ravel criticized Debussy for comparing his opera to Mussorgsky's, and Debussy rebuked Louis Laloy for favorably comparing the *Histoires naturelles* with Mussorgsky's song cycle *The Nursery*.

52. to Theodor Szántó[1]

11 rue Chevallier   June 6, 1908
Levallois (Seine)
Dear Sir,

As I did not have your address, I replied by telegram to M. de Glueck.[2] The telegram was returned to me with the indication "unknown." Fortunately, my letter reached him, as I have recently received his reply. I thank you sincerely for having thought of performing an orchestral work of mine in Berlin. I would be very curious to know the impression that it makes. I'm afraid that the aesthetic orientation of Germany at this time is rather appreciably different from ours. But some sympathetic individuals might be found, and that is what's important. You will receive the *Miroirs* shortly; I'm writing about this to Demets, the publisher.

I'm afraid I won't be able to go to Berlin, despite my keen desire to do so. However, many things may happen between now and then. . . .

At any event, I hope to hear from you occasionally, and in the meantime, please believe me very cordially yours,

Maurice Ravel

La Cloche engloutie is still at the same point. I'm going to get back to it.

1. The Hungarian pianist, conductor, and composer Theodor Szántó (1877–1934) studied with Ferruccio Busoni in Berlin. He enjoyed an international concert career, living mostly in Paris (1905–1913) and Switzerland (1914–1921), before returning to Budapest (1922–1930). Szántó gave the first performance of Delius' Piano Concerto, which is dedicated to him, and introduced the piano music of Bartók and Kodály to

Parisian audiences. His correspondence in the Library of Congress includes 34 letters from Ravel, 45 from Busoni, and 87 letters from Frederick and Jelka Delius.

2. Hermann von Glueck, a German impresario.

53. to Ida Godebska

11 rue Chevallier   June 19, 1908
Levallois (Seine)
Dear friend,

Before writing to you, I wanted to arrange matters with Delage. We weren't able to speak Saturday night at the home of the Morlands,[1] nor upon coming back with the Schmitts.[2] Delage left the next morning for Mary sur Marne, and had made an appointment to see me on Tuesday night at the home of Benedictus.[3]

Monday, I received a card from . . . Bourbonne-les Bains![4] Then, nothing. What's going on?[5]

The day before yesterday, I saw Séverac at a performance of *Pelléas* (small audience—obviously it's less in fashion this year). Déodat intends to visit you one of these days.

Viñes asked to be excused for not being at the Morlands: he had to leave for Lerida as his father is very ill.

I reexamined what was written of *La Cloche engloutie.* Good heavens! how it has aged! It has to be redone. What a miserable business! but it has its charms, as Voltaire would say, speaking about someone else.

If I didn't give you enough details about *Pelléas*, it was out of embarrassment. You can't imagine what has become of it: the Olympia[6] orchestra would accompany more discreetly, and musical clowns would be more believable than the performers. You have to see Périer[7] projecting his voice towards the side of the stage, instead of inflicting it on the public! Maggie Teyte[8] is an adorable doll; she is physically more a Mélisande than Garden,[9] and vocally superior, but she sings the role with a total lack of comprehension.

The others sing at the top of their lungs, and thus they can occasionally be heard above the uproar of the orchestra. This general massacre is truly too painful for those who heard *Pelléas* in the early days.

Boris Godunov will also be butchered later on, along with everything else given in France. That's how it is with everything: we only do it correctly in the very beginning. It's always like that. . . .

The premières continue: the Arts Theater, the New Art Theater. Catulle Mendès[10] says that "the most stupid and the most repugnant of vices" now appear on stage in *The Gentleman with Chrysanthemums.*[11] The old guard is always virtuous.

I will keep you informed about what has been decided just as soon as I speak with our drivers. Affectionate regards to all from yours truly,

Maurice Ravel

1. Probably M. and Mme Jacques Morland, friends of the Ravel family.

2. M. and Mme Florent Schmitt.

3. The French painter and composer Edouard Benedictus (1878–1930) was a member of the *Apaches.*

4. Some 150 miles southeast of Paris.

5. Ravel humorously wrote "Kécèkécèkécèlà?" (= "Qu'est-ce que c'est que cela?" literally, "what is that?"), thus imitating an elfin passage in *La Cloche engloutie.*

6. A Parisian music hall.

7. The French baritone and actor Jean Périer (1869–1954) made his debut in 1892. He created the role of Pelléas and that of Ramiro in *L'Heure espagnole.*

8. The English soprano Dame Maggie Teyte (real name Tate, 1888–1976) performed in Europe and the United States for almost 50 years. In 1908, Debussy chose her to succeed Mary Garden in the role of Mélisande, and she also performed Debussy's songs with the composer at the piano.

9. The Scottish-born soprano Mary Garden (1877–1967) created the role of Mélisande, and enjoyed a long and distinguished international operatic career.

10. Mendès (1843–1909) was a noted playwright, poet, novelist, and critic.

11. This comedy in three acts by M. Armory was being performed at the New Art Theater. The plot, dealing with seduction and homosexuality, centers about three protagonists, each of whom is enamored of another of the trio.

54. to Rudolph Ganz[1]

[Levallois Perret]   September 2, 1908
Dear Sir,

I have just completed 3 poems for the piano, *Gaspard de la nuit,* which will be published by Durand.

I am eager to have you accept the dedication of one of them, "Scarbo." This in token of the gratitude which I would be happy to express to you in person, if you come to Paris someday.

I would be curious to meet the paradoxical virtuoso who expressed interest in a work because it appeared new to him, at a time when our national virtuosi insolently persist in revealing the sonatas of Beethoven.[2]

Dear Sir, believe in my keen sympathy.

Maurice Ravel

1. The Swiss-born pianist and composer Rudolph Ganz (1877–1972) devoted himself to the performance of contemporary music. He settled in the United States in 1901, and later became the president of the Chicago Musical College. He also con-

ducted the St. Louis Symphony Orchestra (1921–27) and the New York Philharmonic's Young People's Concerts (1938–49).

2. Ravel's complaint still has a curiously familiar ring to it.

55. to Ida Godebska

[La Grangette]   [September 1908]
Valvins
Par Avon (S. & M.)
Dear friend,

Received your card upon returning from Avon. I left in Durand's car and returned in the car of Cabarus. Tomorrow, no doubt, I'll go in Tabuteau's car.[1] All in all, bicycles are idiotic!

Upon returning from Paris this morning, I found everyone well. Family life now resumes: laborious conversations with Miss,[2] aided by gestures and dictionaries; stories to tell the kids, not too gloomy in the evening to avoid nightmares, but lugubrious in the morning to stimulate their appetite. There are occasional distractions: on Sunday, a drunkard almost drowned, and there was also a runaway horse (I simply couldn't make Miss understand what that meant).

Mimie and Jean are exhorting me to ask for their donkey.

Have you savored the interview with Gunsbourg in the *Figaro*? He declares that he's a chap just like Mussorgsky: he's composing an opera, both words and music.[3]

No news from Natanson.[4] I'll write to you as soon as I hear anything.

Affectionate regards to you both and to Misia.

Maurice Ravel

I wanted Mimie to write a few words, but she fell asleep on the sofa.

There are 2 cards for Cipa, one from Vuillard,[5] who is in Beg-Meil,[6] and the other from a mysterious, unknown lady: "I am visiting Italy again."

Enclosed are 50 francs: will send you a detailed account tomorrow.[7]

1. The aviator Maurice Tabuteau was a member of the *Apaches*.

2. The English governess of the Godebski children, Miss Hatchell.

3. Raoul Gunsbourg (1859–1955), the Romanian-born impresario, directed opera companies in Russia and Monte Carlo. In an article entitled "Is Music a Science or a Gift?", which appeared in the *Figaro* on September 15, 1908, Gunsbourg stated that music is a gift and not a craft. He told Robert Brussel that he was able to compose only melodies and suggestions for harmony. Just as the orchestration of *Boris Godunov* was completed by Rimsky-Korsakov, Gunsbourg explained, my opera will be orchestrated by Léon Jehin. Gunsbourg's opera *Le Vieil Aigle* (The Old Eagle, based on the fable by Maxim Gorky), was performed at the Monte Carlo Opera on February 13, 1909. In the 1920s, it was at Gunsbourg's insistence that Ravel eventually completed *L'Enfant et les sortilèges*, which was first performed at the Monte Carlo Opera.

4. Probably Thadée Natanson, Misia's former husband.

5. The French painter Edouard Vuillard. Cipa Godebski was painted by another close friend, Henri de Toulouse-Lautrec.

6. In Brittany.

7. Following Ravel's postscript, the Godebski children wrote: "Hello Mama and Papa. Marie   Jean."

56. to Louis-Charles Battaille[1]

Valvins   September 19, 1908
Par Avon (S. & M.)
Dear Sir,

Don't think that I forgot my promise. This summer, I had undertaken several works, some of which are finished.[2] With regard to the quartet, I have selected the poem for it. It is the "Menuet" by F. Gregh,[3] and the music is even thought out, in principle. Now I just have to write it down, and that won't be the hardest part. I believe that I can promise you this work shortly.[4]

Please present my kind regards to Madame Battaille,[5] and believe me, dear Sir,

Very truly yours,
Maurice Ravel

1. Battaille, the son of the celebrated 19th-century French bass Charles Battaille, was a noted professor of voice. He also wrote for the *Courrier musical.*

2. Ravel had recently been working on *Gaspard de la nuit* and *Ma Mère l'Oye.*

3. The French poet Fernand Gregh (1873–1960) was elected to the Académie Française. During his student days, Ravel occasionally visited the poet's home.

4. If there was in fact a setting for 4 voices of Gregh's early poem "La Tristesse des menuets" (The Sadness of Minuets), the manuscript has not yet come to light. Similarly, Ravel planned to write a prelude and incidental music for a poem in verse by Georges Jean-Aubry, *L'Heure fantasque.* Nothing came of that project either (letter to Jacques Rouché, June 22, 1912; autograph in the Music Division of the Bibliothèque Nationale).

5. She was a concert pianist and teacher. In a letter to her written on October 10, 1912, Ravel noted that he would be "delighted" to hear his Sonatine "performed by an artist of your stature" (autograph in the library of the Brussels Conservatory).

57. to M. and Mme Cipa Godebski

[c. November 1908]

Dear friends,

I think that you have excused my silence: apartment hunting, a lucky find, upholsterer, etc. We are moving in tomorrow, 4 Avenue Carnot[1] (near the Place de l'Etoile); a magnificent view, a delightful apartment with everything work-ing, even the electricity. I will try to see you the day after tomorrow. In any case, drop me a note at the new address.

Affectionate regards,
Maurice Ravel

1. Following the death of Joseph Ravel on October 13, 1908, Madame Ravel and her two sons moved to this apartment in the fashionable 17th arrondissement. They lived there until 1917.

58. to Jean Marnold

4 Avenue Carnot   December 22, 1908
My dear friend,

Were it not for the visit of M. Varèse[1] on Sunday morning, I would have prepared to visit you at home in the evening. I was convinced that you had invited us for Sunday evening, and my mother didn't say otherwise. The funniest thing is that Abbé Petit[2] had also written to me, but I thought that you had seen him since. You have forgiven me, haven't you? M. Varèse told me of your desire to have all of us get together another time. We will do it whenever you wish.

Carré has just informed Séverac that *Le Coeur du moulin* will be performed next March. While awaiting a similar decision with regard to *L'Heure espagnole*, I'm finishing the orchestration. The piano-vocal score, which has just been published, will perhaps convince him.

Once again, a thousand and one apologies. See you soon,
Maurice Ravel

1. Edgard Varèse (1883–1965) studied at the Schola Cantorum with d'Indy and Roussel, and at the Conservatoire. Most of his life was spent in the United States, and his legacy consists of some fifteen important avant-garde works.

2. The Abbé Léonce Petit was a member of the *Apaches*.

59. to Charles Koechlin

4 Avenue Carnot   January 16, 1909
My dear friend,

Because of my change of address, I received your letter only on Monday. By then, you already knew that I didn't belong to any committee except for Schmitt's, which was perfectly homogeneous.[1]

Societies, even national, do not escape from the laws of evolution. But, one is free to withdraw from them. This is what I am doing now by sending in my resignation as a member. I presented 3 works of my pupils, of which one was particularly interesting.[2] Like the others, it too was refused. It didn't offer those solid qualities of incoherence and boredom, which the Schola Cantorum baptizes as structure and profundity.

I understand that your music has also been deemed unworthy to join that of Coindreau, Crèvecoeur, and company.[3] Doesn't that make you heartsick?

I am undertaking to form a new society, more independent, at least in the beginning. This idea has delighted many people. Would you care to join us?[4] If so, it would be useful to meet, either at your home or at mine. If you decide to join, you pick the time and place for us to meet.

Give my kind regards to Madame Koechlin, and believe me, dear friend, very cordially yours,

Maurice Ravel

1. Ravel and Florent Schmitt had been serving on the steering committee of the Société Nationale.

2. The piece which Ravel found "particularly interesting" was Maurice Delage's *Conté par la mer,* which was later performed at a recital of the Société Musicale Indépendante.

3. Compositions by Pierre Coindreau and Louis de Crèvecoeur, both obscure figures, had been performed by the Société Nationale. Ravel could not resist punning on the name Crèvecoeur, as he noted that Koechlin's music wouldn't be in the company of "those Coindreaus and other Crèvecoeurs" (= heartbreakers).

4. The founding committee of the Société Musicale Indépendante consisted of Gabriel Fauré, president, Louis Aubert, André Caplet, Jean Huré, Charles Koechlin, Ravel, Jean Roger-Ducasse, Florent Schmitt, and Emile Vuillermoz, with A. Z. Mathot as secretary. Although the organization disbanded in the late 1930s, it proved to be a healthy competitor of the Société Nationale for some three decades. (A photograph of the committee, minus Florent Schmitt, is found in Orenstein, *Ravel: Man and Musician,* plate 9.)

60. to Cipa Godebski

4 Avenue Carnot   March 14, 1909
Dear old chap,

Praised be your mumps, which prevented you from hearing the concert of the Société Nationale![1] Oh, those rotten musicians! They can't even orchestrate, so they fill in the gaps with "Turkish music."[2] Craftsmanship is replaced by fugal diversions, and themes from *Pelléas* make up for the lack of inspiration. And all of this makes a noise! from the gong, tambourine, military drum, glockenspiel, and cymbals, used at random. Inghelbrecht[3] holds the record, with an additional xylophone and Chinese bells. Well now! in Japan . . . it could just as well have taken place in Lithuania. But after all, he is rather skillful: if a bit finicky, at least he gets an occasional response from the audience. A little music and it would be just fine.

Amid all this, Schmitt seemed like an intruder, with his noble inspiration and musical line, his sumptuous and delicate orchestration: everything that the others lacked. One managed to discern these qualities despite a wretched performance and a singer with no voice.

There was one happy note: *Eginéa.* The composer, Mlle B. Lucas, left in the lurch by a prudent singer, performed the work herself. Now that's something I wouldn't do . . . Mlle Lucas has a voice similar to mine, only stronger. At the beginning the audience thought there would be a painful delivery (Gésinéa);[4] it was quickly reassured, however, and took the whole thing in the gayest of spirits. Then, a little scherzo lasting about 35 minutes concluded the program. I sneaked out to avoid the composers and ran to a bistro, where I had a lemon squash and 3 glasses of water—no stimulants.

I was told of the incredible faux pas regarding the presentation of Tabuteau on Sunday night: that's a fine beginning! I'll tell you all about it if you're not up-to-date.

Let me know just as soon as you are well. Until then, my brother's doctor has absolutely forbidden me to see you. It seems that nothing is more contagious than the mumps. Did I leave my umbrella at your home? I couldn't find it at the home of Benedictus, where I thought I had forgotten it.

My brother is well again, except for the fact that he badly crushed his burnt finger.

I am finishing *L'Heure espagnole.* Durand will have the final part of the score tomorrow. Write soon (on balsam paper, with a nitrate pencil).

Affectionate regards to all from the three of us.

Maurice Ravel

1. On Saturday evening, March 13, 1909, the Société Nationale de Musique presented a program of eight orchestral works, all of which were being heard for the first time. Conducted by Vincent d'Indy, Marcel Labey, and several of the composers, the program consisted of the following works:

1) Symphony in D Minor . . . . Marcel Orban
2) Chants d'automne . . . . Pierre Bretagne
3) Le Chevalier Moine et les diables dans l'abbaye . . . . . . Pierre Coindreau
4) La Toussaint . . . . Henri Mulet
5) Two poems for voice and orchestra, sung by Mme Jeanne Lacoste:
   Tristesse au jardin (Laurent Tailhade) and
   Demande (Jean Forestier) . . . . Florent Schmitt

6) Pour le jour des premières neiges au vieux Japon
    (Poème symphonique) . . . . D.-E. Inghelbrecht
7) Eginéa (excerpts from act 2) . . . . Blanche Lucas
8) Symphony in A, third movement: Assez animé . . . . Paul Le Flem

2. A reference to the 18th-century Turkish marching bands, which featured some of the percussion instruments mentioned later in the letter. They were parodied by Mozart in his *Abduction from the Seraglio.*

3. The French conductor and composer Désiré-Emile Inghelbrecht (1880–1965) was a member of the *Apaches* (see Ravel's comments about him in letter no. 77).

4. Apparently a humorous anagram of the title *Eginéa,* deriving from an obsolete noun "gésine," which means lying-in.

61. to Ralph Vaughan Williams

4 Avenue Carnot   April 13, 1909
Dear Sir,

Your invitation is so kind that I simply must accept.[1] I'm all the more grateful to you, because I feel a bit frightened, I confess, of being in a country where I don't know the language.

I'm supposed to arrive in London during the day on the 25th,[2] but I still don't know the exact time. I will write to you between now and then.

Please give my kind regards to Mrs. Williams, and with my sincere thanks to you, believe me,

    Cordially yours,
    Maurice Ravel

1. Vaughan Williams had invited Ravel to stay at his home on Cheyne Walk during a forthcoming concert tour in England.

2. In April 1909 Ravel and Florent Schmitt concertized together in London under the auspices of the Société des Concerts Français. The trip marked Ravel's first concert appearance abroad. An unsigned review appeared in the *Times* on April 27:

> The whole program was full of the liveliest interest, for each composer speaks with a distinct voice of his own, and although they belong to the same school, their works show many points of strong contrast. Some of Mr. Ravel's work is already well known here, and the examples of it which were given were all thoroughly characteristic. The greater part of his contribution to the program consisted of songs sung alternately by Madame Jane Bathori and Mr. Emile Engel. The "Cinq mélodies populaires grecques" are miniatures of the most delicate type, in which the charming melodies given to the voice are supported and intensified by slender piano accompaniments. . . . Mr. Florent Schmitt's songs aim at a fuller type of expression, and, though placed beside Mr. Ravel's they are apt to appear a little labored, their beauty is distinct, and "Tristesse au jardin" was perhaps the most beautiful.

62. to Mrs. Ralph Vaughan Williams

4 Avenue Carnot   May 5, 1909
Dear Madame,

Here I am, once again a Parisian: but a Parisian home-sick for London. I have never before keenly missed another country. Yet, I had left here with a certain fear of the unknown. In spite of the presence of Delage, and in spite of the charming reception of my British colleagues, I still would have felt like a stranger. I needed the warm and sensitive welcome which awaited me at Cheyne Walk to make me feel at home in new surroundings, and to give me a taste of the charm and magnificence of London, almost as if I were a Londoner.[1]

One can't express all of this in the commotion and haste of a departure, so I would like to express my gratitude to you and to Mr. Williams here, just as I feel it.

Please present my respects to your mother, and reiterate my apologies to her and to your brother for not being able to accept their kind invitation.

Please convey my good wishes to Mr. Williams, and, Madame, believe in my respectful friendship.

Maurice Ravel

1. Ursula Vaughan Williams wrote that Ravel

was a pleasant visitor. Ralph enjoyed taking him sight-seeing, and was fascinated to find that he liked English food—the one thing the Cheyne Walk household had foreseen as a problem. But it was no problem at all: it appeared that steak and kidney pudding with stout at Waterloo station was Ravel's idea of pleasurably lunching out. He also wished to be taken to something he described as "Vallasse," which Ralph rightly interpreted as the Wallace collection. (*R.V.W.*, p. 86).

63. Camille Saint-Saëns to Jules Ecorcheville[1]

June 16, 1909

Dear Sir,

You are dissatisfied; I understand and regret it <u>very sincerely</u>. But I am indeed forced to combat a host of people who, under the pretext of serving the highest interests of art, work—unconsciously—to destroy it.

Time alone will judge between these belligerents; but on seeing the solid impression made by *Samson*, written 37 years ago, and the other day in Darmstadt, seeing the reception given to a quintet written by me 50 years ago, I cannot refrain from having some hope in my destiny.

You are young; in about 40 years, you will see how much importance will be attached to *Pelléas* and the *Histoires naturelles.*[2]

Very truly yours,

C. Saint-Saëns

1. The noted French musicologist Jules Ecorcheville (1872–1915) was killed in World War I. He was the editor of the *Revue musicale de la S.I.M.* (formerly the *Mercure musical*, edited by Laloy and Marnold), and among its contributors were Debussy, d'Indy, and Ravel.

2. Although Saint-Saëns (1835–1921) had praised Ravel's 1901 Prix de Rome cantata, he viewed Ravel's avant-garde works (and those of Debussy) as cacophony, an opinion which should be understood in terms of his unusually long career, as well as his fear that their art would lead to a collapse in musical syntax, resulting in chaos. Ravel in turn admired Saint-Saëns' orchestration and his innovations in musical form, but found much of his music overly facile.

64. to Madame René de Saint-Marceaux

4 Avenue Carnot   June 27, 1909

Dear Madame,

I hope that you didn't wait for me too long, today. And yet, last night, I intended to come. But I became so ill that I thought I was going to die. It wasn't anything too serious, but as I am rarely indisposed, if I have the slightest pain I imagine that it's the end.

I must tell you that I've just had an insane week: preparation of a ballet libretto for the next Russian season.[1] Almost every night, I was working until 3 A.M. What complicates things is that Fokine[2] doesn't know a word of French, and I only know how to swear in Russian. Despite the interpreters, you can imagine the flavor of these discussions.

Yesterday, I wanted to reply to your kind invitation, and ask you to count on me, but I simply couldn't find a free minute. I trust that everything worked out well.

Do you expect to remain in Jouy[3] for a while? And may I invite you to lunch one of these days?

Pardon me this time, dear Madame, and kind regards from yours truly,

Maurice Ravel

1. Owing to innumerable problems and delays, *Daphnis et Chloé* was first performed by the Ballet Russe on June 8, 1912, with Vaslav Nijinsky and Thamara Karsavina in the title roles, and Pierre Monteux conducting.

2. The Russian choreographer and dancer Michel Fokine (1880–1942) arranged the libretto and the choreography of *Daphnis et Chloé.*

3. Probably Jouy en Josas, a town near Versailles.

65. to Jules Ecorcheville

4 Avenue Carnot   September 12, 1909
Paris
Dear friend,

   The minuet is tailored.[1] Would you like to stop by my home to try it, or shall I deliver it to yours? In the latter case, please arrange for an appointment towards the late afternoon, or in the evening, because of my frantic work.[2]

   Kind regards to Mme Ecorcheville, and very cordially yours,

   Maurice Ravel

   1. An unusual and bantering way of suggesting that the minuet was "tailored" like a suit—in this case, the "material" being the letters of Haydn's name (H-A-Y-D-N = B-A-D-D-G in musical notation; in German H is equivalent to B♮). This short piano piece entitled *Menuet sur le nom d'Haydn* was commissioned by Ecorcheville for a special issue of the *Revue musicale de la S.I.M.* honoring the centenary of Haydn's death. The other participating composers were Debussy, Paul Dukas, Reynaldo Hahn, Vincent d'Indy, and Charles-Marie Widor.
   2. Ravel was correcting the orchestral proofs of *L'Heure espagnole.*

66. to Theodor Szántó

4 Avenue Carnot   [October 1909][1]
Dear Sir,

   I would be delighted to see Delius once again, whom I haven't seen in years. You can count on me tomorrow at 7:00 P.M. Thank you, and very cordially yours,

   Maurice Ravel

   1. This undated message was written on Ravel's calling card. The envelope is postmarked October 1909.

67. to Chékry-Ganem[1]

                                                      January 23, 1910
Dear Sir,

   I authorize you to negotiate with M. Leduc[2] for the music which will accompany the performances of *Antar* at the Odéon theater.[3] This incidental music comprises:

   1: The symphonic poem *Antar* by Rimsky-Korsakov, and some fragments of this same work specially reorchestrated by me for these performances.

2: A fragment of *Mlada* by the same composer.

3: Fragments of songs by the same composer, orchestrated by me.[4]

Dear Sir, believe me very truly yours,

Maurice Ravel

1. An Arab poet living in Paris, he was the author of *Antar*, a play in five acts based on an oriental fantasy.

2. The music publisher Alphonse Leduc.

3. The first performance took place on February 12, 1910, with Gabriel Pierné conducting the Colonne Orchestra.

4. The manuscript of *Antar* is in the archives of Editions Alphonse Leduc. (55 pages are in the hand of a copyist, and 4 pages are in Ravel's hand. However, the songs, from opus 4 and opus 7, are lacking.) Five additional pages of manuscript are in the Music Division of the Bibliothèque Nationale (MS. 17653). They include Ravel's hastily written piano reduction of parts of act 1, scene 5 (song, op. 7 no. 4, poem by Lermontov), and act 2, scene 1 (song, op. 4 no. 3, poem by I. Nikitin).

68. Marie Ravel[1] to Maurice Ravel

Geneva   January 27, 1910

My dear Maurice,

The end of the month approaches, and the final delay for the exchange of new year greetings as well, and that is why despite the lack of enthusiasm that I feel for writing, I want to assure you that we wish the three of you well all year long. If I send our greetings so late, it is because I am very depressed and tired. This first month of 1910 has made us swallow many great hardships; I am digesting them badly, and they leave a bad taste in my mouth, which is only natural. Then, a certain weariness, a moral torpor set in, which your letter helped to shake off a little, and I thank you for it. Your uncle is well, but his lumbago came back in November and December.

The news from Paris is dreadful; but fortunately you don't run any risk, being on Avenue Carnot. It would be frightful to have to worry about you. Who would have ever imagined that Paris could be inundated, and that the Seine could overflow its elevated banks? Today, the rain and snow stopped here, and I wish that it would happen everywhere, as this respite would allow the waters to subside a little. Destruction and fatalities occurred in our vicinity: Versoix also suffered considerably, but nowhere in Switzerland were there as many catastrophes as in France, and that must be related to the superior construction of our houses.

On Sunday afternoon, we went to see the confluence of the Rhône and the Arve.[2] The Rhône was magnificent, with a very special color which I had never seen in it before, all the prettier as it was unexpected. Even in midsummer, the water flow is not so great; then, the Arve, enlarged by the melting of glaciers, hurls itself violently into the Rhône, barring its path, and allowing it to advance but timidly along its right bank. And now the scene changes: the Arve, although very broad and deep, is held in check in its bed by the Rhône, which passes majestically before it, flowing copiously. Its beautiful blue water doesn't allow the muddy and yellow streams of the Arve to flow into it. If only these games of water[3] could always be so calm! Your *Jeux d'eau*, in any case, was played by Viñes almost a week ago at the Geneva Conservatory, and it was well received. The audience wanted an encore, and I don't know why Viñes didn't play it again; his program was probably a bit too long. Among the young, modern composers, the reviews in the newspapers pointed out only your name with praise. At the same time, I received a clipping from Germany, taken from the *Frankfurt Journal* (always very well informed), which reviewed a concert given by Miss or Mrs. Ethel Leginska.[4] It said among other things: A series of short pieces included the *Jeux d'eau* by Mr. Ravel, which resolved, in an interesting way, the most modern problems of harmony, and proved to us that the pianist attained the summits of <u>authority</u> (in the sense of interpretive authority) as well as pure virtuosity.

I'm very sure that you are not so impressed by the favorable reviews of the critics, but I send them to you anyway.

There still remains a very small place to deplore our nephew Edouard's neurasthenia, and offer him the consolation of our keen sympathy; and to tell your mother of our most affectionate regards, and to thank you, dear Maurice, for occasionally taking the trouble to give us news about the family. Know also that you are working, and are creating beautiful and very artistic things, and this gives your uncle and me great joy. I shake your paw which works so well.

M[arie] Ravel

1. The aunt of Maurice Ravel and wife of the painter Edouard Ravel.

2. This occurs just below Geneva. The Arve river, whose waters rush down from the glaciers of Mount Blanc, is a tributary of the Rhône.

3. In the French, "Jeux d'eau" (fountains, literally "games of water"), which serves as a link to Ravel's composition.

4. The stage name of Ethel Liggins (1886–1970), the English pianist, teacher, conductor, and composer. A pupil of Leschetizky in Vienna, she later studied composition in the United States with Ernest Bloch.

69. to Emile Vuillermoz[1]

[La Grangette]   April 13, 1910

My dear Vuillermoz,

You will soon receive two copies of *Ma Mère l'Oye* from Durand. I thought that the most expeditious thing would be to send them to you directly. Please give them to the 2 kids,[2] unless Chadeigne[3] has already taken a copy for his young student. I will be in Paris next Monday, the 18th, and can be at Mathot's[4] office about 4:30 P.M. If a committee meeting can be arranged for that time, it would be perfect. In any case, it will be necessary to meet with my charming interpreters at that time. I think that if, exceptionally, we could meet at Salle Gaveau, that would perhaps be even better; then, we could rehearse on the piano which will be used for the concert. I myself wouldn't mind trying out the instrument, and I won't hide the fact that this eminent virtuoso is beginning to have the jitters.[5]

A thousand and one excuses for all of these chores.

Very cordially yours,

Maurice Ravel

1. The French music critic Emile Vuillermoz (1878–1960) was a fellow student in Fauré's composition class, and remained a lifelong friend of Ravel (see plate 3).

2. The première of *Ma Mère l'Oye* was given by two young ladies, Geneviève Durony, age 14, a pupil of Marcel Chadeigne, and Jeanne Leleu, age 11, a pupil of Marguerite Long. Ravel had wanted Mimie and Jean Godebski to give the first performance, but the music proved too difficult for them.

3. The pianist Marcel Chadeigne (1876–1926) was a fellow student at the Conservatoire in the class of Professor Charles de Bériot. (A class photo which includes Professor de Bériot, Chadeigne, Ravel, and Viñes, is found in *Ravel: Man and Musician*, plate 2.)

4. The music publisher Albert Zunz Mathot was the secretary of the newly founded Société Musicale Indépendante (S.M.I.). His company was later purchased by Salabert.

5. Ravel was going to play the première of Debussy's *D'un cahier d'esquisses* at the inaugural recital of the S.M.I. (see letter no. 71, note 1).

70. to Mademoiselle Jeanne Leleu[1]

La Grangette   April 21, 1910

Mademoiselle,

When you become a great virtuoso and I either an old fogey, covered with honors, or else completely forgotten, you will perhaps have pleasant memories of having given an artist the very rare joy of hearing a work of his, of a rather special nature, interpreted exactly as it should be.

A thousand thanks for your child-like and sensitive performance of *Ma Mère l'Oye*, and, Mademoiselle, believe in the gratitude of yours truly,

Maurice Ravel[2]

1. Mlle Leleu (1898–1979) began to study at the Conservatoire at the age of nine. A pianist and composer, her cantata *Béatrix* won the Prix de Rome in 1923. She later taught sightreading and harmony at the Conservatoire.

2. The autograph of this letter is reproduced in Marguerite Long's *Au piano avec Maurice Ravel*, plates 4 and 5.

71. to Gabriel Fauré

La Grangette   April 21, 1910

My dear teacher,

How I would have wished to express my joy to you, yesterday, as deeply as I felt it, after the performance of *La Chanson d'Eve*![1] I was too moved, and moreover, how to do it amid the jostling? But you certainly understood. One feels so close at these magnificent moments.

Another joy awaited me after the concert: at the home of friends, I read in *Comœdia* what you had said about your students.[2]

I left Paris very early this morning, and now that I am in my hermitage, I can no longer wait: I must tell you how happy I am, today more than ever, to be among those students and *friends*.

Thank you, my dear teacher, and please continue to believe in the profound affection of your devoted student,

Maurice Ravel

1. The opening concert of the Société Musicale Indépendante took place at the Salle Gaveau on April 20, 1910. This auspicious event consisted entirely of first performances: Fauré accompanied Madame Jeanne Raunay in *La Chanson d'Eve*, *Ma Mère l'Oye* was performed, and Ravel interpreted Debussy's *D'un cahier d'esquisses*. There were also works by Franz Liszt, Maurice Delage, Zoltán Kodály, Jean Roger-Ducasse, and André Caplet (a reproduction of the program is found in *Ravel: Man and Musician*, plate 10).

2. In a front-page interview with Louis Vuillemin, Fauré was quoted in *Comœdia* (April 20, 1910) as follows:

I can only give you . . . my personal opinion, which is that of a completely independent musician, who, for a long time, has been totally uninvolved in the destiny of the Société Nationale. As a former founder, I can assure you that I am happy to learn that the Société Nationale is faring better than ever. With regard to the Société Musicale Indépendante, I could hardly imagine that it would offer competition to anyone at all. Its programs are too eclectic to permit it. Moreover, competition! that term is inadmissable in artistic matters.

Oh, the ingratitude of those young people, and of their elders, too! To tell the truth, don't you find these episodes of schisms, disciples, and scholasticism totally devoid of interest? Here, you know, we are planning to occupy ourselves exclusively with music. That's our only concern. The more societies which flourish with the same goal, the more that art will benefit, and the more we will have to rejoice about. Moreover, it was with genuine pleasure that I agreed to preside over the work of a committee in which I have the utmost confidence, and in which I meet again with my former students, who are now my faithful friends.

72. to Emile Vuillermoz

[La Grangette]   April 22, 1910
[Valvins par Avon (S. & M.)]
My dear Vuillermoz,

We have some tactless friends. I read the article by Vuillemin[1] in yesterday's *Comœdia*. Don't you think that attributing the catcalls and laughter of the crowd to some of our enemies strangely limits the field of combat? Thus, the first hateful words will have been officially pronounced from our side. Obviously, not by you. But how our adversaries will be able to use similar statements against us! You know Vuillemin. Don't you think we could suggest to him that he be responsible for his accusations? Otherwise, if they seem to come from us, how do you expect Séverac and Roussel[2] (who is reserving a *Sérénade*[3] for us, I believe) to have their works performed in a society with such little <u>independence</u>?

All of this is even more unfortunate, as in everyone's opinion the debut of the S.M.I. was a great success. We owe this triumph chiefly to you and Mathot. You can imagine how happy I am about it, and how profoundly grateful I am to both of you. I'm going to ask you a favor, if it wouldn't be too much trouble. Could you send me reviews of the concert—as many as possible. Here, there are 4 local papers, not more. You have to take the train in order to find any other dailies.

For the humorous concert, I insist that you consult Calvo's[4] dossier. I already looked through it, and it is well documented. You might consider the trio of Mozart, whose subtitle I unfortunately don't know.[5]

And you will be the protecting archangel of our little coterie, if you faithfully report your most spiritual exercises to the hermit who sends you his cordial benediction.

Maurice Ravel

1. The critic Louis Vuillemin (see letter no. 217).

2. Albert Roussel (1869–1937) studied with d'Indy at the Schola Cantorum and taught composition there (1902–1914). He was a member of the *Apaches*, and in the

postwar years, together with Ravel, he was internationally regarded as one of France's leading composers.

3. Roussel's *Sérénade* for flute, violin, viola, cello, and harp was not completed until 1925. On October 15, 1925, it was introduced by the Paris Instrumental Quintet at a concert of the S.M.I.

4. Calvocoressi's nickname.

5. Apparently referring to Mozart's Trio in E♭, K. 498, for clarinet, viola, and piano. The subtitle "Kegelstatt" came about as Mozart presumably composed the Trio during a game of ninepins (Kegel).

73. to Cipa Godebski

Valvins par Avon   April 25, 1910
(S. & M.)

Dear old Cipa,

By Jove! yes, you're right about the article in *Comœdia*. We all agree with you, but what can be done? The next day, I received a letter from Vuillermoz, who knows Vuillemin. In good faith, Vuillemin, who's not even half a reporter, saw in our lovely evening nothing but catcalls, screams, slaps, and jujitsu kicks between supporters and detractors of the Schola Cantorum.[1] Such articles can only be disastrous for us, but you also have to consider the newspaper in which it appears. The dream of the editor, and, it seems, of all editors, would be to have duels between Fauré, d'Indy, Debussy, and Ravel, or at least kicks in the belly. We are going to try to exploit these fine intentions, not in such a bellicose way, but, on the contrary, in order to palliate the danger. Have you seen *Comœdia* today? Almost all of the article signed by l'Oeuvreuse,[2] plus a long article by L[ucie] D. Mardrus were devoted to the S.M.I. That dear Lucie compared the Gaveau concert grand to a yawning, gigantic oyster awaiting the tide, which finally appears in the form of . . . Schmitt and Aubert![3] I think that these words must have surpassed the thought of the eminent poetess.[4]

I made a flying visit to Paris just now (like a comet, as Retinger[5] would say); it was very impromptu—otherwise, I would have let you know beforehand. I returned by Melun-Vulaines, which is surely the most picturesque route one could possibly take by train. I found a little sunshine again, which I had left behind—but not enough to dry out the house, by God! If you want to rent it, you'll need some help from the weather. I don't think I told you the other day that someone came on behalf of the would-be renter from Fontainebleau. I gave him a good sales pitch, but I categorically refuse to show the house unless you ask me to do so.

Who didn't get up yesterday to accompany his friend Bonniot to the polling booth? Nevertheless, your Radical-Socialist party was elected.

Bonniot was supposed to come to say good-bye to us, but we didn't see him again. Maybe he dissolved in the downpour. What weather! And on top of that it's so cold. By Phoebus! we were very wrong to break with the Church, as Mariette, our congenial housekeeper, would say.

Fauré had me jointly sign two letters, one to Madame de Saint-Marceaux and the other to Princess de Polignac.[6] His attitude toward us is really first-rate. Write what's new with everyone, including Mimie. Mama's bucolic soul regrets the absence of cabbage in your domain; nevertheless, she sends to all her most affectionate regards. + mine = a lot.

Maurice Ravel

1. Louis Vuillemin's brief but generally favorable review of the opening concert of the S.M.I. appeared in *Comœdia* on April 21, 1910.

2. The review in the "Letter by the Usherette" (Henri Gauthier-Villars) was mixed (*Comœdia*, April 25, 1910).

3. The French composer, pianist, and conductor Louis Aubert (1877–1968) was a fellow student at the Conservatoire, and remained a lifelong friend of Ravel. In May 1911 he played the first performance of the *Valses nobles et sentimentales*, which is dedicated to him. At the inaugural concert of the S.M.I., together with Florent Schmitt, he performed Liszt's transcription for piano 4 hands of the "Chœur des faucheurs" (Chorus of the Harvesters) from his *Entfesseltem Prometheus* (Prometheus Unbound, based on Herder's text), originally for double chorus and orchestra, which was introduced in Weimar on August 24, 1850.

4. Lucie Delarue Mardrus (1880–1945) was a well-known novelist and poetess of the day. Her fertile imagination likened the Gaveau concert grand to a "gigantic black oyster," which opened and closed its mouth between certain pieces. She observed that the hall was packed, with the audience overflowing on to the stage, and concluded her review as follows: "The S.M.I. has been born, like Fauré's *Eve*, and it has been baptized by Ravel's enchantment. We wish it, in complete confidence, long life and great success" (*Comœdia*, April 25, 1910).

5. Probably J.-H. Retinger, a friend of the Godebski family. The library at Montfort l'Amaury contains a copy of his *Histoire de la littérature française* (Paris: Bernard Grasset, 1911) with a dedication to Ravel.

6. During his student days, and well into the postwar years, Ravel attended the elegant salon of Princess Edmond de Polignac (1865–1943), to whom he dedicated the *Pavane pour une Infante défunte*. Born in the United States, her maiden name was Winnaretta Singer. She inherited the Singer sewing machine fortune, and was a distinguished patroness of the arts.

74. to Michel D. Calvocoressi

May 3, 1910

Old chap,

A host of things to ask you: let's proceed in order. First, to the Russophile: if you have some free time, could you do me the great favor of making a draft of an agreement regarding Fokine's royalties? I know that it affects the Russian season, but so very little! It's even in case the ballet would not be given by the imperial company. Then, the following would occur: if *Daphnis* were given at the Opéra, Madame Stichel[1] would receive a third, Fokine another third, and I would have to be satisfied with the rest. Now, <u>under no circumstances</u> would I allow my work to be performed on those terms. We spent (I say *we*, because I worked on it also) many nightly hours writing the libretto, which I later retouched, moreover, and since then I have slaved over the music for many long months. I believe it would be supremely unjust for me to receive only a third. I think you agree. Now, I believe I told you that the agreement with Durand stipulated that should another ballet master intervene, his share would be taken from Fokine's. He requested that this clause be canceled. As we had only thought, in adding it, of performances in the remote future in undetermined countries, I agreed. It had been agreed for the Russian performances that we would divide the royalties in half. At the Society of Dramatic Authors, I was told that it would suffice to write down the agreement on any paper and have it stamped.[2] That's fine; but what if the Russian season doesn't take place? The contract will then be much more difficult to draw up, because it will have to stipulate that under no circumstances will the composer receive less than fifty percent of the royalties. Please make this clear to Fokine or the others. If an agreement can't be reached, I absolutely refuse to allow my ballet to be performed. I'm annoyed to have to bother you with this episode, but it's not very convenient to correspond with chaps who don't know a word of that language which is the envy of Europe.

Another matter, less serious: my student Louis Timal has selected a work by some author from a book of Russian translations in order to set it to music. He doesn't know to whom to write for permission, because, if there is a publisher, it's explained in that lingo which only you can understand. He will send you more details, and it would be most wonderful of you to reply.[3]

Now to the Hellenist: In *Daphnis*, what are the exact names of (1) the very obliging lady (Lycea, I think); (2) the old shepherd who brought up one of the two kids (something like Lammon)?[4] Still to the compatriot of Ganymede:[5] I'm incapable of recalling (neurasthenia) the name of Pan's pipe.[6] Which other instrument, played in the orchestra by an E♭ clarinet, might a shepherd be holding? (No, not the old shepherd, a different one.)

If you manage to clear up all of this, you will merit my admiration, and subsequently my gratitude.

Mama is completely over her cold, and sends you and your mother her best regards. Mine too, respectful to your mother, and affectionate to you, with a handshake to boot.

Maurice Ravel

1. The ballet-mistress of the Opéra.

2. In France, documents may be legalized by affixing special governmental stamps to them.

3. Calvocoressi later recalled that Timal did not write to him, nor could he supply any information whatsoever about him. Timal was probably an amateur composer. Between 1905 and 1928, six of his pieces were published in Paris, mostly by Costallat.

4. In Ravel's score, the names are given as Lyceion and Lammon.

5. In Greek mythology, he was abducted by Zeus to be the cupbearer to the gods.

6. Syrinx.

75. to Jean Marnold

Valvins   Saturday [May 7, 1910]
Par Avon (S. & M.)

Dear friend,

Can't make it for *Salome*.[1] I'm orchestrating ... and it's not going quickly.[2] I will console myself by playing Debussy's *Preludes* once again.[3] They are wonderful masterpieces. Do you know them?

Thank you, and cordially, in haste,
Maurice Ravel[4]

1. Richard Strauss' opera, which was first performed in 1905, was being presented in a French translation at the Opéra.

2. Probably referring to the orchestration of *Daphnis et Chloé* (see the following letter).

3. Book I of Debussy's *Preludes* had recently been published by Durand.

4. The autograph of this letter is reproduced in Chalupt and Gerar, *Ravel au miroir de ses lettres*, p. 12, and Lesure and Nectoux, *Maurice Ravel*, Bibliothèque Nationale, p. 72.

76. to Gabriel Pierné[1]

[c. June 1910][2]

Dear M. Pierné,

I will be able to give you a very considerable fragment of my ballet *Daphnis et Chloé* for the coming season. This fragment (Nocturne and Martial Dance) is for orchestra and mixed chorus. If you think this would be suitable, would you be kind enough to inform Durand directly, so that they can have the material copied or printed in time?

Dear M. Pierné, believe me very truly yours,
Maurice Ravel[3]

1. The French conductor, composer, and organist Gabriel Pierné (1863–1937) studied with Massenet and César Franck. From 1910 until 1932, he was the principal conductor of the Colonne Orchestra (see plate 3).

2. This approximate date is based upon the contents of Ravel's letter.

3. On the first page of Ravel's letter, Pierné wrote a note to himself planning out his strategy: "Meet at beginning of season for audition. See Durand about the chorus. Will the committee agree to pay the expenses?" All of these problems were successfully resolved, and on April 2, 1911, Pierné conducted the first performance of the "Nocturne," "Interlude," and "Martial Dance" at the Châtelet theater.

77. to Jacques Rouché[1]

August 20, 1910

Dear Sir,

Have you already chosen a conductor for the Théâtre des Arts? If not, let me take the liberty of pointing out a remarkable musician, M. Inghelbrecht, who, in my opinion, does not yet have the position which he deserves. I should tell you right away that friendship has nothing to do with this recommendation. For extra-musical reasons, I am on rather cool terms with M. Inghelbrecht. But I have seen him at work sometimes, and recently at an S.M.I. concert. He was called upon at the last minute, and in just 3 rehearsals, he successfully put together different new works, which were rather difficult for the most part. Together with my colleagues, I have been struck by the exceptional skill and understanding of this young man, who, moreover, has a keen feeling for contemporary trends. As this, I believe, is the direction you intend to pursue in the Théâtre des Arts, I thought that Inghelbrecht would be a most useful recruit for you.

Do you still intend to produce *L'Oiseau bleu*?[2] I read this lovely work, and thought, not without alarm, that it calls for music. It would need continuous orchestral music, somewhat atmospheric.[3]

Very truly yours,

Maurice Ravel

1. The distinguished French administrator Jacques Rouché (1862–1957) studied décor and stage production in Germany and Russia. After directing the Théâtre des Arts for several years, he was appointed director of the Paris Opéra in 1914, a position he held until 1945 (see plate 3).

2. *The Blue Bird* was written in 1908 by Maurice Maeterlinck (1862–1949). For a while, it rivaled *Pelléas et Mélisande* in popularity. The play has been described as an allegorical fantasy, portraying a search for happiness in the world.

3. Apparently nothing came of this project. About 1895, Ravel wrote a one-page sketch for a Prelude to Maeterlinck's play *Intérieur*. (Autograph in the private collection of Mme Alexandre Taverne.)

78. to Ida Godebska

4 Avenue Carnot   September 27, 1910
Paris 17
Dear friend,

The last time you wrote I was in bad shape: a boil on my neck had to be opened with a bistoury. Because of the fever, I couldn't do a thing for more than a week. I tried to make up for lost time. Couldn't find a minute to write, because orchestration is much more engrossing than catching shrimps. You don't seem to think so, you fashionable society people, who send me your maledictions through Calvo.

When are you coming back? If you only knew how pretty Paris is at the moment! And besides, you see dirigibles and airplanes all the time. The sun is shining as if it's midsummer. We're leaving on Friday and will spend 3 days in Mary sur Marne. This is to inform you that a gentle rain will fall continually during all of that time.

I wrote to Sert in order to ask for an appointment. He didn't reply. And yet I think it's important that we plan things together.[1] No news from Vienna. I sense some bellicose inclinations. Nor do I hear anything more about *L'Heure espagnole*. If it's going to be performed in November, it's time to get moving.

With their congratulations, Durand sent me a clipping from Germany concerning *Ma Mère l'Oye*, which said: "The most remarkable . . ."[2] in brief, you get the idea: probably the most remarkable children's pieces in existence. What a sensitive and understanding nation!

Octave Maus[3] wrote to me in order to ask where I spent my vacation, what my plans are for the winter, on which days I take my medicine, and other similar matters. It appears that this would keenly interest his readers. I'm replying that I took a cruise to the Indies, and this winter I'm going to hunt grouse in Scotland and begin training for the international car races.

Announce your return quickly, and affectionately to all,
Maurice Ravel

1. They were probably going to collaborate on a project. José Maria Sert (1874–1945) would later be responsible for the scenery and costumes in the Ballet Russe production of Chabrier's *Menuet pompeux*, which Ravel had orchestrated.

2. Ravel copied the German, "Die merkwürdigsten."

3. Maus (1856–1919), a Belgian art and music critic, was the founder of two avant-garde groups, "Les XX" (The Twenty) and "La Libre Esthétique".

79. to Marie Olénine d'Alheim[1]

4 Avenue Carnot   November 3, 1910
Paris
Madame,

By the same mail I am writing to Moscow in order to thank the jury for the pleasant and flattering distinction with which it has honored me.[2]

In this regard, I wish to express my sentiments of gratitude to you personally. Indeed, thanks to your kindness, it was possible for me to take part in the competition.[3]

1. At the invitation of the Russian soprano Marie Olénine d'Alheim (1869–1970), Ravel participated in an international competition sponsored by the Maison du Lied in Moscow. The organization was founded with a threefold purpose in mind: first, to stimulate public interest in folk melodies; second, to increase the repertory of artistically harmonized folk melodies by inviting composers to enter biannual competitions; finally, to encourage young singers by giving them the opportunity to perform folk songs before the public in small recital halls. In 1908, Madame Olénine d'Alheim founded the Maison du Lied with her husband Pierre d'Alheim (1862–1922). A gifted linguist, he carried out many of the organization's translation assignments.

2. Ravel's four prizewinning songs (Spanish, French, Italian, and Hebraic) were first published in Moscow by P. Jurgenson and later by Durand. The Scottish song, based upon a poem by Robert Burns, "The Banks o' Doon," was published by Salabert in 1975. Ravel's two other competition entries, the Flemish and Russian songs, have yet to be recovered.

3. Although this letter is unsigned, Ravel's letter to the jury, which included Madame d'Alheim, undoubtedly contained a formal closing formula and signature.

80. to Désiré-Emile Inghelbrecht

4 Avenue Carnot   February 26, 1911
Paris XVII
My dear Inghelbrecht,

What a pity that the concert is so close! I'm supposed to orchestrate *Ma Mère l'Oye*—at my publisher's request—and it would have been just what you needed. Therefore, the only suggestion I can think of is the *Pavane pour une Infante défunte*, which would require a supplementary pair of nonchromatic horns in G. As this piece is dedicated to the princess,[1] it might interest her to have the first Parisian performance at her home. The publisher is Demets.

With regard to the piece for harp,[2] it is not, properly speaking, a piece for orchestra. There are 7 instruments in all. But it could be arranged: the string quartet could be doubled, or even tripled. And, with the exception of several solos, it would sound even better than the original.

To the best of my knowledge, there is nothing of Debussy except the 2 dances for chromatic harp and strings.[3] I don't believe that the *Petite Suite,* orchestrated by Busser, is for a small orchestra.[4]

Let me know what you decide.

My respects to Madame Inghelbrecht, and very cordially yours,

Maurice Ravel

1. Princess Edmond de Polignac.

2. The *Introduction et Allegro.*

3. The "Danse sacrée" and "Danse profane."

4. Ravel's assumption is correct. Henri Busser (1872–1973) was a prolific composer, conductor, and teacher. A close friend of Debussy, he transcribed several of his works. In an interview with this writer, M. Busser recalled meeting Ravel in 1891 at the Conservatoire, when the director, Ambroise Thomas, presided over the annual distribution of prizes. Ravel won first prize in the preparatory piano division, and Busser received the first prize in fugue. The young prize winners would remain lifelong friends.

81. Erik Satie to Maurice Ravel

Arcueil[1]   March 4, 1911

My good Ravel,

I am writing to Monsieur Ecorcheville that, to my great regret, I will not be able to hear you this evening. It would be too emotional and a strain on my nerves.

I am asking Monsieur Lerolle[2] to be my representative to the head of the household, and to congratulate my interpreters, who are charming.

I thank you, my Good one, for your friendly devotion.[3]

Debussy will conduct the *Gymnopédies*[4] the 25th of this month at Salle Gaveau, at a concert of the Musical Circle. That's something I owe to you. Thanks. Please convey my respects to your mother.

Amicably,

ES

1. Satie lived in the Parisian suburb of Arcueil during the final 27 years of his life. During all of this time, he allowed absolutely no one to enter his apartment. A musical example, among many, of his enigmatic personality may be seen in the piano piece entitled "d'Edriophthalma" from the *Embryons desséchés* (Dried-Up Embryos), in which a simple parody of the slow movement of Chopin's Funeral March Sonata is explained in the score as a quotation from a celebrated Mazurka by Schubert!

2. The Parisian publisher Jacques Lerolle, whose company published most of Satie's music.

3. In addition to this private musicale at the home of Jules Ecorcheville, Ravel was

largely responsible for the S.M.I. concert devoted to Satie's works, which had taken place on January 16, 1911. In the program, Ravel performed the second *Sarabande,* the Prelude to the *Fils des étoiles,* and the third *Gymnopédie.* Furthermore, Ravel wrote the following dedication to Satie in a score of *Ma Mère l'Oye*: "for Erik Satie, grandpapa of 'The Conversations of Beauty and the Beast,' and others. Affectionate homage from a disciple" (this score belongs to Monsieur Max Fontaine).

4. These three forward-looking piano pieces were completed in 1887, and Debussy had recently orchestrated two of them. In addition to conducting his transcription, Debussy accompanied Maggie Teyte in several of his songs, and conducted André Caplet's orchestration of the *Children's Corner* suite.

82. to Cipa Godebski

La Grangette   March 22, 1911

I'm so sorry, old chap, that you waited for me on Thursday. Yet, I had told Koechlin[1] that nothing was definite. The Colonne Orchestra rehearsal went very well, and the performance is set for April 2.[2]

They are working at the Opéra-Comique, but my presence isn't necessary yet. Carré wrote to me that H.[3] would be incapable of conducting a work of this difficulty, so Ruhlmann[4] will take over. He also proposed a small change in the cast. We'll see.

Everything is fine here. It's warmer than last year, and thus a bit more comfortable. Sunday was like a spring day: a host of little birds, still awkward, were preparing their recitals. Edouard came, the fellow who repaired the kitchen stove. The stove repairmen had presumably cleaned it thoroughly this winter. I'm inclined to believe that they put off the job.

You'll probably see me next week when you customarily eat your breakfast: 1:00 P.M. It will depend on the Colonne rehearsals.

Enclosed are my tickets for the 5th Durand concert,[5] the one in which Debussy himself will perform.

They even came here to interview me—by mail, that is. I wrote back nothing but fibs.[6]

The *Rapsodie espagnole* was a success in Lyon.[7] A very kind note from Gédalge informed me about it.

Affectionate regards to all from both of us.

Maurice Ravel

Tell Ida not to make a scene. The next time, it will be her turn.

1. Rather curiously, Ravel wrote "Katalin" by mistake.
2. See letter no. 76, note 3.
3. Louis Hasselmans (1878–1957), who began his career as the cellist of the Capet Quartet. He made his conducting debut in Paris in 1905, and joined the Opéra-

Comique in 1909. He also founded the Concerts Hasselmans in Paris, and conducted extensively in the United States following World War I.

4. François Ruhlmann (1868–1948) was active mostly in his native Belgium and in France. On May 19, 1911, he conducted the première of *L'Heure espagnole.*

5. Following the death of August Durand in 1909, Durand and Company initiated an important series of commemorative concerts, which took place between 1910 and 1913. Among the participating composers were Caplet, Debussy, Fauré, d'Indy, Ravel, Saint-Saëns, and Schmitt.

6. If this interview was printed, it has yet to be traced.

7. The first performance of the *Rapsodie espagnole* in Lyon was conducted by Georges Witkowski on Sunday afternoon, March 19, 1911, at the Société des Grands-Concerts. The program also included the overture to Mozart's *Don Giovanni*, Beethoven's Piano Concerto No. 3 and Rhené-Baton's Variations for piano and orchestra (with one Armande Ferté as soloist), and the Prelude to *Parsifal*. The *Revue musicale de Lyon* (March 26, 1911, pp. 755–57) reprinted five press reviews of the *Rapsodie*: they were mostly negative. Although some reviewers praised the orchestration, the piece was generally criticized for its incoherence, poor taste, and curious sonorities. One critic called the first movement a "joke," and another concluded his review as follows: "Having put up with so much second-rate Wagner, may we now not have to endure second-rate Debussy."

83. to Alfred Bruneau[1]

4 Avenue Carnot   Saturday [April 1, 1911][2]
Paris
Dear Sir,

Permit a young colleague to tell you of the pleasure he experienced at the performance of *Penthésilée*.[3] I believe I told you that through a series of rather peculiar events, I was unacquainted with this work. This morning, therefore, my reactions were completely fresh, and my joy very sincere in encountering a work which contains character, vigor, and . . . music. And this piece, which was written a long time ago, is younger than a host of skillful and insensitive things which we are subjected to daily. Moreover, you know that it's rather in our generation that your importance has been truly appreciated.

Dear Sir, believe in the respectful artistic sympathy of yours truly,

Maurice Ravel

1. The music of Alfred Bruneau (1857–1934) was widely performed during his lifetime. In addition to composing a substantial oeuvre, which includes eight operas in collaboration with his close friend Emile Zola, he was active both as a music critic and music educator (see plate 3).

2. This postmark appears on this special delivery letter. Ravel had attended a Saturday morning rehearsal of the Colonne Orchestra conducted by Gabriel Pierné. In addition to the first suite from *Daphnis et Chloé*, he heard Bruneau's *Penthésilée*. The full

program, performed on Sunday afternoon, also included works by Gluck, Mozart, Haydn, Richard Strauss, and Debussy.

3. Subtitled "Queen of the Amazons," *Penthésilée* is a symphonic poem for voice and orchestra based on a text by Catulle Mendès. Bruneau completed it in 1884, at the age of 27, and Wagnerian influence is evident in this early work.

84. to the Editor of *Le Figaro*[1]

[May 1911]

Dear Sir,

What have I attempted to do in writing *L'Heure espagnole*? It is rather ambitious: to regenerate the Italian opera buffa. However, this work was not conceived of in traditional form. Like its direct ancestor, Mussorgsky's *Marriage*,[2] which is a faithful interpretation of Gogol's play, *L'Heure espagnole* is a musical comedy. Apart from a few cuts, I have not altered anything in Franc-Nohain's text. Only the concluding quintet, by its general layout, its vocalises and vocal effects, might recall the usual repertory ensembles. Except for this quintet, one finds mostly ordinary declamation rather than melody. The French language, like any other, has its own accents and musical inflections, and I do not see why one should not take advantage of these qualities in order to arrive at correct prosody.

The humorous spirit of the work is purely musical: here, laughter must be obtained, not, as in operetta, by the arbitrary and comical accentuation of words, but by the unusual harmony, rhythm, melodic design, and orchestration.

Believe me, dear Sir, very truly yours,
Maurice Ravel[3]

1. Ravel had learned an important lesson as a result of the scandal caused by the *Histoires naturelles,* and he was determined to avoid a similar mishap with *L'Heure espagnole.* Not only did both works exhibit a similar type of conversational melodic line, but Franc-Nohain's witty play about the amorous adventures of a clockmaker's wife had been criticized as too risqué for the operatic stage. Ravel's letter was an attempt to reassure both public and critics. It was printed in *Le Figaro* on May 17, 1911, with the following introduction: "The dress rehearsal at the Opéra-Comique: What is *L'Heure espagnole,* the work by M. Maurice Ravel, based on a libretto by M. Franc-Nohain? In this regard, we have received the following letter."

2. In a letter to the French author and historian Robert d'Harcourt, written on July 27, 1911, Ravel expressed keen interest in orchestrating Mussorgsky's opera *The Marriage.* D'Harcourt had translated Gogol's comedy into French, but the orchestration was never carried out, apparently because of the low fee offered by the publisher Bessel. (See M. Béclard d'Harcourt, "Quelques souvenirs sur Ravel," in *La Revue musicale,* December 1938, p. 229.)

3. Although the autograph of Ravel's letter has not been found, sketches for his statement have been recovered. The sketches, which consist of five pages, were written at the Godebski's summer home, La Grangette. They contain an important paragraph which was not printed in *Le Figaro.* In it, Ravel observed that his goal in writing *L'Heure espagnole* was:

> . . . not to revive the French operetta, which is light, parodic, and at times sentimental, but rather the old Italian buffa. I was thinking about a humorous musical work for a long time, and the modern orchestra seemed perfectly adapted to underline and exaggerate comic effects. On reading Franc-Nohain's *L'Heure espagnole,* I decided that this droll fantasy was just what I was looking for. Many things in this work attracted me: the mixture of familiar conversation and intentionally absurd lyricism, and the atmosphere of unusual and amusing noises which surround the characters in this clockmaker's shop. Finally, the opportunities for making use of the picturesque rhythms of Spanish music.

(Formerly in the private collection of Jean Godebski, the sketches are now in the Pierpont Morgan Library.)

85. to Marie Gaudin

La Grangette   June 27 [1911]
My dear Marie,

I wish to thank you and your mother for all of the trouble you took. We decided to take the Anchochouri rooms.[1] With meals included, Mama won't have to do a thing. We won't be able to chat from window to window, but it will console us to know that you won't be far away.

I have never met William Laparra. It's rather amusing to think that I will have to go to Ciboure to meet the person who designed the costumes for *L'Heure espagnole.*

We will thus have the joy of seeing you soon. I also hope to see a little sunshine in my native region. The weather here is disgusting. For over two weeks we haven't seen the sun. In addition, it rains continually, and we're freezing. We will return to Paris the day after tomorrow, and make all of our arrangements. Barring anything unforeseen, we will arrive in St.-Jean-de-Luz on the 15th.

In the meantime, <u>saspi ehun muchu gusiheri</u>[2] from Mama, Edouard, and yours truly,

Maurice Ravel[3]

1. See the following letter.
2. In Basque, literally "700 kisses to all."
3. A reproduction of the autograph is found in Pierre Narbaitz, *Maurice Ravel,* following p. 96.

86. to Ida Godebska

[28 rue du Quai]   July 19, 1911
Ziburu[1]
Dear friend,

Are things beginning to improve at home? Will you soon rejoin your unique pine forest? And to think that you could have decided to come here, where the ocean front is lined with acacias! And those gentle green hills, covered from top to bottom with oak wreaths, trimmed in the Basque manner. And above all this, the Pyrenees, with their enchanting mauve color. Moreover, there is the light: it's not like the relentless sun found in other parts of the Midi. Here, it is delicately brilliant. The people feel it; they are agile, elegant, and their joy is not vulgar. Their dances are nimble, with a restrained voluptuousness. Religion itself, although devoutly observed, is mixed with a grain of skepticism. But not in the house where we are living, damn it! As soon as we arrived, my mother's old friend Dominica Anchochouri gave notice that she was planning to convert her. Until now, she has been discreet. It is true that Mama cooled this noble zeal considerably by declaring that she would prefer to be in hell with her family, rather than in heaven all alone.

I must stop: I have to go to Donibane Loihilzun (St.-Jean-de-Luz as they say in France) to see Mme Vicq-Challet.[2]

Write quickly, and try to come and see us soon, when you've had enough of Brittany's austere scenery.

Affectionate regards from both of us to all, and, in addition, to you, from yours truly,

Maurice Ravel

(Our address is on the back of the envelope.)

1. The Basque name of Ciboure. It comes from "zubiburu," meaning "end of the bridge."
2. The soprano Gaëtane Vicq-Challet, a concert and operatic singer of the day.

87. to Joaquín Turina[1]

[Spain]   September 8, 1911
Dear friend,

Thank you for the *Revista musical*[2] and for your letter. Am delighted your symphonic poem is progressing.[3] It's not cold here either, but that's to be expected in this region.

Very best wishes from your (or my) fatherland.

Maurice Ravel

1. After his initial musical studies in Spain, Turina (1882–1949) moved to Paris in 1905. Before returning to Spain in 1914, he studied composition with Vincent d'Indy for eight years, and also joined the executive committee of the S.M.I.

2. Turina had written a favorable review of *L'Heure espagnole* in this Spanish journal: vol. 3, no. 6 (June, 1911), p. 151.

3. Apparently a reference to *La Procesión del Rocío* (opus 9), completed in 1912.

88. to Ida Godebska

Irunia [Spain]   September 27, 1911

Don't get nervous. Will write soon. Affectionate regards to all,

   Maurice Ravel

Cordial and unexpected regards from Léon Blum.[1]

And from Gustave P. Samazeuilh.[2]

1. The French statesman Léon Blum (1872–1950) began his career writing criticism for *Comœdia* and other publications. In 1936, he became France's first Socialist premier.

2. The French composer, pianist, and critic Gustave Samazeuilh (1877–1967) met Ravel during his student days and remained a lifelong friend.

89. to Ricardo Viñes

[Fuenterrabia]   October 13, 1911

[Spain]

Dear Ricardo,

   I'm returning home the day after tomorrow and will come over to see you soon.[1] Kind regards to all.

   Cordially yours,

   Maurice Ravel

1. Several excerpts from the diary of Ricardo Viñes (see Gubisch in Bibliography) offer an interesting look at music making in the home. (1) At the salon of Madame de Saint-Marceaux, January 13, 1905: Viñes performs Rimsky-Korsakov's piano concerto accompanied by André Messager, Ravel plays "Oiseaux tristes" and Debussy's *D'un cahier d'esquisses*. (2) At the home of M. and Mme Robert Mortier, June 11, 1907: Viñes and Ravel perform Rimsky-Korsakov's *Antar*, a cousin of Abbé Léonce Petit sings works by Duparc and Ravel, Mme Mortier plays works by Liszt, and Ravel performs his Sonatine. (3) At the home of the critic Magnus Synnestvedt, January 20, 1909: Viñes plays *Gaspard de la nuit*, Debussy's "Poissons d'or" and "Reflets dans l'eau," and Déodat de Séverac performs several of his own compositions. (4) At the home of Calvocoressi, March 8, 1912: Among the guests are Alexander Siloti, Schmitt, Roussel, and Marguerite Babaïan, who sings; Ravel performs the *Valses nobles et sentimentales*.

90. Ravel and Mouveau[1] to Jacques Drésa[2]

Sunday [c. early January 1912][3]

Dear Sir,

I can't tell you how delighted I am with your sketch of the décor,[4] which I have just seen at Mouveau's home. It is enchanting, and, above all, genuine décor. A quick question about a detail: first of all, I thought that the rear curtain was divided into 2 parts. Mouveau has told me that this is not your intention, but he agrees with me that it would improve the décor. One objection stood in the way, which no longer exists: the matter of the book. It bothered me, and I came up with another solution. Here it is: after presenting the banderole to the princess and the audience (the title of the fairy tale will be written on it), the little Negroes will go towards the rear of the stage, and will take—or at least will pretend to take—the rear drop curtain, which will come down in front of the drop curtain of the opening scene. The 3 drop curtains will be brought forward in the same way, always by the little Negroes, who will pull down the strings, which will all be raised together afterwards for the final scene. The drop curtain for the opening scene will therefore remain fixed.

With regard to the tunnel that I spoke to you about, which would hide the sleeping princess, don't be concerned about it. It would spoil the symmetry of the décor. We'll certainly find a different way to do it.

Dear Sir, believe me very truly yours,

Maurice Ravel

Dear friend,

Listen to Ravel. The yellow rear curtain on one level, with the cut out green level in front of it will make the décor a delightful success: take my word for it.

One further item: let me know if you agree that I should modify two of the measurements which I had given to the sceneshifter.

Very cordially yours,

Georges Mouveau

1. The stage decorator Georges Mouveau was a member of the *Apaches*. He worked at the Théâtre des Arts and later at the Opéra.

2. Jacques Drésa (1869–1929) designed the décor and costumes for *Ma Mère l'Oye* and the ballet version of *Valses nobles et sentimentales*.

3. This approximate date is based upon the contents of Ravel's letter.

4. For the ballet version of *Ma Mère l'Oye* (see plate 8).

91. to Madame Paule de Lestang[1]

4 Avenue Carnot   Friday night [January 26, 1912][2]
Paris

Dear Madame,

I am distressed: involuntarily, I am going to cause you a grave injustice. On Monday night, the first performance of *Ma Mère l'Oye* will take place at the Théâtre des Arts. Naturally, I will not be able to attend your recital: I will be obliged to remain in the wings in order to animate the fervor of my birds, pagoda slaves, and little Negroes. But the defection of one of the many composers whose works you will be performing is not such a great calamity. What is more important is that I am going to take away part of your audience.[3] This première was supposed to have taken place tomorrow, but, of course, it was postponed. The date is now definite, alas! and I am asking you to pardon me for this wrong, which, I'm afraid, I have caused you in all innocence.

With my sincere apologies, dear Madame, please believe in my respectful artistic sympathy.

Maurice Ravel

1. See letter no. 31, note 2. In addition to her talents at the keyboard, Madame de Lestang was also a soprano, and she recorded "D'Anne jouant de l'espinette," accompanying herself on the harpsichord.

2. This postmark appears on this special delivery letter.

3. Madame de Lestang's recital on Monday night, January 29, was devoted to the French art song. An interesting aspect of the program was that each song would be accompanied by its respective composer. She sang Ravel's *Sainte*, "Le Cygne" and "La Pintade," as well as works by Louis Aubert, André Caplet, Florent Schmitt, and others.

92. to Jacques Rouché

February 1, 1912

Dear Monsieur Rouché,

Your idea of mounting *Ma Mère l'Oye* enchanted me from the very beginning. For a long time, I have dreamed of writing a work for the Théâtre des Arts, which is the only theater in France today that brings us something new.

However, I didn't dare hope for the total joy, so delightful to a composer, of seeing a work for the theater realized exactly as he had conceived it. The sumptuous and delicate harmony of Drésa's décor and costumes, whose theatrical logic is so fresh and personal, seem to me the most perfect commentary for my musical fantasy. Madame Hugard[1] also proved to be an intelligent and fine collaborator, who took it upon herself to observe my tiniest instructions, and to realize them in an elegant and sensitive manner. All of my interpreters, including the children young and old, brought to their roles, large and small, an artistic integrity which delighted me and touched me profoundly.

As for the musical gifts of my friend Grovlez,[2] I have been aware of them for many years, and I knew beforehand that under the direction of this refined composer, the excellent orchestra of the Théâtre des Arts would flawlessly perform my score, which, however, does contain some very difficult passages.

Above all, dear Monsieur Rouché, I wish to express to you my pleasure at having met an artistic director whose constant concern is to respect the composer's ideas, while assisting him with the kind of intelligent advice that comes from a gentleman of taste.

Please convey my most sincere thanks to everyone, and believe in the keen gratitude of yours truly,

Maurice Ravel[3]

1. The choreographer Jeanne Hugard.

2. Gabriel Grovlez (1879–1944) and Ravel were fellow students at the Conservatoire. In addition to composing, Grovlez gave piano recitals throughout Europe, and conducted at the Théâtre des Arts, the Opéra, and the Chicago Opera.

3. The autograph of this letter has not been recovered, but a typewritten copy of it is found in the Bibliothèque de l'Opéra. Jacques Rouché wrote the following note on this copy: "Yesterday, I received the following letter from Monsieur Maurice Ravel, which I have the pleasure of posting. Together with my congratulations, I wish to express my renewed feelings of gratitude to all of my collaborators."

93. to Ralph Vaughan Williams

February 2, 1912

Dear Mr. Williams,

I am delighted to inform you that the executive committee of the S.M.I. has unanimously decided to include your song cycle with accompaniment for string quartet and piano[1] in the program of the concert on February 29. This concert will be exceptionally brilliant: Fauré will accompany Jeanne Raunay at the piano, and I'm trying to persuade Cyril Scott[2] to come and play his *Suite*, which is on the program. We will certainly have members of the British embassy in the audience, as well as the most prominent members of the British colony.

We thought that your work should be sung by Plamondon, a well-known tenor and an excellent musician, who also sings in English. The Wuillaume Quartet will accompany. If you would like to perform the piano part, that would be perfect. If not, I offer my services.

In any case, I hope that I will have the pleasure of seeing you soon. Your presence would be quite necessary, at least in order to indicate the proper tempos.[3]

Please reply immediately. It's important for the publicity which we are planning for this exceptional concert.

Please convey my respectful friendship to Mrs. Vaughan Williams, and believe me, most cordially yours,

Maurice Ravel

1. *On Wenlock Edge,* a cycle of six songs based on the poetry of A. E. Housman. The songs may also be accompanied by piano alone.

2. The English composer and poet (1879–1970).

3. Vaughan Williams attended the concert, but did not participate in the performance of his song cycle, as may be seen from the program:

1) "Scherzo"—Borodin (Duttenhoffer Quartet)
2) 2nd *Suite* for piano—Cyril Scott (performed by the composer)
3) *La Bonne chanson*—Fauré (Jeanne Raunay accompanied by the composer)
4) Sonata in one movement—Cyril Scott (performed by the composer)
5) A group of five songs—Fauré (Jeanne Raunay accompanied by the composer)
6) *On Wenlock Edge*—Vaughan Williams (Rodolphe Plamondon, tenor, the Duttenhoffer Quartet, and Maurice Ravel, piano.)

94. to Father Joseph Joubert

St.-Jean-de-Luz   August 4, 1912
Dear Father Joubert,

I am far too ignorant about the technique of the organ to risk writing for this instrument. But I intend to study it this winter, and, as soon as it will be possible, I shall endeavor to satisfy your kind request.[1]

Very truly yours,
Maurice Ravel

1. Father Joseph Joubert, an organist at the cathedral of Luçon, was preparing an anthology of contemporary organ music, *Les Maîtres contemporains de l'orgue*. This imposing set was published by Sénart, and it consists of some 1700 pages in eight volumes (1912–14). Although the vast majority of the contributors have remained obscure, there are compositions by Vincent d'Indy, Jules Massenet, Florent Schmitt, and Joaquín Turina. As it turned out, Ravel never composed for the organ.

95. to Ralph Vaughan Williams

St.-Jean-de-Luz   August 5, 1912
Dear Mr. Williams,

Enclosed is a letter which has weighed on my conscience since the day you left Paris. My friend Godebski wrote it to me, asking me to forward it to you.

Since then, every time I saw him, I promised him it would be done the next day, because I myself had to write to you. You must be wondering why I kept putting off the pleasure of congratulating you, and telling you of my sincere joy at your great success. In everyone's opinion, your song cycle was a revelation. I'm planning to write about it in an article which will be largely devoted to you.[1]

My various works which were performed last season, and, above all, *Daphnis et Chloé*, left me in pitiful condition. I had to be sent to the country in order to take care of an incipient neurasthenia. I'm completing my cure in my native region.

I almost went to London last month, but it was so hot there, it appears, that the concerts in which I was supposed to participate were delayed until October. I hope to have the pleasure of seeing you then.

In the meantime, I would be very happy to hear from you and to learn about your work. Please convey my respectful friendship to Mrs. Vaughan Williams, and believe me cordially yours,

Maurice Ravel

Delage, who is here, has asked me to send you his best regards.

1. If this article was ever written, it has yet to be traced.

96. to Jacques Rouché

8 Place Louis XIV   October 7, 1912
St.-Jean-de-Luz
Dear Monsieur Rouché,

I will be in Paris on the 15th of this month. We will thus be able to talk about your project, which is more convenient than corresponding.

As a rule, the undertaking of a new work frightens me a bit. I have to finish a host of things which are scarcely even sketched, but all of this might be cleared up in just a few days.

I believe that the libretto of this ballet has not yet been agreed upon. I would prefer to write it myself, with some guidance. The precedent of *Daphnis et Chloé*, whose libretto was a source of perpetual conflict, has made me extremely reluctant to undertake a similar experience again. But we will talk about all of this next week. I will come to see you as soon as I return.

Dear M. Rouché, believe me cordially yours,

Maurice Ravel

97. to Igor Stravinsky[1]

4 Avenue Carnot   January 19, 1913
Paris XVII
Old chap,

From the three of us, all the best wishes to all of you. They're late in arriving, but I still haven't finished correcting the proofs of *Daphnis*, in which I have discovered things which would make Astruc's hair stand up on end.[2] I heard about you through Delage, who went to seek the antidote which his harmony craved in *The Rite of Spring*. . . . When you just think that M. d'Indy, whose *Fervaal* I heard the other day, is in good health! There is no justice.

Did you know that M...l[3] intended to get a divorce, and that he asked Abbé Petit's opinion about the matter?

I have been assured that Nijinsky no longer wants to hear anything about dancing.[4] Well now, I can see it clearly, M. Poincaré[5] will have to take up choreography.

See you soon. Affectionately,

ΠR

1. Stravinsky (1882–1971) arrived in Paris in May 1910. With the Ballet Russe performances of *The Firebird*, he immediately became an international celebrity, and soon met Debussy, Ravel, and the leading French artistic personalities of the day. His close friendship with Ravel extended into the war years, but during the 1920s their careers went in separate directions. Despite some criticism of each other's works, their artistic and personal esteem remained mutual. In a brief necrology, Stravinsky wrote as follows:

> Ravel's death did not surprise me. I knew that for some time the gravity of his illness was causing extreme anxiety.
>
> I also knew that it was the very nature of this illness which brusquely halted his musical production.
>
> Our friendship goes back many years. I met him when I first made my debut in Paris with *The Firebird*, and I remember that he then played for me fragments of his marvelous *Daphnis et Chloé*, which he was composing.
>
> France has lost one of its greatest composers, whose prestige is recognized throughout the world. History will assure him a place of honor in the domain of music, which he achieved with so much courage and such firm conviction. ("Maurice Ravel est mort," *L'Intransigeant*, December 29, 1937.)

2. The publisher and impresario Gabriel Astruc (1864–1938). Ravel's comment about him is yet another example of his subtle humor. A young Polish pianist, Arthur Rubinstein, met Astruc in 1904, and recalled his manager as follows: "He was a man in his forties whose heavy build and premature baldness made him look older than his age" (*My Young Years*, New York: Alfred A. Knopf, 1973, p. 123).

3. Several of Ravel's personal friends would qualify as the mysterious "M...l."

4. Apparently because of his frustration in choreographing *The Rite of Spring*.

5. The statesman Raymond Poincaré had been elected president of France just two days before this letter was written.

98. to Lucien Garban

Clarens-Montreux   March 28, 1913
Hôtel des Crêtes

So sorry, dear friend. I'll miss you this time as I will only be returning to Paris towards the end of the month. But I do hope that you will be there for the Russian season. You must hear Stravinsky's *Rite of Spring*. I believe it will be as important an event as the première of *Pelléas*. See you soon. Drop me a note if you have the time.

You may know that I am working on a reconstruction of Mussorgsky's *Khovanshchina*.[1]

Cordially yours,
Maurice Ravel

1. This adaptation was carried out with Stravinsky in Clarens, Switzerland during March and April 1913. Diaghilev gave the commission to Stravinsky, who suggested that Ravel collaborate in the project. Essentially, their task was to reorchestrate selected passages of Mussorgsky's opera. In addition, Stravinsky composed a chorus for the finale, based upon a theme which Mussorgsky had notated. This joint version of *Khovanshchina* was performed by the Ballet Russe at the Théâtre des Champs-Elysées on June 5, 1913. (Ravel's manuscript, which consists of 40 pages for orchestra, is now in the Pierpont Morgan Library. It was formerly in the collection of Serge Lifar.)

99. to Madame Alfredo Casella[1]

Clarens-Montreux   April 2, 1913
Hôtel des Crêtes
Dear Madame and friend,

We are all upset at what you wrote about your health. It is true that an operation, today, should be no cause for alarm. Nevertheless, the anxiety of waiting and the prospect of lying flat on your back for several days are extremely disagreeable. Mama—and I, of course—beg you to keep us fully informed. I was going to write to you as soon as I received your letter, but I myself was in pitiful shape, because my work began to resemble a grave illness: fever, insomnia, lack of appetite. At the end of 3 days, a song emerged, based upon a text by Mallarmé . . .[2]

That is what the next page of my letter is about, but it's not for you. Not that the text is improper, but simply that it concerns our very holy S.M.I. I have submitted several projects and suitable observations to interest my honorable colleagues. I still don't know when I will be returning to Paris, perhaps not before the end of April. By then, you will certainly have recovered, and you will be able to resume your wild life, which you will be giving up for a few days. Above all, have Alfredo[3] write to me.

Shake his hand for me, and please believe in the respectful friendship of yours truly,

Maurice Ravel

Best regards from Mama to you both. For three days, Stravinsky has also been meaning to write to you. While awaiting his letter, I can already tell you not to look for an apartment for him, because he will be coming to Paris alone.

Would you ask Alfredo to look at the quartet by M. Arènal,[4] and decide if this work should be presented at the S.M.I.?

The weather, which was improving for 2 days, has again become horrid. It's cold, and raining, and a little higher up it's snowing.

: : :

To the board of the S.M.I., or, instead, M. Gustave Samazeuilh.

I) I will certainly not be in Paris on April 15. It is rather embarrassing, I think, to ask Mlle Hatto[5] to come and sing, without being accompanied by the composer. My songs, moreover, don't even offer the interest of a first performance. The project below (II) seems more interesting to me. For the first concert, have Debussy's *Preludes* (book 2) been considered? Have they been performed at the Société Nationale?

Are Erik Satie's *Pièces froides* on the program of the first concert? It was understood that Viñes would perform them—keep in mind that the Société Nationale is doing everything it can to attract Satie.

Do you recall that a commitment was made to perform M. Milhaud's Sonata at the first concert?[6] No doubt it was done <u>to make him happy</u>, but after all....

II) Stupendous project for a scandalous concert. Perhaps not at the Conservatoire: the Ministers would never permit the same kind of behavior there as they do in the Chamber of Deputies.

Pieces for (a) narrator; (b) and (c) voice and: piano, string quartet, 2 flutes, and 2 clarinets.

(a) Pierrot lunaire: Schoenberg (21 pieces: 40 minutes)[7]
(b) Japanese Songs: Stravinsky (4 pieces:[8] 10 minutes)
(c) 2 poems by S. Mallarmé: Maurice Ravel (about 10 minutes)

(a) and (b) will make the audience howl; (c) will calm them down, and the people will go out whistling tunes—N.B. let me respectfully point out to my honorable colleagues that I know (a) only through hearsay. But we must play this work for which blood is flowing in Germany and Austria. As for (b), they are worthy of their composer, whom I judge to be a genius. For the composer of (c), consult Messieurs Lalo and A. Pougin.[9]

We are writing to Schoenberg in order to obtain his cooperation. The composers will conduct their own works. Thus, in principle, this concert should be scheduled towards the end of May (because of Stravinsky, whose *Rite of Spring* will have been recently performed).[10]

Continuation of the projects for the S.M.I. and . . . for

I think we will have to wait for the first performance of Stravinsky's work, which will not fail to create a stir, even in the heart of Monsieur P. Souday.[11] For that, as well as the other concerts, avoid coinciding with the Ballet Russe, whose dates are already determined irrevocably (make inquiries). Please send me these dates, so we can make arrangements with Schoenberg.

III) Please write to Raoul Bardac, 47 rue de Poissy (St. Germain en Laye) informing him of the deadline for sending or auditioning orchestral scores. Likewise to M. Joaquín Cassado,[12] who wishes to submit a cello concerto. Monsieur J. Cras informs me that he submitted a quartet. If the work is accepted, he would like to be informed as soon as possible of its date of performance, so that he would be able (I did say would be able) to come to Paris.[13]

IV) I have assured Stravinsky that thanks to Inghelbrecht, we have choruses in France capable of singing his recent composition, which is extremely difficult. His piece would be excellent for the orchestral concert[14] (very short, barely 5 minutes).

May Independence protect you in its holy safekeeping! but not too much, right?

ΠR

1. Hélène Kahn, herself a musician, married Alfredo Casella in 1907.

2. "Soupir," the first of Ravel's *Trois Poèmes de Stéphane Mallarmé.* At this point, only two songs were contemplated. The manuscripts and the score of the Mallarmé songs indicate the following: "Soupir" (Clarens, April 2, 1913); "Placet futile" (Paris, May 1913); "Surgi de la croupe et du bond" (St.-Jean-de-Luz, August 1913).

3. The distinguished Italian composer, pianist, conductor, and teacher, Alfredo Casella (1883–1947) studied at the Conservatoire. He remained in Paris until 1914, and served on the board of the S.M.I. In his memoirs, Casella noted the following:

> In the winter of 1900–01 I audited Gabriel Fauré's composition class. A very brilliant class in quality, it included at that time Roger-Ducasse, Charles Koechlin,

Maurice Ravel, and several others of great talent. . . . Ravel and I became close friends at once. . . . As soon as I made his acquaintance, I realized what an intellectual force inhabited that tiny little man and tried to be around him as much as possible. . . . His culture was vast, in literature as well as in music. I owe him my first knowledge of Russian music, including that of Mussorgsky. Once or twice a week we met at the home of Pierre Sechiari, the concertmaster of the Lamoureux orchestra, and read in four-hand arrangements all the operatic and symphonic repertoire of the Russian "Five" and of Glazunov, Liapunov, Liadov, and others. Tchaikovsky was excluded from these sessions, because Ravel detested him. A great impression was made on us by the music of Borodin, Balakirev, and Rimsky-Korsakov. There was developing, at least in the bold and unprejudiced circle headed by Debussy and Ravel, an anti-Wagnerian viewpoint which was also anti-Germanic. This constituted a fact of great importance in the history of music, after so many years of autocratic domination by German art. (*Music in My Time: The Memoirs of Alfredo Casella,* trans. Spencer Norton, Norman: University of Oklahoma Press, 1955, pp. 59–61.)

4. He was apparently an amateur musician. The Music Division of the Bibliothèque Nationale has a short piece by one R. Arènal, a simple waltz in C major entitled *Petit Conte* (Little Story), published in 1913.

5. The French soprano Jane Hatto, who had sung the first performance of Ravel's *Shéhérazade* with Alfred Cortot conducting in May 1904 (see the letter to her, no. 187).

6. Darius Milhaud (1892–1974) composed over 400 works. He met Ravel in 1913, and in his autobiography, Milhaud recalled his reaction to the dress rehearsal of *L'Heure espagnole*: "I found the subtle elegance of this music seductive, but felt some regret at not finding the same depth of feeling in Ravel as in Debussy. From that time on, therefore, I was hostile to Ravel's music, and so I have remained, though I freely confess my attitude was not always justified" (*Ma vie heureuse,* Paris: Editions Belfond, 1973, p. 29). In 1927, Ravel defended Milhaud's opera *Les Malheurs d'Orphée* from the diatribes of Pierre Lalo, which led to a rapprochement between the composers (see letter no. 276).

7. Schoenberg's work was not performed in Paris until 1922. Conducted by Darius Milhaud, with Marya Freund as soloist, it engendered a riot.

8. As there are three songs in this cycle, this is either a slip on Ravel's part, or it is possible that Stravinsky mentioned a fourth song to him.

9. The French writer on music Arthur Pougin (1834–1921), like Pierre Lalo, was frequently critical of Ravel's works.

10. On May 29th, Ravel attended the stormy première of *Le Sacre du printemps,* which one critic solemnly declared to be anti-music and hysteria.

11. The literary critic Paul Souday (1869–1929) wrote for *Le Temps.*

12. The Spanish composer (1867–1926).

13. The French composer Jean Cras (1879–1932) lived in Brest, some 300 miles west of Paris.

14. Stravinsky's cantata for male chorus and orchestra, *Zvezdoliki* (Starface), based on a Russian text by K. Balmont. It was first performed in Brussels on April 19, 1939.

100. to Roland-Manuel

Hôtel des Crêtes   April 3, 1913
Clarens-Montreux

Dear friend,

This is our third day of sunshine. I took advantage of it by catching laryngitis, in the country to which they send people who suffer from it. Not only am I finishing *Khovanshchina*, but I'm also composing 2 songs for voice, piano, string quartet, 2 flutes, and 2 clarinets, based on texts by Mallarmé. Has your book been published?[1] I promised Mr. José de Arriaga,[2] 5 Hurtado de Amezaga, Bilbao, that you would send him a copy of it as soon as it appeared. Don't make a Basque break his word, especially to a compatriot . . . and let me hear from you soon.

Very cordially yours,
Maurice Ravel

1. Roland-Manuel's *Maurice Ravel et son oeuvre,* published by Durand in 1914, was the first of his four books and many articles on Ravel.

2. The library at Montfort l'Amaury contains a book by Arriaga in Spanish and Basque, *Lekobide* (Bilbao, 1913), with the following dedication: "This copy is for M. Ravel, the eminent composer and Basque patriot. Bilbao, February, 1913."

101. to Roland-Manuel

[Hôtel des Crêtes]   April 12, 1913
[Clarens-Montreux]

You have won only a dozen macaroons dear friend: indeed, the first poem is "Soupir." But the superior plated lady's watch was destined for the person who would also guess the second one, which is "Placet futile."[1] The little comment of G.C.?[2] It's not Anatole France,[3] of course, but the intention is there all the same. I understand that ℗ is still < ⌐.[4] Carraud gets even when he can, doesn't he?

Very cordially yours,
Maurice Ravel

I am impatiently awaiting your divertissement.[5] That's precisely what's missing here . . .

1. In his reply to Ravel's letter of April 3, Roland-Manuel guessed that he would set Mallarmé's "Soupir" and "Apparition."

2. The music critic Gaston Carraud (1869–1920), who wrote for the newspaper *La Liberté.*

3. France (1844–1924) was celebrated for his elegant style and won the Nobel Prize in literature (1921).

4. Meaning that Claude Debussy is still "the source of" Maurice Ravel. Writing in *La Liberté* on April 8, 1913, Carraud commented on a performance by Ricardo Viñes at a Société Nationale recital, in which he praised the music of Jean Cras and indirectly criticized both Debussy and Ravel: Viñes "also gave a marvelous performance of the *Poèmes intimes* by M. Jean Cras, which are musical and sincere works, and three recently published Preludes from book 2 by M. Debussy, which clearly illustrate why M. Ravel must now concede that he is Debussy's disciple."

5. In Ravel's parlance, a dry-as-dust academic fugue.

102. to Ida Godebska

Ongi Et[h]ori[1]   July 29, 1913
23 rue Sopite
St.-Jean-de-Luz

The swimming is great, dear Ida! It's hot, and it only rains at night. I finished the corrections of *Shéhérazade*.[2] I only have about 40 more letters to write, and then I'll resume work. When will we see you?

Our affectionate regards to all.

Yours truly,

Maurice Ravel

Which address?

1. In Basque this means "Welcome" (the correct spelling is "Ongi Etorri" or "Ongi Ethori"; see plate 9).

2. Although Ravel's song cycle was first performed in 1904, the orchestral score was not published by Durand until 1914.

103. to Dumitru Kiriac

Ongi Ethori   August 3, 1913
23 rue Sopite
St.-Jean-de-Luz
My dear friend,

Heaven forbid that you be in Paris once more during my absence! Or, in that case, keep going until you arrive here—the largest part of the trip is behind you.

What a disconcerting silence of . . . I don't dare recall how many years! For lack of better, I spoke about you at length with M. Otescu.[1] I am very pleased to learn through you that Béla Bartók has some sympathy for my works. I know some of his, in particular a string quartet which is indeed one of the rare works in recent years that I found striking and moving.[2]

Don't stay out of touch for so long next time. I will try, for my part, to write to you now and then. And if I go to Bucharest some day, I will do my utmost to see you.

My mother sends you her best regards. My dear friend, believe me very cordially yours,

Maurice Ravel

1. The Romanian composer Ion Nonna Otescu (1888–1940), who was a pupil of Kiriac in Bucharest. Between 1908 and 1911 he studied composition in Paris with Vincent d'Indy and Charles-Marie Widor. Otescu later returned to Romania, where he taught composition and served as the director of the Bucharest Conservatory.

2. A reference to Bartók's first string quartet, opus 7. In a letter to Rudolph Ganz, written on April 23, 1910, Bartók wrote: "It just so happens that I do not know anything of Ravel; I will send for his latest piano pieces without fail" (I wish to thank Mrs. Rudolph Ganz for kindly sending me a copy of Bartók's letter).

Ravel and Bartók (1881–1945) met briefly in the 1920s, first in Paris and later on in New York. In a commemorative article, Bartók made the following observations:

... The appearance of an isolated genius, no matter how important, cannot be completely convincing in relation to the musical life of a nation: one might attribute it merely to chance. The discovery of two analogous cases is more convincing, and, in any event, one may conclude from it that a kind of crystallization of a phenomenon is taking place, produced by the social environment of a country. And that is why, from our Hungarian point of view, next to that of Debussy, the genius of Ravel is so very significant. (*La Revue musicale*, December 1939, p. 244.)

104. to Roland-Manuel

Ongi Ethori   August 27, 1913
23 rue Sopite
St.-Jean-de-Luz

If you're not too involved with your biography, dear friend, stop everything: Durand is prepared to accept the proposed scheme, namely, biography by Roland-Manuel, and musical analysis by Vuillermoz. Reply immediately, so that I can write to Vuillermoz. Durand is awaiting my answer in order to make the offer official.[1]

I have just finished "Surgi de la croupe." We will soon witness a Debussy-Ravel match. The other day, our publisher sent me a desperate letter, because Bonniot[2] refused the authorization for "Soupir" and "Placet futile," which Debussy had just set to music. I have settled everything.[3]

Kind regards to all. Cordially yours,

Maurice Ravel

1. For whatever reason, Vuillermoz did not collaborate in the project. He later wrote an important article on Ravel's style in *Maurice Ravel par quelques-uns de ses familiers,* pp. 1–95.

2. Mallarmé's son-in-law was the executor of his estate (see letter no. 51, note 3).

3. In 1913, Debussy and Ravel each set three poems of Mallarmé to music. Through an amazing coincidence, two of their three poems were the same. Ravel asked Dr. Bonniot for permission to utilize the poet's texts, and the required authorization was granted promptly. A short time later, when Dr. Bonniot was approached by Jacques Durand with a similar request, he agreed to the publication of Debussy's setting of "Eventail," but refused "Soupir" and "Placet futile," whose rights had just been granted to Ravel. All ended well, however, as Ravel managed to convince Dr. Bonniot to reconsider, a gesture which is typical of his probity and good will.

105. to Igor Stravinsky

Ongi Ethori   August 28, 1913
23 rue Sopite
Saint-Jean-de-Luz

I'm not criticizing you at all, old chap: I imagine that you are working on *Le Rossignol*[1] day and night. I am rising from the crupper and "leaping,"[2] as our colleague Tcherepnin[3] would say. This means that I have just finished the third Mallarmé poem. I am now going to reexamine the second one, and return immediately to *Zazpiak-Bat.*[4] I'm giving myself one day off, which will be devoted to some 20 letters. Think of all those unfortunate people waiting for more than 2 months for an immediate reply . . . For one of these letters, I need your help: I need to know where the Russians are right now.[5] Since the month of June, those poor devils are simply waiting for my letter in order to send me some money (royalties for the 4th performance).[6] That is for Svetlov.[7] I still have to write to Diaghilev to tell him not to count on me for the Scarlatti ballet.[8] I really have better things to do.

So, write an immediate reply—don't be like me. No need for literature: address of the Ballet Russe—news of your family—Believe me, etc. . . . signature.

My affectionate regards to you and yours.

Maurice Ravel

Furthermore, if you have a moment, write me a long letter.

1. Ravel playfully invented a verb based on Stravinsky's title: I imagine that you are "nightingaling" day and night.

2. Similarly, a bit of juggling with the title of Mallarmé's poem.

3. The Russian composer Nikolay Tcherepnin (1873–1945) spent much of his life in France. From 1908 to 1914, he conducted many of Diaghilev's productions in western Europe.

4. See letter no. 31, note 3.

5. The Ballet Russe had sailed for South America in mid-August.

6. Of *Daphnis et Chloé*.

7. The critic Valerian Svetlov frequently assumed Diaghilev's responsibilities in his absence.

8. Probably a reference to *The Good-Humored Ladies*: based on Domenico Scarlatti's music as adapted by Vincenzo Tommasini (1878–1950), this Ballet Russe production was given in 1917.

106. to Edouard Ganche[1]

Ongi Ethori   August 29, 1913
23 rue Sopite
St.-Jean-de-Luz
Dear Sir,

Your kind letter found me in the midst of preparing to leave Paris. I brought it with me, along with many others, and I intended to answer them as soon as I arrived. But I began working, and it is only today that I am resuming my correspondence. First of all, I would like to thank you for your book. It is the first, to the best of my knowledge, to provide a very complete documentation about the life of Chopin, and I don't have to tell you of the interest I took in reading it.

For *Daphnis et Chloé*, you could extract, if absolutely necessary, 2 or 3 fragments. But I do not believe that my contract would give me the right to extract such a considerable part of it. In any case, you would have to consult with my publisher Durand.[2]

With my sincere apologies for this late reply, dear Sir, accept my best wishes.

Maurice Ravel

1. Edouard Ganche (1880–1945) devoted much of his life to furthering Chopin's art by editing his music, collecting documents, and writing extensively about him. In 1910, he founded a Chopin society, and Ravel agreed to serve as its vice president.

2. Ganche was apparently hoping to perform a piano transcription of *Daphnis et Chloé*.

107. to Roland-Manuel

[St.-Jean-de-Luz]   October 7, 1913
Dear friend,

You have returned home, no doubt. Perhaps you even appreciate the glorious servitude of the barracks. Excuse me for not having written for such a long time. When I received your last letter, I was finishing my 3 poems. Indeed,

"Placet futile" was completed, but I retouched it. I fully realize the great audacity of having attempted to interpret this sonnet in music. It was necessary that the melodic contour, the modulations, and the rhythms be as precious, as properly contoured as the sentiment and the images of the text. Nevertheless, it was necessary to maintain the elegant deportment of the poem. Above all, it was necessary to maintain the profound and exquisite tenderness which suffuses all of this. Now that it's done, I'm a bit nervous about it.

By the same mail—it's high time!—I am writing to Vuillermoz. I think it would be a good idea for you to insist also.[1]

I was forgetting to tell you that when the Mallarmé songs were finished, I traveled in Spain.[2] Since coming back, I've been working on *Zazpiak-Bat* . . . and above all, for 2 days, I've not been doing a thing. The weather is so nasty that I'm thinking of returning to Paris soon.

Give my kind regards to your parents, and believe me very cordially yours,
Maurice Ravel

1. See the opening paragraph of letter no. 104.
2. The Spanish border is just a twenty minute drive from Saint-Jean-de-Luz.

108. to Igor Stravinsky

Comarques, Thorpe-Le-Soken[1]   December 13, 1913
Old chap,

It's been a while since I've heard any sensational news about your health.[2] About 3 weeks ago, I learned of your sudden demise, but, as I received a card from you that very morning, the news didn't affect me in any special way.

Delage must have told you that your "Japanese" songs will be performed on January 14, with his "Hindus"[3] and my Mallarmés. We are counting on your presence. In 3 days I'll be in London, where I hope to hear some news about *Le Sacre du printemps.*[4]

Will *Le Rossignol* be performed soon?[5] Please convey my respectful friendship to Mme Stravinsky. Kiss the children, and believe in the affection of yours truly,
Maurice Ravel

1. In Essex, England.
2. A brief notice in *Comœdia* (October 11, 1913) stated that Stravinsky had been placed in a sanatorium in St. Petersburg. The report was apparently a rumor, and it turned out to be false.
3. Maurice Delage's *Quatre Poèmes hindous,* for voice and instrumental ensemble.
4. Following the Parisian première on May 29, 1913, Stravinsky's ballet was performed three times in London during the summer.

5. The first performance was given by the Ballet Russe at the Opéra on May 26, 1914, with Pierre Monteux conducting (see Ravel's article on *Le Rossignol,* p. 380).

109. to Désiré-Emile Inghelbrecht

[4 Avenue Carnot]   Wednesday evening[1]
My dear Inghelbrecht,

I rushed to the foyer after the concert . . . and didn't have the pleasure of seeing you. What became of you? I would have keenly wished to tell you in person how satisfied I was with the performance of my poems, those of my friend Stravinsky, and those of my illustrious student.[2]

And, it goes without saying, I was a bit nervous: 3 compositions of this sort, with only two rehearsals—there was good reason to be nervous!

I applaud your tour de force, and thank you triply.

Yours truly,

Maurice Ravel

1. Although undated, this special delivery letter is postmarked [Thursday] January 15, 1914. It was written just after the S.M.I. concert on Wednesday evening, January 14.

2. That is, Ravel's *Trois Poèmes de Stéphane Mallarmé,* Stravinsky's *Trois Poésies de la lyrique japonaise,* and Delage's *Quatre Poèmes hindous.*

110. to Alfred Kalisch[1]

January 26, 1914

Dear Sir,

It is with a deep sense of embarrassment that I write to you. For over a month I have been feeling terribly remorseful. As soon as I returned, I wanted to— and had to—fulfill the pleasant duty of expressing my gratitude to the Music Club.[2] But I found a host of commitments which prevented me from doing so until now: the orchestration of a work for a performance in Lyon on January 10;[3] the corrections and rehearsals of my Mallarmé poems, etc. I spent the new year holiday bent over my manuscripts and proofs, and it is only today that I'm beginning to catch my breath.

It is much too late, and yet the memory of the Music Club's friendly welcome is so fresh, and the pleasure it gave me is still so vivid, that in spite of everything, I am venturing to ask you—5 weeks late!—to be my spokesman to the members of your society: beg them to excuse me, and tell them how grateful I am for their kind reception.

I also beg you to excuse me, dear Sir, and believe me, very truly yours,

Maurice Ravel

1. The English music critic Alfred Kalisch (1863–1933) wrote for the *Star,* the *World,* and other British newspapers.

2. The London Music Club, founded by Kalisch, occasionally invited composers to participate in recitals of their music, which were followed by a gala dinner. In addition to Ravel, guests of the Club included Debussy, Schoenberg, and Sibelius. One author has observed that "club members, for the most part, were distinguished by their wealth, advanced age, paunchiness, and stertorous breathing" (Marian C. McKenna, *Myra Hess,* London: Hamish Hamilton, 1976, p. 50).

3. A reorchestrated version of *Noël des jouets,* which Ravel had completed in December 1913. The performance was given at the Concerts Witkowski by Jane Bathori, who was making her debut in Lyon.

111. to Madame Alfredo Casella

St.-Jean-de-Luz[1]   March 21, 1914

Thank you, dear friend, for your kind letter and forgive my persistent silence. I am working on the trio[2] despite the cold, the storms, the thunder, the rain, and the hail. Delighted at Monteux's success.[3] So, modern music doesn't make the public run away?[4] I'm really sorry to have to miss the *Notte,*[5] and sincerely wish it all the success that it deserves. Send me news immediately, and clippings, if possible. Affectionate regards to both of you from yours truly,

ℿℝ

1. The face of this postcard shows the interior of the 13th-century church of Saint John the Baptist, in Saint-Jean-de-Luz.

2. The manuscript of the Trio indicates that it was written in Saint-Jean-de-Luz between April 3 and August 7, 1914.

3. Following his studies at the Conservatoire, Pierre Monteux (1875–1964) went on to establish a brilliant international career. He introduced many contemporary works, among them *Daphnis et Chloé* and *The Rite of Spring,* and later conducted extensively in the United States.

4. On March 1, 1914, Monteux conducted the first concert performance of Stravinsky's *Petrushka* at the Casino de Paris.

5. Alfredo Casella conducted the première of his *Notte di maggio* (May Night, for soprano and orchestra, based on the poetry of Giosuè Carducci) on March 29, 1914, at the Concerts Colonne.

112. to Ida Godebska

St.-Jean-de-Luz   April 8, 1914
Dear friend,

I'm finally back—since Monday, but "I am . . . still . . . completely knocked ou-ou-out."[1] The stay in Lyon, like Geneva, was delightful, but what a trip!

In Lyon, I met with Pierre Haour,[2] who left his regular Tuesday guests—Stravinsky among others—to come see me. Would you do the same on a Sunday night?[3] And they boast about Polish friendship![4]

The concert went well. Of course, there wasn't Londonian enthusiasm, but you have to take meridional coolness into account.

I wrote to you from Geneva to go see Chevillard,[5] as I had forgotten my copy of *The Rite of Spring*[6] at Monteux's home. Apparently it was a triumph.[7] When I think of all those idiots who booed it less than a year ago!

I was forgetting to tell you that at the concert in Lyon, amid the success of the *Histoires naturelles*, 2 ladies were overheard saying, "All the same, it didn't sound like Beethoven."

To conclude, 2 gems taken from the classified section of the *Geneva Journal*, which were pointed out to me by my aunt. I don't remember the others, alas!

For Sale, a mare belonging to a gendarme.[8]

Young Lady, wishing to get rid of a sofa, would be willing to lose something on it.

Write very soon. Affectionate regards to all,

Maurice Ravel

And you know, the owner of the International Hotel in Geneva is the widow Amherd!

1. A humorous allusion to Massenet's *Manon*: her opening aria begins "Je suis . . . encor . . . tout étourdie . . ." (I am . . . still . . . completely dazed . . .).

2. A close friend of Ravel, he was a member of the *Apaches*.

3. The traditional time for the Godebski musicales.

4. Ida Godebska was born in Cracow.

5. See p. 347, note 4.

6. For piano duet; the full score was first published in 1921.

7. Referring to the first concert performance of *The Rite of Spring*, which Monteux conducted at the Casino de Paris on April 5, 1914.

8. Grammatically, a mare fathered by a gendarme! (Une jument provenant d'un gendarme).

113. to Ralph Vaughan Williams

June 7, 1914

My dear friend,

No, alas! I will not be going to London, and the following letter, which I am addressing to the English press, will explain the reason to you.

Sir,

My most important work, *Daphnis et Chloé,* is to be produced at the Drury Lane Theatre on Tuesday,[1] June 9. I was overjoyed; and fully appreciating the great honour done to me, considered the event as one of the weightiest[2] in my artistic career. Now I learn that what will be produced before the London public is not my work in its original form, but a makeshift arrangement which I had accepted to write at Mr. Diaghilev's special request, in order to facilitate production in certain minor centres.

Mr. Diaghilev probably considers London as one of the aforesaid "minor centres" since he is about to produce at Drury Lane, in spite of his positive word, the new version, without chorus.

I am deeply surprised and grieved and I consider the proceedings as disrespectful towards the London public as well as towards the composer. I shall therefore be extremely thankful to offering you my thanks in anticipation, I remain, dear Sir, faithfully yours,

Maurice Ravel

This letter—which should not deceive you with regard to my progress in the English language, because it is only a translation—should appear in the *Times*, the *Morning Post*, the *Daily Mail*, and the *Daily Telegraph*. If you could arrange to have it published elsewhere, I would be extremely grateful. I owe this protest to the English public,[3] which received me in an unforgettable way.

I recommend that you go to see *Le Rossignol* by Stravinsky; musically, it is a genuine masterpiece. The décor and costumes are wonderful.

I want to thank you for the generous offer of your hospitality, which I would have accepted without hesitation, were it not for these unfortunate circumstances.

Please convey my respectful friendship to Mrs. Vaughan Williams, and, dear friend, believe me very cordially yours,

Maurice Ravel

1. In the autograph, "Tuesdy."
2. In the autograph, "veightiest." By copying out an English translation of his letter to the press, Ravel created a unique document. In addition to the two slips previously noted, the final sentence of the letter indicates that French formulas may be confusing when translated literally. The *Morning Post* printed the conclusion of the letter as follows: "I shall therefore be extremely thankful to you if you will kindly print this letter. Offering you thanks in anticipation, I remain yours, etc., Maurice Ravel." (The autograph is partially reproduced in Orenstein, "Some Unpublished Music and Letters by Maurice Ravel," p. 316.)
3. In an article entitled "Composer and Impresario, M. Maurice Ravel versus M. Diaghilev" (*Comœdia*, June 18, 1914), the impresario replied that *Daphnis et Chloé* had been previously performed in Paris with the chorus, which proved to be "not only useless but actually detrimental. I was therefore obliged to beg Monsieur Ravel to write the second version, which was successfully accomplished by the distinguished composer." Ravel in turn replied that *Daphnis et Chloé* would be performed in the future with

the chorus in all major productions, because Diaghilev would now be bound by written, not oral, agreements.

114. to Georges de Feure[1]

4 Avenue Carnot   June 19, 1914
Paris
Dear Sir,

I received your kind letter concerning a project in which you propose that I compose a ballet based upon your argument destined for the Alhambra Theatre in London.

In principle, I would find this project captivating, but a bilateral engagement would have to intervene in this matter, between the management of the Alhambra and me.

This contract, like the one drawn up for Debussy's "Le Palais du silence,"[2] would stipulate the general terms, including the schedule of payments and the delivery of the ballet. Of course, it would still be useful for the management of the Alhambra to come to terms with my publisher regarding the rental of the orchestral material: Durand and Co., 4 Place de la Madeleine, in Paris, the proprietors of all my works. The right of publication would naturally be excluded from the contract between the Alhambra and me.

The premium which the Alhambra will reserve for me should be representative of my royalties in England, and as I must, moreover, defer some important works in progress, it seems to me that its sum should not be less than Fifteen Thousand francs. Moreover, it would be useful to determine the approximate length of the ballet, and the eventual make-up of the orchestra. Furthermore, I would like to read other ballet arguments by you. The areas which I believe would most conveniently suit this project would be an exotic subject, or a French or Italian festival set in the 18th century.[3]

Please examine all of this, dear Sir, and ask the Alhambra management to send me a draft of a contract, which I will examine at leisure.

For your information, I am leaving for St.-Jean-de-Luz (Lower Pyrenees), where I will reside this summer. Here is my address: 23 rue Sopite, in Saint-Jean-de-Luz.

Believe me, dear Sir, very cordially yours,
Maurice Ravel[4]

1. Georges de Feure (1868–1928, the pseudonym of Georges van Sluijters) was a French painter, lithographer, and author.

2. This ballet in one act by Georges de Feure was begun by Debussy in 1914 and left incomplete.

3. Despite Ravel's interest, nothing came out of this project. Feure did submit two

libretti to Ravel. Formerly in the composer's home at Montfort l'Amaury, they are now in the Music Division of the Bibliothèque Nationale: (1) *Le Masque terrible*, which is based on Poe's chilling tale, *The Masque of the Red Death*; (2) *Les Jardins d'Antinoüs* (The Gardens of Antinoüs), which is set in a dreamlike garden on the banks of the Nile. Antinoüs, a jaded tyrant, magnanimously allows the young Bithynian slave Mallinda to be united with her lover, and then drowns himself in the Nile. It is not difficult to see why Ravel rejected these banal libretti, which were on the same level as the texts he had set for the Prix de Rome (See Jean-Michel Nectoux, "Maurice Ravel et sa bibliothèque musicale").

4. A copy of Ravel's autograph is found in the archives of Durand and Company.

115. to Lucien Garban

Ongi Ethori   June 30, 1914
23 rue Sopite
St.-Jean-de-Luz

My dear friend,

I trust that my letter will find you in London, and that you will have heard *Daphnis*—alas! without the chorus—unless my protests published in the English press persuaded Diaghilev to withdraw my work entirely from his programs.

It's been about ten days since I left Paris, and the beautiful sky, the heat, and the flies of my native region have made me neglect to learn the outcome of this controversy.[1]

It's at least 95 degrees, and for relief I'm working on the trio and *Zazpiak-Bat*, despite the numerous diversions: Basque pelota, local fireworks, *toros de fuego*,[2] and other pyrotechnics. The fountain displays[3] will begin the day after tomorrow. The public pool doesn't open until July 1, and I'm waiting for that day with an impatience which the temperature renders legitimate.

Write soon. My mother sends you her good wishes; add to them the cordial regards of yours truly,

Maurice Ravel

1. The first performance in England of *Daphnis et Chloé* took place at the Drury Lane Theatre on June 9, 1914, with Michel Fokine and Thamara Karsavina in the title roles, Pierre Monteux conducting, and the chorus omitted. The other works on the program, Balakirev's *Thamar* and Rimsky-Korsakov's *Scheherazade*, were conducted by Thomas Beecham. When Ravel later completed *La Valse* for Diaghilev, he refused to stage the work, a decision which engendered a permanent rupture of relations between them.

2. Literally, in Spanish, "bulls of fire," referring to a mechanical bull with fireworks shooting out of it which was run in the streets as part of the local festivities.

3. In the French, "jeux d'eau."

116. to Madame Alfredo Casella

St.-Jean-de-Luz   July 18, 1914

Dear friend, may the boldness of these svelt mountain crests bring the affectionate regards of my mother and myself to both of you.[1]

Despite the fine weather, the trio has not progressed in 3 weeks, and it disgusts me. But today, it didn't seem to be so loathsome . . . and the carburetor is repaired.

Alfredo is certainly right to compose for the piano: it goes 3 times faster.

ГГR

1. The face of this postcard shows the mountain crests surrounding Urrugne, which is near Saint-Jean-de-Luz.

117. to Maurice Delage

Ongi Ethori   August 4, 1914
23 rue Sopite
St.-Jean-de-Luz
My dear old chap,

Write to me immediately, if you receive this, so that I can feel the presence of a friend. There are many people here for whom I have a great deal of sympathy. But it's not that. . . . If you only knew how I am suffering! . . . Since this morning, unceasingly, the same horrible, criminal idea . . . if I leave my poor old mama, it would surely kill her. Moreover, France isn't waiting for me in order to be saved. . . . But that's all rationalization, and I feel it falling apart from hour to hour . . . and to hear no more of it, I'm working.

Yes, I'm working; and with an insane certainty and lucidity. But, during this time, the blues are at work too, and suddenly I find myself sobbing over my sharps and flats!

Naturally, when I go downstairs, and am with my poor mama, I have to appear calm, even amusing . . . but will I be able to keep it up?

This has been going on for 4 days, since the tocsin. . . .

Write quickly, old chap, I beg of you.

Affectionately,

Maurice Ravel

118. to Edouard Ravel

Ongi Ethori   August 8, 1914
23 rue Sopite
St.-Jean-de-Luz
Dear Edouard,

Today is August 8, and we still haven't received anything from you. Yet it's likely that you wrote a long time ago! I imagine that you heard some news about us from M. Pavlovsky,[1] who promised me to pass by Avenue Carnot or to phone you at Levallois.

Our situation isn't the most cheerful. There aren't 10 francs in the house. Durand must be closed. The Society of Authors too. Most of our friends, the Piots,[2] La Laurencies,[3] Benoises,[4] and Pavlovskys, are or will soon be in the same financial situation. But everyone is taking it rather gaily. There are more distressing preoccupations. During the 4 days following the tocsin, I suffered like I never did before. And as I felt I was going to go crazy, I took the wisest course: I'm going to enlist. I have already thought of all the reasons that you could possibly object. Above all, our poor mama. . . . But if I become insane, or croak of a heart ailment, it would be even sadder. Besides, I'm not deluding myself. If they take me—and that's far from being definite—I'm not ready to be sent to the front. Of course, our poor mama doesn't know any of this. There will be time enough to tell her when something is definitive. When you write to me about this matter, or anything else that might alarm her, write all of it separately, put it in an ordinary envelope, and have someone else address it. Even better, write two letters, one official, the other . . . unofficial.

As soon as you receive this, go to the Society of Authors at 10 rue Chaptal, and to the Society of Dramatic Authors, on rue Henner, and ask if I am owed any royalties. Enclosed is an authorization. Also, pass by Durand, tell them about my situation, that I'm finishing the trio, and that I'll probably be leaving.

Telegraph your news, if possible.

By the same mail, I'm writing to Bonnet,[5] in case you should be separated by the fortifications.

We embrace you.

Maurice

1. The French writer and journalist Gaston de Pavlovsky (1874–1933) was the editor of *Comœdia*.
2. The painter René Piot (1869–1934) created many décors and costumes for the Théâtre des Arts.
3. The noted musicologist Lionel de La Laurencie (1861–1933).
4. See p. 383, note 9.
5. Monsieur and Madame A. Bonnet were Edouard's business associates and close

friends of the Ravel family. Following the death of Monsieur Bonnet, Edouard married Madame Bonnet.

119. to Cipa Godebski

Ongi Ethori   August 20, 1914
23 rue Sopite
St.-Jean-de-Luz
Old chap,

The day after I wrote to you, I asked for a copy of my birth certificate—just think, it's only across the bridge!—[1] Except for you, everyone criticized me: those who were mobilized, volunteers, and even an officer. You know me well enough to know that neither these criticisms nor your earnest plea will have the slightest influence on my resolution: I will sign up (if they want me) because I want to sign up. But—everyone has his faults; mine is to act only with complete conscience—I know that I'm committing a crime, and don't need everybody to keep reminding me about it.

That's what made me . . . hesitate, as you put it, for 2 days. You certainly don't have to hesitate. . . . But, old chap, our situation is completely different! If you were allowed to sign up, you would only leave behind a young wife and children, who could get along without you if absolutely necessary. Valery Larbaud[2] is leaving behind a mother who is still young. But my mother is a poor old lady who is sustained neither by religion nor by principles, and whose only ideal has always been the love of her husband and children, and who wouldn't be ashamed at all to preserve what she still has. A sort of monster, right? Would that there be more such monsters! And you know how much I love her. I don't know how well she will be able to endure what I am hiding from her: my brother has volunteered as a driver. But I know, I am certain of what will happen when she learns that both of us are leaving: she won't even have to die of hunger. That's why I made a second resolution, in case I return alive, and this resolution is as irrevocable as the other.

And now, if you wish: Vive la France! but, above all, down with Germany and Austria! or at least what those two nations represent at the present time. And with all my heart: long live the Internationale[3] and Peace! That's why I'm signing up,[4] just like Hervé, whose action seems to have surprised you.

Affectionately to you both,

Maurice Ravel

and why not: long live Poland!

1. Ciboure, Ravel's birthplace, is just across the bay from Saint-Jean-de-Luz.
2. The French novelist and critic Valery Larbaud (1881–1957) was an occasional visitor to the Godebski salon.

3. The words of this revolutionary socialist hymn were written by Eugène Pottier in 1871, and set to music by Adolphe Degeyter.

4. Sketches exist for this letter, which break off at this point. Although they do not vary in any significant way from the final version, it is nevertheless rare to encounter them for a letter written to a friend. (The sketches are in the private collection of Mme Alexandre Taverne.)

120. Edouard Ravel to Maurice Ravel

Atelier de Construction Mécanique   August 27, 1914
A. Bonnet
Usine électrique,[1] Téléphone 112
11 et 13, rue Camille-Desmoulins
Levallois Perret, Seine
Dear Maurice,

I received your card and am happy to know that both of you are well. I am also very well, as are the Bonnets. We have settled in Colombes,[2] and I come to Paris and Levallois only on occasion in order to see if there is any mail.

You asked me where I got the funds which I sent to you. I received 253 francs from the Society of Authors and Composers, and 245 francs from the Society of Dramatic Authors and Composers, 498 francs in all. Of this, I sent you 400 francs, and I paid Madame Bonnet what we owed her.

We're impatiently awaiting the end of the month, in order to know if we will receive any money from our various customers, because, like everyone, we understood nothing about the moratorium enacted by the government.

I still haven't been able to see Madame Guys to get some news about poor Richard, who was sent to the front.

Salsbury enlisted in the British army and left yesterday for Rouen. I saw the Broglias; Josephine sent me a card telling me that her husband, who was in Avignon, had just left.

I can't think of anything else to write. The Bonnets send you their best regards.

Love,
Edouard

1. Mechanical Machinery Workshop, A. Bonnet, Electric Plant.
2. A suburb to the northwest of Paris.

121. to Roland-Manuel

Ongi Ethori   September 26, 1914
23 rue Sopite
St.-Jean-de-Luz
My dear friend,

For some time, I've been asking myself what has become of you amid all these events. And I had no way of finding out, as I didn't know your family's address.

Thank you for having reassured me, and also for having given me news of my brother, who decided all the same to write to you. He has finally begun his service, which he says is appalling. I can well imagine that he wasn't sent to look for forget-me-nots on the battle fields.

As you can imagine, it's frightfully calm here. I have never worked so much and so rapidly as this summer, particularly after the mobilization. In 5 weeks, I accomplished the work of 5 months. I wanted to finish my trio before going to enlist, and was disappointed to be found underweight by 2 kilograms.[1] I'm now counting on the general examination of those previously rejected for military service, and if I don't succeed again, I'll try to finagle something when I return to Paris. They'll surely end up being touched by the elegance of my body. This hope encourages me to return to the grind. I'm going to begin a suite of pieces for the piano, as I was obliged to interrupt 2 important works, which, however, were not very timely: *La Cloche engloutie,* in collaboration with Gerhardt Hauptmann, and a symphonic poem: *Vienna*!!![2] . . . which would have progressed during a trip I was supposed to make from the 15th to the 25th of November: Prague (French music festivals), and Berlin (Ballet Russe). How everything works out . . .

I told Mme de Saint-Marceaux of your activities; she is helping the wounded piddle at the local casino.

Go see Pierre Haour, who lives near you, at 5 rue Desbordes-Valmore. You will observe quite a show: our friend with Jean Cocteau,[3] arrayed in a brassard and kepi, leading peaceful herds of milch cows[4] (Cocteau himself described his uniform to me). Moreover, you will be able to obtain the address of our poor Sordes, which Pierre forgot to send me.

You didn't tell me about your brother. Where is he?[5] Write soon.

Yours affectionately,

Maurice Ravel[6]

1. Just over 4 pounds.
2. Ravel wrote the German name "Wien," the original title of *La Valse.*
3. Brilliantly gifted, Cocteau (1889–1963) was a poet, librettist, novelist, actor, film director, and painter. He met Ravel at the Godebski salon, and they were on friendly

terms for a number of years. However, following the war, under Satie's influence, Cocteau, Milhaud, Georges Auric, and Francis Poulenc adopted an anti-Ravel position, but a reconciliation with the younger generation came about, largely owing to Ravel's extraordinary tact and good will (see Cocteau's postcard to Ravel, no. 204).

4. This pastoral scene occurred in Paris' Bois de Boulogne.

5. Roland-Manuel's brother Jean Dreyfus was later killed in the war, and the "Menuet" from *Le Tombeau de Couperin* was dedicated to his memory.

6. In a letter to Maurice Delage, written five days before this one, Ravel mentioned several of the same things he discussed in this letter, and added the following observation about the war:

> Oh God! When I think that they just destroyed Reims cathedral! . . . and that my physical condition will prevent me from experiencing the splendid moments of this holy war, and taking part in the most grandiose, the noblest action which has ever been seen in the history of humanity (even including the French revolution)!

122. to Roland-Manuel

Ongi Ethori   October 1, 1914
23 rue Sopite
St.-Jean-de-Luz

But for heaven's sake, for heaven's sake, of course I know, dear friend, that I am working for the fatherland by writing music! At least, I've been told that enough times in the past 2 months to convince me of it; first, to stop me from signing up, then, to console me for being rejected. They didn't stop anything, and I'm not consoled.

To get some action, will I have to wait for the arrival of 2 German uhlans in my nonexistent garden which surrounds the plans for my villa in St.-Jean-de-Luz? At last, I wrote a trio, like poor Magnard:[1] it's still a beginning.

I'm also caring for the wounded every week, which is rather engrossing: the number, if not the variety of needs which 40 gentlemen can have in the course of one night is incredible!

I'm also writing music: it's impossible to continue *Zazpiak-Bat*, the documents having remained in Paris. It's delicate to work on *La Cloche engloutie*—this time I think it really is ——,[2] and to complete *Vienna*, a symphonic poem. While awaiting the opportunity to resume my old project, Maeterlinck's *Intérieur*—a touching effect of the alliance—I have begun 2 series of piano pieces: (1) a French suite—no, it isn't what you think: *La Marseillaise* will not be in it, but it will have a forlane and a gigue; no tango, however; (2) a *Romantic Night*, with spleen, infernal hunt, accursed nun, etc.[3]

Your letter arrived just in time: I was deciding to write a letter to your mother, which probably would never have reached its destination, any more than your military postcard. It's distressing to mail letters into the void, but I'm going to begin to do it. I can't remain without news of my friends. From time to time, I receive some frightful news, indirectly, which is denied 2 days later. That's how I learned of Captain Marliave's death, and I don't dare write to his wife,[4] any more than to Vaudoyer,[5] who, it's said, lost his younger brother.

Did Delage receive my card written on the 28th? Is he in Bordeaux? No further word from my brother. It is true that he doesn't write in peacetime either.

We no longer have Cécile Sorel[6] here. Nouguès[7] has also left us. . . . Write soon. I thought I understood you to say that your parents were with you. Present my compliments to them, and believe me very cordially yours,

Maurice Ravel

1. The Trio in F for piano, violin, and cello by Albéric Magnard (1865–1914) was published in 1906. On September 3, 1914, he met a tragic death (partially alluded to in Ravel's preceding sentence) defending his villa in Baron, France: German soldiers burned it to the ground.

2. Meaning that *The Sunken Bell* really is sunk.

3. Of all these projects, only two were completed following the war: the "French suite," *Le Tombeau de Couperin,* and *La Valse.* Ravel's quip about the tango apparently alludes to the fact that the archbishop of Paris had recently declared the new, highly popular dance to be lascivious and offensive to public morality. A one-page sketch of the "accursed nun" is all that appears to have survived of the "Romantic Night" (autograph in the Pierpont Morgan Library).

4. The pianist Marguerite Long (see letter no. 202, note 1). The "Toccata" from *Le Tombeau de Couperin* was dedicated to the memory of Captain Joseph de Marliave. He was the author of a book on Beethoven's Quartets, which was published posthumously with an introduction by Gabriel Fauré.

5. The novelist and poet Jean-Louis Vaudoyer (1883–1963).

6. The celebrated French actress (1873–1966).

7. Perhaps the composer Jean Nouguès (see p. 356, note 5).

123. Manuel de Falla[1] to Maurice Ravel

Ponzano, 24   November 6, 1914
Madrid

Dear friend,

I am writing to you, still hoping to receive your news, which I hope is as good as possible in these moments which are so very sad. I wrote similar letters to other friends, but never received a reply, although that doesn't surprise me under the circumstances. I don't have to tell you that my thoughts are always in

France, which I love so much, and to which I am so grateful. I think of so many excellent friends who, like you, were so kind to me.

Is Delage in Paris? I have just written again to Florent Schmitt.

I am now very busy with the rehearsals of *La Vida breve,* whose première in Madrid will take place in a few days at the *Teatro de la Zarzuela.* It is going to be sung, finally! in Spain, and . . . in Spanish. That strikes me as very comical.[2]

Write to me about Madame Ravel, your brother, and our friends. Please give them my sincere good wishes. While awaiting the pleasure of reading your letter, I shake your hand very affectionately.

Manuel de Falla

1. Ravel and Falla (1876–1946) were introduced by Ricardo Viñes in the summer of 1907. Falla had just arrived in Paris from Madrid, ostensibly for a brief visit. As it turned out, he remained in the French capital until the outbreak of World War I. The cordial relationship between the composers is evident in this letter. (A study of their correspondence is found in Orenstein, "Ravel and Falla.")

2. Although *La Vida breve* won first prize in a national competition in 1905, the opera was first performed in a revised version at the Nice Municipal Casino in 1913 (Ravel's review of a performance at the Opéra-Comique is found on p. 373). The library at Montfort l'Amaury contains a piano-vocal score of *La Vida breve* with the following inscription: "For Maurice Ravel, with warm friendship and admiration. Manuel de Falla, Jan. 23, 1914."

124. to Manuel de Falla

4 Avenue Carnot   December 15, 1914
Paris

Dear friend,

I am delighted to learn that *La Vida breve* is finally going to be performed in Spain, and I'm sure it will be a success. You will thus be discovered by your compatriots after having been appreciated abroad; that's always the fate of artists.

We have just returned to Paris, after a stay of 4 months in St.-Jean-de-Luz which was most delightful, as you can well imagine. Here is the news about our friends: Delage enlisted voluntarily with his father's automobile, and spent some time in Bordeaux. He is now being sent on a mission. His general quarters are in Fontainebleau, where I'm supposed to go see him one of these days. I don't know his exact address. Schmitt is with the 41st Territorial Army, 16th company, in Toul. He was sent to the front at his own request, but I believe that he will receive letters sent to the above address. My brother enlisted in the ambulance corps, and writes to us far too rarely. As for me, I went to sign up in Bayonne, and was rejected because I was 2 kilograms underweight. I'm only thinking about effective ways to start all over again. My mother is not very well. Her anguish, in these circumstances, accounts for her condition. Write soon about yourself and your work.

Maurice Ravel

Is your brother in Paris?

125. to Igor Stravinsky

4 Avenue Carnot   January 2, 1915
Paris

Well, old chap, everything was prepared to receive our ally[1] in a dignified manner: a Persian room, with Genoa shades, Japanese prints, Chinese toys— indeed, a synthesis of the Ballet Russe season! There was even a mechanical nightingale. And you're not coming . . . Oh! that slavic fantasy! Is it owing to this fantasy that I received a note from Szántó, who was delighted to learn that I would be arriving in Switzerland at the end of January? As I wrote to you, I'm going to be leaving, but I doubt very much that they'll send me in your direction.[2]

I'm still waiting for news about your brother, yourself, and your entire family. In the meantime, accept our most affectionate wishes for the new year (new style).

Yours truly,
Maurice Ravel

1. A bantering reference to Stravinsky himself.
2. Stravinsky and Szántó were living in Switzerland at this time.

126. Igor Stravinsky to Maurice Ravel

Hôtel Victoria   [January 10, 1915][1]
Château d'Oex
[Switzerland]

Dear old chap, don't be angry with me—I truly had my heart set on coming to see you, but my financial situation didn't permit it. I was counting on receiving some money which didn't arrive. I can assure you that I regret it more than you. Moreover, as my wife was exhausted from household cares, we decided to take the entire family to the mountains, to a small, ordinary pension, in order to spend the best month of the winter—January. Here we are. Then, all of a sudden, Diaghilev implores me to come see him in Rome. All of these things made my trip to Paris impossible.

As for Szántó—the issue was raised of inviting you to conduct half of a concert devoted to the music of Ravel and Stravinsky in Lausanne or Geneva, which was supposed to take place, but which probably won't. There's another example of Hungarian fantasy, thanks to which this hapless people is undergoing so much misery today.

I conclude my card by wishing you all the very best for the new year (old style).[2] Good health to your dear mother.

Ever cordially yours,
Igor Stravinsky
My brother has completely recovered.

1. This postmark appears on Stravinsky's undated postcard.
2. At the present time, the more commonly accepted Gregorian calendar (new style) is 13 days ahead of the Julian calendar (old style).

127. to Ralph Vaughan Williams

4 Avenue Carnot   April 5, 1915
Paris
My dear friend,

What has become of you? After such a long while, I would be happy to hear from you. As for me, I am extremely busy doing nothing very important. After 8 months of applications, I finally managed to enlist in the 13th Artillery Regiment. At the present time, I'm waiting for my appointment to the post of airplane bombardier, which I requested, and which should be granted shortly.[1]

I hope you will drop me a note soon. Convey my respectful friendship to Mrs. Vaughan Williams, and, dear friend, believe me very cordially yours,
Maurice Ravel

1. The appointment was never granted.

128. Edouard Ravel to Maurice Ravel

May 26, 1915

Dear Maurice,

I have just received your letter written on the 18th. You must know from mama that we are no longer at Châlons.[1] I gave mama some details, but I didn't tell her that we now constitute one of the outposts, and naturally that means riding on roads which are riddled with shells. A few days ago, I was on duty in. . . .[2] I had just eaten dinner with the ambulance drivers in the courtyard of a farm which was serving as our post; and as I wanted to smoke, I went out to get my matches which were in my vehicle, when a shell landed next to the table I had just left. We rushed in with the other ambulance drivers and amid all sorts of debris, we pulled out 8 dead and 21 wounded.

I immediately took care of the wounded and transported them to the rear. It was done rapidly of course, in order to avoid being spotted by enemy batteries. This bombardment lasted part of the night, and since then the Boches[3] have recommenced this little game almost every day. Until now, not one of the comrades in my section has been wounded; although a vehicle was hit, nothing happened to the driver. Let's hope it will continue.

I did receive a reply to the request I had made. Unfortunately, it was turned down. The regulations prohibit taking men over the age of 30 on the light or heavy armored cars. Therefore, I can't see what more I can do about it.

We're sleeping here in the open air. It's very pleasant, except when it rains; then we get little drops of water which leak into the tent.

I'm still feeling fine.

Love,

Edouard

1. Châlons-sur-Marne, about 100 miles east of Paris. Some of the bitterest fighting of the war would take place on this western front, in particular the battle of Verdun.

2. French military law forbade soldiers from mentioning their specific places of active duty.

3. Borrowed from the French, this is a colloquial and pejorative term for Germans.

129. Madame Joseph Ravel to Maurice Ravel

[c. early March 1916][1]

Maurice dearest, don't be concerned about me. I couldn't be feeling better, but it's you that I'm concerned about. You cannot imagine how distressed I am to know that you are so sick—I don't sleep and I have nightmares—do everything necessary to get well as fast as possible, because I tell you I am very distressed. I'm sending your pyjamas and 2 nightshirts. I wish you a happy birthday, and embrace you with all my heart. From your mother who thinks of you,

Madame J. Ravel[2]

1. This approximate date is based on the contents of this letter.

2. Written in very light pencil, this letter contains many misspellings (Ravel describes it in the letter to Jean Marnold, no. 132).

130. to Madame Joseph Ravel

Conducteur Ravel   Sunday, March 19, 1916
Convois automobiles
Section T.M. 171
par B.C.M. Paris[1]

Mama dearest, finally, I received Edouard's letter! I won't be able to get the dough until tomorrow. I have 1 penny left, and no tobacco, but I don't give a d[amn]: I have news about you. Write to me, write to me often. You can see that your letters take about 5 days to arrive. And you can't imagine how unhappy I am to feel so far away. I'm not in any danger here, but it's already like being at the front. Although the front is far away, it feels as though it's very close. Everything reminds you of it. The airplanes going there, the convoys filled with soldiers, and at every turn in the road, you see the same sign: V. . . . .[2] and an arrow. Almost every night, zeppelins are reported by the sirens at the factory and the train station. When the region is seriously threatened, they sound the "attention" in town. Then all the inhabitants go out in the street with their noses up, just like in Paris.

The truck which was set aside for me is now being repaired. It was moving only on 3 feet. When it was taken apart, they discovered that a valve was damaged, and only a shaft of the other one was left. As I was anxious to know what had happened to the other valve, they found out that it must have been bouncing around for 2 months in the cylinder, and for that reason the piston was reduced to its simplest state. All of this doesn't mean anything to you, but Edouard had a good laugh about it, and expressed his admiration for the durability of Aster motors.

My assistant was appointed to take the old truck to the hospital, and in the meantime they will give me another one. I'm a "big shot," thanks to the recommendation of Captain Le Lorrain, and also thanks to my name, which is known to the chief second-lieutenant. This morning, he offered me a touring car, and as I modestly refused, he promised me a van! We chatted for 2 hours, to the great admiration of the garage mechanics. You can see that I won't be too unhappy, as long as you write to me often. I will write to you as often as possible.

Love,
Maurice

1. Driver Ravel, Automobile Convoys, Section T.M. 171, c/o Central Military Bureau, Paris.
2. Verdun.

131. to Madame Joseph Ravel

Conducteur Ravel   March 26, 1916
Convois automobiles
Section T.M. 171
par B.C.M. Paris
Mama dearest,

Still no letter! It's already 18 days since I left Paris, and since that time only my friends have written to me. All of them, even those to whom I didn't write.

You know however that you don't have to write literature. Tell me what's new, what you are doing, the visits you receive, what is happening to Edouard. It's not that complicated; you have all the time to do it, and I won't be in this sad situation of a poilu without a family—but with a correspondent,[1] because Madame Dreyfus[2] has adopted me as her godson.

Love,
Maurice

1. In the French "marraine," short for "marraine de guerre," meaning a woman who "adopts" a soldier, sending him packages and letters.
2. The mother of Roland-Manuel. After the death of her husband, Paul Lévy, she married M. Fernand Dreyfus. Monsieur Dreyfus' first wife had died after bearing him two sons, Jean and René, and thus there was no blood relationship between them and Roland-Manuel.

132. to Jean Marnold

Conducteur Ravel   April 4, 1916
Convois automobiles
Section T.M. 171
par B.C.M. Paris

Thank you, my dear friend, for your kind letter—if you only knew the joy with which they are received! Thanks also for the authentic news that you wrote about mama. I myself suspected something, merely by receiving her feeble letters, which are scarcely legible. Obviously, she must see another doctor—not that imbecile who is treating her; all he tells her is that it's very beneficial to bleed from the nose. I wrote to some friends to send her their doctor, in whom they have confidence.

The other day, I was assigned one of those "interesting missions" which you have told me you distrust. It consisted of going to X . . . in order to bring back a requisitioned vehicle; abandoned would be more correct. Nothing troublesome happened to me. I did not need my helmet, and my gas mask remained in my pocket. I saw a hallucinatory thing: a nightmarish city, horribly deserted and mute. It isn't the fracas from above, or the small balloons of white smoke which align in the very pure sky; it's not this formidable and invisible struggle which is anguishing, but rather to feel alone in the center of this city which rests in a sinister sleep, under the brilliant light of a beautiful summer day. Undoubtedly, I will see things which will be more frightful and repugnant; I don't believe I will ever experience a more profound and stranger emotion than this sort of mute terror.

I'm going to write to the abbé;[1] perhaps we'll have an opportunity to meet, as we are almost neighbors. Write often. My kind regards to your family, and cordial greetings to you from yours truly,

Maurice Ravel

I trust that you are completely over the grippe. In the letters I receive, that's all I hear about.[2]

1. Abbé Léonce Petit.

2. The autograph of this crowded postcard is reproduced in Orenstein, "L'Oeuvre de Maurice Ravel."

133. to Jane Bathori

Conducteur Ravel   April 6, 1916
Convois automobiles
Section T.M. 171
par B.C.M. Paris

I very much regret having to miss your little reunion, my dear friend, and I hope that you will excuse me: I'm far away from Paris and far away from music; I'm a poilu, dressed in goatskin, with helmet and gas mask, who drives on forbidding roads, even into the midst of the "gigantic struggle." The service is beginning to get interesting, to the point that I'll end up forgetting about my lovely dreams of aviation.

I would be happy to hear from you. Be sure to tell the friends who will be there on Sunday to write to me often, and that I'll reply when my service permits.

My kind regards to Engel, and the respectful friendship of yours truly,

Maurice Ravel

134. to Lucien Garban

April 6, 1916

Dear friend,

Here is a further example of ridiculous slander. Moreover, if the letter from America hadn't remained in my room, and I wouldn't have forgotten to take it yesterday, you would have received this 2 days sooner. Behold the wonders which the enticement for profits may bring about![1] There is also another reason. It's that I have nothing to do—the axle still hasn't arrived—and I don't know how to occupy my inaction better than by chatting with friends. Moreover, I've been wanting to write to you for a few days. Since you kindly offered to take care of some errands which I couldn't do, being so far away, I'm going to take you up on it quickly and in earnest.

Here's the situation: I am far from having everything settled with the Society of Authors. I believe that through the oversight of my publishers, and above all by my own negligence, quite a few pieces have not been declared. I'm therefore going to ask you to stop by at rue Chaptal, and verify the list of my works (original compositions, separate pieces, arrangements, transcriptions— *L'Après-midi,* the *Nocturnes*—[2]). It's more complicated than you could possibly imagine, because of the different publishers. But this will be greatly simplified by Roland-Manuel's book, which you need only consult. (There are also folk songs published in Russia.) However, you would have to see Durand and Demets for the separate pieces and the arrangements, which I may not know about. (Ask Durand if it wouldn't be a good idea to declare the *3 Chansons pour chœur mixte*[3] without delay.) Another thing: the words of these songs, those of *Noël des jouets,* and the translations of the Hebraic songs are by me.[4] I'm not inscribed as an author, and would therefore lose half of the royalties. In order to be inscribed, one must be able to present a certain number of printed works. I think that my critical writings would suffice. Could you make inquiries, and find out if I must pay for my new inscription immediately, or if the payment could be deducted in advance from the royalties of my compositions already received, or yet to be received? For the articles, the most important ones are in *Comœdia illustré.* I don't know if their office is open (at the Pavillon de Hanovre). You can find that out from the Godebskis, who are in touch with Brunoff.[5]

And that's it. You can see that the one time I avail myself of your kindness, I abuse it. My excuse is my present situation. Obviously, I don't risk being killed at any minute, but after all, I am more exposed than at the Vaugirard garage.[6]

There's my axle arriving. I'm finally going to get back to work. . . .

The Godebskis[7] must have told you about the interesting little excursions that I have already taken. I'll write to you from time to time, but don't wait for me before you write.

Thanks in advance, my dear friend, and believe me very cordially yours,
Maurice Ravel

What are these automobile trips that my mother is supposed to be taking? My brother's military privileges?

Enclosed are (1) the letter from America; (2) the bulletin of declaration for the Trio, which you can deliver to the Society of Authors when you pass by for the information. (Note that it's in 4 movements, not 3.)

1. The letter from America may have contained a commission for a large-scale work.

2. In 1910, Ravel transcribed the *Prelude to the Afternoon of a Faun* for piano four hands. (For the transcription of the *Nocturnes*, see letter no. 6, note 1.)

3. These a cappella songs were completed in 1915; the text of the second song refers to the war.

4. Ravel meant that he arranged the French translations of the Hebraic songs, which were provided by Durand.

5. Maurice de Brunoff, the editor of *Comœdia illustré*.

6. Ravel had previously served at the garage on rue Vaugirard in Paris.

7. Referred to here as "the Cipas."

135. to Lucien Garban

May 8, 1916

My dear friend,

It has been a long time since I have received your letters, which arrive in no particular order and with considerable delay.[1] My various transfers and military duty have left me no time to thank you for all the errands which I owe to your friendship, nor to put all of this complicated red tape in order. You probably know that after a short stay with field hospital 13, an accident forced me to leave the front. After recovering, I went back to the park, which I left almost immediately for the squad which repairs the 75.[2] I went through 5 days—and almost as many nights—of exhausting, insane, and perilous service, which consisted of going to look for damaged trucks over muddy or rough roads, passing over ruts and holes from shells, which put my poor vehicle in such a state that she left me in the lurch in the middle of a forest, fortunately far from the field of operation, and just next to the outdoor kitchen of a truck encampment. I've been waiting 4 days for them to get me out of here, while leading an ancestral existence, freshening up at a nearby spring, living from the benevolence of the cooks, and sleeping in my truck, rolled up in animal skins. The first few days it was all right: the weather was fair. But it has been raining since yesterday, and I was so cold that I could hardly sleep, in addition to the frightful preoccupation of being without any news for 10 days.[3] My compulsory leisure will permit me to try to arrange all of these complicated matters with the Society of Authors. In recent days, I have frequently regretted not having been able to do it sooner. Even more than the fatigue, which I was afraid I wouldn't be able to overcome, there was the element of danger. I don't think that any automobile service, even ambulance duty, could expose anyone more than I was in the 75 section. Several times I drove right through the shells, thinking I had been spotted. In retrospect, I can't restrain a slight shudder, when I think that one hour before my definitive leave, my old truck nearly broke down right in the middle of a road designated as being in a dangerous zone, just in sight of the Boche batteries . . . And I was obliged to remain there and guard the truck!

Well now, let's try to proceed in order. It's not easy; I'm lost amid your letters and the various documents I brought back with me from Paris.

First of all, the short list that you sent:

1) *Adélaïde.* Has the orchestration of the *Valses* [*nobles et sentimentales*] been declared?[4] I believe that this title would only concern the Society of Dramatic Authors. In the concert hall, it would always be performed with its original title (*Valses nobles* etc . . .).

2) *A la manière de*[5] . . . You will find enclosed a bulletin of declaration which I had signed in Paris and forgot to send back. This bulletin also has the declaration of:

3) *Noël des jouets.* Here, it's more complicated. First of all, I see that this piece is listed as being only for voice and piano. However, it was orchestrated, and was performed this way a long time ago in Paris, and in Lyon, at the beginning of 1914, I believe. For a copy of the score, you would have to see Mathot, if you can manage to find him. I've been assured that he was inducted. I'm adding a comment on this bulletin for the Society, and a word for Mathot as well.

4) 2 Hebraic songs.[6] How can this bulletin of declaration be drawn up? Moreover, I couldn't do it from memory. I would need a copy of the first 8 measures of each song, and until I would get it. . . . Couldn't the regulations be modified under the circumstances, so that the declaration of my publisher, for example, would suffice? The unaccompanied themes were not composed by me, and in a work of this sort, it's precisely the accompaniment which counts. These works cannot be considered as a simple arrangement. As for the texts, they were written by me.

5) Spanish song and Hebraic song: there are 2 others, French and Italian.[7] The same observation holds as above. (Find out at Durand what was done for the Greek songs.) I don't know who wrote these texts.

6) *Prélude à l'Après-midi* . . . (arrangement for 4 hands). This time, I couldn't decently take credit for the themes, with or without accompaniment. What should be done?

    (A) And indeed, here is a bulletin which I didn't sign recently, because of the same scruple (Debussy's *Nocturnes* for 2 pianos 4 hands). I had previously wanted to make some inquiries about it, but didn't do so.

    (B) Fragments of *L'Heure espagnole.* It's impossible to remember all of this precisely.[8] Can something be worked out?

(C) I also came upon a very old bulletin (the Levallois address proves it) which has a host of things which were not declared at that time. Since you don't mention them on your list, I imagine that it has been taken care of since.

(D) Declaration of the *Chansons pour chœur mixte*. Would you ask Durand if it is necessary to mention that the second song was published in *Musica* (with the publisher's authorization)? If I had to make a declaration about the words, I would be quite embarrassed about it, particularly with regard to "Ronde."[9] In this case, you would have to send me a copy of the separate text which Durand has. Likewise for a copy of the translations of the Hebraic songs.

I don't believe that Enoch or Hamelle have kept anything. Do you know if the *Vocalise* was published by Leduc?[10] In any event, I never filled out a declaration for it. That would be another thing I would find difficult to write from memory.

And that's it . . . phew! How can I apologize, and thank you for the trouble you have already taken and will continue to take because of all this?

You may speak with Edouard about my adventures. He's up to date. I don't have to tell you that the same doesn't hold true for my mother. . . . My poor mama, how can she feel?

Most cordially yours, my dear friend,

Maurice Ravel

What objection do you think I might have to your reexamining the score of *Daphnis*? I would only thank you once again.

Also enclosed is the application form.

1. Some of the confusion brought about by the war was noted in a letter to Florent Schmitt:

Old chap, it's true that I don't write to you often, but you certainly know how to retaliate! I learned that you were simultaneously in Dijon, by Durand, in Paris, by Madame Clemenceau, and very sensible, by Satie. Similarly, my mother announced to me that Ladmirault was declared missing in action, and Ida Godebska wrote that he's feeling just fine. Another day, I received two letters from home. Edouard reproached me for having upset mama by telling her that I was sick, and mama complained that she learned about it from others. It's enough to drive a fellow nuts. (Letter dated July 8, 1916, in the Music Division of the Bibliothèque Nationale.)

2. A 75-millimeter cannon which was mounted on an armored car.

3. In a letter to Major A. Blondel, Ravel wrote as follows:

For a week, I was driving day and night—without lights—on unbelievable roads, often with a load twice too heavy for my truck. And yet you couldn't drag along, because shells were falling all around. I didn't think it possible for a driver to see so many in so few days. One of them, an Austrian 130, sent the residue of its powder right into my face. Adélaïde and I—Adélaïde is my truck—escaped with only some shrapnel, but the poor thing couldn't hold up any more, and after leaving me in the lurch in a dangerous zone, where parking was forbidden, in despair, she dropped one of her wheels in a forest, where I played Robinson Crusoe for 10 days, while waiting for them to come get me out. . . .

Above all, I would like to thank you profoundly for having been willing, albeit reluctantly, to do your utmost to facilitate a vocation for which I was undoubtedly not destined, because, for 2 years, everything has opposed it: my friends, events, and my health. (Letter dated May 27, 1916, in the Music Division of the Bibliothèque Nationale.)

Before describing the same episode to Jean Marnold, Ravel wrote:

. . . There was a beautiful park, and, in the vestibule of a château, an excellent Erard, on which I played some Chopin one Sunday afternoon. I then convinced myself that he is one of the composers I prefer. It seemed that nothing like this had happened to me for centuries. At night, I was soothed by different sonorities. (Letter dated May 9, 1916, in the Music Division of the Bibliothèque Nationale.)

4. *Adélaïde ou le langage des fleurs* was commissioned by the Russian ballerina Natasha Trouhanova. At the première, in April 1912, four composers conducted their ballets: *Istar* by Vincent d'Indy, *La Tragédie de Salomé* by Florent Schmitt, *La Péri* by Paul Dukas, and *Adélaïde*, which marked Ravel's first important conducting role since he had led the overture to *Shéhérazade*.

5. Ravel's two pastiches for piano "in the style of" Borodin and Chabrier. They were introduced at an S.M.I. recital on December 10, 1913, by Alfredo Casella, who also performed his pastiche of the *Valses nobles et sentimentales*.

6. "Kaddisch" and "L'Enigme éternelle," for voice and piano, composed in 1914.

7. The four *Chants populaires* for voice and piano, composed in 1910.

8. Durand had published four excerpts for voice and piano: the duet of Gonzalve and Concepcion, Concepcion's aria ("Oh! la pitoyable aventure!"), Gonzalve's aria ("Adieu cellule"), and the concluding quintet.

9. Ravel set his own poetry to music on two occasions: *Noël des jouets*, and the *3 Songs for Unaccompanied Mixed Chorus*. The unusual sylvan vocabulary in "Ronde" was partially due to the assistance of Georges Jean-Aubry and Roland-Manuel, and the manuscript indicates that Ravel encountered greater difficulty in arranging the text than in composing the music.

10. These three publishers had each printed one work by Ravel: Enoch, the *Menuet antique* (for piano), Hamelle, *Manteau de fleurs* (voice and piano, poem by Paul Gravollet), and Leduc, the *Vocalise* (voice and piano).

136. To the Committee of the National League
for the Defense of French Music

Military Zone   June 7, 1916

Gentlemen,

A compulsory rest enables me at last to reply to your letter containing the notice and statutes of the <u>National League for the Defense of French Music</u>, which reached me with considerable delay. I beg you to excuse me for not having replied sooner, but my various transfers and active duty have left me very little free time until now.

Excuse me, also, for not being able to subscribe to your statutes: having carefully studied them, and your notice as well, I feel unable to do so.[1]

Of course, I have only praise for your "obsession with the triumph of our fatherland," which has haunted me since the outbreak of hostilities. Accordingly, I fully approve of the "need for action" which gave birth to the <u>National League</u>. I felt this need for action so keenly that I gave up civilian life, although nothing compelled me to do so.

I am unable to agree with you when you assert as a principle that "the role of the art of music is economic and social." I have never considered music, or any of the arts, in that light.

I willingly grant you "cinematographic films," "phonograph records," and "song writers." All of these are only distantly related to the art of music. I would even grant you the "Viennese operettas," although they are more musical and more polished in workmanship than our own productions. These compositions, like all the rest, would be in the "economic" sphere.

But I do not believe that "in order to safeguard our national artistic inheritance" it would be necessary to "forbid the public performance in France of contemporary German and Austrian works not yet in the public domain."

"If it is out of the question for us and for future generations to repudiate the classical masterworks, which constitute one of the immortal monuments of humanity," how much less so should we "discard for a long time" interesting works, which some day may be cited as monuments, and from which we may draw useful lessons in the meantime.

It would even be dangerous for French composers to ignore systematically the productions of their foreign colleagues, and thus form themselves into a sort of national coterie: our musical art, which is so rich at the present time, would soon degenerate, becoming isolated in banal formulas.

It is of little importance to me that Mr. Schoenberg, for example, is of Austrian nationality. This does not prevent him from being an outstanding musician, whose very interesting discoveries have had a beneficial influence on certain allied composers, and even our own. Moreover, I am delighted that

Messieurs Bartók, Kodály, and their disciples are Hungarian, and show it so unmistakably in their music.

In Germany, apart from Mr. Richard Strauss, there appear to be only composers of secondary rank, whose equivalent could easily be found within France. But it is possible that some young artists may soon be discovered, whom we would like to know more about here.

Besides, I do not believe it necessary to have all French music, of whatever value, predominate in France and propagated abroad.

You will observe, Gentlemen, that our views are frequently so disparate, that it is impossible for me to join your organization.

I hope nevertheless to continue to "act as a Frenchman," and to "count myself among those who wish to remember."[2]

Very truly yours,

Maurice Ravel

1. The complete text of the league's notice reads as follows:

National League for the Defense of French Music
Its Predominance in France—Its Propagation Abroad

NOTICE

In all spheres of activity, the obsession with the triumph of our fatherland imposes upon us the duty of collective action and of unity.

The art of music, whose role is economic and social, must remain sympathetic to this precaution of active solidarity.

The *National League* was created because of this need for action.

It is concerned with chasing, then ferreting out the enemy by all possible means, and preventing the return of his disastrous infiltrations in the future.

If it is out of the question for us and for future generations to repudiate the classical masterworks, which constitute one of the immortal monuments of humanity, it is important to condemn Pan-Germanic *modern* Germany to silence.

Our aim, therefore, is to unite and make common cause in order to pave the way for our future and our liberation, by abandoning the petty quarrels of various coteries.

First, to discard for a long time the public performance of *contemporary Austro-German works which are not yet in the public domain,* their interpreters, conductors, and virtuosi, their Viennese operettas, their cinematographic films which swarm over us, their phonograph records which are more or less a camouflage; let us unmask their maneuvers as well as the pseudonyms of their song writers, who, even now, are deceiving our censorship. Let us watch that the enemy "shall not pass."

Then, in order to safeguard the development of our music, let us protect the professional interests of our compatriots; preserve our national heritage without discrimination with regard to style or school; work with all the means available for the predominance of our art in France, for its emergence by publications and public performances; let us create the bases for exchanges with our allies, and welcome their art *as generously as possible.*

Our means of action, depending on circumstances, will be multifarious: coalitions, censure, propaganda, intervening with public authorities, reforms of adjudications and of the bylaws of our schools, the placing of injunctions, communal action favoring French editions, struggles against suspected trusts, subventions, decentralizations, etc., all those things which inspire our firm will to smash the enemy's return.

The League has been constituted according to the law passed at its meeting on March 10, 1916. Its statutes have been fully worked out. Its assessment in principle is insignificant (25 centimes or 1 franc).

Let us adhere to the League, support it willingly and in large numbers; to do so is a patriotic and artistic act. It also means counting oneself among those who wish to remember.

The large trade associations have assured the League of their influential cooperation.

The League calls for the cooperation of all musicians and friends of music, who, within the limits of their means, inspired by the sublime effort of our brothers in the armed forces, are interested in the destiny of our art, wish to set it free from now on, and wish to act as Frenchmen.

French Music for the French

Honorary presidents: Messieurs Camille Saint-Saëns, Théodore Dubois, Gustave Charpentier, Vincent d'Indy, Xavier Leroux, and Charles Lecocq; Paul Meunier and Lucien Millevoye, deputies, presidents of the Parliamentary Group for Art; Jean Poueigh, secretary; Charles Tenroc, president-founder.

2. Shortly before mailing his letter to the League, Ravel sent a copy of it to Jean Marnold, with the following explanation:

... Incidentally, I haven't told you why I am entrusting this copy to you: it's because I'm a very cautious chap. Later on, a friend, even well-meaning, might quote some short fragments of sentences in a careless way, to be chic; and if I weren't there to set matters straight, one can't tell what might come of it. (Letter dated June 2, 1916, printed in *La Revue musicale,* December, 1938, p. 69.)

Ravel's letter to the League underscores his independent thinking as well as his courage in taking an unpopular position on an explosive emotional issue. Despite its many supporters, the National League for the Defense of French Music ultimately failed to achieve its goals. During the first season after the war, in June 1919, Wagner's music was performed at the Tuileries Gardens in Paris. Ravel made it a point to attend, and together with the audience, he applauded enthusiastically.

137. to Ralph Vaughan Williams

Conducteur Ravel   June 18, 1916
15ᵉ section de parc automobile
par B.C.M. Paris
My dear friend,

If this letter arrives, I would be very happy to hear from you. Are you still in England? For several months I have been at the front, at the part which has seen the most action. It seems as if I left Paris years ago. I went through some moving experiences, occasionally painful, and perilous enough to amaze me that I'm still alive. Nevertheless, I hasten to resume this adventurous life. I have been forced to rest for almost a month: my vehicle is being repaired, and I am exhausted. And the existence one leads in these parks is incredibly boring.

I hope that Mrs. Vaughan Williams is in good health. Please give her my kind regards, and, my dear friend, believe in the cordial friendship of yours truly,

Maurice Ravel

138. to Jean Marnold

June 24, 1916

My dear friend,

As soon as my postcard was mailed, I received your reply. I'm answering immediately: now there is swift correspondence.

Thus, I see that we share the same opinion. You'll be thoroughly convinced to devote an article to this League, when fully aware of all its projects . . . and besides, its simpler: here are the documents. Keep them. I don't know what I could do with them here, even though they affect our national defense. . . .

Seriously, this "patriotic" act presents a danger, not only to our common sense, but also to our liberty, judging by this threat from M. Tenroc,[1] the president, if you please.

"I am delighted to learn just how much you appreciate the 'important value' of the musician Schoenberg, and the 'savor' of Messieurs Bartók, Kodály, and their disciples. The National League will be there, at the opportune moment, to warn of your admiration in exchange for an eventual sacrifice, which would be most painful for the public, of your own music." Although the letter is signed the <u>president</u>, I don't consider it official, and I don't believe that extracts could be taken from it for publicity.

In addition, keep in mind the "intervention with public dignitaries," which has been promised by influential and well-known people such as Messieurs Saint-Saëns, d'Indy, Charpentier, Paul Meunier, etc.[2]

My letter? . . . I'm hesitating . . . but I believe that you are right. Obviously, these gentlemen will not publish it, and it is even probable that it will not be read before a meeting; as you observed, they will acknowledge their adherents, but will ignore the names and the reasons of those who protest. After all, it is true that I am as qualified as anyone else to speak in the name of French music. If I have not been in the trenches, I have aided our defense at least as much as those who remained at rue d'Assas.[3] The dangers weren't the same, that's all.

But let's not forget that I am a soldier, and don't have the right to publish anything; what's more, it might very well turn into a polemic. It's unfortunate, because when we return, we might well be obliged to acquiesce before a fait accompli. Well! publish my letter anonymously: a few hints will make your readers realize what it's about. The effect will be the same.[4]

What is regrettable is that these gentlemen will be able to spread their propaganda with complete ease: the *Mercure de France* appeals only to an élite, and they will easily win over readers of the large dailies. However, I would like to point out some remarks made by Tobby in *Le Matin*, 4 or 5 days ago—my landlady kindled a fire with it, not knowing that I wanted to keep it. There was an obvious allusion to the National League. It was said in principle, that, apart from our infatuation with slow waltzes, which come to us from Vienna, lovers of good French music have never been lacking in France; and in spite of all the national powers, there will always exist only two types of music: that which gives pleasure and that which is boring.

After having fought the militarist element of modern Germany, it would be a bit intolerable to return home and have admiration or aversion imposed by decree.

Upon returning, how many trenches we will still have to mop up! For my part, I have decided to return by horse—with 12 horses, right in the middle of a meeting on rue d'Assas.

Could you send me the literary raid of Bombardier Poueigh? And your reply?[5]

Affectionate regards,

Maurice Ravel

When you meet her, send my best to our new Joan of Arc, Saint Rachilde[6] . . .

1. The music critic Charles Tenroc.

2. See letter no. 136, the conclusion of note 1.

3. The headquarters of the League were in Paris, at 16 rue d'Assas.

4. Marnold did not publish Ravel's letter, nor did he write an article about the League.

5. The composer, author, and music critic Jean Poueigh (1876–1958) often used the pen name Octave Séré. Writing in *La Renaissance* on February 4, 1916, he asserted that

Wagner's music should be banned in France after the war. In a stinging reply, Marnold argued that Wagner should be heard both during and after the war ("Polémiques," *Mercure de France,* May 16, 1916, pp. 328–336).

6. A prolific writer and critic, Marguerite Rachilde (1860–1953) was married to Alfred Vallette, the founder and publisher of the *Mercure de France.* The Vallettes were influential figures in French literary circles.

139. to Jean Marnold

Conducteur Ravel   July 24, 1916
38ᵉ section de parc automobile
par B.C.M. Paris

Don't let this new address deceive you, my dear friend: I haven't budged. Sections come and go, but I remain. It will soon be 2½ months since I arrived here, with the hope of leaving at the end of a week. The spare parts finally arrived the day before yesterday . . . then they thought my radiator was a bit shoddy, so another one was ordered. So I'll still be here for some time.

. . . And I don't give a d[amn]. They can put me in the rear, or send me back to the front, or even keep me here: I don't give a d[amn]. This stupid and useless existence has jaded me to the point that nothing interests me any longer . . . except music, and my leave, which doesn't come through. Oh no! a time such as this doesn't make one a philanthropist! And yet I often think of Voltaire's *Vision de Babouc.* You know, that short, charming statuette, composed of precious stones and coarse materials. There are nevertheless some precious stones.[1] Over there, even here, I met some noble, sensitive souls. But what coarse materials, vulgar, or simply stupid! And to read the newspapers! one might well conclude that we have become a nation of imbeciles and cads. 3 days ago, *Le Matin* published a photo of some poor souls dragging themselves toward our trenches: How they surrender. Compare that to the British communiqué issued the same day: "We have taken X number of prisoners, all of whom remained as valiant defenders of the village."

No more news from Delage; the latest report hardly gave any hope for some sort of deal: the entire service is going to be dismantled. Most of these young people will be sent to other places—probably not very far—and replaced by the rabble from the front. Delage dreads being promoted to the rank of officer, and is resisting it with might and main.

The letter from mama saddened me; this frail letter, incoherent, almost illegible, like the ones I received before she saw Netter.[2] The treatment seemed to be successful. Is she still following it? Above all, I'm afraid that she lacks sleep, which she admitted to me one day.

The Boche officer? He was simply an Alsatian, who deserted the day before the mobilization, and had been a lieutenant in the German army. He has been at the front continually as a driver, at his own request, and was awarded a croix de guerre; a very decent chap, but with such an awful accent that I couldn't understand a word he said.

My compliments to Mme and Mlle Marnold, and cordial regards from your

Maurice Ravel

1. Voltaire's philosophic tale was first published in 1748. The story is not unrelated to the book of Jonah: Babouc is sent to Persepolis to see if that Persian city should be destroyed or be allowed to mend its ways. He sees cruelty and stupidity, as well as bravery and generosity. The city is ultimately allowed to continue in its ways, for, as Voltaire points out, "if everything is not good, it is at least tolerable."

2. Madame Ravel's physician.

140. to Jean Marnold

Conducteur Ravel   July 27, 1916
38ᵉ section de parc automobile
par B.C.M. Paris

My dear friend,

Thanks for the better news that you gave me about mama. I don't have to tell you how grateful I am to you for having reassured me.

Still no news about my leave. But things are being arranged for me ... I'll let you know when something happens.

I'm going to bother you—if you have the time, of course—it could be quite a job: could you find me as much information as possible on the folk songs of the Valois region?[1] (No need to bother with the little work by Gérard de Nerval:[2] that's precisely my point of departure.) Texts, music, legends, everything would be fine. If you know a specialist in this type of research, you need only put me in touch with him. That would simplify things for you. Of course, let me repeat, only if you have the time. In any case, thanks in advance.

These things must strike you as far removed from the cannons. I'm also not very close. It is true that I amused myself by writing down bird songs[3] in the Bois-Bourrus.[4] ... Even if I try, I'll never be a chap like Napoleon.

I'm quite sure that in my last letter, I forgot to thank you for the cards and the little notebook. Pardon me, and believe me very cordially yours,

Maurice Ravel

1. Just to the northeast of Paris.

2. The French author (1808–1855) was brought up in the Valois (now Oise) region. His work, *Chansons et ballades populaires du Valois*, first appeared in 1885, with a preface by Anatole Locquin (Paris, Garnier frères, 32 pp.).

3. In a letter to Roland-Manuel, written on June 12, 1916, Ravel congratulated him on his forthcoming marriage, and wrote the following:

> I don't even have the leisure to compose my epithalamium for you. If you wish, you may have this warbler's song, transcribed for the occasion, played on the grand organ:

or, if that doesn't seem joyous enough, use this, which a little bird found so ingenious that he drilled it into my head for half an hour:

(Autograph in the private collection of Claude Roland-Manuel.)

4. A wooded area near Ravel's military post.

141. to Madame Fernand Dreyfus

Hôpital temporaire no. 20   September 29, 1916
Salle 7
Chalôns sur Marne

I received your letter dated the 27th, my dear marraine.[1] You were uneasy about my fate, despite my explanation. I want to tell you immediately how much your sentiment touched me, coming especially from you, who have more serious reasons to be uneasy.[2] But I also want to reassure you. I'm in no danger, or rather in the least danger that one can risk in undergoing an operation. It was suggested, not ordered, by our medical officer, and one hour later, I was in the hospital. You know of my faith, a bit simplistic, but absolute, in surgery.[3] I know—from the example of many comrades here—that I will suffer horribly for some time, but I prefer that to discomfort and pain for the rest of my life. This "sense of suffering" is far removed from that described by M. Bourget in his most recent novel:[4] my soul is not very Catholic!

You have anticipated my need for books, and I am extremely grateful to you for it. During the long days ahead, they will be pleasant, even necessary companions.[5] Contrary to what I had thought, I was allowed to eat today, which suits my cannibal appetite very well.

Nearby, a comrade in my situation, who just returned from the operating table,[6] is moaning pitifully . . . and he claims to be inured to pain. I'm not at all, so what will happen to me? Oh well, I'll have time tomorrow to become inured.

As I will scarcely be in any condition to write a letter, I'm entrusting a comrade to give you the result.[7] Please telephone my brother; I didn't tell him when they would operate on me. As for mama, I didn't even tell her that I was in the hospital; I simply assured her that I was taking a rest.

A second marriage?[8] Not for me. I'm not even looking. But come now! secret marriages no longer take place in our entourage!

This delightful return of summer weather didn't last very long. Since this morning, the yellowish sky and monotonous rain have resumed, which remove every regret at being cooped up. But, one thinks of those who are outdoors, over there . . .

This instant, I was brought a postcard from Roland, sent from Arles. He writes that he should be returning home tomorrow, that is, the day before yesterday.

Continue to write often, my dear marraine. You next letter will undoubtedly find me in bad shape . . .

Affectionate regards to you both from your devoted godson,
Maurice Ravel

1. See letter no. 131, note 1.
2. Madame Dreyfus' three sons, Jean, René, and Roland-Manuel, were serving in the armed forces.
3. The day after writing this letter, Ravel underwent an operation for dysentery.
4. *Le Sens de la mort* [The Meaning of Death], by Paul Bourget (1852–1935). It is a Catholic, philosophical novel dealing with the war, and the ultimate questions which it inevitably raised. In another letter to Madame Dreyfus, Ravel observed that he found the book "interesting, but it irritates me with its mixture of honesty and insincerity" (letter dated September 28, 1916).
5. Other letters to Madame Dreyfus written about this time indicate some of Ravel's literary pursuits:

1) "I'm nourishing my mind: A[natole] France or H[enri] Bordeaux, H[enri] de Régnier or Octave Feuillet, everything is good. The number of insignificant things I've read in recent days is incredible" (September 24, 1916).
2) Ravel asks for a copy of Albert Thibaudet's study, *La Poésie de Stéphane Mallarmé*, noting that "everything which deals with Mallarmé interests me deeply" (September 28, 1916). Soon after, he receives the book, and thanks Madame Dreyfus, noting that it appears "serious and very sincere" (October 3, 1916).
3) Ravel expresses interest in the memoirs of Countess de Boigne. "I glanced through some fragments, which are fascinating" (October 9, 1916).

6. Ravel uses the slang "billard," literally a billiard table.
7. In a letter to Jean Marnold dated October 7, 1916, Ravel wrote:

The operation went very well: all of the comrades in my situation assured me of unthinkable tortures, quasi-Chinese—the agony of the rat—. I'm a chap like the Spartans, no doubt, because I found it very bearable. Moreover, I hold the record for assimilating chloroform; and no colic, headaches, or nausea. On the contrary, as soon as I woke up, I needed a cigarette, because I was dying of hunger.

8. Following the recent marriage of Roland-Manuel.

142. to Lucien Garban

October 8, 1916

I'm all right, my dear friend; I can eat almost everything now—not American style lobster yet—but am obliged to avoid it, which might flatter my instinct for economy, but disturb my instinct for comfort.

The detail of your present preoccupation impresses me: I had difficulty with my Trio. At least, don't change the harmonies.[1]

Hélène Casella wrote to me that she met you upon leaving Madame Clemenceau's home.[2] Thus, she must have heard my latest news.

I have just read *Le Grand Meaulnes*.[3] Have you read it? If not, hurry up. I haven't enjoyed a novel as much in a long time. Although the author was killed, or at least reported missing in action, it doesn't concern war at all, or even this forced patriotism, which led so many of his apostles into the trenches of Dijon or Orléans. That takes away nothing of its charm, despite what Monsieur Fosent of *Le Matin* may think: he believes that books published before the war no longer have any interest.

I was very saddened to learn that from now on, sick leaves will be counted just like regular leaves: I had calculated so carefully that I would get twice as much time off . . . all I needed was this stupid decision to come along and spoil my little plans. Oh well, I'm not giving up hope of finagling something.

In about two weeks, I hope to be able to surprise you with my scalpel in hand, and trust that it won't be too late to save a few pieces of my poor Trio.

In the meantime, believe in the cordial friendship of your
Maurice Ravel

1. Garban was transcribing the Trio for piano, four hands.

2. Madame Paul Clemenceau, née Sophie Zuckerkandl, was the sister-in-law of the French statesman and premier Georges Clemenceau. In the postwar years, Ravel often spent Christmas Eve with the Clemenceaus, at whose élite salon one might encounter Albert Einstein, Paul Painlevé, or Stephan Zweig.

3. The author, Alain-Fournier (pseudonym of Henri-Alban Fournier, 1886–1914), was killed in action during the second month of the war. His only completed novel, which is partially autobiographical, was published in 1913. It centers about the adven-

tures of a seventeen-year-old boy, Augustin Meaulnes, which combine reality and fantasy in a sort of dreamlike world. The author's reputation rests almost entirely on this outstanding achievement. Ravel thought about *Le Grand Meulnes* for many years, contemplating a work for piano and orchestra, or cello and orchestra. Apparently nothing of it was committed to paper.

143. to Serge Diaghilev[1]

1 rue de Chazelles   January 12, 1917
Paris XVII[2]
Tel.: Wagram 59.19
My dear Diaghilev,

In accordance with our conversation yesterday, I agree to compose a ballet based on the libretto you discussed with me, written by the Italian poet Cangiullo.[3] The piano score of this work must be finished by the end of 1917, and the orchestral score by April 1, 1918. The exclusive right to produce this work in all countries will belong to you for a period of five years, to begin from the first performance. For this work, you will pay me the sum of ten thousand (10,000) French francs, half payable upon delivery of the piano score, and the balance upon delivery of the orchestral score.

With regard to the orchestral material, you will come to terms with my publisher, M. Jacques Durand.

I[4] will retain the rights for performance in the concert hall, but only after the ballet has been performed in the city where the concert takes place.

Very truly yours,
Maurice Ravel

1. It has been observed that the genius of Serge Diaghilev (1872–1929) consisted in bringing out the genius of others. As director of the Ballet Russe, he collaborated with Stravinsky, Debussy, Ravel, Matisse, Picasso, Nijinsky, Pavlova, and many other legendary artists.

2. The home of M. and Mme Fernand Dreyfus.

3. Francesco Cangiullo (1884–1977), the Italian futurist poet. Although nothing came of this project, Ravel appears to have had some sympathy for the futurist movement, which sought a "great renovation of music through the Art of Noises." The futurist composer Luigi Russolo recalled that "real battles took place during my concerts. The incomprehension of the very serious principles underlying my music on the part of the public and the critics was exasperating. Only a few musicians of stature— among them Ravel and Stravinsky—understood the value of my innovations, as yet realized only in part" (letter to Nicolas Slonimsky, dated August 24, 1934, quoted in N. Slonimsky, *Music Since 1900,* 4th ed., New York: Charles Scribner's Sons, 1971, p. 239).

4. In the autograph, Ravel first wrote "You," and then wrote "I" over it.

144. to Madame Fernand Dreyfus

February 9, 1917

My dear marraine,

I am writing to you from my landlady's kitchen, because it's really too cold in my room.

The situation is still the same. My papers haven't arrived. Were they sent to Dijon?

Physically, I'm still all right, but it may not last for long: my diet isn't very proper. There's no way to have vegetables other than potatoes.

Spiritually, it's dreadful . . . it was such a short while ago that I wrote to her, and would receive her frail letters, which saddened me . . . and yet, they gave me such joy. I was still happy then, despite the inner anguish . . . I didn't know it would happen so quickly.[1] And now, this horrible despair, the same recurring thoughts. . . . It's not good that I am so far away from my poor Edouard.

My captain keeps telling me that "I've got to snap out of it." He's putting me second in command on a vehicle, and is going to take me a for a ride near the front. I know very well that it won't be enough. More than ever, I am grateful to you for not letting me remain all alone. I am more isolated here than anywhere else, amid kind and cheerful comrades, who are nevertheless so distant from me at this moment . . .

Thank you for your letter, which I received yesterday. Did you receive mine?

Write to me often, and affectionate regards to both of you from your devoted godson,

Maurice Ravel

Please tell Edouard that I embrace him, but I'm not going to write, because I don't want to distress him even more.

1. Mme Ravel died on January 5, 1917.

145. to Charles Koechlin

February 19, 1917

Dear friend,

First of all, pardon me for still not having thanked you for your expression of sympathy, which touched me deeply. I was, and still am, very depressed, and don't have the courage to reply to my friends.

In response to your last letter, which I received here, this is the letter I am addressing to Doire,[1] personally:

My dear Doire, on the first page of the recent *Courrier musical*, Monsieur d'Indy, in the name of music and the sacred alliance, spreads ironic and spiteful remarks concerning some younger colleagues, most of whom, at the moment, are occupied with other tasks. I am astonished that neither of you realized that the right of reply is forbidden to soldiers, and it would therefore have been better to wait before entering into this polemic.[2]

Believe me, etc.

I reserve the right to reply openly later—as I did not long ago, to this distinguished musician, this loyal man, who is so kind to people in their presence, but who cannot bring himself to name them in his sly attacks.

I agree with you about the concerts of the S.M.I. We will be able to talk about it soon: I have a 7-day leave coming up, and will be in Paris the day after tomorrow, the 21st.

You can phone me at 1 rue de Chazelles (W. 59.19).

Kind regards, my dear friend, from yours truly,

Maurice Ravel

1. René Doire, the editor of *Le Courrier musical.*

2. A meeting had been held on December 17, 1916, between representatives of the Société Nationale and the S.M.I. in the hope of having the societies merge. D'Indy explained in a letter to his colleague August Sérieyx that

> it didn't work out at all: Ravel, Koechlin, Grovlez, Casadesus and Company refused, in the name of their "Aesthetics"??? . . . "which can not be the same as ours." I confess that it appeared so funny to me that I'm still laughing about it. . . . Only poor Fauré is sad about it, and would like to get out of that S.M.I. gallery. I really enjoyed myself . . . (letter dated December 18, 1916, printed in *D'Indy, Duparc, Roussel, lettres à Auguste Sérieyx,* Lausanne: Editions du Cervin, 1961, pp. 24–25).

Despite d'Indy's comments, the refusal of the S.M.I. to merge was apparently no laughing matter, for it engendered his malevolent article, appropriately entitled "Aesthetics," which appeared in *Le Courrier musical* on January 15, 1917. The article was essentially an attack on avant-garde composers, without one name being mentioned. D'Indy divided composers into two groups: "there remain those musicians who have something in their heart, and those musicians who have nothing in their heart. The first group is making *music,* the second *is not.*"

Writing on behalf of the S.M.I., Koechlin answered d'Indy's comments in an article entitled "Aesthetics?", which appeared in *Le Courrier musical* on February 15, 1917.

> Along with M. d'Indy and Giacomo [!] Rossini, I would therefore repeat: "There are but two kinds of music: good and bad." . . .
>
> And that brings me back to the words uttered at that historic meeting which united the committee members of the Société Nationale and the Société Musicale Indépendante. I had insisted on this point: with regard to both sides, *we do not have the same taste.* This wasn't a discovery: I believe that everyone knew it before the war. The best intentions (which we have), and the finest theories cannot hide *the facts*:

many works accepted by the Société Nationale would have been refused by our S.M.I. jury; and conversely, I could very easily cite orchestral works (later performed at the S.M.I.) which the steering committee of the Société Nationale turned down (it preferred to program certain compositions whose *musicality* seemed dubious to us).

The Schism was therefore very logical. . . .

And, in my opinion, only two things matter: the heart,—and musicality."

146. to Madame Fernand Dreyfus

St.-Cloud[1]   September 10, 1918

My dear marraine,

I was very happy to receive your kind letter, and furious with myself that it preceded mine. It is true that I have a serious excuse: in recent days, I've been feeling simply horrible. Spanish grippe? I have no idea; 5 days of fever with no other symptoms. But I remained in an unbelievable state of exhaustion and weakness. It strongly resembles neurasthenia: before doing the slightest thing, putting on my slippers, for example, I calculated the effort it would take, and wanted to go lie down again. Moreover, I was sleeping badly. It's beginning to get better now. But I lost an entire month, and the trip to St.-Jean-de-Luz will be postponed till next year. I'm supposed to be leaving shortly for England, where I must present myself as a virtuoso; just thinking about it makes me uneasy.

I have very recent news from Roland—from the 5th—. His morale is good. One of his comrades, who I believe competed with me for the Prix de Rome, informed him that I was managing a gas factory in St.-Denis:[2] the utilization of one's skills . . .

The feathered and hairy races are prospering. But Edouard's boarders are not producing good results: the pair of Russian rabbits have remained resolutely sterile. Each time these peculiar lovers are together, it turns into a rather Homeric[3] boxing match, which ends up with Daphnis in the corner of the feeding trough, and Chloé buried underneath the overturned drinking trough. The pair of "high society" pigeons form an exemplary household. But after having crushed the eggs of 5 coveys, because they were sat upon too conscientiously, they succeeded in producing a single kid, who is ugly.

It will be a joy to see you soon. In the meantime, affectionate regards to all from yours truly,

Maurice Ravel

Warmest good wishes from Edouard and your friends. We're tired of congratulating you on account of René, but still do so with all our heart.

1. On the Seine, it is just southwest of Paris. Edouard and Maurice shared the villa at 7 Avenue Léonie with Monsieur and Madame A. Bonnet. Owing to his poor health and the death of his mother, Ravel had received a temporary discharge from military service in January of 1917. In June 1917, he completed *Le Tombeau de Couperin,* and each of the piano suite's six pieces was dedicated to the memory of a fallen comrade in arms (see letter no. 149, note 4).

2. Just northwest of Paris.

3. That is, noisy, based on the loud, unrestrained laughter which Homer attributed to the gods.

147. to Alfredo Casella

St.-Cloud   November 5, 1918
Old chap,

Nothing is working, alas! All of my activities, perhaps for months, will be reduced to transporting myself from my bed to a chaise longue. In 2 or 3 weeks, I'll devote myself to this violent sport in the mountains—where I'm bored at the end of a week. Work is absolutely prohibited—the elaboration of these few lines is going to raise my temperature—. You can imagine how this chases away my blues. All the same, I prefer to know what's wrong with this confounded right lung, and, above all, how I should take care of it. If I had done so 2 years ago, when I was discharged, I wouldn't be in this situation.

Excuse me, and beg the Academy of Santa Cecilia[1] and Count San-Martino[2] to excuse me also; thank them sincerely for the kind and flattering reception they were preparing for me.

How are both of you feeling? Write soon, and affectionate regards to you both from your

Maurice Ravel

Darn it! I was forgetting! warm congratulations for Trento, Trieste[3] . . . and the forthcoming peace. When will the dress rehearsal take place?[4] I think that it would make me feel a bit better already.

1. The music conservatory in Rome where Casella was teaching.

2. The Italian senator and music patron Enrico San Martino e Valperga.

3. Both cities were ceded to Italy as a result of the war.

4. Perhaps referring to Casella's orchestration of his piano four-hand work *Pagine di guerra* (War Pages), which was first performed in Rome on January 12, 1919.

148. to Ida Godebska

[7 Avenue Léonie]   November 11, 1918[1]
St.-Cloud

Dear Ida, I took a short automobile ride this morning. Edouard drove me to Larboisière's operating table and brought me back—tuberculous ganglions: it's not contagious, so we're counting on all of you next Sunday for lunch. Take the train at 11:22 from the St. Lazare station. Get off at <u>St.-Cloud</u>—not before, not after—on leaving the station, turn right, then right again (rue Gounod), and walk straight ahead until you see Avenue Léonie on your left. Number 7 is at the very end. You'll see a Boche flag—pardon me: a moche[2] flag. Besides, I think that Edouard will go to pick you up. But don't miss the train: he'll be kept waiting for nearly an hour, the roast will be burned, and the cook will take off. Call me to confirm your visit (St.-Cloud 2.33).

Affectionately to all,

Maurice Ravel

1. At 11:00 A.M. on this day, hostilities ceased on the western front, and World War I ended.
2. A colloquialism meaning "ugly."

149. to Ida Godebska

Hôtel du Mont Blanc   January 14, 1919
Mégève (Haute Savoie)
Dear friend,

For the past few days, the sun has been radiant. On my balcony, where I'm doing some chaise longue—as you say in Polish—one would think it's mid-July. At times, a bit of snow falls, just to freshen up the old. Cipa and Mimie would probably shiver, but it's still what I prefer to do in the mountains. I did a little tobogganing, together with some well cushioned flops into the snow. I'm looking at the skiing, while waiting to chance it.

I'm not working yet: the piano has to be changed. The present one is indescribable, and tuned a major third too low: I'm afraid that it might cause a certain lowering of my inspiration.

I'm reading . . . all sorts of things, except newspapers. When there is something sensational in *L'Echo de la Savoie* or in *Suisse,*[1] they tell me about it.

Is it true that Paderewski has been named president of the Polish Republic?[2] After all . . . but I don't see Szántó as a Hungarian Poincaré, or Ricardo Viñes governing the destiny of the future socialist Spanish Republic.

I'm writing to Durand, to tell him of Durey's[3] visit, embellishing it with praises which are only sincere.

Continue to write: I like it. All of my friends don't do as much, alas! Perhaps it is true that there is a shortage of gossipers.

Affectionately to all,

Maurice Ravel

What's become of the architect? Write to me about the first S.M.I. concert. Isn't *Le Tombeau* [*de Couperin*] supposed to be performed?[4]

1. Two local newspapers.

2. The celebrated pianist and statesman Ignacy Jan Paderewski (1860–1941) served as premier and foreign minister of the Polish Republic for some nine months in 1919. On behalf of his government he signed the Treaty of Versailles.

3. See Ravel's letter to Louis Durey, no. 152.

4. The S.M.I. recital on April 11, 1919, marked Ravel's first public appearance following the war, and he acknowledged an exceptionally warm ovation. Marguerite Long's interpretation of *Le Tombeau de Couperin* was greeted with enthusiasm, and the entire suite was encored.

150. to Madame Alfredo Casella

Mégève   January 19, 1919

My dear friend,

You can well imagine how your letter surprised and upset me. After so many years of perfect harmony![1] . . .

Morality . . . this is what I practice, and what I am determined to continue. Artists are not made for marriage. We are rarely normal, and our lives are even less so. Alfredo was one of the best of us—just look around—. Nevertheless, it had to break up. Is it irreparable?

Moreover, you won't remain all alone. Oh! of course I know that nothing can replace certain attachments. But you still have some true friends, who will only love you more.

Life does hurt us, doesn't it?

My letter isn't very comforting: pardon me, I'm doing what I can. I'm not in very good spirits . . . especially here, where I'm alone and no one notices me in a crowd!

Physically, things are better. I'm far from being cured, but I am coughing less and am gaining weight.

Even so, were I to be in perfect health, there would always be something shattered . . .

If only I can resume my work!

Keep your promise to write sometimes, and, dear friend, believe in the sincere affection of your

Maurice Ravel

1. The Casellas separated after eleven years of marriage, and were later divorced.

151. to Madame René de Saint-Marceaux

Hôtel du Mont Blanc   January 22, 1919
Mégève (Haute Savoie)

Dear Madame and friend, here's the village.[1] It is pleasant, and not closed in by the mountains. The view is very lovely, the cold is terrible, but the sun is more radiant than anywhere. After several attempts at taking walks and tobogganing, I have been ordered almost complete rest. Until now, no improvement. Fortunately, I have some charming companions, a family with 3 very active children. But despite everything, what isolation! The mail doesn't arrive every day. In order to get a haircut, I'll have to go by sleigh to Sallanches or St. Gervais.

A brief note, from time to time, will bring much joy to your respectfully devoted

Maurice Ravel

1. The face of this postcard shows a view of Mégève and its surrounding mountains (see plate 10).

152. to Louis Durey[1]

Mégève   January 28, 1919
Dear Sir,

I simply told Durand what I thought about you, which is perfectly natural. I would be genuinely happy to learn that you have come to terms with the only French publisher who takes an interest in music. You have begun a string trio. Among my projects is a duo for violin and cello. Who among our colleagues will compose a sonata for violin alone? As much as I could judge from just one hearing, it would be rather delicate to orchestrate *Carillons*.[2] I can understand that it attracted you for that very reason; I think you have the short treatise by Widor,[3] which is very well done and very useful with regard to instrumental technique. Do you know the wonderful treatise by Rimsky? The examples in it are drawn exclusively from the works of this inspired orchestrator. As experience in this complex art, as in any other, is of great importance, and since you have told me that you are going to undertake the study of orchestration, I place myself entirely at your disposal if you need the tiniest bit of advice, or even detailed information. Don't hesitate: I have all the time; I'm far from being able to resume work. I had started to do some exercise and very little winter sports, but had to stop: there is no improvement in my condition. Heaven only knows how long I will have to remain here, and if they won't send me even higher. I hope therefore to have the pleasure of hearing from you soon, and beg you, dear Sir, to believe in my keen artistic sympathy.

Maurice Ravel[4]

1. Although a member of *Les Six*, Louis Durey (1888–1979) formally withdrew from the group in 1921. He wrote over 100 compositions, but some three quarters of them have remained unpublished.

2. "Carillons," dedicated to Satie, was composed in 1916, and "Neige," dedicated to Ravel, was composed in 1918. Durey's orchestral transcription of these pieces for piano four hands was introduced in 1929.

3. Ravel frequently consulted three standard works on orchestration, the treatises by Berlioz and Rimsky-Korsakov, and Charles-Marie Widor's *Technique de l'orchestre moderne*.

4. This letter is printed in *Louis Durey, l'aîné des Six*, by Frédéric Robert (Paris: Les Editeurs Français Réunis, 1968), pp. 201–02. See Durey's letter to this writer in appendix A.

153. to Jacques Rouché

Mégève   February 20, 1919

Dear friend,

Your letter was so timely: I have been wanting to write to Colette de Jouvenel[1] for a few days (I just lost my address book—it's a disaster) in order to ask her if she still wants me as a collaborator.

It's only recently that I have perceived the possibility of being cured. I'm coughing less, gaining weight, and sense a desire to get back to work, which hasn't happened to me in more than 4 years!

As early as my discharge—in June, 1917—I should have taken care of myself. My condition was not serious. But my negligence aggravated it to the point that it became impossible to do anything at all.—I'm not counting *Le Tombeau de Couperin*, which progressed considerably in 1914—.

I expect to return in April, almost in good health, and the first thing I intend to work on will be Colette's "opera-ballet."

Would you be kind enough to tell her that, and to give me her address? I would like to write to her about our future work—not in order to make cuts; on the contrary—.

Thanks in advance, and very cordially yours,

Maurice Ravel

I'm also thinking of "La Valse," this choreographic poem which I have already spoken to you about.

1. Ravel and Colette were introduced at the salon of Madame de Saint-Marceaux about 1900. During the war, she wrote a libretto for the Opéra, which had been commissioned by Jacques Rouché, who then suggested Ravel as a collaborator. He finally began to work on *L'Enfant et les sortilèges* in 1920, and completed it in 1925 (see p. 37, note 25).

154. to Colette de Jouvenel

Mégève   February 27, 1919

Dear Madame,

While you were expressing your regrets to Rouché about my silence, I was thinking, amid all the snow, of asking you if you still wanted such an unreliable collaborator.

My only excuse is the state of my health: for a long time, I feared that I would never be able to do anything. It appears that I'm improving: the desire to work seems to be returning. Here, it's not possible; but as soon as I return, at the beginning of April, I'm planning to resume work, and will begin with our opera.

In truth, I am already working on it: I'm taking notes—without writing any—; I'm even thinking of some modifications. . . . Don't be afraid: they're not cuts— on the contrary. For example: couldn't the squirrel's dialogue be extended? Imagine everything that a squirrel could say about the forest, and how that could be interpreted in music!

Another thing: what would you think of the cup and teapot, in old Wedgwood—black—singing a ragtime? I confess that the idea of having a ragtime sung by two Negroes at our National Academy of Music[1] fills me with great joy. Note that the form—a single couplet, with refrain—would be perfectly suited to the gestures in this scene: complaints, recriminations, furor, pursuit. Perhaps you will object that you don't usually write American Negro slang. I, who don't know a word of English, will do just like you: I'll work it out.[2]

I would be grateful to have your opinion on these two points, and, dear Madame, believe in the keen artistic sympathy of yours truly,

Maurice Ravel

1. The official name of the Paris Opéra.

2. The black Wedgwood cup was later changed to a Chinese cup, which joins the black Wedgwood teapot in one of the most curious scenes in the operatic repertoire. The libretto calls for English, French, and pseudo-Chinese nonsense, which are set to a ragtime, complete with piano, sliding trombone, xylophone, celesta, wood block, and a cheese grater.

155. Colette de Jouvenel to Maurice Ravel

69 Boulevard Suchet   [March 5, 1919][1]
Paris XVI
Dear Sir,

Why certainly a ragtime! Why of course Negroes in Wedgwood! What a terrific gust from the music hall to stir up the dust of the Opéra! Go to it! I am glad to know that you are still thinking of "Divertissement for my Daughter."[2] I despaired of you, and was told that you were sick. Do you know that orchestras in cinema houses are playing your charming *Mother Goose* suite, while they show American westerns? If I were a composer and Ravel, I think I would derive much pleasure from learning that.

And the squirrel will say everything you wish. Does the "cat" duo, exclusively meowed, please you? We'll get acrobats. Isn't the Arithmetic business a polka?

I wish you good health, and shake your hand impatiently.

Colette de Jouvenel[3]

1. This postmark appears on the envelope of Colette's undated reply.

2. One of the original titles of the opera. Ravel also rejected "Divertissement for My Granddaughter" and "Ballet for My Daughter," saying that he had no daughter.

3. Other letters and commentary about the opera are found in Orenstein, "L'Enfant et les sortilèges."

156. to Georges Jean-Aubry

St.-Cloud   May 24, 1919
My dear Aubry,

At the same time as the autograph, and even the day before, I had sent you a letter. Your reply indicated that you hadn't received it. I was about to write to you again, when Madame Godebska informed me that you were returning to Paris. Since then, it's been impossible to get any precise information: you were in Paris, London, Scotland, Holland . . .

Finally, I know where you are, and you see how quickly I'm writing:

1) Don't count on me as a collaborator: I've hardly begun working again—how difficult it is to get back!—I've got 4 years of work, and it has to be ready in one![1]

2) If you think it necessary, I'll go to England and Holland, but only to accompany. I'm absolutely incapable of playing anything at all. Last year, I tried to get back to the piano. I was horribly fatigued and made no progress. So, I let it go. . . .

Can you tell me as soon as possible when I would have to leave?

Very cordially yours,

Maurice Ravel

You included Lord Berners among continental musicians, but isn't he English? What a delightful musician! Could you arrange to have me sent the scores of his pieces which have been performed at the S.M.I.?[2]

1. Probably a reference to *L'Enfant et les sortilèges*.

2. The English composer Lord Berners (Gerald Tyrwhitt, 1883–1950) had recently performed his *Fragments psychologiques*, for piano, at an S.M.I. concert on April 25, 1919.

157. to Ida Godebska

7 Avenue Léonie   May 24, 1919
St.-Cloud

Dear Ida,

I hope to begin working next week. I won't be here for anyone, I'll pick up the telephone saying "Go to h...," and I won't answer any letters. And I'll forget about concerts. Only music, by God! Concerts, rehearsals, auditions; and this will continue . . . it won't stop this year, you'll see. The weather is tropically hot: that stimulates the organizers. Three quarters of the concert halls are empty, but they still insist on arranging new performances.

Piano examinations at the Conservatoire last Thursday—from 9:00 till 6:30—. They won't get me again.

So you've got fine weather, right? Here, it's a bit stormy. Nevertheless, I don't think that you will see me at Carantec,[1] although Mme Bonnet and Edouard would like to see me go there. Edouard thinks that I'm partying too much. I'm not convinced that it's really true: despite the rehearsals of *Alborada*,[2] concerts, and examinations . . . (see above), I managed to orchestrate Chabrier's *Menuet pompeux* for Diaghilev[3] and I'm finishing *Le Tombeau de Couperin*[4] . . . for Durand. . . . But, all the same, I'm getting slimmer. I know that Jean is getting fatter. He wrote to me, and kindly invited me to spend my free time at his château. Mimie also invited me to have tea at a friend's home. That's the only place she could think of to see me. And you? are you getting fatter?

I have to stop: I must shave, get dressed up, and go to a banquet in honor of Mr. Damrosch,[5] the American conductor. I'll come back drunk, and won't budge—like I said—all summer.

Love to all,
Maurice Ravel

1. In Brittany. The Godebskis frequently vacationed there.

2. The orchestration of *Alborada del gracioso* had just received its first performance on May 17, with Rhené-Baton conducting the Pasdeloup Orchestra.

3. The Ballet Russe gave the first performance in London's Alhambra Theatre on July 18, 1919, with choreography by Léonide Massine, décor and costumes by José Maria Sert, and Ernest Ansermet conducting. The ballet, entitled *Les Jardins d'Aranjuez,* consisted of Fauré's *Pavane,* Ravel's *Alborada del gracioso,* and the *Menuet pompeux.*

4. That is, an orchestration of the "Prélude," "Forlane," "Menuet," and "Rigaudon." The suite was first performed by Rhené-Baton conducting the Pasdeloup Orchestra on February 28, 1920, and was later mounted by the Swedish Ballet, directed by Rolf de Maré ("Forlane," "Menuet," and "Rigaudon," conducted by Désiré-Emile Inghelbrecht, November 8, 1920).

5. The German-American conductor, composer, and music educator Walter Damrosch (1862–1950). He was later awarded the Legion of Honor for his active role in furthering Franco-American musical ties.

158. to Ida Godebska

7 Avenue Léonie   September 2, 1919
St.-Cloud
Dear Ida,

When I received your letter and Mimie's, I planned to go to Carantec, and then to Lyons.[1] Soon after, I decided not to go to Carantec; a bit later, I decided not to go to Lyons. Finally, I decided not to go anywhere. Then, I had to go to Geneva, as my aunt suddenly died of pneumonia, leaving my poor uncle in a deplorable state. Fortunately, he was perfectly lucid, and well taken care of, but there were also heirs looking after his interests, who were chiefly concerned with their own. I managed to straighten things out.

These hesitations, travels, preoccupations, and occupations prevented me from resuming my work and my correspondence. You were certainly aware of that, and will excuse me, won't you?

. . . Today is the 8th, and I still haven't finished my letter. During this time, I think that Poulenc[2] would have written at least 3 sonatas, and Darius Milhaud 4 symphonies.

L'Heure espagnole was performed last month in London at Covent Garden: 17 curtain calls, and according to the press, the greatest success in the lyric theater in 30 years.[3] Gheusi[4] is supposed to present it this winter: will *L'Heure espagnole,* after its English success, merit the same fate in France as *Carmen* and Perrier?[5]

I hope that your return letter will contain good news. Here, it depends: M. Bonnet is a bit under the weather, and Mme Bonnet is completely out of sorts: she has to undergo an operation. Edouard claims that he's fine. I'm not up to par . . . for 3 days: don't know what's the matter.

Affectionate hugs to all,
Maurice Ravel

1. Lyons-la-Forêt, some sixty miles northwest of Paris, where M. and Mme Fernand Dreyfus had a summer home.

2. Francis Poulenc (1899–1963) was already making his reputation as a composer and pianist. The young musician met Ravel in 1917 through his piano teacher, Ricardo Viñes. Poulenc recalled being bowled over by Ravel's contradictory opinions, and soon adopted an anti-Ravel posture. Indeed, one may wonder if Ravel himself believed everything he told Poulenc—that Mendelssohn's *Songs Without Words* were far superior to Schumann's *Carnaval,* that Debussy's late works didn't amount to much, that Saint-Saëns was a genius, and that Chabrier was unable to orchestrate his own music. After Satie's death in 1925, Poulenc's attitude changed, and his admiration for *L'Enfant et les sortilèges* led to a reconciliation (see Poulenc, *Moi et mes amis,* Paris: La Palatine, 1963, pp. 173–86). Although Ravel was upset by the criticisms of Auric, Milhaud, and Poulenc, his reconciliation with them largely stemmed from his admiration for their music and his realistic yet somewhat paradoxical outlook. "The youngsters are right to criticize me," he told Cipa Godebski. "In their place I would do the same thing."

3. The performance was conducted by Percy Pitt, with the leading roles performed by Pauline Donalda (Concepcion) and Alfred Maguenat (Ramiro).

4. Pierre Barthélémy Gheusi was the director of the Opéra-Comique from 1914 to 1918 and from 1932 to 1936.

5. *Carmen* and Perrier mineral water began their careers with great difficulty in France, but enjoyed marked success later on. The same would indeed happen to *L'Heure espagnole.* By 1919, Bizet's masterpiece had already been performed some 1500 times in France, and was rivaled in popularity only by Gounod's *Faust.* With regard to Perrier, about 2 million bottles were sold in 1914, mostly in England and the United States, but by 1922, some 6 million bottles were sold worldwide, and over 2 million in France alone (documentation kindly supplied by Perrier, Inc.).

159. to Ralph Vaughan Williams

St.-Cloud   September 18, 1919
Dear friend,

I am very late in replying, and don't even have the excuse of work: I still haven't been able to get back to it. Yet my winter stay in the mountains did me a great deal of good. Now it's my morale which must be cared for, and I don't know how to do it.

Convey my apologies to Mr. Fox-Strangways:[1] I was already imprudent enough to promise my collaboration for a journal. They're still waiting for my first article!

Won't you be coming to Paris soon? I would be very happy to see you after so many terrible years. I was supposed to go to England next season, but I think that it would be preferable to work, if I'm still capable of it.

Please convey my respectful friendship to Mrs. Vaughan Williams, and believe me cordially yours,

Maurice Ravel

1. The English musicologist and critic Arthur Henry Fox Strangways (1859–1948) was the founder and first editor of *Music and Letters*, which began publication in January 1920. Ravel had probably promised to write an article for this issue, but it turned out that he never contributed to the journal.

160. to Manuel de Falla

St.-Cloud   September 19, 1919
My dear friend,

Aubry[1] told me that you were in London;[2] I asked him to send you my cordial regards, and then, I heard nothing from you.

And now Stravinsky has informed me of the terrible misfortune which compelled you to leave London hastily.[3]

I'm going to revive your pain, and yet I cannot let you think me indifferent. I haven't forgotten your kind letter, which you sent to me in the same circumstances, and which received such a late reply.

A terrible thing has happened to us, my dear friend. From that moment on, life is transformed. One can still feel its joys and emotions, but no longer in the same way; a bit like when one hasn't slept, or when one has a fever. Perhaps it will finally subside in the long run.

I still haven't pulled myself together. Although my stay in the mountains did me a great deal of good, and my health is almost back to normal, I still haven't been able to resume work. And yet I feel that doing so would in any case be the best consolation, rather than forgetting, which I do not desire.

Try to be stronger than me, my dear friend. I wish it to you with all my heart, and send you my deepest sympathy.

Maurice Ravel

1. Georges Jean-Aubry.
2. Falla was in London for the première of *The Three Cornered Hat* (July 22, 1919).
3. Falla's mother became gravely ill, and died only a few hours before his return.

161. to Georgette Marnold[1]

[Lapras par Lamastre][2]   December 8, 1919
[Ardèche]
Dear friend,

Thanks for the cigarette lighter: if only I had asked you for my razor strap! I'm still waiting for it, and only have to choose between letting my beard grow, making my face bleed, or losing an entire day to go get a shave in Lamastre. I've tried each way, and don't know which one I prefer. Thanks for the caramels— for the delightful caramel. The ones in the tin foil weren't as good; yet, I ate almost every one of them—with good reason—.

I sent Durand the orchestration of the Hebraic melodies yesterday. I'm going to move on to another genre.

Moreover, I've finally found my vocation: I was made to be a hermit.

Cordial regards to you and yours,

Maurice Ravel

Have you heard the *Madrigaal Vereeniging*,[3] which sang "Nicolette" on the 5th at Salle Gaveau?

1. The daughter of Jean Marnold.

2. Ravel spent the winter of 1919 in the home of an old friend, André Ferdinand Hérold (see letter no. 19, note 5). Here, some 350 miles southeast of Paris, in total isolation, Ravel painstakingly began to recapture his former creative enthusiasm. He orchestrated the accompaniments to "Kaddisch" and "L'Enigme éternelle," hoping thereby to stimulate his creative faculties, and soon after he began the writing of *La Valse*, which was completed in Lapras.

3. "Madrigal Society," in Dutch. In addition to Ravel's song, this a cappella choir from Amsterdam sang a program ranging from the Renaissance (Jannequin, Josquin, Lassus) to contemporary French works (Debussy, Paul Le Flem).

162. to Nicolas Obouhov[1]

Lapras   December 21, 1919
Dear Sir,

I received your 1st letter the day before yesterday; today, the 2nd, and yesterday, your manuscript. I am doubly happy, first of all, for the good news which will enable you to work without preoccupation, and secondly, for the genuine progress which I have observed in your work. Now you must begin to understand the orchestra. Continue to follow the Pasdeloup orchestral rehearsals assiduously: there are no better lessons than that. I will return your manuscript, with annotations, tomorrow or the day after. Let me now recommend an excellent assignment: without following the score, listen attentively to a simple, classical work, <u>after having carefully studied the piano transcription</u>. Try to orchestrate what you heard, and then compare your orchestration with that of the composer. Please thank Madame Obouhov sincerely for her kind words, which touched me deeply, and convey my compliments to her.

Very cordially yours,
Maurice Ravel

1. The Russian composer Nicolas Obouhov (1892–1954) emigrated to France in 1918. Soon after his arrival, he began to study composition and orchestration with Ravel, who was particularly helpful in furthering his career.

163. to Ida Godebska

Lapras   December 27, 1919
Dear Ida,

Your new year wishes came at a nasty moment!—I don't thank you any less for them—a maddening headache (I never get them). I had forgotten that Christmas Eve had passed. My New Year's Eve will be grim. I'm thinking of those in former years, in the charming apartment on Avenue Carnot, where I was so happy. I'm thinking that it will soon be 3 years since she has departed, and my despair increases daily. I'm thinking about it even more, since I have resumed work, that I no longer have this dear silent presence enveloping me with her infinite tenderness, which was, I see it now more than ever, my only reason for living. Mimie and Jean still can't know that: one always learns it too late. They mustn't do as I have done! I'm in gay spirits to wish you a happy new year, no? Nevertheless, I wish it to you affectionately, and embrace all of you.

Maurice Ravel

164. to Ida Godebska

Lapras   January 15, 1920
Dear Ida,

Today is the day devoted to . . . what's the name of the Muse who presides over the art of letter writing? I'm a bit uneasy thinking about the pile of letters awaiting a reply for several days. There are even the papers to fill out for "my candidacy for the Chevalier's Cross of the Legion of Honor, having been submitted"—by whom?[1]

Hurry up and congratulate me: you'll never have the chance again.[2]

And I'm working: on December 31, I began the orchestration of "Wien." I hope to finish it towards the end of this month. I wrote to Misia that Diaghilev could hear it any time after that, but I would prefer to postpone the audition until mid-February. At that time, I will have to interrupt my intensive work in order to spend several days in Paris: 1st performance of *Le Tombeau* [*de Couperin*] at the Pasdeloup concerts,[3] and 1st performance of the Hebraic songs, likewise at the Pasdeloup concerts.[4] I'm even rather ill at ease: these few days will be terribly busy. I'll be forced to get up at Cévennes mountain time[5] in order to arrive at the rehearsals. I don't think that anything has changed since my departure, so I won't be able to find a hotel room anywhere. If you hear about something, let me know.

I'm feeling rather out of sorts, and sleeping less and less. No doubt my morale has a lot to do with it. I spoke with Pierrette Haour,[6] an atheist like myself,[7] about what you had written concerning the benefits of religion. You're quite correct, but there's nothing to do about it, right? There might well have been a chance to do something—which would have established a record!—Abbé Petit was supposed to visit me towards the end of the year; but he didn't come.

Do you occasionally see Réalier-Dumas?[8] If so, ask him for the address of Jean Laurent. He's a delightful young fellow, whom I remember with affection. He helped me, over there, to get through those moments of terrible depression, whose cause, which I didn't dare admit to myself, was the approach of my misfortune.[9]

Tell Misia to hurry up with her letter, which I'm waiting for, in order to reply myself to Baton.[10]

Love to all,

Maurice Ravel

1. Léon Bérard, the minister of public education, had submitted Ravel's name, after being told by a colleague that the nomination would be accepted.

2. Ravel's refusal to accept the Legion of Honor created an uproar. Many newspapers supported his position in this new "affaire Ravel," and in a press interview in Saint-Cloud, Edouard Ravel explained that his brother had refused the decoration in principle, as he was opposed to all honorary awards. Nevertheless, Ravel subsequently accepted many honorary citations, and thus there can be no doubt that he still harbored resentment against the very same official circles which had refused him the Prix de Rome on five occasions. On April 2, the hotly debated episode was officially closed; Ravel's nomination was formally revoked by André Honnorat, the new minister of public education, and Paul Deschanel, the president of the French Republic.

3. See letter no. 157, note 4.

4. They were performed by mezzo-soprano Madeleine Grey, with Rhené-Baton conducting, on April 17, 1920.

5. That is, the time that Ravel would customarily wake up at Lapras—early in the morning.

6. The wife of Pierre Haour.

7. In a conversation with Roland-Manuel, I pointed out this passage and asked for his reaction to it. He expressed surprise, observing that Ravel was certainly not an atheist, but rather a confirmed agnostic. His reasoning, Roland-Manuel explained, was as follows: since he could not fully understand the workings of his own mind, Ravel found it impossible to accept or reject the existence of a Supreme Being.

8. The sculptor Maurice Réalier-Dumas (1860–1928).

9. Referring to the death of Madame Ravel.

10. The French conductor and composer Rhené-Baton (pseudonym of René Baton, 1879–1940), who was the principal conductor of the Pasdeloup Orchestra between 1916 and 1932.

165. to Lucien Garban

Lapras   January 16, 1920
My dear friend,

Don't be surprised to find the enclosed circular. It's not to bother you with a new translation. There's no hurry: it's probably of no interest. If you see something of value in it, you can tell me so in two words.

Thanks for the letter from Schoenberg. What an admirable fellow: while dying of hunger, he manages to find a way to popularize interesting works![1] I haven't answered him yet: I'm waiting to receive the French text of *Pierrot lunaire,* and see if it can be arranged.[2] At that time, I will ask you to make Jacques understand the beauty of this gesture, and have certain works forwarded to him which I will think about. It will be laborious, I have no doubt. . . .[3]

I imagine that you have returned home, and that you spent a joyous holiday season over there; certainly gayer than mine. . . . Finally, I'm working, and that's the essential point.

I was amazed at the silence of Franc-Nohain, whom I asked to write back immediately: he went to Warsaw to look for his son, who is a sergeant—that doesn't make us look any younger—.

Write soon, and affectionate regards to you both from your
Maurice Ravel

Would you please forward a copy of the ITR brochure[4] to Mr. E. Lonsdale Deighton (that's what you said), 24 Portland Road. Finsbury Park. N.4 London? That will save me the trouble of looking up everything I have written for voice. Tell Jacques that I'll write to him one of these days.

1. At this point in his career, Arnold Schoenberg (1874–1951) was still struggling against considerable indifference and hostility. In 1918, he had founded the *Verein für musikalische Privataufführungen* (Society for Private Musical Performances) which intro-

duced the music of Bartók, Debussy, and Stravinsky, among many others, to Viennese audiences. Schoenberg's letter was most likely about the program that his Society was planning to devote to Ravel's music in October of 1920 (see letter no. 172, note 3).

2. The original French text of *Pierrot lunaire* was written by the Belgian symbolist poet Albert Giraud, and Schoenberg had set the German translation by Otto Erich Hartleben. Jean Wiéner organized the first performance of Schoenberg's work in Paris in a French translation by Benoist-Mechin, on December 15, 1921 (part 1 only) and January 12 and March 10, 1922 (complete cycle) with Marya Freund as soloist and Darius Milhaud conducting. See J. Wiéner, *Allegro Appassionato* (Paris, 1978), and letter no. 217 below. Marya Freund performed the cycle in German with the composer conducting at an S.M.I. Schoenberg Festival in Salle Pleyel on December 15, 1927.

3. Durand was apparently planning to publish works of contemporary German and Austrian composers, which naturally had been unavailable in recent years. The project did not materialize.

4. This brochure, published by Durand, was periodically updated; it listed Ravel's work by category, as well as transcriptions of his music.

166. to Roland-Manuel

Lapras   January 22, 1920
Dear friend,

I'm beginning to laugh—it's high time—. This affair[1] has all the elements of a comedy by Calderón.[2]

What's not funny are the postal communications between Paris and Lapras: this morning, I received your two letters, one dated the 17th, the other, the 19th. Your telegram arrived on the 19th; I gave my reply to the mailman. It is true that he could only have it sent from Lamastre in the afternoon. So, if you die, inform me the day before.

Now on to the comedy: I had telegraphed my refusal on Sunday. Monday morning—no mail delivery on Sunday—I receive a letter from Jacques,[3] telling me that I will receive the information sheets, and asking me to be sure to sign them. I had received them on the 12th. To convince me, no doubt, he confided to me, under an oath of secrecy, that it was Garban who cooked up this whole thing, through a highly placed cousin. You can imagine my despair. I bungled my orchestration all day long, and had a dreadful night. The next day, I received Garban's letter, and replied by telegram, as you know.

It was therefore only to avoid serious repercussions to Garban—just think: the highly placed cousin!—that I let everything subside. And now, you tell me that it's Jacques who. . . . I'm writhing, above all to think that my reply—in spite of myself—will be taken as a cartload of blame. I had reminded him, among other things, that several years ago, I had asked him not to propose my candidacy in the way it was presented. Have you noticed that "legionnaires" are similar to morphine addicts, who use any means, even deceit, to have others share their passion, perhaps in order to legitimatize it in their own eyes?[4]

I think that the solution I'm indicating is rather elegant: "in place of Maurice Ravel, read Maurice Rostand."[5] The readers of the "Officiel"[6] will rectify it themselves.

I would indeed like to have some news: has your uncle recovered? Is M. Dreyfus continuing to feel better?

Affectionate regards to all,

Maurice Ravel 𝄪 ✡ 𐤟[7] & other orders.

Tell Suzanne[8] that her reasoning is fundamentally incorrect: a legionnaire no longer has the right to be a bolshevik, and their victory, all the same, is no reason to abandon them.

1. That is, Ravel's refusal to accept the Legion of Honor.

2. The Spanish author Pedro Calderón de la Barca (1600–1681) wrote over 100 comedies, which were particularly popular in France.

3. Durand.

4. As a faithful student of Baudelaire's writings, Ravel was well acquainted with a passage from the *Intimate Journals* dealing with the Legion of Honor: "If a man has merit, what is the good of decorating him? If he has none, he can be decorated, since it will give him distinction."

5. The dramatist was then 28 years old. His father, Edmond Rostand, was the celebrated author of *Cyrano de Bergerac.*

6. The French government's "Official Journal," which published the list of nominations and promotions for the Legion of Honor.

7. Respectively, the orders of the cross, the palm, and the elephant.

8. Roland-Manuel's wife (see plate 2).

167. to Hélène Jourdan-Morhange[1]

Lapras   March 1, 1920
Dear friend,

For 3 days, I haven't received any letters or newspapers. To complete this horror, I'm quite sure that I lost my address book, and I seem to have misplaced your letter. So, my letter may remain in Lamastre, or Tournon, or if it arrives in Paris, perhaps you will never receive it.

. . . And I have to ask you some rather urgent information—it's not about the concerto yet—.[2]

In order to play chromatic scales in glissando, nothing is simpler, naturally, on one string alone. The disadvantage is that it begins to sound a little thin in the upper register. Can this be done? (I'm deliberately taking an example which neither begins nor ends on an open string):

And, if it is possible, would there be several ways of doing it, that is, of changing strings? Would it be necessary to indicate the string changes for an orchestra, or should it be left to the discretion of the performers?—if there are several ways, of course—.

If it's not too much trouble, I would appreciate an immediate reply. Letters take at least 3 days to arrive here. I don't dare think how long this will take to reach you.

I am working like I haven't been in many years, in total isolation, despite very poor health, which has been confirmed by radioscopy, and which obliges me to take very good care of myself.

A thousand thanks in advance. I apologize for the time I am going to make you lose, but console myself in thinking that in this way, I will hear from you. Dear friend, believe me very cordially yours,

Maurice Ravel

1. The violinist Hélène Jourdan-Morhange (1888–1961) met Ravel following a performance of the Trio given during the war, in which she appeared with pianist E. Robert Schmitz and cellist Félix Delgrange. Her first husband, the painter Jacques Jourdan, was killed in the war. Almost thirty years later, she married another painter, Luc-Albert Moreau (the pseudonym of Albert Lucien Moreau, 1882–1948), who had made many sketches of Ravel, and also drew the interpretive lithographs found in the score of the *Chansons madécasses*. Ravel dedicated the Sonata for Violin and Piano to Madame Jourdan-Morhange, and undoubtedly would have wished her to introduce the work, but her brilliant career was tragically cut off by the onset of motor cramps. Because of her friendship with Colette, she became interested in writing, and completed an important book of memoirs, *Ravel et nous* (see plate 6).

2. Ravel apparently never began to sketch a violin concerto. He often told Madame Jourdan-Morhange that the most beautiful violin concerto of all had been composed by Mendelssohn.

168. to Georgette Marnold

Lapras   April 13, 1920

Dear friend,

Phew! I finished last night[1]—it's 75 pages—accompanied by a downpour with frightful thunderclaps. I still have to reexamine my manuscript—that will take all day—reply to some of the 50 letters which have been waiting for more than a month, and pack my bags. I'm leaving on Thursday, will spend the night in Lyon, and if the express train from Marseilles isn't canceled, I'll arrive in Paris on Friday at 2:50 P.M. I'll send you a telegram from Tournon or Tain, where I hope to get some information. Thanks for the tobacco: I think I have enough for the trip. More tobacco is now arriving. Thank you—enough! enough!

My discreet refusal was rather successful. I have a cartload of clippings here, which "Argus" and other press agencies have been sending me over the past 3 days. They're really letting me have it! There is a poor soul writing in *L'Ordre public*—what's that?[2]—who managed to say exactly what shouldn't be said (a host of courageous men wearing a red ribbon in their buttonhole). *L'Humanité* made an intelligent statement.[3]

Even if it was all in vain, I am nevertheless from now on "the eminent composer" . . .

The "personal reasons" which Edouard attributed to me intrigue those gentlemen very much.

As you can see, I wrote this on the envelope. I stopped the minute I was about to put the address on the card.[4]

Affectionate regards to all,

Maurice Ravel

I only informed the Dreyfuses and Garban about my arrival.

1. The orchestral holograph of *La Valse*, which is now in the Pierpont Morgan Library.

2. This morning newspaper began publication in February 1919, and went out of business sixteen months later. An article in it mentioned that in 1920 there were a total of 2071 nominations for the Legion of Honor: 4 for the Commander's Cross, 328 for the Cross, and 1739 for Chevalier, the lowest order.

3. An unsigned article entitled "The Legion of Honor" appeared on April 8, 1920, in *L'Humanité*, the official organ of the French Communist party. It said that

> One of the most brilliant representatives of our younger musical school, Maurice Ravel, was promoted to Chevalier of the Legion of Honor last January 15. He refused to be decorated, however, for personal reasons. . . . Maurice Ravel is satisfied: the red ribbon will not bleed on his buttonhole. This distinction deserves another one.

4. This letter was written on a plain card inserted into an envelope; Ravel momentarily confused the two.

169. to ?[1]

la Bijeannette[2]   May 21, 1920
Saint Sauveur
(Eure et Loir)
Dear friend,

The one time I write to you, there is an ulterior motive: I need to have some information. Do you know the works of James Elroy Flecker, "one of England's most highly regarded young poets," I have been told, who died in 1915?[3] He left an oriental drama which his literary friends consider his masterpiece, and it is supposed to be given soon in London. The director of the theater which is supposed to produce the play, Basil Dean, requested the poet's widow to ask me if I would be willing to write incidental music for the performance.[4] In order to accept, I await, first, any tips that you can give me, then, to know the importance of this work. For over 5 years, I was unable to do anything. It is true that this winter, I managed to get back to the grind, and compose 100 pages for orchestra in 4 months.[5] But, I'm half dead from it . . . and I've hardly begun a work which the Opéra has been waiting for since 1916.[6] I heard about you recently through Mme Benett.[7] I would be very pleased to be more up to date. But if you don't have the time—I know what it is—give me your opinion about J[ames] E[lroy] F[lecker] in a few words. Convey my respectful friendship to Mme Benett, and believe me, dear friend, very cordially yours,

Maurice Ravel

1. The addressee was apparently an English friend who was well acquainted with the contemporary literary scene.

2. The elegant château of M. and Mme Pierre Haour, in Châteauneuf-en-Thymerais, some sixty miles southwest of Paris.

3. Flecker (originally Herman Elroy Fleckner, 1884–1915) studied oriental languages in England and served in the diplomatic corps in Turkey and Beirut. He died of tuberculosis in a Swiss sanatorium.

4. For whatever reason, Ravel did not undertake this assignment. Flecker's verse play, *Hassan*, was performed in London in 1923 with incidental music by Frederick Delius.

5. *La Valse.*

6. *L'Enfant et les sortilèges.*

7. Ravel's spelling; probably Mrs. Arnold Bennett, the wife of the English novelist.

170. to Lucien Garban

la Bijeannette   July 3, 1920
My dear friend,

I think that the manuscript of *La Valse* for 2 pianos will arrive at Durand and Co. on Monday.[1] I would have done just as well to begin everything anew: I spent more time erasing, cutting out, and pasting than writing the transcription. Enclosed are some observations, mostly about doubtful passages which I discovered in the rough draft of the orchestral score.[2] Perhaps they have been corrected on the copy.

. . . No time to send it today. I need the piano part for the observations. So, I'll mail it out on Monday.

But I'm sending this to you anyway, for the following reason: Dr. Vidal telephoned just this minute to say that Geiger[3] is asking me not to forget the recommendations to the jury members for the piano competition on the 7th: a message from Garban. What competition? What jury? Send a telegram or telephone 24. Châteauneuf-en-Thymerais (Eure & Loir).

In haste . . . affectionate regards to both of you.

Maurice Ravel

1. This manuscript is now in the Robert Owen Lehman Foundation, on deposit at the Pierpont Morgan Library.

2. Formerly in the collection of Roger Désormière, this manuscript is now in the Music Division of the Bibliothèque Nationale.

3. Ravel's physician, Dr. Raymond Geiger.

171. to Henry Prunières[1]

[la Bijeannette]   August 18, 1920
Dear Sir,

I am sending you, by registered mail, the first movement of the duo for violin and cello.[2] Please return the manuscript as soon as the printer no longer needs it,[3] as my rough draft does not conform entirely to the copy.

Don't forget to ask my publisher for permission to reproduce this fragment.[4]

Very truly yours,

Maurice Ravel

Pardon me for not having thanked you sooner for your article, which I did receive.

1. The distinguished French musicologist and critic Henry Prunières (1886–1942) was the founder and first editor of *La Revue musicale*, which began publication in November 1920. Under his leadership, important recitals of contemporary chamber music were presented at the Vieux Colombier theater.

2. The title would later be changed to the Sonata for Violin and Cello. Prunières also commissioned two other pieces which were first printed in *La Revue musicale*, the *Berceuse sur le nom de Gabriel Fauré*, for violin and piano, and the song *Ronsard à son âme*.

3. It appears that the manuscript was not returned. Thus, in the three extant autographs of the Sonata for Violin and Cello, each one begins with the second movement.

4. The movement was published in a special supplement of *La Revue musicale* (December 1, 1920), as part of a commemorative issue devoted to Debussy. Together with a frontispiece by Raoul Dufy, musical contributions were also written by Bartók, Dukas, Falla, Eugene Goosens, Gian Francesco Malipiero, Roussel, Satie, Schmitt, and Stravinsky. All of the compositions were performed at an S.M.I. recital on January 24, 1921.

172. to Roland-Manuel

la Bijeannette   August 30, 1920
My dear friend,

We are leaving the day after tomorrow, but with such apprehension![1] Moreover, we are living in continual anguish. Nevertheless, I'm working . . . incidentally, I have to reply to your 2 letters. Thus, I'm working for Rouché. Some inside information . . . I can still assure you that this work, in 2 parts, will be distinguished by a mixture of styles which will be severely criticized, which leaves Colette indifferent and me not caring a d[amn].[2] I'm also working on the duo for violin and cello, in 4 movements. The only thing I'm not working on is the piano, and I'm afraid that I won't arouse the enthusiasm of the Viennese with my virtuosity.[3]

You didn't understand a thing about the neurologist: it's probably my fault. I wanted to point out to you, for M. Dreyfus, a surgeon who has written remarkable studies on the nerves, and who performed miracles during the war. As no one here recalls his name, I wanted to know who was the specialist taking care of your father-in-law, who was perhaps the same doctor, but it turned out that he wasn't. I'm supposed to see Leriche soon, who will give me the information. I seem to recall answering your first letter. So you owe me another one, that's all. Perhaps I'll see you soon.

Affectionate regards to all,
Maurice Ravel

1. Pierre Haour was seriously ill and died shortly after.
2. Ravel's prediction was partially fulfilled some five and a half years later, when *L'Enfant et les sortilèges* was performed at the Opéra-Comique. Writing in *La Liberté* on February 3, 1926, Robert Dezarnaux observed that the opera "is not convincing. It seems void of music! Why? Because the music never has the opportunity to expand. . . . The rapid succession [of differing styles] bewilders the mind, fatigues the ear—and, what is worse, is not amusing." Writing in *Le Temps* on the same day, Henry Malherbe came to the opposite conclusion:

> The most refined of our contemporary composers and the most penetrating of our
> authors have united in order to create a work of incomparable enchantment. . . . It
> is impossible, indeed, to enumerate all the carefully selected riches, all the subtle

notations, the rhythmic forms, all the tours de force of this classical and spiritually sensual score, which is so ingeniously reconciled with contemporary taste.

3. Ravel's first concert appearances in Vienna, which took place in October 1920, were sponsored by the French embassy. In one recital, he accompanied Marya Freund in the *Histoires naturelles* and the Mallarmé poems. Another concert, with Oskar Fried conducting the Vienna Symphony Orchestra, featured two performances of the *Rapsodie espagnole*, at the beginning and end of the program, the second suite from *Daphnis et Chloé*, and, with Marya Freund as soloist, *Shéhérazade* and the *Deux Mélodies hébraïques*. Arnold Schoenberg's Society for Private Musical Performances in Vienna presented a concert in Ravel's honor on Saturday afternoon, October 23, 1920. In addition to works by Schoenberg, Berg, and Webern, *Gaspard de la nuit* was performed by Eduard Steuermann, and Ravel and Alfredo Casella performed the two-piano version of *La Valse* (mistakenly entitled *Valses nobles et sentimentales* in the program). Schoenberg could not be present, as he was living in Amsterdam, and Berg, after assisting Ravel considerably, suffered a severe asthma attack the day before the concert, and thus did not attend. In a letter to Schoenberg, dated October 28, 1920, he wrote:

> *Previously,* I had been in frequent contact with Ravel, had—as your representative, so to speak—invited him and attended to his wishes. . . . Because Ravel proposed to me that he wanted to honor you and the *Verein* [Schoenberg's Society] by playing his latest work with Casella on two pianos and because Mme Freund decided to sing at the very *last* moment, the concert grew to three hours in length, with short intermissions and unbroken interest on the part of all those present. I mention this because a friend of Ravel's (Clemenceau) had informed me before the concert to keep it as short as possible, since Ravel is known in Paris for leaving every concert before its conclusion. But *here it was just the opposite.* In other ways as well this concert provoked attention and generated good propaganda. . . . There is no interest among people of wealth and society for the music of Ravel. (His own two concerts were *very* poorly attended in spite of the French embassy, etc.) Artistically, however, our concert proved very satisfactory.

With regard to Ravel's "leaving every concert before its conclusion," it should be explained that he often stepped out for a cigarette, and would then return to his seat (see Donald Harris, "Ravel Visits the *Verein*").

173. to Abbé Léonce Petit

Le Frêne   September 21, 1920
Lyons-La-Forêt
Eure
My dear friend,

   Before receiving your letter, I already knew that the misfortune which struck us[1] was even greater for you, because of the loss of your uncle. I didn't write to you immediately: you know at what moment your news arrived, and you certainly didn't think me indifferent. Although you have some hope, which I lack, your sadness cannot be any less profound. I embrace you fraternally. Convey my deep sympathy to your cousin, which makes me share in her grief, which I have felt myself, and which the years have not attenuated.

From Mouveau's explanation, you understood why I did not reply immediately to your letter. I wasn't able to see him before my departure. I would have liked to discuss with him, then with Pierrette, the delicate matter of Roger's[2] education. You know that the doctors think the poor fledgling should be taken away from the unhealthy climate of Paris. So what should be done? No doubt, his mother could also live in the country, but she would never agree to live there continually. Moreover, for Roger, there is the important question of physical education, which is much more efficacious when done collectively. At first, the Roches school seemed to be an elegant solution. Upon reflection, I saw, like you, many dangers . . . and I have no solution.

Although in principle, I'm supposed to remain here until next Tuesday, I will return to Paris, if necessary, as soon as Mouveau asks me to. If you have an idea, help us with your counsel.

I must stop, if my letter is to leave today. My dear old Léonce, believe in the profound affection of your

Maurice Ravel

1. The death of Pierre Haour.
2. The son of Pierrette Haour. Ravel wrote him an amusing letter; no. 305.

174. to the Directors of the Théâtre de la Monnaie[1]

Le Belvédère[2]   February 28, 1921
Montfort l'Amaury (S. & O.)
Dear Gentlemen and friends,

This is the first letter I have been able to write since leaving Brussels: and I was planning to send it to you the second day after I left! Since then, I have been occupied with moving. And it's far from being finished. I'm encamped in a corner of the house, trying to activate the slowness of masons, painters, carpenters, etc., and shuttling between Montfort and Paris, with the days fleeing at a distressing pace. Although it is undoubtedly very late, I wish to thank all of you, without exception, for the great joy which I experienced at the perfect performance—why seek another epithet?—of *L'Heure espagnole* at the Théâtre de la Monnaie.[3]

I trust that you will be indulgent with me, and, dear Gentlemen and friends, believe in the profound gratitude of yours truly,

Maurice Ravel

1. The three directors were Messieurs Jean Van Glabbeke, Paul Spaak, and Corneil de Thoran.

2. See p. 8.

3. The opera was performed 12 times in Brussels during the 1920–21 season, with the première taking place on January 27, 1921.

175. to Christian Cornélissen[1]

Le Belvédère   March 10, 1921
Montfort l'Amaury (S. & O.)
Dear Sir,

I returned yesterday to Montfort, after a stay in Paris, during which I was counting on going to see you: a host of activities, among them the Obouhov matter, didn't leave me a free moment.

But everything is arranged, and this is how things stand; treasurer: Monsieur Louis Hauser. 10 rue Lafayette.

Subscribers: Madame J[osé] M[aria] Sert——— 100 francs per month
              Madame Paul Clemenceau, 1000
                  francs paid, making a total
                  for 10 months of——————— 100   "   "   "
              Madame Denichov——————— 300   "   "   "
                              total 500   "   "   "

The rest (500 francs per month) has been guaranteed by Messieurs Léo Sachs[2] and Léonard Rosenthal.

This took quite a few requests on my part, and it didn't help my installation, which is far from being completed. But you must understand that I don't regret a thing. I'm planning to go to Paris about the 20th, and I will come to see you in order to give you all the details. You can imagine with what joy I'm going to write to Obouhov, to whom I haven't replied yet, as I was awaiting a definitive outcome.

Very truly yours,
Maurice Ravel

1. This is Ravel's only letter to him which has come to light. Judging from the contents, he may have been a lawyer or a banker.

2. An obscure composer (1856–1930) who was active in the S.M.I.

176. to Jacques Rouché

Le Belvédère   March 16, 1921
Montfort l'Amaury (S. & O.)
Dear friend,

Very happy at the good news.[1] I agree with you completely with regard to Bakst's[2] décors and costumes. The décor for the second act, in particular, is one of his most beautiful.[3]

I'm not working, or at least I'm working on getting settled. And it's interminable!

Cordially yours,
Maurice Ravel

1. That *Daphnis et Chloé* would be performed at the Opéra. It was given on June 20, 1921, with the leading roles performed by Michel Fokine, who was responsible for the choreography, and his wife Vera Fokina, with Philippe Gaubert conducting.

2. Léon Bakst (pseudonym of Lev Samoylovich Rosenberg, 1866–1924) was the chief set designer for the Ballet Russe, and had created the décor and costumes for the original production of *Daphnis et Chloé* in 1912.

3. Bakst's model for this décor is reproduced in Lesure and Nectoux, *Maurice Ravel*, Bibliothèque Nationale, following p. 24.

177. to Charles Koechlin

Le Belvédère   March 18, 1921
Montfort l'Amaury (S. & O.)
My dear friend,

I have persuaded Viking Dahl, the Swedish composer,[1] whose remarkable *Maison de fous*[2] you may have heard, that it's necessary to work. I wasn't able to convince him to study counterpoint and fugue, which he considers useless, indeed detrimental. So it's up to you to convince him, if you could take it upon yourself to direct an artist who is truly worth the trouble. I can't do it: teaching exhausts me dreadfully. And after looking carefully, I see no one but you. If you wish to accept, please write to him at 3 rue Bonaparte, in order to make an appointment.

Please take note of my new address, and, my dear friend, believe me cordially yours,

Maurice Ravel

1. Dahl (1895–1945) was a pupil at the Stockholm Conservatory and later studied dancing with Isadora Duncan.

2. At the Champs-Elysées theater, the Swedish Ballet was performing Dahl's work on the same program with *Le Tombeau de Couperin* (the "Forlane," "Menuet," and "Rigau-

don"). The ballets were choreographed by Jean Borlin and Rolf de Maré, the artistic director of the company, and were conducted by Désiré-Emile Inghelbrecht.

178. to Alfred Cortot[1]

Le Belvédère   June 27, 1921
Montfort l'Amaury (S. & O.)
My dear Cortot,

I hope that you won't hold me strictly accountable for my silence; your letter arrived at Montfort during one of my too frequent absences: rehearsals at the Opéra,[2] at the Champs-Elysées theater,[3] and, above all, this laborious installation which has been going on for almost 4 months, and which is still not completely finished.

Jacques Thibaud[4] was supposed to come take me last Tuesday to the Conservatoire, in order to hear the rehearsal of my Trio. I waited for him in vain. But I'm not worried. I hope to be able to hear you on the 30th.[5]

In this regard, I received a desperate letter from Madame Jacques Hermant. She was unable to get a ticket, and, for lack of something better, she is asking to be allowed to stand. Is it possible? Once again, pardon me. See you Thursday, most likely, and believe in the cordial fellowship of your

Maurice Ravel

1. The eminent pianist, conductor and pedagogue Alfred Cortot (1877–1962) was a fellow student at the Conservatoire.

2. Of *Daphnis et Chloé*.

3. Of the ballet *Le Tombeau de Couperin*.

4. The French violinist (1880–1953) was also a fellow student at the Conservatoire. Cortot, Thibaud, and Pablo Casals formed their celebrated trio in 1905 (see plate 3).

5. On Thursday, June 30, 1921, at 4:00 P.M., the Cortot, Thibaud, Casals trio performed a recital of works by Beethoven (opus 70 no. 2), Ravel, and Schumann (opus 110) at the Mogador theater in Paris.

179. to Henry Prunières

Le Belvédère   July 18, 1921
Montfort l'Amaury (S. &. O.)
Dear Monsieur and friend,

I'm thinking of going to Paris[1] before the end of the month, and inviting you to lunch, as you kindly invited me. Thus, I am going to begin musical criticism anew[2]—it's not too pressing? As for the theme to vary, I'm writing to Schmitt and Koechlin. We'll find a theme between the three of us.[3]

If I pointed out Bardac to you, it is, above all, because he is a sensitive musician; but he's also one of the oldest students of Fauré, who had great affection for him. If he is not very well known, it's really due to his personality, which, if not overly modest, is at least very distant.

I'm enclosing a letter for Ansermet. I don't recall his exact address in Geneva, and he may not even be there at this moment.

Thanks in advance, and very cordially yours,

Maurice Ravel

1. Ravel uses the slang "Panam" for Paris.

2. Ravel's last article had been written about seven years before. Prunières was planning a special issue of *La Revue musicale* honoring Gabriel Fauré. It was published in October 1922, with a musical supplement containing works by Fauré's former pupils, Georges Enesco, Louis Aubert, Schmitt, Koechlin, Paul Ladmirault, Jean Roger-Ducasse, and Ravel. All of the pieces were introduced at an S.M.I. recital on December 13, 1922. (See Ravel's article on Fauré's songs, p. 384.)

3. The theme which was chosen was based upon Fauré's name. As notes are labeled from A to G (in English and French), H became A, I became B, and so on, thus giving the following theme:

G	A	B	R	I	E	L		F	A	U	R	E
G	A	B	D	B	E	E		F	A	G	D	E

(A similar procedure had been followed for the *Menuet sur le nom d'Haydn*.)

180. to Ernest Ansermet[1]

Le Belvédère   July 18, 1921
Montfort l'Amaury (S. & O.)
Dear friend,

I don't know how long it's been since I should have written to you. Some assured me that you were in London, others, in Rome, in America, who knows? You might say that I could have addressed my letter to Geneva. I know very well that you live on Boulevard des Tranchées, but I no longer remember the number. In any event, I'm sending this in care of Madame Sert. But I've got a better idea! I'm going to send it to Prunières.

The situation is as follows: Madeleine Grey,[2] whose address is 48 rue des Martyrs, Paris 9, has asked me if it would be possible for her to be engaged in Geneva for next season—I'm quite sure that's when, in order to sing my works. I recommend her with pleasure: she is a most remarkable performer; a pretty voice, rather strong (the voice), and very clear. And, what is appreciable, perfect diction. Thanks to her, *Shéhérazade* was heard without sounding like a symphonic poem. She sang the première of my 2 Hebraic songs in Hebrew.[3]—I couldn't vouch for the purity of her pronunciation, but I was assured that it was good.—Fauré entrusted the first performance of his latest songs to her,[4] G[eorges] Hüe[5] as well. This is to let you know that she can sing other things beside Ravel.

Is it too late? I would have terrible remorse. It is true that in addition to the above reasons, I have been frightfully busy. And my installation still isn't finished! Nevertheless, I'm going to resume work.

I have just read your article on Stravinsky.[6] It confirmed to me that musicians are the ones who speak best about music, when they take the trouble to study it thoroughly—were I to state this publicly, I would be attacked by writers on music and even by Jean Cocteau.

Please present my compliments to Mme Ansermet, and, my dear friend, believe me very cordially yours,

Maurice Ravel

1. The Swiss conductor Ernest Ansermet (1883–1969) was particularly gifted in the interpretation of twentieth-century music (see plate 6). His close friendship with Stravinsky led to a distinguished tenure with the Ballet Russe (1915–1923), and his name is inextricably linked with the Orchestre de la Suisse Romande, which he conducted from its inception in 1918 (see p. 544).

2. The French mezzo-soprano (1896–1979). In the postwar years, she toured and recorded with Ravel (see plate 6).

3. Actually, neither song is in Hebrew. "Kaddisch" is in Aramaic, and "L'Enigme éternelle" is in Yiddish.

4. *Mirages,* a cycle of four songs, which Madeleine Grey introduced at a Société Nationale recital on December 27, 1919.

5. See p. 347, note 6.

6. Entitled "L'Oeuvre d'Igor Stravinsky," Ansermet's article appeared in *La Revue musicale,* July 1, 1921, pp. 1–27.

181. to Marie Gaudin

Le Belvédère   August 10, 1921
Montfort l'Amaury (S. & O.)
My dear Marie,

I'm replying immediately; and it's the 1st letter that I have written in more than 2 weeks.

My installation is far from being finished. However, I abandoned everything in order to resume work.—It's close to a year since I stopped!—So, I can go to Donibane,[1] where I will continue to plug away; I hope so, at least, because of the return to those years which were so happy, and so long ago . . .

In any case, I'm making arrangements: I'll certainly bring along my bathing suit, but no dinner jacket.

Edouard still hasn't returned from Vichy. I don't think they will go as far as St.-Jean-de-Luz. They were intending to take a trip to the Creuse valley, and should be returning very shortly. I have received no news, except for a card from Châtelguyon,[2] with 3 signatures.[3]

I expect to be arriving in the beginning of September, perhaps before.

Moreover, thanks very much in advance for your kind hospitality. Without you, I would never have had the courage to return.

I embrace all of you very affectionately.

Maurice Ravel

1. St.-Jean[-de-Luz], in Basque.
2. A spa in central France, in the same general area as the Creuse valley and Vichy.
3. Those of Edouard and the Bonnets.

182. to Ernest Ansermet

Le Belvédère   October 20, 1921
Montfort l'Amaury (S. & O.)
Dear friend,

Your letter found me in St.-Jean-de-Luz, knocked out by a southerly wind which brought on a splendid case of inertia.

And now I'm back; I'm going to try to finish the duo for violin and cello. As for my correspondence, I've given up all hope of catching up.

Madame Doire[1] has indeed sung *Shéhérazade* in various places. I have never heard her, and therefore cannot give you an opinion.

Your understanding of *La Valse* is perfect. I could never get that rhythmic suppleness in Paris. I have resigned myself to be present at the first performance in Vienna—which is supposed to occur this season—. Don't forget to have the programs mention that this "choreographic poem" is written for the stage. I believe it is necessary, judging from the surprise which the concluding frenzy has evoked from some listeners, and, above all, from the fantastic comments of several music critics. Some situate this dance in Paris, on a volcano, about 1870,[2] others, in Vienna, before a buffet, in 1919.[3]

Please convey my respectful friendship to Madame Ansermet, and believe me very cordially yours,

Maurice Ravel[4]

1. The wife of René Doire.
2. Suggesting that the "concluding frenzy" relates to the Franco-Prussian war.
3. A play on words. The French idiom "danser devant le buffet," literally "to dance before the buffet," means having nothing to eat, as in postwar Vienna.
4. The autograph of this letter is reproduced in Jean-Louis Matthey, *Ernest Ansermet* (Lausanne, 1983), p. 123.

183. to Florent Schmitt

Le Belvédère   October 29, 1921
Montfort l'Amaury (S. & O.)
Dear old chap,

I took your card to St.-Jean-de-Luz with the intention of answering it there. I brought it back with the same intention. However, anything can happen.

Why did you see some irony in my congratulations?[1] I don't like snails, but if you did, and were to receive a basketful of them, I would be very happy for you. On the other hand, I wouldn't allow them to be shoved into my mouth against my will. My logic? There's nothing surprising about it: it's to do only what I want, according to what appeals to me. People tell you off, but who gives a d[amn], right?

See you soon, at the S.M.I. or at Prunières' home.

Affectionate regards to the three of you,

Maurice Ravel

I'm cold, which doesn't prevent me from grinding away, even less from being bored. Timal[2] would like to show me his compositions. Would that interest you? In this regard, I persuaded Miss Ethel Leginska[3] that your teaching was indeed superior to mine. Have you heard this young Yankee?

1. Schmitt had recently accepted the Legion of Honor (which Ravel had refused). The remainder of the paragraph deals with this episode (see plate 11).

2. See letter no. 74, note 3.

3. See letter no. 68, note 4.

184. to Jacques Rouché

Le Belvédère   December 8, 1921
Montfort l'Amaury (S. & O.)
My dear friend,

You were aware that until Monday, I doubted the successful outcome of this venture: it turned out that you were right.[1]

It is true that in addition to the audacity of presenting my opera buffa at the National Academy of Music, you also gave it the cast and the stage settings which suited it.[2] This perfect ensemble led to its success, for which I am doubly grateful to you.

Cordially yours,

Maurice Ravel

1. On Monday, December 5, 1921, *L'Heure espagnole* was presented for the first time at the Opéra, with Fanny Heldy (Concepcion), Henri Fabert (Gonzalve), Robert Cou-

zinou (Ramiro), Albert Huberty (Don Inigo Gomez), Gaston Dubois (Torquemada), décor by André Mare, and Philippe Gaubert conducting. Both the opera and *Daphnis et Chloé* fared considerably better with the public and press on this occasion than at their original productions.

2. In a letter to Rouché written on June 30, 1921, Ravel thanked him for planning to present *L'Heure espagnole* at the Opéra: "I'm afraid of only one thing: the proportions of the house . . . and of the work. But you have undoubtedly considered this disadvantage yourself. Thus, it's agreed."

185. to Tristan Klingsor[1]

Le Belvédère   January 5, 1922
Montfort l'Amaury (S. & O.)
Dear friend,

The *Humoresques* will be most welcome, and my sincere thanks in advance. Didn't you receive my new address, about a year ago?

Excuse me for Sunday. I'm not planning to go to Paris until I have finished my duo for violin and cello, which has been dragging on for too long.

Most affectionate regards to the three of you from your
Maurice Ravel

1. The pseudonym of Arthur Justin Léon Leclère (1874–1966), French poet, painter, art critic, and composer. Klingsor was a member of the *Apaches*, and in 1903 Ravel set three of his poems from the collection *Schéhérazade*. Among his other important works are *Humoresques* (1921) and *Cinquante Sonnets du dormeur éveillé* (1949). In 1959, he was awarded a Grand Prix in poetry by the Académie Française.

186. to the Director of the Music Academy of Stockholm

Le Belvédère   January 24, 1922
Montfort l'Amaury
Sir,

Upon returning to Montfort, I found your letter, as well as the diploma and the certificates of the Music Academy of Stockholm.[1]

With my sincere thanks, believe me, Sir, very truly yours,
Maurice Ravel

1. In addition to Ravel, the Academy had recently honored Paul Dukas and Gabriel Pierné (see *Excelsior*, December 3, 1921). Ravel later accepted many honorary awards, among them the Cross of the Order of King Leopold of Belgium (1926), the Cross of King Carol II of Romania (1932), both of which were presented by the respective kings, and a degree of Doctor of Music, *honoris causa*, from Oxford University (1928).

187. to Madame Jane Hatto[1]

Le Belvédère[2]   January 31, 1922
Montfort l'Amaury (S. & O.)
My dear friend,

You can imagine how happy I will be to see you again, after such a long time. My duo for violin and cello will certainly be finished before the 18th.[3] I must tell you that this duo has been dragging on for a year and a half, and I made a vow—not at the altar of Saint Cecilia,[4] because then I would have had to go to Paris—not to leave Montfort until it is completed. So, see you soon—I'll telephone—and believe in the old friendship of your

Maurice Ravel

1. Ravel spelled her first name Jeane. It appears most often as Jane, and sometimes Jeanne.

2. The following address is crossed out at the top of this letter: 7 Avenue Léonie, St.-Cloud (S. & O.), Tel.: 233.

3. On Saturday evening, February 18, 1922, Mme Hatto presented a recital at Salle Pleyel with the French composer and pianist Max d'Ollone. The program, which included works by Franck, Fauré, d'Ollone, and Chausson, concluded with Ravel's *Shéhérazade.*

4. The patron saint of musicians.

188. to M. D. Calvocoressi

Le Belvédère   February 3, 1922
Montfort l'Amaury (S. & O.)

Well now, my dear friend, I owe you another apology! I didn't know that both of you had come to see me,[1] and simply thought that I was wanted on the telephone. I'm sleeping a little better these past few days—not much—. Today, I'm a bit dazed: the effects of Dial.[2] I rarely use this method, as a single tablet suffices to knock me out.

The duo was finished. Then I thought that the scherzo was much too extended, and moreover shoddy. I'm going to begin it all over again.

Still no news from the Vienna Opera, for whom the 1st performance of *La Valse* has been reserved,[3] as you may know. Frau Gustav Mahler[4] and several others are trying to stir things up. When I think of the millions of crowns this production will cost, my head spins, and I can't foresee it taking place. Please apologize to Madame Calvocoressi for me, convey my compliments to her, and believe me very cordially yours,

Maurice Ravel

I reopened my letter. That's evident. This is why: I was expecting a copy of *Pictures at an Exhibition,* in Mussorgsky's original edition.[5] Now, this minute I received a notice that it cannot be procured. Do you have one, and could you lend it to me for a while? Or do you know anyone who could do me this favor? I would very much appreciate a reply as soon as possible. Thanks in advance.

ΠR

I should also write a book about musical criticism.[6] It would really be amusing . . .

1. Calvocoressi and his wife.

2. Short for Dialdéhyde, a drug to induce sleep.

3. That is, the first performance with choreography. The first performances in Vienna and Paris were given by Ida Rubinstein's troupe.

4. Née Alma Schindler (1879–1964). Ravel and Casella were guests at her home during their visit to Vienna in October 1920.

5. Ravel had been commissioned by Serge Koussevitzky to orchestrate Mussorgsky's work, and he wanted to use the original edition, not the first edition (1886) which Rimsky-Korsakov had edited. Calvocoressi recalled that he was only able to give Ravel the Rimsky-Korsakov edition. Ravel's copy of this score is now in the Music Division of the Bibliothèque Nationale.

6. Calvocoressi was writing a book on the subject, entitled *The Principles and Methods of Musical Criticism.* It was published by Oxford University Press in 1923.

189. to Roland-Manuel

February 3, 1922

Dear friend,

Enclosed is the letter of introduction. If it's not suitable, tell me how it should be revised.

No more news from Lyon, nor from Marseilles. In principle, the Marseilles recital is set for March 17, and the other for the end of April.[1]

The duo was finished. And then, I thought that the scherzo was much too extended, and moreover shoddy. I'm going to begin all over again, with new material; it will delay my leave, but I still hope to be in Montfort in order to receive your visit and that of Suzanne & Co. Give me some notice, so I'll order a meal fit for the occasion—sauerkraut, pudding, goose, tripe—.

I replied to Siohan[2] that I would meet him in Paris. I intend to receive him one day, when I have lunch at rue de Chazelles.[3] May I do so without indiscretion? Are you on good terms with him? Is what he's doing interesting?

Affectionately to the two and a half of you.[4]

Maurice Ravel

1. The recital in Marseilles marked Ravel's first concert appearance there. Sponsored by the Marseilles Chamber Music Society, the program included a performance of the String Quartet, and Madeleine Grey singing the *Histoires naturelles*, the Hebraic songs,

and *Shéhérazade,* accompanied by the composer. Another Ravel festival took place in Lyon on May 3, with Madeleine Grey and the composer performing the same works as above, and a performance of *Ma Mère l'Oye* by Paul Gayraud and Ravel.

2. Robert Siohan (1894–1985), the French music theorist, conductor, writer, and composer.

3. The home of M. and Mme Fernand Dreyfus.

4. Ravel's *Berceuse sur le nom de Gabriel Fauré* was of course intended to honor his teacher, but the gentle lullaby also celebrated the birth, on June 20, 1922, of Claude Roland-Manuel, to whom the piece is dedicated.

190. to Jacques Durand

Le Belvédère   March 23, 1922
Montfort l'Amaury (S. & O.)
My dear friend,

Upon returning, I found a letter from M. Dommange,[1] dated the 16th, concerning the dedication of the Sonata for Violin and Cello.

I don't recall having discussed this matter with him last Sunday. Please convey my apologies to him for not replying directly: I was going to write to you about this very work . . . and about other matters.

I) The dedication, which I did forget to inscribe at the head of the manuscript, should read: <u>to the memory of Claude Debussy.</u>

II) In the 2nd movement (<u>very lively</u>), in the 17th measure after the

in the violin part, the cello has this:

each *d* must be replaced by an *e,* as follows:

thus reestablishing the first version,[2] which, to my great surprise, seemed unplayable, on a bad cello, it is true. . . .

III) A telegram from Ansermet, asking for some clarifications about the tempi in the 2nd suite from *Daphnis,* allowed me to ascertain—which I had already partially done—that complete lunacy presided over the tempo indications: at 176 (very slow) there is: ♩ = 66. It should read ♪ = 66 (in the piano score as well). Further on, in the 4th measure before 180 add a tempo, and in the following measure add twice as fast: ♩ = the preceding ♪. Therefore, at 180 (lively) ♩ = the preceding ♪ (same for the piano).

At 194 (animated) there is no metronomic indication for the orchestra. The piano has one, alas! ♩ = 68; and, more aggravating: Andante! It should be 168.[3] One day, I must reexamine this unfortunate score from beginning to end.

IV) (This has nothing to do with music publishing.) Go see Caligari.[4] Cinema has finally been created. Some may regret that this film was made by the Boches, who have never invented anything, as we all know.

See you soon, and affectionate regards to both of you.

Maurice Ravel

1. René Dommange (1889–1977), a cousin of Jacques Durand, later became the head of Durand and Co.

2. This correction is found in the score.

3. Only the correction at rehearsal number 180 appears in the piano and orchestral scores of *Daphnis et Chloé*. It should be pointed out, however, that Ravel himself made all of these errors in the manuscripts.

4. "The Cabinet of Doctor Caligari," a celebrated German expressionistic avant-garde film made in 1919, directed by Robert Wiene. It deals with psychiatric disorders, and has been described as being a premonition of German racial policies in the 1930s. (Dr. Caligari hypnotizes a young patient, Cesare, turning him into a robot and forcing him to commit sadistic murders. Cesare dies, Caligari is exposed and committed to an insane asylum.) The leading roles were played by Werner Krauss (Caligari) and Conrad Veidt (Cesare).

191. to M. D. Calvocoressi

Le Belvédère   March 24, 1922
Montfort l'Amaury (S. & O.)
My dear friend,

Don't think that my long delay in replying to your letter announcing the arrival of the *Pictures* [*at an Exhibition*], which I indeed found at Montfort, was intended as an act of retaliation. I was in Paris when it arrived; intending to stay 4 or 5 days, I remained there almost a month. Then I came back to Montfort, packed my valise, and left immediately for Marseilles. Now I'm at Le Belvédère till the end of the month, when I must return to Paris to supervise the final rehearsals of the duo, which, in agreement with Durand, and in light of the proportions of this work, is going to be entitled "Sonata for Violin and Cello." The first performance will take place on April 6.[1] This business for two instruments may not seem like much, but there's close to a year and a half of work in it. During that time, Marius—called Darius—Milhaud, would have found a way to compose 4 symphonies, 5 quartets, and several settings of lyric poems by Paul Claudel.

You can reassure Mr. Mead:[2] I'm presently working on 5 piano pieces (still counting the Sonatine as only 2),[3] am busy finding a better pianist than myself for the 5 others,[4] and will have everything ready for the month of June. I haven't informed him of this yet, because I don't know exactly when I will be able to go. I'm not asking Ricardo for 2 reasons: first, I think he's supposed to be in Spain about that time; second, I would especially like to have *Gaspard de la nuit* recorded, and Viñes never wanted to perform these pieces, in particular "Le Gibet," according to the composer's intentions. I did say <u>wanted</u>: I don't know if you were ever present at one of those discussions in which he assured me that if he observed the nuances and the tempo that I indicated, "Le Gibet" would bore the public. And nothing would make him change his mind.

Thus, it's set for June. As soon as the date for the trip is set, I'll write to Mr. Mead.

A thousand thanks for the *Pictures,* ten thousand apologies for turning your library upside down—I hate that—and very cordially yours,

Maurice Ravel

1. The performers were Hélène Jourdan-Morhange and the French cellist Maurice Maréchal.

2. Alfred Mead, the representative of the Aeolian Company, for whom Ravel was planning to record his piano pieces (the text of their contract is found in Appendix E).

3. In 1913, Ravel had made a piano roll of the first two movements of the Sonatine for Welte-Mignon.

4. The pianist would be Robert Casadesus.

192. to E. Robert Schmitz[1]

Le Belvédère   March 25, 1922
Montfort l'Amaury (S. & O.)
Dear friend,

When your letter arrived, I was finishing—with such fury!—a Sonata for Violin and Cello, which required almost a year and a half of work.

You can understand—and will certainly excuse me—that during this intense period, I couldn't even think of answering any letters.

The piece was finished a few days ago; I've given myself a convalescent leave, and, if it isn't too late, let me assure you that I would be very pleased to join the advisory board of the Franco-American Musical Society.[2]

The Basque concerto, *Zazpiak-Bat*—how long it takes for news to reach

America!—I had in fact begun it . . . in 1913. Its 3 movements were even rather developed, when, suddenly, I abandoned everything.

I have a new project: *Le Grand Meaulnes*, a fantasy for piano and orchestra. I hope that I'll be able to complete this one, and many others; although I am not at all well—morally, above all—I feel that I'm getting back to work.

I hope to see you during your next stay, and, in the meantime, send you my most cordial regards.

Maurice Ravel

Thanks for the programs and the reviews.

1. The French pianist, author, conductor, teacher, and entrepreneur Elie Robert Schmitz (1889–1949) was an indefatigable champion of contemporary music. In the 1920s and 1930s, the organization he had founded, Pro-Musica, Incorporated, had over 40 chapters in North America, Europe, and even Honolulu and Shanghai. In addition to Ravel's tour of North America in 1928, Schmitz was responsible for similar tours by Prokofiev, Bartók, Roussel, Milhaud, and many others.

2. The name was soon changed to Pro-Musica, Incorporated.

193. to Henry Prunières

Le Belvédère   March 29, 1922
Montfort l'Amaury (S. & O.)
Dear friend,

Thank you for your kind invitation. I was supposed to leave Paris on the 7th, but will remain one more day. Of course I will go to hear Bartók's Sonata.[1] Will he be in Paris on the 6th? I would be delighted if he were able to hear the duo at the S.M.I. I think that Vuillermoz is aware that it's being played that day. If you should see him, would you please remind him of it? The duo is now called "Sonata for Violin and Cello."

Please present my compliments to Madame Prunières, and believe me cordially yours,

Maurice Ravel

1. On Saturday, April 8, at 5:00 P.M., the concerts of *La Revue musicale* presented a program of works by Bartók, Kodály, and Ravel. Bartók performed his own piano pieces, among them the Suite (opus 14), and the 2 burlesques (opus 8), as well as piano works of Kodály, and, with Jelly d'Aranyi, his First Sonata for Violin and Piano (opus 21). Ravel's brief contribution to the program consisted of the Hebraic songs, sung by one M. Slivinsky. The recital was followed by a dinner and musicale at the home of Henry Prunières, in which Jelly d'Aranyi and Bartók played the Sonata once again. Among the guests were Ravel, Stravinsky, Poulenc, and the Polish composer Karol Szymanowski (1882–1937).

194. to Cipa Godebski

Le Belvédère   April 11, 1922
Montfort l'Amaury (S. & O.)
Old chap,

Above all, don't see the slightest irony in this, as Schmitt did: I learned that my Sonata for Violin and Cello didn't please you, and that you had the courage to say so. And I'm very pleased about it, because it proves to me—which I didn't doubt at all—that it's not because of friendship or snobbism that you like my other works. And I prefer this spontaneous impression to the one I received in a letter from a fine society lady: after congratulating me for my "modesty," she called my new work "original" and "spiritual," which is what she had previously told me about my Trio.

I was so busy Friday and Saturday—didn't even have the time to visit Georgette Marnold, which must have struck her as completely gauche—that I wasn't able to inform you that Pruneton[1] had allowed me to take you in on Saturday for the Bartók recital at the Vieux Colombier. His Sonata is splendid.

It's agreed for Easter? You'll all come? I can put all of you up, you know. I even think you will inaugurate the bathroom. An attempt was made yesterday, and I saw blackish water flowing delightfully in the bathtub.

You can see that I'm not hiding the attractions.

I await the confirmation of your visit.

Affectionately to all,

Maurice Ravel

1. Ravel's nickname for Henry Prunières.

195. to Marie Olénine d'Alheim[1]

Le Belvédère   April 12, 1922
Montfort l'Amaury

The name of Pierre d'Alheim marks an important era in my life as a musician. I cannot forget the day, so long ago, when, with him, you came to reveal Mussorgsky's music to us.[2] It is with deep emotion that I beg you to accept my most profound sympathy.

Maurice Ravel

1. See letter no. 79, note 1. This letter of condolence was written the day after Pierre d'Alheim's death.

2. Madame Olénine d'Alheim made her debut in Paris in 1896, and for some forty years she specialized in singing the music of Russian composers, particularly Mussorgsky, as well as folk songs from many nations. The d'Alheims also gave many lecture-recitals devoted to Mussorgsky's music, which was virtually unknown in western Europe.

196. to Serge Koussevitzky[1]

Le Belvédère   May 1, 1922
Montfort l'Amaury (S. & O.)
My dear friend,

The "Great Gate of Kiev" is finally finished. I started at the end, because it was the least interesting piece to orchestrate. But you wouldn't believe how much work such a simple thing demands. The rest will go much faster.[2]

Here are some useful indications:

1) I numbered the pages provisionally.

2) I represented the rehearsal numbers with frames □. This is for the copyist, who will merely have to add the numbers when the score is finished.

3) At the last measure of page 7 and the first of page 8: the organ effect can die away: in this case, there is a caesura. Or else—I prefer this interpretation—the organ effect is suddenly cut off by the entry of the bell. In that case, the notes and the slurs written in pencil would have to be added.[3]

There are certainly changes in tempo which were not indicated by Mussorgsky. Thus, when the theme of the "Promenade" returns, it seems to me that the tempo should be much faster. This explains my orchestral interpretation. Perhaps this livelier tempo should even commence at the entrance of the bell—page 8—[4] that's why, at the end of page 11, I wrote the scale in eighth notes, and not sixteenths.[5] If one doesn't make an accelerando before, these 8 measures should be performed twice as fast. At the end of this passage, I even added an ascending and descending scale, which won't do any harm, and which, I hope, won't have me accused too much of "vandalizing" Rimsky-Korsakov's style.[6] With an inner pedal point, played by the bell[7]—which Mussorgsky certainly anticipated—that's all I permitted myself.

I'm leaving for Lyon the day after tomorrow in the morning, and will leave there the same night, so that I will have the pleasure of seeing you on Thursday evening. To gain time, I'm mailing you the "Great Gate" in a registered package.

Please give my kind regards to Mrs. Koussevitzky, and, my dear friend, believe me very cordially yours,

Maurice Ravel

1. In Paris, and as conductor of the Boston Symphony Orchestra for 25 years, Koussevitzky (1874–1951) commissioned many outstanding works, among them Honegger's *Pacific 231*, Stravinsky's *Symphony of Psalms,* and Copland's Third Symphony. Earlier in his career, he began a publishing firm in Moscow, devoted to Russian music. His annual concerts in Paris in the 1920s were a highlight of the musical season.

2. Ravel's orchestral holograph of *Pictures at an Exhibition* is on deposit at the Library of Congress from Boosey & Hawkes. Consisting of 98 pages, it is signed and dated May

1922. This date, however, only applies to "The Great Gate of Kiev," and the remainder of the work was completed by the fall of 1922. The manuscript contains many corrections in pencil by Ravel together with many blue crayon markings, undoubtedly by Koussevitzky, and was used as a conductor's score. Koussevitzky led the first performance at the Opéra on October 19, 1922, and his publishing firm printed the score in 1929.

3. Corresponding to rehearsal number 110 and its preceding measure (in the Eulenburg Miniature Score, no. 1303. The "organ effect" refers to rehearsal numbers 109 to 110.) Ravel's original orchestration

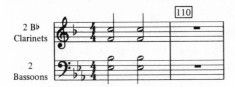

was modified as follows:

4. At rehearsal number 110.

5. Corresponding to rehearsal number 114. Ravel later changed his mind: in the score, the four measures between rehearsal numbers 114 and 115 contain sixteenth notes, but in the manuscript there are eight measures of eighth notes.

6. Corresponding to the measure before rehearsal number 115, which does not exist in Mussorgsky's piano piece.

7. The pedal point extending from rehearsal numbers 110 to 114.

197. to Hélène Jourdan-Morhange

Le Belvédère   May 9, 1922
Montfort l'Amaury (S. & O.)
Dear friend,

No doubt you're astonished that I didn't answer you. Once again, Mme Mauvernay is to blame. At first, she set the date for the concert in Lyon for May 4, then the 7th. At the last minute—and only because I asked her to please tell me the exact date—she informed me that the recital was put back to its original date . . . the 3rd! I just had enough time to pack my valise, take the 8:00 A.M. train, arrive at Lyon at 4:00 P.M., and leave there at midnight, because the next day I had to see Koussevitzky, and Friday I had to be at the charity auction of Madame Clemenceau.

I returned to Montfort only on Sunday, by auto. Your letter awaited me there, in the company of many others. Instead of replying, I spent all of yesterday sleeping. And yet, I had to write to you about the Sonata for Violin and Cello.

1) It seems that the first performance, according to what I presumably said—I've never been told to whom—was a "massacre." And everyone knows my opinion, even you, and no doubt Maréchal[1] also. I think that this revelation didn't sadden either one of you too much. Moreover, I have learned of my departure for Africa and of my forthcoming marriage—I don't know which of these events is supposed to precede the other—.

2) Thursday night, Aubert,[2] to whom I had spoken about the possibility of having a 2nd performance of the Sonata, told me that the issue had been raised, and that the Sonata was requested again. I was going to write to you about it when I received the program for the 16th. It only remains for me to thank you, and to ask both of you to excuse me for letting myself be governed by events. I am already so behind in completing the work I have undertaken, that I'm afraid I won't be able to be present at the new "massacre." If you don't see me Tuesday evening, don't attribute my absence to any other reason.[3]

In order to visit houses,[4] come any day you wish except Thursday, when I'll probably be out for part of the day. You need only tell me beforehand, take the train at 9:00 A.M., and have lunch here, which will be much more convenient for you.

Cordial regards from your grateful victim,

Maurice Ravel

1. The French cellist Maurice Maréchal.

2. See letter no. 73, note 3.

3. The Sonata was performed again at an S.M.I. recital on Tuesday evening, May 16. The program included the first performance of Maurice Delage's piano piece, *Schumann*, played by Henri Gil-Marchex, and works by Charles Koechlin, Jean Huré, and Alexandre Tansman.

4. Madame Jourdan-Morhange and Luc-Albert Moreau later bought a summer home in Les Mesnuls, a village just two miles away from Montfort l'Amaury.

198. to Maurice Delage

Le Belvédère   May 19, 1922
Montfort l'Amaury (S. & O.)

Old chap,

The other evening, I wasn't able to tell you everything that I thought about *Schumann*—it's a bit your fault, you deserter. First of all, I like it very much, and it's perfectly successful. But that's not the point. You can no longer write like that.[1] It would be too long to explain a host of things here which you must have perceived as well as I. However, you must get out of your impasse. If I managed to do so, it isn't, as you think, due to my natural talent. Before finishing my String Quartet—which is far from being perfect—I knew even less than you.[2] Do you want to work? There is still time.

Will you be joining the company next Monday—there will be enough food to go around. . . . Delighted if Mme G. D. D. could come also. On account of the Calvos[3] and M. and Mme Casadesus, Mme Dreyfus would only have to tell me: "I took the liberty of bringing our young lady friend, etc." In a few words, I can make you understand what would be impossible for me to explain in 8 pages. Understood?[4]

Cordial regards,
Maurice Ravel

1. Delage's piano piece is a rather lengthy, virtuoso work played without pause, which mingles Schumannesque elements with more contemporary passages.

2. An excessively modest statement. The first edition of the String Quartet was published by Gabriel Astruc in 1904. Six years later, at Ravel's request, the rights were ceded to Durand, and a "new edition reviewed by the author" was published. Aside from two minor corrections, both scores are identical.

3. Calvocoressi and his wife.

4. Madame G. D. D. was obviously a friend of Delage, and Ravel suggests that he introduce her as Madame Dreyfus would have done in an analogous situation.

199. to Jean Jobert[1]

Le Belvédère   June 8, 1922
Montfort l'Amaury (S. & O.)
Sir,

Allow me to defer my reply for several days. Although it would be a pleasure to orchestrate these two pieces, and particularly the "Sarabande," I would first like to have the authorization of Madame Claude Debussy.[2]

Very truly yours,
Maurice Ravel

1. The French publisher Jean Jobert (1883–1957) had written to Ravel, asking him to orchestrate Debussy's *Danse* (1890), and "Sarabande" from *Pour le piano* (1901).

2. The authorization was granted promptly, and the transcriptions were completed in the winter of 1922. Paul Paray led the Lamoureux Orchestra in the first performance on March 18, 1923.

200. to Madame Claude Debussy

Le Belvédère   June 8, 1922
Montfort l'Amaury (S. & O.)
Dear Madame and friend,

Here is the letter that I received yesterday.

It is certain that these two pieces, and particularly the "Sarabande," are very orchestral. Unfortunately, it is also certain that the publisher has the right to entrust them to Heaven only knows who!

Nevertheless, I will do nothing without your authorization.

I sincerely regretted not having been able to see you the other evening. When Marguerite Long told me that you were in the lobby of Salle Gaveau, I rushed downstairs, but you had already left.

I hope that you will be in Paris toward the 25th of this month, and that I will have the pleasure of meeting you there. I'll be passing through on the way to London, where the Aeolian company is supposed to record the precious wrong notes which I will assuredly add to my works.

Dear Madame and friend, please believe in the respectful friendship of yours truly,

Maurice Ravel

201. to Roland-Manuel

Le Belvédère   June 9, 1922
Montfort l'Amaury (S. & O.)
Dear friend,

Damn it! I don't have the address of Casadesus.[1] Would you tell him that I said we would be arriving in London on the 29th? —Recording session on the 30th—. And tell him to inform me immediately if these dates don't suit him. I also have to find a day when we can put the finishing touches on *Gaspard de la nuit.*

Furthermore, could you tell me if a soldier's registration and an expired passport would suffice in order to go to an allied country?

Thanks in advance—and my apologies—. I trust that this won't coincide with the arrival of the little darling.[2]

Affectionately to you both,

Maurice Ravel[3]

1. See letter no. 203, note 1.

2. Claude Roland-Manuel, who was born on June 20, 1922.

3. The autograph of this letter is reproduced in Roland-Manuel, *A la gloire de Ravel* (Paris: Editions de la Nouvelle Revue Critique, 1938), plate 24, following p. 204.

202. to Marguerite Long[1]

Le Belvédère   June 12, 1922
Montfort l'Amaury (S. & O.)

Pardon me, my dear friend, for not having replied immediately. Pardon me also for not being able to accept your kind invitation: there is a task that I must finish before leaving for London—at the end of the month—.

However, I will be coming to Paris on Tuesday evening for the homage to Fauré.[2] Perhaps I will see you there.

Above all, don't tell anyone that I wrote to you! I would receive a thousand and one insults from neglected correspondents.

With respectful friendship from your
Maurice Ravel

1. The eminent French pianist and pedagogue Marguerite Long (1874–1966) wrote three books of recollections, each entitled *Au piano avec* [At the piano with]: *Fauré, Debussy,* and *Ravel.* She played the first performance of *Le Tombeau de Couperin* and the Piano Concerto in G Major, which is dedicated to her. Following the première of the Concerto, with Ravel conducting, on January 14, 1932, they undertook a triumphant three-month tour, performing it in some twenty cities throughout western and eastern Europe.

2. On June 20, an all-Fauré program was given at the Sorbonne under the patronage of the president of the French Republic. The concert included songs performed by Mesdames Claire Croiza and Jeanne Raunay, the *Ballade* for piano and orchestra with Alfred Cortot, and the *Elégie* with Pablo Casals as soloist. In a glowing review, Henry Prunières paid homage to Fauré's distinguished contributions both as teacher and composer, and called the evening an "apotheosis" . . . for the "great musician, whose works will live like those of Berlioz, Gounod, or Debussy." (See "Hommage national à Gabriel Fauré," *La Revue musicale,* July 1, 1922, pp. 71–72.)

203. to Robert Casadesus[1]

Hôtel d'Athènes[2]   Tuesday [June 20, 1922]
21 rue d'Athènes
Paris 9
Dear Sir,

Am in Paris for 2 days. Today, at 1:30 P.M., Conservatoire. Tomorrow, at 4:30 P.M., American Foundation.[3] The rest of the time, I have a host of errands to take care of, but will do so depending on the time that you can see me. If you could come this afternoon at the end of the competition for composers—I don't know at what time, we could make arrangements. This evening, I'm having dinner at the home of Madame Jourdan-Morhange, where you can call me (WAG. 30.51), and then I'll be going to the Fauré concert, where we can meet in the foyer at the conclusion. —And if it's impossible for us to meet in Paris, I'll wait for you on Sunday.

Your uncle told me that you were going to take care of the arrangements for the trip. If you are prevented from doing so, please call here (GUT. 0.28), and your message will be transmitted to me.[4]

1. The celebrated pianist, pedagogue, and composer Robert Casadesus (1899–1972) made his recital debut in 1917 (see plate 6). In a career spanning some 55 years, he performed over 3000 recitals throughout Europe, North Africa, and North and South America. In addition to composing over 60 works, he made many recordings, and those of the complete piano works of Ravel won the Grand Prix du Disque. His trip to London with Ravel marked the beginning of a warm friendship (see Orenstein, "La Correspondance de Maurice Ravel aux Casadesus").

2. When in Paris, Ravel frequently stayed at the Hôtel d'Athènes, near the St. Lazare train station, which was just across the street from the apartment of the Godebskis.

3. Ravel served on the board of the American Conservatory of Fontainebleau, which was cofounded in 1921 by Francis Casadesus (Robert's uncle) and Walter Damrosch. Now in existence more than half a century, it remains a vital, creative program of cultural exchange.

4. This is a rare example of an unsigned letter.

204. Jean Cocteau to Maurice Ravel

Pramousquier   [August 29, 1922][1]
par Lavandou (Var)
My dear Ravel,

While I was infirm, Ida[2] told me that you had asked about me and were even thinking of coming to see me. After a long cure in the sun, my hand is now strong enough to shake yours, and I wish to thank you for your interest. Paris is a city of misunderstandings. We should see each other precisely when everyone is far away from everyone else, and when it's the heart which judges.

Your   Jean Cocteau
No longer have your exact address.[3]

1. This postmark appears on Cocteau's undated postcard.

2. Godebska.

3. Sent to Durand and Co., Place de la Madeleine, Paris, this card was subsequently forwarded twice, first to Montfort l'Amaury, and then to Lyons-la-Forêt, where Ravel finally received it.

205. to Alfredo Casella

Le Frêne   September 18, 1922
Lyons-la-Forêt
Eure
Dear friend,

I have been working here, in a season which is generally referred to as summer. Perhaps I'll find the sun in Amsterdam towards the end of the month,[1] but I don't dare hope to take in some of its last rays in Milan, where we will undoubtedly meet soon. I've had no further word from the Istituto del Convegno[2] since I asked them to set the date for the recital in which I am supposed to participate.

There is one question to which I still haven't replied: that of the fee. I'm going to ask for your advice in this delicate matter. I wouldn't be at a loss at all if it were Chicago, but in defending Right and Justice, your country is less prosperous than mine. What do you think that I should request for all expenses—travel and stay—?

I would be very grateful for your help in resolving this perplexing matter, and that will also give me the pleasure of hearing from you.

See you soon, dear friend, and affectionate regards to both of you[3] from yours truly,

Maurice Ravel

1. In September 1922, Ravel participated in a festival of contemporary French music held in Amsterdam. A performance of *La Valse* given by the Concertgebouw Orchestra led by Willem Mengelberg was greeted with acclaim, and in another recital, Ravel accompanied Claire Croiza in several of his songs. The entire festival, which included works by Debussy, Lili Boulanger, Fauré, Roussel, Milhaud, and Schmitt, was a brilliant success (see Ravel's interview, on p. 423).

2. The Convegno Institute and its journal *Il Convegno* sponsored an all-Ravel program in Milan on November 1, 1922. The program featured the first performances in Italy of the *Berceuse sur le nom de Gabriel Fauré* and the Sonata for Violin and Cello.

3. Casella remarried in July 1921; his second wife was a former student, Yvonne Müller.

206. to Maurice Emmanuel[1]

Le Belvédère   October 14, 1922
Montfort l'Amaury (S. & O.)
Dear Sir,

Upon returning to Montfort, I found your kind letter as well as that of M. Bleuzet.[2]

The score that you will receive clearly indicates the composer's intentions, and they are the only ones which should be taken into account. This "choreographic poem" is written for the stage. The première has been reserved for the Vienna Opera, which will perform it—when it can. I believe that this work needs to be illuminated by footlights, as it has elicited so much strange commentary. While some discover an attempt at parody, indeed caricature, others categorically see a tragic allusion in it—the end of the Second Empire, the situation in Vienna after the war, etc.—

This dance may seem tragic, like any other emotion—voluptuousness, joy— pushed to the extreme. But one should only see in it what the music expresses: an ascending progression of sonority, to which the stage comes along to add light and movement.[3]

I think that Durand must have sent you Roland-Manuel's brochure, in which you will find all the information which M. Bleuzet asked me on your behalf explained better than I possibly could.

Dear Sir, please believe me cordially yours,

Maurice Ravel

1. The French composer Maurice Emmanuel (1862–1938) studied with Léo Delibes at the Conservatoire, and was appointed professor of music history there in 1909. From 1910 until the last year of his life he wrote program notes for the Société des Concerts du Conservatoire on a voluntary basis, and in this capacity he asked Ravel for some clarification with regard to *La Valse*.

2. He was the secretary of the Société des Concerts du Conservatoire. Founded in 1828 by François Antoine Habeneck, the Society is still in existence. In 1967, it was renamed the Orchestre de Paris.

3. In 1928, Ravel would compose an even stricter "ascending progression of sonority," the *Boléro*.

207. Gabriel Fauré to Maurice Ravel

32 rue des Vignes   October 15, 1922
[Paris 16]
Dear friend,

I was very touched that despite all your work, you willingly participated in the special issue of *La Revue musicale*, which will certainly be the most beautiful jewel in my crown. Everything you brought to it was cordial and exquisite, in word and in music; it touched me deeply and I thank you for it with all my heart.

I'm thinking of your growth, dear friend, since the faubourg Poissonnière,[1] and I am happier than you can imagine about the solid position which you occupy and which you have acquired so brilliantly and so rapidly. It is a source of joy and pride for your old professor.

Believe me always very affectionately yours,

Gabriel Fauré

I trust that your health is as good as possible.

1. During Ravel's student days, the Conservatoire was located at 15 rue du faubourg Poissonnière.

208. Henry Prunières to Maurice Ravel

La Revue musicale   October 16, 1922
3 rue de Grenelle
Paris VI
My dear friend,

I don't know if this letter will still find you at Montfort l'Amaury. I am extremely embarrassed to write this reply.[1] Indeed, it was wrong of me not to raise the question of money at the outset, when asking for your collaboration for the musical homage to Fauré. Given the nature of this offering, I did not foresee any payment for the seven musicians who were kind enough to write pieces based upon Fauré's name; I had informed the six others from the beginning, and they accepted with no objections. Several of them wrote articles in the same issue, and I paid them for their literary collaboration, but not musical, as the enormous cost of printing, plus the outlay for the copyright, which I had to pay, sufficed to absorb and even go beyond the funds which I had earmarked for this musical supplement. I don't have to tell you that this issue was not an undertaking for *La Revue musicale*; were we to succeed in paying our expenses, that would be wonderful. One doesn't become wealthy by publishing a journal like *La Revue musicale,* as you can well imagine.

I trust, my dear friend, that you won't hold me strictly accountable for my avarice, and please believe me most cordially yours,

H. Prunières

1. On September 17, Ravel had written to Prunières requesting him to decide upon a fee for the *Berceuse sur le nom de Gabriel Fauré.* The fee, Ravel explained, was not for himself, but would be given to Nicolas Obouhov.

209. Richard Strauss to Maurice Ravel

Staatsoper[1]   December 7, 1922
Vienne
Dear Sir![2]

In reply to your letter of November 14, I inform you that we already hope to perform your delightful *Ma Mère l'Oye* next January in the Salle de la Redoute. But I do not believe that it will be possible to produce your waltzes[3] this season. And for this reason, we cannot expect you to reserve for us the right to the first performance for such a long time.

On the other hand, a fine success in the concert hall would increase the chances for a performance in the theater.

With the assurance of my high esteem,

Yours truly,

Richard Strauss[4]

1. From 1919 to 1924, Strauss was the codirector of the Vienna State Opera.

2. This letter was written in French.

3. That is, *La Valse*.

4. In a letter excerpted in *La Revue musicale* (December 1938, p. 287), Strauss reiterated his high regard for Ravel's "mastery," and expressed his regret at being too little informed about the details of Ravel's music and career to write an homage. The composers met briefly during the first decade of the 20th century, when Strauss came to Paris on several occasions to conduct his works. In his *Fragments de journal,* Romain Rolland discusses a dinner at the home of Jean Marnold, which took place on May 22, 1907. The only other guest was Ravel, who expressed his view that *Salome* and *Pelléas et Mélisande* were the most striking works in European music written during the past fifteen years. Later in the evening, Marnold, Ravel, and Rolland attended a performance of *Pelléas et Mélisande,* where they were joined in their loge by Strauss. According to Rolland, Strauss listened attentively, but failed to grasp the essence of the music (see *Cahiers Romain Rolland,* 3, *Richard Strauss et Romain Rolland,* Paris: Editions Albin Michel, 1951, pp. 157–65).

210. to Alfred Françaix[1]

Le Belvédère   January 10, 1923
Montfort l'Amaury (S. & O.)
Sir,

During the past five months, I have neither stopped traveling nor remained 8 consecutive days at home.

These continual trips have forced me to neglect my correspondence.

I have reproached myself for a long while for not having replied to your kind letter and the package containing the very interesting manuscript of your son.

Among the gifts of this child, I note above all the most fruitful that an artist can possess, that of curiosity. From now on, these precious gifts must not be stifled, at the risk of letting this youthful sensibility wither. Technique is indispensable; but harmony, counterpoint, fugue, the principles of composition, and the detailed analysis of scores can only be studied usefully when his musicianship has already been developed. First of all, he must be allowed to assimilate the materials of music instinctively. To accomplish this, he should study a polyphonic instrument, such as the piano—the organ poses some risk—which will help him to become intimately acquainted with all the classical or modern works which attract him. The grammar and rhetoric will come later. Above all, have him continue his academic studies: today, more than ever, a musician should not only be a musician.

. . . And now, you can advise your son to summon up his courage in order to pursue the "pleasurable" career upon which he has embarked.

Very truly yours,
Maurice Ravel

1. For many years, Alfred Françaix was the director of the National Conservatory of Music and Dramatic Arts in Le Mans. As his ten-year-old son was particularly interested in Ravel's music and in composition, he wrote to Ravel for advice, sending him one of Jean Françaix's earliest compositions.

211. to Jean Jobert

Le Belvédère   February 8, 1923
Montfort l'Amaury (S. & O.)
Dear Sir,

By the same mail, you will receive the corrected proofs in a registered package. They gave me a lot of trouble. It's not that the engraver wasn't careful enough. On the contrary, what made me lose the most time were the indications a2, solo, unison, divisi, etc. needlessly repeated on each new page. This won't help the proofreader at all, who may suppose that the solo or the a2 begins on that page, which can only complicate the printing of the parts.

A double error—mine first, and then the engraver's, will necessitate at least a partial resetting of page 23 [1] (the bassoon part was omitted, and the horns and bassoons were put in the place of the trumpets and horns).

At no. (I no longer remember) a fortunate error by the engraver (G$\sharp$ instead of G$\natural$) in the harp part, drew my attention to an incorrect change in key signature, which should appear later on, as I indicated.

In the penultimate page (no. [42]), I restored Debussy's indication $\stackrel{}{\downarrow} = \stackrel{}{\downarrow}$ and added <u>poco allargando</u>,[2] which was certainly the composer's intention.

I believe that the tempo indication at the beginning: $\stackrel{}{\downarrow} = 144$, which I set with the metronome, will be best after all.[3]

Very truly yours,

Maurice Ravel

1. Corresponding to page 23 of the Jobert orchestral score of *Danse*. All of the references in this letter are to this transcription.

2. The printed score indicates "Allargando."

3. Debussy's piano piece is marked "Allegretto." In his manuscript, Ravel wrote $\stackrel{}{\downarrow} = 120$, which he then crossed out, replacing it with $\stackrel{}{\downarrow} = 144$. The final decision, however, is found in the printed score: $\stackrel{}{\downarrow} = 132$ (the manuscripts of "Sarabande" and *Danse*, formerly in the private collection of Mme D. Jobert-Georges, are now in the Frederick R. Koch Foundation Collection on deposit in the Pierpont Morgan Library).

212. to Hélène Jourdan-Morhange

Le Belvédère   February 20, 1923
Montfort l'Amaury (S. & O.)
Dear friend,

I received a telegram from Bathori. For her ΠΡ recital on March 5, I had promised her to ask for your collaboration and that of Maréchal for the Sonata and the *Berceuse*, in which you will finally be accompanied by the composer. I was planning to ask you in person. But then I didn't think that March 5 would arrive so quickly—perhaps it's because of my birthday, which is so close to that date—.

I'm no longer sure just what to do: I am leaving for Pau and St.-Jean-de-Luz next Friday.[1] Would you reply directly to Bathori, at 10 rue Oudinot? What's more serious is that I don't have Maréchal's address, not even the number on rue Biot. Therefore, I will ask you to find out if he would be willing to participate in this little festival.

You will no doubt receive an invitation to a new ΠΡ festival given by Jean Duhem at the Salle d'Athènes.[2] Don't be upset if you have something else to do. I myself can't be there: I'm leaving on Friday, one half hour before the concert. I've had no luck with these festivals, except for Henriette Faure's recital.[3] The two upcoming festivals, on March 5 and 6, are the only ones I can attend—and with good reason—.[4]

I hope it will be O.K. for Bathori's recital. Thanks in advance, and many apologies!

Cordially yours,

Maurice Ravel

1. A recital in Pau was followed by a brief vacation in St.-Jean-de-Luz.

2. On Friday evening, February 23, the pianist Jean Duhem performed at the Salle des Agriculteurs, on rue d'Athènes, which Ravel telescoped to "Salle d'Athènes."

3. Following a number of coaching sessons with Ravel, the 19-year-old prodigy Henriette Faure (1904–1985), sister of the French statesman Edgar Faure, played the complete piano works on January 12, 1923, at the Champs-Elysées theater. This was apparently the first all-Ravel piano recital ever given (see p. 558).

4. At an S.M.I. recital on March 6, Ravel performed *Ma Mère l'Oye* with Robert Casadesus, accompanied Madeleine Grey in a number of his songs, and conducted the *Introduction et Allegro.*

213. D. G. Kiriac and C. Brailoiu to Maurice Ravel

Bucharest   February 20, 1923

My dear old friend,

While rummaging through my old papers, I found some of your letters. I remembered Avenue Trudaine, our long nocturnal conversations at the Auberge du Clou and the Café de Clichy. A few years have passed since. . . . Just now, I've been telling my friend Brailoiu—my compatriot whom you met in Paris, and who brought me back your regards several times—about your beginnings: Pessard's class, your first appearance with the little orchestra at the seashore (I no longer recall the locality),[1] your first appearance as a composer and conductor at the Colonne concerts,[2] our Saturday meetings at the Molards in Montparnasse,[3] the concerts of the Société Nationale, then the kind publisher Demets. I also remembered the Basque country and Switzerland, which you often spoke about. What beautiful memories the years of our youth leave behind, with their ideals and their gropings.

And now you should rejoice, seeing yourself above the crowd. You are present everywhere, remembered by cultivated people in Budapest as in London, in Bucharest as in Vienna, in America as in Japan, perhaps. Here in Romania, you are the idol of our musical youth. They appreciate you very much and admire you.

As for me, I have spent my time popularizing music for the common people, chiefly choral and folk music. I have tried to provide simple but proper nourishment to both the poor and rich. Such is our native soil; I have planted seeds which can sprout in our virgin soil.

My dear friend, I'm still the same (at least I think so): a good fellow, modest and indulgent toward others. Deep down, I haven't attached too much importance to life; I consider our accomplishments like childrens' toys, which give pleasure for the moment. I have now come to the most morose season of life, with white mustache and grey head. It's a pity that the Creator is so harsh to his dear child, man. . . . He pushes him to hold on to many things down here, and one fine day . . . crack! . . . he is banished, despite himself. But I shouldn't go on too much with philosophy (an old habit), and I'll pass the pen to my friend Brailoiu. His youth will certainly make him write happier things.

I still preserve the fondest memories of you, and although very far away, I shake your hand in warm friendship.

A little note from you will give me much pleasure.

All the best,

D. G. Kiriac

My address: Professor at the Conservatory of Music, Bucharest, Romania.

Dear Monsieur Ravel,

The letter which you have just read is the end result of many conversations. How many times my good teacher Kiriac and I have spoken of you! And how many times we have jointly agreed to write to you! In addition, my good teacher's arranging of his papers yesterday was but a pretext whose time had come (so to speak). Don't believe everything that you have just read. Your friend Kiriac hasn't aged at all. Perhaps at another time he had black hair . . . I didn't know him then. I only know that he is still at work, still devoted to everyone, still interested in things—in a word, he's very young in spirit.

But on the other hand, you should believe what he wrote about you, of the admiration we all have for your music, and your influence on many of us. It is rare that your works aren't played at a musical soirée, or at a gathering of musicians—whether sung or played (even on two pianos)—or that your name is not mentioned. And your more recent disciples are no less fervent than I am.

Last summer, when I spent 3 months in Paris, I sincerely regretted not being able to see you there. You were away. I had to content myself with two performances of *La Valse*, which we had often read through in Bucharest, and whose orchestral sonority I found amazing.

I don't want to overburden my good teacher's letter with an overly long postscript. Please believe that you are keenly remembered here, and I would be happy to see you again or to hear from you. In addition, believe in my complete devotion.

Constantin Brailoiu[4]

<u>Same address: Professor at the Conservatoire, etc.</u>[5]

1. Granville; see letter no. 2, note 1.

2. A slip for the Lamoureux concerts, where Ravel conducted *Adélaïde, ou le langage des fleurs* in April 1912.

3. M. and Mme William Molard, who entertained at 6 rue Vercingétorix in the Montparnasse section of Paris. Molard was a student in Pessard's harmony class, and in

the spring of 1894, he invited several of his classmates to meet Edvard Grieg at his home. The background of this little-known episode has been explained as follows:

> Grieg was in Paris that April for a performance of one of his works and evidence points to his being together with Delius quite often then. His visit to the Molards must surely have been engineered by Delius, their intimate mutual friend. While the bright-eyed company discussed music, Ravel quietly went over to Molard's piano and began to play one of the master's Norwegian Dances. Grieg listened with a smile, but then began to show signs of impatience, suddenly getting up and saying sharply: "No, young man, not like that at all. Much more rhythm. It's a folk dance, a peasant dance. You should see the peasants at home, with the fiddler stamping in time with the music. Play it again!" And while Ravel played the little man jumped up and skipped about the room, to the astonishment of the company. Perhaps it was on a rather later occasion, when Delius was in the company of Ravel and some other French musicians, that the question was raised as to what sources modern French music was especially indebted. The French consensus view was that it was to Rameau, Couperin and Lully, etc., but Delius felt differently: "Nonsense! Modern French music is simply Grieg, plus the third act of *Tristan.*" To which Ravel replied: "That is true. We are always unjust to Grieg".
>
> Florent Schmitt, incidentally, is on record as saying that William Molard's musical theories had had a considerable influence on both Ravel and himself. How interesting it might prove to be if the manuscript of Molard's only known work, *Hamlet,* were one day to come to light. (Lionel Carley, *Delius, the Paris Years,* p. 56.)

4. Brailoiu (1893–1958), an ethnomusicologist and composer, had studied in Paris for two years just prior to World War I. In 1929, he was awarded the French Legion of Honor.

5. Ravel's reply to this letter is below, no. 216.

214. to Charles Koechlin

Le Belvédère   February 21, 1923
Montfort l'Amaury (S. & O.)
Dear friend,

You have upset me: I'm wondering if I didn't receive that circular, and if I didn't join that organization without examining its statutes carefully. I receive so many of those things. I would have to waste time justifying my refusal to join, so I generally look over the information, join, and never show up. But here, it would be more serious. Would you try to find out from Prunières—or better yet, from someone else—if I accepted? There would always be time to submit my resignation, and justify it this time. I'm afraid that we'll also be obliged to quit the I.S.C.M.,[1] which perhaps is not so International after all. It's simply leaning in the other direction, which is no less stupid.

As soon as you have some information, please let me know. From next Friday on, until March 4, here is my address: 41 rue Gambetta, St.-Jean-de-Luz (Lower Pyrenees).

Cordially yours,
Maurice Ravel

1. Founded in 1922, the International Society for Contemporary Music sponsored annual festivals, which offered an important cross section of modern European and American music. Despite Ravel's criticism of the I.S.C.M., he did not resign his membership, and served as a member of the jury in December 1928, in Geneva.

215. to M. D. Calvocoressi

St.-Jean-de-Luz   February 27, 1923
Dear friend,

Forgive my very late reply. I have been so busy during the past 2 months— the installation of central heating at Montfort, painting, touch-ups, coming and going—that I took advantage of a concert in Pau to come here for a week and recuperate.

It is possible, later on, that I will write if not a treatise, at least some notes on orchestration.[1] For the moment, I have no ideas on the subject. In the meantime, I will keep the publisher's proposal in mind.[2]

I trust that we will meet soon in London. I'm supposed to arrive there on the 12th, returning from Italy. My kind regards to Madame Calvocoressi, and very cordially yours,

Maurice Ravel

1. One such jotting has been preserved (autograph in the private collection of Mme Alexandre Taverne): "Nuances, accents, and slur marks can and must often be distinguished in an orchestral transcription. — doesn't mean >" (a stress doesn't mean an accent).

In a conversation with this writer, Georges Auric recalled that about 1925, Ravel asked him to act as his secretary for a small volume on orchestration. Unlike Rimsky-Korsakov's treatise, which pointed out model passages from his own works, Ravel was going to present a series of examples with commentary, taken from his own compositions, showing how not to orchestrate by highlighting passages which were bungled! This project came to nought, as did another tantalizing one that Ravel contemplated at the same time: a small volume explaining his relationship with Debussy.

2. Oxford University Press was the interested publisher.

216. to Dumitru Kiriac

Le Belvédère   March 13, 1923
Montfort l'Amaury (S. & O.)
My dear friend,

It was a great joy to receive your letter, which arrived just as I was leaving St.-Jean-de-Luz, where I had spent a week. Because of my departure, I didn't reply at once. I was going to spend two days in Paris; as usual, I stayed there over a week, doing nothing more than trying to get rid of a fit of the blues which just doesn't want to go away. In addition, it's been more than a year since I have written anything, and I have no reason to believe that the desire to resume work will ever return. So, like a young Englishman of 1830, I'm traveling—that's the extent of my Romanticism—and it changes nothing.

Won't you be coming to Paris sometime? If so, let me know beforehand. Perhaps I'll go to Bucharest one day.[1] I will soon be represented there by *La Valse*, which Morin[2] is supposed to conduct there shortly.

Let's not stay out of touch for such a long time.

Would you please convey my very good wishes to Constantin Brailoiu and tell him that I intend to write to him one of these days?

See you soon, and warmest regards from your
Maurice Ravel

1. Ravel visited Bucharest in 1932, during his tour with Marguerite Long.

2. Probably referring to the French conductor Henri Morin. In addition to touring widely, he studied conducting with Arthur Nikisch and composition with Vincent d'Indy.

217. Ravel, Roussel, Caplet, and Roland-Manuel
to the Editor of *Le Courrier musical*[1]

[c. March 1923]

The musicians who have sympathetically followed Monsieur Jean Wiéner's efforts since last year, were painfully taken aback by an article which they read in *Le Courrier musical* on January 1, 1923, written by Monsieur Louis Vuillemin.[2]

The undersigned have neither the right nor the desire to interfere in a personal dispute between Messieurs Vuillemin and Wiéner. However, by declaring that certain persons expressed their approbation to him, Monsieur Louis Vuillemin places several of his friends in the position of having to state publicly in turn that they in no way agree with his position concerning the so-called "alien concerts."

Monsieur Vuillemin's independence and impartiality are so well known to them, that they are convinced that the eminent critic's good faith was taken aback under the circumstances. In any event, they affirm their delight in having been able to hear Arnold Schoenberg's *Pierrot lunaire*, thanks to Monsieur Jean Wiéner, as well as a series of new works, French and foreign, whose tendencies are open to discussion, but whose interest is certainly not.[3]

They would like to take this occasion to express the hope that patriotism err a bit less in an area where it has nothing to gain, but everything to lose.[4]

Maurice Ravel, Albert Roussel,
André Caplet, Roland-Manuel.

1. This letter was printed in *Le Courrier musical*, 25 (April 1, 1923), p. 123, with a reply by Louis Vuillemin.

2. In this article, entitled "Alien Concerts," without naming anyone specifically, Vuillemin noted in vehement terms that such concerts were taking place in Paris, organized by "musical Dadaists," who were supported in their "intrigues" by "cosmopolitan fools." His comments revealed the same kind of jingoism and xenophobia which Ravel had decried in his letter to the National League for the Defense of French Music.

3. Jean Wiéner (1896–1982) performed over 2000 piano recitals of jazz, classical and popular music with his colleague Clément Doucet, and was active as a composer and impresario. He referred to his "Concerts Jean Wiéner" as salads—that is, a deliberate attempt to mix the most disparate elements. The first recital, in December 1921, featured works by Milhaud and Stravinsky, which were preceded by Billy Arnold's jazz group. Following the recital, Ravel went backstage and congratulated Wiéner warmly.

4. Vuillemin's inept reply contained an attack on *Pierrot lunaire*, with an acknowledgment of the importance of Austro-German music through Wagner.

218. to Hélène Jourdan-Morhange

14 Holland Park   April 16, 1923
London, W.11[1]
Dear friend,

My spare time in London enables me to send you even more cards, especially today, when I'm supposed to have lunch at the embassy at 1:30 P.M. I was finally able to sleep last night—10 hours—I was beginning to miss it.

Ma Mère l'Oye and *La Valse* went very well the day before yesterday.

According to the newspapers, I am, if not a <u>great</u> conductor, at least a <u>good</u> one. I didn't expect as much.[2] . . . The weather is unpleasant, no more so than in Rome.

Of course, it's still O.K. for May 8.

And Madame Alvar thanks you for your regards, and sends you hers in return.

Cordial regards from your
Maurice Ravel[3]

1. During his visits to London in the 1920s and 1930s, Ravel often stayed at the elegant home of Mr. and Mrs. Charles Copeley Harding. Mrs. Harding, a soprano, whose professional name was Louise Alvar, was born in Sweden and died in London in 1966 at the age of 82. She concertized with Ravel in Scandinavia in 1926 (see plate 2). In their salon Ravel would meet many outstanding artists, among them Hugo von Hofmannsthal, Joseph Conrad, and Paul Valéry, as well as many English musicians.

2. This comment may have been based upon an unsigned review which appeared in *The Times* on April 16:

> M. Maurice Ravel was most cordially received, as was natural. Since the death of Debussy he has represented to English musicians the most vigorous current in modern French music. . . . His baton is not the magician's wand of the virtuoso conductor. He just stood there beating time and keeping watch, getting everything into the right place. The orchestra did their very best for him, not because they were charmed into it, but because he showed them so clearly what he wanted each member to play, when, and how. *Ma Mère l'Oye* has never sounded so simple and childlike; the introduction to *La Valse*, with its flitting scraps of waltz rhythm on bassoons and deep-toned instruments, had an unusual clarity, and both pieces were immensely enjoyed.

The remainder of the program at Queen's Hall, conducted by Sir Henry Wood, consisted of Schubert's Symphony in C Major (the Great) and Saint-Saëns' Piano Concerto No. 4, with one Mr. Pouishnoff as soloist (see p. 596).

3. The autograph of this letter is reproduced in Rollo H. Myers, *Ravel* (London: G. Duckworth, 1960), pp. 64–65.

219. to Désiré Defauw[1]

14 Holland Park   April 17, 1923
London, W.11
Dear Sir,

The enclosed envelope will explain to you how your kind letter took 10 days to reach me.

I imagine that you didn't wait for my reply in order to arrange your program.[2] But anyway, let me recommend to you:

1) The Sonata for Violin and Cello, if, of course, you have artists who have already worked on this piece, my most recent work, which is very difficult.

2) Either the String Quartet or the Trio (piano, violin, cello), without the participation of the author, who would be absolutely incapable of playing the piano part.

3) With a singer whom I would accompany, and several piano pieces which I would perform very badly, it seems to me the program would be complete.[3]

I expect to be in Brussels towards the 24th.

Until then, I will remain in London, where you can write to me if you need further information.

Very truly yours,
Maurice Ravel

1. The Belgian violinist, conductor, and impresario (1885–1960).

2. Defauw was organizing a recital of Ravel's chamber music, which took place in Brussels at the Théâtre du Marais on April 26, 1923.

3. The program included the String Quartet (performed by Désiré Defauw and MM. Waersegers, Miry, and Doelsaerd), *Shéhérazade* (sung by Mme Delacre accompanied by Ravel), and the *Introduction et Allegro* conducted by the composer (Miss G. Mason, harp, M. Borlée, flute, M. Adam, clarinet, and the above mentioned string quartet). In addition, Ravel performed his *Pavane pour une Infante défunte*, "La Vallée des cloches" (*Miroirs*), the "Menuet" from *Le Tombeau de Couperin*, and the Sonatine. Despite Ravel's self-deprecating remark, the critic of *L'Indépendance belge*, Ernest Closson, was favorably impressed by his performance: "His playing is exactly as we would imagine it, precise, discreet, very refined, of extraordinary distinction, at times bordering on preciosity. The delighted audience applauded the performers, but gave a genuine ovation to the composer, whose slender appearance and smiling affability, perhaps a bit ironic, were also wonderfully evocative of his refined art" ("Chronique musicale— M. Maurice Ravel au Marais," *L'Indépendance belge*, April 28, 1923, article signed "E. C.").

220. Rudolph Mayer to Maurice Ravel

Daniel Mayer Company Ltd.   June 12, 1923
Grafton House, Golden Square
Piccadilly, London, W.1
My dear Mr. Ravel,[1]

I have not had the pleasure of seeing you now for two years, since I met you in Paris. The reason for my writing to you is that I think there is a good possibility that I may be able to secure you a first class engagement as guest conductor in America to conduct the big orchestras there.[2] I shall be glad to hear from you at your earliest convenience if this proposition would interest you, the period that would suit you best and what your terms would be (your terms of course, to be subject to my commission). If you would reply by return I shall at once get to work and would soon be in a position to let you know something definite.

Kind regards,
Yours sincerely,
DANIEL MAYER COMPANY, LTD.
Rudolph Mayer

1. This letter was written in English.

2. This proposal was one of several which Ravel had received in 1923. In a reply to E. Robert Schmitz, written on March 14, he noted:

> You will excuse me for hesitating: I still haven't despaired of resuming work, and no matter how flattering the success might be, it doesn't seem to me worth the loss of 3 or 4 months. You won't fail to draw my attention to another aspect of the matter [the fee], and I certainly agree with you. But from this point of view, you can't blame me for comparing the advantages before giving you a definitive reply.
>
> I promise to give you one very soon. At the beginning of next week, I'm going to spend 2 days in Paris solely for this purpose.

Ravel finally turned down all of the proposals. His only concert tour in North America would take place in 1928.

221. to Edouard Mignan[1]

Le Belvédère   June 20, 1923
Montfort l'Amaury (S. & O.)
My dear colleague,

Please find enclosed the copyright declaration,[2] and pardon the incongruities of my pen, which I remedied as best I could.

I thank you sincerely for the copy of your *Rapsodie,* which I did receive, and which I found very charming, as much as I could judge from an uncertain reading.[3]

I may tell you that I also discovered a paradoxical element in it, in the way your numerous whole-tone scales accompany the theme, written by the one contemporary composer who has never used the whole-tone scale.[4]

Please don't see any bitterness in this observation, which, I think, you will find as amusing as I do, and, my dear colleague, believe in my sincere artistic sympathy.

Maurice Ravel

1. Mignan (1884–1969), a French composer and organist, studied at the Conservatoire with Paul Vidal (composition) and Charles-Marie Widor (organ). In 1923, he composed a *Rapsodie* for chromatic harp based on the opening theme of the minuet from Ravel's Sonatine. Published in Paris by Evette and Schaeffer, the piece was intended for the Conservatoire's annual harp competition.

2. As the composer of the Sonatine, Ravel had to sign the copyright declaration together with Mignan.

3. Ravel was suffering from a painful foot inflammation.

4. A slight exaggeration: after his youthful infatuation with the whole-tone scale (in the overture to *Shéhérazade* and *Si morne!*), Ravel hardly ever used it again.

222. to Manuel de Falla

Le Belvédère   June 26, 1923
Montfort l'Amaury (S. & O.)
Dear Falla,

As I wrote to Princess de Polignac, it was truly impossible for me to hear your work last night,[1] although I hoped to do so until the last minute. I trust that you will excuse me, and that you won't leave without seeing me. I certainly won't be able to budge from here until Saturday. Won't you be able to come one of these days and partake of a luncheon which won't even be frugal because of the poor season? I'm inviting the princess to come with you. If she is unable, and if your car is being repaired, you need only take the 9:13 train at the Invalides station (check the timetable), and at Montfort l'Amaury the bus will bring you into town. So I'll see you very soon, won't I? and very affectionately yours,

Maurice Ravel[2]

1. Falla's marionette play *El Retablo de Maese Pedro* (Master Peter's Puppet Theater) was commissioned by Princess Edmond de Polignac, and the first staged performance, conducted by Vladimir Golschmann, was given at her salon on June 25.

2. In a brief note dated July 1, 1923, Falla expressed his regret at not being able to visit Ravel, and observed that he hoped to see him soon, "here or in Granada, where I will also have a frugal meal to offer you, together with my very affectionate friendship."

223. to Igor Stravinsky

Le Belvédère   June 26, 1923
Montfort l'Amaury (S. & O.)
Dear Igor,

Your *Noces* is so beautiful! And how I regret not having heard it—and seen it—more often! But it was apparently very unwise of me to have gone the other evening: my foot swelled up considerably and I had to return to rest it once again, until next Sunday at least.[1]

Thanks old chap, and very cordially yours,
Maurice Ravel

1. In another letter written on June 26, Ravel explained to Roland-Manuel as follows: "I heard *Les Noces* last Thursday, doped up by Desjardins, who shot cocaine into my foot. You were right: it is a splendid work. I even believe that it's Stravinsky's master-piece to date, and the production is also one of the masterpieces of the Russian season. I must thank you: were it not for your insistence, I would have missed this great joy."

224. Igor Stravinsky to Maurice Ravel

"Les Rochers"   July 14, 1923
Biarritz
My dear Ravel,

I was very touched by your kind letter, and I'm also delighted that my *Noces* ... pleased you so much. Too bad you didn't also hear it in the early days, when it was played so well. How goes it with your foot? Please keep in touch, and write (in general) a bit more often to your old friend

Igor Stravinsky

225. to Piero Coppola[1]

Le Belvédère   August 4, 1923
Montfort l'Amaury (S. & O.)
Dear Sir and friend,

I was very touched by your kind gesture in dedicating one of your songs to me; they indeed pleased me very much.[2] Perhaps I will have the pleasure of thanking you in person, if, as I'm planning, I go to Paris on Monday or Tuesday.

After a year and a half of inactivity, I was going to resume work, but was prevented from doing so by a stupid accident: two fingers were crushed by the legs of a chaise longue, almost 3 weeks ago. The doctor was able to reassure me only today: the skin is improving on the left hand, and the middle finger, still numb, finally appears to be on the road to recovery.

While awaiting the pleasure of seeing you, if not in Paris, at least in London in October, please believe me most cordially yours,

Maurice Ravel

1. The Italian conductor and composer (1888–1971) was active in Paris during the 1920s and 1930s (see p. 552).

2. Coppola's *Dix Poèmes arabes* for voice and piano were based on the "Jardin des caresses" by Franz Toussaint. They were published in two collections of five songs each, dedicated respectively to Ravel and Henry Prunières. These brief songs occasionally evoke the oriental sensuousness found in Ravel's *Shéhérazade*.

226. to Jacques Durand[1]

Saint-Jean-de-Luz   September 8, 1923

Sonia Pavlov, of the Opéra-Comique, has asked me to write a ballet for her, based on a scenario by Henry Malherbe,[2] and, if I don't have the time, which is the case, to try to adapt several of my Spanish works to this libretto (the subject is inspired by the *Pavane pour une Infante défunte*). I think I have found the way, with ten measures of composing at most, to do this little job à la Diaghilev, which would combine the *Pavane*, the "Alborada [del gracioso]," and the *Rapsodie espagnole*. Of course, this <u>olla</u> <u>podrida</u>[3] would not be published, and I don't think you would find any objection to it. I await your authorization in order to begin (and to finish, which won't take long) this Castilian mosaic.[4]

1. The text of this letter is virtually complete, save for the opening and concluding formulas. Some sixty letters from Ravel to Jacques Durand were in the archives of Durand and Co., 4 Place de la Madeleine, Paris, where I consulted them in 1966. They were subsequently misplaced, and have yet to be recovered.

2. Probably the music critic of *Le Temps* (see letter no. 172, note 2).

3. Meaning a medley or stew, literally, in Spanish, a rotten pot.

4. The manuscript of this work was virtually unknown until 1977, when it briefly surfaced in Paris and was purchased by a private collector. The ballet is entitled *Le Portrait de l'Infante* [The Portrait of the Infanta] and the scenario is set in Madrid about 1670. The score of 25 pages includes 11 pages for piano solo in Ravel's hand, the remainder being excerpts from the printed scores of the three pieces mentioned by Ravel. This ballet was apparently never performed.

227. to Marcelle Gerar[1]

Le Belvédère   November 25, 1923
Montfort l'Amaury (S. & O.)
Madame,

From what Roland-Manuel and many others have told me about your remarkable talent, please believe it is with great regret that I cannot attend your recital on December 6.[2] But having been unable to compose anything for two years, I have resolved not to leave Montfort the entire winter.

With sincere thanks, and many apologies, believe me, Madame, very truly yours,

Maurice Ravel

1. The French lyric soprano Marcelle Gerar (1891–1970, her professional name being a partial anagram of her true name, Regerau) was for many years a professor of voice and vocal pedagogy at the Ecole Normale de Paris. She made her debut in Paris in 1921, and devoted herself to the interpretation of contemporary French song. In the 1920s, she toured with Ravel in England, Spain, and throughout France. In addition to Ravel, many composers dedicated their vocal works to her, among them Honegger, Jacques Ibert, Milhaud, Roussel, and Schmitt.

2. In addition to Madame Gerar, this all-Ravel program was performed by several other artists, among them Jane Bathori, the pianist Henri Gil-Marchex, and the Vandelle String Quartet. Commentary on the music was provided by Roland-Manuel.

228. to Georges Jean-Aubry

Montfort l'Amaury December 13, 1923
My dear friend,

Immersed in work,[1] I'm in Paris so rarely that I don't know if you are in London at the moment.

If you are, please convey my apologies to Monsieur W. A. Chevery, who wrote me a letter at the end of October (a very busy time for me),[2] asking my opinion about Safonov's *La Nouvelle formule*.[3] Since receiving this work, I haven't had the time to study it very carefully, and I think it merits it. Now that I'm working, even practicing the piano, I'll be able to examine it. What an achievement if I become a great virtuoso thanks to this method! Unfortunately, my fingers do not respond very well.

Would it be possible to receive a copy of *Les Noces?* Many other things too: I don't have *Le Boeuf sur le toit*,[4] nor Poulenc's *Promenades*,[5] nor other works which are undoubtedly interesting, but I don't know if they have been published. Try to look into it.

The score of *Carrosse* has been at the Opéra-Comique for some time.[6] During my next visit to Paris, I'll pass by there and ask what they think of it.

Would you let me know if Madame Alvar will be in London towards Xmas? I have a little thing to give her and don't want it to get lost.

You'll reply soon, won't you? and very cordially yours,
Maurice Ravel

1. In January 1924, Ravel completed an orchestral version of the Hebraic folk song "Mejerke mein Suhn," which had been set in 1910, and the song *Ronsard à son âme*.

2. During this month Ravel concertized in Amsterdam and London, thus letting his mail accumulate.

3. Vasily I. Safonov (1852–1918), the Russian conductor, pianist, and teacher, studied with Leschetizky, and among his pupils were Josef Lhevinne and Alexander Scriabin. His piano method, *Novaya formula* (Moscow, 1916), appeared in English as *A New Formula for the Piano Teacher and Piano Student* (London, 1916).

4. Darius Milhaud's ballet, based on the scenario by Jean Cocteau.

5. A suite of ten short piano pieces composed in 1921 and published in 1923.

6. *Le Carrosse du Saint-Sacrement*, a one-act opera by Lord Berners, based on the comedy by Prosper Mérimée. It was introduced at the Champs-Elysées theater in 1924.

229. to Manuel de Falla

Le Belvédère   January 11, 1924
Montfort l'Amaury
My dear friend,

I should have written to you long before receiving your good wishes. But I was waiting for some news from Barcelona's Association of Chamber Music, with whom I have been negotiating for several weeks regarding a concert whose date was originally set for February 24, but which I wanted to postpone for a few days. I have just received a telegram informing me that the concert has been postponed until February 27.

I would be very happy if you could arrange something in Madrid about that time, as close as possible to that date, because even if Spain is the country that I wish to know most keenly, and particularly the city to which I owe so much[1] (at the moment, I owe it no gratitude), I prefer to wait for a more favorable time to remain there.

From February 15 on, I'm traveling: London, Brussels, etc. I immediately accepted the Barcelona date because it fell in the period I had set aside for a rest. I was thinking of finishing my sonata for violin and piano toward the beginning of February. I have just abandoned it. The above parenthesis will explain the main reason: a most wonderful resumption of the blues. The only thing I can do is to set to music an epitaph by Ronsard, which rather corresponds to my state of mind. Prunières will be delighted, however, because I had only given him slight hope of collaborating on his *Ronsard* issue.[2] But I had promised London the first performance of my sonata!

I impatiently await your news, my dear friend, and send you my most affectionate thoughts.

Maurice Ravel

And also my best wishes, no less affectionate, even though late.

ՈՌ

1. Ravel's mother spent her youth in Madrid, and met her future husband there.

2. This issue of *La Revue musicale* (May 1924) commemorated the four-hundredth anniversary of the poet's birth. The other composers participating in the homage to Ronsard were Louis Aubert, André Caplet, Maurice Delage, Paul Dukas, Arthur Honegger, Roland-Manuel, and Albert Roussel.

230. to Robert Casadesus

Le Belvédère   January 24, 1924
Montfort l'Amaury (S. & O.)
My dear friend,

Pardon me in advance for the confusion of this letter: Barcelona, London, and Brussels are joining forces to drive me crazy.

On December 28, in reference to abandoning an arrangement with Aeolian,[1] which, fortunately! I still hadn't spoken to you about, Mr. R. Mayer[2] wrote to me: "To what extent will this have an influence on the appearance of M. Casadesus, who is supposed to perform here on February 16? In case he does not come, would you like me to engage M. Gil-Marchex?"[3]

I replied affirmatively, and, a few days later, Mayer having written that he had engaged Marchex, I therefore concluded that you couldn't go to London, which didn't surprise me, since you had said some time before that you expected to be in Spain about that time, and it was agreed that you would participate in a concert of my works in Barcelona on the 24th, at the end of your tour.

Wait; that's not all: I wasn't thrilled about the 24th. In order to be in Barcelona that day, I would have to go there directly from Brussels. Therefore, I asked for a later date, if possible. They replied that it would depend on your trio.[4] January 11, a telegram: they proposed February 27, which I accepted. Today, another telegram: "Impossible to have Casadesus trio" and a proposition for another trio and other dates on which I will not be free.

Meanwhile, in Brussels, Defauw[5] was corresponding with Mlle Sanderson[6] (and with me, alas!) in order to juggle the dates of the concerts in Belgium, and finally postpone the one with my Sonata[7] until later, because it has been abandoned for the time being following a fit of the blues which innumerable distractions have failed to dissipate.

And on my advice, Mayer has acted similarly, postponing the recital to April 26, and has informed Ritter-Ciampi,[8] Jelly d'Aranyi,[9] and Gil-Marchex, who cannot be abandoned now, of course.

I trust that you will explain some of the mysteries of London and Barcelona on January 30. The day before yesterday, Roland-Manuel and I made up plans to go to the concert of Marcelle Gerar after hearing your Sonata. The program change you described will facilitate this considerably.[10]

Till Wednesday, then, and very cordially yours,
Maurice Ravel

1. Apparently a recording session.
2. The English impresario Rudolph Mayer.
3. The French pianist Henri Gil-Marchex (1894–1970; see p. 564).

4. The Casadesus trio, consisting of Robert, his uncle Marius Casadesus (violin), and Maurice Maréchal (cello).

5. Désiré Defauw (see letter no. 219, note 1).

6. An impresario in Belgium.

7. The Sonata for Violin and Piano, begun in 1923 and finally completed in 1927.

8. The French soprano Gabrielle Ritter-Ciampi. She was replaced by Marcelle Gerar, who thus sang the première of *Ronsard à son âme* accompanied by Ravel at the London recital on April 26.

9. *Tzigane* was dedicated to the brilliant Hungarian violinist Jelly d'Aranyi (1895–1966), who gave the première in London accompanied by Henri Gil-Marchex.

10. On Wednesday evening, January 30, 1924, Ravel attended two concerts: he heard the opening work at an S.M.I. recital, the Sonata for Cello and Piano by Robert Casadesus, and then he went to a recital given by Marcelle Gerar, who performed several of his songs.

231. to Marcelle Gerar

Le Belvédère   February 7, 1924
Montfort l'Amaury (S. & O.)
Dear Madame,

Did Roland-Manuel forget the errand?[1] He was entrusted: (1) to send you the manuscript of the song;[2] (2) to ask you if it were possible to perform it for my publisher on Saturday, between 3:00 and 4:30 P.M. at the latest, because he leaves the office at 5:00 P.M.

If you still haven't written to me, don't: I will have left Montfort before the mail arrives. But I will ask you either to call me at Jacques Durand's home from noon until 1:30 P.M. (Ségur 73-54), or send me a special delivery letter there (5 Avenue Sully-Prudhomme, Paris VII), and if you cannot come, have the manuscript dropped off at the store on Place de la Madeleine, as I don't have another copy of it.

Obviously, the song will be less effective if performed by the composer . . . I trust that my publisher's imagination will make up for the deficiencies.

With my sincere apologies for so much bother, dear Madame, please believe in my keen artistic sympathy.

Maurice Ravel

1. Roland-Manuel had faithfully transmitted Ravel's message to Mme Gerar in a letter to her written on February 5.

2. *Ronsard à son âme.*

232. to Cipa Godebski

Le Belvédère   February 14, 1924
Montfort l'Amaury (S. & O.)
Old chap,

I received a card and some good news from Mimie. But that young scatter-brain forgot to include her address. Please send it to me.

The blues have been relatively quiet for a few days; but the Sonata still hasn't progressed. By Jove! I'll get it despite everything!

I may go to Paris on Monday. If so, we'll see each other in the evening, at the Roland-Manuels.

Enclosed are the tickets for Janine Weill's concert. She is a delightful musician, who performs my Sonatine as I would like to play it. Moreover, the program is very intelligently arranged.[1]

See you perhaps on Monday. Affectionately to all,
Maurice Ravel

1. On Friday evening, February 22, Madame Janine Weill (1903–1983) presented a program of classical and modern works, performing both as soloist and as a partner in chamber music. The latter included Mozart's Quintet for piano, oboe, clarinet, horn, and bassoon (K. 452), Milhaud's Sonatine for flute and piano (opus 76), and Joseph Jongen's *Rapsodie* for piano and wind quintet (opus 70). In addition, several Schubert Impromptus were performed, and Ravel's Sonatine, *Jeux d'eau,* and "Alborada del gracioso."

233. to Mimie Godebska

Le Belvédère   February 28, 1924
Montfort l'Amaury (S. & O.)
Dear Mimie,

As soon as I received your letter, I wrote to your father in order to get your address, which you didn't mention (in my day, you know, there weren't "sump-tuous hotels" in Mégève). Of course, I wanted to answer you immediately. But I had resumed my Sonata, which the blues had made me abandon. As it wasn't progressing, I took a well-known measure: I wrote to London not to count on it for the April 26 concert. Now it's Mr. Mayer who won't be able to sleep.

You could have just as well convalesced at Le Belvédère: I'm blockaded by snow, and don't know how I'll be able to return to my room shortly.[1] The central heating doesn't seem to be working. Not now! I'm thinking of going to Paris the day after tomorrow, no doubt by sled.

I know that you're feeling better. In that air, it's inevitable. Are you tobogganing? It's really delightful, especially when you forget to turn and go right into the snow. Skiing is idiotic: I wasn't allowed to do it.

Embrace Esther and Lydia for me. Go say hello to the owners of the "Mont Blanc," if they are still the same. And to an old friend, warmest regards from a young maître.

Maurice Ravel

1. Ravel's bedroom was one flight below the rest of the house, and could only be reached by going outside. He later eliminated this inconvenience by having a staircase built which connected the kitchen and his bedroom.

234. to Lucien Garban

Le Belvédère   March 10, 1924
Montfort l'Amaury (S. & O.)
Dear friend,

It would be most kind of you to send me Liszt's *Hungarian Rhapsodies* as soon as possible. I've forgotten quite a few of them. I think that they appeared in the Classic Edition.[1]

And then, have my photo sent to "Menschen und Menschenwerke," Porzellangasse 16, Vienna 9. For 2 months, this encyclopedia has been asking for it, and the photographer on rue de Bourgogne[2] has been promising it to me. I'll simply look younger with Durand's photo.

Till Friday, probably, at Salle Gaveau (Le Roi David).[3] In the afternoon, I don't know where or when, some songs by Roland[-Manuel] are to be performed. He was supposed to let me know. Can you tell me?

Affectionate regards to both of you,
Maurice Ravel

1. Published by Durand.
2. That is, Roland-Manuel.
3. On Friday evening, March 14, Honegger's oratorio *King David* and Fauré's *Requiem* were conducted by Robert Siohan.

235. to Jelly d'Aranyi

Le Belvédère   March 13, 1924
Montfort l'Amaury
Dear Mademoiselle,

Would you have the time to come to Paris in 2 or 3 weeks? If so, I would like to speak to you about *Tzigane,* which I am writing specially for you,[1] which will be dedicated to you, and which will replace my sonata, temporarily abandoned, in the London program.

This *Tzigane* must be a piece of great virtuosity. Certain passages can produce brilliant effects, provided that it is possible to perform them—which I'm not always sure of.

If there is no other way, I will submit them to you by mail. Obviously, this would be less convenient.

While awaiting the pleasure of seeing you again, at the very least on April 26, dear Mademoiselle, please believe in my great artistic sympathy.

Maurice Ravel

1. In an interview with this writer, Mme Robert Casadesus recalled a private musicale which took place in London in 1922, in which Jelly d'Aranyi and Hans Kindler performed the Sonata for Violin and Cello. Late in the evening Ravel asked the Hungarian violinist to play some gypsy melodies. After Mlle d'Aranyi obliged, the composer asked for one more melody, and then another. The gypsy melodies continued until about 5 A.M., with everyone exhausted except the violinist and the composer. That evening was to mark the initial gestation of *Tzigane.*

236. to Roland-Manuel

Le Belvédère   March 25, 1924
Montfort l'Amaury (S. & O.)
Dear friend,

Germaine Tailleferre[1] reminds me that I must write to Ida Rubinstein about her ballet.[2] She doesn't know that I forgot to speak to Koussevitzky about her concerto![3]

I console myself in hoping that my recommendation will be all the more effective precisely because it is tardy.

Would you put the address on the envelope and mail the letter?

Almost nothing of *Tzigane* is written. Yet I am convinced that it will be finished on time.

Cordial regards,
Maurice Ravel

1. Mme Tailleferre (1892–1983) began her studies at the Conservatoire in 1904. Cocteau compared her music to that of the Parisian artist Marie Laurencin, whose paintings are noted for their charm and elegance. Mme Tailleferre was the last surviving member of *Les Six.*

2. Probably *Le Marchand d'oiseaux,* first performed in Paris by the Swedish Ballet in 1923.

3. Mme Tailleferre performed the première of her Piano Concerto with Koussevitzky in 1924.

237. to Jean Jobert

Le Belvédère   April 14, 1924
Montfort l'Amaury (S. & O.)
Dear Sir and friend,

It's agreed then: I will conduct "Sarabande" and *Danse* in Madrid on May 5. Please send the material to the Philharmonic Society of Madrid, Carretas, 27 and 29, Madrid, as soon as possible.

The orchestra and its conductor, Señor Perez Casas, wishing to keep these pieces in their repertoire, would like to know your terms.

I still haven't thanked you for the scores which I received. Excuse me: I am distracted by this damn violin piece, which is supposed to be played in London, and which still isn't finished.

Dear Sir and friend, believe me cordially yours,
Maurice Ravel

238. to Lucien Garban

14 Holland Park   April 24, 1924
London, W.11
Dear friend,

I finally managed to arrive in London on Monday night, not without difficulty: no seats were available on the noon train; I had to fight to get one on the 4 o'clock train, which arrived an hour and a half late.

I had anticipated that I wouldn't be able to see your in-laws: I was working till the last minute and arrived in Paris by car on Sunday evening.

I forgot—among other things—to take the proofs of the song.[1] I had scarcely glanced at them when I discovered a serious error: Gerar with an accent on the e, which would dismay the dedicatee. There are probably others, perhaps also some nuances, which I will determine tomorrow with the interpreter. Have another proof sent to me in Madrid, c/o the Philharmonic Society of Madrid, Carretas, 27 and 29. I will arrive there on the 28th at night, directly from London.

Affectionately to both of you,
Maurice Ravel

1. *Ronsard à son âme.*

239. to Constantin Brailoiu

14 Holland Park   April 25, 1924
London, W.11
Dear Sir and friend,

Your special delivery letter arrived at Montfort when I was finishing a rhapsody for violin and piano: *Tzigane*, whose première has been announced here for tomorrow.

I was thinking of going to see you before leaving for England, but I only passed through Paris on Sunday morning. Once here, I continued to work (proofs, corrections, rehearsals with the violinist), and it's only today—the day before the concert—that I found a few moments to ask you to excuse me, and to express my sincere regret at not having been able to see you again and speak with you about our friend Kiriac.

Won't you be returning to Paris soon? I'm leaving London next Sunday and will go directly to Spain. I'll be back at the beginning of June, and intend to remain in Montfort l'Amaury the entire summer and work. I would be happy to receive you (9 o'clock train from the Invalides station; at Montfort, take the bus into town).

I trust that you will give me this pleasure and send you my most cordial regards.

Maurice Ravel

240. to Manuel de Falla

Hôtel de Paris   April 30, 1924
Madrid
Dear friend,

You know that I am in Madrid. Don't you have to come here shortly?

I would certainly like to go and see you, but 22 hours in a train is really a lot. Moreover, on the 18th, I'm supposed to be in Barcelona, and thanks to a 3-hour delay, I had to spend 2 nights on the train, from which I am still exhausted.

I have just rehearsed *La Valse*, and Debussy's "Sarabande" and *Danse*, which I orchestrated. Fortunately, the orchestra is composed of excellent musicians who are very kind; otherwise, I don't know how I would have managed with the few words of Spanish, Italian, and pidgin French that I can put together.

At the hotel, it produced some disastrous results: when I asked for some stationery, they brought me a hot chocolate. It finally got straightened out. . . .

I was requested to send you fond regards from the Copeley Hardings[1] and Aubry, who, moreover, was supposed to write to you.

Nevertheless, I still hope to see you. Until then, accept my most affectionate regards.

Maurice Ravel

1. See letter no. 218, note 1.

241. to Robert Casadesus

Le Belvédère   June 18, 1924
Montfort l'Amaury (S. & O.)
Dear friend,

I should have written to you a week ago: one of my oldest friends sent me a letter which he had received from Tokyo. In it, M. Mishio Ishimoto wrote of his wife's interest in coming to France—she is a student at the Tokyo Music Academy—in order to study the piano, either with you or with me. It seems to me that you are much more qualified.

If you accept, would you reply directly to my friend, at the following address?:

Count Austin de Croze
Avenue Mac-Mahon, 7   Paris, XVII

And here are some of the addresses of the singers. Unfortunately, I'm almost certain that the 1st will be in Aix-les-Bains, and the 2nd in St.-Jean-de-Luz.[1]

Very cordially yours,
Maurice Ravel

Did I tell you, the other night, that *Jeux d'eau* (among other pieces) has never been played so well?[2]

1. These names and addresses were written on a separate sheet, which has been lost.
2. On June 11, 1924, Robert Casadesus played an all-Ravel program at Salle Pleyel. The recital was broadcast on the radio, a pioneering event whose revolutionary technology was duly noted by the critics. (See *Le Ménestrel*, vol. 86, no. 25, June 20, 1924, pp. 276–77.)

242. Manuel de Falla to Maurice Ravel

Granada   July 7, 1924
Dear friend,

Ernesto Halffter has asked me to write you a letter of introduction, and I do so with great pleasure.[1]

As you know, he is a young man with uncommon musical gifts. He has the greatest admiration for you—which is perfectly natural; and this is another reason why I admire him. Welcome him kindly. He needs your precious counsel. I have great hope in Halffter's future, for in addition to his natural gifts, he has a strong desire to develop them as much as possible through serious study.

He is also the conductor of the new Bética Chamber Orchestra,[2] which we have organized in Seville. I have already spoken to you about it. They are, moreover, working enthusiastically on your wonderful *Mother Goose.*

I keenly regretted not being able to see you during your stay in Spain, and was also touched by your great kindness towards me on that occasion.

Heartfelt thanks, dear friend, together with my warmest regards.

Your

Manuel de Falla

1. Halffter (1905–1989) would become Falla's most important disciple. At Falla's request he orchestrated the accompaniments to the *Seven Spanish Folk Songs,* and he later completed *Atlántida,* the imposing posthumous oratorio that Falla had worked on during the last eighteen years of his life.

2. This group traveled throughout Spain, introducing audiences to works by Monteverdi, Alessandro Scarlatti, and Haydn, as well as Stravinsky, Ravel, and the modern Spanish school.

243. to Georgette Marnold

Le Belvédère   August 29, 1924

Montfort l'Amaury (S. & O.)

Dear friend,

My news is simple: I'm neither getting fatter nor thinner. I'm working a great deal and producing little. And I have no regrets at having been forbidden to take a vacation, as I have learned from everyone that it rains as much at Montfort as it does, I think, in Normandy. And besides, they are demolishing my house, which is not tidy; they're going to reconstruct it, which will be even less so.[1]

If the name of your landlady is badly misspelled, the postmarks alone are to blame for it.

Affectionately,

Maurice Ravel

1. See letter no. 233, note 1.

244. to Theodor Szántó

Le Belvédère   September 27, 1924
Montfort l'Amaury
Dear friend,

Thank you for *Taifun*,[1] which just arrived. I hope to find a free moment to examine your score: I quit the grind only to take some nourishment, or to walk several kilometers in the forest when I feel that my head is going to split. Of course, I haven't left Montfort all summer.

If we don't see each other before, I hope to see you on October 15 at Salle Gaveau: first performance at the S.M.I. of *Tzigane*.[2] I will have a copy of it sent to you.

Cordial regards to you both.

Maurice Ravel

1. *Typhoon* is based upon a German libretto by Melchior Lengyel and subtitled "a Japanese tragedy in three acts." The opera had recently been published by Universal Edition.

2. The performers were two young American artists, violinist Samuel Dushkin and pianist Beveridge Webster. Credit should also be given to the page turner, Maurice Ravel. For this performance, the piano was fitted with a special attachment called a "luthéal," which produces the approximate timbre of a Hungarian cimbalom or a harpsichord. The luthéal was invented by Georges Cloetens, a Belgian organ builder, who patented it in 1919. By 1925, however, it was rapidly becoming obsolete. Ravel used the luthéal for the last time in *L'Enfant et les sortilèges*, but also suggested an alternate method of approximating its timbre.

245. to Charles Koechlin

Montfort l'Amaury   October 21, 1924
Dear friend,

I am still a bit tired: I'm recovering from a grippe which was thought to be rather serious, but which suddenly dissipated. Nevertheless, it made me lose 4 days. And my lyric fantasy,[1] which is far from being finished, must be completed by the end of the year! This is a continual preoccupation, and not a clever preparation for an excuse: I will, nevertheless, come to Villers[2] on the 20th, but will ask you for complete details in order to gain as much time as possible.

At what time will the concert take place? Of course, rehearsals will be unnecessary: Fournier[3] plays the Sonata by heart and Bathori knows my songs better than I do, as she can sing them while accompanying herself, which I would be incapable of doing.

What is the train schedule? If the concert is in the afternoon, could I leave immediately afterwards?

I did indeed read the article by Monsieur J. R. Bloch: it's an incoherent chattering, no sillier than so many others.[4] Didn't I represent to the critics for a long time the most perfect example of insensitivity and lack of emotion? That was of no importance. And the success they have given me in the past few years is just as unimportant.

Thanks in advance for the information, and warmest regards,

Maurice Ravel

1. *L'Enfant et les sortilèges.*

2. Koechlin had a country home in Villers-sur-Mer, on the coast of Normandy, about 110 miles northwest of Paris.

3. The Sonata for Violin and Cello was performed by violinist Robert Krettly and the brilliant cellist Pierre Fournier, then 18 years old.

4. Jean-Richard Bloch's article, "Une Insurrection contre la sensibilité," appeared in *Le Monde musical* (September 1924, pp. 303–04), and was promptly challenged by Koechlin's "Au sujet de l'insurrection contre la sensibilité et de l'article de M. J.-R. Bloch" (*Le Monde musical,* October 1924, pp. 323–24). Although praising Honegger's music, Bloch criticized Stravinsky's *Rite of Spring,* and noted that "love, tenderness, and poetic revery" had been expunged from modern music. "We have witnessed a genuine surgery of sensibility," he wrote. Koechlin refuted Bloch's criticism of Stravinsky, pointed out examples of sensibility in contemporary music, and noted that Ravel had interpreted the romanticism of *Gaspard de la nuit* "with the qualities of a classic."

246. to Marcelle Gerar and family

Le Belvédère   [late October, 1924]
Montfort l'Amaury (S. & O.)

Warmest good wishes, dear friends, on the arrival of young Ariel,[1] who, let's hope, won't be too naughty an angel.[2]

ᒪᖆ

1. The younger of Mme Gerar's two sons, who was born on October 28, 1924.

2. This message is written on Ravel's calling card (see plate 8).

247. to Marcelle Gerar

Le Belvédère   November 21, 1924
Montfort l'Amaury (S. & O.)

Abandon all hope, dear friend. On that day, I must indeed go to Paris in order to rehearse *Tzigane* with Pierné,[1] but I will take the 4 o'clock train. As I'm writing to my old friend de Croze, I was supposed to leave at 7 o'clock in order to come for lunch; and you wouldn't believe how important 9 hours are for me at this moment.

I also won't go to the Châtelet theater the following Sunday. I'm not budging, or moving quickly, as you see; and I'm seeing no one but my frogs, Negroes, shepherdesses, and various insects.

Cordial regards to all, including the saint and the sinner,[2] from yours truly,

Maurice Ravel

1. The first orchestral performance of *Tzigane* was given by Jelly d'Aranyi, with Gabriel Pierné conducting the Colonne Orchestra on November 30, 1924.

2. A bantering reference to Mme Gerar's young sons.

248. to Madame René de Saint-Marceaux

Le Belvédère   December 8, 1924
Montfort l'Amaury (S. & O.)
Dear Madame and friend,

L'Enfant et les sortilèges will be performed this winter in Monte Carlo; I must deliver the score by the end of this month . . . and it's far from being finished. I'm working on it continually.

But as I am conducting *La Valse* at the Châtelet theater on the 21st,[1] and have a rehearsal on Saturday, I would only have to leave Montfort the previous evening. I can therefore come on Friday, though not for dinner: the train arrives in Paris only at 10:30, so I could be at your home about 11:00 P.M.

Dear Madame and friend, believe in the very cordial and respectful friendship of yours truly,

Maurice Ravel

1. Ravel shared the podium with two old friends, André Caplet and Gabriel Pierné. Caplet conducted his *Miroir de Jésus*, and, following *La Valse*, Pierné led the Colonne Orchestra in *La Damoiselle élue* by Debussy and *The Sorcerer's Apprentice* by Dukas.

249. to Jacques Durand

Hôtel de Paris   March 16, 1925
Monte Carlo
Dear friend,

Pardon me for not having written sooner: since my arrival, I have been occupied with rehearsals and also, alas! with corrections—every note has an error—. Thanks to a marvelous orchestra, which loves the work, and a conductor <u>the like of whom I have never before encountered</u>,[1] everything has worked its way out: this evening, a complete run through. The roles are remarkably performed. Mlle Gauley[2], the Child, looks like a six-year-old, and has a delightful voice. The cat duet will never be meowed better than by Madame Dubois and Warnery, who, moreover, sings the Clock's air to perfection. By the same mail, I am writing to Colette. Till Thursday, and warmest regards to you both.

Maurice Ravel

1. The Italian conductor and composer Victor de Sabata (1892–1967) led the première of *L'Enfant et les sortilèges* (see p. 438, note 6).

2. The French soprano Marie-Thérèse Gauley created the role of the Child in Monte Carlo and in Paris (at the Opéra-Comique, February 1, 1926).

250. to Colette de Jouvenel

Hôtel de Paris   March 16, 1925
Monte Carlo
Dear friend,

When are you arriving? Despite the disastrous state of the material—it's my fault . . . tsk . . . tsk . . .—, they managed to decipher the score, thanks to a superior orchestra and a truly extraordinary conductor.

There is a <u>complete run through</u> tonight, and the première is set for the 21st (next Saturday).

The orchestra, chorus, soloists, and the ushers—I was forgetting Gunsbourg—are enthusiastic: it's a good omen.

Come quickly: your suite awaits you at the Hôtel de Paris, where the food is carefully prepared and indigestible.

And if you have a few minutes before leaving, send Durand a second couplet for the celebrated aria: "You, the heart of the rose . . ."[1] which awaits only you in order to be launched by our publishers.

See you soon. With kind regards and gratitude,

Maurice Ravel

1. The Child's aria (Durand piano vocal score, p. 50).

251. to Lucien Garban

Le Belvédère   April 20, 1925
Montfort l'Amaury (S. & O.)
Dear friend,

The commission from America . . . I intend to begin work on it tomorrow.[1] Until now, I have been nursing a colossal case of laziness. I feel as if I have aged 10 years: it's always like that after each job. Fortunately, I haven't written much!

I have matters to take care of in Paris all day Saturday and may go there on Friday—I don't know when (it depends on my work). If so, I will be at Durand's office about 3 o'clock, or will come to your home in the evening. I don't suggest that you invite me for dinner, because I couldn't arrive at your home before 8 o'clock. Have the score with you: you spoke about some doubtful passages— there are more than you would believe!

At any event, I'll see you on Saturday. Affectionate regards to the three of you,

Maurice Ravel

1. This would be the *Chansons madécasses*, which were commissioned by Mrs. Elizabeth Sprague Coolidge (see letter no. 259, note 1).

252. to Lucien Garban

Le Belvédère   May 1, 1925
Montfort l'Amaury (S. & O.)
Dear friend,

I have just looked over the "excerpts"....[1] Damn it! you can sense the haste:

I) <u>The Clock</u>: there's no danger of an error regarding the missing sharp in the score. A superb natural sign has taken its place.

II) <u>The Fire</u>: in the 6th measure from the end, the chord has disappeared: yet it's not a pearl necklace!

III) <u>The Shepherds</u>: when a <u>contralto</u> sees what is asked for beginning from the 1st measure, it's certain that she won't bother with it. Second: in the penultimate measure, the note is <u>d</u>, not <u>e</u>:

A————dieu!

IV) <u>Ragtime</u>: "for mezzo-soprano <u>or</u> tenor" . . . Indeed, nothing indicates that it's not for 2 mezzos or 2 tenors. And besides, there is a misalignment in the 1st measure of the last line on page 3.

V) <u>The Child</u>: more slurs are needed following measure 6. This would be serious only when a shortwinded singer felt warranted in taking a breath between each note.

Enclosed is a receipt which I would ask you to give to whom it may concern. Furthermore, I no longer have a score. Was I given 3 of them? One was for my brother, one for Mme Casella: I should still have one. Perhaps I inadvertently gave it away to a beggar.

I began working productively only today: it's high time!

Affectionate regards to the three of you; and my compliments to Mme Varlez,[2] if she is still with you.

Maurice Ravel

1. Of *L'Enfant et les sortilèges.*
2. Garban's mother-in-law.

253. to Georges Jean-Aubry

Hôtel d'Athènes   May 23, 1925
21 rue d'Athènes
Dear friend,

I'm writing to Madame Alvar (informally and a bit late) to tell her of my forthcoming trip to London (reception of Mrs. Coolidge) and to request her hospitality. If she won't be in London, could you let me know immediately?

Bathori proposed that we perform a recital during our stay (at a private home of course, tell Mayer). Do you think it would be possible?

I'm counting on your prompt reply (to the 1st question) as I'm planning to leave on Wednesday morning.

Thanks in advance and cordial regards,

Maurice Ravel

254. to M. D. Calvocoressi

Le Belvédère   July 31, 1925
Montfort l'Amaury (S. & O.)
Dear friend,

That's one, two, three replies I owe you. This one will be all the more "consequential," because I don't owe it to you. Let's proceed in order.

1) Your letter of January 9/25: at the time, I was sleeping 3 to 5 hours a night, with one sleepless night a week (more or less). That lasted for 3 months. Your 1st letter, therefore, shared the same fate as my other mail: I read it with one eye while orchestrating with the other, and thus ran the risk of becoming cross-eyed. I still intend to reply to M. Georges Marchand, if he is still at the same address: 2 rue de Gros Murger (is that right?) Does it mean that this starving writer died of indigestion?[1]

2) Your letter of May 1/25: I was in Paris, occupied with rehearsals of the "Chanson Madécasse," which was also going to be performed in London a few

days later.[2] You must have learned that the matter you spoke to me about did not materialize.

3) Your telegram of May ?/25: when you got mine, didn't you go to meet me at the Gare du Nord? That morning, just as I was leaving to go there, I discovered that my passport had expired. I rushed over to the Foreign Office; a secretary accompanied me to the passport office and everything was hurried through in fifteen minutes. But I missed my train and only left in the afternoon. I intended to send you an apology from London, then from Paris, and finally from Montfort. Impossible: I remain petrified in front of a pile of unanswered letters. The only thing I can do is to rearrange them once a week. And this prevents my getting back to work: a huge job, to be followed by another big one, which I recently promised to deliver by the end of the year.[3] How many nights of hard work lie ahead!

4) In reply to Eschig[4] (for your trouble, please let him know I gave you the information directly): "Une Barque sur l'océan" was orchestrated in 1907, and the "Alborada [del gracioso]" in 1918. As for the *Pavane* [*pour une Infante défunte*], I have no idea.[5] Isn't it in Roland-Manuel's book? It's a very useful thing. Don't you have a copy? I'll arrange to have Durand send you one.

Will you be coming to Paris soon? I'm not budging: I'm going to try to get back to the grind.

Affectionate regards to you both,

Maurice Ravel

1. Calvocoressi recalled that Marchand was a young French musician who wished to organize some performances of Ravel's music ("Ravel's Letters to Calvocoressi," p. 16). "Ravel was not the only one to be struck by the peculiar street-name [meaning "Large" or "Stout" Murger] and to wonder what relation it bore to the author of *La Vie de Bohème*." (Puccini's *La Bohème* is based on the work by Henri Murger.)

2. Referring to "Aoua!," the middle song of the cycle, which was the first to be completed.

3. In addition to the *Chansons madécasses,* Ravel was working on the Sonata for Violin and Piano, and was planning to write an operetta based on a text by Mayrargues, with Maud Loty in the leading role. The operetta remained in the planning stages.

4. The publisher Max Eschig.

5. Composed in 1899, the *Pavane* was orchestrated in 1910.

255. Berg, Honegger, Gieseking, et al. to Maurice Ravel[1]

[Austria]   [August 11, 1925][2]

It was a great joy to hear some of your charming music once again.

Alban Berg

The Duo[3] was a triumphal success. We are very happy about it.
   Arthur Honegger[4]

Kind regards from Vaura.[5]

Respectful greetings from your admirer
   Walter Gieseking[6]

   1. This postcard, sent from Austria, was addressed to the summer home of Roland-Manuel's parents in Lyons-la-Fôret. Some ten other musicians signed their names, among them Egon Wellesz, Hermann Scherchen, and Paul Hindemith. Berg's message is written in German, and the others are in French.
   2. This postmark appears on the postcard. The face of the card shows a panoramic view of Salzburg.
   3. That is, the Sonata for Violin and Cello.
   4. See Ravel's appreciation of Honegger (1892–1955) on p. 446.
   5. Honegger's wife, the pianist Andrée Vaurabourg (1894–1980).
   6. One of the foremost pianists of his time, Gieseking (1895–1956) was particularly noted for his interpretations of Debussy and Ravel. Mme A. Colassis, the pianist's daughter, kindly informed me (letter dated July 23, 1985) that Gieseking and Ravel never met, nor was she aware of any other correspondence between them.

256. to Hélène Jourdan-Morhange

Le Belvédère   August 15, 1925
Montfort l'Amaury (S. & O.)
   Definitely not, dear friend: I will not come to applaud you. One must be reasonable: I'm resuming work—with difficulty. If I stop–I know myself—I'll have to start all over again.
   Pardon me—you have no choice: the Sonata!—and believe me very affectionately yours,
   Maurice Ravel

257. to Madame V. Pavlovsky-Borovick[1]

Le Belvédère   December 11, 1925
Montfort l'Amaury (S. & O.)
Madame,
   Away from home since last Monday, I found your kind letter upon returning to Montfort. I trust that my reply will still find you in Paris.
   I am unaware of the existence of this transcription, and am certain that my

publisher is also unacquainted with it. I think that you should consult with him in this matter, and with my sincere apologies, believe me very truly yours,

Maurice Ravel[2]

1. A Russian soprano, she came to Paris in 1925 to study voice. In Paris she heard a transcription of "La Flûte enchantée" from Ravel's *Shéhérazade* for voice, string quartet, and flute, and, wishing to perform it, she wrote to Ravel for permission. (The transcription, apparently illegal, was never copyrighted.)

2. Ravel's autograph is reproduced in A. Gosenpud, *Pis'ma zarnbežnyh muzykantov iz russkih arhivov* [Letters of foreign musicians in Russian archives], (Leningrad: Musika, 1967), plate opposite p. 365.

258. to Alexandre Tansman[1]

Le Belvédère   December 18, 1925
Montfort l'Amaury (S. & O.)

Dear friend,

I was just about to leave for Alsace when I received your 2nd letter. After visiting with our friends the Clemenceaus, I was counting on answering you from there. Naturally I didn't have the time, and upon returning, I found a huge amount of mail.

On the basis of our conversation, I saw that our friends shared my opinion completely: the article is perfidious, all the more so because one cannot reply to it. Whether or not Marya Freund sings Schoenberg better than Debussy is a matter of personal taste.[2]

All of the rest is true (but there is a way of presenting it), or it is impossible to prove the contrary.[3]

No doubt, it would have been more justified to confer the Legion of Honor upon Mme Vuillemin: at least that distinction would have been approved by *Comœdia* and the *Courrier musical* . . . and I can assure you that I would not have protested.[4]

Very cordially yours,
Maurice Ravel

1. The noted French composer and pianist of Polish origin (1897–1986) was born in Łódź and studied at the Conservatory there (1902–14). In 1919, he came to France and soon after met Ravel, who gave him artistic counsel and encouraged him.

2. The soprano Marya Freund (1876–1966), of Polish origin, specialized in singing contemporary works, and frequently performed Schoenberg's music with the composer.

3. In a combative article entitled "Rougeurs!" [Blushes!], which appeared in *Le Courrier musical* (27, November 1, 1925, pp. 501–02), Louis Vuillemin complained that many foreign artists were awarded the red ribbon of the Legion of Honor, but many

deserving French musicians had been overlooked. Thus, he explained, Theodor Szántó and Marya Freund had been decorated, but Louis Aubert and Gabriel Grovlez had not.

4. Another example of Ravel's ironic humor: Lucy Vuillemin, the critic's wife, had performed minor roles at the Théâtre des Arts, the Opéra-Comique, and the Théâtre des Champs-Elysées.

259. to Mrs. Elizabeth Sprague Coolidge[1]

Le Belvédère   December 19, 1925
Montfort l'Amaury
Dear Madame,

I did not leave Montfort all summer, thereby hoping to be able to finish the 2 Chansons madécasses which I had promised you, and a sonata for violin and piano which I began almost 2 years ago.

I had to abandon these projects: all of my time was occupied correcting the orchestral proofs and then directing the rehearsals of *L'Enfant et les sortilèges*, which the Opéra-Comique will present on January 23.[2] The next day, I will be leaving on a journey which will last more than 2 months.[3]

You can imagine how very sorry I am to have broken my word. Of course, this is only a delay, and as soon as I return—towards April—I'm counting on resuming work.[4]

I trust that you will pardon me, and believe me, dear Madame, very truly yours,

Maurice Ravel

1. The American patroness Elizabeth Sprague Coolidge (1864–1953) commissioned an imposing number of chamber works from composers such as Bartók, Copland, Hindemith, Prokofiev, Schoenberg, and Stravinsky, among many others. In addition, she sponsored recitals of contemporary chamber music in the United States and Europe (see her letter to Ravel, no. 322).

2. The date was later postponed to February 1.

3. Ravel's concert tour took him to Belgium, Germany, Scandinavia (Copenhagen, Oslo, Stockholm), England, and Scotland. A number of lecture-recitals were presented with his good friends Georges Jean-Aubry and Louise Alvar (see p. 439).

4. Completed in April 1926, the *Chansons madécasses* were performed in Paris on June 13, 1926, with soloists Jane Bathori, Alfredo Casella (piano), M. Baudouin (flute), and Hans Kindler (cello). The program, which consisted entirely of chamber works commissioned by Mrs. Coolidge, including Ernest Bloch's Suite for Viola and Piano, and Charles Loeffler's *Cantique au soleil*, for soprano and chamber orchestra, which had been specially composed for the inauguration of the new music room in the Library of Congress. (M. Baudouin replaced Louis Fleury [1878–1926], who died just before this recital. See letter no. 268, note 2.)

260. to Madame A. Bonnet

Montfort   January 11, 1926
Dear Madame Bonnet,

Here is the monogram for the handkerchiefs.[1] I'm afraid there won't be enough time to embroider it before my departure (on the 24th).

I'll telephone Edouard tomorrow morning.

Affectionately to all,

Maurice Ravel

1. On a separate sheet, Ravel enclosed a copy of his monogram.

261. to Hélène Jourdan-Morhange

[Copenhagen]   February 4, 1926

These are the only minutes—on the verge of leaving for Oslo—that I found to write to you, dear friend. Give the above address[1] to our friends, asking them to pardon me, and write to me about yourself (and about *L'Enfant* [*et les sortilèges*], which, according to *Le Temps,* seems to me to have received a slap).[2]

Affectionately,

Maurice Ravel

Were you able to hear *L'Enfant?*

1. The following address, written in another hand, appears at the top of this post-card: Dehn Pensionat
   Strandvägen 7ª
   Stockholm

2. Another example of Ravel's ironic humor. Henry Malherbe's review (*Le Temps,* February 3, 1926) was ecstatic from beginning to end. Roland-Manuel called Malherbe's article a "stupid dithyramb" (see letter no. 264).

262. to Madame Maurice Delage

Oslo   February 6, 1926

It's really winter here. As in Paris, beams are placed against the houses in order to prevent people from passing on the sidewalk, but here it's to protect them from blocks of ice which can tumble down from the roofs.

There are all kinds of vehicles: trolleys, cars (with chains), sleighs, skis . . .

I hope to find a letter from you in Stockholm.

Affectionate regards to you both,

Maurice Ravel

263. to Madame Fernand Dreyfus

London   February 23, 1926

I haven't written to you often, my dear marraine. It isn't that I'm taking revenge for the persistent silence of my pupil, for which you are not responsible, but because of the little free time afforded by my comings and goings from London to the country. I was a bit out of sorts from the Scandinavian diet. But I miss the snow, the sun, and the skies of Sweden, although England surprised me with a delightful spring: crocuses amid the grass, verdant shrubs, nightingales. I'm leaving tomorrow morning for Glasgow and Edinburgh,[1] and will be back in early March.

Affectionate regards from your
Maurice Ravel

1. In several recitals of chamber music performed in England and Scotland, Ravel accompanied the twenty-year-old violin prodigy Zino Francescatti, who played the *Berceuse sur le nom de Gabriel Fauré* and *Tzigane*.

264. Roland-Manuel to Maurice Ravel

[42 rue de Bourgogne]   February 23, 1926
[Paris]
Dear friend,

Pardon my delay (the blues; personal vexations; a thousand things which diminish one's zest for living and acting, rendering friendship mute but in no way altered). Excuse me: I'm telling you too much or not enough. That's all for today.

It is difficult to give you a thorough account of the actions and reactions which *L'Enfant* has aroused. The family circle naturally applauded. The Institute cursed you until the seventh generation. Henri Février[1] declared that the production of your work is a scandal, and a generator of scandals. He maintains that Marnold slapped Rouché's face for the hidden reason that Rouché had refused to produce *L'Enfant* (sic).[2]

Your work is performed every night in a lively, scandalous atmosphere. Everyone is delighted that it is always possible to hear the music, particularly the performers. "We're having a good time," Roger Bourdin[3] confided to me, "we're living through historic moments."

Whether your work is greeted with praise or with reservations, the critics are stammering a bit more stupidly than usual with regard to you. The composer's fame bothers them and they are disconcerted. For example: the stupid dithyramb by Malherbe.[4] There was very keen praise from Raymond Douches (in

L'Avenir); a short article in *Paris-Midi* with a picture of the film producer Ravel (Gaston)[5]; a very pleasant article by Vuillermoz. Finally, a characteristic thrashing by Messager in *Le Figaro*. I spoke with Messager about his review. His opinion is categorical: by removing every element of sensibility from your music, you condemn yourself to composing nothing more than imitative music, which in his view is intolerable.[6] The serious error in his article, in my view, is that he claims you sacrifice everything for some orchestral effects, when it seems to me that *L'Enfant* is the least orchestrated but the most orchestral work you have written. That was the main point of my article in *Le Ménestrel.*[7]

I wrote a detailed review of *L'Enfant* in an article published in *La Revue Pleyel*[8] which I am sending to you, and which gave me a great deal of difficulty. I forced myself to be objective and not follow the dictates of my heart, which always pushes me, when I speak about you, in the direction of poetic enthusiasm "which ain't worth the trouble" and which doesn't concern anyone since I have no father confessor. To you, however, I can say that I am filled with affectionate admiration when I see you walking on a tightrope. I love to see you enclose yourself in your clocks, without even missing those slippers—as Inigo does—which so many of the young bourgeoisie put on after you.

I call bourgeois, says Fargue,[9] anyone who renounces combat and love—for personal safety. There are many passages in *L'Enfant* in which you renounce yourself in order to discover this other identity, which eternity will not change. There isn't one passage in which you renounce combat—or love, despite Messager, this sophisticated man, who although best qualified to understand you, doesn't hear you.

From everything I have written, you can infer that *L'Enfant* did not receive a "slap" at all, as you said. It is even claimed that the success of the work is due to the claque which you employ to imitate the cat at the end of the first scene. Therefore, I promise to imitate the cat the next time I go to hear *L'Enfant et les sortilèges*, but I will be less successful at it than your music.

I trust that your tour is concluding pleasantly, and I hope to see you among us soon. We will take you to hear *L'Enfant et les sortilèges* at the Opéra-Comique; we will imitate the cat, and Malherbe will fall into your arms shedding gentle tears.

Very cordially yours,
Roland-Manuel

1. The French composer (1875–1957). His son, the pianist Jacques Février (1900–1979), was one of Ravel's favorite interpreters.

2. This incident took place at the dress rehearsal of *L'Enfant et les sortilèges*. According to a front-page article in *Paris-Midi* (February 3, 1926), a brief scuffle broke out, and Marnold challenged Rouché to a duel. (Whatever the precise aftermath of this episode,

there were, fortunately, no fatalities.) The events leading up to this episode were as follows: In his monthly column in the *Mercure de France*, Marnold had criticized some décors carried out by one Valdo Barbey. It turned out, Marnold explained, that Barbey was Rouché's son-in-law, and the director of the Opéra had retaliated by canceling his press privileges. This led to a heated personal attack, in which the charge that Rouché was "completely devoid of musical culture" was one of Marnold's milder statements (see the *Mercure de France,* December 1, 1925, pp. 512–22).

3. The French baritone (1900–1974). He performed the roles of the Clock and the Cat at the Opéra-Comique, and Ravel later dedicated the "Drinking Song" from *Don Quichotte à Dulcinée* to him.

4. See letter no. 172, note 2.

5. Writing in *Paris-Midi* on February 2, 1926, André Coeuroy gave *L'Enfant* a glowing review. His article contained two photographs, one of Colette, and the other of Ravel—the film producer Gaston Ravel!

6. André Messager's review appeared in *Le Figaro* on February 4, 1926. He tempered his criticism as follows: "To sum up, a very fine effort which brings credit upon the new management of the Opéra-Comique" (see p. 483, note 13).

7. This article appeared in *Le Ménestrel* on February 5, 1926, pp. 60–61.

8. This article appeared in *La Revue Pleyel* on February 15, 1926, pp. 10–12. In his review, Roland-Manuel aptly observed: "We know that a curious discretion always pushed Ravel to grant more of a heart to clocks than to clockmakers, more of a soul to trees than to humans. *L'Enfant et les sortilèges* illustrates this aesthetic even more than *L'Heure espagnole*."

9. One of Ravel's last songs, *Rêves,* was set to a poem by his old friend Léon-Paul Fargue (1876–1947).

265. to Robert Casadesus

Le Belvédère   March 20, 1926
Montfort l'Amaury (S. & O.)
My dear friend,

A sonata for violin and piano, half finished, which my publisher is waiting for; 2 Chansons madécasses scarcely begun, which I promised to finish by the end of April; an operetta which is supposed to be performed at the beginning of next season, whose first note has yet to be written; and I will have to go to Milan soon for the final rehearsals of *L'Enfant et les sortilèges*.

I wanted to take refuge in Saint-Jean-de-Luz. Upon reflection, I decided to cloister myself in Montfort, like last year.

Therefore, convey my apologies to Mlle Fity,[1] and while awaiting a more favorable time, believe me most cordially yours,

Maurice Ravel

A thousand thanks for the *Préludes* and for the dedication.[2] I found them upon returning home the day before yesterday, and of course haven't had the time to examine them.

ПR

1. An Italian impresario.

2. Composed in 1924, the *24 Préludes* by Robert Casadesus, opus 5, were dedicated to Ravel and published by Eschig in 1925.

266. to Mrs. Louise Alvar

Le Belvédère   March 31, 1926
Montfort l'Amaury
Dear friend,

To think that I had promised to give you an account of the 2 staged versions of *L'Enfant* . . . as soon as I had seen them!

How restful the Scandinavian countries seemed in comparison with Paris!

I returned to Montfort dead tired, having accomplished nothing of what I had intended to do. But I know all of the hit operettas: I never heard so many of them at one time (professional duty!).

Let's discuss *L'Enfant*: at the Monnaie theater, the realization was charming, a bit "Art Deco." At the Opéra-Comique, it wasn't "Art Deco" at all. And I was so satisfied with the staging that, two days later, I spent an entire day changing everything; but it's still not perfect.[1]

The type of success is also different: there, the audience awaits the end of each scene and applauds with all its might. Here, they whistle,[2] applaud, meow, and shout oaths nonstop.

Now I'm cloistered here—I decided that Le Belvédère would make a better monastery than the Pergola in St.-Jean-de-Luz.[3] I'm working on the Chansons madécasses. The operetta will follow, and then the sonata for violin and piano: you can see that my subjects of meditation are varied.

For the moment, I'm going to lie down; I'm exhausted: it's probably a cold. Note that for 2 days, the weather has been magnificent.

Happy Easter to all, and affectionate regards from yours truly,
Maurice Ravel

1. At the Théâtre de la Monnaie in Brussels, the décor and production were carried out by Jean Delescluzes and M. Dalman respectively; their counterparts at the Opéra-Comique were Raymond Deshays and M. Arnaud, and Georges Ricou.

2. In France, a sign of disapproval.

3. The local casino!

267. to Hélène Jourdan-Morhange

Le Belvédère   April 21, 1926
Montfort l'Amaury (S. & O.)
Dear friend,

The nougat has just arrived. I'm interrupting my work (no more 8-hour days: I'm also on the night shift).

You will see me next week: it will mean that I have finished the [*Chansons*] *madécasses.*

A thousand thanks and affectionate regards,
Maurice Ravel

268. to Madame Alfred Madoux-Frank[1]

Le Belvédère   April 23, 1926
Montfort l'Amaury (S. & O.)
Dear Madame and friend,

I am so sorry that I must refuse the brief vacation whose itinerary, however, seemed so delightful! But, I really must: upon returning to France, I had decided to leave for St.-Jean-de-Luz; and then, I thought I would be better off here, but on condition that I seclude myself. At the moment I am finishing the *Chansons madécasses,* whose 1st performance is supposed to be given in Rome on May 8, and several days later, I believe, in Brussels.[2] As soon as the songs are finished (next week) I will direct the rehearsals in Paris and will return immediately to isolate myself till the end of the summer.

I'm even having a telephone installed, despite its disadvantages, so that I can avoid going to Paris.

Please excuse me; Defauw will also pardon me, I hope.

I'm getting back to work; perhaps I'll spend all night at it. Please convey my most cordial regards to M. Madoux, and, dear Madame, kindly accept my respectful friendship.

Maurice Ravel

1. When visiting Brussels, Ravel often stayed at the elegant home of M. and Mme Madoux-Frank. He was the owner and editor of the newspaper *L'Etoile belge.*

2. The first performance of the *Chansons madécasses* took place at the American Academy in Rome on Saturday afternoon, May 8, 1926. The performers were Jane Bathori, Alfredo Casella (piano), Louis Fleury (flute), and Hans Kindler (cello). The song cycle was performed soon after at the Egmont Palace in Brussels, and the Parisian debut occurred on June 13.

269. to Jean Huré[1]

May 4, 1926

My dear Huré,

Would you, and could you without troubling yourself too much, instruct Manuel Rosenthal,[2] who has a great deal to learn, particularly counterpoint and fugue, and who is far from being a millionaire?

I don't need to recommend him to you because you are acquainted with his endeavors, and have judged them favorably, and rightly so. If you have the spare time to drop me a note about this matter, I would also be glad to learn about your activities, which I haven't kept up with for a very long time.

Yours affectionately,

Maurice Ravel

Did I ever thank you for your book and its contents?[3]

1. Huré (1877–1930) was a gifted composer, organist, pianist, pedagogue, and writer on music.

2. The French conductor and composer Manuel Rosenthal (b. 1904) was educated at the Conservatoire. He later studied counterpoint and fugue with Jean Huré, and composition with Ravel. Thus, following Maurice Delage, Ralph Vaughan-Williams, and Roland-Manuel, he became the last member of what Ravel enjoyed calling "the school of Montfort." In the 1930s, with Ravel's approbation, Rosenthal orchestrated the accompaniments of the *Histoires naturelles* as well as three of the *Five Greek Folk Songs*. Two of them had been transcribed by Ravel many years before, and it was agreed that a complete set would be useful. Ravel observed that he would have carried out these transcriptions himself years ago, but somehow never found the time to do so (see p. 584).

3. Possibly Huré's *Introduction à la technique du piano* (Paris, 1910). (The autograph of this letter has not been traced. A copy of it is in the private collection of the author.)

270. Alexander L. Steinert[1] to Maurice Ravel

[18 rue Matignon]   May 24 [1926]
[Paris]

Dear Maître:

In sending you the photos I spoke about, I want to tell you at the same time how happy I was to see you again the other day at Montfort, and how grateful I am for everything you told me about the music you played for me and the music I showed to you. It seems to me that in two minutes you discovered the shortcomings which have always disturbed me. I wish to thank you once again for the kindness which you have shown to me.

I hope to have the pleasure of seeing you soon, and perhaps I will have the honor of receiving you one day in the near future at 18 rue Matignon.

With my deep admiration, dear Maître, believe me very truly yours,

Alexander L. Steinert

1. The American composer and pianist (1900–1982). Following his initial studies in Boston, Steinert settled in Paris and worked with Charles Koechlin and Vincent d'Indy. He later wrote film music, and was active in Hollywood as a conductor and arranger.

271. to Alexander L. Steinert

Le Belvédère   May 28, 1926
Montfort l'Amaury
Tel.: 89. Mt. l'Amaury
    Dear friend,
    Since I have abandoned my operetta, I am more often in Paris than in Montfort. I will be there again on Saturday, but so busy that I'm afraid I won't be able to accept your kind invitation. But I promise to do my utmost. If I don't come, excuse me. See you soon: perhaps on June 1 (concert of the *Revue musicale*),[1] or the 13th (the Coolidge soirée),[2] or again on the 25th (at the Ministry of Finance, where I will prop up the franc).[3]
    Very cordially yours,
    Maurice Ravel

1. This all-Ravel program at Salle Gaveau was sponsored by *La Revue musicale*. It included the *Miroirs,* performed by Robert Casadesus, the String Quartet (Pro Arte Quartet), and concluded with the *Introduction et Allegro* conducted by the composer, with Lily Laskine (harp), Marcel Moyse (flute), M. Hamelin (clarinet), and the Pro Arte Quartet.
    2. See letter no. 259, note 4.
    3. Ravel's quip reflected the financial crisis which occurred in France in 1926 when the franc fell precipitously against the dollar and the British pound. In 1921, the pound equalled 55 francs, but in 1926 it soared to 240 francs.

272. to ?[1]

La Musique vivante[2]   September 22, 1926[3]
20 Avenue de L'Opéra
Paris (1 er)
    [I do not desire a second performance, after thirty years, of my *Sites auriculaires.*][4]

I see no objection to have my *Sites* heard again [and the score will be at your disposal]⁴ if I can recover the manuscript.

(Signed):

With cordial regards from

Maurice Ravel

1. This document is a draft of a letter.

2. La Musique vivante [Living Music] was a weekly concert series which often combined music and slides of the period in which the music was written, with commentary by Léon Vallas. For the opening recital of its second season, on October 22, 1926, it had been widely publicized that *Sites auriculaires* would be performed for the second time, following a lapse of 28 years. The performance, however, did not take place (see *Le Guide du concert*, 13, October 1 and 8, 1926, pp. 64 and 83).

3. In the autograph, this date is written in another hand.

4. Ravel crossed out the words enclosed in brackets.

273. to Alfred Perrin¹

Hotel Bristol   November 20, 1926
Bern

Dear Alfred,

I will be in Geneva on the 25th, arriving from Basel. My concert takes place on the 26th, and I expect to remain in Geneva at least 3 days. I therefore hope to have the pleasure of seeing all of you. If I cannot contact you before the evening of the 26th, perhaps you can make arrangements to be free for this "festival".² In any case, 3 tickets will be put aside for you at the box office in your name (I believe the concert is at the Conservatoire). At any event, I will not leave Geneva without seeing you.

I had lost your old address. Madame Ansermet managed to give me the new one. Even though the address is incomplete, I trust that my letter will reach you. If you receive it in time, and write to me immediately, I'll receive your reply in Bern, which I am leaving Wednesday morning.

As soon as I arrive in Geneva, I'll go to the Alhambra³ where, if I don't find you, I will leave the address of my hotel.

See you soon, dear Alfred, and very affectionate regards to all,

Maurice Ravel

1. Alfred Perrin (1880–1957) was a first cousin of Maurice Ravel; his mother, née Louise Ravel, was the composer's aunt.

2. This all-Ravel program, organized by the Swiss pianist Franz-Josef Hirt, was presented under the patronage of the French ambassador Jean Hennessy. Ravel performed the *Pavane pour une Infante défunte* and the Sonatine. The program also included

the Trio, played by Franz-Josef Hirt, his brother Fritz Hirt (violin), and Lorenz Lehr (cello), the *Berceuse sur le nom de Gabriel Fauré,* and *Tzigane.*

3. Perrin was a violinist in the orchestra of the Alhambra music hall.

274. to M. and Mme E. Robert Schmitz

Le Belvédère   January 18, 1927
Tel.: 89 Montfort l'Amaury (S. & O.)

Received your letters and cablegrams, dear friends, before, during, and after my trip to Switzerland. Since my return, at the beginning of December, I haven't been at Montfort often; and as you can easily imagine how my time is spent in Paris, I trust that you will excuse my silence. I cabled you last Thursday, during my most recent stay. I left 10 days ago, returned there two days later, and have just returned home this minute to find your letter of January 4, which arrived this morning. It's fortunate therefore that I didn't have the time to send you a letter announcing my telegram. My reply is thus all the more complete:

First of all, I cannot negotiate with Welte-Mignon, as I am engaged by Aeolian (Duo-Art).[1] Recently, I had to refuse to enter into a contract with Pleyel, for the same reason.

With regard to the concerto, as I cabled you, don't count on it any more: I discovered that *Le Grand Meaulnes* had nothing to do with the piano; if Euterpe[2] permits, it will become a fantasy for cello. Furthermore, my sonata for violin and piano, which is far from being finished, must be completed by May 30, the date set for the première in Paris. And I am planning to write a grand opera,[3] which might have far-reaching consequences.

You should therefore only count on me to conduct. If you consider it sufficient, I am confirming that, for the 1927–1928 season, I give you the exclusive right to negotiate with organizations for a series of 10 concerts, in return for a guarantee of ten thousand dollars (10,000).

I didn't quite understand the passage concerning Mayer: is it up to me to specify "that it is by special agreement with him that I . . . am appearing with you"? If so, I think that other terms would be necessary.

If you need to cable me, please do so, if possible, "via Commercial" (The Commercial Cable Company): I have an account there, and telephone my messages directly to them.

Accept my most cordial regards, dear friends.

Maurice Ravel

I'm happy to have your telegraphic address written distinctly at last; till now, it has been transmitted much too capriciously.

1. See Appendix E.

2. In Greek mythology, the Muse of music and lyric poetry.

3. See p. 499.

275. to Jean Jobert

Le Belvédère   February 21, 1927
Montfort l'Amaury (S. & O.)
Dear friend,

Indeed, I was close by the other day, but occupied, and regretted it very much. I hope that you have pardoned me, and above all that you're still not waiting for me to begin your meal.

"Sarabande" and *Danse* went very well in Lyon. I discovered an error in the "Sarabande" which had escaped me until now: at rehearsal number ⑨, in the harp part and the full score, a treble clef is missing in the left hand, and consequently a bass clef 4 measures later. I imagine that the performers made the corrections instinctively,[1] or else I would have to resign myself to composing a 9th symphony.

Perhaps I will see you Thursday evening at *Les Burgraves*,[2] and certainly on Friday (afternoon) at the Bériza performance.[3]

My most cordial regards to you and Madame Jobert.

Maurice Ravel

1. In the Jobert score, on p. 10, the treble clef is missing, but a bass clef does appear four measures later. Such an oversight would indeed by corrected instinctively.

2. An opera by Léo Sachs based on the trilogy by Victor Hugo. It was presented at the Opéra on Thursday, February 24, 1927, as a gala fund-raising event for the Victor Hugo Foundation.

3. The French soprano Marguerite Bériza sponsored a series of private performances in which she sang. She performed the role of Eurydice in *Les Malheurs d'Orphée* by Milhaud, which was coupled with Florent Schmitt's *Fonctionnaire MCMXII*, a humorous pantomime subtitled "inaction en musique." (It portrays a civil servant who successfully manages to accomplish nothing at his job.) Both works were conducted by Vladimir Golschmann.

276. Darius Milhaud to Maurice Ravel

10 Boulevard de Clichy   [April 2, 1927][1]
[Paris]
My dear friend,

Allow me to tell you how touched I was by your comments about my little *Orphée* in your interview in *Les Nouvelles littéraires*.[2]

Only your judgment had the necessary authority to put M. Lalo's opinion in its place. It is extremely important to all of us that you were willing to intervene in this quarrel.

My dear friend, please believe me your very cordially devoted
Milhaud

1. This postmark appears on the envelope of Milhaud's undated letter.
2. See p. 446.

277. to Marcelle Gerar

Le Belvédère   April 21, 1927
Tel.: 89. Montfort l'Amaury (S. & O.)

May 23, dear friend? May it please our good Euterpe that my sonata be on the road to completion, and that Enesco[1] won't have to sight-read it a week later!

Don't hold it against me, and believe in the sincere friendship of your
Maurice Ravel

Don't forget to enroll yourself for the 30th.[2]

1. The eminent Romanian violinist and composer Georges Enesco (1881–1955) was a fellow student at the Conservatoire, and spent most of his life in France. He introduced the Sonata for Violin and Piano with Ravel on May 30, 1927, in a recital sponsored by Durand and Company (see p. 557).
2. That is, for the Durand recital on May 30.

278. Paul Morand[1] to Maurice Ravel

3 Avenue Charles Floquet   June 12, 1927
Paris 7ᵉ

Dear friend,

If you have some errands to take care of in Paris, try to do them on June 30 (Thursday).

And on June 30, come to lunch at my home at 1 o'clock, 3 Avenue Charles Floquet, in complete privacy with M. Edouard Herriot and his pipe.[2]

Yours very faithfully,
Paul Morand

1. Morand (1888–1976) was a versatile author as well as a widely traveled diplomat. In 1932, he provided Ravel with three short texts, *Don Quichotte à Dulcinée*, which turned out to be the composer's swan song. The texts were part of a film, *Don Quixote*, directed by George Pabst, with the celebrated Russian basso Feodor Chaliapin in the title role.

As Ravel was late in completing his score, the assignment was turned over to his younger colleague Jacques Ibert, who hurriedly composed the background music and five songs for Chaliapin.

2. An erudite political figure, Herriot (1872–1957) also wrote a biography of Beethoven. His pipe, like Neville Chamberlain's umbrella, was proverbial.

279. to Henry Prunières

9 rue Tourasse   September 7, 1927
Saint-Jean-de-Luz
My dear Prunières,

I was convinced I had told you that from August 1 on, I would be in Saint-Jean-de-Luz.

Moreover, it seems to me that an "interview" format would add nothing to your article. As for my feelings about America, it would be better to limit yourself to the strict truth: never having been there, I would be happy to see it. If it would give pleasure to your readers, you may add that I like jazz much more than grand opera.

With regard to my family tree, its essence is so complex that I have never found the spare time to analyze it: my mother, who was born in Ciboure, came from a family of sailors, like almost all of the Basques on the coast. There must have been a bit of everything, from captains of trading vessels to simple fishermen. Most of these ancestors departed for "the Americas" and never returned.

On my father's side: he was born in Versoix, and consequently a Swiss subject, as the canton of Geneva was no longer part of France at that time. I am unable to give you any more precise information. I hope that you will use much less of this information, and that your readers will find other points of interest in your article.[1]

Be sure to send me your article before it is published, and I will return it to you immediately.

I'm staying here until the 28th, as I have to be in Amsterdam on October 1.
With most cordial regards,
Maurice Ravel

1. If this article was printed, it has yet to be traced.

280. to Léon Leyritz[1]

Rue Tourasse   [September 1927]
Saint-Jean-de-Luz
Dear friend,

It's already a month since you wrote to me. Some letters arriving late, a bit of work, and above all, the pleasant idleness induced by my native region have prevented me from replying earlier to your charming letter.

Thanks for the news about my Siamese cats, and about my bust. (If you could send me a photo of it before my departure, I would be very happy to show it to all those friends whom I've interested in seeing it.)

I'm leaving Saint-Jean on the 26th in the morning, will stay only a few days in Paris before going to Amsterdam,[2] and will finally return home on October 4.

I trust that you are in a region where the sun is thriving—here, it is less visible than usual.

My kind regards to Madame Leyritz, and very cordially yours,
Maurice Ravel

1. The French sculptor (1888–1976) met Ravel at the home of Marcelle Gerar, and soon after expressed interest in making a bust of the composer. Ravel agreed, on condition that he never pose. When the bust was finished, he remarked, "It's my best portrait!" (Leyritz's stone bust of Ravel is in the Paris Opéra; see plate 12.) In 1935, thanks to the behind-the-scenes generosity of Ida Rubinstein, Leyritz traveled with Ravel to Spain and North Africa (see letters 338 and 339).

2. For a recital of chamber music sponsored by Mrs. Coolidge, who had commissioned all of the works on the program. The *Chansons madécasses* were performed by Madeleine Grey, with Marcel Moyse (flute), Hans Kindler (cello), and the composer at the piano. The program also included works by N. T. Berezowski, Francesco Malipiero, and Gabriel Pierné.

281. to Ernest Ansermet

Le Belvédère   October 15, 1927
Montfort l'Amaury (S. & O.)
Dear friend,

Your letter arrived this minute, via Montfort, St.-Jean-de-Luz, the hotel d'Athènes, and Montfort. In another fifteen minutes, it would have returned to Paris, which is what I'm about to do. Therefore, please excuse this hasty reply.

It's impossible to perform the entire work without a pause.[1] You could present most of it by linking separate numbers. Decide for yourself which pieces can do without scenic gestures. With regard to the 1st suite, the *a cappella* choral part is orchestrated. It's a makeshift arrangement, but I still believe it preferable to an interruption.

A concert performance of *L'Enfant*? There too, I would be afraid that this work, which is rather short in the theater, would appear very long without movement, or rather without the kaleidoscopic succession of animated movement. You can always try . . .

Excuse me: the train's official timetable doesn't wait.[2] Very cordial regards from your

Maurice Ravel

I'm leaving toward the end of November for the United States.

1. Meaning a concert performance of *Daphnis et Chloé*.

2. A humorous reference to Torquemada's concluding line in scene two of *L'Heure espagnole*: "the official timetable doesn't wait."

282. to Mrs. Louise Alvar

14 Holland Park   October 27, 1927
London, W.11

Dear friend,

I sincerely regret having come to London during your absence. There was no way to postpone the recording sessions:[1] the date which I selected, the 18th, had to be changed because of the Pleyel inauguration.[2] Moreover, I'm supposed to be leaving for the United States in about two weeks.

I'm as pampered as anyone could be: even the cook, touched by the strictness of my diet, adds a little milk to my tapioca in the morning!

Nothing is lacking . . . except your presence.[3] Will I have the pleasure of seeing you before you return to London, either in Paris or Montfort? I hope so; if not, we will meet in "the other world," if you go there this winter, or else upon my return.

Transmit my handshake to Jean-Aubry, and, dear friend, believe in the sincere affection of yours truly,

Maurice Ravel

1. In another letter to Madame Alvar, dated October 14, 1927, Ravel noted that he would be coming to London toward the end of the month in order to record for Brunswick. These recordings, however, were apparently never issued (unpublished autograph in the Charles Alvar Harding Collection, on deposit at the Pierpont Morgan Library).

2. Some of Ravel's earliest works were introduced at Salle Pleyel, at 22 rue Rochechouart. On October 18, 1927, a new concert hall bearing the identical name was inaugurated at 252 rue du faubourg St. Honoré in the presence of Raymond Poincaré,

the president of France, and many other dignitaries. For this gala event, Philippe Gaubert conducted the Orchestre du Conservatoire, sharing the podium with Ravel, who conducted *La Valse*, and Stravinsky, who led the orchestra in the *Firebird* suite. The new hall held about 3000 people.

3. Madame Alvar was vacationing in France.

283. to Bernard R. Laberge[1]

Le Belvédère   November 11, 1927
Montfort l'Amaury (S. & O.)
Dear Mr. Laberge,

In order to answer you, I was waiting for the letter mentioned in your first cable, and then the second one. As you have learned from my "Weekend Letter," I will embark on December 28.

Here are the details about the artists under consideration:

I) Madame Esther Dale[2] told me in London, where I met her recently, that she is highly regarded in the United States. She has performed *Shéhérazade* with orchestra in New York and Boston, and is making a special trip to Paris the day after tomorrow in order to sing it for me. I have informed her that she must write to you directly.

II) A letter from M. de Valmalète[3] arrived just after my departure from Saint-Jean-de-Luz. Through an oversight it was not forwarded, and therefore I became aware of it only recently. He proposed that I perform a recital in New York with Nina Koshetz.[4] I telephoned immediately to Valmalète and gave him your address.

III) The same reply to Gaston Elcus, who would like to organize a chamber music series in Boston. He is the only one of these three artists that I know, and about whom I can give an opinion: an excellent musician, he is in Koussevitzky's orchestra, and together with several French colleagues in the orchestra, he has formed the following group: Elcus, 1st violin; Mayer, 2nd violin; Lefranc, viola; Zighera, cello; Motte-Lacroix, piano.

Here is the definitive list of works to be programmed.

Orchestra

Introduction et Allegro, for harp and 6 instruments.
Pavane pour une Infante défunte.
Le Tombeau de Couperin.
Ma Mère l'Oye.
"Prélude" and "Danse du rouet." (I'm quite sure that we didn't speak about this piece when making up the programs. It can be played separately or placed at the beginning of *Ma Mère l'Oye*, of which it is the Introduction.)

Symphony in G Minor (Mozart).[5]
"Sarabande" and *Danse* (Debussy, orchestrated by M. R.)
Rapsodie espagnole.
Daphnis et Chloé.
"Alborada del gracioso."
Valses nobles et sentimentales.
La Valse.

Be sure to let me know which orchestral material I will be responsible for.
I will prepare a brief talk for the concert in Cleveland.[6]

Don't forget about the <u>very important</u> matter of the tobacco;[7] after making inquiries, let me know if I would be certain to find it throughout the United States, or, as Robert Schmitz has assured me, if it can be sent to me from France.

Also, keep in mind the advance of 1000 dollars.

In your next letter, please include a complete itinerary, so I will be able to have my mail forwarded.

With best wishes,

Maurice Ravel

In rereading my letter, I noticed that I had forgotten to include the list of piano pieces which I will perform. Here it is:

Menuet antique.
"Habanera."
Pavane pour une Infante défunte.
"Oiseaux tristes" [*Miroirs*].
Sonatine (3 movements).
Le Tombeau de Couperin (Prélude, Forlane, Menuet, Rigaudon).
"La Vallée des cloches" [*Miroirs*].
Prélude.[8]

ПR[9]

1. The Bogue-Laberge concert management in New York, and France's Association Française d'Expansion et d'Echanges Artistiques handled all the technical matters of Ravel's North American tour.

2. The American soprano. She later performed with Ravel during his North American tour.

3. Marcel de Valmalète, the Parisian impresario.

4. The Russian mezzo-soprano (see p. 568).

5. Mozart's Fortieth Symphony; see p. 440, note 4.

6. See p. 49, note 3.

7. Ravel was a heavy smoker of Caporal cigarettes.

8. A short, lyrical piano piece composed in 1913 for the women's sight-reading competition at the Conservatoire.

9. The autograph of this letter has not been traced. A typewritten copy of it is in the private collection of Mrs. Monique Leduc.

284. Paul Paray[1] to Maurice Ravel

Concerts Lamoureux   November 16, 1927
2 rue Moncey
Paris
Dear Sir and friend,

I received Monsieur Theodor Szántó and acknowledged the letter which you had asked him to deliver. I read it to my committee, which, as you can well imagine, would be eager, as I would, to oblige you. Unfortunately, it is impossible for me to program one of Monsieur Szántó's works at the time he desires, that is to say before Christmas. If things can work out more agreeably at a later date, I would be happy to give you satisfaction.[2]

Dear Sir and friend, believe me very truly yours,
Paul Paray

1. The French conductor and composer Paul Paray (1886–1979) studied at the Conservatoire and won the Prix de Rome in 1911. He later conducted the Lamoureux Orchestra, the Monte Carlo Orchestra, and was the principal conductor of the Colonne Orchestra and the Detroit Symphony.

2. In a letter to Theodor Szántó, written from Le Belvédère on December 13, 1927 (autograph in the Library of Congress), Ravel enclosed a copy of this letter, adding the following explanation:

Dear friend,

I thought I had communicated this letter to you a long time ago. Excuse me: I'm rather out of sorts and must follow an energetic treatment—injections of cyto-serum, pituitary and adrenal extracts, etc. [all of these drugs are stimulants]—so that I can embark at the end of the month.

Affectionate regards to you both,
Maurice Ravel

285. to Henry Prunières

Le Belvédère   December 6, 1927
Montfort l'Amaury (S. & O.)
Dear friend,

Please excuse me: I will not be able to accept your kind invitation, or attend the Schoenberg concert,[1] or so many other gatherings at which I would have been happy to see my friends before departing. I am in a state of extreme fatigue (blood pressure: 110/50), and under doctor's orders, I must abandon my prescribed diet, overeat and rest in order to be in condition to embark on the 28th.

Please convey my apologies to Madame Prunières, and kindest regards to you both,

Maurice Ravel

1. See letter no. 165, note 2.

286. to Cipa and Ida Godebski

Le Belvédère   December 14, 1927
Tel.: 89. Montfort l'Amaury (S. & O.)
Dear old friends,

I hope you won't let me depart from the old world without saying good-bye. I am inviting you, Friday evening at 8 o'clock.

I had requested jackets, but as everyone insisted on tuxedos, we'll have to dress up.

Affectionate regards,
Maurice Ravel

287. Darius Milhaud to Maurice Ravel

10 Boulevard de Clichy   [late December 1927]
[Paris]
My dear friend,

I sincerely regretted not being able to attend the *Chantecler*[1] banquet in your honor, but in addition to the première of *Le Pauvre Matelot*,[2] I had to be at Madame Janacopulos' recital, in which I accompanied my Hebraic songs at the beginning of the program.[3]

I trust that your health is improving. I have such great confidence in homeopathy that I would like to see all of my friends adopt it!

I sincerely hope that your concert tour in America won't fatigue you too much, and I wish you bon voyage and a happy new year, because 1928 is approaching!

Very cordially yours,
Milhaud

1. A Parisian weekly devoted to the arts.

2. Milhaud's opera, based on the libretto by Jean Cocteau, was introduced at the Opéra-Comique on December 16, 1927.

3. The remainder of Madame Vera Janacopulos' recital at Salle Gaveau on December 16 consisted of songs by Honegger and Stravinsky. Milhaud's six *Chants populaires hébraïques* were published by Heugel in 1925.

288. to Nelly and Maurice Delage

aboard the "France"   December 31, 1927

Happy new year, dear old friends, We are supping joyously in a dance hall which is hardly level: jazz, paper streamers, balloons, champagne, a Russian quartet, drunk Americans—all the local color of Montmartre.

January 3, 1928

We are supposed to drop anchor tonight and disembark tomorrow. The crossing has been very pleasant until now.

A photo of my studio is on the other side. I have an entire "de luxe suite" to work in . . . and I'm hardly abusing it.

Affectionate regards,

Maurice Ravel

289. to Roland-Manuel

aboard the "France"   January 3, 1928

Dear friend,

We arrive in New York tomorrow. I'm quite sure there has never been a more pleasant crossing at this time of year. Write to me—and don't forget the lecture[1]—at the following address: c/o Bogue-Laberge, 130 West 42nd St., Suite 1201, New York.

Affectionate regards to all,

Maurice Ravel

1. "Contemporary Music"; see part 1.

290. to Edouard Ravel

The Copley-Plaza   January 13, 1928

Boston, Massachusetts

My dear little Edouard,

If I return to Europe alive, it will prove that I am long-lived! In short, until now, I've survived, and my manager assures me that I have gone through the worst. As soon as we arrived in the harbor, a swarm of journalists invaded the boat, with cameras, movie cameras, and cartoonists. I had to leave them for a moment in order to see our entry into the port: it was even a bit too late, but splendid all the same.

I wasn't even able to practice the piano a little during my stay in New York (4 days which seemed like 4 months). As soon as I settled down at the Langdon Hotel, a little nothing of a hotel which has only 12 stories (I was on the 8th), and delightfully comfortable (an entire apartment), the telephone didn't stop ringing. Every minute they would bring me baskets of flowers, and of the most delicious fruits in the world. Rehearsals, teams of journalists (photographs, movies, caricaturists) relieving one another every hour, letters, invitations to which my manager replies for me, receptions. In the evening, relaxation: dance halls, Negro theaters, gigantic movie houses, etc. I hardly know New York by day, cooped up in taxis in order to go to appointments of all sorts. I was even in a film, with make-up 2 centimeters thick. . . .[1] I was forgetting the concert which the Boston Symphony played in New York, devoted to my works. I had to appear on stage: a standing audience of 3500; a tremendous ovation, climaxed by whistling. Sunday evening, a private concert and a gallop in evening dress for the train to Boston.

January 14, 1928

I continue: I have been relatively undisturbed here during the day between orchestral rehearsals (a marvelous orchestra). The day before yesterday a concert at Cambridge, yesterday at Boston: a triumph (they thought I looked English!) Koussevitzky told me that I was the greatest living French conductor. . . . When I think that I had to conduct the *Rapsodie espagnole* at sight! I'm doing it again tonight, returning immediately to New York for tomorrow's concert,[2] setting out again for Chicago where I will remain a few days, and from there on to Texas. Several free moments have enabled me to write to you: today, no receptions.[3] Those at Cambridge and Boston were less exhausting than the one given by Mrs. Thomas Edison[4] in New York: 2 or 3 hundred persons filing before me speaking English, and more often French (it's amazing how many people speak our language here).

As in New York, in the evening, relaxation: dance halls, Chinese theater, etc. Attached are several clippings. Keep them. Affectionate regards to all.

I embrace you,

Maurice[5]

1. This film has not been recovered. On the other hand, Alexander Steinert took some extraordinary home movies which have been preserved. These silent films include footage of the Godebski family, Arthur Rubinstein, Vladimir Horowitz, and Ravel at Le Belvédère. (Copies of these films are in the private collection of the author.)

2. This recital was devoted to chamber music. The program included the String Quartet, the Sonatine, the *Introduction et Allegro*, and the Sonata for Violin and Piano.

The Sonata was performed by Joseph Szigeti, who made the following perceptive observation:

> Ravel was somewhat nonchalant about his piano-playing; "unconcerned" might better describe his attitude. It was the confidence of the creative artist that determined his stand with respect to our task. It was as if he said: "What of it, whether we play it a little better, or in a less polished and brilliant fashion? The work is set down, in its definitive form, and that is all that *really* matters." (Szigeti, *With Strings Attached*, 2d ed., New York, Knopf, 1967, p. 139.)

3. Following the January 15 recital in New York, a reception was held in Ravel's honor at an exclusive Madison Avenue apartment. Among the guests were Mr. and Mrs. Fritz Kreisler, Mr. and Mrs. Edgard Varèse, Béla Bartók, and George Gershwin. At Ravel's request, Negro artists presented a program of interpretive dancing and Negro spirituals (see the unsigned article, "M. Ravel Honored at Large Reception," in the *New York Times*, January 16, 1928).

4. The wife of the famous inventor.

5. The autograph of this letter is reproduced in Orenstein, "Some Unpublished Music and Letters by Maurice Ravel," pp. 333–34.

291. to Edouard Ravel

from New York to Chicago   January 16, 1928

My dear little Edouard, I'm writing this in the club car of the express train to Chicago. Left New York at 2:45 P.M. and I arrive tomorrow at 9:45 A.M.—just less than 20 hours. The concert in New York went well. Flattering reviews, at times an entire page.[1] Only the French newspaper in New York didn't write about me.

Affectionate regards to all,

Maurice

It was like spring in New York, as in Boston. Now there is snow along the way.

1. Writing in the *New York Times* on January 16, the noted critic Olin Downes commented:

> Nothing could have been more typical of the precision, economy and refinement of this music than the slight, aristocratic, gray-haired and self-contained gentleman who bore himself with such simplicity on the platform; presenting his music with a characteristic reticence and modesty; well content, as it were, to give an accounting of what he had done, and to leave his listeners to their own conclusions. And, indeed, his achievement speaks for itself.
>
> Never to have composed in undue haste; never to have offered the public a piece of unfinished work; to have experienced life as an observant and keenly interested beholder, and to have fashioned certain of its elements into exquisite shapes of art

that embody the essence of certain French traditions, is a goal worth the gaining. Mr. Ravel has pursued his way as an artist quietly and very well. He has disdained superficial or meretricious success. He has been his own most unsparing critic. The audience was appreciative of the opportunity to welcome the man and the composer.

292. to René Polain?[1]

San Francisco Overland Limited   January 30, 1928
Chicago & North Western Ry.
Union Pacific System
Southern Pacific Lines
My dear friend,

Since arriving in the United States, this is the first opportunity I have had to write. I hasten to take advantage of it in order to ask you to be my spokesman to your colleagues, to tell them of my joy in hearing my works performed with such perfection by an orchestra which is rightly considered to be the world's finest, and whose conscientiousness in capturing the spirit of my music touched me profoundly.

This beautiful performance, to a large extent, was responsible for the public's unforgettable reception both in Boston and Cambridge; I apologize to all of you for being unable to express my deep gratitude sooner.

Maurice Ravel

1. This letter and the following one may have been written to René Polain, a member of the first violin section of the Boston Symphony, who had acted as an interpreter for Ravel. The second letter, which seems to be an extended afterthought, begins with a note of personal thanks, which Ravel had omitted in the first letter.

293. to René Polain?[1]

San Francisco Overland Limited   January 30, 1928
Chicago & North Western Ry.
Union Pacific System
Southern Pacific Lines

And I personally wish to thank the kind Mentor, fortunately less severe than the original one,[2] who helped me so much to appreciate the charm of Boston.

Everything went well in Chicago and Cleveland; here, the orchestra's task was particularly difficult: the program was completely unknown to most of the musicians.

I raced through *La Valse* in 4th gear. The *Valses nobles* [*et sentimentales*] sounded perfect, and you know that it is one of my most difficult works to interpret. In this regard, I'm writing directly to Koussevitzky to thank him for his kindness, which saved the day. I trust that his orchestral material was returned promptly.

See you soon in France, perhaps, I hope, once again in America.

Don't forget to telephone Paris first: Gutenberg 0-28, before requesting number 89 in Montfort.[3]

My dear friend, believe me very cordially yours,

Maurice Ravel

1. See the preceding letter.

2. In Greek legend, Mentor was the friend of Odysseus. The name passed into common usage after being popularized in Fénelon's *Les Aventures de Télémaque* (1699), in which Mentor is portrayed as the wise counselor of Odysseus' son Telemachus.

3. The telephone numbers, respectively, of the Hôtel d'Athènes and Le Belvédère.

294. to Edouard Ravel

Los Angeles Biltmore   February 7, 1928
Los Angeles

this hole represents my room[1]

My dear little Edouard, now it's like summer: 95 degrees. A brilliant sun; a large city in full bloom, with flowers which grow in greenhouses in France, and tall palm trees which grow here naturally. . . . Took an excursion to Hollywood, the film capital. Various stars: Douglas Fairbanks, who fortunately speaks French.* The trip from San Francisco to Los Angeles was very pleasant, and I spent it almost entirely on the rear platform: eucalyptus forests, tall trees which might be taken for oaks, but which are in fact hollies; variegated mountains, which are rocky or magnificently green. It's annoying to think that I'll soon be back in the cold weather. A pile of letters awaited me here: everyone wrote except you. Tomorrow night, a concert.[2] In the afternoon, I'm going to visit the lion factory for the movies.[3]

Affectionate regards to all.   I embrace you   Maurice

*I was supposed to have lunch with Charlie Chaplin, but I didn't think it would be any more amusing for him than for me: he doesn't know a word of French.

1. The face of this postcard shows the Los Angeles Biltmore Hotel. Ravel must have enjoyed pointing out that his room was close to the top of this imposing skyscraper.

2. On February 8, 1928, the Los Angeles chapter of Pro-Musica presented an all-Ravel program in the Biltmore Hotel Ballroom. The program was as follows:

1) Sonata for Violin and Piano, performed by Calmon Luboviski and the composer (following prolonged applause, the "Blues" movement was repeated).

2) *Shéhérazade* (complete), sung by the young American soprano Lisa Roma, accompanied by Ravel.

3) Sonatine, performed by the composer.

4) *Histoires naturelles* (complete), Lisa Roma and Ravel.

5) *Pavane pour une Infante défunte*, "Habanera," performed by the composer.

6) *Introduction et Allegro*, conducted by Ravel, with Alfred Kastner (harp), the Luboviski Quartet, Jay Plowe (flute), and Pierre Perrier (clarinet).

3. A humorous reference to the Metro-Goldwyn-Mayer studios, Hollywood's "Home of the Stars," whose trademark was a roaring lion.

295. to Hélène Jourdan-Morhange

Southern Pacific Lines   February 10, 1928
Dear friend,

Thanks to Mme Schmitz, I received your letter in Los Angeles—95 to 104 degrees, palm trees, and hothouse plants lining the avenues. You still hadn't received my letter—or letters, I no longer remember; but how is it that you didn't have my address? Edouard promised me to give it to you.

Another night on the train (that makes two; from Chicago to San Francisco there were 3), and I will arrive in Seattle, then Portland, Vancouver, Minneapolis, and back for the 3rd time to New York, where I'm really afraid of finding cold weather.

I am seeing magnificent cities and enchanting regions, but the triumphs are exhausting. In Los Angeles, I slipped away from the people; besides, I was dying of hunger.

Do write again.

Affectionate regards,

Maurice Ravel

I hope that my brother is still alive: till now, I have received only one cable from him.

296. to Edouard Ravel

Union Pacific System   February 21, 1928
The Overland Route
from Denver to Minneapolis

Left Denver last evening. Had a good night: slept 9 hours. We arrive in Omaha soon (at 3 o'clock) in order to change trains. Will leave tonight about 10 o'clock, after having heard Omaha's jazz, which is famous. I spent 3 days in Denver, a city situated at an altitude of 1600 meters[1] (gold and silver mines). The air is very pure. Always bright sunshine. It looks like it's becoming overcast. I'm afraid of finding cold weather in New York next week.

Affectionate regards to all.

I embrace you,

Maurice

1. About 5,250 feet.

297. to Nadia Boulanger[1]

The Biltmore   March 8, 1928

New York

Dear friend,

There is a musician here endowed with the most brilliant, most enchanting, and perhaps the most profound talent: George Gershwin.[2]

His world-wide success no longer satisfies him, for he is aiming higher. He knows that he lacks the technical means to achieve his goal. In teaching him those means, one might ruin his talent.

Would you have the courage, which I wouldn't dare have, to undertake this awesome responsibility?[3]

I expect to return home in early May, and will come to see you in order to discuss this matter.

In the meantime, I send you my most cordial regards.

Maurice Ravel

1. Mlle Boulanger (1887–1979) received her training at the Conservatoire (1897–1904), where she met Ravel. She went on to enjoy a distinguished career as a teacher of composition, and as a lecturer and conductor. A list of her pupils would include many of the leading American and European composers of the twentieth century: Sir Lennox Berkeley, Elliott Carter, Aaron Copland, David Diamond, Jean Françaix, and Walter Piston, to name but a few.

2. Ravel and Gershwin (1898–1937) met on several occasions in New York in 1928. In a conversation with this writer, Alexandre Tansman recalled acting as their interpreter when they spent some evenings together listening to jazz in Harlem. On March 7, 1928, the mezzo-soprano Eva Gautier (1885–1958) gave a dinner party in New York in honor of Ravel's 53rd birthday. She recalled the evening as follows:

> The menu consisted of all the things he liked to eat, and especially plenty of red meat, which he loved—he really preferred it raw to the point of being purple—as his complaint was that all meats here were overcooked. The late George Gershwin was one of the honored guests, since Ravel had expressed a great desire to meet

him and hear him play the "Rhapsody in Blue," "The Man I Love," etc. It was a memorable evening. George that night surpassed himself, achieving astounding feats in rhythmic intricacies, so that even Ravel was dumfounded. George was very keen to study with Ravel, but the Frenchman's answer was that "you might lose that great melodic spontaneity and write bad Ravel." ("Reminiscences of Maurice Ravel," *New York Times,* January 16, 1938.)

3. Gershwin would continue his studies with the American composers Henry Cowell and Wallingford Riegger, and also with the theorist and composer Joseph Schillinger.

298. to Madame Fernand Dreyfus

Crescent Limited	Pennsylvania Railroad	April 4, 1928
New York. New Orleans	Southern Railway	
	West Point Route	
	Louisville & Nashville R.R.	

<u>En Route</u> (sic)

My dear marraine,

Your letter reached me in New York, where I spent 3 days once again. On Monday, I was in Boston, where I slept in a stable bed. Returned to New York for 5 hours. Now it's time for the little concluding leg: New Orleans, where I will arrive tomorrow morning, merely to cast a tender glance at this old French colony, and taste the "Pompano en papillotes,"[1] washed down with French wines (why yes . . . if you knew what prohibition is!). I leave there at night for Houston: 2 concerts,[2] and an automobile trip to the Gulf of Mexico. Thus, 3 nights on the train. From there, on to the Grand Canyon: 2 days of rest; no concerts (from Houston to the Grand Canyon, 2 nights). Then I leave Arizona and go directly to Buffalo and New York (4 nights this time). New York, Montreal, and back to New York for embarkation on the "Paris" which leaves at midnight (I arrive at 10:30 P.M.) on the 21st.

And I won't be dead tired: as you know, I have never felt better than during this crazy tour. I have finally discovered the reason: it's because I have never led such a rational existence.

You forgot to tell me about your health. Don't bother to do so now: your letter would arrive after my departure. I'll check up on you in person.

The weather was very lovely in New York and Boston; but upon awakening this morning, I found myself in the midst of spring (up north, the flowers bloom later) and in the heat of midsummer. In my compartment, I could only survive in my shirtsleeves, with all of the ventilators open and the fan in high position. It was hardly any cooler on the rear terrace. What will happen in Texas?

It's almost 11:00 P.M., and the club car is beginning to empty out. I'm going back to my compartment, at the other end of the train.

See you soon, and kind regards from your
Maurice Ravel

1. That is, a fish cooked and served in a wrapping of buttered parchment paper or aluminum foil (cooking fish in paper bags appears to have originated in New Orleans in the early 1900s).

2. See *Ravel: Man and Musician,* plates 13 and 14.

299. to Cipa Godebski

The California Limited   April 14, 1928
Santa Fe

From the Grand Canyon to Buffalo

10 days of excursions, with 6 nights spent in the train—it was worth it. Wisely obeying the text below, I will not attempt to describe the Grand Canyon:[1] you have to see it. Only 7 more days and I'm off (unless the train from Montreal is blocked by snow for an hour and a half).

See you soon, old chap.
Affectionate regards to all,
Maurice Ravel

1. The text of this picture postcard of the Grand Canyon reads: "The finest effects at the Grand Canyon are altogether uncommunicable by brush or pen. . . . Here even silence seems to have dimension and color."

300. to Madame Isaac Albéniz

9 rue Tourasse   June 27, 1928
St.-Jean-de-Luz
(Lower Pyrenees)
Dear Madame,

Ida Rubinstein has asked me to orchestrate 6 pieces from *Iberia:*[1] "El Puerto," "Fête-Dieu à Séville," "Rondeña," "Triana," "El Albaicin," and "El Polo."

However, I have just learned that most of these pieces have already been orchestrated by Arbós,[2] and I have every reason to believe that you would refuse the authorization I must seek, which I would find legitimate.[3]

Nevertheless, I would be grateful for a reply as soon as possible, whether favorable or not, as these pieces have been selected to be danced at the Opéra at the beginning of next season.

With kind regards, dear Madame, believe me very truly yours,
Maurice Ravel

1. Isaac Albéniz (1860–1909) worked on the twelve piano pieces comprising his suite *Iberia* from 1906 until shortly before his death. A virtuoso pianist, he concertized widely and is largely remembered for his brilliant keyboard works. After studying composition in Spain with Felipe Pedrell, he moved to Paris in 1893, where he met Ravel and was influenced by Vincent d'Indy and Paul Dukas.

2. The Spanish violinist, conductor, and composer Enrique Arbós (1863–1939) was a close friend of Albéniz.

3. Copyright law forbade anyone else from transcribing the pieces that Arbós had orchestrated. Upon learning about Ravel's predicament, he graciously offered to renounce his exclusive copyright. But now Ravel changed his mind and decided to orchestrate one of his own compositions. Finally, he composed an original work for Mme Rubinstein, initially entitled "Fandango." The title was later changed to *Boléro.*

301. to Robert Casadesus

Le Belvédère   August 10, 1928
Montfort l'Amaury (S. & O.)
My dear friend,

I could just as well have replied sooner: the beginning of this season, which is so complicated for me, is still far from being settled. The only thing I'm sure of is that at the end of November I will be in Spain,[1] and simultaneously at the Opéra, where Ida Rubinstein will present *La Valse* and "Fandango," a new work which perhaps will be finished.[2] Note that in the 2nd half of October, I have to go to Oxford in order to receive the title of "Doctor of Music honoris causa,"[3] and that the management of Bordeaux's Grand Théâtre is honoring the 3 vice-presidents of the S.M.I.[4] with one of its afternoon chamber music recitals in December.[5]

Can you figure this out better than I can?
Very cordially yours,
Maurice Ravel

I was forgetting certain concerts in Holland, whose dates have not yet been determined.

1. Setting out on November 6, Ravel concertized in Spain with Madeleine Grey and violinist Claude Lévy, appearing in nine cities in just over two weeks.

2. The new work, *Boléro,* was introduced at the Paris Opéra by Mme Rubinstein's troupe on November 22, 1928, with Walther Straram conducting, décor and costumes

by Alexandre Benois, and choreography by Bronislava Nijinska. In addition to *La Valse*, the program also included music of Bach transcribed by Honegger, and works by Schubert and Liszt orchestrated by Milhaud.

3. On October 23, 1928, Ravel appeared in academic garb at Oxford University, which conferred upon him the degree of Doctor of Music. Speaking in Latin, the public orator compared his achievements to "colors worthy of Parrhasius," and referred to the composer of *Daphnis et Chloé* as a "charming artist, who persuades all cultured people that Pan is not dead, and that even now Mount Helicon is green." Following the ceremony, the guest of honor conducted the *Introduction et Allegro* before a large outdoor gathering, as part of an all-Ravel program given in front of the Town Hall.

4. The two other vice-presidents were Léo Sachs and Florent Schmitt.

5. The chamber music recital in Bordeaux was organized by pianist Paul Loyonnet, who performed *Gaspard de la nuit*, and, with the Calvet Quartet, Florent Schmitt's Quintet (opus 51). The vocal works included five songs by Léo Sachs and the *Chansons madécasses*, with Madeleine Grey, M. Bergeon (flute), Paul Mas (cello), and Ravel at the piano.

302. Jacques Durand to Maurice Ravel

A. Durand & Son, Publishers   August 13, 1928
Durand & Company
4 Place de la Madeleine
Paris (VIII)
My dear Maurice,

I won't hide the fact that your letter gave me great pleasure—I was a bit sad to see you tied down with "recomposing" the music of Albéniz!

You wrote that you are occupied with a "Fandango" of your own—I applaud it in advance, while blessing Arbós! But, you will have to work at top speed, because we must have your work (<u>piano</u> and <u>orchestral score</u>) by October 15 <u>at the very latest</u>, and some excerpts before then, if you can.

I received your letter upon arriving at the office this morning, and one hour later, the secretary of Mme Ida Rubinstein was shown in.

We had a long chat, and I presented your terms. She seemed a bit upset, but she will transmit them to Mme Rubinstein, who is in Palermo.

For *La Valse*, which advantageously is already well known, I realized that you would like to see it presented in accordance with your ideas, and therefore made the terms ultrasweet for Mme Rubinstein.

For "Fandango," it's different: there is a restriction for 3 years in the theater, and 1 year in the concert hall—which is considerable. I therefore requested a forfeit of <u>twenty-five thousand francs</u>, from which you will receive your share for performances abroad.

The secretary complained loudly, pointing to the case of Honegger and of . . . Stravinsky! Both had received only a fixed sum of 3000 francs, plus royalties from eventual performances.

Knowing the whims of this celebrated artist as I do, it will be better to be patient, rather than hasty. I assume that she is going to give you a bonus.

So now, let's await future developments, and, above all, your manuscript.

Very fond regards, my dear Maurice, from your old friend,

J. Durand

303. to Roland-Manuel

Le Belvédère   October 4, 1928
Montfort l'Amaury (S. & O.)

This, dear friend, is what I wish to speak to you about on the telephone Friday, at lunchtime.

I would be pleased if you could accompany me to the Aeolian Company, where I have made an appointment for Saturday at 2:30 P.M., after which I will return to complete a "Boléro," using the same material that you assured me Prokofiev employed in *Le Pas d'acier.*[1]

Affectionate regards,

Maurice Ravel

Whether M. Dubois[2] likes it or not, the <u>interview</u> format will have to be adopted.

1. Prokofiev's ballet, *The Steel Leap,* completed in 1925, was introduced in Paris by the Ballet Russe on June 7, 1927. Roland-Manuel was apparently referring to the throbbing, ostinato rhythm found in the part entitled "Fabrika" (The Factory).

2. See p. 29.

304. to Marcelle Gerar

Le Belvédère   October 29, 1928
Montfort l'Amaury (S. & O.)

Dear friend,

Occupied with reexamining the *Boléro* until Saturday night, I returned Sunday and immediately sat down at the piano in order to try to recapture my American virtuosity. Thus, if you want to have the composer's approbation, you will have to postpone your recording until my return—from November 28 on.[1]

It's all right for the ahs! in the <u>Fire's aria</u>.[2] You won't be the first. But don't add (spoken): "and you understand me perfectly well . . .". For the <u>coda</u>, look at the aria published separately, which you will be given at Durand's shop upon going there on my behalf.

Why no, the trill isn't on *a* and *b*: means , trill with the

lower neighbor. Didn't you know that?

Till the end of the month. In the meantime, I will light a candle for you at Notre Dame del Pilar,[3] will climb the steps of Saint Jacques of Compostela on my knees, and will drink a glass of port[4] to your health in its country of origin.

Affectionate regards,

Maurice Ravel

1. See p. 563.

2. In *L'Enfant et les sortilèges.* Mme Gerar wanted to take some quick breaths in the long phrases at the end of the aria (Durand piano vocal score, pp. 28–29). Her second question, about the trill, relates to the same passage.

3. In Zaragoza, Spain. The cathedral is named for the Virgin of the Pillar, the patron of Spain.

4. This wine originated in Oporto (Portugal), hence its name. Ravel's November 1928 tour in Spain originally included several cities in Portugal, but this part of the trip was later canceled.

305. to Roger Haour

Le Belvédère   December 4, 1928
Montfort l'Amaury (S. & O.)
Dear Chicky,[1]

Upon returning from Spain, I found your chicken scratch.[2] I brought back a whopping cold from there, caught under the coconut palms of Malaga.

It is true, as Pierrette says, that I am the biggest idiot around, but, since I finished the *Boléro,* on October 15 precisely, I haven't stopped running around, exchanging a toga for a cape,[3] and a pull-over for a tuxedo, this in a sleeping car, in order to arrive just in time for the final performance of my ballet[4]—an excellent performance, but picturesque, which wasn't appropriate.

I can only see December 31 for us to get together—between two hangovers. Come to the Hôtel d'Athènes (21 rue d'Athènes) about noon. We'll have a cocktail to wake up and gorge ourselves afterwards. O.K.? If you wish to reply, write to me here; your letter will be forwarded: I'm leaving the day after tomorrow for Geneva (jury of the I.S.C.M.).[5] From there, I will go to Saint-Jean-de-Luz to relax for 5 or 6 days.

Affectionate pecks and hugs[6] to both of you.

Maurice Ravel

1. Literally, "Dear Fowl." This unusual letter contains puns, slang, some translation-defying vulgarity, and bubbling good spirits.

2. In the French, "poulet," literally a chicken, colloquially a letter.

3. A playful description of going from academic garb (Oxford) to the land of the bullfight (Spain; Ravel uses the Spanish word "capa"—"a cape").

4. *Boléro*, as interpreted by Ida Rubinstein's troupe.

5. See letter no. 214, note 1.

6. Literally, "pops on the kisser."

306. Béla Bartók to Maurice Ravel

Rome   March 15, 1929

Dear Monsieur Ravel,

Allow me to present Mr. Zoltán Székely,[1] a young violinist who is absolutely first-rate. He plays all of your works for the violin, and would like to play them for you and have your advice with regard to their interpretation. Very cordially yours,

Béla Bartók

1. The noted Hungarian violinist (b. 1903) frequently performed Bartók's music with the composer at the piano.

307. to Marcelle Gerar

Le Belvédère   May 13, 1929

Montfort l'Amaury (S. & O.)

Dear friend,

Did Leyritz deliver your message? In such a moving way that I shed tears! But here's the situation: I had to remain in Paris the entire week without even taking time off to sleep—I caught up last night: 11 hours straight—.

And it's starting again this week: on Wednesday, the dress rehearsal of works by Ibert and Roland-Manuel.[1] Thursday, I conduct the *Boléro*.[2] Would you like to come? It may be the only way for us to meet.

I have 10 tickets: don't publicize it! You need only pass by rue d'Athènes and take two of them, one for you and the other for Leyritz.

Or else, drop me a note at the Hotel d'Athènes: I will arrive there Wednesday morning.

Affectionate regards,

Maurice Ravel

1. The works performed at the Opéra on May 15 were *Persée et Andromède*, an opera in two acts by Jacques Ibert, libretto by M. Nino, based on the "Moralités légendaires" by Jules Laforgue, and Roland-Manuel's ballet *L'Ecran des jeunes filles*, based on a scenario

by Jacques Drésa. (M. Nino was the pen name of Michel Veber, who was Jacques Ibert's brother-in-law.)

2. Ravel conducted the Straram Orchestra (see p. 588).

308. to Serge Koussevitzky

MONTFORT L'AMAURY   JULY 2, 1929

I WAS HOPING TO BE ABLE TO COME HONOR THE FRIEND & THANK THE GREAT ARTIST TO WHOM MODERN MUSIC OWES SO MUCH. IMPOSSIBLE. URGENT WORK. SEND YOU PROFOUND REGRETS & GREAT AFFECTION.

RAVEL[1]

1. This telegram was sent to the Restaurant Laurent in Paris, where a gala soirée marked the conclusion of Koussevitzky's European engagements and his departure for the United States. Ravel's "urgent work" was chiefly the piano concerto for the left hand.

309. to Marie Gaudin

Le Belvédère   August 19, 1929
Tel.: 89. Montfort l'Amaury (S. & O.)
Dear Marie,

This time, I do believe that it's you who owe me a letter. . . . It is true that I didn't send you greetings for your Saint's day,[1] and while I'm thinking of it, I recall that I also forgot Mme Bonnet, whom I saw yesterday. But after all, considering my situation, one has to be indulgent: I am gestating a concerto (I'm at the vomiting stage).

You probably know that we will see each other soon: the posters by Foujita[2] must have announced the grand ΠR festival in Biarritz (at 200 francs a seat, it's fortunate that I can get in for nothing).[3] If my room and piano in Saint-Jean are available, I will move in on the 8th or 9th for a week, and—but I don't expect it—if they can leave me alone, I will stay much longer. Hurry over to Mme Galichet[4] and beg her on your knees to throw out the intruders, if there are any. This, of course, after you have distributed several "units" of thousands of kisses,[5] keeping at least one for yourself.

Maurice Ravel

1. The Feast of the Assumption, celebrated on August 15.
2. The French artist of Japanese origin Foujita Tsuguharu (1886–1968).
3. The festival took place on September 11, with assisting artists Marcelle Gerar, Robert Casadesus, and soprano Marcelle Denya.
4. A local resident who rented rooms.
5. Ravel uses the Basque "muchus," meaning "thousands of kisses."

310. to Michel D. Calvocoressi

9 rue Tourasse   October 3, 1929
Saint-Jean-de-Luz

Sorry, old chap: I have been here for almost a month and plan to stay here until the 15th, perhaps till the end of October. I came here to work on my concerto. But there were proofs to correct: the *Boléro* and *Pictures at an Exhibition*. Finally, that's finished.

Why yes, you must have read an obituary notice about Mme Cruppi some 3 years ago; her life was so sad till the very end.[1]

I was going to write to tell you of another misfortune, thinking that you were probably unaware of it. I learned about it the other day, and still don't know the details: our unfortunate friend, Casa-Miranda died rather suddenly in a sanatorium in Cambo, I believe, where he was supposed to undergo a rather benign operation. His wife was also ailing for a long time, and hadn't left San Sebastián;[2] struck by this terrible news, she died 2 days later.

The mail will be collected soon. Fortunately, I have no other bad news to communicate, and send my affectionate regards to you both.

Maurice Ravel

1. Ravel had dedicated the "Fugue" from *Le Tombeau de Couperin* to the memory of her son, Second Lieutenant Jean Cruppi.

2. Cambo-les-Bains and San Sebastián are a short distance apart, the former in southwestern France and the latter in northwestern Spain.

311. to Cipa Godebski

Le Belvédère   November 15, 1929
Tel.: 89. Montfort l'Amaury (S. & O.)
Old chap,

Franek[1] won't have a chance: Schmitt and other well-known composers are presenting their works—probably Schmitt's piece will be accepted—.[2]

It would be better if you were to tell Franek the unpleasant news. I wouldn't dare do it.

Will we perhaps see each other the day after tomorrow at the Opéra-Comique? (Watch out! 1:45 P.M.)[3] It will be the only opportunity: I am arriving tomorrow, but will leave my bag in the checkroom, and will arrive at the hotel just in time to go to sleep.

Affectionate regards to all,

Maurice Ravel

1. The nickname of Franz Godebski, an elder brother of Cipa and Misia. A composer and violinist, he was for many years the director of the Conservatory in Perpignan.

2. For an S.M.I. recital.

3. The work performed was Chabrier's *Le Roi malgré lui*. Ravel's reaction to the opera is found in the next letter.

312. to Madame Bretton Chabrier[1]

Le Belvédère   December 4, 1929
Montfort l'Amaury (S. & O.)
Dear Madame,

The other day, at the performance of *Le Roi malgré lui*, a work which I can play by heart from beginning to end, and which I was seeing for the 1st time, I noticed certain imperfections in its inspired orchestration, and during the performance, I could not help thinking of certain adjustments which would increase its effect tenfold.

You know of my great sympathy for the one musician who has influenced me above all others. I am therefore asking you for the authorization to attempt this enhancement, for there is certainly no question of seriously revising the orchestration, in which everything is indicated, if not always perfectly realized.

Although extremely busy with important projects, I could temporarily examine one of the principal scenes: the waltz from act 2.

I would be only too happy if I could contribute to increasing the overly belated success of one of the most brilliant works in our lyric theater, and would make it a point to refuse any compensation from the publisher, or any royalties whatsoever.[2]

In the hope of receiving a favorable reply, dear Madame, please believe me very truly yours,

Maurice Ravel

1. The composer's daughter-in-law. (See plate 11.)

2. For whatever reason, this project was not carried out. Thus, Ravel's only direct homage to Chabrier was his orchestration of the *Menuet pompeux*, done for the Ballet Russe in 1919.

313. to Serge Koussevitzky

Le Belvédère   December 20, 1929
Tel.: 89. Montfort l'Amaury (S. & O.)

But, my dear friend, it is impossible for me to sign this contract![1] As soon as my concerto is finished, as I told you, I must take it around the world. The only thing I was able to promise is to reserve the 1st performance for you "in the world."[2] You will certainly concede that I cannot defer my tour for 2 or rather for 3 years and expect my publisher to agree to this delay.

Moreover, this concerto is far from being finished. As always, I'm working on several things at the same time: on another concerto, this one for the left hand, and, even, for several days, on a symphonic poem.[3] Perhaps this outsider will cross the finish line first. In that case, you could have a 1st performance as well as exclusive rights, but only for one season (there is always the matter of the publisher).

My dear friend, I send you my most cordial regards.

Maurice Ravel

1. The proposed contract between Ravel and the Trustees of the Boston Symphony Orchestra is in the Koussevitzky Collection in the Library of Congress. It reads:

The said Ravel hereby agrees to compose a concerto for symphony orchestra and piano, the score, solo piano part, and a complete set of orchestral parts in manuscript to ɹe delivered to the Boston Symphony Orchestra, Inc., at Symphony Hall, Boston, not later than September 20th, 1930, said manuscript to be the property at all times of the Boston Symphony Orchestra, Inc.

The said Ravel also agrees that the Boston Symphony Orchestra shall have the first world performance of said concerto, and further that the Boston Symphony Orchestra shall have the sole rights of performances in America of this work during its Fiftieth Anniversary season of 1930–1931 and without the payment of any performance fees or other charges. . . .

In consideration of the performance of the above by the said Ravel the said Trustees of the Boston Symphony Orchestra, Inc., agree to pay to the said Ravel or authorized representative Three Thousand ($3,000) Dollars, Fifteen Hundred ($1,500) Dollars of which are to be paid on the receipt of this contract duly signed by the said Ravel and the balance of Fifteen Hundred ($1,500) Dollars to be paid on the receipt of the complete score and parts of said concerto.

2. The autograph reads "in the Vorld."

3. Probably a reference to *Dédale 39* (Labyrinth 39), which did not go beyond the planning stage (see p. 469, note 4).

314. to Piero Coppola

Montfort   January 5, 1930

Dear friend,

I am conducting the Lamoureux Orchestra on Saturday and Sunday.[1] The rehearsals are Thursday and Saturday. I have to go to Paris on Wednesday . . . and I have just caught a cold which feels like the flu. I am confiding this letter to my brother, in order to ask you to excuse me tomorrow morning.

Would you like me to visit you Wednesday, in the late afternoon? I think that the record will still not be definitive.[2] Write to me or telephone Gutenberg

0-28, where I will arrive Wednesday. Your message will be forwarded. My apologies once again, and very cordially yours,

Maurice Ravel

1. On Saturday afternoon, January 11, Ravel shared the podium with Albert Wolff, who conducted works by Falla, Mozart, and Roussel. Ravel conducted the *Pavane pour une Infante défunte* and *Boléro.* In addition, Mme Lotte Schoene sang Lieder by Schubert and Schumann with piano accompaniment. The same artists performed a different program the following afternoon, with Ravel conducting "Alborada del gracioso" and *Boléro.*

2. Coppola conducted the very first recording of the *Boléro* in Ravel's presence, and the next day, Ravel recorded it with the Lamoureux Orchestra (see p. 540).

315. Jean Wiéner to Maurice Ravel

Le Manoir de la Juste Pie[1]   April 16, 1930
Orgeval (S. & O.)
Dear friend,

I am in the country for a few days with my wife and children, the car and my phonograph—no more sleeping cars for a few weeks, thus a bit of something resembling tranquility—and—taking your advice, I bought the Polydor records of *Boléro.* As ridiculous as it may seem, and as unnecessary, I am writing to you anyway, simply to tell you that I have been living with this *Boléro* since yesterday: it is a sort of marvel; in itself, it is wonderful, and that you wrote it is even more wonderful—in brief, I send you the most enthusiastic and the most profoundly cordial bravo which can be sent, and with it my very devoted friendship.

Jean Wiéner

Would you come here one day to have lunch with us, before the 27th, if I were to pick you up by car?? If so, write or telephone. Again, THANKS.

1. Wiéner called his country home "The Manor of the Truly Pious."

316. to Ida Godebska

Le Belvédère   May 8, 1930
Montfort l'Amaury
Dear Iduchu,[1]

And do you think that my presence isn't essential here? I was already beginning to curtail my sleep. If I was seen at the Opéra, it's because I knew that Toscanini was taking a ridiculous tempo in the *Boléro,* and wanted to tell him so, which disconcerted everyone, beginning with the great virtuoso himself.[2] I will also be seen at the Clemenceaus on Monday, because Painlevé[3] will come to take me from Versailles and will bring me back early. Although it is really impractical, I think that I'm going to take refuge in Saint-Jean-de-Luz.

Wittgenstein must have his concerto at the end of next month, and it's far from being finished![4]

I'm sure that Falla will not blame me. Should I doubt your indulgence?

Affectionate regards to all,

Maurice Ravel

1. A Polish diminutive which is used as a term of endearment.

2. In May and June 1930, the New York Philharmonic led by Arturo Toscanini (1867–1957) gave a series of highly acclaimed concerts in Europe. The tour began in Paris at the Opéra, and the program on May 4 included the *Boléro.* An uproar occurred when Ravel did not acknowledge Toscanini's gesture to his box, and in a heated discussion backstage, he told the Maestro that his tempo was ridiculously fast. Although the men eventually shook hands, the *Boléro* had now become a *cause célèbre* (see the letter to Toscanini, no. 318).

3. Ravel and Paul Painlevé (1863–1933), the noted French mathematician and statesman, were mutual friends of M. and Mme Paul Clemenceau.

4. The Austrian pianist Paul Wittgenstein (1887–1961) commissioned the concerto for the left hand.

317. to Charles Mapou[1]

Le Belvédère   July 24, 1930
Tel.: 89. Montfort l'Amaury (S. & O.)
Dear Sir and friend,

Thus, it's agreed for August 24. I will accompany my Sonata for Thibaud, the *Chansons madécasses* and other songs for Madeleine Grey, and if the program isn't too long, I will play *Ma Mère l'Oye* with Robert Casadesus.

I thank you sincerely for the kind offer of your hospitality, which, to my great regret, I cannot take advantage of: I do not wish to interrupt my work, and in order to accomplish this, it is more sensible to move into my flat[2] on rue Tourasse, where I will once again find my piano, my bathing suit, and my set ways.

Should you happen to meet my compatriot Dongaitz, please tell him that I am deeply touched by his gracious participation in the pelota match,[3] which, I hope, will take place during the last week in August—my only vacation of this season.

Once again, thank you for all the trouble you have taken to organize this festival, excuse me for only being able to assist you very little, and, dear Sir and friend, believe me cordially yours,

Maurice Ravel

I reopened my letter: yours just arrived.

But there was never any question of my accompanying Mademoiselle Lamballe![4] Moreover, I would be incapable of doing it.

Casadesus is supposed to return to Paris tomorrow: as soon as I have telephoned him and Madeleine Grey, I will send you a detailed program.

I will rehearse with Thibaud in Saint-Jean-de-Luz.

ℿℝ

1. Mapou organized a special Ravel festival which took place in Ciboure and Biarritz on August 24, 1930. The village of Ciboure paid homage to its eminent native son, as a commemorative plaque was placed on the composer's birth house, formerly at 12 rue du Quai, now on the newly inaugurated Quai Maurice Ravel. Following the ceremonies, a pelota match was played before the large outdoor gathering. The proceeds of the evening recital, held in Biarritz, were donated to charity (the program is essentially outlined in the opening paragraph of Ravel's letter). Following the recital at the Hôtel du Palais, the evening ended with a gala dinner dance.

2. In English in the autograph.

3. See letter no. 319, note 1.

4. Mlle Lucienne Lamballe, accompanied by Mlle Mordant, performed choreographic interpretations of "Alborada del gracioso" (from *Miroirs*, and well beyond Ravel's technical ability) and the "Rigaudon" from *Le Tombeau de Couperin*.

318. to Arturo Toscanini

Le Belvédère   September 9, 1930
Montfort l'Amaury (S. & O.)
My dear friend,

I have recently learned that there was a Toscanini-Ravel "affaire." You were probably unaware of it yourself, even though I have been assured that it was mentioned in the newspapers: it seems that I refused to stand during the applause at the Opéra in order to punish you for not having taken the proper tempo in the *Boléro*.

I have always felt that if a composer does not participate in the performance of his work, he should avoid the applause, which should be directed only to the performer or the work, or both.

Unfortunately, I was badly or rather too well situated for my abstention to remain unnoticed. However, not wishing my attitude to be misinterpreted, turning toward you, I feigned a gesture of applauding and thanking you.

But, isn't it so?—for "sensational" news, maliciousness is more useful than the truth.

I trust that such news will not have altered your confidence in the admiration and the profound friendship of your

Maurice Ravel[1]

1. Ravel's autograph is reproduced in Piero Weiss, ed., *Letters of Composers Through Six Centuries* (Philadelphia: Chilton, 1967), plates 9 and 10 following p. 318.

319. to Charles Mapou

Le Belvédère   September 24, 1930
Tel.: 89. Montfort l'Amaury (S. & O.)
My dear friend,

It wasn't easy (in principle, one should not relinquish royalties), but I managed to obtain the maximum: 50%. It's hardly less than what I should have received after the distribution.

Therefore, please write directly to the Society of Authors, 10 rue Chaptal (Paris IX), reminding them that at my request, they led me to expect this refund.

And furthermore, don't be angry with me: I should have written what I said to you in person about my deep joy and sincere gratitude to you, to the municipality, to Dongaïtz,[1] the chorus, and to all who contributed to the complete success of this manifestation, which will surely be the most touching of my entire career. But, since my return, I have plunged into work without respite, or almost so: half an hour for each meal; an hour to walk 6 kilometers at the end of the day; 5 to 6 hours of sleep. I am finishing the orchestration of the Concerto for the left hand. 3 months remain to finish the other one, which I am supposed to take around the world. Provided that I hold up!

You will excuse me, won't you? and don't think you have been forgotten by your grateful

Maurice Ravel

1. The father and son pelota team of Léon and Frédéric Dongaitz played against MM. Haitce and Titi during the festivities.

320. to Georges Vriamont[1]

Le Belvédère   December 5, 1930
Montfort l'Amaury (S. & O.)
Dear Monsieur Vriamont,

At the rate it was going, the concerto should have been finished soon. I hadn't counted on the fatigue which suddenly overwhelmed me.

Under the threat of dire repercussions: cerebral anemia, neurasthenia, etc., I have been ordered to rest, and above all to sleep—I was beginning to lose that habit entirely.

I will be able to resume work soon, but with greater moderation. I have to make my decision: the concerto will not be ready for this season.[2]

I am sorry about it and can only ask you to pardon the feeble limits of my "productivity."

Dear Monsieur Vriamont, believe me very truly yours,
Maurice Ravel

1. He was a Belgian impresario, piano dealer, and music publisher.
2. Vriamont was hoping to arrange for the first performances in Belgium of the G Major Piano Concerto. He accomplished that goal in 1932.

321. to Madame Alfred Madoux-Frank

Le Belvédère   February 5, 1931
Montfort l'Amaury (S. & O.)
Dear Madame and friend,

Please excuse me: your kind letter written in December did reach me, but I was in such pitiful condition that the previous month they had to forbid me to do any work, or anything else except sleep, which I had been deprived of almost entirely for a year. Owing to this restriction, my concerto[1] should have been finished at the end of January. But suddenly, at the beginning of November, I came to the realization that human endurance has its limitations. I am only now beginning to resume work on the concerto, but naturally it won't be ready this season. Nevertheless, the concert will take place—without the concerto—and I will be very happy to accept your thoughtful invitation.[2]

Would you please ask M. Van der Moylen[3] to get in touch directly with M. Boquel,[4] at 69 Boulevard de Clichy? I don't believe that my manager's contract gives him exclusive rights.

So I'll see you soon, dear Madame and friend. Once again, a thousand pardons, a thousand thanks, and please accept my warm and respectful friendship.

Maurice Ravel

1. The Piano Concerto in G Major.

2. In March 1931, Ravel participated in a program of his works, a benefit concert for Belgium's disabled war veterans, held in the Palais des Beaux-Arts in Brussels. At an elegant soirée given in his honor, Ravel was introduced to Ottorino Respighi, and the following day he was the guest of honor at an afternoon tea sponsored by the Society of Phonic Arts and Sciences. In the presence of a large audience, recordings of the *Menuet antique*, *Introduction et Allegro*, *La Valse*, and *Boléro* were heard, as well as excerpts from *Shéhérazade*, *L'Heure espagnole*, *Ma Mère l'Oye*, and *Daphnis et Chloé*.

3. A Belgian impresario.

4. A Parisian impresario.

322. Elizabeth Sprague Coolidge to Maurice Ravel

Los Angeles, California   April 6, 1931
My dear M. Ravel,[1]

I hope you will not think that I am forthputting if I appeal to you again to write for me for an important concert which I am planning to give in Paris next fall, probably in the early part of November. I feel that it would add enormous prestige to such a concert if I might give the premiere performance of a work by you, and I am, therefore, venturing to offer you $1,200.00 for a string quartet to be played in your city by the London String Quartet whom I have already engaged for the purpose.

I am choosing this form of composition for several reasons, hoping that it will not be an unwelcome plan to you, and I am sure that the whole musical world would be delighted and grateful to have at hand another quartet by Maurice Ravel after the lapse of twenty-five or thirty years since your first one was written.[2]

It is needless to say that I shall hope for a favorable answer and shall look forward to seeing you again in dear Paris. May I ask you to send your reply to me in the enclosed self-addressed envelope.

I am, with unaltered esteem and most friendly regards,

Yours very sincerely,

Elizabeth Sprague Coolidge

1. This letter was written in English.

2. Like Debussy, Ravel composed but one string quartet. At Oxford University in 1928, he was presented with a document signed by Professor Hugh P. Allen and 135 other musicians. It stated:

We, Musicians of Oxford, whose privilege it was to share in the welcome accorded to M. Maurice Ravel by the University when he was admitted to the degree of Doctor of Music (honoris causa), venture to express our earnest hope that he will commemorate the event by giving to us and to posterity the benefit and delight of another string quartet. (Autograph in the Music Division of the Bibliothèque Nationale, Dossier Ravel, no. 34.)

323. to Mrs. Louise Alvar

Le Belvédère   June 22, 1931
Tel.: 89. Montfort l'Amaury (S. & O.)
Dear friend,

Aubry telephoned me this morning. Immediately after, your letter arrived: I cannot tell you how much it touched me . . . and delighted me. I promptly forgot my remorse.

Thus, I hope to find you in London, because the 2 performances which I am supposed to conduct will be given on July 7 and 8.[1] I will arrive the 6th on the "Golden Arrow" and will leave the 9th in the morning: 4 days taken from my concerto!

Thank you again, excuse the haste of these few lines, and affectionate regards to all from your
Maurice Ravel

1. Ravel conducted *La Valse* and *Boléro* at Covent Garden for Ida Rubinstein's troupe.

324. to Henri Rabaud[1]

Le Belvédère   November 20, 1931
Montfort l'Amaury (S. & O.)
My dear friend,

Please excuse me for the Osiris competition:[2] my concerto is finished, but I'm not far from being so myself and would risk falling asleep at the first candidate. I have been ordered complete rest and am being treated with injections of serum. I will have to be content to conduct for Marguerite Long on January 14.[3]

Accept my regrets and believe me very truly yours,
Maurice Ravel

1. The French composer and conductor Henri Rabaud (1873–1949) succeeded Gabriel Fauré as director of the Conservatoire, a position he held between 1920 and 1941 (see plate 3).

2. A special competition for students who had already received a Premier Prix in tragedy, comedy, or operatic studies, named in memory of the French financier and philanthropist Daniel Illfa Osiris (1828–1907).

3. In the all-Ravel program given on January 14, 1932, the composer shared the podium with the Portuguese conductor Pedro de Freitas-Branco, who was making his Parisian debut. Emile Vuillermoz tempered his enthusiastic review as follows:

Once again, I wish to protest against the habit, more and more frequently indulged in, of attempting at all costs to bring a composer before the public in a part which he is incapable of filling. M. Ravel is continually brought out as a pianist or as a conductor, whilst he cannot possibly shine in either of these two specialities.... His *Pavane* was unutterably slow, his *Boléro* dry and badly timed. And the accompaniment of the concerto lacked clarity and elasticity. . . . :

But there is only praise for the composer of all these delicate, subtle works, the orchestration of which abounds in amusing and profound inventions, and which is really of inimitable originality of writing and of thought. The new concerto is worthy of the other masterpieces that we owe to Ravel. . . . The work is very easy to understand and gives the impression of extreme youth. It is wonderful to see how this master has more freshness of inspiration than the young people of today who flog themselves uselessly in order to try to discover, in laborious comedy or caricature, a humor that is not in their temperament.

Vuillermoz summed up by calling the concert "the finest artistic manifestation of the season" (*Christian Science Monitor,* February 13, 1932).

325. to Jane Bathori

Bonnet Machine Shop   Levallois, September 15, 1932
Factory & Offices:
11 & 13, rue Camille Desmoulins
Telephone: Péreire 01-12
Levallois Perret (Seine)
Dear friend,

When you informed me (in your letter dated July 20!) that *L'Heure espagnole* was going to be performed in Buenos Aires, I wanted to reply immediately. Unfortunately, I was immersed in a project which I should never have undertaken and which made me lose more than 3 months needlessly.[1] I had taken my work with me to Saint-Jean-de-Luz, together with your letter and many others. I brought back all of the letters without replying. Finally, I'm beginning with yours.

Is there still time to make several very important recommendations with regard to the character of this light and good-natured work,[2] which is never obscene, as it has sometimes been interpreted, particularly abroad?

The roles of <u>Concepcion</u> and <u>Ramiro</u> demand a great deal of tact, the latter in particular, a gruff fellow without malice, but not without modesty, and occasionally poetic (in his monologues). As for <u>Gonzalve</u>, who should have a pleasant tenor voice, he should exaggerate the vocalizations.

The two other roles are easier to understand, if not to realize.

If all of these suggestions are taken into account, the interpretation of *L'Heure espagnole* will be the best "in the Walk."[3]

I hope this won't reach you too late, and that you and your colleagues will excuse my involuntary delay. Dear friend, believe in the great affection of your

Maurice Ravel

I'm returning shortly to Montfort.[4]

1. Referring to the film music for *Don Quixote* (see letter no. 278, note 1). Despite serious financial problems, the film was eventually completed. According to an article in *Paris-Midi* (June 13, 1933), Ravel sued the film company for damages, but apparently nothing came of the matter.

2. Ravel's very late reply probably arrived just in time, as the program in the Teatro Colon was given on September 24. Jane Bathori sang the role of Concepcion with Juan José Castro conducting. The program also included the *Boléro* and an opera by Franco Casavola, *El Jorobado del Califa* (The Hunchback of the Caliph), based upon a libretto by Arturo Rossato.

3. Written in English in the autograph, this is another attempt to write "in the world."

4. Ravel's autograph is reproduced in *Ars: Revista de arte*, 27, no. 104 (1967), no pagination.

326. to Guido Gatti[1]

Le Belvédère   January 5, 1933
Montfort l'Amaury (S. & O.)
Dear Signor Gatti,

I have learned that Madeleine Grey, who had been chosen to sing the *Chansons madécasses* at the Florence Festival, must be replaced by another singer: I find this upsetting, as you realize.

In fact, since Bathori's perfect first performance, quite a number of years ago, this very difficult work has been taken up by many other distinguished artists: not one has expressed its character as faithfully as Madeleine Grey. I designated her recently when the Polydor Company asked me to record these 3 pieces, allowing me to select the performers.

If you consider my particular preference for this work, you will understand that I wish it to be performed as closely as possible to my intentions.

I am still hoping that the jury will reverse its decision, which would make me extremely grateful.[2]

Dear Signor Gatti, believe me most cordially yours,

Maurice Ravel

1. The Italian critic and musicologist (1892–1973).

2. Madeleine Grey's performance was canceled owing to the anti-Semitic policies of fascist Italy.

327. to Manuel de Falla

Le Belvédère   January 6, 1933

Tel.: 89. Montfort l'Amaury (S. & O.)

Dear Falla,

Roland-Manuel upset me with the news that you had been ill.

I was going to write to you: you anticipated me and reassured me because you have resumed work, which is the best sign of health.

I am just beginning to resume my work. The accident, however, was not very serious:[1] a bruised thorax and some facial wounds. And yet, I was unable to do anything but sleep and eat. There remains only an irrational fear of taxis, which I use only as a last resort.

See you soon, dear Falla: will I have the joy of seeing you again on the coast, towards autumn, if not before? In the meantime, warmest good wishes from your

Maurice Ravel

1. On October 9, 1932, Ravel was injured in a taxi collision in Paris. Although he endured considerable pain, his condition was not serious, and in December he felt well enough to participate in a concert of his works given in Basel.

328. to Alfred Perrin

Le Belvédère   February 7, 1933

Montfort l'Amaury (S. & O.)

Dear Alfred,

I bless M. Casanelli for having given me the opportunity to write to you: I really didn't know how to go about it. Finally, thanks to that kind young man, I have some news which I wouldn't have dared to ask about, as he must have told you.

The news about my cousin saddened me, but she is still so young! She still has her entire life ahead of her.

As for me, I have been rather busy: first, a project without respite for close to three years (2 concertos). An extended tour in Europe was genuinely restful, and a sojourn in my native region was a bit less so, as always. Upon returning, I began 3 Spanish songs[1] and an Arabic pantomime[2] (more travels).

This stupid accident was enough to knock me out for 3 months. It's only during the past few days that I have been able to resume work, and with some difficulty.

Now I have 3 concerts which I had to accept, and then I'm going into seclusion.[3]

My apologies to all, and despite my frequent silence, believe in my deep affection.

Maurice Ravel

I really must write to Marc[4] one of these days, but first I must have his address.

1. *Don Quichotte à Dulcinée.*

2. *Morgiane,* a ballet commissioned by Ida Rubinstein, was based on the tale of Ali Baba and the Forty Thieves. Virtually none of it was committed to paper.

3. The three concerts were as follows: 1) On Sunday afternoon, February 12, 1933, an all-Ravel program was performed at the Champs-Elysées theater by the Pasdeloup Orchestra conducted by the composer (G Major Piano Concerto with Marguerite Long, and *Boléro*), and Manuel Rosenthal (*Ma Mère l'Oye, La Valse,* and excerpts from *Daphnis et Chloé*). 2) Ravel led an amateur orchestra in a performance of *La Valse.* 3) Ravel was planning to conduct the Piano Concerto for the Left Hand with Paul Wittgenstein in Monte Carlo, but Paul Paray replaced him. (See letter no. 330, notes 3 and 4.)

4. The son of Alfred Perrin. He was a trombonist in the Orchestre de la Suisse Romande.

329. to Madeleine Grey

Le Belvédère   February 8, 1933
Montfort l'Amaury (S. & O.)
Dear friend,

I had carefully put these 2 pieces aside: I found them there. They didn't have the sense to join you all by themselves.

We hadn't thought about the laws of fascism, neither you, nor Kiesgen,[1] nor I.

Polydor recently sent me the *Madécasses* (they had forgotten me). It's perfect. It is true that my Thomson is excellent.[2]

Sincere apologies for the delay, and best wishes,
Maurice Ravel[3]

1. The impresario Charles Kiesgen was Mlle Grey's manager.

2. Ravel's phonograph may still be seen at Le Belvédère.

3. This autograph is reproduced in Vladimir Jankélévitch, *Ravel* (Paris: Editions Rieder, 1939), plate 14 following p. 130.

330. to David Diamond[1]

Le Belvédère   April 6, 1933
Montfort l'Amaury (S. & O.)
Dear friend,

Excuse me: Prix du Disque,[2] P.T.T.[3] (I conducted *La Valse*), etc., etc.
Returning to Montfort, I only had time to begin packing, finish at Levallois, and
hurry off to Monte Carlo.[4]

Outside of that, I have just finished *Don Quichotte à Dulcinée*, and am
beginning *Morgiane*, the devil take the shock![5] See you soon, dear friend.
Believe in the affection of your

Maurice Ravel

1. The noted American composer (b. 1915) met Ravel in Cleveland in 1928. They
were introduced by the young musician's violin teacher, André de Ribaupierre, an old
friend of Ravel. The composers occasionally met in the 1930s, when Mr. Diamond
continued his studies in France.

2. The Grand Prix du Disque began to distribute its coveted awards in 1931, and
Ravel had been a member of the jury since its inception.

3. An amateur orchestra largely composed of postal workers. P.T.T. (Post, Telegraph,
Telephone) is the French abbreviation for a post office.

4. Ravel had intended to conduct the Piano Concerto for the Left Hand in Monte
Carlo with Paul Wittgenstein, but owing to deteriorating health, he asked Paul Paray to
replace him. He did attend the performance, however, and acknowledged an exceptionally warm ovation.

5. That is, the "shock" of going from the chivalrous Don Quixote to a den of thieves!

331. to Marie Gaudin[1]

La Floride   August 2, 1933
Le Touquet
Pas-de-Calais   Tel.: 639
Dear Marie,

You won't see me this year at Saint-Jean, alas! Feeling rather washed-out for
quite a long time, I continued nevertheless to work, but without any results. I
had undertaken a pantomime: *Morgiane*, which is supposed to be performed
next March at the Opéra.[2] Increasingly tired, I went to see Vallery-Radot:[3]
blood pressure, rather low. Blood test: the doctor was concerned about a rather
large accumulation of urea. Now it's satisfactory. But the anemia continues.
Medication: a bewildering host of drugs, complete rest, which is hardly possible in my native region, and it's too hot anyway: the seashore in the North
department is more invigorating.[4]

Some charming friends offered me their hospitality.[5] In 1 month all of the symptoms disappeared. Vallery would like to compel me to stay here till the end of September, but as soon as I feel stronger, I'm going to try to skedaddle and work at Montfort, without tiring myself out too much.

I hope you will pardon my silence, having learned the reason for it, and that you will send me good news about everyone.

I embrace all of you gochoqui[6]

gochot[6]

1. This letter, which contains many erasures, is written in ink and pencil. A poignant document, it shows the beginning stages of Ravel's final illness, in which his ability to write deteriorated sharply. Written on the recto sides of two pages, the first verso side contains many capital M's and R's (Ravel laboriously practicing the writing of his initials), the indication Allegramente, and the opening theme (3 measures) of the Piano Concerto in G Major. The verso of page two contains the beginning of a letter to Marie Gaudin, written in light pencil: "Dear Marie, I'm feeling much better," . . .

2. Despite the erasures, one can distinguish a slightly different version of these sentences: "For a rather long time, I felt rather washed-out. Nevertheless, I continued to work, but rather poorly. I had undertaken a rather important work: *Morgiane*," (etc.).

3. Dr. Pasteur Vallery-Radot was a trusted friend of both Debussy and Ravel (see his letter to Hélène Jourdan-Morhange, no. 333).

4. Dr. Théophile Alajouanine, who examined Ravel over a period of two years, described his patient's condition in *Brain*, a journal of neurology, and his comments are quoted in full.

It is a Wernicke aphasia of moderate intensity, without any trace of paralysis, without hemianopia, but with an ideomotor apractic component. The cause, though indefinite, belongs to the group of cerebral atrophies, there being a bilateral ventricular enlargement; but it is quite different from Pick's disease. Oral and written language are diffusely impaired, but moderately so, without any noticeable intellectual weakening. Memory, judgment, affectivity, æsthetic taste do not show any impairment to repeated tests. Understanding of language remains much better than oral or written abilities. Writing, especially, is very faulty, mainly due to apraxia. Musical language is still more impaired, but not in a uniform manner. There is chiefly a quite remarkable discrepancy between a loss of musical expression (written or instrumental), and musical thinking, which is comparatively well preserved. With the help of two musicians, a favourite pupil of the master and a neurologist with great musical ability we could study as precisely as possible musical tune recognition, note recognition (musical dictation), note reading and solfeggio piano playing, and dictated musical writing (copied or spontaneous). I apologize for giving such an analysis, but it seems to me essential in respect of the value of such a case-history.

Recognition of tunes played before our musician is generally good and prompt. He recognizes immediately most of the works he knew, and anyway he recognizes perfectly his own works. That recognition is not a vague one, for he is able to evaluate exactly rhythm and style as shown by the following facts. He immediately notices the lightest mistake in the playing; several parts of the "Tombeau de Couperin" were first correctly played, and then with minor errors (either as to notes or rhythm). He immediately protested and demanded a perfect accuracy. When playing the beginning of "La pavane de ma Mère l'Oye" which contains two exactly similar bars, one was omitted. The patient immediately stopped the pianist. He succeeded in explaining, in his halting speech, that the first bar was to link with the preceding part. The same is true for rhythm: if played too fast, he protests and has the music played again with its exact rhythm. Another remark: during these studies on musical interference of aphasia, my piano—because of the dampness of the winter—had become somewhat out of tune. The patient noticed it and demonstrated the dissonance by playing two notes one octave apart, thus showing again the preservation of sound recognition and valuation.

On the contrary analytic recognition of notes, and musical dictation, are quite faulty, or seemingly so, since he could name only some notes hesitatingly and with difficulty. His numerous mistakes are due, very likely, to aphasia itself, and to the difficulty of finding the name of a note, a trouble exactly similar to name designation for common objects. The fact that reproduction of notes played on the piano, without giving their name, is quite good, seems to confirm this opinion.

Note reading is extremely difficult. From time to time a note is read exactly. Most often reading is impossible. The same is true for solfeggio. The trouble of name-finding may partly explain the failure. But there is something more, since piano playing is almost impossible after reading. A component due to apraxia supervenes therein. Anyway a quite definite discrepancy is noted between deciphering musical signs, and their visual recognition. If an analytic deciphering is almost impossible, on the contrary the patient is able to recognize at first glance whatever piece he has to find, and that without any error.

Piano playing is very difficult, since in addition to difficulty in reading, our aphasic patient has to search for the location of notes on the keyboard. He sometimes misplaces notes without being aware of it. For instance he plays the *mi–mi* instead of the *do–do* arpeggio, and plays it again and again, until his fingers are placed on the proper keys. He plays scales quite well, both major and minor ones. Diesis and flats are well marked. There is just a praxic difficulty. He can play with only one hand (the right one) the beginning of "Ma Mère l'Oye." With both hands, he cannot decipher. He needs many exercises to play in that way. In spite of numerous exercises during a whole week he cannot succeed in playing the beginning of the "Pavane" [from *Ma Mère l'Oye*], even with separate hands. On the contrary he has a greater performance ability when he plays by heart pieces of his own composition. He suddenly gives a right idea of the beginning of "Le Tombeau de Couperin" which is, however, too difficult to finish. Seven or eight bars are played almost perfectly, and he plays them, transposing to the lower tierce, without any error. When attempting an unknown piece he finds a much greater difficulty: he cannot play more than two or three notes of a piece by Scarlatti, which he did not previously know.

Musical writing is very difficult, although better preserved than plain writing. He writes dictated notes slowly and with numerous errors, but copying is almost impossible and requires from the patient enormous effort. On the contrary, writing by heart a portion of his "Entretiens de la belle et la bête," though difficult and slow, is better performed than the other tests. Notes are better and more quickly placed, and he seems mainly disturbed by writing apraxia. Singing by heart is correctly performed for some of his works, but only if the first note or notes are given. He says that tunes come back quite easily, and that he can hear them singing "in his head." Musical thinking seems comparatively better preserved than musical language itself.

Though all artistic realization is forbidden to our musician, he can still listen to music, attend a concert, and express criticism on it or describe the musical pleasure he felt. His artistic sensibility does not seem to be in the least altered, nor his judgment, as his admiration for the romantic composer Weber shows, which he told me several times. He can also judge contemporary musical works.

Thus, in our musician, because of aphasia, and as already mentioned, because of a simultaneous apraxia, musical reading, piano playing, use of musical signs are much more impaired than expression and recognition of musical themes. Severe disturbance of realization, and difficulty of expressing a relatively preserved musical thinking, while affectivity and æsthetic sensibility are almost intact, are the main features of our composer's case-history. They explain why his work has been completely arrested by his cerebral affection. (Théophile Alajouanine, "Aphasia and Artistic Realization," *Brain*, vol. 71, part 3, September, 1948, pp. 232–234.)

5. Ravel was staying at the villa of Jacques and Françoise Meyer in France's North department (see her telegram to Dr. Robert Lemasle, no. 345).

6. In Basque, "goxoki," meaning "tenderly."

332. to Anatole de Monzie[1]

December 3, 1933

Sir,

It is true that my work, my frequent absence, and above all, for over a year, the state of my health hardly permit me to attend the meetings of the Conservatoire's Advisory Board.

While fully regretting this, I have no doubt that a juror who is so deficient will be advantageously replaced.

With my apologies, Sir, please be assured of my high esteem.

Maurice Ravel

1. From June 4, 1932, until January 30, 1934, Anatole de Monzie (1876–1947) was France's minister of National Education. He had written to Ravel, asking him if he would continue to serve on the Conservatoire's Advisory Board (letter in the National Archives).

333. Dr. Pasteur Vallery-Radot to Hélène Jourdan-Morhange

49 bis, Avenue Victor Emmanuel III   January 30, 1934
Paris (8)
Telephone: Elysées 21-16
My dear Hélène,

It has been a very long time since I have seen you. I hope to see you soon, but you know that I am increasingly pressed for time.

If you see Maurice Ravel's brother, tell him (but without alarming him too much because he strikes me as extremely emotional) that I am very uneasy about his brother. I have had him undergo numerous examinations in order to be certain that there isn't any lesion whatsoever: there isn't; but he does indicate a state of intellectual fatigue which is very disturbing. It is absolutely necessary—and insist on this to Maurice Ravel—that he rest completely for many weeks, and in order to do it, he would be better off visiting with friends in the Midi or going to the mountains.

Very affectionately yours,
Sioul[1]

1. Dr. Vallery-Radot's nickname.

334. to Edouard Ravel[1]

[Switzerland]   [c. March 1934]
My dear little Edouard,

I believe that I have done the best thing by following the advice of Professor Michaud, whom Desjardins[2] had recommended, as well as Madame Dommange,[3] in her letter: <u>Mon</u> <u>Repos</u>[4] is maintained by nuns, like Blomet. Every night, they prepare my hot bath with fir milk in order to make me sleep. In the morning, after breakfast, a hot shower.

Maurice Ravel

1. This document, written in light pencil, is a draft rather than a letter, properly speaking. It is written on the back of a bill (dated 1934) presented to Maurice Ravel by F. Georges, haberdashers on Boulevard des Capucines (Paris). At the top of the page, Ravel practiced writing the word "petit" (misspelled "petti" in the draft), and signed his name in ink well below his comments. (The bill, which comes to 658 francs, is for shirts, collars, and cuffs.)

2. Dr. Abel Desjardins, one of Ravel's physicians.

3. Mme René Dommange (see letter no. 190, note 1).

4. Literally, "My Rest." It was a rest home in the mountains overlooking Vevey, Switzerland.

335. to Marie Gaudin

[Mon Repos]   March 12 [1934]
[Switzerland]
Dear Marie,[1]

Thanks to the invigorating mountain air, I'm beginning to be able to write, more or less. I should have taken care of myself over 2 years ago: now, I have cerebral anemia. Finally, all of the doctors, including the specialists, assure me of being cured, but it's taking so long!

I have moved into an establishment maintained admirably by French nuns. I'm thinking of staying here at least another month.

Let's talk business: as I still hope to return to Saint-Jean, I think it would be more convenient to leave the cash there, in the Société Générale bank. As I'm not very skilled in business terminology, could they send me a letter which I would only have to sign? Thanks in advance, and love to all. Write me sometimes. I will try to answer you although it costs me entire days of torture to do so: I began this letter over a week ago.

Maurice Ravel

Address your letters here, otherwise they are sent to the Durand company, which answers them or forwards them to Edouard.

1. See plate 13.

336. to Lucien Garban

April 22, 1934
Dear friend,

It is true that I entrusted the manuscript of *Don Quichotte à Dulcinée* to Singher[1] so that he could work on these three songs and give the 1st performance with orchestra. I was even thinking of conducting them myself. But I never dreamed of having them recorded first, which incidentally would be contrary to my agreements with Durand. Obviously, Singher is unaware of all this as he doesn't know about my condition. I will see him soon: I'm returning at the end of this month to move into Malmaison with our eminent statesmen:[2] it's an end like any other.

As for the Broadcasting Commission,[3] I hardly think that I will be able to attend for a long time. It would be best to ask the minister to excuse me, bringing him up-to-date about my situation.

See you soon. Affectionate regards,

Maurice Ravel

1. The French baritone Martial Singher (b. 1904). See his letter to this writer in appendix A.

2. Not to be taken literally for Napoleon's famous château, this is a bantering reference to the neighboring clinic in Rueil-Malmaison, just west of Paris, where, among many other dignitaries, Paul Deschanel, a former president of the French republic, had undergone treatment.

3. Probably the Radio Broadcasting Commission, which was under the aegis of the Ministry of Communication.

337. Durand & Co. to Maurice Senart[1]

Paris, January 16, 1935

Sir,

Maître Maurice Ravel, who has been prescribed complete rest by his doctors, begs us to tell you that at the request of M. Obouhov, he willingly authorizes you to utilize the following statement for the publication of M. Obouhov's two pieces which you are about to print:

"Obouhov performed fragments of his *Le Livre de Vie* for me. I was struck by the emotional power, truly inspiring, of this unusual work. It is written in his new notation, which considerably simplifies the writing of music."[2]

Very truly yours,

A. Durand & Co.

1. The French music publisher.

2. By using different shaped note heads, Obouhov's system eliminated the need for sharps and flats. (See Raymond Petit, "Introduction à l'oeuvre de Nicolas Obouhow," *La Revue musicale*, 290–291, 1972, pp. 27–39.) Although fragments of Obouhov's work have been recorded, the score has yet to be printed.

338. Léon Leyritz to Madame Maurice Delage

La Mamounia   Wednesday, March 6 [1935]
Hôtel Transatlantique
Marrakech [Morocco]

We received your letter last night, dear Madame, which was mistakenly sent to Fès! Yes, we visited the Escorial[1] as well as Goya's chapel outside the walls,[2] and we also found some denicotinized tobacco! Everything is thus working out for the best—the trip, obviously, was a bit long and tiring, but despite the excitement here, a marvelous aura of peace and calm prevails, which is certainly beneficial. The comb was found easily, and the cuff links are fastened as if by magic. The result of all this is that he is presently writing to his brother! all by himself! slowly, to be sure; but it's a fact! We avoid invitations which appear to be taxing, but some, like the one we accepted yesterday were very interesting in their own right. We drove four hours high up in the mountains (2,000–2,400 meters)[3] to find a young and charming prince in an enchanting palace, who displayed all of the pageantry at his command and presented a magnificent spectacle of dance and music which fascinated Maître Ravel—thirty tambourines with their deep, vibrant sound, accompanying one hundred female dancers dressed in festive costumes laden with jewels and embroidery—it was very beautiful.

We occasionally go to the terrace of the Café de France, from where one can overlook Djemar el Fra, which we have explored thoroughly. We don't pass there without thinking of you, which is to say very often! We exchange many telegrams with Madame Rubinstein, who is so charming—we expect to see her descending from heaven one day soon!

My wife has told me how kind you were to her, and I sincerely thank you for it.

Please accept my most respectful compliments, dear Madame, as well as my kind regards to your husband.

Maître Ravel embraces you very affectionately and thanks you for your thoughtful letter.

Léon Leyritz

1. The sixteenth-century palace and monastery just northwest of Madrid.
2. The church of San Antonio de la Florida, in Madrid.
3. About 6,550–7,850 feet.

339. Léon Leyritz to Hélène Jourdan-Morhange

La Mamounia   Saturday the 9th [March 1935]
Hôtel Transatlantique
Marrakech
Dear Madame,

I just received your charming letter which touched me deeply. Your dear "Ravelito" is working at this moment—despite the inevitable slight fatigue, I believe that this trip will prove beneficial, above all, precisely from the point of view of this confidence in the future, which you wrote about. Perhaps you won't find a big change at first, but I can tell you that he often speaks to me about his music, no longer as something unrealizable, as he recently did, but as something which is possible—difficult, but possible. He has whistled some melodies for *Morgiane*, and has spoken to me about his views of the staging. All of this augurs well. Of course, he is not yet capable of actually writing the music. He has been happy and in good spirits during our stay here, and I would like to arrange for him to remain longer.

We had the opportunity to meet your friends the Lapiduses at a reception on behalf of a charity given at our hotel by General Catroux.[1] Indeed, they were introduced to Maître Ravel as being your friends, and they invited him to an Arabic dinner with other doctors and their wives. But Ravel was afraid of upsetting his diet too much, and he declined the invitation. It is regrettable that despite the introductions, they thought it necessary to ignore my presence. I could very well have arranged everything—tell them what sort of invitation they could make, keep it intimate, and it would have worked out very well— they must have taken me for some kind of secretary-valet!

Dear Madame, we are leaving Marrakech tomorrow for Fès and its environs. We will return at a leisurely pace and will be back in Paris on the 20th at night. Maître Ravel embraces you very affectionately. We often speak of your pretty eyes! Kindly allow me to offer you my most respectful compliments.

Leyritz

1. The French general Georges Catroux (1877–1969) served for many years in Indochina and North Africa.

340. Mademoiselle René Perret to Madame Maurice Delage

Mlle R. Perret   May 4, 1936
Pension "Mon Port"
Tel.: 25416
Lausanne [Switzerland]
Dear Madame,

It has been 10 days since you left your friend M. Ravel, and as I promised, I will now bring you up-to-date. M. Ravel has settled into a routine, as much at our institution as elsewhere, and he appears to be happy. On Sunday, April 26, M. Ravel took an automobile trip with M. d'Alexandrie from 5:30 to 7 o'clock, and then, as M. André Germain had sent him a fresh bouquet of flowers, M. Ravel wished to receive him in order to recall their last meeting, which had taken place on May 1; the gentlemen then went to the Lausanne Palace. Yesterday, we took a lovely promenade atop the city, visiting the orchards in full bloom; M. Ravel was beaming, and imitated bird calls for us. Evenings are spent pleasantly, chatting and listening to a fine radio; M. Ravel still has difficulty recalling proper nouns, but given confidence, he talks about his travels or relates anecdotes about artists; I am not alone in finding that M. Ravel expresses himself with more facility. On Thursday, I will be at the doctor's office when he explains to M. Ravel the reasons for the treatment which he is following; our dear M. Ravel must recover, and in order to accomplish that, he must rediscover faith in himself and in his recovery, don't you think? M. Ravel is also sleeping better, and his appetite is also good. He did indeed receive several undergarments and his bathrobe, and I believe it would be useful if you could send him his raincoat.

I will send you further news at the end of the week. Please believe me, dear Madame, very truly yours,

René Perret

341. to André Dezarrois[1]

Le Belvédère   Paris, June 17, 1936
Montfort l'Amaury (S. & O.)
Dear Sir,

It is impossible for me at the present time to participate in the deliberations for the awarding of a scholarship to a musician, but if a mail ballot is admissible, I would be grateful to you if you would inform my colleagues on the jury that M. Emile Passani[2] seems to me, by virtue of his musical talent as well as his financial situation, worthy of being the winner of the prize in musical composition for 1936.

Very truly yours,
Maurice Ravel[3]

1. He was the secretary-general of the American Foundation for French Art and Thought.
2. The French composer, pianist, and choral conductor (b. 1905).
3. This letter was typewritten for Ravel, but he managed to sign it himself.

342. to Hans Brückner[1]

[May 1937]

Sir,

I am extremely surprised to learn that you have included my name among the Jewish musicians listed in your publication entitled *Judentum und Musik*. Now I am a Catholic, having been baptized in the month of my birth, March 1875, in Ciboure (Lower Pyrenees), and I descend from Catholic parents and grandparents.

I absolutely insist that you <u>have</u> <u>my</u> <u>name</u> <u>removed</u> <u>from</u> <u>every</u> <u>copy</u> without further delay, and that a rectification be published in the newspapers. Furthermore, I request that you send me a justificative copy of the corrected volume, and some of the insertions in the press. Otherwise, I will feel obliged to take all necessary measures.

Very truly yours,[2]

1. A publisher and writer in Munich. With Christa Maria Rock, he was the co-author of *Judentum und Musik* (Judaism and Music), a book of some 250 pages which lists Jewish and non-Aryan musicians in alphabetical order, together with a thumbnail sketch of their careers. The book's despicable racism calls for no further commentary.

2. A copy of the autograph is in the archives of Durand and Company. The original document was certainly signed, either by Ravel or for him, and the following letter is Brückner's reply.

343. Hans Brückner to Maurice Ravel

Das Deutsche Podium   May 21, 1937
Fachblatt für Unterhaltungs-Musik
    und Musik-Gaststätten
Kampfblatt für deutsche Musik
Hans Brückner Verlag
München[1]
Dear Meister Ravel![2]

I have received your letter, for which I thank you very much, with reference to your entry in the book *Judentum und Musik*; I inform you most politely that this entry was taken from the 39th edition of the *Handbuch der Judenfrage*.[3] Furthermore, at the time my book was published, in many places in Germany there was no uniform opinion concerning your ancestry.

However, I myself have taken pains to clarify all doubts, and I inform you most politely that before your letter arrived, I had already removed the entry from the forthcoming 3rd edition of my book. I will also rectify the entry in future supplements to the previous editions, and will inform the appropriate official authorities of the matter.[4]

Yours very truly,
Brückner

1. The German Podium, Professional Journal for Light Music and Musical Cafés, Combat Sheet for German Music, Hans Brückner Publisher, Munich.

2. This letter was written in German. A copy of it is in the archives of Durand and Company.

3. *Handbook of the Jewish Question*. This work does not seem to be listed in any bibliography, and it may have been circulated privately.

4. A directly related question—the performance of Ravel's music in Germany—was the topic of an exchange of letters between André François-Poncet, the French ambas-

sador to Germany, and Joseph Goebbels, the German minister of propaganda. On November 21, 1936, the ambassador inquired if it were true that Ravel's works were boycotted in Germany. Replying on December 3, the minister of propaganda asserted that he had ordered an investigation into the matter, the result being that Ravel's music was not boycotted, either in the concert hall or on German radio. In all, he maintained, Ravel's works were performed 36 times by various stations during the 1935–36 season, and he requested that this information be forwarded to the composer. (Copies of these documents are in the archives of Durand and Company.)

344. to Ernest Ansermet

Paris, October 29, 1937

My dear friend,

I cannot tell you how touched I am by your very prompt decision: your self-denial permits the realization of a project which was dear to me. Allow me to express my very sincere gratitude.[1]

To my knowledge, Jacques Février is the only one, I believe, who presently knows my concerto well enough to perform it immediately;[2] for several reasons which you will easily understand, I don't dare mention Alfred Cortot, who, I have been told, is supposed to play it at a date which I do not know.[3]

But, if a delay of three weeks doesn't strike you as impossible, Jacques Février, upon his return from America at the end of November, would be pleased to play the concerto for you whenever it would be most convenient; he would thus express his joy in performing my work under your distinguished baton, and acknowledge his gratitude to your audiences in Geneva and Lausanne. I trust that you will find this suggestion acceptable.[4]

In renewing my grateful friendship to you, please believe me, my dear friend, very truly yours,

Maurice Ravel[5]

1. This episode has remained obscure.

2. Février had studied the Piano Concerto for the Left Hand with Ravel, and performed it several times in Paris in 1937: on March 19 under the baton of Charles Münch, on October 17 with Philippe Gaubert, and on December 5 with Albert Wolff. He also played the Concerto in Boston (November 12 and 13) and New York (November 20) with the Boston Symphony Orchestra under the baton of Serge Koussevitzky.

3. Ravel's falling out with Cortot was somewhat analogous to the one with Ricardo Viñes (see letter no. 191). In this case, Cortot insisted on playing the Concerto for the Left Hand with both hands, which Ravel found totally unacceptable. (Cortot performed the Concerto with Paul Paray conducting the Colonne Orchestra on December 19, 1937.)

4. It turned out that the Swiss pianist Jacqueline Blancard performed the première of

the Concerto in Lausanne and Geneva on November 8 and 10, 1937, with Ernest Ansermet conducting the Orchestra de la Suisse Romande (see the *Journal de Genève,* November 12, 1937).

5. This letter was typed for Ravel, who signed it himself. Written just eight weeks before his death, it is his last known letter.

345. Françoise Meyer to Doctor Robert Lemasle[1]

PARIS   DECEMBER 28, 1937

HOUR OF DEPOSIT: 07:45

    IT'S OVER

        FRANÇOISE[2]

1. A physician and personal friend of Ravel.
2. This telegram was sent some four hours after Ravel's death at a clinic on rue Boileau in Paris. He was 62 years old.

346. Edouard Ravel to Jacques Rouché

Mayatza   February 19, 1940
Saint-Jean-de-Luz
Dear Sir,

I received your letter dated the 13th, as well as the scenario which you forwarded to me. Let me reply to the question you raised in the following way:

My brother admired everything which was mechanical, from simple tin toys to the most intricate machine tools. He would thus spend entire days, around the new year, on the main boulevards, in front of street vendors' stalls, and was delighted to come with me to factories or to expositions of machinery. He was happy to be in the midst of these movements and noises. But he always came out struck and obsessed by the automation of all these mechanisms.

He never spoke to me of his plans for scenarios, but often, when passing by Le Vésinet,[1] he showed me "the Boléro factory." Personally, knowing Leyritz's integrity, and his admiration for my brother, I have no doubt that the ideas expressed in the model and the scenario derive from the conversations which they had during their trip to Morocco and Spain.

I hope that this information will enable you to make a well-informed decision.[2]

Believe me, dear Sir, very truly yours,
Edouard Ravel[3]

1. A suburb to the west of Paris noted for its mechanical industry.
2. A new production of the *Boléro* was presented at the Opéra on December 29, 1941,

with choreography by Serge Lifar, décor and costumes by Léon Leyritz, and Louis Fourestier conducting. The principal roles were danced by Serge Lifar and Suzanne Lorcia.

3. In the sixteenth division of the small cemetery at Levallois Perret, there is a simple gray granite tomb with the following inscription:

Joseph Ravel 1832– October 13, 1908
Marie Delouart Ravel 1840– January 5, 1917
Maurice Ravel—composer— 1875– December 28, 1937
Edouard Ravel 1878– April 5, 1960

Edouard Ravel married late in life and left no descendants. With his death, this branch of the Ravel family passed into eternity.

Articles

(listed in Selected Bibliography)

I : : :

Wagner and Today's Musicians: The Opinions of Messieurs Florent Schmitt and Maurice Ravel—Conclusions[1]

Louis Laloy:

"M. Maurice Ravel is perfectly willing to render justice to Wagner, but does not wish the progress of music to be stopped in his name: indeed, it is known that the usual tactic of the conservative party, here as everywhere else, is to condemn new institutions, but to cling to them with a strength born of despair when they grow old."

Maurice Ravel:

"Truly, there would be far too much to say about it. See first in Wagner what he was above all, a magnificent musician.

It's too late. After Nietzsche,[2] Catulle Mendès, and M. Joséphin Péladan,[3] one would seem to be creating a paradox.

. . . Is the wish so strange?[4] Not really! I rediscovered it in an old article. There is 'Wagner' instead of 'Debussy,' and 'Rossini' in place of 'Wagner.' It's signed: Scudo."[5]

NOTES

1. Louis Laloy, *La Grande Revue* (May 10, 1909), 13(9):160–64. In an article entitled "Wagner et nos musiciens" (*La Grande Revue*, April 10, 1909, pp. 558–566), Laloy cited a recent comment by Pierre Lalo in *Le Temps*, who observed that the younger generation was wrong in breaking with Wagner and seeking a more "pernicious" (Debussyian) influence. "The art of these young people," Lalo wrote, "amounts to the exploitation of some formulas; and it is becoming increasingly trivial, trivial, trivial. One would almost wish to restore Wagnerian influence in France." Laloy thought it would be interesting to consult "these young people" themselves, and hear their reactions to Lalo's suggestion. Among the twelve respondents were Alfredo Casella, Jean Huré, Raoul Laparra, Mme Armande de Polignac, Albert Roussel, Déodat de Séverac, and, finally, two late replies by Schmitt and Ravel. Laloy concluded his article as follows: "Every influence is beneficial for the gifted, and demoralizing for the mediocre. If our country is as sterile as

the eminent critic of *Le Temps* seems to believe, not in musicians, but in music, it isn't Wagner who will save it" (*La Grande Revue*, May 10, 1909, p. 164).

2. See p. 378, note 3.

3. Péladan (1858–1918), a poet, novelist, theologian, and occultist, was a fervent Wagnerian, as was his colleague Catulle Mendès (see letter no. 53, note 10).

4. That is, the wish to return to Wagnerian influence in France. As Debussy's "Golliwogg's Cake Walk" (1908) parodies *Tristan und Isolde*, the notation "Wagneramente" in Ravel's "Fanfare" for the ballet *L'Eventail de Jeanne* (1927) suggests a good-natured poke at the composer of *Götterdämmerung*, who apparently could be ridiculed, but not ignored.

5. The French critic Pierre Scudo (1806–1864, also known as Pietro, Paulo, or Paul Scudo) was celebrated for his extremely conservative views. He admired Mozart, but attacked Berlioz, Liszt, and Wagner, and showed almost no enthusiasm for modern music (that is, music written after 1830).

The Polonaises, Nocturnes, Impromptus, the Barcarolle—Impressions[1]

"Nothing is more hateful than music without hidden meaning."
—FRÉDÉRIC CHOPIN

This profound statement is relatively unknown. Even though Chopin proclaimed it constantly in his music, the contrary was understood. Hidden meanings were discovered in his music later on! Until Chopin, music was addressed to the emotions. Now it was to be transferred to the intellect, a notion which Chopin found irrelevant.

Music for *musicians*. This is the true meaning of Chopin's idea. Not for professionals, hang it! A *musician*: composer or dilettante, to be sensitive to the rhythm, melody, harmony, and the atmosphere which the sounds create. To thrill to the linking of two chords, just as one would to the juxtaposition of two colors. In all the arts, the *subject* is of primary importance, for everything flows from it.

Comparisons with architecture are inane. There are rules for making a building "stand up," but there are none for constructing modulations. Yes, there is but one: inspiration. I know that there aren't enough rules in today's music. One sets out needlessly, with anything at all, hastening to modulate in order to appear daring. Here, some chords reputed to be modern, and there, a so-called Chinese scale. It's like fashioning a hat, but less skilled. The piece concludes at random. Was it necessary to begin?

The architects draw up great plans: all of the modulations are established beforehand, and if less daring than in the works previously mentioned, they are just as useless. Inverted themes, retrograde canons, clear or obscure modulations—you don't understand this? Don't worry, neither do I. Despite all of this industry, if the music doesn't strike you as coherent, it's because you aren't a craftsman! What is lacking in all of this is having something to say: Chopin's hidden meaning.

Some examples: the dance, before Chopin, exhibited grace, gaiety, and occasionally some feeling. It was all a bit shallow, even in Schubert's *Ländler*, which, nevertheless, are delightful works.

Chopin's contribution is obvious in the Polonaises: before him, the polonaise was a festive march, solemn, brilliant, and thoroughly superficial (see Weber,[2] Moniuszko,[3] etc.). Only one polonaise by Chopin is in this traditional style (A Major, opus 40 no. 1). Yet how superior it is to those of his contemporaries in inspiration and harmonic richness. The *Grande Polonaise* in E♭[4] is already in another realm, with its heroic vehemence, and its splendid rhythmic drive in the middle section. Often, Chopin introduced a sad, poignant element in these dances, which was hitherto unknown (C♯ Minor, opus 26 no. 1).[5] At times, this tragic feeling attains such sublime heights that one may discover an entire epopee in the music (*Polonaise-Fantaisie* in A♭ Major, opus 61). The sincerity of expression, whether sorrowful or heroic, averts pomposity.

Critics have already analyzed the Nocturnes and Impromptus with keen perception. It is the nature of genuine music to evoke, even indirectly, feelings, landscapes, and ideas.

Chopin was not merely satisfied to transform pianistic technique. His inspired passage work may be observed amidst brilliant, exquisite, and profound harmonic progressions. There is always hidden meaning, which is often conveyed by an intense poem of despair.

The material is even more condensed in the Nocturnes. The sensitivity of the listener is aroused, and is often satisfied. So much the better. But what can be performed after that? Only an artist of genius would know which pieces to perform after Chopin's music. A frequent reproach is heard that Chopin did not evolve. Agreed. If not evolutionary, the splendid flowering of his art is found in the *Polonaise-Fantaisie*, the posthumous *Prelude* (opus 45),[6] and the *Barcarolle* (opus 60).

The *Barcarolle* synthesizes the expressive and sumptuous art of this great Slav, who was nurtured on Italian music. This attractive Latin school, joyfully vibrant, somewhat melancholy, sensual, but of lamentable facility, willingly abandons, if not its soul, like Molina,[7] at least its inspiration, in the worst places, so that it may recapture its supreme excellence more rapidly. Chopin achieved everything that his teachers had expressed only imperfectly, through negligence.

In the *Barcarolle*, the theme in thirds, supple and delicate, is continually arrayed in dazzling harmonies. The melodic line is continuous. At one point, a gentle melody appears, remains suspended, and subsides softly, underpinned by magical chords. The intensity increases. A new theme of sumptuous lyricism appears, thoroughly Italianized. Calm is restored. A delicate, fleeting passage arises from the bass, which hovers above exquisite, tender harmonies. One thinks of a mysterious apotheosis. . . .

NOTES

1. *Le Courrier musical* (January 1, 1910), 13:31–32. This special issue of *Le Courrier musical*, honoring the centenary of Chopin's birth, contains thirteen brief articles dealing with various aspects of the composer's life and works. Ravel frequently performed Chopin's music during his student days, and retained a lifelong admiration for his art. It is only fair to warn the reader that the text of this article is partially unreliable. In a letter to René Doire, the editor of the magazine, Ravel complained bitterly of the cuts and changes made in his article on Chopin, and stated emphatically that he would have no further dealings with *Le Courrier musical* (excerpts from Ravel's letter are in the Fonds Montpensier, Music Division of the Bibliothèque Nationale).

2. Carl Maria von Weber (1786–1826) composed two polonaises for the piano, the *Grande Polonaise* in E♭ (opus 21) and the *Polocca brillante* in E (opus 72).

3. A marked nationalistic quality is found in the work of Stanisław Moniuszko (1819–1872), who composed the Polish national opera *Halka*.

4. Inadvertently "Grande Polonaise in D♭" in the text. The work in question is the *Andante spianato et Grande Polonaise brillante*, opus 22.

5. Inadvertently "C Minor, opus 26" in the text.

6. Inadvertently "opus 46" in the text.

7. The Spanish Jesuit theologian Luis de Molina (1535–1600), whose doctrine, called Molinism, attempted to reconcile grace and free will.

3 : : :

What Should Be Set to Music?

Good Poetry or Bad, Free Verse or Prose?[1]

Opinions presented by Fernand Divoire

The opinion of Maurice Ravel:

It seems to me that for truly poignant and emotional situations, free verse is preferable to regular verse. The latter, however, can produce very beautiful things, on condition that the composer wishes to disappear entirely behind the poet and agrees to follow his rhythms step by step, cadence by cadence, without ever displacing an accent or even an inflection. In a word, if the musician wishes to set regular verse, his music will simply underline the poem and sustain it, but will be unable to interpret it or add anything to it.

I believe that if one is specifically dealing with emotion and fantasy, it is preferable to adopt free verse. Indeed, it seems criminal to me to "spoil" classical verses.

Why in *Faust*, for example, there are some verses which are absolutely massacred:

> Ah! je ris de me voir
> Si belle en ce miroir.[2]

The composer wanted a waltz. He counted the number of feet in these lines and found twelve. From that moment, nothing else mattered to him, neither the rhyme, nor any detail of form: he wanted his waltz; the librettist wanted his twelve syllables; you know the result

> Ah! je ris
> De me voir si belle
> En ce miroir.

And you know how the strong accentuations fall. It would really have been preferable there to use free verse or prose. The same would apply when the composer puts vocalizations in the middle of the text. They are pretty, fresh, and give a certain élan and crystalline quality to the melody. But the Ah! Ah!

Ah! Ah! Ahs! . . . situated in the middle of an Alexandrine give it a variable length, between seventeen and twenty-five feet, which is not useful.

Prose is sometimes very pleasant to set to music, and there are circumstances in which it is marvelously appropriate to the subject. Thus, I selected several of Jules Renard's *Histoires naturelles;* they are delicate and rhythmic, but rhythmic in a completely different way from classical verses.

Pelléas et Mélisande could only have been set to prose. Nothing else would have permitted Debussy to render the stylized naïveté and simple affectation of these missal- or tapestry-like characters with such delicacy.

NOTES

1. *Musica* (February and March 1911), pp. 38–40 and 58–60. Ravel's comments appear on pp. 59–60. Among the nineteen replies to the inquiry were those of Debussy, Dukas, Fauré, d'Indy, and poets Pierre Louÿs and Henri de Régnier.

2. Marguerite's "Jewel Song" from act three of Gounod's *Faust* (1859), libretto by Jules Barbier and Michel Carré:

> Ah! I laugh to see myself
> So beautiful in this mirror.

4 : : :

The Lamoureux Orchestra Concerts[1]

I t seems odd that musical criticism is rather infrequently entrusted to professional musicians. No doubt, it is assumed that they have better things to do, and with some brilliant exceptions, which are works of art themselves, a review, even if perspicacious, is of necessity inferior to a composition, however mediocre it may be. Moreover, one may fear that professionals, however honorable their motives, aren't always capable of judging with complete independence, and that their opinions may be sullied with passion, if not worse.[2] One must acknowledge, however, that the judgments of critics who are not professional musicians may not always be exempt from this passion. Quite often, a vehement ardor in the attack skillfully masks the incompetence that a more modest opinion would lead one to suspect.

The four most recent concerts given this month by the Lamoureux Orchestra offered an exceptionally varied program. To tell the truth, there were no first performances, except for an important scene from *Eros vainqueur*, a French opera of great musical distinction, which foreigners may enjoy in its entirety, while we are condemned to savor it in fragments.[3] But most of the other pieces were so little known, that it was interesting to have them performed once again.

By an irony of fate, the first piece which I must evaluate is my own *Pavane pour une Infante défunte*.[4] I feel no constraint in speaking about it: it is old enough to let me retreat from composer to critic. From such a distance, I no longer see its virtues. But, alas! I perceive its shortcomings very well: the excessive influence of Chabrier, and its rather poor form. The remarkable interpretation of this imperfect and unadventurous work contributed a great deal, I think, to its success.

Many in the audience who applauded the *Pavane*, demonstrated against Liszt's brilliant tone poem *Les Idéals*.[5] No doubt, this work of genius may seem a bit long on first hearing. But is it really longer than the final scene of *Götterdämmerung*, whose success at the same concert was unanimous?

Of course, I know that the finale was sung by Lucienne Bréval[6] in such a way as to make us forget the most renowned Wagnerian singers we have heard until now at our concerts. And that, despite Ernst's disconcerting gibberish,[7] in which this great artist was obliged to express herself. I also admit that the audience's rapture over this extraordinary performance was more than justified. But as everyone knows, the finale, as well as the rest of the opera, was not received with the same enthusiasm at its creation. It must have seemed even longer than *Les Idéals*.

Furthermore, of what importance are the shortcomings of this piece, or of all the works of Liszt? Are there not enough good qualities in this tumultuous ebullition, in this vast and magnificent chaos of musical material, which several generations of illustrious composers have imbibed?

It is in large part due to these shortcomings, it is true, that Wagner owes his overly declamatory vehemence, Strauss, his weighty enthusiasm, Franck, the heaviness of his elevation, the Russian school, its occasionally gaudy picturesqueness, and the present French school, the extreme coquettishness of its harmonic charm. Yet do not these composers, who are so dissimilar, owe the best of their good qualities to the musical generosity, truly prodigious, of this great precursor? Within this form, often clumsy, always effusive, doesn't one distinguish the embryo of the ingenious, facile and limpid development of Saint-Saëns? And the dazzling orchestration, with its powerful yet light sonority, has it not exercised considerable influence on Liszt's most avowed opponents?

There is a certain irony in the fact that most of these opponents were pupils of Franck, who, among his contemporaries, owed the most to Liszt. Franck's disciples were careful not to follow the example of their teacher, whose colorless and heavy orchestration often spoils the beauty of his ideas.

This reproach does not apply to any of the three composers of the Franckist school whose works were recently heard. M. Witkowski ably uses a brilliant palette in his Second Symphony, but the colors seem artificial.[8] This is because he appears to have been guided by will alone in this composition. Several brief sequential passages, treated in academic fashion (augmentation, inversion), form the basis of the melody. The harmony is almost always the result of contrapuntal encounters; the rhythm, of industrious deformations. Thus, the three elements of music, whose conception should be simultaneous and above all instinctive, are elaborated separately, and are linked, one might say, by purely intellectual workmanship.

The academic techniques which abound in the three movements of this symphony make it all too clear that M. Witkowski imposed upon himself the task of presenting an idea and developing it in a particular manner, come what may. How far this repulsive intellectual logic is from sensibility! Nevertheless, behind this dour mask, one discerns a profound, vibrant musician at every moment—one who could not easily have accepted the discipline and the vexations imposed upon him in the name of I-don't-know-what absurd dogmas.

Ernest Chausson's *Poème de l'amour et de la mer*[9] is altogether different: from the outset of this piece, inspiration sustains the melody and the harmony, which form a unity. A mood of gentle enchantment is revealed, whose memory will be happily preserved during the needless and clumsy confusion found in the thematic development, which weakens this otherwise very musical work. The orchestration, if at times a bit heavy, is always captivating, interpreting the landscapes evoked by the poet with remarkable skill.

The orchestral talents of M. Pierre de Bréville are likewise superior to those of his teacher. His elegant harmony and distinctive melodic color are revealed in shimmering sonorities of tranquil picturesqueness.[10] I might reproach this work for a certain tameness of inspiration. In some passages, I would have preferred a more dramatic expression, somewhat crude, which can move even the most fastidious audience. But should one reproach this artist for excessive modesty, and for disdaining those facile "tricks," by means of which some of his colleagues achieve notoriety?

I seem to be making the same mistake that I was complaining about in others. What's the use of looking for imperfections in a work which I found utterly delightful? Do I always have to be such a *professional*?

NOTES

1. *Revue musicale de la S.I.M.* (February 15, 1912), 8(2):62–63. In the autograph, the title of this article ("Lamoureux Concert") is written in another hand. However, Ravel mentions that he is reviewing four (Sunday afternoon) concerts. He could not of course comment on every piece, and among the other works which were performed, we may note the following: Beethoven's 7th Symphony, Debussy's *Nocturnes*, Mozart's Piano Concerto in C Minor, Rimsky-Korsakov's *Scheherazade*, Schumann's 4th Symphony and his *Overture, Scherzo, and Finale*. The programs were conducted by Camille Chevillard.

2. For whatever reason, a controversial paragraph was deleted from Ravel's article, which would have been inserted at this point.

> In fact, I have just received an article written by M. Gaston Carraud concerning a short work of mine which was recently produced. The article contains the most serious accusation which can be brought against an artist: the lack of sincerity. In the critic's own words, my works aim, in general, to "wow" the public. No less a person than a colleague dared to make such a statement. (See plate 14.)

Writing in *La Liberté* on January 30, 1912, Carraud explained that he would review the ballet version of *Ma Mère l'Oye* the following day, and called it a "very pleasant tiny choreographic fantasy." The review on January 31, however, was highly negative, and Carraud even suggested that Ravel should have written a new score, rather than orchestrate an old one. "For the first time," he noted, "M. Ravel indicates something natural, and a greater desire to amuse himself and us discreetly, rather than 'wow' us."

3. *Triumphant Eros,* an opera in three acts, with libretto by Jean Lorrain and music by Pierre de Bréville, was first performed with great success at the Théâtre de la Monnaie in Brussels on March 7, 1910. Its Parisian debut finally took place at the Opéra-Comique on February 8, 1932. Two excerpts from the opera were performed, the ballet music from act 2, and the aria of Eros, sung by the celebrated French mezzo-soprano Claire Croiza (1882–1946).

4. Composed in 1899, the *Pavane* was orchestrated in 1910.

5. Based on Schiller's poem *Die Ideale.* Rather curiously, Ravel consistently misspells Liszt's name as "Listz."

6. The noted French soprano (1869–1935) enjoyed a distinguished international career.

7. The French critic Alfred Ernst (1860–1898), a passionate Wagnerian, translated six of Wagner's libretti into rhythmic French prose.

8. Georges-Martin Witkowski (1867–1943) studied composition with Vincent d'Indy at the Schola Cantorum. His Second Symphony was published by Durand in 1910, and from 1924 to 1941 he was the director of the Conservatory in Lyon. He was also active in Lyon as a conductor, directing the Société des Grands-Concerts and the Concerts Witkowski (see letter no. 82, note 7).

9. Chausson's piece (1882–90, revised in 1893), for voice and orchestra, is set to the poetry of Maurice Buchor. It was sung by one Madame Bloomfield-Zeisler.

10. Referring once again to the excerpts from Bréville's opera.

5 : : :

The Lamoureux Orchestra Concerts[1]

That *long patience*, or will, in which, unfortunately, Buffon[2] believed he had discovered the very essence of genius, is only, in fact, a useful assistant. The principle of *genius*, that is of artistic creation, can be established only by instinct, or sensibility. What was in Buffon's mind perhaps nothing but a whim, has given rise to a more serious error, which is relatively modern—the assumption that will alone can direct artistic instinct.

An artist's will should only be the attentive servant of his instinct: a robust, lucid servant, who must intelligently obey the orders of his master, yielding to his slightest caprice, facilitating the pursuit of his path, never attempting to detour him from it; helping him to adorn himself magnificently, but never selecting any garment from his cast-off clothing, no matter how sumptuous. Sometimes, however, the master is so weak that the servant is obliged to support him, even guide him. The results of this halting association are rather paltry, at least in the domain of music. Certain listeners, who are rather insensitive themselves, nevertheless appear satisfied with these results.

In these tedious works, one is particularly tempted to esteem what is called "craft." Now, in art, *craft*, in the absolute sense of the word, cannot exist. In the harmonious proportion of a work, and in the elegance of its flow, the role of inspiration is virtually unlimited. The will to develop can only be sterile.

This is what appears most clearly in the majority of Brahms' works. It was evident in the Symphony in D Major, which was recently performed at the Lamoureux concerts. The themes bespeak an intimate and gentle musicality; although their melodic contour and rhythm are very personal, they are directly related to those of Schubert and Schumann. Scarcely have they been presented than their progress becomes heavy and laborious. It seems that the composer was ceaselessly haunted by the desire to equal Beethoven.

Now the charming nature of Brahms' inspiration was incompatible with his vast, passionate, almost extravagant developments, which are the direct result of Beethovenian themes, or rather, themes which spring from Beethovenian inspiration. This craft, which his predecessor Schubert was deprived of *natu-*

rally, was acquired by Brahms through study. He did not discover it within himself.

Does a similar phenomenon account for the disappointment one experiences with each new hearing of César Franck's Symphony? Probably so, even though these two symphonies are very different, as much in their themes as in their development.[3] Their faults, however, emanate from the same source: a similar disproportion between the themes and their development. With Brahms, a clear and simple inspiration, sometimes playful, sometimes melancholy; learned developments which are grandiloquent, complicated, and heavy. With Franck, melody of an elevated and serene character, bold harmonies of particular richness; but a distressing poverty of form. The structure of the German master is skillful, but one perceives too much contrivance. In Franck's work, there is at best an attempt at structure: groups of measures up to entire pages are repeated, transposed textually; he awkwardly abuses out-of-date academic formulas. Brahms' superiority is clearly seen in one respect, namely, his orchestral technique, which is extremely brilliant. In Franck's work, on the contrary, the errors in orchestration accumulate. Here, the double basses drag along clumsily, weighing down an already lusterless passage for the strings. There, noisy trumpets double the violins. Just when the inspiration is at its peak, one is disconcerted by extraneous sonorities.

It is not surprising that in Germany, just as in France, Brahms and Franck were singled out in order to combat Wagnerian influence—they, whose flaws often elicit reactions of indifference and boredom. This very peculiarity of their genius designated them as precipitators of the inevitable movement of reaction.

Wagner's extraordinary spontaneity, which synthesized all the sensibility of the nineteenth century, must have disturbed even those who were among the first to have experienced its powerful attraction. Even today, when one hears the resounding Venusberg music, which is one of the most representative examples of Wagner's art, it is understandable that after this explosion of joy and passionate suffering, after this roaring outburst of pagan vitality, the need must have been felt for a peaceful, even austere, retreat.

In France, this meditation produced various results: first, from the Franckist cloister, there emerged a solemn procession of composers who were devotees of the artist's will, and their faith in it became only stronger. Then, a less organized group of young, free-spirited people appeared, who were guided much more by their instinct; their sensibility strove to perceive its slightest external manifestations profoundly, and with more subtlety than their predecessors.

Recently, M. Chevillard[4] reintroduced *Saugefleurie*, by Vincent d'Indy, the leader of the first group. In this symphonic poem, one can already ascertain the principles which guide the composer's artistic behavior. The orchestration is rich and colorful, the form is clear. But one discovers a disdain of natural harmony, of spontaneous rhythm, of free melody—in a word, of everything not in the domain of pure will. This principle, pushed to its limits, must give, as a final result, that musical abstraction, d'Indy's Sonata for piano.

The second group may be legitimately linked with the Russian school, which contributed significantly to the blossoming of our generation's musical sensibility. Two of the most characteristic works of this school were performed in recent programs: Borodin's *In the Steppes of Central Asia*, an ingenuous work, whose musicality and *impressionism* are so penetrating; and *Islamey*, by Balakirev,[5] orchestrated by Alfredo Casella.

I would venture to call *Islamey* a masterpiece. The original conception of this work being purely pianistic, the need for an orchestral transcription seemed odd to certain people. Some even cried "sacrilege," yet they accept a piano transcription or even a paraphrase of an orchestral work without complaining. Personally, I must admit that I thoroughly enjoyed hearing this piece in its new form. It would have been practically impossible, and probably rather fruitless, to reproduce pianistic effects in the orchestra. While scrupulously respecting the work's musical material, M. Casella chose to interpret it boldly, rather than simply transfer it. The complex orchestration, very full, nevertheless light, transformed a brilliant fantasy for the piano into an equally brilliant orchestral piece.

At the same concert, the ballet music from Georges Hüe's lyric drama *Le Miracle* was performed, which I had previously heard at the Opéra.[6] I was pleased to reencounter the feeling of spontaneity which had first impressed me in these lilting, folklike dances, with their ingenious and varied rhythms. Once again, I was delighted to savor one of the most attractive orchestral sonorities imaginable, which occurs, I believe, in the second variation of the "Bear's Dance."[7]

On February 25, the Colonne concert presented its first performance of Florent Schmitt's *Psalm XLVI*, an important and highly distinguished work.[8] That very day, the finest, most curious, and the most artistic public in the world eagerly rushed to the Lamoureux concert in order to acclaim M. Emil Sauer.[9] This pianist, who has been applauded on several occasions—he is, moreover, an extraordinary virtuoso—gave a brilliant rendition of Liszt's Concerto in E♭, a work as beautiful as it is well known.

It is not customary to grant composers the same attention as interpreters. That is why the public responded with less enthusiasm to the *Children's Corner* by Claude Debussy, orchestrated by André Caplet with subtle refinement. These short pieces are obviously nothing but a great artist amusing himself. But there is more music in a single measure of this work than in all of *Les*

Impressions d'Italie, that interminable suite written by a grateful winner of the Prix de Rome, which formerly earned its skillful author the touching esteem of the Institute's most venerable members.[10]

NOTES

1. *Revue musicale de la S.I.M.* (March 1912), 8(3):50–52.

2. The eminent naturalist Georges-Louis Leclerc, Comte de Buffon (1707–1788), is best remembered for his imposing *Histoire naturelle,* published in 44 volumes (Jules Renard borrowed Buffon's title for his animal sketches). Buffon's observations about patience and genius appeared in the first discourse of the *Histoire naturelle,* "How to Study and Deal With Natural History," published in 1749.

> Natural History, taken in its broadest sense, is an immense History, embracing all of the objects found in the Universe. This prodigious multitude of Quadrupeds, Birds, Fish, Insects, Plants, Minerals, etc., presents a vast spectacle to the curiosity of the human mind, whose totality is so great that its details seem and are in fact inexhaustible. . . . The most skillful Observers, after working for several years, have only produced rather imperfect sketches of the excessively multiple objects which the particular branches of Natural History contain, which they have examined minutely. However, they did what they could, and far from blaming these Observers for the meager advancement of Science, we cannot sufficiently praise their assiduity and their patience; we must accord them even nobler attributes, for there is a sort of force of genius and of intellectual courage to be able to envision Nature, without being amazed, in the innumerable multitude of its manifestations, and to believe oneself capable of understanding and comparing them.

3. Brahms' Second Symphony dates from 1877, and Franck's Symphony was completed in 1888.

4. Camille Chevillard (1859–1923) studied composition with Chabrier, but is best remembered as the principal conductor of the Lamoureux Orchestra. In this capacity, he conducted the first performance of *La Valse.*

5. Ravel was particularly impressed by Balakirev's oriental fantasy *Islamey* (1869, second version in 1902), which was generally thought to be the ultimate in keyboard virtuosity. Nevertheless, he informed Maurice Delage that *Gaspard de la nuit* would be even more difficult to play, which in fact it is.

6. This opera in five acts with libretto by P.B. Gheusi and A. Mérane was introduced at the Opéra on December 30, 1910. Hüe (1858–1948; see plate 3) studied at the Conservatoire, won the Prix de Rome in 1879, and went on to compose a large body of music which enjoyed considerable popularity during his lifetime (a ballet-pantomime, *Siang Sin,* was performed over one hundred times at the Opéra).

7. This passage, marked Allegro brillante, indicates the influence of Rimsky-Korsakov's colorful orchestration, with an active percussion section (especially the tympani, bass drum, and cymbals), closely spaced writing for the brass, fleeting

arpeggios in the clarinets, and the melody mostly in the strings. The texture is light throughout.

8. The French text of this piece is taken from Psalm 47 (46 in the Vulgate). Completed in 1904, this massive, dramatic work calls for a large orchestra, organ, mixed chorus, and soprano soloist.

9. The German pianist Emil von Sauer (1862–1942) trained with Nicholas Rubinstein at the Moscow Conservatory, and studied briefly with Liszt.

10. See letter no. 6, note 4.

6 : : :

Symphonic Scenes *by Monsieur Fanelli*[1]

"An unrecognized genius." "A French Wagner." "Incomparable and sublime." "Everyone: rendezvous at the Colonne concert next Sunday."

The daily press is truly abusing its almighty power! If it wants to be involved in launching a wonder drug, well and good. If it attempts to provoke international conflicts for its own financial self-interest, or to revive a defaulting industry by means of so-called patriotic subscriptions, that is its right, if not its duty. We have already relinquished politics, commercial ventures, and even the theater to it. But, at least, the press should leave art to us!

For more than a week, the daily papers have continuously written about M. Fanelli,[2] who was too little known until now. We were informed each day how he struggled to earn his living as a copyist, barely having enough to eat, and how his daughter was working in order to obtain a teaching diploma. We learned about the poignant emotions which his score engendered in M. Gabriel Pierné and the Colonne Orchestra, as well as Mme Judith Gautier[3] and M. Benedictus.[4]

These demeaning journalistic techniques, presented in installments like a second-rate novel, produced a most ridiculous and distressing manifestation: for a quarter of an hour, a mid-Lenten crowd repeatedly screamed "Fa-ne-lli!, Fa-ne-lli!", until the poor man had to be dragged on stage. This consoling ovation rectified nothing; M. Fanelli deserves better than that.

This American-style advertising should certainly excite the fans of Nick Carter.[5] On the other hand, it provoked the distrust of composers as well as critics, whose profession requires prudence. Some of the critics were courageous enough to maintain their prejudices. Nevertheless, this composer's case is remarkable: completely isolated in 1883, he devoted himself to researches which are commonly labeled *impressionist,* at a time when no one in France was concerned with *impressionism.*

This impressionism is certainly very different from that of present-day composers. In his youth, M. Fanelli was probably unaware of certain works by Liszt, and was surely unacquainted with the works of Rimsky-Korsakov, Balakirev, Mussorgsky, and Borodin, which inspired the younger French school. M.

Fanelli's impressionism derives more directly from Berlioz, whose perception of the sounds of nature is hardly stylized. The melodic and harmonic interest is hardly more satisfying than the *Roman Carnival* overture, or certain passages of *Romeo and Juliet.*[6]

Be that as it may, and above all, placing oneself in the time it was written, M. Fanelli's composition is of the greatest interest. One may note the overly dense atmosphere at the beginning of the first part, the strident whining of the lammergeiers, and the slave's lament in the distance, despite its somewhat conventional orientalism; in the second part, the dazzling effect of a fleet of motley ships; in the third part, the ceaseless rolling of rumbling chariots accompanied by bursts of fanfares—all of this was expressed, it seemed at least on first hearing, by the most picturesque orchestration alone, which would have amazed the audience, had the Colonne Orchestra performed this symphonic poem in time. The reception probably would not have been so unanimous; but the performers, rather than shedding tears, would have at least smiled. The same audience would only have applauded more enthusiastically for the brilliant *Fireworks* by Igor Stravinsky. Perhaps it would simply have cried hush!, as at the first performance of *The Afternoon of a Faun,* which it encores today.[7]

Above all, the investigations of the young Fanelli could not have diminished those of his colleagues. It is peculiar that these investigations, which until now were considered negligible by some, suddenly assume extraordinary importance because their embryo is discovered in a work written thirty years ago. This noble courage, which consists of crushing the innovations of troublesome contemporaries with the innovations of their predecessors, has uncovered the source of Claude Debussy's *impressionism* in M. Fanelli's piece.

One critic, carried away by his own enthusiasm, even thought it necessary to state point-blank that in this symphonic poem, "the conception and the harmonic language are clearly Debussyian, or rather pre-Debussyian," no doubt because "M. Fanelli abuses *successions of major thirds,* which, in 1883, was a discovery and a novelty." By that, the honorable critic means chords based upon the whole-tone scale. Now he was apparently unaware that about the middle of the last century, this technique was already used, first by Liszt,[8] and then by Dargomijsky, who did more than abuse it: an entire act of *The Stone Guest* is based on this scale.[9]

It is customary for M. Debussy to undergo a yearly attack of this sort. We already knew that the discovery of his harmonic system was entirely due to Erik Satie, that his stage works derived from Mussorgsky, and his orchestration from Rimsky-Korsakov. We now know the source of his impressionism. Despite this paucity of invention, Debussy only remains the most important and profoundly musical composer living today.

As for M. Fanelli, I do not know many French musicians of his generation who could be compared with him in 1883, as much for his orchestral boldness as for the power of his inspiration.[10]

NOTES

1. "Les 'Tableaux symphoniques' de M. Fanelli," *Revue musicale de la S.I.M.* (April 1912), 8(4):55–56.

2. Ernest Fanelli (1860–1917), a pupil of Léo Delibes, composed a handful of works. Although his music and personal career became a cause célèbre, both are now virtually forgotten.

3. Mme Gautier (1850–1918), the daughter of Théophile Gautier, was an important author in her own right, whose essays and novels reflected her particular interest in orientalism and music. Fanelli's piece, which is dedicated to her, is based on Théophile Gautier's *Le Roman de la momie* (The Novel of the Mummy). Completed in 1883, the symphonic poem was first performed in 1912.

4. Edouard Benedictus had set several of Judith Gautier's poems to music (see letter no. 53, note 3).

5. This fictional American detective was the hero of more than 1,000 dime novels written by various authors.

6. Although he called Berlioz a "genius," Ravel's enthusiasm for his music was limited (see p. 461).

7. Despite Ravel's observation, Debussy's work was repeated at its première on December 23, 1894. In his memoirs, the Swiss conductor Gustave Doret (1866–1943) recalled the Société Nationale concert as follows:

> The hall is packed. An impressive silence reigns when our marvelous flutist Barrère reveals his opening theme. Suddenly, I feel behind my back—it is a special ability of certain conductors!—a completely captivated public! The triumph is so complete that despite the rule forbidding encores I do not hesitate to break the rule. And the orchestra, delighted, joyfully repeated the work it had loved and had imposed upon the conquered public. (Gustave Doret, *Temps et Contretemps*, Fribourg: Editions de la Librairie de l'Université, 1942, p. 96.)

8. Successions of major thirds appear in the opening passage of Liszt's *Faust Symphony* (1854).

9. Alexander Dargomijsky (1813–1869) left this opera incomplete at his death. It was finished in 1872 by César Cui, with orchestration by Rimsky-Korsakov.

10. Another critique of Fanelli's piece was written by Claude Debussy, who observed the following:

> For the moment he is rather too concerned with obeying that familiar spirit which demands that he should pile more and more notes on top of one another without concerning himself with the overall proportions. He is very aware of the decorative aspect of music, which sometimes leads him to concentrate too much on the

description of minute details; he forgets that music can be persuasive in its own right. Let us hope that he will have time to take stock of himself: life owes him that. Meanwhile, we should afford him our generous support. (*Revue musicale de la S.I.M.*, March 15, 1913, pp. 48–49; translation taken from François Lesure, *Debussy on Music*, trans. Richard L. Smith, New York: Knopf, 1977, p. 285.)

7 : : :

The Witch *at the Opéra-Comique*[1]

The underground caverns of the Inquisition. On the wall, an impressive representation of Christ, wrapped in the Spanish manner in a black velvet loincloth. On the stage, instruments of torture. An inquisitor and his assistants are clad in leather aprons, which, by inexplicable reserve, appear unsoiled by bloody stains. A demented witch fills the theater with hysterical laughter and hideous shrieks. Cardinal Jiménez[2] himself does not hesitate to take part in wringing the defendants' wrists in order to expedite confessions. The lofty philosophical scope of the opera is then revealed: Zoraya, a Moorish maidservant, cries out in a Voltairian tirade on the incompatibility of torture and the teachings of the gospel. A program note specifically mentions that "Victorien Sardou's[3] personal belief, based upon meticulous study, reflection, and scientific research," led him to discover that there are but two types of witches: neurotic and simple-minded. At the outset of the twentieth century, the boldness of this conclusion is truly astonishing.

Despite all the thrilling elements lavished upon the fourth act, most of the audience was disappointed when the curtain fell: the instruments of torture were not used.

Several years ago, the Gaîté-Lyrique theater presented an operatic spectacle whose least shortcoming was the absence of lyricism. At one point, M. Périer[4] had to spit out his tongue in a torrent of blood. The composer, M. Nouguès, specifically omitted music in this delicate scene, perhaps intentionally.[5]

But M. Erlanger[6] is a musician, and cannot conceal this fact even for a moment. Thus, unless he decided beforehand to sacrifice his natural gifts for the facile effects of *verismo* horror, it is difficult to understand his reasons[7] for composing an opera based upon this melodrama, which, strictly speaking, could have served as a pretext for the obsolete formulas of bygone operas.

No doubt, the first three acts offered the composer some obvious, but attractive situations: in the first act, the apparition of Zoraya in the moonlight, and the scene which follows; the prelude and beginning of act two, whose enchanting musical color features the voice mingling harmoniously with the ringing of bells; the Spanish and oriental atmosphere, which, in my opinion, M.

Erlanger could have taken advantage of with greater abandon. These poetic and picturesque elements are treated successfully most of the time.

But one senses that the restless audience accepts these three acts of music as an overly slow preparation for the expected torture. Attracted by the scenes of the Inquisition, which are reproduced in the program, young ladies, who are customarily escorted to the Opéra-Comique, expected a foretaste of the Grand-Guignol,[8] where they will be able to go without fear, once married. From this long awaited fourth act until the dénouement of the opera, in which the emotionalism of the stake lies in store for the audience, one's attention is riveted by a spectacle in which music can only seem alien.

In general, this music seemed more natural than M. Erlanger's other works. The rhythms are more direct, and the overall conception is clearer. The vocal writing, however, is extremely scabrous. I admit that this shortcoming is neither peculiar to this work, nor even to other works by M. Erlanger. One finds it in almost all of the vocal music written in our time. It is to Wagner's dangerous example that we owe this sort of contempt—which affects most of today's composers—for the most expressive of sonorous instruments.

M. Erlanger pushes this contempt to the extreme. Nothing less than Mlle Chenal's powerful and brilliant voice would have been heard above the orchestration, which, although often picturesque, was uniformly too heavy, thereby prohibiting any gradations of color. Without respite or apparent fatigue, this extraordinary artist performed the most perilous leaps required by the composer.

The vigorous accents of the German language, and particularly those of Wagner's idiom, account for this animated declamation. Applied to the French language, it becomes paradoxical, and the comprehensibility of the text, which is necessary in the theater, can only suffer as a result. Even M. Périer, whose clarity of diction is exceptional, did not always succeed in making every word intelligible. As for M. Beyle, whose ardent and musical voice is well known, Mlle Vallin, whose moving performance was achieved by the simplest of means, and the other artists who performed their secondary roles perfectly, one was satisfied if, by chance, one occasionally managed to discern some words with correct prosody.

With regard to the role of Afrida, the hysterical witch, one need not grasp the subtleties of her lines. Mlle Espinasse, who performed this role at the dress rehearsal, laughed, shrieked, and gesticulated with such vehemence, that she justly merited the ovation offered by a horrified, entranced audience.

The Opéra-Comique's excellent orchestra, which M. Ruhlmann[9] conducted with expert control, brilliantly performed its role, which is extremely important in this score.

I find myself very embarrassed: mustn't I discuss the décor and the production? Unfortunately, it turns out that both of these important components of theatrical art run counter to all of my aesthetic aspirations. To be sure, ingenuity and picturesqueness are lavished upon the décor. Thus, in the first act, all the products of nature and of human industry are meticulously represented: trees, hills, crags, rivers, bridges, illuminated cities, and what not? But in this microcosm, which is too cramped on the stage of the Opéra-Comique, and would be so even in a more spacious setting, one searches in vain for the most essential attribute of theatrical décor: style.

The great nineteenth-century scenery painters mastered this style, and, moreover, they modified it in accordance with the work being presented: act two of *Les Huguenots,* the cathedral in *Faust,*[10] etc. The obsolete techniques of these masters—nowadays made trivial and complicated—still serve their inferior successors, who apply them indifferently to any work ancient or modern, or to whatever nationality or school a composer may belong.

This approach to décor, one must admit, still gratifies the taste of many amateurs, whose artistic penchants appear loftier in other situations. Among the spectators who let out a gasp of admiration when the curtain rose on a Moorish garden displaying a jumble of colors, how many would be pleased to have a similar painting in their own drawing room?

: : :

At the Théâtre des Arts: Act Three of *Idomeneo* and
La Source Lointaine [The Distant Source]

I could not resist comparing the feeble décor of *The Witch* with M. Piot's[11] beautiful décor, executed by M. Mouveau, for the performances of the third act of Mozart's *Idomeneo* at the Théâtre des Arts. The simple, spacious format of the scenery enlarges the proportions of this tiny stage in a curious way. The color scheme is bold and captivating, without useless variegation. The décor is one of the finest that the Théâtre des Arts has presented, and it is the best that I have seen on a Parisian stage in a long time.

Moreover, M. Rouché must be thanked for having mounted this splendid fragment, whose sublime character is scarcely equaled in the art of music, and in which tragedy is achieved by musical expression alone. There are none of those "tricks" which Gluck brought to the lyric theater, whose futility has been demonstrated so often by his successors.[12]

Despite the youthful voice and the refined art of Mlle Lucy Vauthrin, the power and nobility of M. Ghasne, and the genuine talents of their colleagues, perfection was not achieved. Here, as elsewhere, it will not be possible to achieve it for a long time. As long as those facial expressions and realistic gestures—which are so remote from tragic beauty—hinder the clear projection of the voice, and as long as the stage is filled with unimportant, superfluous activity, which destroys the thread of the plot, lyric art, which today has been reduced to the level of pretentious entertainment, will be unable to regain its lofty path.

Poets, musicians, and painters must all unite in restoring the grandeur and the plenitude of theatrical emotion. But in order to achieve this, the assistance of theater directors is necessary. In France, until now, this assistance has been furnished only by M. Rouché.

Together with *Idomeneo,* the Théâtre des Arts is presenting a ballet suggested to M. de Goloubev by a Persian legend, *The Distant Source.* The music is by Mme Armande de Polignac.[13] The form of this composition is at times a bit vague. On the other hand, one frequently encounters innovations, chiefly harmonic discoveries, whose daring does not exclude charm. It would be absurd to blame Mme de Polignac for her unrelenting creative concern, which is the noblest endowment that a sincere artist can possess.

Although conducted by that sensitive musician M. Gabriel Grovlez,[14] the orchestra did not always seem properly balanced. The fault lies with the small size of the hall, and with the composer, who was caught unawares by these unusual proportions.

The principal performer is Mlle Napierkovska. Her supple grace is well known, and the elegance of her arm movements is rarely encountered even among ballerinas.

M. Doucet's[15] scenery and costumes reveal a very rare sensitivity for color. The scenery and costumes are, so to speak, nothing but enlargements of Persian miniatures, but their interpretation is flawless. This quality is indispensable, as much for theatrical décor as for any work of art.

NOTES

1. *"La Sorcière* à l'Opéra-Comique," *Comœdia illustré* (January 5, 1913), 5(7):320–23. The opera is by Camille Erlanger (see note 6).

2. The Spanish cardinal, grand inquisitor, and statesman Francisco Jiménez de Cisneros (1436–1517) rose from humble beginnings to become the religious and political adviser to the Spanish throne.

3. In addition to *The Witch,* Sardou (1831–1908) wrote some seventy works for the stage. His melodrama *Tosca* was the basis of Puccini's famous opera.

4. See letter no. 53, note 7.

5. Jean Nouguès (1876–1932) composed the opera in question, *Quo Vadis* (1909).

6. Camille Erlanger (1863–1919) studied at the Conservatoire with Léo Delibes and won the Prix de Rome in 1888. He composed mostly vocal music, including nine operas, the most successful of which was *Aphrodite* (1906), based on the novel by Pierre Louÿs,

which received almost two hundred performances at the Opéra-Comique. *The Witch* was introduced on December 18, 1912, with some of the major roles performed by Mesdames Marthe Chenal (Zoraya) and Ninon Vallin (Manuella), and Messieurs Jean Périer (the Cardinal) and Léon Beyle (Don Enrique). François Ruhlmann conducted, with décor by Lucien Jusseaume and M. Bailly, and production by Albert Carré.

7. Literally, "the reasons of the composer of *Saint-Julien-l'Hospitalier*," another opera by Erlanger, based on Flaubert's short story.

8. This celebrated theater in the Montmartre section of Paris opened its doors in 1897. Its productions featured terrifying episodes of bloodcurdling horror, so much so that the noun "Grand-Guignol" entered the French language as a synonym for horrifying.

9. See letter no. 82, note 4.

10. Respectively by Giacomo Meyerbeer (1792–1864) and Charles Gounod (1818–1893). Ravel's opinion of Meyerbeer was similar to his view of Berlioz: while praising their orchestration, he found relatively little else to admire in their music. (An appreciation of Gounod is found on p. 384.)

11. See letter no. 118, note 2.

12. Some of Debussy's criticisms of Christoph Willibald Gluck (1714–1787) were most likely shared by Ravel. In "An Open Letter to Monsieur le Chevalier C. W. Gluck" (*Gil Blas*, February 23, 1903), Debussy wrote:

And between you and me, your prosody is awful: you turn French into an accented language when it is really a language of nuances. (Yes, I know you're German.) Rameau, who helped to form your genius, had some examples of fine and vigorous declamation that could have been of use to you—but I will not bother you with what a marvelous musician Rameau was, lest you suffer by comparison. We must acknowledge that it was you who made the action of the play predominate over the music. But was that such a good thing? On the whole, I prefer Mozart to you; he was a fine man who ignored your influence completely, thinking only of music. (François Lesure, *Debussy on Music*, p. 124.)

13. Mme Polignac (1876–1962) studied with Fauré and d'Indy. She composed several ballets based on exotic subjects, and also wrote songs, operas, and instrumental works.

14. See letter no. 92, note 2.

15. Jacques Doucet (1853–1929), the famous couturier and Maecenas.

8 : : :

Fervaal[1]

When *Fervaal* was produced at the Théâtre de la Monnaie, in 1897, it was generally reproached for being "Wagnerian." M. d'Indy's admirers were not excessively alarmed at this accusation. At that time, to be sure, no work could appear without its author being accused of Wagnerism. After disregarding Wagner's genius for a long time, the critics, disgruntled and powerless, realizing the futility of their efforts, used his glorious name in an attempt to crush all new productions.

A superficial examination sufficed in order to discover everything that a disconcerting unknown work might contain of familiar elements. If a single measure presented a certain formula, everyone, dilettantes and music critics alike, rose up, animated by chivalrous zeal, in order to denounce the plagiarism and take the defense of an artist whose genius, however, sufficed to shield himself. Bizet, Lalo, and Massenet, all pupils of Gounod, and Chabrier, the most profoundly personal, the most French of our composers—not one of them managed to avoid these absurd attacks.

The appearance of Claude Debussy renewed these fruitless struggles. Soon, no doubt, some innovator, as yet unscathed, will serve as a pretext for additional battles.

It is equally true that at all times, important artists have been influenced by certain original masters to the point of involuntarily renouncing their own personality. We have, and will continue to have "Debussyian" works. The passage of time enables us to ascertain that works do exist which are entirely Wagnerian. Among these, *Fervaal* is the most important.

This "music drama" is Wagnerian by the very essence of its music, by its theatrical scheme, its philosophy, the realization of this philosophy, by the symbolic role of the characters and their obscure language. The musical prosody of the dialogue recalls, at times rather disagreeably, that which Wagner's French translators felt obliged to adopt. In fact, the tonic accent, rather weak in our language, is marked vigorously, which is all the more distressing as it is frequently misplaced. For no reason, phrases are interrupted by rests, rather brief, but which suffice to evoke the short-winded declamation of the heroes in *Tristan,* the *Ring* cycle, and *Parsifal,* in the adaptations of Wilder or Ernst.[2] This fault is purely external, but for the listener, it is all the more striking.

The philosophy of *Fervaal* offers an even more profound analogy. Some have tried to show that, far from arising out of Wagner's philosophy, d'Indy's tended, on the contrary, to destroy it. However, time has shown that the monastic ideal of *Parsifal* is not very far removed from the Christian principle of love developed in *Fervaal.*

Moreover, as Wagner's philosophical system is no more original than M. d'Indy's, no great harm would occur if their similarities were more pronounced. What is regrettable is that in order to present this philosophy, the characters in the French drama use the same means as their counterparts in the essentially Germanic work of Wagner. All of the characters reveal themselves by their words, more often than by their actions. One notes the same situations, whose symbolism is asserted with a thoroughly Germanic persistence, the same personalities, and the same obscure, childish dialogue. Mime and Siegfried, Parsifal and Kundry, Wotan and Erda constantly come to mind.

Far superior to the libretto, the music of *Fervaal* is no less influenced by Wagner. First of all, Wagnerian principles of form are deliberately adopted. No doubt, as Ernest Chausson has remarked, "Wagner not only discovered the form which best suited the nature of his genius; he was an innovator, indicating a new direction for the theater. The dramatic revolution realized by him was too universal to remain isolated, without importance and consequences for the future."

But was it necessary to apply these principles so rigorously? Not only are the leitmotifs developed and modified precisely according to the Wagnerian scheme, but their very character, their melodic and rhythmic structure, and the general harmonic language, though less sumptuous, obviously proceed from this system, or rather from its inspiration.

One should not expect a composer's works to be entirely personal creations, offering no analogy whatever with the achievements of his predecessors. These analogies are even inevitable, and a work devoid of them would be nothing but a monstrous exception. But one feels some uneasiness in observing so many of these analogies, all coming from the same source and all reunited in the same work.

Wagner's own work offers the most complete example of assimilation on the grandest scale. Uniting the most diverse materials, this giant constructed a splendid and original palace, whose dimensions were proportioned to his stature. M. d'Indy moved into this grandiose edifice, carefully shutting its doors and windows. The fiery sun, which the architect allowed into his abode, was replaced by candles of exceptional clarity, but of less heat. In this artificial light, objects become tarnished, taking on a moribund appearance. The symbol of Fervaal proclaiming the victory of life and love while bearing a woman's corpse toward the heights is more significant than M. d'Indy intended it to be.

Nevertheless, if this drama does not and cannot possess the inspired brilliance of its models, it must take its place among the most proudly honorable productions of the French musical theater. If it lacks the audacity of certain contemporary works, or even previous ones such as Chabrier's *Gwendoline,* or M. Bruneau's *Le Rêve,*[3] it is exempt from the inherent clumsiness found in all artistic experimentation. The writing is meticulous, exhibiting nobly sustained musicality. At a time when even our subsidized theaters are overrun by untalented amateurs and unscrupulous professionals, we must profoundly admire the example of such integrity.

Under the direction of M. Messager,[4] the orchestra gave a perfect rendition of this richly sonorous score, which is complex but always clear; d'Indy's orchestration owes nothing to that of Wagner, and even surpasses it in lightness.

The shortcomings of Messieurs Delmas and Muratore are those of almost all the lyric artists of our time. Let us then consider only their virtues: the powerful voice and clear diction of the former, and the warm timbre of the latter, struggled victoriously against the acoustics of the hall.

After an announcement, Mlle Bréval, who was seriously indisposed, proved her admiration for the composer by not hesitating to confront the hostile, unappreciative audience at the dress rehearsal. Despite her obvious discomfort, this great artist honorably acquitted herself from an ordeal which any other performer would have found fearsome.

The choral part, which is treated brilliantly, is of great importance in this work. Although difficult to perform, it was admirably done. The ardor of the chorus' acting, however, did not always match the music's vitality.

The scenery showed obvious effort. Although perfection was surely far from being achieved, one could discern progress toward a less constrained style. In the second act, the "tricks" which accompanied Arfagard's incantations were as successful as possible. They only gave further proof of our theatrical poverty.

In my next article, I will discuss the new musical production at the Théâtre des Arts, which proved to be a brilliant success at its dress rehearsal.

NOTES

1. *Comœdia illustré* (January 20, 1913), 5(8):361–64. The article is subtitled "A Music Drama in Three Acts and a Prologue: Libretto and Music by Vincent d'Indy." First produced in Brussels in 1897, *Fervaal* was heard in Paris one year later at the Opéra-Comique. Ravel was reviewing a performance given at the Opéra, in which the

leading roles were sung by Mesdames Lucienne Bréval (Guilhen) and Lise Charny (Kaïto), and Messieurs Lucien Muratore (Fervaal) and Francisque Delmas (Arfagard).

2. Like Alfred Ernst, the Belgian music critic Victor van Wilder (1835–1892) was a fervent Wagnerian. He translated all of Wagner's libretti from *Lohengrin* on into French.

3. Ravel was probably thinking of the harmonic "audacity" found in *Gwendoline* (Brussels, 1886), with its many unresolved seventh and ninth chords, and with regard to *Le Rêve* (Paris, 1891), he told Calvocoressi that it contained "significant examples of chords that were pure resonances, laid out without any regard to part-writing" (Calvocoressi, "Ravel's Letters," p. 18).

4. See p. 483, note 13.

9 : : :

At the Théâtre des Arts[1]

The second series of musical productions at the Théâtre des Arts is successful in every respect. At the dress rehearsal, the success was so great that the audience expressed its desire to have the final work repeated. The performance consists of three works: a modern operetta, a Baroque lyric work, and a recent ballet. The scenic realization of these works, which are so different in nature and chronology, is obtained by artistic means as varied as the works themselves, and each time the result is a perfect adaptation. However, there is an underlying unity present in the ensemble—that of taste. In many theaters which are more influential, one would be happy to observe this single characteristic.

Une Education manquée by Emmanuel Chabrier is only an operetta, and it has the great merit of not aiming beyond that. Nevertheless, there is more genuine music in this little work than in many full-length operas. In the shortest couplet or romance, one can recognize the unique personality of the composer of *Gwendoline, Le Roi malgré lui,* and *La Sulamite.* In these works, one finds the same musical material, more extended, but just as delightful. How much light music, even recently composed, seems out-of-date in comparison with *Une Education manquée,* which, however, is only thirty-four years old. Unfortunately, the libretto has not retained the same freshness,[2] and the inferiority of the text forms a distressing contrast with the originality, character, and delicate orchestration of this charming score.

The vocal part, which at times is perilous, is in very capable hands, thanks to the bravura of Mlle Rachel Launay, the charm of Mlle Marxelle Coulomb, and the winning buffoonery of M. Bourgeois. Certain passages would have gained by being performed with greater vivacity, as for example in the duet between Pausanias and Gontran, in which the tutor pitilessly enumerates the variety of attainments he has inculcated in his pupil, while the pupil laments his feelings of inadequacy.

M. Farge's décor and costumes are adapted to this very simple plot with restraint and commendable taste, without attracting attention by means of trifles available in a secondhand shop. The stagehand responsible for producing the thunder performed his task with such verve, that the composer, no doubt, would have preferred greater discretion.

The prologue of *Thésée*, as everyone knows, is suitably sumptuous, intending to celebrate the campaign in Flanders.[3] The gods of Olympus descend respectfully on the stage in order to talk about the king's bravery, to compliment him on the success of his weapons, the abundance of his favors, and even the choice of his mistresses. Lully's majestic inspiration becomes supple in the cantilenas of Venus and Ceres. At moments like this, I must confess, I am more receptive to the charm of this musicality than to the orderly and somewhat dry ingenuity of Rameau.[4]

One might think that the stage of the Théâtre des Arts is a bit small to encompass such a grandiose pageant. However, the elegant architecture of the décor and the sumptuousness of the costumes are such a joy for the eye to behold, that one overlooks this disproportion.[5]

In a French garden, illuminated by lampions and a beautiful bronze candelabrum, the gods and heros march past in their courtly apparel. The felicitous mixture of the most splendid fabrics, the bold yet delicate variety of the colors, and the nobility of the lines accord perfectly with the music of this prologue. A rare and sumptuous harmoniousness emanates from all of this.

One recalls the tragic bareness of the décor that M. Dethomas created for Dostoyevsky's haunting drama, *The Brothers Karamazov.* This remarkable artist has just proved, even more than in *Dominos,*[6] or *Salomé* by Florent Schmitt, that he can intelligently adjust the resources of his art to the most disparate theatrical requirements.

The interpretation is extremely polished: a choir of youthful voices accompanies the excellent soloists, Mesdames Lucy Vauthrin and Vuillemin, and Messieurs Ghasne and Moisson.

Dolly, by M. Gabriel Fauré, has once again raised the question of the advisability of transferring a piece of absolute music to the stage. Everyone knows this suite for piano four hands, in which a great artist, in homage to childhood, has lavished all of the tender charm and harmonic grace of his unique musicality. M. Laloy had the felicitous idea of having these short pieces illustrated for the stage,[7] and M. Henri Rabaud[8] orchestrated them with the most ingenious tact and suppleness. Thereupon, certain critics and amateurs, guardians of the temple of Music, once again cried "sacrilege." Would the goddess inspire less respect on the altar than in the sacristy? The fact remains that composers are never aroused as much as dilettantes about these transcriptions, which every musical work may undergo, on condition that good taste presides. Certain composers, myself included, have devoted themselves to profaning their own music. And I believe that the composer of *Dolly* was aware of the fact that this new villainy had just been perpetrated. Besides, for those who are excessively affected by the enormity of this defilement, there is always the recourse of purifying the work by performing it at home in its original form.

I would venture to express one reservation with regard to *Dolly,* concerning the opening "Lullaby": the contrast is too obvious between this gracious, slow, and subdued melody, and the angry stamping of a little girl, the pirouettes and slaps in the face of the two Pierrots, the Foottit brothers,[9] who, between two caprioles, pester Mme Varaille, a frolicsome nurse. But except for this detail, the action is adapted so skillfully to the music, that the music seems to have been composed in order to illustrate it. Miss Eva Reid,[10] as Dolly, was full of childish charm, and M. Aveline performed the figurant role of the nimble Dancer with great skill. Joined by M. Pieri Sandrini, they performed one piece as a brisk waltz,[11] whose rhythm lent itself perfectly to this interpretation. The same was true of the "Spanish Dance," whose character was effectively captured by M. Miralès' national ardor. And how can one resist the joyful emotion which overtakes one the moment the curtain rises on Miss Lloyd's curiously stylized landscape, in which one sees beautiful multicolored birds perched on the most unlikely flowers, and when a large fluffy rabbit, M. Marcel Héronville, crosses the stage, pushing a carriage overloaded with red balloons?

M. Grovlez was also one of the more important acrobats of the evening. Followed by his orchestra, he jumped from one genre to another and leaped over several epochs with the greatest of ease.

However, this performance, so successfully varied and so warmly received, will be presented only eight times! M. Rouché, the director of the Théâtre des Arts, thus presents us with a paradoxical situation: in all countries, in Germany and even in Russia, considerable research of the greatest artistic interest is being pursued which seeks nothing less than to renew the principles of theatrical décor. But in France, where directors' efforts focus upon perfecting the stereoscope in color and refining out-of-date scenery, a gigantic effort is being made on a solitary, minuscule stage. In this overly narrow spot, the most diverse dramatic and lyric talents have come together, and their art is appreciated with complete justification. The most brilliant painters of the young French school furnish the sketches for the costumes and the décor. Their realization is entrusted to professional artists of great distinction such as M. Mouveau, for example. The décor and costumes are always works of art. If at times their realization is not perfect, they never fail to attract attention by their innovations in color or style. Sometimes of complex opulence, sometimes of tragic or delicate simplicity, the attempt is made to adapt the décor and costumes to the character of the story. Whatever the expenses necessitated by the works, and whatever their success, the performance is continually renewed. The weak point of this noble enterprise is the dilemma of the director also being a patron, a unique situation in our day. It greatly contributes towards making this undertaking overly exceptional and restricting its scope. A long run of performances of the same work—and this opportunity is frequently offered to M. Rouché—would do more to enhance the reputation of the Théâtre des Arts than all the funds lavished on mounting so many different pieces. Public opinion, now indifferent to this endeavor because of ignorance, would finally realize the benefit to be gained by this approach. And perhaps, weary of the overblown scenes and dreary banalities continually imposed upon it, French taste, so long dormant with regard to the theater, will finally wake up and oblige the directors of our important theaters to give it satisfaction.

NOTES

1. *Comœdia illustré* (February 5, 1913), 5(9):417–20.

2. The librettists were Eugène Leterrier and Albert Vanloo. This one-act operetta is about a young man, Gontran de Boismassif, whose tutor, Master Pausanias, instructs him in science and art, but fails to teach him what to do on his wedding night. Happily, a thunderstorm breaks out, which drives Gontran's terrified bride into his arms. Nature, rather than Pausanias, will thus instruct the young groom.

3. *Thésée*, a "lyric tragedy" in five acts with a prologue, by Jean-Baptiste Lully (1632–1687) and libretto by Philippe Quinault, was first performed before Louis XIV in January 1675. The prologue is set in the garden at the palace of Versailles.

4. Jean-Philippe Rameau (1683–1764), like Lully, was the leading French composer of his time. In addition to his influential theoretical writings, his harpsichord pieces and operas are particularly significant.

5. The décor and costumes were by Maxime Dethomas (1867–1929).

6. Based on the music of François Couperin (1688–1733), with a scenario by Louis Laloy.

7. Laloy recalled that *Dolly* was a "sort of dancing sketch," which combined "the burlesque qualities of the circus and the music-hall." (*La Musique retrouvée*, p. 198.)

8. See letter 324, note 1.

9. The celebrated English clown George Foottit (1864–1921) and his companion Chocolat, a Spanish Negro, made their reputation in Paris. They were befriended (and immortalized) by Debussy ("Minstrels," "Golliwogg's Cake Walk") and Toulouse-Lautrec.

10. "Miss" is used in French for an American or English young lady.

11. "Kitty-Valse," the fourth of Fauré's six short pieces. Completed in 1896, *Dolly* was named for and dedicated to Dolly Bardac, the young daughter of Emma Bardac, who later became Debussy's second wife.

Regarding Claude Debussy's Images[1]

. . . Man is an envious and jealous sort of animal, above all the man of letters, or he who excels in one of the ingenious attainments which we call the fine arts. It always seems to us that the reputation of people in our profession tarnishes our own luster, and chiefly the luster of those who are our contemporaries, or close to it . . . Thus, the jealousy which one feels toward the moderns is often the better part of the admiration which one shows for the ancients . . .
—ANTOINE BAUDERON DE SÉNECÉ, 1687

Notable improvements have recently been made in the methods of musical criticism. The objective of its official representatives has always been, as is known, to weaken the younger generation, whose tendencies appear dangerous to them. The rapidity with which various schools have followed one another during the past half century necessitates a more expeditious approach. It no longer suffices to lament the aesthetics of the older masters, or to feign incomprehension, anger, or hilarity with respect to the pursuits of the young: old and young are contemporaries. The point is to convince people that the older masters are in good health, whereas the vigor of the younger composers is already in decline.

Two distinct schools exist at the present time: the older one consists of César Franck's disciples, whereas M. Claude Debussy is justly considered the principal innovator of the new one.

Generally, composers' opinions are rather moderate, at least in their writings. Thus, the leader of the Franckist group, M. Vincent d'Indy, wisely recognizes the importance of certain young colleagues, and limits himself to fearing that future generations will follow them, rather than retrogress (*Revue musicale de la S.I.M.*, November 1912). The dirty work is left to a small group of music scribblers headed by Messieurs Pierre Lalo and Gaston Carraud. We owe to these two personalities the latest improvements in musical criticism.

As soon as *Pelléas et Mélisande* appeared, they placed themselves at the head of Debussy's partisans, yet from that moment on, they planned the opera's downfall. As the work was disturbing, they declared it to be sublime, but exceptional. The word "impasse" was pronounced, and then everyone waited.

PLATE I

A portrait of Marie Delouart Ravel
by Edouard Ravel (1885). Photograph
in the Music Division of the
Bibliothèque Nationale

A portrait of Pierre Joseph Ravel
by Marcellin Desboutin (1896).
Photograph in the Music Division of
the Bibliothèque Nationale

PLATE 2

Ravel and Roland-Manuel in Lyons-la-Forêt (1923). Photograph in the private collection of Claude Roland-Manuel

Ravel, Maurice and Nelly Delage, and Suzanne Roland-Manuel (c. 1923). Photograph in the Music Division of the Bibliothèque Nationale

Louise Alvar, Ravel, and Georges Jean-Aubry (1924).

A professional portrait of Ravel dedicated to Mme Louise Alvar (1924) with a humorous postscript: London, April 2024.

Both photographs in the Charles Alvar Harding Collection on deposit at the Pierpont Morgan Library. Reproduced with the kind permission of Charles Alvar Harding

PLATE 3

Standing, left to right: Pablo Casals, Jacques Thibaud, and Alfred Cortot; seated: Gabriel Fauré (1923). Photograph in the Music Division of the Bibliothèque Nationale

Jacques Rouché (c. 1910).
Photograph in the Music Division of
the Bibliothèque Nationale

At the Fontainebleau Conservatory (c. 1930). Left to right: X, X, Gérard
Hekking, X, Ravel, Emile Vuillermoz, Charles-Marie Widor, Isidor Philipp,
Georges Hüe, Henri Rabaud, Alfred Bruneau, Jean Chantavoine, and Gabriel
Pierné. Photograph in the Music Division of the Bibliothèque Nationale

PLATE 4

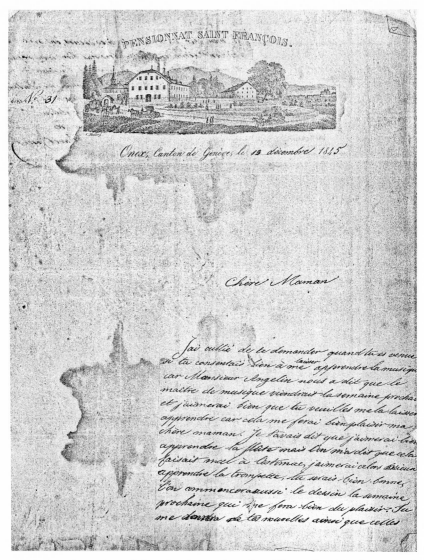

Letter from Pierre Joseph Ravel to his mother, dated December 12, 1845.
Autograph in the private collection of Mme Alexandre Taverne

de mon cher papa et de mes soeurs, en me
rendant réponse. Tu embrasseras bien mon papa
et mes soeurs tu donneras aussi le bonjour à
Monsieur le Curé à monsieur et madame Dalouche,
adieu qu'à la tante. Adieu ma chère maman
je t'embrasse de tout mon coeur adieu

          Ton respectueux fils
              Ravel joseph

cut here
across

PLATE 5

Ravel and Ida Godebska in the Basque
country (c. 1930). Photograph in the
collection of the author

A garden party at Le Belvédère, June 1928. Ravel conversing with Jane Bathori
and Cipa Godebski. To Ravel's left, the Spanish composer Joaquín Nin.
Photograph in private collection

Germaine Tailleferre,
Francis Poulenc, Arthur
Honegger, Darius
Milhaud, Jean Cocteau,
and Georges Auric
(c. 1922). Photograph in
the private collection of
Mrs. Monique Leduc

M. and Mme Lucien
Garban and Ravel
(c. 1921). Photograph in
the private collection of
Mme G. Dallan

PLATE 6

Robert Casadesus (c. 1925). Photograph in the private
collection of Mme Gaby Casadesus

Ravel, Hélène Jourdan-Morhange, and Ricardo Viñes in Saint-Jean-de-Luz
(1923). Photograph in the Music Division of the Bibliothèque Nationale

Ernest Ansermet (1919).
Photograph in private collection

Ravel and Madeleine Grey (c. 1930).
Photograph in private collection

PLATE 7

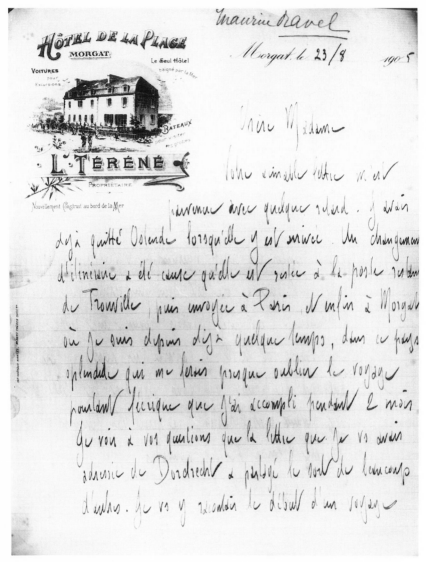

Letter from Ravel to Mme René de Saint-Marceaux, dated August 23, 1905
(letter no. 23). Autograph in the private collection of B. de Saint-Marceaux

magnifique à travers la Belgique, la Hollande, et les bords du Rhin jusqu'à Francfort, par fleuves, canaux et mers, dans le yacht de mes amis Edwards. J'ai vu des choses inoubliables dans ces conditions merveilleuses. Je n'ai pas produit deux mesures durant tout ce temps, mais j'ai emmagasiné une foule d'impressions, et j'espère que cet hiver va être extraordinairement productif. Je n'ai jamais été aussi heureux de vivre, et je crois fermement que la joie est bien plus fertile que la souffrance. C'est une opinion comme une autre. Nous verrons cet hiver si je me suis trompé. En attendant le plaisir de vous apporter le fruit de ces travaux considérables, je serai très heureux que vous me donniez de vos nouvelles. Veuillez me rappeler au souvenir de M. de Saint Marceaux, et croire, chère Madame, à la respectueuse amitié de votre dévoué

Maurice Ravel

PLATE 8

Ravel's return from the United States: with Marcelle Gerar at Le Havre, April 1928. Photograph in the collection of the author

A calling card sent to Marcelle Gerar and family in October 1924 (letter no. 246). Collection of the author

Ma Mère l'Oye at the Théâtre des Arts (1912): Cupid unites Prince Charming and the Princess. Décor and costumes by Jacques Drésa. Photograph in the Music Division of the Bibliothèque Nationale

PLATE 9

Postcard from Ravel to
Ida Godebska, dated
July 29, 1913 (letter no. 102).
Collection of the author

PLATE 10

Postcard from Ravel
to Mme René de
Saint-Marceaux, dated
January 22, 1919
(letter no. 151). Autograph
in the private collection
of B. de Saint-Marceaux

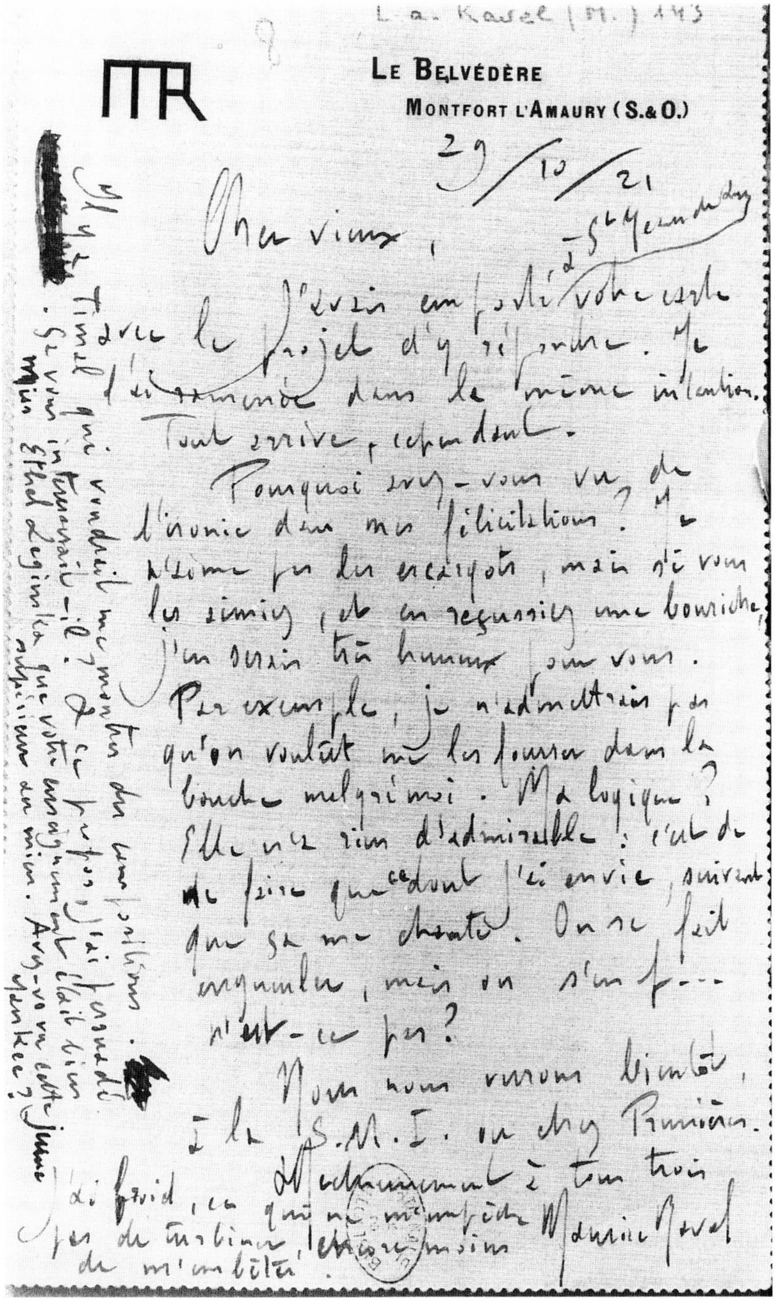

PLATE II

Letter from Ravel to Florent Schmitt, dated October 29, 1921 (letter no. 183).
Autograph in the Music Division of the Bibliothèque Nationale

PLATE II

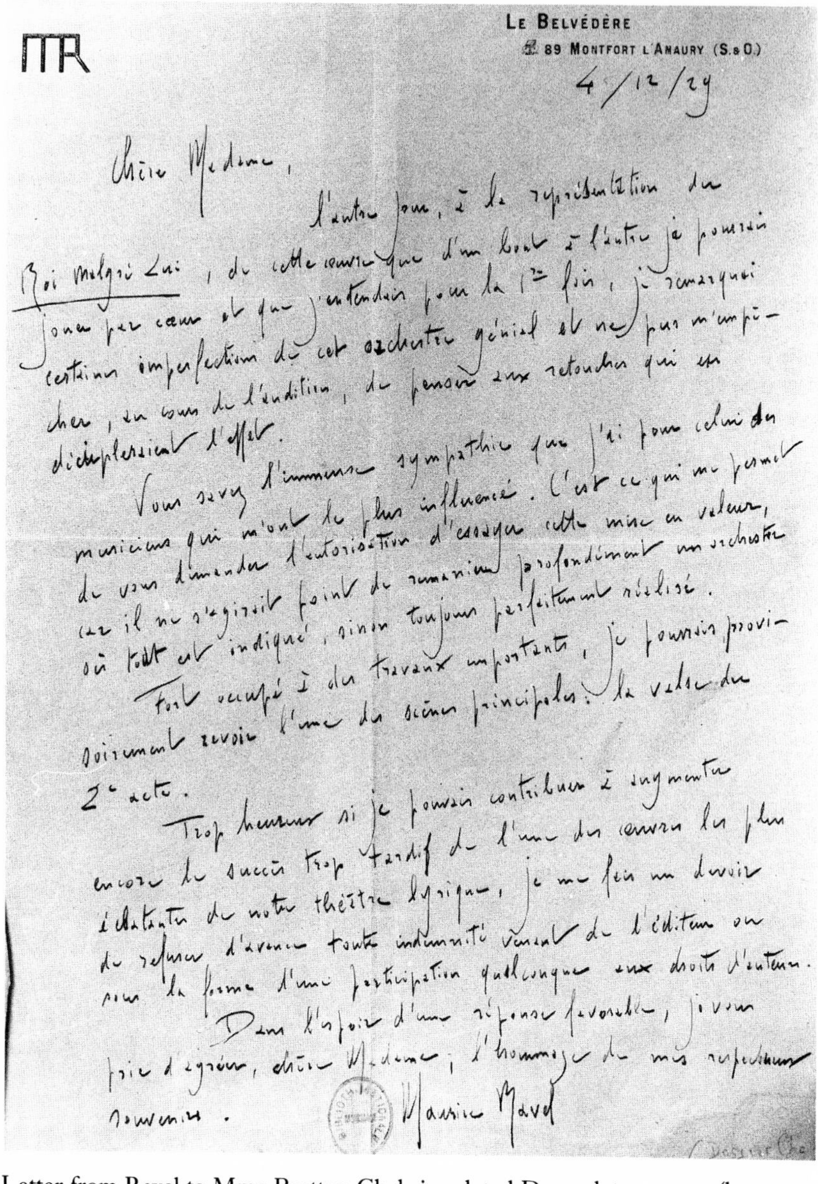

MR

LE BELVÉDÈRE
89 MONTFORT L'AMAURY (S.&O.)

4/12/29

Chère Madame,

L'autre jour, à la représentation du Roi malgré lui, de cette œuvre que d'un bout à l'autre je pourrais jouer par cœur et que j'entendais pour la 1re fois, je remarquai certaines imperfections de cet orchestre génial et ne pus m'empêcher, au cours de l'audition, de penser aux retouches qui en décupleraient l'effet.

Vous savez l'immense sympathie que j'ai pour celui des musiciens qui m'ont le plus influencé. C'est ce qui me permet de vous demander l'autorisation d'essayer cette mise en valeur, car il ne s'agirait point de remanier profondément un orchestre où tout est indiqué, sinon toujours parfaitement réalisé.

Fort occupé à des travaux importants, je pourrais provisoirement revoir l'une des scènes principales: la valse du 2e acte.

Trop heureux si je pouvais contribuer à augmenter encore le succès trop tardif de l'une des œuvres les plus éclatantes de notre théâtre lyrique, je me fais un devoir de refuser d'avance toute indemnité venant de l'éditeur ou sous la forme d'une participation quelconque aux droits d'auteur.

Dans l'espoir d'une réponse favorable, je vous prie d'agréer, chère Madame, l'hommage de mes respectueux souvenirs.

Maurice Ravel

Letter from Ravel to Mme Bretton Chabrier, dated December 4, 1929 (letter no. 312). Autograph in the Music Division of the Bibliothèque Nationale. Photograph D. Tomitch

PLATE 12

A model of Léon Leyritz's stone bust of Ravel found in the Paris Opéra. It is signed by the sculptor with a dedication to the author. Photograph of bust in the collection of the author

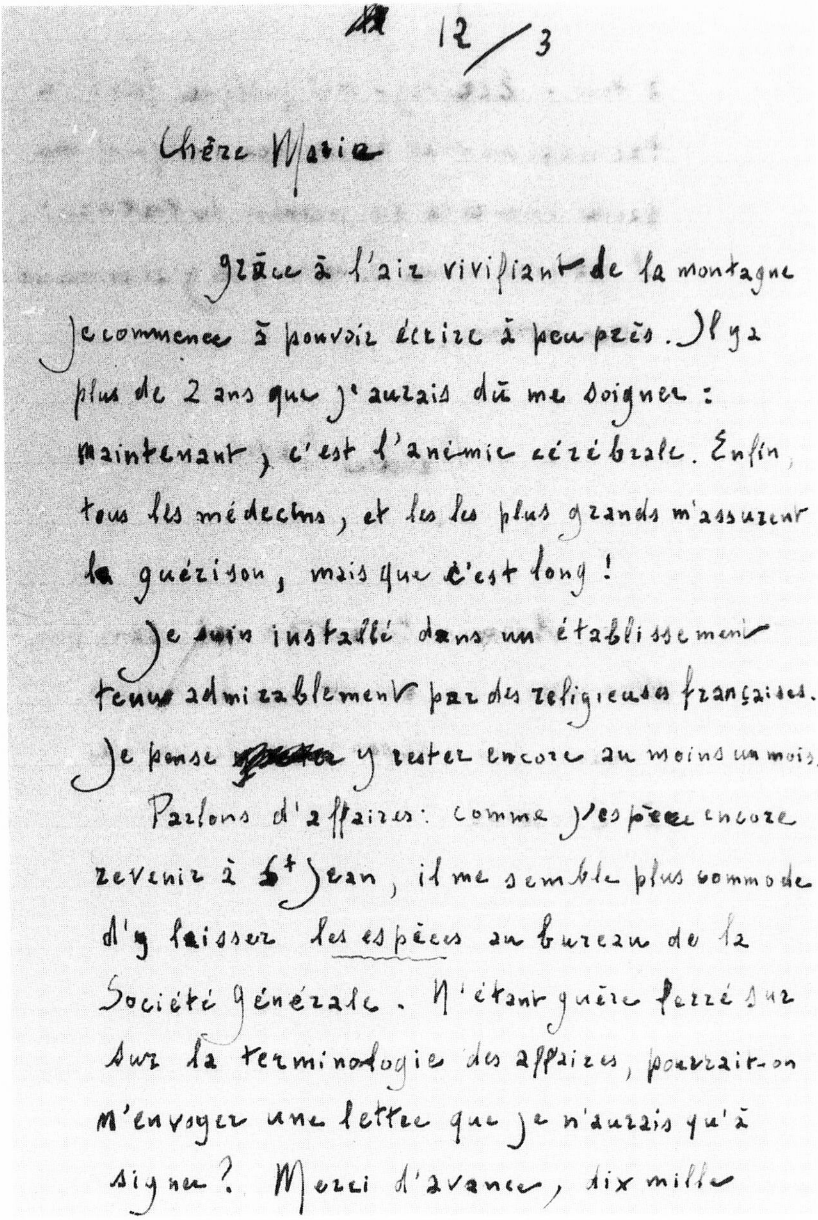

PLATE 13

Letter from Ravel to Marie Gaudin, dated March 12 [1934] (letter no. 335).
Autograph in the private collection of Pierre Courteault

à tous . Ecrivez - moi quelque fois : je
tacherai de vous répondre quoiqu'il me
faille pour cela des journées de tortures :
il y a plus d'une semaine que j'ai commencé
cette lettre .

Maurice Ravel

Adressez tes lettres ici, sans quoi
~~toujours~~ elles passent par la Maison
Durand qui y répond ou les envoie
à Edouard.

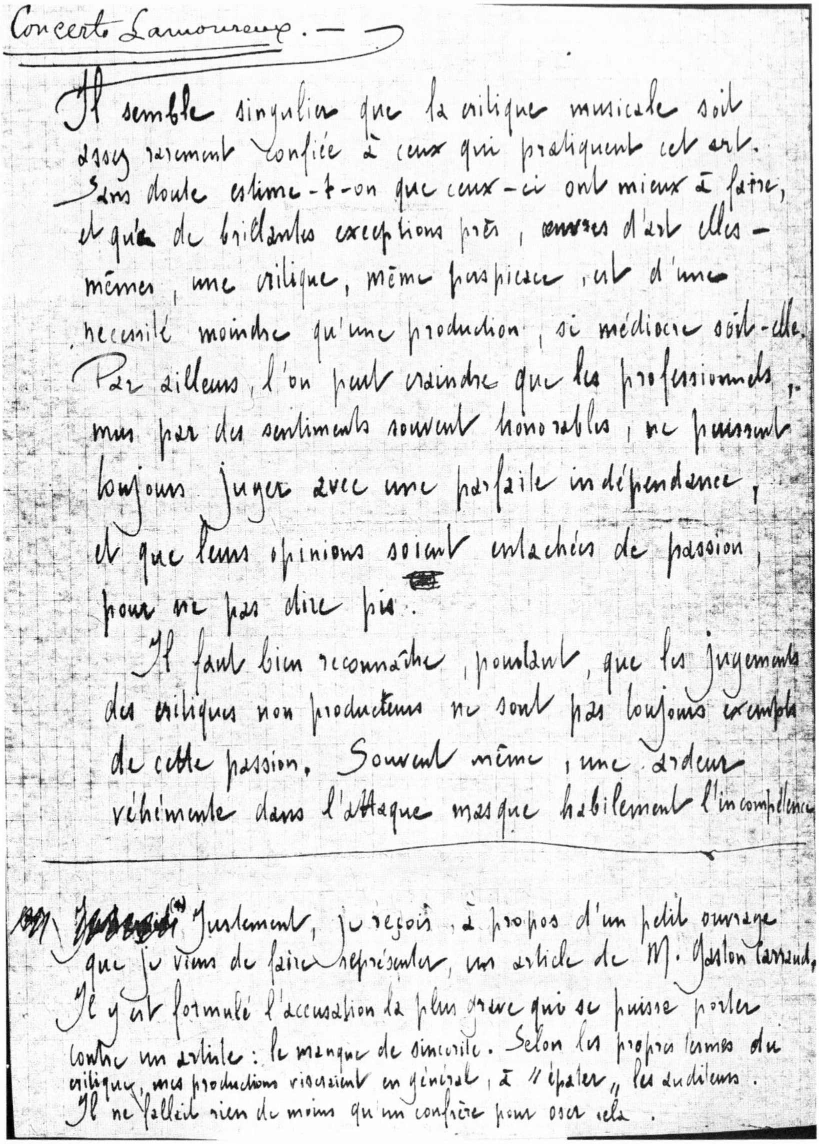

PLATE 14

Manuscript of a concert review (p. 1) published in February 1912. Autograph in the private collection of Claude Ecorcheville

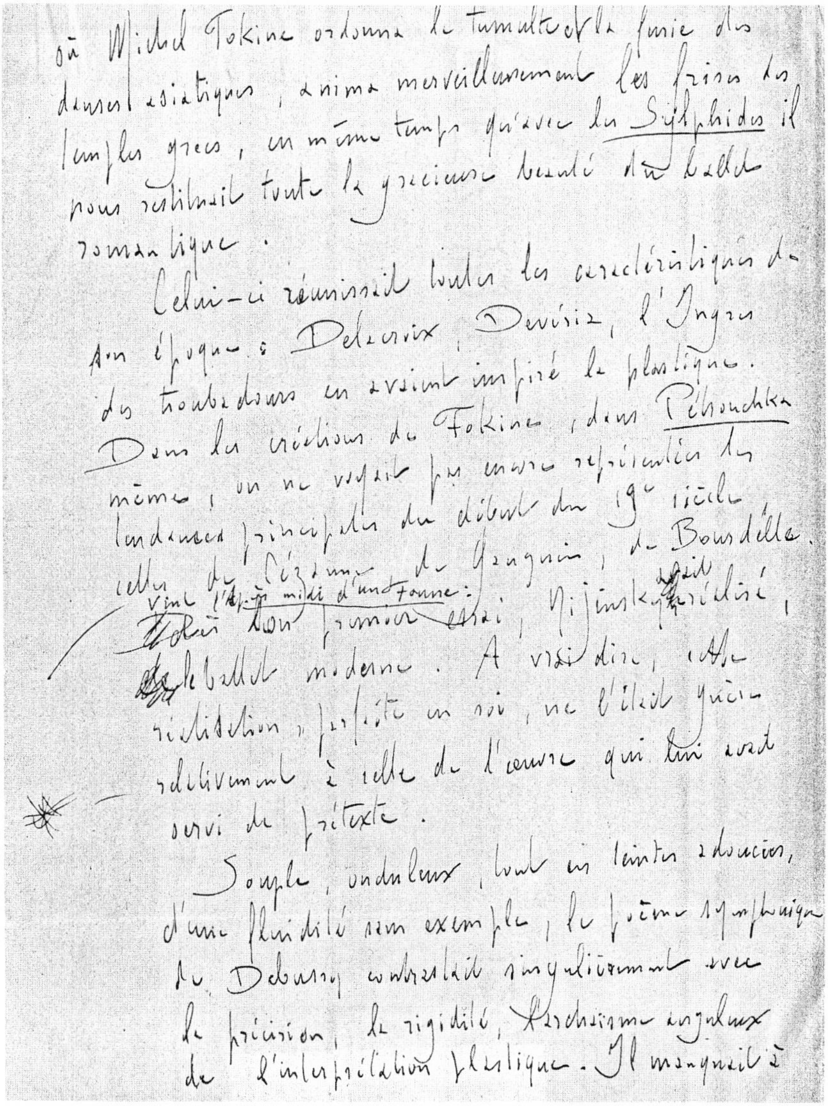

PLATE 15

Manuscript of an article (p. 2) on Nijinsky. Autograph in the private collection of Mme Alexandre Taverne

PLATE 16

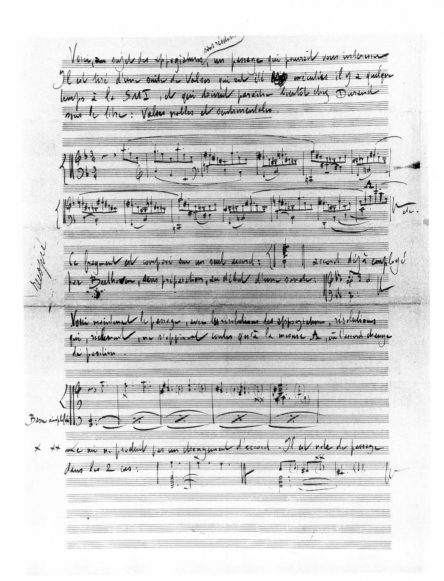

Manuscript of Ravel's analysis of a passage from the *Valses nobles et sentimentales*, sent to René Lenormand. (See appendix D. The word "recopié" was added by Lenormand.) Autograph in the Bibliothèque de l'Opéra

Thereupon, many young people ventured to confirm the critics' assertions, and discovered beyond the impasse a wide open gateway to a splendid, altogether new land. They frolicked freely, impervious to the threats of M. Lalo, who stood at his doorway brandishing a rod borrowed from M. Faguet, his colleague at *Le Temps*. As punishment, the merciless pedant attempted to force them to imitate Wagner, but in vain (*Le Temps*, September 1908). They refused to do it. M. Lalo then realized that they had grown up and it was time to use other tactics, if not nobler, at least more cunning. Summoned to help, M. Carraud and his colleagues responded with alacrity. They tried to sow dissension among these young artists. They tried to turn them against their revered master, and he against them. That noble maneuver hardly succeeded.[2] Hesitation was no longer tolerated: the sedition-monger himself had to be attacked. Just at this moment the *Images* appeared.

Writing in the *Revue musicale de la S.I.M.* on April 15, 1910, M. Gaston Carraud noted with profound sorrow that "at the Châtelet theater, the reception given to 'Ibéria' was as mixed as the audience itself," and that "at Salle Gaveau, where I was among musicians, one could feel a certain constraint in the success of 'Rondes de printemps,'[3] and the applause was directed more to the composer than to the work itself."[4] M. Carraud continued: "One must surely admit that everything M. Debussy has written after *Pelléas et Mélisande* has disappointed most of his early admirers. Others, it is true, evince a growing enthusiasm for him, to the point of affirming that only now has he begun a period of conscious maturity. . . . But one can explain these diverse opinions by distinguishing among those who admire M. Debussy, on the one hand musicians and sensitive listeners, and on the other, painters and writers (I am speaking, of course, not only of professionals, but of all those who think and feel like musicians, painters, or writers). Musicians and sensitive listeners are now retreating from their favorite composer."

You have indeed understood, you, who foolishly succumbed to the remarkable enchantment and exquisite freshness of "Rondes de printemps"; you, who felt moved to tears by the flowing quality of "Ibéria," by the profoundly moving "Les Parfums de la nuit"; by that harmonic richness, so original and delicate; by all of that intense musicality; you are nothing but a writer or a painter. And you fully understand the contempt these terms convey. I too am only a writer or a painter; and with me, Messieurs Igor Stravinsky, Florent Schmitt, Roger-Ducasse, Albert Roussel, and a host of young composers, whose output, however, isn't negligible. M. Gaston Carraud, to whom we owe three songs and a short symphonic poem, M. Camille Mauclair,[5] who has become known precisely through his literary and art criticism, and M. Pierre Lalo, who has composed absolutely nothing—they alone are musicians and sensitive listeners.

M. Lalo evaluated Debussy's new work in approximately the same terms: "Picturesque sensations, descriptions or suggestions of landscapes—it is curious that so many of our musicians believe this to be music's only raison d'être, when it is certainly subordinate, superficial, and ephemeral. There comes a time when these trifles cease to amuse" (*Le Temps*, February 26, 1910).

Whom? Morose incompetents, who have never felt the ardent passion inspired by these landscapes and this picturesqueness, and who cannot discover the musical expression of that passion in a composition.

"This music is so refined, that it succeeds in making one lose one's taste for any other.... While the magic lasts, it is still only half bad. But, what if someday we lose our taste even for Debussy—what will remain for us?" (*ibid*).

Very little, indeed. M. Camille Mauclair will remain to proclaim the genius of M. Isidore de Lara,[6] and Messieurs Carraud and Lalo will overwhelm M. Albéric Magnard[7] with their affection.

For these *sensitive listeners,* the innocuous mania will still remain of gradually closing their eyes before the rising sun, while loudly proclaiming that night is falling.

NOTES

1. *Les Cahiers d'aujourd'hui* (February 1913), pp. 135–38.

2. See letter no. 41.

3. Here Ravel added as a footnote: "The piece was encored."

4. Carraud was reviewing the first performances of two parts of the *Images*: on February 20, 1910, Gabriel Pierné led the Colonne Orchestra in a performance of "Ibéria," and on March 2, Debussy conducted "Rondes de printemps" in a concert sponsored by Durand.

5. See letter no. 33, note 4.

6. The pseudonym of Isidore Cohen (1858–1935), the English composer. He studied with Edouard Lalo in Paris, and devoted himself to the theater, where his light music briefly enjoyed international popularity.

7. See letter no. 122, note 1.

11

Boris Godunov[1]

The brilliant revival of *Boris Godunov*[2] made me relive—if only through recollection—the feverish, combative moments of 1908. It was this work which initiated the enterprise of Russian performances before the Parisian public.

Less than three weeks before the première, a fiasco was feared; M. Serge Diaghilev was wavering with regard to the scene in the snow. Thanks to the insistence of the organizer, M. D. Calvocoressi, the scene was preserved, and someone was bold enough to beg Rimsky-Korsakov to restore certain passages which this great musician had suppressed because of "musical improprieties."[3] At one point, all appeared lost when the scenery arrived: the novel brilliance of those boldly painted canvases astounded the administration of the Opéra, which finally became accustomed to them. Gradually, confidence and then exaltation overtook even the stagehands.

And the opera was a triumph. The public admired everything: improprieties, scenery, performers, the chorus, and supernumeraries. Simultaneously, it appeared to the dilettantes that Claude Debussy had discovered nothing, and that Rimsky-Korsakov was simply a spiteful maniac . . . One week later, these two victims of legitimate fervor resumed their positions of esteem among their contemporaries.

We are now far from those heroic times. Mussorgsky's work has lost none of its splendor. But it no longer belongs to us: even before the composer's version of the work was known, it was classified as a masterpiece. One flattering acknowledgment was lacking: the censure of *Le Temps*. It has just been obtained.

A powerful "tradition" has now taken hold. M. Chaliapin remains the greatest lyric artist of our time, and even though I admire, among other virtues, his manner of interpreting the recitative by almost speaking while fully observing the melodic flow, he is beginning to abuse this technique. In *Boris Godunov*, there are purely lyrical passages in which singing is mandatory, and in which Mussorgsky's tempos must be respected. There is nothing which necessitates the addition of those sinister sneers or cavernous groans, whose effect is so gruff and so unmusical. Mme Nicolaeva, who, as Marina, seemed to me superior to the creator of the role with respect to theatrical facility, also had her little shortcomings. The fourth scene, which takes place in Poland, derives its character chiefly from the national rhythms which underlie Marina's replies. However, it is precisely these rhythms which Mme Nicolaeva seems to disregard completely. M. Damaev's brilliance did not make one overlook M. Smirnov's gentler but more affecting charm.[4] I only wish that the noble monks and crafty villains of our lyric theater could exhibit the tact, intelligence, and the dramatic simplicity of Messieurs Semenov, Strobinder, and Nicholas Andreyev.

With the exception of the Polish scene, in which M. Bakst's sumptuous orientalism is revealed, a young painter, M. Juon, is responsible for the scenery and the costumes. They are dazzlingly opulent and beautifully harmonious. However, I missed the barbaric grandeur and the bold solemnity of the première. I also missed the wonderful conviction of the chorus members and the supernumeraries, which overwhelmed the public in 1908; that lesson has yet to be learned by their French colleagues.

Despite these reservations, I must admit that until now, not one of our important theaters has presented as artistic a production, and one which so closely approaches perfection. Still, it is surely not Mussorgsky's genuine work which has been presented. Would it appear overly unreasonable to wish for a partial restitution of the real *Boris Godunov*?

M. Diaghilev is going to restore the scene at the inn, which has never been performed in France. Why not dare a bit more? In the fifth scene, why not reinstate the episode of the escaped parrot, and the terrifying apparition of the automaton, without which the music performed at that time, which is purely descriptive, becomes incomprehensible? Why suppress the very brief, yet important role of the Jesuit Rangoni? Finally, why continue to destroy the theatrical significance of the work—whose main character is the people—by reversing the order of the final two scenes?

Of course, I know that in accordance with good theatrical succession, as it is understood by our entrepreneurs, it is advantageous to have the curtain fall on the final words of the renowned M. Chaliapin. But M. Serge Diaghilev's artistic enterprises are on a higher level, as he has proven many times.

When will we finally see this inspired and ill-fated work produced in a form closer to its original version?[5] Must we wait until it becomes public domain? Or until a blundering commercial publisher is finally dispossessed of all those masterpieces over which he assumed exclusive ownership by means of macabre hocus-pocus?[6]

NOTES

1. *Comœdia illustré* (June 5, 1913), vol. 5, no. 17; no pagination.

2. It was first performed at the Champs-Elysées theater on May 22, 1913, with Feodor Chaliapin in the title role. Chaliapin (1873–1938) also sang the title role in the 1908 production.

3. Calvocoressi recalled a conversation in which Diaghilev pointed out that Mussorgsky's version of the opera could not be performed, because the soloists and choir only knew the Rimsky-Korsakov adaptation. Calvocoressi noted that "a singer who has studied the one version would find it well-nigh impossible to be at home in the other. The pitfalls are too many: Rimsky-Korsakov tampered with keys and time-signatures and harmonies and modulations, and even, though more seldom, with melodies. Diaghilev's argument was unanswerable" (*Musicians Gallery*, p. 178).

4. These artists had performed the role of Dimitri: Damaev in the 1913 production, and Smirnov in 1908.

5. Thanks to questions such as this, which reflected Calvocoressi's thinking, a campaign to restore the original *Boris Godunov* was launched. Progress, however, was slow. In 1928, the Russian State Music Publishing Company, with Pavel Lamm as editor, began its urtext edition of Mussorgsky's complete works, including variants and extensive critical commentary. Lamm's edition of *Boris*, however, was a conflation of differing sources. Finally, in 1975, some 105 years after Mussorgsky completed *Boris Godunov*, his orchestral score was faithfully printed by David Lloyd-Jones (Oxford University Press). The second volume of this edition contains critical commentary and musical appendixes.

6. Referring to the Russian music publisher Vasily V. Bessel (1843–1907), who printed works by many of the leading Russian composers of the day, among them Tchaikovsky and members of The Five (see p. 435, note 17).

12

At the Opéra-Comique: Francesca da Rimini *and* La Vida breve[1]

In recent years, two important works, among others, were refused at the Opéra-Comique: *Eros vainqueur* by M. Pierre de Bréville,[2] and *La Forêt bleue* by M. Louis Aubert.[3] Orchestral excerpts of these works were performed in the concert hall and were favorably received. Rejected by a national theater, which receives a government subsidy specifically intended to promote works by French composers, the first opera found refuge in Brussels, and the second in Boston, then Geneva. Whatever their shortcomings may be, both works emanate from musicians who are justifiably esteemed, and in full command of their craft.

It was probably about the same time that the Opéra-Comique accepted M. Leoni's *Francesca da Rimini.*[4] The composer, an Italian residing in London, was completely unknown, not only by the public, but by his French colleagues as well. Thus, one might hope that M. Carré would be fortunate enough to discover a genius, or at least an unrecognized talent: what a great disappointment!

All of the platitudes and the undisguised cunning tricks which characterize the art of the Italian *verismo* school are reencountered in this work. The vigorous expression which this wretched school of amateurs claims to derive from its inspired forebears is squandered in *Francesca da Rimini* with the very same lack of conscience. However, one does note somewhat less clumsiness, greater care in the writing, and more appropriate harmony.

As in the work of M. Puccini, certain modern techniques, such as successions of augmented fifths, harp glissandi, and abuse of the celesta, cover up, to some extent, the shortcomings of inspiration or of orchestration.[5] Alas! None of this is *effective*. Perhaps what this work needs is the valuable collaboration of a shrewd publisher: cinema publicity adds a great deal to the reputation of a lyric drama.

Mlle Geneviève Vix, one of the finest and most musical of our lyric artists, M. Francell, elegant and ardent, M. Boulogne, as solemnly tragic as possible, and the charming voices of Mme Billa-Azéma and M. de Creus—all did their utmost to vindicate this dismal legacy from the previous management of the Opéra-Comique.

: : :

Eight years ago, in Madrid, an important musical competition was inaugurated. A very young composer, M. Manuel de Falla, won the first prize with *La Vida breve*. It appeared obvious that the prize-winning work would be performed immediately at Madrid's Royal Theater. But this privilege could only be granted if the text were translated into Italian . . . and, no doubt, if the composer were not Spanish.

That is why, just like his French colleagues whom I previously named, M. Falla found it necessary to present his art abroad: Nice, and then Paris had the honor of presenting the first performances of a work by a composer, who, several years before, had been awarded a prize by his compatriots.

It is not only in the theater, moreover, that M. Falla appears to be neglected in his native land. When the Madrid Symphony Orchestra performed in Paris last November, it was astonishing not to find both his name and that of M. Granados[6] in the program along with their colleagues. Yet, at the present time, they are the two composers who appear to affirm most profoundly and elegantly the distinctly national character of the modern Spanish school.

Together with M. Turina,[7] who appeared a little later, they are the most brilliant disciples of Isaac Albéniz.[8] Exempt from the clumsiness, frequent monotony, and the laborious workmanship which often encumber the work of this innovator, they inherited, in return, his sensitivity for rhythm, harmony, and color.

Among his compatriots, M. Falla offers the closest affinity with present-day French musicians. Yet his origin is revealed even in his less important works, to the point that certain individuals perceive a shortcoming in this respect: *La Vida breve* has been reproached for the frequent recurrence of certain melodic turns, which are characteristic of Andalusian song. One might just as well deplore the fact that the performers are adorned in embroidered shawls, or have their heads covered with mantillas. Has any complaint ever been lodged against Massenet for having squandered some excessively French formulas in *Manon*?

Furthermore, it would be wrong to conclude that local color is obtained solely by means of these melodic turns, or that local color alone accounts for the importance of this work. Certainly, the composer has brilliantly taken advantage of the picturesque episodes, which happily possess very little plot: the march of the fruit peddlers, a folk wedding, and gypsy dances. But, in the scenes which call for other talents, one discovers a sincerity of expression, as well as an abundance and freshness of inspiration which are thoroughly delightful. The expression of passion, although less tumultuous, is more musical than in the works of the *verismo* composers, and it is no less vibrant. Mme Marguerite Carré's frantic waddling could, if absolutely necessary, give an inkling of Andalusian ardor. M. Francell's vocal and theatrical charm were more effective here than in *Francesca da Rimini.* M. Vieuille and Mlle Brohly were both dramatic and melodious. A malagueña was sung poetically by M. Vigneau, and the orchestral performance was faultless.

The opening scene's décor, which is very ingenious, presents Granada lit by the sun, then by a thousand lights, a blacksmith's shop, tenements, drying rags, hanging onions, and a host of local accessories: nothing is lacking, except genuine color.

The décor of the second scene, which is more sober, would have made a fine impression, but for the execrable taste of placing wretched artificial plants in the foreground.[9] The costumes are most picturesque, and the production is as rousing as one could hope for.

NOTES

1. *Comœdia illustré* (January 20, 1914), 6(8):390–91. Both works were sung in French, produced by Albert Carré, and conducted by François Ruhlmann. The article contains a list of the performers and a synopsis of the libretti, which were probably added by an editor.

Francesca da Rimini

Mmes G. Vix (Francesca)	MM. Francell (Paolo)
Billa-Azéma (first woman)	Boulogne (Giovanni)
Marini (a page)	de Creus (the gardener)
	Deloger (a soldier)
	Donval (an old servant)

Married to a swarthy, lame, and deformed Malatesta, Francesca prefers her brother-in-law, the fair, elegant, and lovesick Paolo. Her husband surprises the lovers and runs them through with a single sword thrust.

La Vida breve (Life is Short)

Mmes M. Carré (Salud)	MM. Francell (Paco)
Brohly (grandmother)	Vieuille (Sarvaor)
Syril (Carmela)	Vigneau (the singer)
Carrière (salesgirl)	Vaurs (Manuel)
Camia (salesgirl)	Donval (a voice)
Jeutel (salesgirl)	Deloger (a vendor)
Billa-Azéma (salesgirl)	

Dancers:
Mlle Malaguenitas
M. Rafael Pagan

The gypsy Salud is seduced by Paco, who abandons her in order to marry a young lady of his rank. Salud appears in the midst of the wedding celebration. Rejected by her former lover, she is overcome by grief and dies.

2. See letter no. 3, note 3 and p. 340.

3. See letter no. 73, note 3. Aubert's opera, *The Blue Forest*, based on the children's stories of Charles Perrault, was first performed at the Opéra-Comique in 1924.

4. Based on a work by the English playwright Francis-Marion Crawford, in a French translation by Marcel Schwob, the musical setting by Franco Leoni (1864–1949) was performed but seven times at the Opéra-Comique. The première took place on December 30, 1913, with the title role performed by Geneviève Vix, who had created the role of Concepcion in *L'Heure espagnole*.

5. Despite this criticism of Puccini, in the course of a lesson with Manuel Rosenthal, Ravel warmly praised the innovative harmony and orchestration found in *Tosca*. "I did the same thing in *Le Tombeau de Couperin*," he explained. "This economy of means, in which two instruments alone produce such striking effects in Puccini's orchestration—this is the mark of a great artist."

6. Enrique Granados (1867–1916), like Albéniz, was a composer and virtuoso pianist.

7. See letter no. 87, note 1.

8. See letter no. 300, note 1.

9. The décor was by M. Bailly, who had arranged the décor for the original production of *L'Heure espagnole*.

13 : : :

Parsifal[1]

iterature has played a large role, if not in the work, at least in the history of the work of two illustrious composers: Beethoven and Wagner. Perhaps it was their own fault.[2] This is all but true in the case of Wagner. I am convinced, however, that he would be surprised, and dismayed, to learn about the victories—and the defeats—of his army of commentators. From philosophy to reporting, from important lyric poetry to boudoir aesthetics, from Nietzsche to Pierre Lalo, passing by Catulle Mendès, Wagner's theories have been the object of so much learned discussion, that nothing has remained for musicians to do. It must be admitted that if one had to wait for the approbation of musicians, the genius of this great artist would have remained unrecognized for a long time. Fortunately, alas! there was in Wagner's art—may I call it a defect?—in any case, an extramusical part, which immediately captivated everyone who remained unsatisfied by the charm and richness of the music alone.

Thus, it was among writers that the first neophytes were recruited. And it is from their ranks that we also find the first iconoclasts. Nietzsche's writings on Wagner seem to prove that he was by turns the leader of these two sects.[3] But, like recent Wagnerism, anti-Wagnerism has also degenerated. Its peripatetics have invaded the salons, artistic cabarets, and the newsrooms of our daily papers: before long, *Siegfried* will be ranked alongside *Robert le Diable.*[4]

One might object that some twenty years ago, an anti-Wagnerian movement became conspicuous among our young musicians. Pardon me! We had the right to express ourselves, and even the duty to do so. Wagner's musical influence might have become disastrous in our country. One need only examine the important works written at that time: *Fervaal, Le Roi Arthus,*[5] and even *Gwendoline,* in order to see a Wagnerian imprint here and there. Above all, one need only recall the deplorable multitude of theatrical works, chamber music, and songs, whose disproportion, heaviness, and sadness were so uninspired, that they have not survived these twenty years. Our inflexible position is therefore understandable.

Nevertheless, not one of us ever proposed to deny Wagner's prodigious

376

creativeness and profound musicality. If we find fault with him, or find his art long-winded, we admit that these faults, which may be virtues, are inherent in his race, and that this long-windedness is never entirely without significance. And it was certainly not our reticence which authorized our amiable socialites and diligent reporters to yawn openly when speaking about the Ballet Russe, whose artistic importance we surmised before they did.

Parsifal, no doubt, is less entertaining than *La Vie parisienne.*[6] All the same, it is less annoying than the *Missa solemnis,* that inferior work by Beethoven, of which, however, so many good things have been said at social gatherings.

Was it right to disregard the last will and testament of a deceased composer? I cannot answer this question, as I have never been in Bayreuth. It appears that *Parsifal* is performed there somewhat like the Eleusinian mysteries.[7] Here, it takes on the importance of a Parisian première, which is very different. This leads me to believe that it would hardly be possible to wish for a musical realization superior to that of the Opéra, whether at Bayreuth or elsewhere. Not only are the leading roles superbly performed—Mlle Bréval (Kundry), Messieurs Franz (Parsifal), Delmas (Gurnemanz), Lestelly (Amfortas), Journet (Klingsor), A. Gresse (Titurel)—but the chorus sings in tune with a sonority, precision, and a sense of style which we have not often encountered. The scene of the flower maidens was a delight to hear. It should be noted that these very ugly flowers—I'm speaking of their corollas—were chosen from among the prettiest voices at the Opéra. Under the distinguished baton of M. Messager, one of the finest orchestras in the world performed, as it can, to perfection. One might be tempted to make some reservations about the occasional harshness and heaviness in the brass. But this fault is imputable first of all to Wagner, whose splendid orchestration is not exempt from imperfections, and above all, to the location of the orchestra, which in Bayreuth, as is known, cannot be seen.[8]

I have been assured that the Bayreuth production was inferior to that of the Opéra, which, however, is not good. The same apparently holds true for the décor.[9] This doesn't surprise me: even less than the *Ring* cycle, *Parsifal* cannot be realized with the theatrical techniques which have been used until now. (Will the attempt be made one day to carry out the ideas of M. Adolphe Appia, which have been explained in his book, *Die Musik und die Inszenierung?*)[10]

Wherein lies the magic of this music, which in spite of everything makes us accept conventional stage effects, and the supposedly noble poses of our highly gifted singers? Even the most outmoded and insensitive taste would be completely taken aback by the overly precise changing scenes: the "modern style" flower maidens, in their abominable colors, turning around in a mid-Lenten castle; the fellow in a shirt taking his foot bath in the middle of a trite stage set, while the marvelous Good Friday music arises from the orchestra; the impaled dove suspended by overly visible wires, descending toward the ciborium at the most sublime moment in the music.

Perhaps what we need is nothing less than a rehabilitation of the theater, which, in that case, would not be such an inferior genre, since it does permit us, even in our present-day situation, to endure four hours of wonderful music without too much fatigue.

NOTES

1. *Comœdia illustré* (January 20, 1914), 6(8):400–03. A subtitle reads as follows: "Sacred Drama by Richard Wagner, French Version by Alfred Ernst, Performed for the First Time at the Opéra on January 1, 1914."

2. It should be kept in mind that the music of Beethoven and Wagner was performed incessantly in France during Ravel's lifetime. His complex and somewhat contradictory attitude toward these "philosophical" composers combined elements of respect, awe, and jealousy, coupled with a marked rejection of their influence on French composers.

3. In the preface to *Der Fall Wagner* (The Case of Wagner, 1888), Nietzsche explained as follows:

> I am writing this to relieve my mind. It is not malice alone which makes me praise Bizet at the expense of Wagner in this essay. Amid a good deal of jesting I wish to make one point clear which does not admit of levity. To turn my back on Wagner was for me a piece of fate; to get to like anything else whatever afterwards was for me a triumph. Nobody, perhaps, had ever been more dangerously involved in Wagnerism, nobody had defended himself more obstinately against it, nobody had ever been so overjoyed at ridding himself of it. A long history!—Shall I give it a name?—If I were a moralist, who knows what I might not call it! Perhaps a piece of *self-mastery*. . . . I can perfectly well understand a musician of today who says: "I hate Wagner but I can endure no other music." But I should also understand a philosopher who said: "Wagner is modernity in concentrated form." There is no help for it, we must first be Wagnerites. (*The Complete Works of Friedrich Nietzsche*, vol. 8, trans. Anthony M. Ludovici, New York: Russell & Russell, 1964, pp. xxix–xxxi.)

4. Meyerbeer's grand opera, first produced in 1831, was based on a libretto by Eugène Scribe. Professor Grout has described the story as "a jumble of medieval legend, romantic passion, grotesque superstition, and general lunacy" (Donald J. Grout, *A Short History of Opera*, New York and London: Columbia University Press, 1947, p. 316).

5. Ernest Chausson composed the music and wrote the libretto of this opera, which was introduced at the Théâtre de la Monnaie on November 30, 1903.

6. The scintillating operetta by Jacques Offenbach, introduced in 1866.

7. These secret religious rites of ancient Greece celebrated the annual death and resurrection of nature.

8. Ravel stated the following in an interview: "The basis of orchestration is the isolation of timbres. Wagner never troubled himself to highlight a clarinet or a violin. *Le Prophète* [by Meyerbeer] is orchestrated infinitely better than *Lohengrin*" (Georges Devaise, "Raveliana," *Gringoire,* January 14, 1938).

9. The décor at the Opéra was arranged by Messieurs Simas (acts 1 and 3) and Rochette (act 2), with Paul Stuart in charge of the production.

10. *Music and Staging* (1899). Appia (1862–1928) was a Swiss stage designer whose theories were influential on 20th-century theater. In *Music and Staging,* he urged the adoption of a three-dimensional setting rather than a flat backdrop; lighting which would blend the actor and the setting into a unified whole, and the use of lighting effects as an interpretive and visual counterpart of the music.

14 : : :

New Productions of the Russian Season:
The Nightingale[1]

I t is distressing to observe that at a time when French composers have liberated music from a large number of prejudices, in this country where logic and lucid enthusiasm could elevate criticism to the rank of a nobly useful art, a multitude of incompetent amateurs, who consider themselves writers on music, strive to extol hallowed masterworks, most often when they are in their decline, and to struggle blindly against any sort of innovation. All of their refinement is applied to finding new means of attack. So much ingenuity, however, remains sterile: to the great joy of their readers, these valiant soldiers transform themselves into acrobats in order to execute an impressive pirouette together.[2] This is what happened to *The Rite of Spring*. It will soon happen again to *The Nightingale*.

In order to disparage the significance of *The Nightingale*—may I venture to assert along with M. Emile Vuillermoz that it is a masterpiece?—the critics gave up boxing, which was used against *The Rite of Spring*, and which proved to be such a failure. They returned to their sly jiujitsu, whose maliciousness is beginning to wear thin, although they still seem to have confidence in it.

While the most violent epithets were hurled at *The Rite of Spring*: barbarity, a hoax, hysteria, antimusicality—what do they know about this?—now there were only murmurs, innuendoes, and petty jibes. Indeed, *The Nightingale* does not make a great deal of noise, and everyone knows that for a majority of the public, and for most critics, noise, coupled with some well-tested formulas, is necessary for greatness. "It touches neither mind nor heart!" says one critic. Another writes: "The effect of this deliberate dissonance, while amusing in many passages, appeared much more superficial than in *The Rite of Spring*." No doubt, one cannot be touched by the expression of a language which one doesn't understand, and what one doesn't feel can only be considered superficial. I could cite but few theatrical works which offer more moving passages than the concluding scene of *The Nightingale*.

I rejoice in being different from the critic, who, already blasé about an art which he has never savored, informs us that "the results were beneath my expectations," that "nothing wears out more quickly than innovations which are repeated without being renewed," and that "after *The Rite of Spring*, M. Stravinsky's poetics (in *The Nightingale*) appeared, if not yet reactionary, already stationary,"[3] an observation which will stupefy all musicians.

In fact, musicians were precisely struck by Stravinsky's fresh innovations, and by the musical conception, whose embryo was only discovered in *The Rite of Spring*. I am referring to this absolute contrapuntal liberty, this audacious independence of themes, rhythms, and harmonies, whose combination, thanks to one of the rarest musical sensibilities, offers us such a fascinating ensemble. Stravinsky's new work is mainly related to the most recent style of Arnold Schoenberg, but the latter is harsher, more austere, let us say the word: more cerebral.

Stravinsky's evolution vividly struck another critic, who declared point-blank that "*The Rite of Spring* seems like Meyerbeer in comparison with the two concluding scenes of *The Nightingale*." I should point out that this critic is also a composer, which must give him greater authority to evaluate his colleagues. I must also say, alas, that his confraternity is most often expressed by bitterness. Thus, until now, he alone has reproached Stravinsky for not having rewritten the opening scene, which dates from 1909. Furthermore, he doesn't hesitate to participate in the favorite game of amateurs: discovering musical reminiscences.[4]

Stravinsky must surely have been aware of the fact that one of his themes slightly resembled Debussy's "Nuages," but even more so a certain song by Mussorgsky.[5] I think he considered it unnecessary to change one or two notes of his theme in order to disguise this similarity. More serious and more frequent examples of this are found in the works of the classical masters. And if he did not rewrite the music of the opening scene, it is because he saw the difficulty, even the impossibility, for "an artist who is truly an artist," to compose entirely new music to the same text. It would have been easier, but less honorable, to retouch the former version and rejuvenate it by some tricks of the trade.

I previously mentioned the insight and the moving exaltation of the concluding scene. Less sober and more brilliant, the second scene is in no way inferior. It would be difficult to convey through words or imagery, the roaring tumult, disturbing, but always musical, at the beginning of this scene, the orchestral enchantment of this strange and powerful march whose Far-Eastern quality engenders a more profound feeling, truly, than that of simple curiosity, and the uncommon charm of the mysterious timbres which depict the mechanical nightingale.

The disparity between the scenes, which seems to have shocked certain listeners, might perhaps have astonished them less had they known that the opening scene was composed five years before the others. I personally did not find the difference so enormous. The composer's technique had merely evolved.[6] The inspiration and orchestration of the opening scene are worthy of the composer of *The Firebird*, whose personality is closely related to that of Mussorgsky after his evolution. And if it is true that *The Nightingale* did not create a scandal, nevertheless, I believe that I must reassure my fellow critic, who seems to have experienced such keen anxiety about the fate of this music.

The prodigious effort of the Opéra orchestra and M. Monteux's[7] unusual skill were necessary to produce a creditable performance of this work, which was accorded only five rehearsals. M. Strauss had obtained fifteen rehearsals for *Joseph*,[8] a much less difficult work.

I believe that I have never seen more perfectly harmonious costumes and scenery. To the Asiatic splendor of his compatriots, M. Alexandre Benois[9] joins his exquisite taste, whose moderation derives perhaps from his French origin.

NOTES

1. "Les Nouveaux Spectacles de la saison russe: *Le Rossignol*," *Comœdia illustré* (June 5, 1914), 6(17):811–14. In a letter to the English critic Edwin Evans, dated May 31, 1914, Ravel observed that he would send his colleague a copy of this article, "which is less a review of the music than a critique of those who claimed to have reviewed it" (unpublished autograph in the Frederick R. Koch Foundation Collection, on deposit at the Pierpont Morgan Library).

2. Besides being a technical term in ballet, "pirouette" in French suggests a brusque change in direction. Ravel thus ridicules the critics who gracefully "pirouette" from censure to praise.

3. These comments, by the French musicologist and critic Jean Chantavoine, appeared in *Excelsior* on May 28, 1914 (see plate 3).

4. The critic was Gaston Carraud, whose comments on *The Nightingale* appeared in *La Liberté* on May 28, 1914.

5. The opening theme of *The Nightingale* is almost identical to the piano accompaniment (measure 17) in the third song, "Okonchen prazdnïy, shumnïy den'," (The festive, noisy day has ended) of Mussorgsky's cycle *Bez solntsa* (Sunless). The rhythmic accentuation, however, is completely different.

6. Professor Eric Walter White has observed that in the interim between 1909 (act 1) and 1914 (acts 2 and 3), Stravinsky's musical language "had developed almost beyond recognition." The author summed up as follows:

The idiom of Acts II and III is certainly more original and mature than that of Act I, and the difference between the two parts must have disconcerted some of the early listeners; but with the passage of time this gap has narrowed and the variations in style now seem to be much less of a flaw than they at first appeared. It is the nature of the work that it is built up out of contrasted musical styles, and its weaknesses are to be found, not in stylistic disparities, but in the imperfect fusion of the operatic, balletic and narrative elements. (Eric Walter White, *Stravinsky,* 2d ed., Berkeley: University of California Press, 1979, p. 227.)

7. See letter no. 111, note 3.

8. Richard Strauss' *Josephslegende* (Legends of Joseph) was commissioned by Diaghilev and completed in 1914. Just before the outbreak of World War I, Strauss conducted the ballet in London and Paris.

9. An important figure in the creation of modern ballet, Benois (1870–1960) was active as a scenic designer and ballet librettist. Together with Diaghilev and Léon Bakst, he founded a Russian magazine, *World of Art,* which proved to be an important factor in the creation of the Ballet Russe.

15 : : :

The Songs of Gabriel Fauré[1]

Indispensable and pressing tasks prevented M. Maurice Ravel from writing the article which he intended to contribute to La Revue musicale. *As a result, I interviewed him at his home in Montfort l'Amaury. While illustrating the songs of his teacher at the piano, M. Ravel commented on them freely, and I have attempted here to relate this informal talk faithfully.*
—ROLAND-MANUEL

"Although Villiers is already highly praised, and his name launched, destined for consummate renown for all time, we nevertheless classify him among the *poètes maudits* (accursed poets), *because he is not sufficiently glorified* by his contemporaries, who should bow in reverence before him."[2]

These lines, which Verlaine devoted to Villiers de l'Isle-Adam, could be applied as well to the composer of *La Bonne Chanson*, whose reputation, distinguished as it may be, is far from being proportional to his stature as one of France's greatest composers.

One could not better evaluate the importance of Gabriel Fauré than by studying his songs, which bestowed on French music the hegemony formerly enjoyed by the lied.

The Austro-German lied is essentially folk; one discovers the authentic sources of Schubert's wonderful lieder in the refrains of student songs. In France, folk song did not evolve from its remote origins, so to speak, and it infiltrated only superficially into the classical repertoire. At any event, French folk song did not influence the lied at all.

The true founder of the art song in France was Charles Gounod. The composer of *Venise, Philémon et Baucis,* and the shepherd's song in *Saphô,* rediscovered the secret of a harmonic sensuousness which had been lost since the French harpsichord school of the seventeenth and eighteenth centuries. In fact, the musical renaissance which occurred in France about 1880, had no more valid precursor than Gounod. The true godfathers of the generation of 1895, Fauré and Chabrier, both continued Gounod's work. Following them,

Bizet, Lalo, Saint-Saëns, and Massenet, and later Claude Debussy—all more or less partook of Gounod's beneficial influence.[3]

Fauré, who studied with Saint-Saëns, appears to have been more attracted to the obvious Gounodlike color of certain works by his young professor, than to his research with respect to form, which for Saint-Saëns was a constant preoccupation.[4] Fauré's songs do not bear the slightest imprint of the continual pursuit of architectural design found in the shortest works of Saint-Saëns, who truly *created* new techniques of development. In Fauré's art, structure is never deliberate, but spontaneous; it is not the end, but the supple means.

It is possible that the innovations of a Chabrier influenced Fauré's style to some extent. This influence, however, is rather vague, and more in spirit than in letter. As for Duparc,[5] who cannot be overlooked, his songs, although imperfect, exhibit genius, and occasionally they are related to Fauré's songs. However, it is difficult to determine which composer influenced the other.

Fauré's personality is conspicuous in his earliest songs; one notes in astonishment the date of composition of his opus 7, *Après un rêve*, written in 1865. Then came *Nell*, in which Gounod's influence appears in a delightful way, and *Automne*, which serves as a prelude to *Les Berceaux*. Although success has debased this celebrated song, it remains a moving and profound work.

Le Secret is one of Fauré's most beautiful "lieder." In this piece, the enchantment of the melodic line matches the subtlety of the harmony. Unusual, equivocal resolutions, and modulations to distant keys which return to the tonic by unexpected paths—these are among the perilous techniques that Fauré employs masterfully from the very outset. Chabrier uses these techniques analogously, but each musician adapts them in his own way: Chabrier, with more refined pointedness, Fauré, with more aristocratic reserve. Where Chabrier exaggerates the effect, Fauré will smooth out the edges, and sometimes he goes even further.

Clair de lune, composed in 1887, is one of the most beautiful songs in all of French music. Many musicians have been attracted to Verlaine's celebrated poetry. Fauré alone understood how to interpret his poetry in music. This masterpiece seems to have been written in a burst of inspiration, with no effort apparently necessary. Ignoring the various images suggested by the poem, the melodic line is chiefly inspired, one might say, by a single verse, which could be inscribed as an epigraph: "Et sangloter d'extase les jets d'eau" (And brings sobs of ecstasy to the fountains). The song flows along undisturbed by the vicissitudes of the bergamask players; its serene continuity is exemplary. The same calm atmosphere will be reencountered in a wonderful scene from *Pénélope*: "Ulysse fier époux" (Ulysees, proud husband). Have you noticed that the words "sur le mode mineur . . ." (in the minor mode) lead into an arpeggio which paradoxically outlines a *C major* chord, adding an ineffable melancholy illusion to the lunar landscape?

Au cimetière presents an unusual mood. A feeling of pathos is projected, which is extremely rare in Fauré's work. Note how his tragic inspiration rises far above the limited, indeed weak, effects found in the poem.[6] One might compare *Au cimetière* with *Ich grolle nicht*, in which Schumann likewise surpasses the confines of his intimate lyricism. Although the poem of *Au cimetière* reveals a greater and more deliberate contrast than that found in *Ich grolle nicht*, the mood of Fauré's somber and animated setting does not relent for an instant.

In *La Bonne Chanson*, one can detect the origins of a fresh style, which is clearly distinguished by the importance that harmony will henceforth assume in the musical language. Far from being restricted by this richer harmonic scope, the melody exhibits even greater suppleness and freedom. Everything is admirable in *La Bonne Chanson*, this incomparably harmonious work, whose nine songs are ordered and balanced to form a vast, lyrical poem, which is moving and perfect.

Le Parfum impérissable is likewise inspired by its harmonic atmosphere. At the verse: "Sur le sable qui brûle on peut l'épandre toute" (On the burning sand it can be completely poured out), Fauré deliberately modulates far from the tonic key, letting us think that he has abandoned it in earnest, only to return suddenly by an unforeseeable path. What would elsewhere be considered a diverting bit of legerdemain, responds here to a sort of intimate and profound need. Fauré never cultivated technique for its own sake: the setting down of his inspiration was his primary concern.

Le Parfum impérissable, *Prison*, and *Soir* share the same aesthetic, whose origin is found in *Philémon et Baucis*, but which evolved in a thoroughly personal manner in Fauré's music. This supreme purity and delicate sensualism continued to be expressed over the years, in an art which preserves not only all of its subtlety, but also all of its freshness: *La Chanson d'Eve*, *Mirages*, and the recent *L'Horizon chimérique* offer valuable and very touching proof of this.

At a time when composers were no longer greatly concerned with the exigencies of singing, Fauré's songs had the almost unique merit of being truly written for the voice. His vocal writing is always justified and perfectly apt. His declamation, which is appropriate and of exquisite grace, appears much more precise than in the works of his colleagues; it does not turn into recitative, and disdains the facile procedure of brusquely passing from psalmody to lyrical élan, an expedient which was dear not only to Massenet.[7]

Fauré's declamation, always melodic, manages to capture the fleeting music of the French language, which is less obvious for example than Italian, but how much more delicate, and therefore more precious!

If the limpid grace of Fauré's songs recalls the most beautiful arias of

Mozart, their lyricism also bears comparison with the lieder of Schumann. Indeed, "In Paradisum" from the *Requiem*—to take an example outside our topic—is quite naturally related to the third act of *Idomeneo;* Fauré's sensuality, however, is more meridional than Mozart's, and the composer of *Le Parfum impérissable*, unquestionably an Attic musician, is less Grecian on the whole than the Salzburg master.

Schumann's music reflects the life of the German bourgeoisie in the nineteenth century. Fauré is certainly more discreet than Schumann with regard to personal disclosures and passionate outbursts. Nevertheless, though probably not considered a great lyric composer in the eyes of Germany, Fauré is a great French lyric artist: his nostalgic, tender lyricism, unobtrusive and free from superfluous outcries, knows how to achieve—particularly in *Le Secret*—a poignant, powerful emotion.

The techniques of Gabriel Fauré are as personal as they are subtle. He proposed no formulas to his pupils, urging them, on the contrary, to beware of stereotyped workmanship. His penetrating individuality, more subtle than innovative, always loathed convenient artifices, and it offers no reward to epigones. The materials of Fauré's oeuvre are uniquely his own, and will remain useless in the hands of imitators or plagiarists. In fact, Fauré's mysterious techniques captivate us even more and fatigue us less, owing to their subtlety and quiet demeanor; their discretion is their strength.

It is truly in his songs that Fauré offers us the flower of his genius. In the song, this intimate form of musical expression, access to the most humble home is possible. Quietly and unobtrusively, the songs of Fauré gradually superseded the romances of the salon, and they have contributed significantly to the favorable transformation presently occurring in the public's taste.

Fauré's art, in essence too aristocratic to function in a popular capacity, is rather one of subtle and delicate innovation. One notes with emotion the profound influence of these songs, which indicated "the most charming path" to the younger composers of 1895, and which remain today the discreetly eloquent ambassadors of the French sensual tradition, which they have greatly helped to restore.

NOTES

1. *La Revue musicale* (October 1922), 3:22–27.
2. Paul Verlaine's short biographical studies, *Les Poètes maudies* (1884), attempted to stimulate interest in six poets whom Verlaine considered unjustifiably neglected: Tristan Corbière, Marceline Desbordes-Valmore, Villiers de l'Isle-Adam, Stéphane Mallarmé, Arthur Rimbaud, and "Pauvre Lelian"—Verlaine's anagram of his own name.
3. Literally, "partook of the beneficial influence of the composer of *Mireille.*"

4. Literally, "which for the composer of the Trio in F was a constant preoccupation."

5. Henri Duparc (1848–1933) studied with César Franck. His reputation rests on some fifteen songs written between 1868 and 1884. Owing to a nervous disorder, he virtually ceased composing after 1885.

6. "Au cimetière," from the collection *La Mer* (1886), was written by Jean Richepin (1849–1926), whose poems and plays enjoyed considerable vogue during his lifetime.

7. Massenet's expedient of repeating several low notes which suddenly rise to a dramatic high note may also be seen in the early songs of Debussy ("De fleurs," from *Proses lyriques*) and Ravel (*Un Grand Sommeil noir* and *Si morne!*).

16 : : :

On Inspiration[1]

All that I am able to affirm is that in 1924, when I undertook the Sonata for violin and piano,[2] which has just been completed, I had already determined its rather unusual form, the manner of writing for the instruments, and even the character of the themes for each of the three movements before "inspiration" had begun to prompt any one of these themes.

And I don't think that I chose the easiest way.[3]

NOTES

1. Reply to an inquiry conducted by L. Dunton Green in *The Chesterian* (January–February 1928), 9(68):105–118. Ravel's comments appear on page 115. Among the eleven respondents were Sir Arthur Bliss, Alfredo Casella, Paul Dukas, Sir Eugene Goossens, Albert Roussel, and Franz Schreker. Other composers, among them Sir Edward Elgar and Ildebrando Pizzetti, observed that they were unable to make any comments regarding the nature of musical inspiration.

2. The initial work on the Sonata actually began in 1923.

3. In addition to these comments, Ravel often quoted Baudelaire's aphorism: "Inspiration is decidedly the sister of daily work" (*L'Art romantique*). Inspiration was thus considered a by-product of unremitting labor, and therefore an artist who waited for it was on the wrong track. There was, of course, no simple solution to this vexing problem, as Ravel observed in a letter to Jacques Durand, written in June 1918: "I went through some terrible moments, convinced that I was drained, and that neither inspiration nor even the desire to work would ever return. And then, a few days ago, it returned." Another comment about inspiration was made during a rehearsal of the Sonata for Violin and Piano with the French violinist André Asselin. When asked about the role of inspiration in the Sonata, Ravel answered as follows: "Inspiration—what do you mean? No—I don't know what you mean. The most difficult thing for a composer, you see, is choice—yes, choice," and with a gesture he emphasized the term. "With regard to the performer, his task is never to forget that the line between the letter and spirit of a work is very narrow, and must remain so" (unpublished typescript by André Asselin, entitled "Nostalgie," kindly communicated to this writer by Jean Touzelet; see p. 549).

17 : : :

Take Jazz Seriously![1]

You Americans take jazz too lightly. You seem to feel that it is cheap, vulgar, momentary. In my opinion it is bound to lead to the national music of the United States. Aside from it you have no veritable idiom as yet. Most of your compositions show European influences, either Spanish, Russian, French, or German—rather than American individuality. Nor do I believe that those who claim that this is due to the admixture of foreign peoples who comprise the American people. *Pas du tout. C'est ridicule, ça!*[2]

Look at the *mélange* we have in France. In one section you will find Frenchmen who resemble Germans, in another some who resemble Italians more closely than the French. Besides we have Arabs, Algerians, expatriated Americans and intermarried Americans. Still who would deny that our music is characteristically French?

Mais non.[3] The two most important influences on art are climate and language. The first is perhaps more easy to comprehend than the second, which, however, I believe I can make clear. Glance for a moment at the English authors. *Par exemple,*[4] Joseph Conrad[5] and Michael Arlen,[6] the former a Pole, the latter an Armenian, yet both are outstanding names in the English world of *belles lettres. Et pourquoi?*[7] Because their medium of expression was the English language.

I could sit down and play you some French music written about 1849 that you would take for jazz, so characteristic is it, so syncopated in rhythm, *néanmoins,*[8] it retains a French flavor. What is more, it is considered as classical music.[9]

Abroad we take jazz seriously. It is influencing our work. The Blues in my sonata, *par exemple,* is stylized jazz, more French than American in character perhaps, but nevertheless influenced strongly by your so-called "popular music."

Personally I find jazz most interesting: the rhythms, the way the melodies are handled, the melodies themselves. I have heard some of George Gershwin's works and I find them intriguing. *Malheureusement,*[10] I am not acquainted with the compositions of your ultra-modern *enfant terrible,* George Antheil. He has piqued my curiosity because people either praise him to the skies or condemn him to the ends of the earth. There is never any in-between. A composer who can arouse such positive likes and dislikes must have something to him.[11]

We have some ultra-modern composers among our young group also. I don't know yet what it will amount to. Nevertheless, if you ask me if we have an impressionist school of music I must admit that I never associated the term with music. Painting, *ah, ça c'est autre chose!*[12] Monet and his school were impressionists. But in the kindred art there is no counterpart of this.

Music in France today is the contrary of impressionism. The composers know where they are going. While the Italians are groping for new terms of expression and the Germans are reacting against Wagner and the sentimental music of Schumann, we have our object in view: to follow the line of conduct set by Gounod.

Fauré is greatly beloved by our young musicians for his *préciosité* of harmony and equivocation of his melody. As you probably know, I was deeply impressed by Debussy. Nevertheless, I started the reaction against him in favor of the classics because I craved more will and intellect than his music contained. Paul Dukas belongs to an older group. He was influenced by Liszt and Saint-Saëns. His compositions did not affect me. The one who made a more profound imprint on me than Debussy was Chabrier, and the latest to move me Erik Satie. *Voilà un vrai musicien!*[13]

When it comes to my own works, my favorite is always the most recent one. Just at present I like my Chansons Madécasses (Songs of Madagascar) the best. *Mais,*[14] I am conceiving a concerto, an operetta based on a libretto by Bousquet that is rather Pirandelloesque in style, and I intend to write an opera. When they are finished, *qui sait?*[15]

Opera in France today is *l'opéra romantique.* The composers are looking for nothing new. They are content with the products of Lalo,[16] such an opera as Meyerbeer's Le Prophète, and even with Wagner.

The age we live in is an auspicious one for composers. We are experiencing an economic upheaval, a polite revolution. Internationalism is developing parallel to nationalism, constructive measures are being adopted alongside of destructive ones. We devise methods of hygiene and instruments of war. One part of the world was never so civilized; other portions seem more uncivilized than ever. The world is changing and contradicting itself as never before.

I am happy to be living through all this and to have the good fortune of being a composer.

I am also happy to have come to America at last and although I have hardly been out of doors I can testify that Broadway After Dark is *ravissant.*[17]

NOTES

1. *Musical Digest* (March 1928), 13(3):49 and 51. This article, which is in English, may have been translated by a writer for the *Musical Digest*.

2. Not at all. That's ridiculous!

3. Of course not.

4. For example, . . .

5. See p. 241, note 1. The library at Montfort l'Amaury contains several of Conrad's short stories which were translated by Georges Jean-Aubry and published in Paris in the 1920s.

6. He was born Dikran Kouyoumdjian (1895–1956) and changed his name upon becoming a British subject. *The Green Hat* (1924), a witty novel about London's high society, was phenomenally successful, and made Arlen an international celebrity.

7. And why?

8. . . . . nevertheless, . . .

9. Referring to the piano pieces of Louis Moreau Gottschalk (1829–1869), with their ingratiating Latin-American and Creole rhythms. Born in New Orleans of an English father and Creole mother, Gottschalk was a child prodigy. He toured widely in Europe and the Americas, often performing his own elegant and brilliant salon music.

10. Unfortunately, . . .

11. It appears that the composers never met. Antheil (1900–1959) aptly entitled his autobiography *Bad Boy of Music* (1945). He studied with Ernest Bloch in New York, was a member of the Parisian avant-garde in the 1920s, and later wrote traditional film music in Hollywood. His *Ballet mécanique* (Mechanical Ballet), written for some twenty percussion instruments, including four pianos, "airplane propellers," and electric bells, created a sensation in Paris (1926) and New York (1927).

12. . . . . ah, that's another matter!

13. There's a true musician!

14. But, . . .

15. . . . . who knows? (Of these projects, only the piano concerto in G would be completed. See p. 455, note 4.)

16. Edouard Lalo's opera *Le Roi d'Ys* (1888) still holds the stage in France.

17. . . . . enchanting.

18 : : :

Memories of a Lazy Child[1]

For me, there are not several arts, but only one: music, painting, and literature differ only in their means of expression.
Thus, there aren't different kinds of artists, but simply different kinds of specialists. This specialization becomes increasingly necessary
as technical knowledge increases, for even in art, nothing can be achieved
without study. Moreover, it has become impossible to follow the example of
Leonardo da Vinci, who succeeded in being an amateur in everything . . . even
in painting!

As for me, I was certainly born a musician; but if I do not write, it's because of
a lack of training: I realize, for example, that I read in a thoroughly professional
manner, as if I were a writer. The same holds true for painting: I cannot look at a
painting as an amateur, but rather as a painter. This may stem from the fact that
as a child, I was gifted in many areas—which, of course, worried my parents
very much. It particularly worried them because in addition to my numerous
propensities, I was also extremely lazy. I worked only like a taxi; that is, in order
to make the slightest effort, I had to be paid. The only subject which attracted
me a little was mathematics, to the great joy of my father, who was an engineer.
My mother, who was Basque, and a musician like all her compatriots, would
have liked me to be more disciplined at the piano; but I truly found it excessively
boring. Moreover, I learned that the performance of a piece, particularly if it is
slow, like Chopin's "Funeral March," for example, demands the expenditure of
physical force amounting to an impressive number of kilograms. And in retrospect, that seems to legitimize somewhat my lack of enthusiasm for work.

However, as soon as I began to compose, everyone realized that I was on the
right path. I even enjoyed it! . . . which isn't so strange after all, as my inclination
for mathematics surely helped me a bit in that direction, to such an extent that
the inveterately lazy person that I had been up to then began working even at
night—a habit which I have always maintained, unfortunately for my health.
My teacher, Charles René, had me writing composition exercises when I was
scarcely sixteen or seventeen, but it was only three or four years later that I
devoted myself to my first genuine compositions, which by the way I was careful
to keep hidden. I had also entered the Conservatoire as a pianist, in the class of

393

Charles de Bériot, who did not fail to recognize my "artistic" nature, but also noted that I possessed a minimum of zeal as a performer.

However, I enthusiastically applied myself to the study of fugue, counterpoint, and harmony; and even though I had composed very little, I already felt a strong urge in this direction. It was at this time that I began to make incessant discoveries in the works of my favorite composers, while concomitantly feeling that there were other things to be said. The influences that I underwent at the time confirmed my opinion that there are not different kinds of art: of course, I was influenced above all by a musician: Chabrier, who moreover still does not have the recognition he deserves, for all of contemporary French music stems from his work. His role was as important as that of Manet in painting. Incidentally, it was Chabrier who owned the most beautiful Manets, like *Le Bar des Folies-Bergère*, for example.

If the Debussyian revelation did not touch me deeply, it's because I was already conquered by Chabrier; nevertheless, I was influenced by Debussy, but voluntarily so, and I always reacted to his music at certain passages. At any event, I never accepted Debussyian principles; I believe this to be so obvious that no one can doubt it.

To return to the connection which, in my view, exists between Chabrier and Manet, it is not restricted to the influence which they exercised on their respective arts. This connection strikes me as more profound: I discovered the same impression created by Chabrier's music in Manet's *Olympia*, which gave me one of the most beautiful emotions of my adolescence, and which I still regard as a wonderful painting. In *Olympia*, I always had the feeling of rediscovering the essence of Chabrier's *Mélancolie*, simply transferred to another medium.

As for technique, my teacher was certainly Edgar Allan Poe. The finest treatise on composition, in my opinion, and the one which in any case had the greatest influence upon me was his *Philosophy of Composition*. No matter how much Mallarmé claimed that it was nothing but a hoax, I am convinced that Poe indeed wrote his poem *The Raven* in the way that he indicated.

Naturally, I fully realize that the influences which I underwent are partially related to the time in which I grew up. I am keenly aware that the works I love best have occasionally become outdated. This is true of *A Rebours*: I can't help but consider it of major importance, and yet I know that, justifiably, it no longer retains that importance. Nevertheless, it still rings true for me. I believe that my entire generation found itself in *A Rebours*,[2] even those who, like myself, didn't care for Huysmans' other works. I must say, in addition, that I read it at a very young age. And what joy it is for youth to discover, as I did, for example, Rimbaud, who was still unknown!

This need to discover is not limited to youth alone—I still have it. I have even cultivated it. It's what gives me this eternal desire to renew myself. I let go of a work only when I am certain that I cannot improve upon it in any way. And that is the most wonderful moment. But then I abandon it definitively.

I have never limited myself to a "Ravel" style. When I create a new way of expressing myself, I leave it to others. They may throw my former works back at me, but I know that a *conscious* artist is always right. I say *conscious* and not *sincere*, because in the latter word there is something humiliating. An artist *cannot* be sincere. Falsehood, taken as the power of illusion, is the only superiority of man over the animals; and when it can claim to be art, it is the only superiority of the artist over other men. When one allows oneself spontaneity, one babbles and that's all.

In art, everything must be thought out. Massenet, who was so gifted, squandered his talents by an excess of sincerity. He truly wrote everything that came into his head, the result being that he always repeated the same thing: what he thought were innovations were nothing but reminiscences.

The truth is, one can never have enough control. Moreover, since we cannot express ourselves without exploiting and thus transforming our emotions, isn't it better at least to be fully aware and acknowledge that art is the supreme imposture? What is sometimes called my insensibility is simply a scruple not to write just anything.

As for reproaching me for writing only "masterpieces," that is, works which allow me to say nothing after them, I can only simply reply that if it were true, I would have surely been aware of it, and nothing would remain for me but to cease and to die . . . despite the example of God, who rested after having created the world, and wrongly so!

NOTES

1. *La Petite Gironde,* July 12, 1931, p. 1. The authenticity of this article was challenged by Edouard Ravel shortly after it appeared in the newspaper *Paris-Soir* on January 4, 1938. (See the *Revue de musicologie,* May–August 1938, p. 107.) In place of Maurice Ravel's name as the author, the article is signed "Copyright Opera Mundi Press Service," thereby suggesting some collaboration with an unnamed journalist. Nevertheless, the article's essential authenticity has been convincingly defended by François Lesure (see *Musical,* June 1987, 4:10.)

2. Des Esseintes, the hero of Huysmans' novel *A Rebours* (1884), tries to overcome his profound ennui, but his elaborate experiments with sensual pleasures leave him jaded and pessimistic. A modern writer has observed that the novel has retrospective importance as a compendium of *fin-de-siècle* tastes and interests, for which English comparisons might be found in Oscar Wilde's *Picture of Dorian Gray.* It is interesting to note that the hero's greatest pleasure comes from reading Mallarmé, whose writings, in 1884, were little known.

19 : : :

Concerto for the Left Hand[1]

Next Tuesday, the Paris Symphony Orchestra will give the first perfor-
mance of a concerto for piano and orchestra by M. Maurice Ravel. This
concerto falls into a special category, having been written for the left
hand alone. Before conducting it himself next Tuesday, M. Maurice
Ravel kindly agreed to introduce his work to our readers.[2]

The initial idea for the concerto for the left hand, which I will soon conduct with the Paris Symphony Orchestra, dates from a trip I made to Vienna three years ago.

During my stay in Vienna, which was occupied by rehearsals at the Opera of *L'Enfant et les sortilèges* and by Mme Ida Rubinstein's performances in which I conducted *La Valse* and *Boléro,* I had the occasion to hear the Austrian pianist Wittgenstein. His right hand had been amputated following a war injury, and he performed a concerto for the left hand alone by Richard Strauss.

A severe limitation of this sort poses a rather arduous problem for the composer. The attempts at resolving this problem, moreover, are extremely rare, and the best known among them are the *Six Etudes for the Left Hand* by Saint-Saëns. Because of their brevity and sectionalization, they avoid the most formidable aspect of the problem, which is to maintain interest in a work of extended scope while utilizing such limited means.

The fear of difficulty, however, is never as keen as the pleasure of contending with it, and, if possible, of overcoming it. That is why I acceded to Wittgenstein's request to compose a concerto for him. I carried out my task with enthusiasm, and it was completed in a year, which represents a minimum delay for me.

In contrast to the Piano Concerto in G Major, first performed last year by Marguerite Long, which calls for a reduced orchestra, the Concerto for the Left Hand utilizes a full orchestral complement. The concerto is divided into two parts which are played without pause:

The work begins with a slow introduction, which stands in contrast to the powerful entrance of theme one; this theme will later be offset by a second idea, marked "espressivo," which is treated pianistically as though written for two hands, with an accompaniment figure weaving about the melodic line.

The second part is a scherzo based upon two rhythmic themes. A new element suddenly appears in the middle, a sort of ostinato figure extending over several measures which are indefinitely repeated but constantly varied in their underlying harmony, and over which innumerable rhythmic patterns are introduced which become increasingly compact. This pulsation increases in intensity and frequency, and following a return of the scherzo, it leads to an expanded reprise of the initial theme of the work and finally to a long cadenza, in which the theme of the introduction and the various elements noted in the beginning of the concerto contend with one another until they are brusquely interrupted by a brutal conclusion.

NOTES

1. *Le Journal,* January 14, 1933.
2. The Paris première of the Concerto for the Left Hand took place on January 17, 1933, with Paul Wittgenstein as soloist (see p. 593).

20 : : :

Finding Tunes in Factories[1]

For centuries man has been inspired by music that owes its inception to the works of Nature. The rippling stream, the rustling leaves, songs of birds, and cries of beasts, all have been interpreted into music of enduring beauty.

But all of these are now established. We cannot continue to use them as the inspiration for new works, for the time would surely come when the world would so tire of hearing new themes based upon old inspirations that all music would suffer an eclipse.

Inspiration from Noise

In our search for fresh inspiration we cannot overlook the appeal of modern life. Our cities are said to "hum" with traffic, machinery to "purr," and although these sounds may seem pleasant or unpleasant, there is no reason why they should not be interpreted into great music.

Unquestionably the mechanics of this age will leave their imprint on music that will be handed down through generations, and more and more of our composers will find inspiration in what some now regard as mere noise. In the past battles have been made the themes of world-famous symphonies, and surely the sound of battle is no more inspiring than the hum of a vast machine.

Tchaikovsky's *1812* and Von Suppé's *Light Cavalry* had their birth, not in the ordered sounds of the parade ground, but in the chaotic clash of arms and the irregular thunder of cannon.[2] Beethoven composed a symphony based on the life of Napoleon; why should not a modern composer base a similar work on the life of a great captain of industry?

Business Man as Hero

It is the tendency of the age to look to our industrial leaders, rather than to our politicians and soldiers, for our advancement. This can very naturally be interpreted into music, and must be done if the music of this age is correctly to represent the life of our peoples.

The strange, disordered sounds of a great motor vehicle pulling up a steep hill may not impress with their beauty, but when translated into music they would have a different appeal. The song of the nightingale in the forest is very different from the musical interpretations that have found their way into our scores; similarly, the agitation of a great engine set to music would be quite unlike the actual sounds of the struggle.

To set such sounds to music is true art. Of course the music does not necessarily suggest the noises, but it can tell in music the story of the machine and interpret the machine's works.

Beauty in Industry

Let us consider the factory. Set on a great plain, or in the heart of a crowded industrial city, it is the life, the home, the entire being of thousands of workers. Throughout the day its mighty engines turn and turn and turn. Clanging bells punctuate its ordered progress, piles of finished goods pay tribute to the efficiency of the mechanism and to the greatness of the brain that conceived it.

At dusk the clash and clang and thunder of toil is stilled. The great gates open and the air rumbles with the voices of thousands of workers pouring out and back to their homes. A little later the last lights are extinguished, and where a few hours before was noise and toil is stillness and desolation.

Music of Machines

What a musical story there is in that factory![3] Musicians, together with historians and writers of fiction, must carry on the tale of the mechanics of this age to our children and our children's children.

We have had nature, war, and a hundred other themes in music, and it amazes me that musicians have not yet captured the wonder of industrial progress.

Honegger, Mossolov, Schoenberg, and others have gained much of their inspiration from machinery.[4] My own *Bolero* owed its inception to a factory. Some day I should like to play it with a vast industrial works in the background.

An Airplane Symphony

The airplane, which has done so much to bring greater convenience, faster travel, and to facilitate discovery in these times—what a theme for a symphony it would make![5] Great flights showing the epic courage of our aviators, the perils of earth, sea, and sky, could all be interpreted into music which would be a monument to our heroes of the air. A modern liner putting out to sea with her complement of many hundreds of souls on board, the coming of a storm, man's conquest of the elements—all these could be epitomized into musical story. The ordinary, everyday sounds of our railways could be made into works which would tell of our progress, which would show how we had overcome the obstacles of nature and permitted the ingenuity of man to triumph.

But over all would be the triumph of the machine, the vast monster that man has created to do his bidding. What a noble inspiration! Surely one that will in future years be felt by hundreds of our composers, who will bring into being music that will faithfully and beautifully reflect the spirit of the age in which machinery struggled to lighten the burdens of man.

NOTES

1. *New Britain,* August 9, 1933, p. 367. This article, which is in English, may have been translated by a writer for *New Britain.*

2. These celebrated overtures were completed respectively in 1882 and 1866.

3. See letter no. 19, note 5.

4. Apparently referring to Honegger's *Pacific 231* (1923), Alexander Mossolov's *Zavod* (Iron Foundry, 1927), and Schoenberg's drama with music *Die Glückliche Hand* (The Golden Touch, 1924), whose third scene takes place in a grotto, described in the score as "something between a machine shop and a goldsmith's workshop."

5. See p. 469, note 4.

The Aspirations of Those Under Twenty-Five: Musical Youth[1]

I t is still premature, in my opinion, to try to define the tendencies of today's musical youth. Isn't it always a bit indiscreet, moreover, to wish to formulate a synthesis before devoting oneself to slow and patient analysis? This is the principal error of what one might call "teachers' training" music criticism, in other words, of very ingenious views of the intellect which have acclimatized us to so many fascinating theories, which are very clear and very logical, but which do not sufficiently take into account the musical phenomenon, properly speaking.

In aesthetics, one always tends to create an overly rigid framework, specifying to excess the characteristics of a school in which, somehow, for the needs of the cause, one includes artists whom nothing has predestined for this specialization. We do not have the necessary perspective to encompass the entire picture of present-day French musical life. However, the attentive observer can gather, here and there, some instructive information. When speaking of today's "young people," one must distinguish between two generations, whose paths are beginning to take divergent directions. There are the postwar "young people," in other words, the restless, rash, and somewhat aggressive adolescents, who had to begin afresh the work of musical civilization on a completely topsy-turvy planet. Their task was difficult and ungrateful. They felt an instinctive need to break violently with the traditions of their elders. They found themselves in social and intellectual conditions so different from those which existed before 1914, that they were led, almost automatically, to adopt the attitudes, methods, and the style of iconoclasts. In all revolutions, there is a period devoted to destruction. For a while, we had, in music, demolition squads. And success came to them immediately. Some of them were exceptionally gifted, but the violence of their reaction was, too often, calculated.

After a period in which their approach was continually analyzed, the main representatives of this generation became dispersed and ceased to pursue the same objectives. Their task was accomplished. They had publicly broken with the luxurious art of prewar impressionism, and had attempted to guide contemporary sensibility towards a harsher, more rugged, more robust ideal. They openly repudiated sensibility and tenderness. By their own admission, they were writing "cruel" music, and let's not forget that Serge Diaghilev himself sought to obtain what he called "mischievous" scores.

And now, there comes the generation, which, after clearing the ruins of the former edifice, is going to build anew.[2] This generation offers the keenest interest to the observer. It is little known. It consists of music students and composition pupils who are barely over twenty years old. They are truly "young people," whose early works must be closely watched.

Their teachers detect many common tendencies in them. They clearly part company with the group of pioneers and "underminers" which preceded them. They are far more preoccupied than their predecessors with solidly learning their craft and perfecting their writing. In addition, they have stopped writing music which throws punches. They work more than their immediate elders, producing less and orienting themselves increasingly towards a rather curious type of neoclassicism. These very young people no longer have the same aversion as their elders to expressive pursuits, and they even profess a firm commitment to sensibility. It is still very difficult to fathom the mysterious objectives toward which their instinct directs them. However, one can recognize in their works a concern for clarity, precision, sincerity, a love of life and of knowledge, and a sort of inner joy whose courage is highly commendable. One doesn't find any preconceived manner of writing among them.[3]

What will these young people do? Their situation is particularly distressing. Most of the important forms of musical expression are forbidden to them by circumstances. The lyric theater, in its traditional form, is moribund. Throughout the world, people are turning away from this type of spectacle, which must be revived at all cost. Present economic conditions no longer warrant the composing of large symphonic works, and even less those which require the addition of large choral groups. All of that is too expensive today. Chamber music attracts but few faithful followers. The hour is difficult for composers. In order to reach out to the general public, only the innumerable sounds of the loudspeaker remain. Only the phonograph recording, the sound track film, and the radio can save music, which is now in jeopardy. Unfortunately, producers of recorded music have other preoccupations. They have earmarked the phonograph recording exclusively for commercial success, instead of commissioning new works written especially for it. The sound track film, which could be the most important form of lyric expression in today's art, spurns the collaboration of genuine musicians, and permits very little access to its studios. There remains the radio, which has also been indifferent to this problem until now, but which will have to deal with it in the future.

To sum up, I admire the optimism and the fine sense of balance with which my younger colleagues are approaching the struggle against widespread indifference. Their present state of mind enables us to place our complete confidence in them. It is gratifying to think that the need to conquer the terrible obstacles which accumulated on their way will lead them to discover new and bold solutions to this fearsome problem, solutions which we cannot even surmise at the present time.

NOTES

1. *Excelsior,* November 28, 1933.

2. Having discussed the generation of French composers born about 1890 (*Les Six,* etc.), Ravel now compares them with the generation born about 1910, which would include names such as Jean Françaix, André Jolivet, and Olivier Messiaen.

3. Ravel expressed his preference for this approach to composition in a conversation with the Austrian critic Paul Stefan. Mozart, he explained, understood that "music does not need to be philosophy; it must simply remain music.... I have attempted to compose in this way. My art has nothing in common with 'programmatic' composers who toy with the profundity of universal ideas, or who wish to be revolutionaries at any cost" (*La Revue musicale,* December 1938, 19:277).

22 : : :

Nijinsky as Ballet Master[1]

For half a century, the art of choreography had stopped developing. The same groupings, the same steps, and the same gestures which had been inspired by romantic art, somehow accompanied productions whose style increasingly deviated from romanticism. Soon, the dancers, authors, scene-painters, and musicians felt obliged to dissociate themselves from this morose, hackneyed work, which only a few exceptional virtuosi, who became increasingly rare, were still able to endow with some distinction.

In Russia, these out-of-date traditions seem to have preserved some freshness, thanks to the solid technique of its ballet masters. The imperial theaters of Moscow and Saint Petersburg produced individuals who would renew the art of the Dance, which some isolated attempts could not have brought about.

One cannot forget *Scheherazade,* the dances in *Prince Igor,* and *Daphnis et Chloé,* in which Michel Fokine directed the tumult and fury of Asiatic dances, marvelously brought to life the friezes of Greek temples, while at the same time, in *Les Sylphides,* restoring all of the graceful beauty of romantic ballet.

Les Sylphides united all the characteristics of its time: its plastic art was inspired by Delacroix, Devéria,[2] and Ingres' neogothic works.[3] In Fokine's creations, even in *Petrushka,* one still did not see the principal tendencies of the early 20th century[4] portrayed—those of Cézanne, Gauguin,[5] and Bourdelle.[6] Then came *The Afternoon of a Faun*: with his very first attempt, Nijinsky had created modern ballet. In truth, this realization, perfect in itself, was hardly so in relation to the work which had served as its pretext. Debussy's symphonic poem, supple, undulating, gently tinted, and of unprecedented fluidity, stood in singular contrast to the precision, rigidity, and angular archaism of its choreographic interpretation. This ensemble lacked the necessary cohesion which was revealed several days later in *The Rite of Spring.*

In this work, the intimate collaboration between composer and choreographer was obvious: the monumental construction of sonorous masses and compact groups; the obsessive quality of the rhythms and the movements; the tragic violence of the timbres and the gestures; the implacable expression of the plastic and musical lines—all of these concentrated elements seized you from the outset, transporting you incessantly into splendid and terrible regions from which you were brusquely hurled, panting from spiritual anguish.

All of the interesting choreographic achievements which followed *The Rite of Spring* proceeded more or less from it.[7] As often happens, the most successful of these achievements made the detractors of Nijinsky's choreography realize that his most important work was a masterpiece.

NOTES

1. If this article was published, it has yet to be traced. The holograph, consisting of three pages, is in the private collection of Mme Alexandre Taverne (see plate 15).

2. Achille Devéria (1800–1857), the French painter, lithographer, and engraver.

3. One might contrast the classical outlook of Ingres (1780–1867) and Mendelssohn with the sweeping romanticism of Delacroix (1798–1863) and Berlioz.

4. In the autograph, "early 19th century," an obvious error.

5. Cézanne (1839–1906), the "father of modern painting," and Gauguin (1848–1903) were influential figures in the emergence of Fauvism and Cubism.

6. The vigorous sculpture of Antoine Bourdelle (1861–1929) showed the influence of his teacher, Auguste Rodin.

7. Following the 1913 Ballet Russe season, Nijinsky (1890–1950) broke with Diaghilev temporarily and formed his own company. Thereupon, at Nijinsky's request, Ravel orchestrated Schumann's *Carnaval* and Chopin's *Les Sylphides* for his troupe.

IV

Interviews

(listed in Selected Bibliography)

I : : :

Maurice Ravel's Opinion of
Modern French Music[1]

t was a great pleasure to interview Maurice Ravel in his home. His charming amiability, his simplicity of manner, his refined personality, mark him as one of the fine gentlemen of today. Upon the piano I found a ballet of his called *Daphnis et Chloé.* It was begun for the last Russian ballet season but was not finished on time and will now be given in 1912, when the Russians return to Paris. March 19, fragments from this ballet—a Nocturne, Interlude and Danse Guerrière—will be given at the Colonne concert. The artists of the Opera Comique are now working on an "Opera Bouffe" (musical comedy) called *L'Heure Espagnole* (The Spanish Hour) which will probably have its first performance in May. M. Ravel wishes the music in this work to exaggerate the "bouffe" element indicated by M. Franc-Nohain, the librettist.

Because Ravel is one of the leading men in the modern French school of music, I have gathered some of his views on the subject: The school of today is a direct outgrowth of the Slavic and Scandinavian school, just as that school was preceded by the German, and the German by the Italian. The word "maladif" (ill – neurasthenic) which one often hears in regard to this modern music, is a favorite expression, in all art, of those who have developed ideas up through the past generation and then have stopped still. The new ideas give these people a great surprise, a shock; therefore they have not the same satisfied feeling in regard to a modern composition which they have after hearing a well-known composition by Mozart or Beethoven. Instead of being decadent, the music of today marks the beginning of a new life. Beethoven can be considered a decadent Mozart from the point of view that he brought to its height and to its close the life which Mozart's music expresses, just as the Byzantine Art can be called a decadent Greek art because it brought to a close the Greek Art. Mozart in music, like Raphael in painting, possessed a certain perfection which was marked, nevertheless, by a certain dryness. Beethoven, who was less perfect, was also less dry. Does the new school lack spontaneity and simplicity? No man can be spontaneous to the degree of writing down anything just as it occurs to him. All artistic work goes through a tremendous amount of refining process. The work done in France today is by far more simple than the music by Wagner, his followers, his greatest disciple, Richard Strauss. It has not the gigantic form of Beethoven and Wagner, but it possesses a sensitiveness which other schools have not. Its great qualities are clearness and order. It is intensely rich in musical matter. There is more musical substance in Debussy's *Apres-Midi d'un Faun* (which M. Ravel considers a masterpiece) than in the wonderfully immense Ninth Symphony by Beethoven. The French composers of today work on small canvases but each stroke of the brush is of vital importance.

In speaking of the word genius conventionally defined as a force which appeals to all nations, to all classes of people, and belongs to the whole world, M. Ravel says "genius is that which brings something new." The French music of today is strictly national and personal. That is perhaps its great strength. Erik Satie is the originator of the present form of expression. M. Ravel considers *Pelléas et Mélisande* (Debussy) a masterpiece. However he doesn't understand this particular Maeterlinck play in the same way that Debussy does.

It was with absolute joy that M. Ravel said, "I am happy that I am alive today. I wouldn't care to have lived during any of the other periods in history. I love our modern life; the life of the city, of the factories as well as the life among the mountains and at the sea-shore. I find beauty in all things; the great and the small, the humble and the powerful. Beauty is what all modern artists endeavor to develop to the highest possible degree."

NOTE

1. Unsigned interview in *The Musical Leader* (March 16, 1911), 21(11):7.

2 : : :

L'Heure espagnole[1]

"It's a Comic Opera," Says M. Ravel, the Composer of This Work, Which Will Be Performed Tomorrow.

BY R. BIZET[2]

Knowing that he belongs to our French musical avant-garde, and having heard, a long time ago, the plaintive chords of the *Pavane pour une Infante défunte*, I pictured M. Ravel, whose *L'Heure espagnole* will be performed tomorrow at the Opéra-Comique, as a young master, serious and austere.

I saw that I was mistaken as soon as the composer answered my first question about his work: "I have just written a type of comic opera." M. Ravel then explained his ideas to me in a mordant voice, which is not at all surprising in view of his sinewy and mobile face, coupled with his short height and rapid gestures, which link him to the most impetuous Castilians. "I have written a comic opera, which I would like to think will prove to be a fresh source of inspiration. Note that in France, this musical genre doesn't exist. Offenbach wrote parodies of opera; today, Terrasse,[3] with delightful verve, distorts rhythms and amuses with his unexpected orchestration, but it isn't the music which makes one laugh. I wanted the chords, for example to seem funny, like puns in language. If I may put it this way, I 'heard funny.'

"Franc-Nohain's story is delightful. I changed virtually nothing in it: the wife of the clockmaker Torquemada, in Toledo, awaits her lover, a student, and finally—I'm summing up briefly—submits to a muleteer. That's the plot of this short one-act play. Apart from the student, who sings serenades and cavatinas in a deliberately exaggerated manner, the other roles, I imagine, will give the impression of being spoken. This is what Mussorgsky wished to do in setting Gogol's *Marriage*, which by the way the composer left incomplete.

"You should also understand that I did my utmost to make my work express Spain, and that the numerous rhythms of the jota, habanera, and the malagueña will underpin my musical phrases. Moreover, I have the greatest admiration for Spanish music, and was cradled in my youth by habaneras which I have never forgotten. The very meticulous décor presents a clockmaker's shop in Toledo, and the costumes are copies of models by Goya."

But in relation to your other works, what importance do you attach to *L'Heure espagnole*?

"This undertaking is very important for me. Besides making my debut in the theater tomorrow, I am bringing a rather personal conception to it, and the scenic realization of what I had previously attempted in the *Histoires naturelles*, which were preliminary studies for this comic opera. How will the public react? I believe it will be a bit disconcerted at first, but I'm expecting that. I will continue to work according to my own ideas. I'm adapting a sad work, Hauptmann's *La Cloche engloutie*, and another large-scale comic work. Above all, I attempt to work on things which are very different. No principles, no principles which impose stereotyped formulas. That is what has always been inside of me, and with it, or at times without it, I have written my music."[4]

He thus concluded, it seemed to me, with a courageous statement, which is indeed that of a young man with bold ideas, yet secure in his craft, from a musician who currently represents one of the finest hopes of the French school, and whose talent increasingly seeks to express the frankness, naturalness, and the gaiety inherent in our race. And that is not a trivial ambition, nor is it of little merit.

NOTES

1. *L'Intransigeant,* May 17, 1911.

2. The library at Montfort l'Amaury contains a volume of poetry by René Bizet (*Une Histoire,* Paris, 1910), with a personal dedication to Ravel. Bizet sent the book in appreciation for a performance by Ricardo Viñes of *Gaspard de la nuit.* Touched by this gesture, Ravel accorded some interviews to the critic.

3. The French composer Claude Terrasse (1867–1923) collaborated with Franc-Nohain on several operettas, and in 1906, he introduced his colleague to Ravel.

4. In another interview, Ravel made the following points:

L'Heure espagnole, or "the hour of the muleteer," as the Spanish say, is the comedy of Franc-Nohain exactly as it was performed at the Odéon theater. . . .

L'Heure espagnole contains little staging. With Franc-Nohain's consent, while the clocks chime their mischievous hubbub, I added some grotesque automatons: some dancers, musical marionettes, a soldier, a cockerel, an exotic bird, whose mechanical movements add to the illusion. . . .

As for the interpreters, they convey charming gaiety. M. Jean Périer is a comedian of remarkable flexibility; his Boulevard de la Villette [i.e., Montmartre] accent couldn't be funnier. Mlle Vix sings and plays the role of Concepcion delightfully. Please express my gratitude to the musicians of the orchestra; in this work, which is extremely difficult to perform, they not only gave an excellent rendition, but also evinced artistic devotion beyond all praise. M. Rulhmann, their conductor, is an unusually skillful and gifted artist. . . .

And I believe that the public will be pleased to become acquainted with a humorous Spain, a Spain seen from the heights of Montmartre, with neither mysticism nor truculence. (Charles Tenroc, "Les Avant-Premières: 'Thérèse' et 'L'Heure espagnole' à l'Opéra-Comique," *Comœdia*, May 11, 1911.)

3 : : :

Ma Mère L'Oye[1]

It's a Short, Very Original Ballet by M. Maurice Ravel

BY R. BIZET

This article should begin with a "Once upon a time . . . ," a bit old-fashioned, perhaps, but always evocative of charming fairy tales. M. Maurice Ravel would no doubt take me to task for this, as his intention was not to write a pastiche of ballets from the past, but rather a modern work, and it is well known that the sensibility of the composer of *L'Heure espagnole* is one which brings the highest honor to our young school. *Ma Mère l'Oye*, which will be performed tomorrow at the Théâtre des Arts, gives additional proof of this.

"A while ago, I wrote a collection of short piano pieces entitled *Ma Mère l'Oye*," he said. "They were written for children: 'Pavane of Sleeping Beauty,' 'Tom Thumb,' 'Laideronnette, Empress of the Pagodas,' 'Conversations of Beauty and the Beast,' and 'The Enchanted Garden.' I then transcribed these short musical fantasies for a small orchestra of 32 performers. I added some dances, and everything is held together by an argument, which, although fragile, no doubt, is sufficient to communicate my thought.[2] Princess Florine dances, pricks herself, and falls asleep; a fairy renders her sleep more pleasant by conjuring up lovely dreams for her. Prince Charming comes to awaken her, and leads her into the enchanted garden. The curtain falls.

"I wanted everything to be danced as much as possible. Dance is a wonderful art, and I have never been more keenly aware of it than through observing Mme Hugard arrange the choreography. Mlle Hugon, who will be the princess, has herself devised some unusually graceful figures, some of which are found in her choreographic interpretation of 'The Awakening of Sleeping Beauty,' which is exquisite.

"I cannot sufficiently thank M. Rouché, the director, M. Drésa, the scene-painter, and all those who helped to enhance the presentation of my work."

M. Ravel would not have allowed me to add my good wishes for the success of his ballet. He is among those sincere artists who write original works, somewhat lofty, full of color and life.

And this too is almost a fairy tale. "Once upon a time there was a musician. . . ."

NOTES

1. *L'Intransigeant,* January 28, 1912.
2. See appendix B.

4 : : :

"The Lynx": Maurice Ravel in the Country[1]

BY GEORGES LE FÈVRE

At Montfort l'Amaury, in a house with a terrace and a beautiful view overlooking the valley, where one must knock on the door vigorously, I am introduced to a musician who is at work.

Short, smooth-shaven, an astonishingly youthful gaze underneath his graying hair, Ravel walks toward me with a mischievous smile.

—You've come so far to tell me bonjour?[2]

—Rather bonsoir![3] *Bonsoir* would like to know about your plans for the winter, your ideas on the present crisis in operatic music; *Bonsoir* seeks to resolve a serious problem, which, in the name of the Parisians . . .

—May I say . . . , he replies, perhaps the Parisians are not very musical. That's where one must seek the root of the problem. If, in other branches of art, they show innate, perspicacious, and even refined judgment, you must concede that they lack this profound faith in music, the love, a bit jealous and almost religious, which rouses the devotees of Bayreuth, or this secular but keen passion which sings in the heart of every Viennese. The French are dilettantes.

"Moreover, when I am told that new works are very costly to mount, that the budget of our National Academy of Music incurs a deficit, the subsidy is insufficient, and the demands of the syndicates are excessive, I think of my stay in Vienna, from where I returned several months ago, when two concerts were given there in which my works were performed.

"I recall seeing lyric dramas mounted with unerring and perfect taste, with very simple, very sober décors; I recall hearing impeccable singing and an incomparable orchestra.

"I also recall that after the performance, one evening, several members of the reparations commission who were present gave the musicians, as a token of their satisfaction, four pounds of flour per person, and I concluded that one can be a good musician, show it, and be dying of hunger. But one must be an artist and not an artisan. That's my opinion.

"When they played my works, I found my Viennese interpreters accustomed to my orchestral writing, my style, my technique, and everything went smoothly; it had to, incidentally."

His chin in his hand, Ravel added:

—Rehearsals, Sir, which come to 200,000 crowns!

"I don't believe that France is capable of such a sacrifice, even though, in my opinion, the public which is interested in great art is growing every day. In Vienna, there is a full house at the opera every night; here, with three performances a week, they don't meet their expenses. Let them show motion pictures the other days. Why not? Why not at least give concerts again? What do we have as concert halls in Paris? Salle Gaveau, which everyone agrees is too small;[4] as for Salle Pleyel[5] and Salle Erard,[6] they are dreary and out-of-date; Salle des Agriculteurs[7] is not a concert hall, any more than the Vélodrome[8] or the Trocadéro."[9]

At this moment, in the fields, the lament of a bugle sounded.

—My projects? Maurice Ravel exclaimed. There is an opera in progress, a fantasy based on a libretto by Colette, but it's not fully worked out. I am presently finishing a piece for cello and piano,[10] which is giving me a lot of trouble, but I love difficulty. Come see . . ."

I thought he was going to open the piano; not at all. He took me through a maze of corridors, opening doors, leading me behind him.

I saw a Chinese salon, a kitchen with ochre and sepia tile flooring and Directory chairs; I saw the study, in which the grand piano, next to the desk, was overloaded with bibelots in 1830 gothic style, which the Maître confessed he was passionately fond of; I saw another salon, a small library still unfinished, and then we went down to the garden; I passed by the summer bedroom, the winter bedroom, I climbed three stairs and found myself, without quite knowing how, on the balcony.

—My home isn't bad, right?, he asked. I myself designed all the plans. It's I who . . . I adore puttering about . . .

Leaning on the wooden guardrail, we saw the old church at our feet, ringing the hour of vespers, and, extending as far as the wooded horizon, in gentle sunlight softened by airy clouds, the countryside.

—What calm! I said. How well you must be able to work in this solitude.

—Yes, he sighed, but I miss Paris a little, my friends, my more active life. But in Paris I can't do any work.

—Whereas here, I replied, amid the trees . . . Oh! listen . . . the bells . . .

—The bells? It's obvious that you're not accustomed to them.

—They go well with the landscape.

—Yes, but it's too much, especially on Sunday!

—Yet, I replied, they are melancholy, serene, musical . . .

—Perhaps.

And he reshut the window somewhat brusquely.

—But there are moments when—what shall I say?—they annoy me . . .

NOTES

1. *Bonsoir,* October 8, 1920.

2. . . . good day?

3. . . . good evening!

4. Located at 45 rue de la Boétie, it has about 1200 seats.

5. Referring to the old Salle Pleyel on rue Rochechouart (see letter no. 282, note 2).

6. Located at 13 rue du Mail, this concert hall is now an office building. A plaque at the entrance reads as follows: "In this house Franz Liszt was received by the Erard family from 1823 to 1878."

7. Formerly at 8 rue d'Athènes (just across the street from the Hôtel d'Athènes), this hall was recently demolished and has been replaced by a modern office building.

8. A stadium in Paris.

9. The Palais de Chaillot (1937) now stands on the site formerly occupied by the Palais du Trocadéro, which was built for the International Exposition of 1878. Its large hall held about 5000 people and was famous for its echoic acoustics.

10. An obvious slip on the interviewer's part for the Sonata for Violin and Cello, begun in April 1920, and finally completed in February 1922 (Ravel never composed a work for cello and piano).

5 : : :

Viennese Impressions of a French Artist[1]

(FROM A CONVERSATION)

Vienna, October 28 [1920]

Maurice Ravel, the leader of France's youngest generation of composers, is leaving our city this Saturday as an apostle of the musical city of Vienna and its musically enlightened public. He is enthusiastic about the appearance of the city and all he has seen and experienced in Vienna, and he is grateful to the public for its complete understanding and generous reception of his works, which, as he is well aware, are not calculated to appeal to every musical ear.

I am experiencing genuinely festive days in Vienna, Ravel said today in a conversation with one of our editors. One feels that the entire atmosphere is permeated with music, that the city, basking in the brilliant autumn sun, breathes music. Also, to the French, Vienna has always symbolized a positive attitude to life, a spiritual, charming cheerfulness. It is all the sadder, then, to learn about the suffering of this beautiful city, for which, please believe me, the French people feel the fullest and sincerest sympathy.

What deep respect must one have for a population, that, despite so much hardship, has preserved its taste for the arts, and particularly for music. It is precisely this ancient culture that sets Vienna apart from other cities. I had many dealings with musicians here; each one was a great artist. Right away at the rehearsals, immediate comprehension. Personal rapport was established at once. It was a rare joy for me to hear my works performed in such a way.

I went to the opera, where I saw Puccini's three one-act works[2] and Richard Strauss' *Die Frau ohne Schatten*.[3] I am thrilled with the accomplishments of this wonderful orchestra, this excellent roster of singers, the great art with which the stage is decorated, in brief, with everything one sees and hears there. Every creative artist should consider himself fortunate to have his work performed at such an institution, whose artistic excellence is incomparable.

Unfortunately, I was unable to hear an opera by Mozart. Mozart! To us, adherents of the younger modern school, he is the greatest musician, the musician par excellence, our god! The elder generation swears by Beethoven and Wagner. Our artistic creed is Mozart. On my trip back to Paris, I'm planning to spend a day in Salzburg, tracing Mozart's footsteps, visiting his home and the birthplaces of his immortal works.

Of the Viennese composers, Johann Strauss is and still remains the most popular in France. I admire and love his waltzes, which everybody in our country knows. Unfortunately, the symphonies and lieder of Gustav Mahler have not penetrated our important musical centers.[4] On the other hand, the works of Arnold Schoenberg are being performed.

Among the younger composers, those who are writing operettas are appreciated. I have heard Lehár's *Blaue Mazur,*[5] which is light, but genuine music. I am glad it is going to be performed in Paris, and I'm certain it will be a big success. Among Viennese operetta composers, Oscar Straus is also known in France— particularly his *Walzertraum*[6]—and so is Leo Fall.[7]

I cannot sufficiently express my admiration for the concert-going public in Vienna, for whom music is innate. True, each music has its motherland, but its natural calling is to be international and to bind all nations with the bond of harmony. May music also infuse the spirit of reconciliation into every heart. Once again, please let me reassure you that we in France harbor sincere sympathy for Vienna, and trust that the fate of the Viennese and Austrian people will soon improve. When there was or is talk of "anti-German currents," Vienna and Austria are never meant to be included in the expression.

NOTES

1. *Neue freie Presse,* October 29, 1920.

2. Puccini came to Vienna in October 1920 for the first Viennese productions of *Il Trittico* and *La Rondine.* His visit overlapped with Ravel's, and it is thus possible that the composers met.

3. "The Woman Without a Shadow," first performed in Vienna in October 1919. The fantastic libretto, by Hugo von Hofmannsthal, is a spiritual descendant of Mozart's *Magic Flute,* with the action taking place in an imaginary empire of the Southeastern Islands in an imaginary time.

4. Mahler (1860–1911) conducted his Second Symphony in Paris in April 1910. Ravel would probably have evaluated his symphonies as he did the songs of Duparc: imperfect, but exhibiting genius.

5. It was first performed in Vienna in May 1920. Franz Lehár (1870–1948) is best remembered for his operetta *The Merry Widow* (1905).

6. *A Waltz Dream* (1907), which brought Straus (1870–1954) international fame.

7. Together with Lehár and Straus, Fall (1873–1925) was one of the leading composers of the golden age of Viennese operetta.

6 : : :

Ravel and Modern Music[1]

The French Composer Talks

(FROM A CORRESPONDENT)

"Yes; things are alive now. On commence à se battre."[2] It was Ravel speaking of music in Paris today in the clear-cut, aphoristic French phrase, which loses its raciness in translation. A small, spare man, with eager eyes and regular features, his personality has that same intellectual quality which distinguishes his art. Yet he will not allow that his music is intellectual, and quotes Poe to the effect that art is as far removed from the intellect as from the sensibility. As he hovers over the wide fields of European music, one wishes one could take down his conversation verbatim.

M. Ravel labels himself as an anti-Debussyist, while he places Debussy as the great creative influence in modern French music. Gounod and Chabrier, with Liszt, he said, were the sources from which the main stream of French music was derived. He would not describe Debussy as an impressionist, for impressionism was a term borrowed from a sister art, which had very little application to music. Debussy had shown a *négligence de la forme*;[3] he had achieved through intellectual perception what Chopin had done from inspiration or intuition. Thus, in the larger forms he showed a lack of architectonic power. In a masterpiece like the *Après-midi d'un Faune*, where he achieved perfection, it was impossible to say how it had been built up.

Ravel and Debussy

M. Ravel said that he followed Debussy in the ideal of economy of material, but he was at odds with him in his respect for forms. Indeed, in his view of melody, the melodic line, as distinct from the *thème développé*,[4] he looked upon himself as a Mozartian. He was now engaged on writing a *Fantaisie Lyrique*,[5] which would be a mixture of every style from the music-hall to the purest lyricism. He believed that opera in the old sense was dead, and the future lay in the direction indicated by the *Coq d'Or*.[6]

Nationalism in Music

Before he had been induced to speak in a more personal vein, he had made some interesting observations on the future of music. While we might be moving again to a social internationalism, music was becoming more and more national. Vaughan Williams, for instance, was a composer leagues removed from the influences of the French school, and Schoenberg, "one of the greatest figures of the time," as a German followed a line of development which had hardly reacted at all on the essentially Latin nature of French music. Only at second hand through Stravinsky had the French school felt this new force. Nor did he think that there was anything analogous in France to the movement in England for drawing inspiration and material from the folk-song. French music had always been more subject to literary influences; music in France had never been a popular art.

As for the Parisians, they had recovered from the musical apathy into which they had fallen after the war, when they applauded Ambroise Thomas[7] and Schoenberg indiscriminately. "At that time," M. Ravel said, "I was near despair. Now that we have likes and dislikes, we are alive again. Enfin, on commence à se battre."[8]

NOTES

1. *The Morning Post,* July 10, 1922.
2. "We're beginning to fight."
3. . . . negligence with regard to form;
4. The developed theme, that is, a theme which contains the germ of developmental unfolding. Beethoven's architectural themes are examples par excellence.
5. The "lyric fantasy" *L'Enfant et les sortilèges.*
6. *The Golden Cockerel,* Rimsky-Korsakov's fairy tale opera, takes place in a mythical land. An analogous aura of make-believe enchantment is found in *L'Enfant et les sortilèges.*
7. Thomas (1811–1896) is largely remembered for his opera *Mignon.* He studied at the Conservatoire, won the Prix de Rome in 1832, and later joined the faculty. He was Massenet's composition teacher, and served as director of the Conservatoire during the last twenty-five years of his life.
8. "Finally, we're beginning to fight."

7 : : :

The French Music Festival[1]

An Interview with Ravel

hose who only know Ravel from portraits, especially the ones that appeared in Roland-Manuel's short monograph about him, with his high, uniformlike collar, imagine him as a tall, slim man. On the contrary, he is short, with an overly small proportioned body and a face set like a woodcut. He is simple, likable, and spry. I had a short interview with him, and he talked as easily as if we were having coffee together, speaking very freely. When he has a reservation, he makes it modestly; he is neither aggressive nor controversial in his judgments.

We talked about Ravel's *La Valse*, which he had not yet heard played by our orchestra, and about which he was very curious. "They don't play it well in Paris. They make it sound too much like a Viennese waltz," he said. I said that *La Valse* is explained differently in Holland, and I wanted to hear his own interpretation.

I asked, "Did you compose *La Valse* based on impressions during your visit to Vienna?" (Ravel was in Vienna the year before last at the invitation of *Der Anbruch*.)[2]

"No, it was composed and finished before that time. It doesn't have anything to do with the present situation in Vienna, and it also doesn't have any symbolic meaning in that regard. In the course of *La Valse*, I did not envision a dance of death or a struggle between life and death. (The year of the choreographic argument, 1855, repudiates such an assumption.) I changed the original title "Wien" to *La Valse*, which is more in keeping with the aesthetic nature of the composition. It is a dancing, whirling, almost hallucinatory ecstasy, an increasingly passionate and exhausting whirlwind of dancers, who are overcome and exhilarated by nothing but 'the waltz.'"

"Are you planning to write other ballet music? Do you believe in the future of the ballet?"

"No, the ballet of today is in decline, and the Ballet Russe isn't as good as it used to be. Yes, if you go back to the 18th century."

"What about the 'spectacle-concert,'[3] which appeals so much to the young?"

423

"That's a self-contained art form. It has something, undoubtedly, but I think that the cinema has the best future. Music can coordinate with it in a useful manner. Honegger started something like that with a regulated synchronization between film movement and music."

"What's your opinion about the younger composers, *Les Six*, for example?"

"After impressionism, new trends came about. The younger people strive for other things than the impressionists, who had already found their master in Debussy. Milhaud and Poulenc are undoubtedly composers of great talent. For them, Debussy is not the master, but Erik Satie."

"Do you consider Satie a musician of great importance?"

"Satie is a spiritual influence, but he is not completely sincere. The most important quality of a composer, in my view, is sincerity.[4] Stravinsky's influence, in a technical sense, has been much more profound for our youth."

"You recently spoke very favorably about Schoenberg. Do you consider him the greatest modern composer?"

After some reflection, Ravel said, "Yes, he is a sincere musician. His *Pierrot lunaire* is superb."

"The Dutch public does not like his music," I remarked.

"I can understand that. It is the same in France, although the young people do appreciate and study him. His music will not influence them, however, as it has too little affinity with the French mind."

I changed the subject to the French Music Festival, which is taking place right now. "Do you have the impression that the composers who are present are pleased with the interpretation of their works as performed by our orchestra conducted by Mengelberg?"

"The Amsterdam orchestra plays admirably and Mengelberg is a great musician.[5] Everyone is full of praise. Roussel was very pleased with the interpretation of his *Pour une fête de printemps* on Thursday evening. But the brass could have been a bit more tempered." (Good grief, I thought, that's the old criticism of Mengelberg's excessive use of the brass.)

"Isn't it a pity that the younger people haven't been represented more, and the elder composers a little less? Wouldn't it have been better to include a work by Roland-Manuel or Honegger in the program?"

"Well, perhaps," Ravel said. "The young people are our 'petits oiseaux.' "[6]

"And what are you working on right now?", was my last question.

"I am working on a fantasy for piano and orchestra, based upon the book *Le Grand Meaulnes*. It's a short novel about a little boy who dreams about great things, and who finally becomes the director of a small museum."

NOTES

1. *De Telegraaf,* September 30, 1922. The article is initialed "C. v. W."

2. This monthly journal devoted to contemporary music was edited by the Viennese critic Paul Stefan.

3. A presentation in which music was combined with lighting, improvisation, etc. Schmitt's pantomime *Fonctionnaire MCMXII* would fall into this category (see letter no. 275, note 3).

4. See Ravel's comments about sincerity on pp. 38 and 395.

5. Willem Mengelberg (1871–1951) was the principal conductor of the Amsterdam Concertgebouw for over four decades (see p. 575).

6. . . . 'fledglings.'

8 : : :

M. Ravel in London[1]

(FROM A CORRESPONDENT)

M ost good Frenchmen are supposed only to be able to enjoy themselves in Paris. M. Ravel, greatest of contemporary French composers and one of the most striking figures in the world of music, is an exception. He did not go back to Paris on Sunday, his labors of Saturday over and his guerdon of praise won. On the contrary, he spent the weekend quietly, as a good Englishman does, though I don't believe he plays golf, and is still engaged in enjoying himself in London. When I met him yesterday I have never seen him looking sprucer or in better spirits.

He likes London almost as much as Londoners (to judge from Saturday's reception at the Queen's Hall) like him. And he was loud in praise of the Queen's Hall Orchestra.[2] "Quite first class," he said, "and very quick to seize a point. I could not ask for a finer body of players." I hinted that French critics were apt to find our strings lacking in polish and smoothness of tone. But M. Ravel would have none of it. He added that he was particularly struck with the seating arrangements of the Queen's Hall Orchestra. He liked the violins placed together and the harps well to the front on the left. Though he talks no English, he had found an admirable translator amongst the 'cellists.

Plans and Prospects

M. Ravel talked of many things; of the marionettes, whom he had found entrancing—we discussed the possibility of their playing the *Ma Mère L'Oye* suite, but he dismissed it on the ground that the story was the Sleeping Beauty over again—of a possible visit to America, and another here next year, when some chamber concerts of his works might also be arranged. He was not a conductor, however. Asked about his work, he laughed. For a year he had written nothing. Why, he did not know. "Je m'ennuie,"[3] with another laugh and a shrug of the shoulders that contained a world of meaning in so fastidious a craftsman, so careful an artist. He had been making some orchestral arrangements of Debussy, however[4]—a few of them had been played by Koussevitzky at the London Symphony Orchestra's concert he had conducted.

The masterpieces still to come, for he is yet on the sunny side of fifty, he appeared to regard as objectively as the cigarette he held between his fingers. It is clear that M. Ravel, as a sensible man, only creates when the desire to do so becomes too imperious to resist.

NOTES

1. Unsigned interview in the *Morning Post*, April 18, 1923.
2. Its conductor was Sir Henry J. Wood, see p. 596.
3. "I'm bored," . . .
4. The transcriptions of Debussy's "Sarabande" and *Danse.*

9 : : :

Famous French Composer in London[1]

M. RAVEL ON JAZZ
WRITTEN BY BEST MEN — NOT TO BE DESPISED
A GOOD WORD FOR BRITISH MUSIC
FAMOUS FRENCHMAN'S NEXT WORK TO BE OPERATIC

A little man with a keen, intellectual face, and hair, just going grey, brushed back, wearing a blue shirt with a big soft blue collar, a light brown Norfolk jacket, and purple slippers, and talking French with great volubility, came downstairs and joined a *Star* representative at breakfast at a house in Holland Park this morning.

He was Maurice Ravel, the composer, who is worshiped in the French musical world just as Richard Strauss is in Germany and Stravinsky in Vienna.

Thinking for Two Years

He has been brought over here by Major R. Mayer and is conducting a special orchestra at the Queen's Hall on Thursday afternoon in a festival of his own music.

"Am I working?" he asked. "I haven't composed a note for two years.

"When I do compose—and I'm thinking about a lyrical operatic fantasy, a real departure from the conventional and the traditional, which I hope will be the work of my life—I'll go and bury myself at Rambouillet,[2] for it is impossible to create in Paris."

A New World Tour

"Why?" asked the innocent interviewer.

"Because people don't leave me alone in Paris. Authors, composers, conductors all seem to be pursuing me, so I hide in the forest to escape them.

"Next year I am going right away by invitation to conduct the orchestras in the New World—New York, Philadelphia, Chicago, Boston, Pittsburgh, and St. Louis."

428

Musical France

"How do you find music in Paris and London after the war?"

"Oh," said Ravel, "France has developed an intelligent interest in music since the war. She is really musical now. During the war she listened to anything, inspired or not.

"The new rich rushed to the concert room because they thought it the correct thing. It was snobbish if you like, but being French they soon acquired a taste for music, and now (laughing merrily) they even know how to grasp Schoenberg.

British Reputations

"As for music in England, you are developing a school of your own in a way that has not been done since Purcell.[3]

"Elgar[4] is international. Bax,[5] Holst,[6] Lord Berners,[7] Arthur Bliss,[8] and Vaughan Williams[9]—particularly Williams—are all doing individual and different work, but they are all helping to create a definite English style, assisted, no doubt, by French, Russian, and Italian influences."

English Banana Music

M. Ravel would not be drawn on the theme of banana music, beyond saying that melodies that were popular ought not to be ridiculed.

"Jazz from America," he said, "is not wholly to be despised.

"The best jazz is written by good musicians and contains essential harmonies. They come from the Negroes, no doubt, but I'm not sure their real origin is not partly English and partly Scotch.

"You may be sure that when popular music becomes national there is at least nothing artificial about it."

Some Ravel

Ravel has quite taken the place of Debussy and Saint-Saëns. His *Rapsodie espagnole* is a classic, and so are *Daphnis et Chloé*, the ballet, *Ma Mère l'Oye*, and his *Valses nobles et sentimentales* and the great *La Valse* are part of every musician's knowledge.

NOTES

1. Unsigned interview in *The Star*, October 16, 1923.
2. The forest near Montfort l'Amaury.

3. Henry Purcell (1659–1695), the most important English composer of the seventeenth century.

4. The works of Sir Edward Elgar (1857–1934) stimulated the development of a twentieth-century English musical renaissance.

5. Sir Arnold Bax (1883–1953).

6. Gustav Holst (1874–1934).

7. See letter no. 156, note 2.

8. Sir Arthur Bliss (1891–1975).

9. Together with Elgar, the most important of the contemporary English musicians listed.

10

The Great Musician Maurice Ravel
Talks About his Art[1]

BY ANDRÉ RÉVÉSZ

P hysically, Ravel strongly resembles Stravinsky. The same small, thin, and light body, the same large mouth, prominent nose, and an interesting face with the identical reflections of culture and intelligence.

Ravel receives me in a room at the Hôtel de Paris. Wearing black silk pyjamas, he is seated at a table working on a composition. It is 11:30 in the morning; the sunlight and the noises of the Puerta del Sol[2] penetrate through the open window.

—How is it possible, I ask him, that you aren't taking advantage of this splendid weather to enjoy Madrid? Are you working on something that is so urgent?

Ravel and Spain

"Indeed, it is urgent; my publisher is waiting for it. It is a virtuoso piece for violin[3] in the style of Sarasate."[4]

—Do you know Madrid so well that you aren't interested in going out at this hour?

"No, I don't know it; this is my first time in Spain.[5] In fact, I'm being rather ungrateful, since without Madrid I probably wouldn't exist. My parents met in Madrid. My father was a railroad engineer of French nationality, and my mother was a Basque from Saint-Jean-de-Luz, but probably of Spanish origin. My mother used to lull me to sleep singing guajiras.[6] Perhaps it's because of this link that I feel so attracted to Spain and its music."

—What have you visited so far?

"Only the Prado Museum. One hour after arriving in Madrid I rushed to the Prado. What a great painter Ribera is! And the Velázquez room is so beautiful! I have to go back to the Museum to look at the works of El Greco and Goya more carefully.

His Favorite Composers

—Who are the contemporary musicians you like the best?

"Perhaps Arnold Schoenberg. He was an enormous influence on German composers, and even on French musicians through Stravinsky. Schoenberg is Viennese and Jewish, and therefore he is less cold, less cerebral, less abstract than a purely German composer such as Reger.[7] Schoenberg's *Pierrot lunaire* left me with the most delightful yet terrible and painful feelings. Strauss is a Romantic genius, typically German, and very different from us. Among the Russians, I like Stravinsky and Prokofiev[8] very much. In France we have Darius Milhaud, not the Milhaud of *La Brebis égarée*,[9] which was written when he was very young, but the composer of *Protée*[10] and the *Cinq Etudes* for piano and orchestra.[11] We also have Poulenc and Auric,[12] and Madame Germaine Tailleferre, whose work is full of feminine charm, not at all an unworthy quality in music. Finally, we have Honegger, whose roots come from the German part of Switzerland, but who was born and educated in France, and whose art derives from France and Germany; and because of his Germanic background he has a predilection for the colossal. In Spain you have Manuel de Falla, one of the greatest musicians in the world."

—Among the preceding generations, who are your favorite composers?

"I think Gounod has had an enormous and positive influence on all of French music. The composer of *Faust* and *Philémon et Baucis* was also the teacher of Chabrier, Bizet, Lalo, Fauré, and many others. Without Gounod, perhaps there wouldn't be any modern French music. I love Fauré's *Pénélope* very much, with its nontheatrical but purely musical effects. Among the French classics I prefer Couperin to Rameau. The latter lived in an extremely intellectual period and his work reflects the aridity of his century."

—What is your opinion about Wagner?

"Today, now that we are free, and the terrible influence of Wagner doesn't disturb us anymore, we can talk about him without prejudice and proclaim that he was a very great musician, with equally strong virtues and defects. His major shortcoming is his orchestration, which doesn't proceed from Berlioz and Liszt as people incorrectly believe, but rather from Meyerbeer, with the difference that Meyerbeer happened to be more skilful than Wagner in this kind of military music."

—And Verdi?

"I only like the earlier Verdi, the composer of *La forza del destino* and *Un ballo in maschera*.[13] Later on, he becomes excessively vulgar, and frankly I think it's bad when in order to be up-to-date, he begins to imitate Wagner. In any event, I consider Verdi inferior to Bellini."[14]

Talking about the Russians, I translate to Ravel the interview that I had one month ago with Stravinsky, and ask Ravel his opinion about Stravinsky's admiration for Tchaikovsky and scorn for Rimsky-Korsakov.

"Stravinsky's fanaticism for Tchaikovsky," Ravel answers, "is a paradox. *The Nutcracker* is a charming and very fine piece, but less important, for example, than *Coppélia* or *Sylvia* by Delibes.[15] Tchaikovsky is the least Russian of the Russians, and for this reason he is the least interesting to us. Mussorgsky is far superior to him. As for Rimsky-Korsakov, I think that Stravinsky is rather ungrateful to the man who was his teacher. Rimsky's *Maid of Pskov* was written at the same period and at the same desk as Mussorgsky's *Boris Godunov*,[16] and some passages have the same inspiration. Today, it would be difficult to determine which of the two composers influenced the other. And don't forget that it was Rimsky who orchestrated most of the works of 'The Five'."[17]

—In your opinion, who is the greatest of all composers?

"For me it is Mozart. Mozart is perfection: he is Grecian, whereas Beethoven is Roman. The Greek is great, the Roman is colossal. I prefer the great. There is nothing as sublime as the third act of Mozart's *Idomeneo*."

His Self-Criticism

—. . . . . . .?

"Unlike politics, in art I'm a nationalist. I know that I am above all a French composer: I furthermore declare myself a classicist. I also know that I have the virtues and defects of French artists. We neither want nor do we know how to produce colossal works; we are always somewhat cerebral, but within these limits we very often reach perfection. I consider sincerity to be the greatest defect in art, because it excludes the possibility of choice. Art is meant to correct nature's imperfections. Art is a beautiful lie. The most interesting thing in art is to try to overcome difficulties. My teacher in composition was Edgar Allan Poe, because of his analysis of his wonderful poem *The Raven*. Poe taught me that true art is a perfect balance between pure intellect and emotion. My early stage was a reaction against Debussy, against the abandonment of form, of structure, and of architecture.

"This is, in a few words, the essence of my theories. If you wish, I will now tell you about my works. I have a predilection for my *Trois Poèmes de Stéphane Mallarmé*, which obviously will never be a popular work, since in it I transposed the literary procedures of Mallarmé, whom I personally consider France's greatest poet. In the Sonata [for violin and cello], which is a truly symphonic work for two instruments, I achieve new and interesting effects. In the final movement of this piece I imitate a rondo by Mozart. My opera buffa in one act, *L'Heure espagnole*, written with Franc-Nohain, is very popular. Now I am working with Colette on a very original piece, a kind of lyric fantasy in which there is a mixture of styles ranging all the way from great lyricism to the music hall."

—What is your opinion of *La Valse*, and its interpretation by Koussevitzky?

"Koussevitzky is a great virtuoso who always has a very personal style of interpretation, sometimes admirable, but sometimes mistaken. I don't think his interpretation of *La Valse* is successful. Some people have seen in this piece the expression of a tragic affair; some have said that it represented the end of the Second Empire, others said that it was postwar Vienna. They are wrong. Certainly, *La Valse* is tragic, but in the Greek sense: it is a fatal spinning around, the expression of vertigo and of the voluptuousness of the dance to the point of paroxysm. *La Valse* is meant for the stage, but I want to save the première for Vienna, the city of Romantic waltzes."

NOTES

1. *ABC de Madrid*, May 1, 1924, p. 19.

2. The main plaza in Madrid, literally "the gate of the sun."

3. Referring to *Tzigane*. See letter no. 235.

4. The noted Spanish violinist Pablo de Sarasate (1844–1908) went to Paris at the age of twelve and studied at the Conservatoire for several years.

5. Ravel had visited the northernmost part of Spain in 1911 (see letter no. 89), but this was his first trip to Madrid.

6. A dance of Spanish-Cuban origin, characterized by a continual shift in meter from $\frac{6}{8}$ to $\frac{3}{4}$ or $\frac{2}{4}$. Ravel's "Chanson romanesque" (from *Don Quichotte à Dulcinée*) is based on the rhythm of the guajira.

7. Max Reger (1873–1916) was greatly influenced by Bach and Beethoven, and above all by Brahms.

8. In a commemorative article entitled "Maurice Ravel," Prokofiev wrote:

. . . For us Soviet musicians it is especially gratifying to know that, like Debussy, Ravel was not only keenly interested in Russian music but was influenced by it, and primarily by Mussorgsky and Rimsky-Korsakov. This influence can be traced in many of Ravel's compositions, in his *Daphnis* for example, and his superb symphonic transcription of Mussorgsky's *Pictures at an Exhibition* is striking evidence of Ravel's interest in Russian music, as is the very fact that he chose the subject of *Scheherazade*, although he treats it in an entirely different aspect than Rimsky-Korsakov. . . .

I first met Ravel in 1920 in Paris. It was at a musicale attended by Stravinsky, Ansermet and some other prominent musicians. A little man with sharp, distinctive features and a mane of hair beginning to turn grey entered the room. It was Ravel. Someone introduced me to him. When I expressed my pleasure at the opportunity of shaking hands with as distinguished a composer as himself and called him *maître* (a form of address commonly used in France in addressing noted artists) Ravel snatched away his hand as if I had been about to kiss it and exclaimed, 'Oh, please do not call me *maître.*'

I do not doubt for a moment that Ravel was perfectly aware of his great talent, but he hated any sort of homage and did whatever he could to avoid all attempts to honour him. . . . There was a time shortly after the war when a group of young musicians in France—Honegger, Milhaud, Poulenc and several others—declared that Ravel's music had outlived its time, that new composers and a new musical idiom had appeared on the scene. The years passed, the new composers have taken their allotted place in French music, but Ravel still remains one of the leading French composers and one of the most outstanding musicians of our time.

S. Prokofiev, *Autobiography, Articles, Reminiscences,* trans. Rose Prokofieva (Moscow: Foreign Languages Publishing House, n.d.) pp. 107–110.

9. "The Stray Sheep" (opus 4, begun in 1910, when Milhaud was eighteen, and completed five years later), an opera in three acts based on a libretto by Francis Jammes. It was first performed at the Opéra-Comique on December 10, 1923.

10. Referring to the incidental music for Paul Claudel's *Proteus* (opus 17, composed 1913–19). In 1954, Milhaud composed incidental music for the second version of Claudel's play (opus 341).

11. Composed in 1920 (opus 63).

12. The noted composer (1899–1983) and member of *Les Six.* (See letter 215, note 1.)

13. First performed respectively in 1859 and 1862, when Verdi (1813–1901) was in his late forties.

14. Several operas of Bellini (1801–1835) still hold the stage, among them *La sonnambula* (1831), *Norma* (1831), and *I Puritani* (1835). Professor Grout has observed: "In the Italian opera of the 1830's, Bellini holds a place apart by reason of a certain purity of style and melodies of incomparable elegance, often filled with elegiac, melancholy expression. He is the aristocrat of opera as Chopin is the aristocrat of the piano." (Donald J. Grout, *A Short History of Opera*, New York and London: Columbia University Press, 1947, pp. 341–42.)

15. Ravel's French perspective is obvious in his evaluations of *Coppélia* (1870), *Sylvia* (1876), and *The Nutcracker* (1892).

16. Rimsky-Korsakov's opera in four acts, based on his own libretto after L. A. Mey, appeared in three versions between 1868 and 1892. First composed in 1868–69, Mussorgsky's opera was rewritten in 1871–72. After Mussorgsky's death, Rimsky-Korsakov prepared a thoroughly revised version of *Boris Godunov.* (See Ravel's article on p. 000.)

17. The group of five Russian nationalist composers known as *moguchay kuchka* ("the mighty handful"): Balakirev (1837–1910), Borodin (1833–1887), Cui (1835–1918), Mussorgsky (1839–1881), and Rimsky-Korsakov (1844–1908).

11

Dress Rehearsal[1]

At the Monte Carlo Opera: L'Enfant et les sortilèges, *Poem by Mme Colette, Music by M. Maurice Ravel*

A work resulting from the collaboration of two such individual artists as Mme Colette and M. Maurice Ravel stimulates curiosity in advance, and one is already certain that however profoundly innovative this work may be, it cannot fail to elicit charm of the most delicate imagination.

L'Enfant et les sortilèges is a naive fairy tale, not without irony, a dream which has an element of nightmare, and if, at times, it appears to be a tiny drama, it is always a most gracious comedy; the fantastic intermingles with reality only because it is a logical consequence of it: one might say it is a very pretty series of illustrations[2] designed and colored by miniaturists of genius.

As for the poem, Mme Colette had only to give free rein to her imagination and sensibility.

With regard to the music:

—More than ever, M. Maurice Ravel said, I am for melody; yes, melody, bel canto, vocalises, vocal virtuosity—this is for me a point of departure. If, in *L'Heure espagnole*, the theatrical action itself demanded that the music be only the commentary on each word and gesture, here, on the contrary, this lyric fantasy calls for melody, nothing but melody—incidentally, without the slightest scholastic dogma. The score of *L'Enfant et les sortilèges* is a very smooth blending of all styles from all epochs, from Bach up to . . . Ravel! . . .[3] It moves from opera to American operetta, with a bit of jazz band. The penultimate scene, to cite but one detail, is a deliberate combination of ancient chorus and music hall. The fantasy of the poem would have served no purpose had it not been sustained, indeed accentuated by the fantasy of the music. But, enough said of a work which, until the curtain rises, remains purely and simply the subject of our theatrical production. I cannot sufficiently express my profound gratitude to Raoul Gunsbourg. Without him, this piece, begun in 1920, but interrupted, would not have been completed so soon. But, last spring, he came to ask me for a sequel to *L'Heure espagnole*, putting the exceptional resources of his theater at my disposal, and indeed, that convinced me.[4] For in order to mount *L'Enfant et les sortilèges,* you need a theater like the Monte Carlo opera house and a producer like Gunsbourg. Our work requires an extraordinary production: the roles are very numerous, and the phantasmagoria is constant. Following the principles of American operetta, dancing is continually and intimately mingled with the action. Now the Monte Carlo Opera possesses a wonderful troupe of Russian dancers, marvelously directed by a prodigious ballet master, M. Balanchine.[5] The role of the Child has found an ideal interpreter in Mlle Gauley. And all of the fantastic roles, the Cat, Squirrel, Armchair, Pendulum, Fire, Arithmetic, the Princess, etc., are realized by artists whose equal has rarely been assembled in one company: Mesdames Bilhon, Foliguet, Dubois-Lauger, Orsini, Messieurs Warnery, Lafont, Fabert, Dubois. And let's not forget an essential element, the orchestra, which plays with rare perfection, and its conductor M. Victor de Sabata, who, fortunately for the musicians, is himself a remarkable musician. His collaboration at the rehearsals of *L'Enfant et les sortilèges* not only showed his great talent, which I admire, but also his absolute devotion, for which I am very grateful to him.[6]

NOTES

1. Unsigned interview in *Le Gaulois,* March 20, 1925.
2. In the French, "image d'Épinal." See p. 475, note 9.
3. In another interview about the opera, Ravel stated:

Contrast is necessary in dramatic music, and we must get away from the formulas of Romantic opera, of which Meyerbeer was the great master. Isn't life itself a series of actions and reactions? . . . The theater, be it literary or musical, cannot be compared with any other art form. It has its own laws and exigencies, to which one must submit, without, however, abandoning one's personality in any way. I wanted to write a work which was very "theatrical." (Pierre de Saint-Prix, "Ce qu'est l'oeuvre nouvelle de M. Maurice Ravel: 'L'Enfant et les sortilèges,' " *Excelsior,* July 10, 1925.)

4. Further biographical details about *L'Enfant et les sortilèges* appeared in an interview published in a Monte Carlo newspaper:

Colette sent me her libretto when I was still at the front, at Maison-Rouge, near Verdun. But I didn't receive it, having changed my section. Then, like so many others, I contracted a serious illness, and was discharged in 1917. The libretto finally reached me a little later. I began work on it in the spring of 1920. And then . . . I stopped. Was it the difficulty of producing it, or my poor health which motivated this interruption? In a word, I stopped working on it; and yet, I didn't stop thinking about it all the time. When suddenly, last spring, Gunsbourg descended on my home like a bomb: bombs no longer impress me, but Gunsbourg did.

"Your *L'Heure espagnole,* he told me, was a triumph at Monte Carlo. Give me something else quickly!"

And that is how it came about that I worked on *L'Enfant et les sortilèges* during the past six months, and finally finished it. (Jules Méry, "Opéra de Monte-Carlo, avant-première, L'Enfant et les sortilèges," *Petit Monégasque,* March 21, 1925.)

5. Then 21 years old, the Russian-born choreographer and dancer George Balanchine (Georgy M. Balanchivadze, 1904–1983) went on to enjoy a brilliant international career. After working with the Ballet Russe, he went to the United States and choreographed over 170 works for Hollywood, Broadway, and the New York City Ballet. Balanchine's Russian-French-American career paralleled that of his close friend Igor Stravinsky. His choreography for the Stravinsky (1972) and Ravel (1975) ballet festivals in New York was greeted with particular acclaim.

6. Ravel told another interviewer that twelve hours after Sabata had received the score of *L'Enfant,* he knew it by heart (André Arnoux, "Avant-Premières, Opéra de Monte-Carlo").

12 : : :

Maurice Ravel's Arrival[1]

A Conversation with the Great and Humorous Composer

M aurice Ravel, the great French composer, whom we will hear tonight for the first time in Copenhagen, arrived yesterday evening from Hamburg, where he was honored with ovations last Thursday. Ravel arrived on the 7 o'clock Gedser[2] train with the Swedish-born singer Louise Alvar, who will perform his songs at recitals here with the composer at the piano, an honor not granted to many singers.

Madame Alvar is as tall and blond as Ravel is short and dark.

M. Ravel, a rather informal man, starts off, as he leaves the train, by telling us of his admiration for Madame Alvar. He cannot praise her ability, stamina, and talent enough. We observe that since M. Ravel has chosen her, there can be no doubt as to Madame Alvar's talent as a singer.

"I am not at this moment referring to her singing, but to her talent for languages. It is incredible to travel with such a person; wherever we travel she can communicate with people. She knows every language, in addition to that of Music."

What will we be hearing this evening?

"What is being performed?" M. Ravel asks the music historian Jean-Aubry and the manager Wilhelm Hansen, who are both at the station to greet the composer. M. Jean-Aubry helpfully replies: "The concert will begin with Ravel's famous String Quartet, which the Hamburgers greeted with ovations last Thursday. Ravel will perform his Sonatine and accompany Madame Alvar in the four *Chants populaires*. Madame Alvar will also sing 'Nicolette,'[3] another composition by Ravel, and perhaps an aria from Ravel's latest work, the opera *L'Enfant et les sortilèges*."[4]

Is that the opera now scheduled for the Opéra-Comique and the Théâtre de la Monnaie in Brussels?

"Yes," Ravel answers. "I was able to attend only one rehearsal before my departure. The opera was previously staged in Monte Carlo."

What type of opera is it?

"Call it what you will. A lyrical fantasy, an adventure. It is about a naughty child's experiences during his confinement. Colette has written the libretto and the music passes from operatic style to the music hall. I love to work freely and without prejudice. I have always done that. Therefore I do not belong to any school, or to any particular party. I have always been free. Of course, I have learned my craft. From the age of seventeen, I have had teachers such as Gabriel Fauré, Charles de Bériot—the singer Malibran's son—[5]and André Gédalge, to whom I owe my technical training.

"When it comes to composing on request, such as when I was competing for the Prix de Rome as a young man, it doesn't work. I wrote the most terrible thing and was only awarded a third prize. The last time I entered a competition I was rejected because I had submitted a parody-cantata entitled 'Sardanapalus' Favorite Slave,' at a time when I had already composed my Quartet and *Shéhérazade*.[6] But that's the way I have always been," M. Ravel sighs—and laughs.

What do you consider your greatest composition?

"My most important works are *Ma Mère l'Oye* and *Daphnis et Chloé*, both ballets. The latter was successfully staged by Fokine. I have written a lot of chamber music, an opera, *L'Heure espagnole*, and *Adélaïde*. *L'Heure espagnole* is a comic opera that has been produced both at the Opéra-Comique and the Opéra. My latest opera will also be given at the Opéra-Comique: you should hear *L'Enfant et les sortilèges* in Copenhagen. It is said to be in the style of H. C. Andersen,[7] which I myself couldn't vouch for. I love H. C. Andersen, but I like all adventures. I like to tell adventures in music!"

NOTES

1. Interview (in Danish) initialed X. M., *Berlingske Tidende*, January 30, 1926.

2. A port in southern Denmark.

3. The first of the *Three Songs for Unaccompanied Mixed Chorus* (1914–15). Ravel had transcribed them for solo voice and piano.

4. At a concert given in Copenhagen on February 2, 1926, Ravel led a performance of Mozart's Fortieth Symphony, thus marking a rare occasion in which he conducted the music of another composer. The performance was greeted with enthusiasm, as was the remainder of the program which consisted of *Ma Mère l'Oye*, the transcriptions of Debussy's "Sarabande" and *Danse*, *Shéhérazade*, with Mrs. Alvar as soloist, and *La Valse*.

5. The noted French contralto Maria Malibran (1808–1836) married the Belgian violinist Charles-Auguste de Bériot (1802–1870) shortly before her death. His son, Charles-Wilfride de Bériot, was Ravel's piano teacher at the Conservatoire (see p. 34, note 8).

6. Referring to the cantata *Myrrha* by Fernand Beissier (based on Lord Byron's

Sardanapalus), which was composed for the 1901 Prix de Rome. Ravel's chronology (or the journalist's interpretation of it) is incorrect, as the cantata was composed before the String Quartet and *Shéhérazade* (see p. 61, note 3).

7. The celebrated Danish author of children's stories Hans Christian Andersen (1805–1875).

13 : : :

Scandinavian Influence on French Composition[1]

We recently had the opportunity to make the acquaintance of one of the best known and prominent modern composers when M. Maurice Ravel, accompanied by the Swedish-born singer Madame Alvar, arrived in Stockholm to visit the Chamber Music Society. This Thursday he will conduct some of his own works at the Concert Society.[2]

"This is the first time I have been in Scandinavia," M. Ravel said during a conversation with one of *Svenska Dagbladet*'s representatives. "The visit, however, will be brief, as within a week I will continue my tour in England and Scotland. Then I am heading home again—to work."

By work, M. Ravel of course means composing.

"Since I was twelve years old," he continued, "and until now, at the age of fifty, I have done nothing but compose. I studied the piano with Bériot and composition with Gabriel Fauré. Who inspired and influenced me? I loved Mozart and admired Debussy—and still do! What else?"

Is Scandinavian music appreciated in France?

"I am sorry to have to say it, but as far as the music public at large is concerned, hardly. But what I have noticed is that Grieg[3] and Svendsen[4] seem to have had a considerably larger influence on French composition than on Scandinavian in general.[5] Among your modernists here in Sweden, I know only one of the young composers, Viking Dahl, whose *Maison de fous* was performed some years ago by the Swedish ballet.[6] His music seemed to me most interesting, and strongly influenced by French style." In talking about modern music in general and Arnold Schoenberg in particular, M. Ravel does not hide the fact that he considers the controversial Viennese professor the greatest living composer outside France. "Even Stravinsky," M. Ravel says, "is influenced by Schoenberg. As far as Russia is concerned, I do not believe in the dogma about musical renewal from that direction. Italy, however, will certainly be able to create a new musical style of its own within a not too distant future. I trust that it will be realized by Puzelli."[7]

With regard to France, M. Ravel mentions the names of Honegger, Milhaud, and Georges Auric as the most promising among the young modernists, and thus the discussion turns toward his own work and his latest operatic achievement, *L'Enfant et les sortilèges,* that only a few days ago had its première at the Opéra-Comique in Paris and for which the libretto was written by the celebrated Parisian authoress Madame Colette Willy. "It's quite simply a story about a disobedient child in confinement," Monsieur Ravel says laughing, "told in the style of an adventure with talking animals, toys, and furniture, just like the Dane Andersen does. It is now being produced in Brussels, and its Italian première will take place on March 1 at La Scala in Milan."

Any new compositions after the adventure story?

"None.[8] I didn't compose anything all of last year, and was totally occupied correcting the notes for the opera so that it would be ready in time. I can tell you that it hasn't been an easy task. But I hope it pays off. Perhaps my opera will be performed here some time, and then you can judge for yourselves."

NOTES

1. Unsigned interview (in Swedish) in *Svenska Dagbladet,* February 9, 1926.

2. The programs were similar to those given in Copenhagen (see preceding interview).

3. See letter no. 213, note 3.

4. The eminent Norwegian composer Johan Svendsen (1840–1911).

5. Some additional remarks on this topic were printed in an interview with a Dutch journalist.

The Scandinavian public is certainly strongly influenced by German music. Composers in the Scandinavian countries appreciate Brahms a great deal. They are inspired more by German music than by the delightful and picturesque music of Grieg and Svendsen, which is perhaps a great pity. French musicians are influenced more by Grieg and Svendsen than the compatriots of these two great artists. That is a startling phenomenon. But I am delighted to note the Scandinavian public's genuine understanding of French music. My works received a most cordial reception. ("Een Onderhoud met Maurice Ravel," unsigned interview in *De Telegraaf*).

6. See letter no. 177.

7. Apparently a typographical error for the Italian composer Ildebrando Pizzetti (1880–1968). In a commemorative article, Pizzetti recalled meeting Ravel in Paris in 1913, when his incidental music for Gabriele d'Annunzio's drama *La Pisanella* was performed at the Théâtre du Châtelet. The composers also met briefly in the postwar years, and their relationship was marked by cordiality and mutual artistic esteem (Ildebrando Pizzetti, "Italie—Souvenir de Maurice Ravel," *La Revue musicale,* December 1938, pp. 245–248).

8. Ravel's projected works are mentioned in his letter to Robert Casadesus, no. 265.

14

Maurice Ravel and Recent French Music[1]

BY ROLAND-MANUEL

For some thirty years, M. Pierre Lalo has fulfilled the indispensable role of an influential critic. He is moreover so perfectly destined for this role, that during the time he was away, it must be said that no one replaced him to the satisfaction of traditional music lovers. These dilettantes, having first recognized him as one of their own, also esteem the art which he makes use of to express their own feelings, which he then imposes so well on the credulous mass of newspaper readers.

For M. Pierre Lalo, who is surely not a heavy prose writer, is nevertheless a weighty critic. Heir to a name which resonates pleasantly in every musical ear, the columnist of *Le Temps* is a talented journalist. His style has a rather deliberate quality, which marvelously simulates stateliness, conferring on everything he expresses an air of nobility and the illusion of dignity. If M. Lalo doesn't always have the sensitive erudition of a Louis Laloy, or the intimate knowledge of music which results in the felicitous imagery of an Emile Vuillermoz, or even the impeccable and suavely florid language of a Camille Bellaigue,[2] he does possess his very own style of brutality, which is the least engaging form of frankness. For M. Lalo hates travesties, and if for twenty-five years he has chosen to play the role of Cassandra,[3] he has done so as a male.

After all, the gift of prophecy is assuredly not the one which distinguishes him from his colleagues, and one could make up a rather delightful collection of blunders by counting the number of misfortunes that he didn't wait for Milhaud to predict for Orpheus.[4]

M. Pierre Lalo thinks about contemporary music what the poet of *Sanglot de la terre*[5] thought about life: he called it "banal." May we tell M. Lalo that his criticism is hardly less banal:

On June 13, 1899, he urged Maurice Ravel "to think more often of Beethoven."[6] One shudders to imagine the music that a Ravel would have composed if by chance he had followed this advice. On March 24, 1908, M. Pierre Lalo asked: "When will these young people remove the mutes from their trumpets?"[7] Neither these young people, nor Negro jazz performers have indicated any eagerness to obey until now. In 1907, the critic of *Le Temps* "ceaselessly" perceived in Ravel's *Histoires naturelles,* "the particular echo of M. Debussy's music." Twenty years later, the critic of *Comœdia* reproached Marcel Delannoy for reinvesting "in his work, all the withdrawals in the Ravelian account." Here, the procedure is obvious. It is so obvious that one might well question the value of the summary judgments which M. Pierre Lalo has unfailingly brought upon France's finest musicians since he has wielded authority. Indeed, since 1902, when by felicitous inspiration he judiciously ruled in favor of *Pelléas et Mélisande,* the corpses which Pierre Lalo has slaughtered are doing quite well. Their names are Debussy: the Debussy of *La Mer, Images, Le Martyre de Saint Sébastien.* Ravel: the complete works. And finally, Honegger, Darius Milhaud, and Marcel Delannoy. If you believe that these diverse names sum up some of the most important and most productive tendencies found in today's music, it wasn't I who selected them.

Recalling that there is always a presumption in favor of authority, I thought it necessary to appeal to a higher authority. Unaware of any better choice than the musician who is regarded throughout Europe as embodying the particular virtues of French music, and who is its most distinguished representative since the death of Gabriel Fauré, I took the liberty of interviewing M. Maurice Ravel. M. Pierre Lalo himself advised me to do so, as he could not deny the testimony of a man about whom he wrote not too long ago: "just as he knows his art, he respects it and maintains it." M. Pierre Lalo adds: "you won't find him, like so many of his contemporaries and rivals, worrying about 'paying dues' to so-called advanced parties, and bringing to music the morality of politics. . . ."

The composer of *Daphnis et Chloé* willingly made the following statement, giving his express consent to have it published.

"This isn't the first time," Maurice Ravel said, "that M. Pierre Lalo has assumed the posture of saving music: let's hope that he will fail to save it once again. . . . M. Lalo, who is a rather well surrounded dilettante (when I say *well,* it's a manner of speaking), has constantly served the interests of a sect of which I do not wish to speak ill, but which fights in the name of a Franckist and Wagnerian ideal which is naturally incompatible with the traditional virtues of our music.

"M. Lalo's tactical procedures are as invariable as his aesthetic, and as music progresses, this steadfastness produces some amusing results. For my part, I had occasion to observe this procedure in 1913, in *Les Cahiers d'aujourd'hui*: 'It no longer suffices,' I then wrote, 'to lament the aesthetics of the older masters, or to feign incomprehension, anger, or hilarity with respect to the pursuits of the young: old and young are contemporaries. The point is to convince people that the older masters are in good health, whereas the vigor of the younger composers is already in decline.' You see, M. Pierre Lalo's days follow one another—and are all alike. Speaking of Claude Debussy's marvelous *Images,*

M. Lalo wrote in 1910 that 'there comes a time when these trifles cease to amuse.' At that time, M. Lalo tried to crush Debussy under Wagner, as he later sought to crush me under Debussy, and as he now seeks to crush under poor me that charming musician Marcel Delannoy.

"I heard *Le Poirier de misère*,[8] the debut of an exceptionally gifted composer, whose personality is striking. How can one in good faith call this score a 'pharmacy of sonorous substances,' and 'a weak, old-fashioned work,' when the piece, which is not irreproachable—far from it—exhibits sparkling verve and ingenuous vivacity despite its faults, which are due to the composer's very young age?

"M. Lalo's attitude with regard to Arthur Honegger is equally unacceptable. Honegger is a great musician. I have not heard *L'Impératrice aux rochers*,[9] but where does an amateur like M. Lalo, who is ignorant of so many things in music, get the right to abuse a composer so lightly, particularly one who serves his art with such eloquence, prudence, and loyalty as Honegger does? And I am astonished that a critic who has attempted for a long time to spread Germanic tendencies in France, would find no grounds for sympathy in the work of a musician who, for his part, has never disregarded the legacy of Richard Wagner.

"But it is with respect to Darius Milhaud and his *Malheurs d'Orphée*[10] that M. Lalo attains the height of impertinence. Here is a moving, magnificent work, Milhaud's best, and one of the finest achievements that our young school has produced in a long time. M. Lalo seeks in vain for 'something vibrant and expressive.' He complains that 'the progression is almost always slow,' while at every moment I find rapid progressions which indicate extraordinary rhythmic inventiveness. The orchestration of *Les Malheurs d'Orphée* is always very skillfully balanced. M. Lalo declares it to be abominable, and contrasts it with the instrumental combinations found in Stravinsky's *Les Noces*.[11] Please note that *Les Noces* appeared while M. Lalo was away. Now that the work is famous and classified, he can approve of it without remorse and without any danger. He places his bet after the ball drops: it's safer.

"Actually, all of this is more amusing than tragic: criticism can hardly be of greater value than the critic, and, as the saying goes, one can't stop a river from flowing. . . . When an Edgar Allan Poe, a Baudelaire, or a Delacroix becomes involved with music, it is marvelous: their ignorance of our technique doesn't bother us at all; they grasp its spirit, and sometimes much better than we ourselves. M. Pierre Lalo is certainly too modest to let himself be compared with these masterful artists and geniuses. . . . As for the rest, he is truly not professional enough to furnish his readers with information of any great objective value, and when I hear him speak, as he does, of 'polytonal formulas,' indeed, of a 'harmonized fanfare—or disharmonized—at the interval of the second' (*sic*), it makes me want to tell him what a musician, according to Racine's testimony, said to Philip, King of Macedonia, who maintained that a song did not conform to the rules: 'Heaven forbid, my lord, that you ever be so unfortunate as to know those things better than I!' "[12]

NOTES

1. *Les Nouvelles littéraires*, April 2, 1927.

2. An influential critic, Bellaigue (1858–1930) wrote for the *Revue des deux mondes*, and was the author of some twenty books.

3. In Greek legend, she was given the gift of prophecy by Apollo, but in a fit of anger he caused her dire predictions to be disbelieved. Pierre Lalo's prophecies of doom would similarly be rejected.

4. Playing with the title of Milhaud's opera *Les Malheurs d'Orphée* (The Misfortunes of Orpheus; see note 10 below).

5. "The Sob from the Earth," by the 19th-century symbolist poet Jules Laforgue.

6. In a largely negative review of the overture to *Shéhérazade*.

7. In a negative review of the *Rapsodie espagnole*.

8. "The Pear Tree of Misery," a comic opera by Marcel Delannoy (1898–1962), set to a libretto by Jean Limozin and André de la Tourasse, was introduced at the Opéra-Comique on February 21, 1927. A copy of the score, in the Music Division of the Bibliothèque Nationale, contains the following dedication signed by the composer: "For Maurice Ravel, another 'youngster,' with very sympathetic respect and admiration. Paris, July, 1926."

9. The subtitle of Honegger's incidental music for the drama *Un Miracle de Notre Dame* (1926), by Saint-Georges de Bouhélier.

10. Milhaud's brief opera in 3 acts, based on a contemporary adaptation of the Orpheus myth by Armand Lunel, was introduced in Brussels on May 7, 1926. A chamber orchestra is called for, consisting of 13 instruments.

11. *The Wedding*, subtitled "Russian Choreographic Scenes with Song and Music." The four soloists (S.A.T.B.) and chorus (S.A.T.B.) are accompanied by 17 percussion instruments, including 4 pianos.

12. From the preface to Racine's *Bérénice* (1670), based on Plutarch's discussion of "how one can distinguish a flatterer from a friend."

15

Maurice Ravel, Man and Musician[1]

*Unique Personality of French Composer Who Comes to America Next
Season: His Views on Contemporary Music*

BY OLIN DOWNES

Paris, July 20 [1927]

Something much older than himself looks from the eyes of
Maurice Ravel. It is the spirit of an experienced and ironical
race. He is urbane, Parisian, and very swift. He came into the
room before one knew he was there, examining everything, the furniture, the
ceiling—everything seemingly except his company, which he was examining
closest of all, talking very rapidly the while to the air.

His dress was exceedingly plain, fastidious, exotic. And now he sat in a very
charming garden known to a few, fussing with his food, sampling a Ravelian
liqueur, saying the most monstrous things, in phrases that cut so swiftly that
seconds flew by before the full and awful import of the words sank into a slower
brain. A real Parisian, an artist, French to the bottom of his soul, on his native
heath, and in the most capital fettle. A humming bird would have been
maladroit in his company! M. Ravel grinned behind his lips, shot quick glances,
which took in everything, guyed the millennium and roasted the universe. It is
unfortunate that so much of his conversation must go unquoted. Alas! for
pidgin French, hence imperfect communication. Alas! above all, for the inability to reduce the suavity, the politesse, the glitter of Maurice Ravel to dull
and ponderous Anglo-Saxonism. It is a violence, a crime, and besides, an
impossibility, since this Ravel is as incorrigibly himself as Paris or France,
which, whatever their outward semblance, change in nothing essential. What
they know they knew before our age was in swaddling clothes. They are not
going to change all that for any new-fangled bourgeois contraptions. Just try to
instruct Ravel. His guest looked and listened, finding it difficult to take eyes
from a face which had at moments the very look of some old portrait of a
Rameau or Voltaire, or to keep from shouting at the Gallic felicity, the Gallic

irony, breeding and point and smack of him. That's what he was—in his kind a complete and supreme creation!

: : :

But we are here to talk about music, and when there is talk of music and Ravel it is time to be serious. How still he has stood, yet how far he has traveled, in the last several decades. How deliberately he has fashioned his style, and followed his self-appointed path, this most conscious, most naturally artificial of composers! Ravel has achieved by degrees a style always more isolated from other influences, yet true to itself, although he has gone to various sources for his materials. Nothing passed him that he wanted, and nothing came from his hands without the stamp of a new mind and a fresh artistic purpose upon it. The nature behind the purpose? That's another matter, and Ravel would say that it had nothing to do with the composer.

We made some remark about a composer's sincerity. He regarded us with fatigue. "I don't particularly care about this 'sincerity.' I try to make art." He said he had been working four years at the violin and piano sonata which he will play next season in America—three years in taking out the notes that weren't necessary. "And now for something else." There is a piano concerto in the making, but Ravel has never in his life hurried himself in his work, and it will not be finished in time for America. He will be heard in compositions of a more intimate nature.

"Of course," he added, "if I ever did a perfect piece of work I would stop composing immediately. One just tries, and when I have finished a composition I have 'tried' all I can; it's no use attempting anything more in the same direction. One must seek new ideas."

: : :

The violin and piano sonata has a second movement of "blues." "And I take this 'blues' very seriously," he said with an air of engaging candor. And then, becoming serious: "Why have not more of the important American composers turned to this 'blue' material and to other music of popular origin which has come to you from so many different sources? . . . I don't agree with those who say that this or that music which may have originated on another continent isn't American or English or French or whatever the case may be. If history is examined it will be found that national music is usually an accumulation from many sources. This is even true of your 'jazz,' which could come from no country but America, in spite of influences from Africa and Spain which have contributed to its making.

"You have so many musical strains. You have Scottish, Irish, Spanish, Jewish—an enormous number of influences at work in your country's art. The serious composer, of course, uses the popular melody in his own manner, takes it as his creative point of departure. I don't see why more of you don't do it."

"As you did, for example, with Spanish popular music in the *Rapsodie espagnole*'!"

"That is one method." He regarded us with blandishment. "Do you know my early sources of musical education? They were several. You know, I was born near a border, and that I have Spanish as well as French blood. . . . Well, in my childhood I was much interested in mechanisms. Those machines fascinated me. I visited factories often, very often, as a small boy with my father. It was these machines, their clicking and roaring, which, with the Spanish folksongs sung to me at night-time as a berceuse by my mother, formed my first instruction in music!

"Now, my third teacher was an American, whom we in France were quicker to understand than you. I speak of the great Edgar Poe, whose esthetic, indeed, has been extremely close and sympathetic with that of modern French art. Very French is the quality of 'The Raven' and much else of his verse, and also his essay on the principles of poetry."

: : :

He talked then of French poets. We begged humbly for elucidation of the curious verses which Ravel has clothed with tone in his *Trois Poèmes* (for voice) *de Stéphane Mallarmé.* "Useless to explain," he answered. "The poetry speaks to you or it does not. It is very obscure, and if once it seizes you— marvelous! I consider Mallarmé not merely the greatest French poet, but the *only* French poet, since he made the French language, not designed for poetry, poetical. It is a feat in which he stands alone. Others, even that exquisite singer Verlaine, compromised with the rules and the boundaries of a most precise and formal medium. Mallarmé exorcised that language, magician that he was. He released winged thoughts, subconscious reveries, from their prisons."

There came up the question of "symbolism" and impressionism in French music. Did he feel that Debussy's impressionism was counter to the essential spirit of the Gallic muse?

"Certainly not," replied Ravel. "No more than the symbolism of Mallarmé was counter to it. Some, in the interest of schools, 'tendencies,' 'nationalism,' as you call it, in art—in which, by the way, I profoundly believe, since I do not believe that any art lives which has not roots in national consciousness—would deprive the individual composer of his personal soul, were such a thing possible, which fortunately it is not. Each creative artist, bound by insoluble ties to his people, has within him laws peculiar to himself. Debussy was one incomparable artist, one individual of the most phenomenal genius, in French music. Do they think we are so narrow that we are nothing but him, and he nothing but us? On the contrary. Nor must one fail to observe that underneath his surface Debussy was extremely precise, 'stylisée,' and that in his last days there were signs of an evolution in his music that might have resulted in operas quite different from *Pelléas et Mélisande*, had he lived to write them.

"Early nineteenth century impressionism[2] was a phase of French art which had already passed through a similar phase in painting, and was reacting violently against the Parnassians in its literature. We are perhaps today in the process of another reaction, but this reaction, which will balance itself, is in the direction of our oldest traditions, from which we will never turn.

"A man has died not so long ago whom you knew. He was Erik Satie, more an innovator, a pioneer, even an extremist, than one who left substantial masterpieces. Yet he was sensitive and obedient to a racial intuition. He anticipated Debussyan impressionism, passed through it in his thinking, and was one of the leaders in the direction away from it—a direction which I myself, as I think I can say, have consistently followed.

"With the profoundest admiration of Debussy, I have not been by nature completely sympathetic to his course, and although he was precious and inspiring to me as man and artist, I have gone on a different path. This is likewise true of the young French composers of today. But that doesn't mean that they turn from Debussy, who is a part of our immortal heritage. It only means that they are artists of a rising generation, and that we are approaching another epoch."

: : :

Ravel has admiration for the later Stravinsky. "He is, happily, never content with his last achievement. He is seeking. His neo-classicism may be somewhat of an experiment, but don't think that Stravinsky has stopped. His last work, *Oedipus Rex*, showed that while he plays with old forms, he is actually finding something new."

Of Ernest Bloch: "A powerful and passionate nature; a true musician. I do not take his emphasis of Judaism too seriously; it is the most superficial aspect of him as a composer."[3]

Of Sibelius: "A magnificent talent—I do not say a supreme artist, but a composer strong in feeling and color and inspired by his vast and sombre north."[4]

He said of Schoenberg that this gifted musician had worked deep into a maze of complexities of his own working, and that to a French artist such a course was inconceivable as a source of progress. Nor did he think the direction taken by Vincent d'Indy one to which French composers would rally. Among the young men he found Milhaud one of the most promising; the remark had the flavor of politeness. Of Vaughan Williams, the Englishman, and surely a leader of the English school, who worked with Ravel for a period, he said:

"A real artist, who only realized his richness when he learned to be English!"

Not bad for a supposedly chauvinistic Frenchman!

: : :

Times change. Only a few years have gone by since the first performances in America of a certain piano piece, *Jeux d'eau*, by the young Maurice Ravel. This piece was regarded by some tolerantly, by others with distrust and suspicion. Today, already, others are young, and Ravel in a position which some describe as "classic."

It makes one blink. *Jeux d'eau* indeed! The wonder is not that ears surfeited with discords unimagined at the time of its appearance find the piece an antitoxin, but that it retains for us so much of its early iridescence; another testimony to the facture and distinction of Ravel's art. He has left that far behind, so far as evolution of style is concerned, yet not for an instant has he severed the connecting thread. For *Jeux d'eau* read now "Ondine," that shimmering love picture which is the fulfillment of the youthful idea, and hardly surpassable in its genre, with the newer departures (anticipated nevertheless in certain of the *Miroirs*) of "Le Gibet" and the Hoffmannesque[5] "Scarbo" from *Gaspard de la Nuit.*

Fantastic as you please, but always form, form, form, present in the small works as in the biggest and freest ones—in the macabre shadow and blaze of the orchestral *Rapsodie espagnole*; in the satirical opera, *L'Heure espagnole,* or the big piano trio, or the songs great or little. And whether or not we agree with these works, or find in all of them the same measure of inspiration, we are certain to discover an artist of sovereign conscience and clearness of aim, who has never repeated himself, or written a careless or redundant measure.

It is a great deal to say.

: : :

As for the latest Ravel, he will be heard and estimated this Winter. It will be worth while, as the phrenologists say, to examine his bumps! How he will appear to the future is a question that is happily for others to decide. Ravel has survived notably those rapid and feverish fluctuations of musical taste and fads which follow each other in Paris as quickly and unreasonably as the changes in hats, and in the period of post and ante Debussy finds himself secure and distinguished in his métier. A rising and belligerent generation, after flinging a few missiles at him, Parisian fashion, is now inclined to render respect. It would have been otherwise had Ravel been a romantic or an impressionistic. In that case the present day in Europe would have been chilly for him; but a romantic he never was. As it is, his environment is neither hostile nor unpropitious. Perhaps it is the reproach of a period of hardness and cerebralism that this is so: it is a matter to be seen. But it is something to be as secure, as imperturbable, as consistent in direction as Ravel has proved to be. He has said little, worked, and followed his destiny. There are not many such craftsmen, artists of such firm traditions and conscience. Technically he is amazing; creatively he is seen in some widely differing manifestations. He belongs, at heart, to the thin and proud ranks of those ancestors who learned and forgot nothing.

NOTES

1. *New York Times*, August 7, 1927.
2. A slip for "Early twentieth century impressionism."
3. Despite Ravel's observation, Judaism and Jewish thought deeply influenced the art of Ernest Bloch (1880–1959).
4. Bloch's throbbing Romanticism is also found in the work of Finland's greatest composer, Jean Sibelius (1865–1957).
5. Referring to the macabre and supernatural tales of E. T. A. Hoffmann (1776–1822), the German author, critic, and composer.

16

Ravel Says Poe Aided Him in Composition[1]

French Musician Asserts He Was Influenced by Poet's Theory of Form

Maurice Ravel, France's leading composer, who is here for a three months' tour as recitalist and guest conductor of half a dozen of our foremost orchestras, said yesterday that his "greatest teacher in composition was Edgar Allan Poe." The American poet's "Philosophy of Composition,"[2] M. Ravel declared, wherein he relates in detail the methodical and almost scientific process which he brought to the conception and development of "The Raven," influenced the French composer more than any other artistic creed in deciding to abandon the vagueness and formlessness of the early French impressionists in favor of a return to classic standards.[3]

Despite his recent statement that he intended to cease his labors of composition to gain renewed inspiration from study of Mozart and the other classic masters, M. Ravel announced that he was planning two lyric works for the stage, one an operetta based on a libretto by Fernand Bousquet,[4] author of "The Mannequin," and an opera of more ambitious character inspired by a work of another French author whose name he would not divulge. "As a matter of fact," he added, "the author himself does not yet know of my intention to use his book."[5] The lighter work, he said, would be somewhat in the spirit of the Italian playwright Pirandello.[6]

As an example of his deliberate and studied method of composition M. Ravel cited his sonata for piano and violin, which has a second movement of "blues." The work, he said, was clearly outlined in his mind before the themes of the first and third movements had taken shape. "One night," he continued, "while I was in a cabaret something in what I heard suggested the themes which later I employed."

Modern composers must steer a middle course between emotion and intellect if they are to create significant and lasting music. "Poe proved that art must strike a balance between these two extremes, for the first leads only to formlessness and the second to the dry and abstract."

American composers are as yet little known in France, said M. Ravel. Jazz has been widely used by musicians throughout the world, he added, and should furnish American composers with a wealth of material for the development of a national school.

M. Ravel will make his first appearance in Boston as guest conductor of the Boston Symphony. His first public appearance here will be on January 15 at the Gallo Theatre.

NOTES

1. Unsigned interview in the *New York Times,* January 6, 1928.
2. Ravel read Poe's essay, which was first published in 1846, in the translation by Baudelaire, *La Genèse d'un poème.*
3. Poe wrote:

Most writers—poets in especial—prefer having it understood that they compose by a species of fine frenzy—an ecstatic intuition—and would positively shudder at letting the public take a peep behind the scenes, at the elaborate and vacillating crudities of thought—. . . at the cautious selections and rejections—at the painful erasures and interpolations. . . . It will not be regarded as a breach of decorum on my part to show the *modus operandi* by which some one of my own works was put together. I select *The Raven* as most generally known. It is my design to render it manifest that no one point in its composition is referable either to accident or intuition—that the work proceeded step by step, to its completion, with the precision and rigid consequence of a mathematical problem.

A somewhat similar defense of objectivity is found in Diderot's *Paradoxe sur le comédien* (1773–78, published in 1830), which Ravel often praised. In brief, the paradox is that to move an audience, the actor must himself remain unmoved and possess "a cool head, a profound judgment, an exquisite taste—a matter for hard work, for long experience, and for an uncommon tenacity of memory."
4. This operetta remained in the planning stage, and the libretto in question has not been identified. Bousquet, an obscure critic, was a next-door neighbor of the Ravel family when they lived on rue Victor Massé (c. 1887).
5. The writer was Joseph Delteil, author of *Jeanne d'Arc* (see part I, "Autobiographical Sketch," note 28.
6. Perhaps referring to the Ravelian spirit of contradiction and irony found in Pirandello's *Six Characters in Search of an Author* (1921).

17 : : :

Mr. Ravel Returns[1]

The French Composer-Pianist and His Contacts with America:
Certain Contrasts

BY OLIN DOWNES

W hen a little, subtle man with a rapier meets a big and loud-voiced man with a bludgeon the little man may survive the meeting. This reflection is occasioned by the visit of Maurice Ravel to America, by conversations with him, by glimpses of him on the concert platform. Mr. Ravel is neither young nor robust. His mentality, which is acute and highly developed, is not that of a youthful, ebullient people, or, perhaps, of any modern civilization. Like his art, he is delicately and fastidiously organized. Living cannot be easy for him. Yet his qualities maintain him. The rapier withstands the onslaught of the bludgeon.

Other European visitors, with more physique than Mr. Ravel, and apparently better geared to the exigencies of the young civilization, have not withstood it so well. But that is Mr. Ravel's quality. He has traveled America under the auspices of the Pro Musica Society from coast to coast. Americans in large numbers have examined him. More will examine him this afternoon. Mr. Ravel has courteously and curiously returned the examination—this without rancor or misunderstanding, but, on the contrary, with cognizance of the richness of a future that contrasts formidably with the boundaries of his present and past. The thought would make some artists of Mr. Ravel's years and sensibilities uncomfortable; but he is too sure and aware of himself and his background for that. A characteristic product of ideas refined and re-refined by centuries of an aristocratic culture, he has been watching with coolness and curiosity the formation of a new and cruder society and its gropings in the field of an expressive art. He has surely felt the pressures, the potencies and the swirling forces of a young, impulsive people. But he has stood against other inundations than the one which now sweeps against his defenses, and for the present, at least, he holds his own. If he and his school are to be overwhelmed they will be gay and debonair in the passing. As the swords of aristocrats were once broken on the pikes of a clamorous crowd, so may the esthetic of Ravel and his fellows be overborne by a new and strident epoch. But the aristocrat, swamped and outnumbered, will ply his blade. When he falls he will leave something behind him, something precious, something traditional, not to be extinguished by a hundred revolutions.

His Defenses

One thinks of these things as he considers Mr. Ravel or listens to him, and watches a face which might be that of a Rameau or a La Fontaine—only the wig is missing to create the perfect illusion—and reflects upon the nature of his music. It is all of a piece. The man and his music are one, and they combine for the purposes of self-preservation. It is amazing to examine his scores—his defenses. They are structures of consummate logic and refinement. By virtue of facture and the most delicate balances, and not by solidity or ponderousness, do these intangible edifices resist the action of the elements. Within the subtle circle with which he surrounds himself, in a self-appointed and self-created kingdom, this man has found an invisible refuge from reality. It is an entirely arbitrary and artificial realm, but it has its secret entrances, and its laws, and its own glamour and magic. Perhaps the kingdom is only of papier-mâché, painted. But for the nonce it is there, though created from nothing. Is this art the fruition, or the last vestige, or the mere mirage of a defeated and vanishing culture? We do not have to decide that, for the future will save us the trouble. But Mr. Ravel, like a few other distinguished artists before him, has convinced us, at least momentarily, of the existence of his realm, and left us no doubts of his absolute sovereignty in it. His victory is as immaterial as a victory can be and retain relationship with human existence. It is the sheer triumph of mind and will over the stupidity of obstructive matter. This, of course, is true of all art that arises, but particularly true and, in view of the immense and inevitable obstacles that stood in his path, particularly thrilling to behold on the part of an epigone and descendant of an ancient society.

The Modern Classicist

For Ravel is a true and proud French artist. Always a confirmed stylist, he is today, in spite of his advanced technique, a classic. His conceptions of form would show this, if nothing else did. Three years before he composed his last piano and violin sonata he told a London journalist what the form of its three movements would be. The contents came later. The form was completely and conclusively established. He told us last Summer in Paris that he had been years composing the sonata, and another year taking all the notes that were not essential from it! He follows an inherent demand for clarity, logic, proportion, which has always been characteristic of the "best minds" of his country. The more astonishing, and highly creditable to the breadth of his mind, are his genuinely interested and appreciative comments upon art in America, where there is anything but economy, order or classic tradition. Chauvinism, indeed, would have been pardonable in him. For that, however, he is too intelligent. Therein he is exceptional. Has the reader attempted to discuss music in France and America with a Parisian? If he has the frankness and absence of provincialism in Ravel would be surprising and delightful. Ravel is the man who told the English composer Vaughan Williams that in his music he was not sufficiently English—this many years ago, before Williams had gained his present position at the head of the English school of composition. Ravel, a Frenchman of Frenchmen, applies to others the principle that he applies to himself as an artist, and insists, first of all, upon the expression of racial consciousness. Speaking of music as he has found it in America, he made a just distinction between our executive and creative functioning in that field. For instance, of American orchestras.

American Orchestras

"Your orchestras are the best anywhere. This is because of their international membership, and the standards of individual excellence demanded of the players. Your brass choirs have the depth and richness of tone that ours lack, because of the prevailing superiority of the instruments themselves and the fact that most of the players of these instruments are Germans. They produce a certain nobility of tone of which musicians of other nations are seldom capable, and when you hear a trumpet it is not a cornet-à-piston. Your wood-wind choirs, in a majority, are predominantly French, and the French wood-wind players are the best in the world. The same principle of selection obtains all through the representative American orchestras. Reports of the standards of performance are only now being really credited in Europe.

"But in the field of composition I have found my earlier impressions of American music confirmed. I think you have too little realization of yourselves and that you still look too far away over the water. An artist should be international in his judgments and esthetic appreciations and incorrigibly national when it comes to the province of creative art. I think you know that I greatly admire and value—more, I think, than many American composers—American jazz. I have used jazz idioms in my last violin and piano sonata, but from what point of view? That, of course, of a Frenchman. Fascinated as I am by this idiom, I cannot possibly feel it as I would if I were an American. It is to me a picturesque adventure in composition to develop some ideas suggested by American popular music, but my musical thinking is entirely national—unmistakably so, I fancy, to the most casual listener. I am waiting to see more Americans appear with the honesty and vision to realize the significance of their popular product, and the technic and imagination to base an original and creative art upon it."

Cultural Reciprocities

When his interviewer remarked that this was an astonishing opinion from a classicist and the inheritor of an ancient culture, M. Ravel raised his eyebrows. "No, it isn't strange. It is only logical. It is not the developed artistic culture which fails to comprehend the significance of a culture and civilization different from itself. On the contrary, a developed artistic consciousness implies such appreciation. If we in France, for instance, listen to German music we wish it to be fundamentally German. The thing we are inclined to reject is the German music which leans toward that of the French. It is precisely the same with the good German criticism. Criticism in that country, when it is not a matter of prejudice or chauvinism, is the criticism that recognizes immediately, and appraises at its full value, what is essentially the expression of the spirit of another race. You are most courteous and receptive to the ideas of your neighbor when you are most certain of the quality and the value of your own. There are musicians, I am happy to say, who feel that way in Germany and in France. A world brotherhood of art should include—must, indeed, imply—the confident affirmation by the creative spirits of national and racial consciousness. It is surely time for the American to look about him and found his own art traditions."

Imagine the man who has said these things, surrounded by friends, concert agents, trunks, porters and noise, in New York, discoursing of America and the humanities. Transport yourself, then, to a hillside at Montfort-l'Amaury, forty miles out of Paris. Here is Mr. Ravel's garden, where he makes a specialty of certain floral phenomena and monstrosities, including varieties of enormous, hideous, pimpled squashes. His life there is secluded; it is almost monastic. He works. He curiously examines the products of his garden. His old housekeeper bullies him; she interrupts the conversation peremptorily. "Mr. Ravel, will you please help me with this can opener?" and Mr. Ravel, submissive, obediently assists. The dishes are simply and especially prepared. The farm faces a thirteenth century monastery and cloister on a hillside opposite, with gorgeous stained-glass windows of the purest old workmanship and design. Inside the house is one room most rigidly appointed in Empire style, with all the gimcracks of that period. Each room has its own consistent style. There are walls of a deep blue and objects of lighter but harmonious shades set against this background. There are paintings, some of them highly modernistic; books, principally of the modern period, and especially of Mallarmé, Poe, Pirandello and Joseph Conrad, whom Ravel warmly admires. There are six curious Siamese cats, to whom the composer is attached—exotic creatures, none too affectionate, but affectionately cherished by their owner. He has his own odd fantasy, his own humor. He has probably found animals much more honest and endurable than men. He accepts the facts of life, with a Gallic grin, and no time wasted in attempts at conciliation. He lives here virtually alone, happy in the fact that he is too far from Paris to be bothered by casual callers and secure in his simply but fastidiously appointed surroundings. He has very few intimates, and they are less likely to be musicians than painters or writers. His surroundings are not the result of eccentricity or affectation. They are the carefully worked-out tastes of one of the most genuine but sophisticated of men. They are the outposts of his defenses. Imagine this man transplanted to New York or those vast expanses denominated by the poet as "the great open spaces"! Do you think they pulled him from his perch? Not an atom! Not when he was fatigued, most worn by travel or most diffident on the concert platform. For a virtuoso he was never intended. No! He remains imperturbably, noiselessly, inimitably Ravel, a miniature of a man, an unshakable tower as an artist. One grows to immensely admire the triumphant formalism of this man and the keenness and subtlety of his intellectual weapons. How must it be to inhabit that skin? It must have been sink or swim with him. Well, he found the secret of self-defense. He carries it blandly, mockingly and with invincible valor, even into his art. "In art," Ravel has said, "nothing is left to chance." The same is true of his daily life and his self-possession and ironical poise and humor in America.

NOTE

1. *New York Times*, February 26, 1928.

18 : : :

Maurice Ravel on Berlioz[1]

An Interview

BY M. D. CALVOCORESSI

Ravel, when he last visited London, created something of a sensation by describing Berlioz as "a composer of great genius, but deficient in musicianship." A misunderstanding having ensued as to his reasons for this statement, I availed myself of his presence here to suggest that he should explain his views more fully—to which he readily agreed.

"Of course," he said, "when speaking of the unsatisfactory quality of Berlioz's harmonies, I was not thinking of 'correctness' according to school rules. In fact, I cannot conceive anybody thinking of harmonies in terms of school rules: one must think of it in terms of music pure and simple, or leave the matter alone. My contention is that Berlioz was the only composer of genius who conceived his melodies without hearing their harmonisation, and proceeded to discover this harmonisation afterwards. Something of the kind is noticeable, occasionally, in Gluck's music;[2] but with Berlioz it is the rule, not the exception. The point cannot be demonstrated or explained. It must be felt, and only musicians can feel it. When I say that Berlioz's basses are generally 'wrong,' or his modulations 'clumsy,' I am not referring to the 'rightness' and 'elegance' that text-books profess to teach. Chopin has countless examples of harmonies that are unusual, and perhaps theoretically 'wrong'; but to the musical ear they are always appropriate, and exactly in the right place. There are a few striking harmonies in Berlioz's music; but as often as not what I feel about them is that they have happened by accident, so to speak, and not in accordance with a well-weighed purpose. In the 'Valse des Sylphes,' for instance, there are one or two delightful things—very similar to Glinka's favourite and most effective harmonies;[3] but I doubt very much whether Berlioz actually 'heard' them. One is the result of a pedal point which Berlioz seems to have kept going simply because he did not quite know how to get rid of it.[4] But I do not wish to make my point in terms of technique. One thing I wish to add is

461

that when I spoke of his not being capable of harmonising even a simple waltz suitably (not 'correctly'), I used the word 'waltz,' as is the custom in France, to connote 'the simplest type of tune.' I was not thinking of the 'Valse des Sylphes,' nor of the waltz in the *Symphonie Fantastique* in particular.

Rimsky-Korsakov's "Corrections"

"Nor could there in any case be any question of 'correcting' the harmonies of Berlioz. Mr. Ernest Newman[5] is quite right in saying that a composer's harmony is part of his style, and therefore of himself. You cannot alter a composer's harmonies without altering the trend of his music. Rimsky-Korsakov, for instance, when he imagined himself to be correcting Mussorgsky's harmonies, was really substituting music according to his own conception for music according to Mussorgsky's conception. Incidentally, notice that ninety-nine times out of a hundred Mussorgsky's alleged incorrections are sheer strokes of genius. They are very different from the blunders of a writer lacking the sense of the language, or of a composer lacking the harmonic sense. In the matter of harmonic sense a composer may be deficient: so can any kind of professional musician, or a teacher, or a music critic. And, of course, no explanation, no tuition, can make the deficiency good. I consider that, with all the theory he learnt and practice he had of his craft, Berlioz never acquired the capacity to *hear* harmonies—a point which, I repeat it, must be felt and cannot be explained.

"Chopin is reported to have said to Delacroix—who was endowed with keen musical sensitiveness, and accordingly capable of understanding the utterance in the right spirit: 'The one flaw in Beethoven was that now and then he ignored certain eternal laws of music.' The same could be said, and said more truly, of Berlioz."

I then asked Ravel to give me a few of his impressions on contemporary music, and more especially on French currents.

French Tendencies

"In France," he said, "as in the whole musical world, we are witnessing an attempt towards a general readjustment of values—the horrible word 'revalorisation' is very much in fashion just now. In France and in Germany, as everybody knows, a violent reaction against romanticism is taking place. That something of the kind should occur in France is very natural; for, after all, French romanticism was always rather artificial and deliberate, and had no deep roots in the French mentality and outlook. But in Germany, on the contrary, it is the reaction that is deliberate. There is ample justification for the idea that music has suffered much from the excesses of both emotionalism and sensationalism. Yet, nowadays, a good many German composers are going to the other extreme, and writing music which is purely intellectual, altogether abstract. I would almost say that, having decided to follow a certain path, they deliberately don blinkers so as never to be tempted to swerve right or left. A case in point is a symphony by a young composer, named Butting, which I recently read in manuscript.[6] It is an interesting work, one of the most abstract I know.

"It is curious that this anti-romantic tendency should give birth to works as different from one another as this symphony by Butting, Stravinsky's latest compositions, and my own Violin Sonata. So far as I can see, it would be impossible to find any common measure between these three types.

The Younger Germans

"Schoenberg's abstractness is something rather different. In certain respects, quite undeniably, he has been a leader of the movement, an initiator. But his sensitiveness, at bottom, is Eastern; and, do what he may, he remains romantic. It is the younger German composers who really achieve the abstractness they aim at. And there is another feature which strikes me as very curious in the most recent German music: the sharp division between music that aims at popularity and music which is purely scientific, intended for the initiates only. I can think of no other instance of so marked a contrast—so far as regards, of course, music of a certain standard; let it be quite clear, lest I am again represented as saying something quite different from what I really said, that I am not alluding to differences such as exist between a shop ballad and a string quartet!

"In France there is a certain danger of the anti-romantic tendency leading to an excess of simplicity—to fragility and lack of substance. Among the younger French composers, an interesting one (not yet known in England) is Manuel Rosenthal,[7] a disciple of Erik Satie. Satie of late has been both praised to excess and shortsightedly derided; but it must be acknowledged that he has exercised an influence on several generations of French composers: on Debussy, on myself, on the so-called group *Les Six,* and on many younger ones, among whom, with Rosenthal, Delannoy[8] deserves special mention."

Ravel ended by confirming that at present he is at work on a piano concerto and on a musical play, *Jeanne d'Arc,* derived from Delteil's book of the same name.

NOTES

1. *Daily Telegraph,* January 12, 1929.

2. See p. 357, note 12.

3. Michael Glinka (1804–1857), the founder of the Russian national school, was on friendly terms with Berlioz, whom he met when the young composers were students in Italy.

4. A pedal point on *D* in the cellos and basses is found throughout the 108 measures of the "Ballet des sylphes," from the second part Berlioz's *Damnation of Faust.*

5. The pen name of William Roberts (1868–1959), the English music critic and author.

6. Among his other works, the German composer Max Butting (1888–1976) wrote ten symphonies. Ravel had studied his First (1922), Second (1924), or Third Symphony (1925).

7. See letter no. 269, note 2. Rosenthal did not study with Satie.

8. See p. 447, note 8.

Problems of Modern Music[1]

From a Conversation with Maurice Ravel

I f we are to talk of the "birth of 19th-century music," we must keep two factors in mind: the triumphant progress of Italian opera and the music dramas of Wagner. These two musical genres best reflect the spiritual culture of that epoch. The perspective in which the future can be contemplated will depend upon the artists of the present period.

In the past century, individuality set the fashion, which many philosophers would today call anarchy. After the great political liberation came freedom of thought and of the individual, and its task was to make the former hierarchic, social, and political structures conform to the spirit of a new epoch. Liberated from the traditional literary and artistic norms, the younger generations gave free rein to their imagination, and thus Romanticism was born.

Following the World War, a period began in which the ideas of the 19th century lost a great deal of their luster. This doesn't mean that mankind today is becoming less nationalistic or has less propensity for Romanticism, but it is quite certain that its ideas have lost much of their attraction. The solidly-built edifice philosophy and art had constructed began to totter, and thereupon began what is customarily referred to as the "crisis in Art."

In cultural history there is no separation between events based on real life and those phenomena that are only to be sought in the realm of the spirit, despite their frequently fundamental differences. It is said that only art experiences its crises. Yet the same holds true for parliamentary government, for economic institutions, and for individual nations in their relationships with one another. We may therefore justifiably assert that if there is a genuine crisis afoot, its chaos is not confined to art. Reputable authorities assert that such crises do not exist, yet equally well-known authorities maintain the opposite. The truth is surely to be found somewhere in between.

So-called crises have always existed, and their origins are easier to explain than is commonly believed. Contemporaries can almost never judge the deeper significance of artistic and literary movements with absolute certainty. Their perspective is chronologically limited, and so they speak of a crisis where only a change is taking place. It has always been this way. It is very easy to judge a work retrospectively when a century has elapsed since its birth, but it is surely more difficult to predict whether a contemporary work will retain its admirers in the next century.

We have just alluded to the causes of all temporal crises. But we must not forget meanwhile that the World War has conjured up the greatest of all revolutions. The World War has altered our *Weltanschauung* and, in many ways, our artistic perceptions. Our task is therefore doubly difficult: while our *Weltanschauung* of everything else has matured and crystallized, our artistic maturity is still in a developmental phase.

People often assert today that *jazz* dominates our epoch as a "philosophical Weltanschauung," representing the "spirit" of this epoch in music. In jazz rhythms, it is often said, the pulsation of modern life is heard. We live in the century of the machine, of technology, and we don't want to return to the past, this approach tends to say. I believe this to be absolutely correct. But technology, machinery, and industry, in their contemporary incarnation, can also be interpreted by artistic means, and for that purpose we certainly don't need the deafening noise of jazz. It would be unfortunate if only the ultramoderns were right: Jazz might serve many of us as entertainment, *but it has nothing in common with art.* Humanity was seeking, also in music, loud or deafening media, and it accepted the first, best means Europe could import from the New World. In unenlightened cultural epochs the same process will always take place.

We live at a time of searching, of experimentation, but not in the least in a crisis with fatal consequences. Let us only recall the Renaissance or the French Revolution! It is only a matter of time and patience, and I am sure that future artists of genius will manage to give a new race of humanity an art whose life, yearning, and striving will be revealed in its highest perfection. Then there will no longer be any crises.

NOTE

1. Unsigned article in *Der Bund*, April 19, 1929 (a newspaper published in Bern, Switzerland).

20 : : :

Maurice Ravel and His Bolero[1]

BY JOSÉ ANDRÉ

Paris, January 1930

Ten o'clock in the morning. The old Bal Bullier[2] on rue de l'Observatoire looks discolored and tired from the all-nighters surprised by the first rays of the sun. All the cheapness of its gilt and the showiness of its nocturnal illumination now reveal a poor and dirty reality which are obviated by memories of better times. The Bal Bullier, however, is one of the most famous spots in Paris, fresh and vibrant, and well suited for a work of art. It is here that the Lamoureux Orchestra, with its excellent conductor Albert Wolff,[3] intends to record Maurice Ravel's latest work, the *Boléro*, which made its debut last year at the Opéra with Ida Rubinstein, and was performed later with great success at the Lamoureux concerts. The composer has stated that he will come to conduct his work. He is awaited. Ravel appears, punctual and elegant, wondering at finding himself at such an early hour in such a place.

"This is just fine for what we intend to do," he exclaims.

"Weren't you acquainted with this hall?" somebody asks him.

"I have never set foot in it. You forget that I have always lived on the other bank of the Seine," he adds.

And whoever is familiar with the irony of his fine wit suspects a sort of aesthetic allusion in this reply. Very short and thin, with a white head of hair, rosy complexion, a restless and penetrating look, his entire being reveals an extraordinary interior animation, which translates into a constant mobility and a precise concern for every detail of the work at hand. Albert Wolff introduces me. "Ah, yes, Argentina, La Nación," Ravel says, stressing the *c*, "a great newspaper, I know it. I'm planning an extended tour that will take me from North America through the Antilles and terminate in the republics of South America. The date depends on when I finish the two works I have pending: a symphonic work, a description of a flight,[4] and a piano concerto which I will perform myself. As far as the *Boléro* is concerned, if it interests you, I would like to say, to avoid any misunderstanding, that in reality there is no such bolero, that is, I have not given this piece the typical nature of this Spanish dance, intentionally so. Its theme and rhythm are repeated to the point of obsession without any picturesque intention, in a Moderato assai tempo. This theme, introduced by the flute, accompanied by the constant rhythm of the drum, flows successively through the different instrumental groups in a continuous crescendo, and after being repeated, always in C major, breaks out towards the end in E major. Both theme and accompaniment were deliberately given a Spanish character. I have always had a predilection for Spanish things. You see, I was born near the Spanish border, and there is also another reason: my parents met in Madrid," he says, laughing.

Albert Wolff interrupts the conversation. The recording of the *Boléro* is about to begin. Ravel mounts the podium. The orchestra welcomes him cordially. At a signal from the recording engineer, Ravel begins a rigid three quarter beat, with short, crisp gestures, as nervous and precise as the notation of his music. As the first part concludes, a string of a double bass snaps with a loud noise. The recording engineer looks furiously at the poor musician who stammers his excuses. "He obviously didn't do it on purpose," says Ravel; "it has been a long time since I have had a surprise like that from a double bass." They begin again. This time everything goes well, except for an involuntary blow against the music stand at the end of the piece, a detail easily corrected. We immediately audition the recording, which came out very well according to Emile Vuillermoz, who is present at the session; he is a great authority, as everyone knows.[5]

And not only the excellence of the recording but the music on it as well, I believe, will immediately assure it worldwide diffusion. The theme of the *Boléro*, repeated over and over, is one of those memorable themes that the public sings without wanting to, and the persistence of its obsessive rhythm constitutes an admirable feat of orchestral technique. It doesn't have any of those effects of local color, of Spanish castanets and tambourines, or any of the known recipes associated with Iberian music; nevertheless, it has a profoundly Spanish flavor. It is one of those things that only Maurice Ravel's incomparable talent can create.

It is 12:30. We leave the Bal Bullier and take a taxi; I take advantage of the trip to pick up some impressions of the great musician. It is not difficult, because Ravel, despite being an artist who needs solitude to create, is a delightful conversationalist in society, who handles this extraordinary paradox with the same ingenuity as his orchestral timbres. Thus, in answer to my question about contemporary music, he replies: "I believe, in fact, that present-day music is seeking new direction. To achieve this we must intensify our thinking with the aim of freeing ourselves from the heavy Romantic burden that was weighing us down. This will be the only way to find the expression which will fit in with the sensibility of our time. For us French, it is becoming easier to achieve this because we do not have a past weighted down by Beethoven, Schubert, Schumann, and Wagner. But in Germany I see that present-day composers, despite their desperate efforts, are still struggling against the great Romantic tradition. The best example is Hindemith, who is a fine musician.[6] I do not believe, though, in this return to Romanticism that we are talking about, in these composers. What is happening, simply, is that they have not yet been able to free themselves from it." Ravel, in turn, asks me about musical developments in Argentina. "I do know they are doing very interesting things," he tells me. "And I want very much to go there. But everything depends, as I told you, on my finishing my work. I am also writing a piano concerto for the left hand of a disabled person, and, believe me, it is not easy."

We arrive at Albert Wolff's house. I say goodbye to Ravel and while extending my hand to him he says, "I hope we will see each other again soon to continue talking about those things which are of interest to us." But it is difficult to track Ravel down. He is in Paris only for a couple of days at a time, where he is constantly being sought after by his admirers. He lives in Montfort l'Amaury, a small town not far from the capital, where in a charming retreat he composes with the meticulousness of a laboratory technician and the nobility of a great artist, whose admirable works appear from time to time in concert programs and then travel around the world.

NOTES

1. *La Nación,* March 15, 1930 (a newspaper published in Buenos Aires).

2. A well-known dance hall on the left bank of the Seine.

3. See p. 475, note 7.

4. In a letter to Manuel de Falla written on March 6, 1930, Ravel mentioned a project entitled "*Dédale 39,* which as you can guess is an airplane—and an airplane in *C.*" Another projected work inspired by aviation was to be a symphonic poem, *Icare* (unpublished letter to Manuel Rosenthal). It appears that both works were not even partially sketched.

5. For another eyewitness account of this recording session, see p. 535.

6. At this point in his career, Paul Hindemith (1895–1963) was internationally regarded as the foremost German composer of his generation.

21

An Interview with Ravel[1]

—. . . .

I admire Schoenberg's school a great deal: they are simultaneously romantic and strict. Romantic, because of their strong desire to smash the "old tablets of the law"; strict, by virtue of the new laws which they accept, and because they know how to distrust hateful sincerity, which is the source of rambling and imperfect works.

It is curious and a shame that an all but solid wall separates their goals from those of French musicians. Even when one believes one has discovered a kinship, it is more likely the general influence of Richard Strauss.

— . . .

—Mahler, whom they love, passionate, ingenious, and clumsy, is considered an amateur of genius—somewhat like Berlioz. They detest Strauss (who hates them as well), but they owe a great deal if not to Strauss the composer, at least to Strauss the musician.

In contrapuntal writing, boldness is as old as the organ or the violin. The decorative "wrong" note is already found in the works of ancient masters (see Scarlatti).[2] But Strauss was the first to superimpose lines which were harmonically incompatible. Look at this chord in *Salome*,

which stubbornly resists any cadential analysis—it is at best understood as a simultaneous use of different tonal areas. That is surely one of the sources of Schoenberg's so-called atonal style.

— . . .

—One should never be afraid to imitate. I myself turned to the school of Schoenberg in order to write my *Trois Poèmes de Stéphane Mallarmé*, and above all, the *Chansons madécasses,* in which, like *Pierrot lunaire,* there is a very strict contrapuntal underpinning. If my music doesn't completely sound like Schoenberg's, it's because I am less afraid of the element of charm, which he avoids to the point of asceticism and martyrdom.

— . . .

—Perhaps precisely because he is Viennese, in reaction to the musical sensuousness of the environment, which is evident, by the way, in his earliest works.[3]

— . . .

—They are seeing their experiments through. It is always a good thing, in Art, to realize the work that one wishes to construct with precision. Furthermore, they have swept away quite a few assumptions. . . .

After all, whether desert or promised land, God will recognize His own.

NOTES

1. *La Revue musicale* (March 1931), 12: 193–94. This unsigned interview was probably granted to Henry Prunières. The interviewer's questions, which deal with Schoenberg and his school, are omitted in the original text.

2. Referring to the keyboard sonatas of Domenico Scarlatti (1685–1757), with their appoggiaturas and incisive acciaccaturas.

3. Schoenberg's earliest songs are tonal and Brahmsian, and the sensuous influence of *Tristan und Isolde* is evident in *Verklärte Nacht* (1899).

22

A Visit with Maurice Ravel[1]

His Opinion about the Radio and Phonograph
The Musical Recluse of Montfort l'Amaury: About His Piano
Concerto and Plans for a New Opera

(BY OUR SPECIAL CORRESPONDENT)

Paris, March [1931]

It is not easy to find the hiding place of Maurice Ravel. Trying to escape inquisitive people, the composer has retired to a back corner of the Île-de-France. In Montfort L'Amaury, whose name conjures up warring knights and courtly love from the Middle Ages, we are told that the recluse lives in a villa called Le Belvédère, up on the hill.

A ring . . . no answer. Once more . . . no luck again. The gate is locked. A charming gray-headed housekeeper leans over from an upstairs window and looks down.

We are admitted to a Japanese vestibule, then we pass along a series of rooms, each one having a beautiful view. We feel as if we are in a Chinese curio shop, in which a century of playful exoticism has been exposed. The style is half Pompeian, half Empire. Everything looks neat, expensive and polished. In the last room, resembling a square paper die, we meet Maurice Ravel amid his Siamese cats: he too is small, neat and polished. Knee-deep in manuscripts and letters, he is busy packing his things.

After we apologize for our visit, Ravel says that he is surprised to have been discovered.

"I'll be leaving tomorrow with my friend, the composer Delage, who will drive me in his car to Monte Carlo. I am tired, very tired, and I need to get away for a while. I finished my piano concerto for the left hand, which I wrote for Paul Wittgenstein, who was wounded during the war, but unfortunately, I had to interrupt my new piano concerto."

—The whole world is so curious about this new concerto, that I'm sure you wouldn't mind making a few comments about it.

"It is a divertissement, in which two rapid outer movements circumscribe a slow movement. The treatment of counterpoint and harmony is balanced, so that one does not overpower the other. Note that it is entitled 'divertissement,' or musical diversion. One should not make pretentious assumptions about this concerto which it cannot satisfy. What Mozart created for the enjoyment of the ear is perfect, in my opinion, and even Saint-Saëns achieved this goal, although on a much lower level. Beethoven, however, overacts, dramatizes, and glorifies himself, thereby failing to achieve his goal.

"I hope to perform the new concerto myself everywhere. Just like Stravinsky, I reserve the first performance rights for myself. The orchestral parts will not be published yet, and the score will appear only in a two-piano version. Marguerite Long will be allowed to play the concerto a year and a half from now. In the meantime, I will have performed it in five continents; Amsterdam will be hearing it in the fall, and even Java will get its turn.[2] Batavia[3] does not have an orchestra, but the conductor Dirk Fock[4] assured me that it wouldn't take much to put one together."

—Aren't you especially attracted by Java because of your musical relationship with the Orient?

"Yes, I yearn to see the country of the gamelan.[5] I consider Javanese music the most sophisticated music of the Far East, and I frequently derive themes from it: 'Laideronnette,' from *Ma Mère l'Oye*, with the tolling of its temple bells, was derived from Java both harmonically and melodically. Like Debussy and other contemporaries, I have always been particularly fascinated by musical orientalism."

—Were you not also overwhelmed by jazz?

"No one can deny the rhythms of today. My recent music is filled with the influence of jazz. The 'fox trot' and 'blue' notes in my opera *L'Enfant et les sortilèges* are not the only examples. Even in my new piano concerto, one can recognize syncopation, although it is refined. But jazz influence is waning. Gypsy music has returned to Paris, together with the whirling waltz, which I have often paid homage to."

—What is your opinion of neoclassicism, which nowadays divides the music world into two camps?

"After our extreme modernism, a return to classicism was to be expected. After a flood comes the ebb tide, and after a revolution we see the reaction. Stravinsky is often considered the leader of neoclassicism, but don't forget that my String Quartet was already conceived in terms of four-part counterpoint, whereas Debussy's Quartet is purely harmonic in conception."

—How do you feel about Stravinsky's postwar compositions, which have proven so controversial?

"I was deeply impressed by the *Symphony of Psalms:* the broadening at the end is something great, almost supernatural. There's no doubt that the *Sym-*

phony of Psalms is a successful *Oedipus Rex*. But I appreciate *Oedipus* much more than the many dry, clear-cut styles of exercise which this Russian composer previously offered us!"[6]

—How do you think your *Boléro* should be conducted? And how do you answer the conductors and critics who disagree with your opinion?

"I must say that the *Boléro* is rarely performed the way I think it should be. Mengelberg speeds up and slows down excessively. Toscanini conducts it twice as fast as it should go, and broadens out at the end, which is not indicated anywhere. No: *Boléro* must be performed at one tempo from beginning to end, in the whining and monotonous style of Spanish-Arabian melodies. When I mentioned to Toscanini that he took too many liberties, he replied: 'If I don't play it my way, it will be without effect.' Oh, those incorrigible virtuosi, who go about daydreaming as if composers don't exist."

—In this secluded spot, are you in touch with the musical world by means of the radio?

"Please, spare me the radio! It is painful to hear my music so distorted. No, I prefer the phonograph, which is improving very rapidly. My *Boléro*, recorded on the Polydor label, is completely satisfactory. It is more difficult to record *La Valse*. The conductor Wolff[7] exaggerated the opening pianissimos on purpose, but the recording is still not what it should be, so I am now writing a separate orchestration specially for the phonograph.[8] This simply means that in spite of the improvements, microphone recordings still aren't ideal."

—What are your plans for the future?

"I have been thinking about *Jeanne d'Arc*. The well-known novel by Delteil inspired me, and it is almost mapped out musically. The various episodes in the Saint's life will follow each other 'cinematographically,' or if you wish, as 'images d'Épinal.'[9] This epic about a heroic French girl has won me over completely. Nature and humanity, closely knit together, offer innumerable possibilities for musical interpretation."

We ask the composer if we may examine his sanctum. Several layers of sheer curtains permit some light to enter. This Biedermeier studio somewhat resembles a dark blue grotto. After our eyes get used to the surroundings, we recognize hundreds of miniatures on and around the grand piano: minuscule boats under glass, neogothic clocks, little dancing dolls, elegant glass-cut flowers, and also fashion prints showing crinoline clad ladies, like those popularized in Offenbach's *La Vie parisienne*. Everything breathes a genuine 1830s atmosphere, the same period that Ravel interpreted so beautifully in his precious and poetic *Valses nobles et sentimentales*.

Going from room to room, the composer showed us his subtle art treasures. When he opened the last door, for a moment we were dumfounded. From the balcony, as on a ship's deck, suspended above nature, we view the entire Île-de-

France. Almost unnoticed, the fields and gardens flow on from the mossy roofs of this old cathedral town, then descend very deeply and rise once again, reaching a wooded hill as they round off like a gentle melody. Birds are singing, and the light plays softly with the hazy sky, as in a painting by Corot.

Ravel bends over the guardrail and shows us his last creation: the garden, descending in terraces, with a marble water basin, and in the distance, a small, lovely rock pond.

"Don't you think that it slightly resembles the gardens of Versailles, as well as a Japanese garden?"

Doesn't this remark reflect upon the entire man, on the one hand, filled with memories of the stately, joyous century of Couperin and Rameau, yet on the other coupled with a refined sensitivity and miniature workmanship which conjure up Japan?

NOTES

1. *De Telegraaf,* March 31, 1931.

2. Ravel's tour was limited to Europe; see letter no. 202, note 1.

3. Now called Jakarta.

4. Fock (1886–1973) was born in Batavia, Java, where his father was the governor general of the Dutch East Indies. He studied conducting and composition in Holland and Germany, and conducted in Europe and the United States.

5. The Javanese orchestra, which consists of various types of chimes, a two-stringed violin, a psaltery, and flutes (the melody section), and single gongs and drums (the percussion section).

6. Probably referring to the element of pastiche found in *Pulcinella* (based on the music of Giovanni Battista Pergolesi, 1710–1736), and *Mavra* (which Stravinsky dedicated to the memory of Pushkin, Glinka, and Tchaikovsky). Both works were introduced by the Ballet Russe at the Paris Opéra, the former on May 15, 1920, and the latter on June 3, 1922 (Ravel's criticism of Stravinsky's Concerto for Piano and Wind Instruments of 1924 is found on p. 493).

7. The French conductor and composer Albert Wolff (1884–1970) studied at the Conservatoire. He conducted at the Opéra-Comique, was the principal conductor of the Pasdeloup Orchestra, and also toured widely in Europe and North and South America (see p. 595).

8. This project was never carried out.

9. Literally, "pictures from Épinal"; this town on the Moselle river in eastern France became famous in the 18th and 19th centuries for its colored picture prints.

23 : : :

M. Ravel Discusses His Own Work[1]

The Boléro Explained

BY M. D. CALVOCORESSI

The announcement, some time ago, that Ravel was engaged in composing two piano concertos (one for left hand only, the other for both hands) may have aroused a measure of curiosity in music circles, if only for the reason that he practically never seems to care to write more than a single work of any genre more special than the song, the piano piece, or the orchestral piece. His output comprises, for instance, one string quartet; one septet for strings and harp; one violin sonata; one sonata for violin and cello; one piano trio; one comic opera, *L'Heure espagnole;* one fantastic opera, *L'Enfant et les Sortilèges;* and one ballet, *Daphnis et Chloé;* the other ballets, *Ma Mère l'Oye* and *Adélaïde, ou le Langage des Fleurs*, are adaptations of works first written for the piano. His next play is to be a lyric drama, *Jeanne d'Arc.*

It was to be presumed, therefore, that if he had started work on two piano concertos simultaneously, there would be, between the two, a far greater differentiation than is implied, in principle, by the fact that one was to be written for the left hand only.

And indeed Ravel, in an interview which I have just had with him, has confirmed this natural surmise.

Why Tour Will Not Include Russia

"I have just finished," he said, "the concerto for the left-handed pianist, Paul Wittgenstein. I have left aside, for the time being, my *Jeanne d'Arc,* and am working against time at my other piano concerto, which I must finish by November. I shall play the piano part first in Paris, then start on a tour through Germany, Belgium, Holland, North and South America, Japan, and perhaps Java if—as the conductor, Dirk Fock, tells me—it is possible to recruit there an orchestra for the performance. The tour will not include Russia, because, my agents tell me, artists engaged in that country are compelled by law to spend in it the fees which they receive, and that would mean my having to purchase, say, furs or ikons for which I should have no use."

Two Contrasting Concertos

"Planning the two Concertos simultaneously was an interesting experience. The one in which I shall appear as the interpreter is a Concerto in the truest sense of the word: I mean that it is written very much in the same spirit as those of Mozart and Saint-Saëns. The music of a Concerto, in my opinion, should be lighthearted and brilliant, and not aim at profundity or at dramatic effects. It has been said of certain great classics that their Concertos were written not 'for,' but 'against' the piano. This remark I consider entirely true.[2] I had thought at first of entitling my Concerto 'Divertissement.' Then it occurred to me that there was no need to do so, because the very title 'Concerto' should be sufficiently clear in the matter of characterisation.

"In certain respects this Concerto is not unrelated to my Violin Sonata. It has touches of jazz in it, but not many.

"The Concerto for the left hand is in one movement, and very different. It contains a good many jazz effects, and the writing is not so light. In a work of this kind it is essential to give the impression of a texture no thinner than that of a part written for both hands. For the same reason I resorted to a style which is much nearer to that of the more solemn kind of traditional Concerto.

"A special feature is that after a first part in this traditional style, a sudden change occurs and the jazz music begins. Only later does it become evident that this jazz music is really built on the same theme as the opening part."

I asked Ravel whether he had any particular remarks to offer on his *Boléro*, which had been made the subject of heated discussions in England as elsewhere. His reply was: "Indeed, I have. I am particularly desirous that there should be no misunderstanding about this work. It constitutes an experiment in a very special and limited direction, and should not be suspected of aiming at achieving anything different from, or anything more than, it actually does achieve. Before its first performance, I issued a warning to the effect that what I had written was a piece lasting seventeen minutes and consisting wholly of "orchestral tissue without music"—of one long, very gradual crescendo. There are no contrasts, and there is practically no invention except the plan and the manner of the execution.

"The themes are altogether impersonal—folk tunes of the usual Spanish-Arabian kind. And (whatever may have been said to the contrary) the orchestral writing is simple and straightforward throughout, without the slightest attempt at virtuosity. In this respect no greater contrast could be imagined than that between the *Boléro* and *L'Enfant et les sortilèges*, in which I freely resort to all manners of orchestral virtuosity.

"It is perhaps because of these peculiarities that no single composer likes the *Boléro*—and from their point of view they are quite right. I have carried out exactly what I intended, and it is for listeners to take it or leave it."

These last sentences are most characteristic of Ravel. He may now and then pay attention to what his fellow-composers (and especially those whose music he loves) may think of his achievements; but what critics have to say—be it praise or blame—leaves him utterly cold.

NOTES

1. *Daily Telegraph*, July 11, 1931. In his article in the *Musical Quarterly* (January 1941, p. 17), Calvocoressi quoted part of this interview, inadvertently misdating it July 16, 1931.

2. Ravel was thinking of the piano concertos by Brahms (see p. 494).

24 : : :

An Interview with Maurice Ravel[1]

BY JOSÉ BRUYR

Maurice Ravel has just completed his second masterpiece. Don't tell me right off that you already know a good half dozen of them. So do I. But I can't be sure that this one isn't his favorite.

Will posterity judge Maurice Ravel to be the maître of Ciboure, or of Montfort l'Amaury? We know, don't we, that he settled in Montfort in an unpretentious home, but one which overlooks a vast, variegated landscape; those whom he has admitted have pointed out its Louis-Philippe round tables and its Second Empire desks. Adélaïde could relax there while dreaming of the language of flowers . . .

But yesterday, at a concert, encountering this man who is considered unseizable, I seized the occasion to ask him for an interview.

—"Tomorrow," he replied immediately, "tomorrow, at this time and place . . ."

Don't look for it in the phone book of high society, near Passy or Monceau Park.[2] In a nearby suburb, Maurice Ravel lives in a hotel whose facade is squeezed between the graceless walls of a factory:[3] don't forget that his father was a distinguished engineer, a builder, inventor. . . . It is natural that the profession still remains in the family.

Once inside, I soon leave the entrance hall, and, following the maître, I climb a narrow staircase.

—"Here," he tells me, "some beautiful photos by Man Ray will be hung, from among those which magically approach the limits of the absurd."[4]

A padded landing. A silent door. Here is the study, cell or dream room, a box of dark grey ply wood, with a high border of precious Japanese prints.

—"A new type of stained-glass window will replace this window, which will hide this odious landscape of the industrial suburbs to the point of making one forget it."

Another silent door: we enter the studio. There are reflections from the clear wainscot, the nickel of the elbow rests, from the mirrors and the windows.

A large library rises above a spacious couch.

—"It won't be big enough to contain my collection of memorialists," the maître says. He then shows me his treasures: Viennese crystal, bibelots brought back from Arizona ("Doesn't it look like a Picasso?"), a delightful miniature village from a toy box for a fairy godchild.

His bust by Leyritz is near the entrance, with its broadly hewn face, thick eyebrows, chiseled nose, and distinct lips curled in an ironic smile. In each human profile, the painter David looked for that of an animal. Who referred to Ravel as a fox-cub? In any event, it was Colette who wished to draw him as a squirrel. Moreover, he was sketched many times, by Favory,[5] d'Espagnat,[6] Ouvré,[7] and Luc-Albert Moreau.[8]

—"But it is still Leyritz who has captured me best," he says. "As for this, done by Natanson, it may well be the most beautiful surrealist tableau of all. . . ."

How can one describe it? Under a globe, overlapping strips of glass are lit by a small tinted bulb of glaucous blue or emerald green, revealing the bottom of the sea, in which the volute of a shell and the lacework of an alga are spun out.

—"This finally? . . ."

But it's only a mechanical toy. Ravel winds it up: a puppet seizes a marble, throws it with a gesture toward a "numbered box," as in Satie's song[9]—and does it again.

But it suddenly strikes me that the mechanical toy and the surrealist tableau thus placed side by side illuminate all of Ravel's oeuvre. Ariel[10] and Vaucanson:[11] isn't this how Roland-Manuel—his most penetrating biographer— explained it?

—"I am stopping my little pelota player," Ravel says.

But this word suffices to transfer my thoughts back to Ciboure, near Saint-Jean-de-Luz, to Ciboure, which honored him last summer.

His mother was Basque. His father was from Versoix, the small port which Voltaire had established on blue Lake Geneva. Ravel has also been called "the most perfect of Swiss clockmakers"—or the most enchanting of Iberian magicians: think of *L'Heure espagnole.*

But *L'Heure espagnole* is in the past, and Ravel is interested in speaking about his coming projects. Thus a conversation begins by fits and starts, with phrases surrounded by a bit of silence—and some cigarette ashes. Nervously, Ravel gets up and flicks them into an ash tray.

The future? The next project is the Concerto for the left hand. The farthest one is a *Joan of Arc.*

—"Exactly, based on Delteil," he says. "Indeed, why not? All of our theatrical works have remained essentially Romantic, from the *Huguenots* to Milhaud's *Cristophe Colomb*: there is no lack of Romanticism in Claudel."[12]

Neither in Delteil, I imagine . . .

—"Because there is bad taste. But there is also a fresh opportunity for me to get away from it. Nothing is written yet: I'm trying to establish the outline, and make cuts in this luxuriant work, for as you can well imagine I am writing the libretto myself. French choirs cannot be asked to participate in a performance. It's not the same as in Brussels. There, my animals in *L'Enfant et les sortilèges* got into their respective skins so well that they became quite 'bruised.' I thus pursued an idea that I had formerly given to Diaghilev, which he successfully used in *Le Coq d'or*: the choirs will be placed on each side of the stage. In this book, there are some similarities and contrasts which are very amusing to try to stage—between the two battles, for example: there is Joan of Arc the child, and Joan the leader. I will therefore need two interpreters: only two—I rejected an infant! Obviously, such a work will call for a new form. But this is a constant, absolute necessity: to renew oneself. Thus, I am now also trying to find the form for the operetta projected with Bousquet. The subject is delightful, with a dash of Pirandello. But there too, one must do something which is neither like Messager (I am told that an operetta which is presently a triumph was inspired by him. But then it's not worth the trouble!)—therefore, something which is unlike Messager,[13] Offenbach, or Chabrier."

The influence of Chabrier's *Trois Valses romantiques* on the young Ravel was undeniable, but this didn't prevent him from achieving a personal style in his earliest compositions. The "Habanera" (1895) is an early work: he will be able to introduce it thirteen years later without changing a note into the *Rapsodie espagnole*, one of the scores, which, despite scandal and squabble, established his reputation. And nothing will prevent his oeuvre from acquiring a sublimated reflection of Chabrier (*Pavane pour une Infante défunte*), Satie (*Ma Mère l'Oye*), indeed, of Schoenberg: the Mallarmé poems may be, or may have been called, neutralized Schoenberg.

—"Chabrier," he resumes: "one of France's great musicians, but he continues to be plagued by bad luck. Debussy, who admired him with some reservations, almost didn't have a small street named for himself in the back part of the Batignolles district.[14] Chabrier doesn't even have that, as far as I know.[15] And his music continues to be ignored. People still talk about its vulgarity. A strange defect in a musician whose imprint can be identified in any three measures of his work. I saw this poor great man for the last time at a performance of *Gwendoline*; he was already indifferent to everything, even to his own music. As for *Briséis*, which is an uneven score, I was asked to complete it. But what for? To write some Chabrier? Besides, this type of posthumous collaboration rarely succeeds. *The Tales of Hoffmann* is a notable exception, in which the elegant style of Ernest Guiraud is apparent.[16] There is also another master, Offenbach, and young musicians willingly identify with him. He represents French clarity and the French spirit: for music has never been so national. Never has 'French music' been spoken of so much since the war. Although the most internationalist of men, I am very nationalistic in art, but only in art. Richard Strauss said to me one day in Vienna: 'Of all German musicians, am I not closest to the French?' After the *Alpine Symphony*, with its wind machine, it makes you wonder![17] Some may admire *Salome*, which is so perfectly orchestrated, and I agree—for Strauss orchestrates well, much better than Wagner! But it lacks so much of Wilde's irony. No matter, the young people hardly care for my music . . ."

—But maître . . .

—"But what? By Jove, they are perfectly right! In art, one must have some bad faith. Honegger is a great worker; Milhaud's *Malheurs d'Orphée* is all the same a fine work, even if a bit unsingable; Ibert, it is said, is freeing himself from Ravelian influence; Roland-Manuel has such a lucid intelligence; I admired Delannoy's *Le Fou de la dame* (a fine subject, this tragedy about a chess game!), and even young Manuel Rosenthal asked me for some advice while writing his *Rayon de soieries*. . . .[18] That's a splendid group. Others, the very youngest, still have to learn: they will learn to forget and to find themselves."

—So this is the great lesson that you and Stravinsky are preaching, following Nietzsche?

—"I like the *Symphony of Psalms* very much and said so to Igor. *Les Noces* is like *The Rite of Spring*, without the tiny imperfections. All the same, there are failures in Stravinsky's works, such as *Mavra* or even *Apollon musagète*, which the Ballet Russe performed together with a certain tedious story based on music by Handel . . ."

—*Les Dieux mendiants* . . .[19]

—"That's it: as a classical work it was boring! Only Mozart is never so. Mozart is absolute beauty, perfect purity. Music would have died with him, died from decline or from that purity, if we hadn't had Beethoven, who was deaf. And what we admire of his most is the unplayable Ninth Symphony. Then came Berlioz. Berlioz was the genius who knew everything instinctively, except what all Conservatoire students master in an instant: how to harmonize a waltz correctly."

—. . . .

—"And now, what am I going to do? Relax, perhaps by traveling around the world. Because here, I work a great deal and hardly sleep two hours a night. Now human resistance has definite limits. Yet all of life's pleasure consists of getting a little closer to perfection, and expressing life's mysterious thrill a little better."

And I think of a verse by Tristan Klingsor, whose *Schéhérazade* Ravel garlanded with such lovely music, and who should really write a book about "his" musician:

> "And the ironic and tender heart which beats under
> The velvet vest of Maurice Ravel . . ."[20]

NOTES

1. *Le Guide du concert* (October 16 , 1931), 18: 39–41. Bruyr reprinted this interview with several modifications in his book *Maurice Ravel* (Paris: Editions Le Bon Plaisir, 1950), pp. xi–xviii.

2. Respectively in Paris' fashionable 16th and 8th arrondissements.

3. At Levallois Perret. The apartment is also described on p. 487, and two photographs of it are found in Lesure and Nectoux, *Maurice Ravel* (Bibliothèque Nationale), p. 70.

4. An American photographer and painter, Ray (1890–1976) was active in the Dada and surrealist movements. He lived in Paris in the 1920s and 1930s.

5. A sketch of Ravel by Favory is found in *La Revue musicale* (April 1, 1925), p. 83.

6. Georges d'Espagnat's painting, "Réunion des musiciens chez M. Godebski" (1910), which is in the Paris Opéra, is reproduced in Orenstein, *Ravel: Man and Musician*, plate 7.

7. Two portraits of Ravel by Achille Ouvré are discussed in Lesure and Nectoux, *Maurice Ravel* (Bibliothéque Nationale), plates following p. 24 and p. 30.

8. See letter no. 167, note 1.

9. Referring to a humorous image in "La Statue de bronze" (poem by Léon-Paul Fargue), the first of Satie's *Trois Mélodies* (1917).

10. The airy Spirit in Shakespeare's *Tempest*, thus referring to the Ravelian world of magic and enchantment.

11. The mechanical precision found in Ravel's art, represented by Jacques de Vaucanson (1709–1782), who was a prolific inventor of robot devices (see Roland-Manuel, *A la gloire de Ravel*, Paris: Editions de la Nouvelle Revue Critique, 1938, p. 231).

12. Several of Milhaud's operas were based on texts by the noted playwright and poet Paul Claudel (1868–1955).

13. André Messager (1853–1929), the French composer, conductor, pianist, opera administrator, and critic. His ballet music and operettas were widely performed. In 1902, he conducted the première of *Pelléas et Mélisande* at the Opéra-Comique.

14. A working-class neighborhood in the 17th arrondissement.

15. A Square Emmanuel Chabrier is now adjacent to the Square Claude Debussy.

16. Guiraud (1837–1892) successfully completed works by two of his friends, Jacques Offenbach and Georges Bizet. He provided the recitatives and orchestration for *The Tales of Hoffmann*, and also inserted the famous barcarolle, taken from Offenbach's *Die Rheinnixen* (The Rhine Spirits). In addition, he composed the recitatives for the grand opera version of *Carmen*.

17. Strauss' tone poem (1911–15), which calls for a mammoth orchestra, contains several "impressionistic" passages.

18. Delannoy's *The Queen's Bishop*, a chanson de geste in one act (libretto by Jean Limozin and André de la Tourrasse), and Rosenthal's *Shelf of Silk*, a comic opera in one act (libretto by M. Nino), were introduced together at the Opéra-Comique on June 3, 1930.

19. "The Gods Go A'Begging," a ballet in one act, with libretto by Boris Kochno, choreography by George Balanchine, and Handel's music arranged by Sir Thomas Beecham.

20. From the poem "Jeux d'eau," in the collection *Humoresques* (1921).

25 : : :

Some Confessions of the Great Composer
Maurice Ravel[1]

*The Maître Speaks about His New Piano Concerto, Whose Première
Will Be Given Shortly after the Concerto for the Left Hand Which He
Wrote for the One-Armed Virtuoso Paul Wittgenstein*
    A Moving Homage to Debussy, Whose Prelude to the Afternoon
of a Faun *"Is a Unique Miracle in All of Music"*

BY PIERRE LEROI

The great French musician Maurice Ravel—who, abroad, is
considered the greatest living composer—spent his summer
at Montfort l'Amaury working ceaselessly to complete a second concerto for piano and orchestra.

At the request of the one-armed pianist Paul Wittgenstein, he composed a
piano concerto for the left hand; but even when this work was commissioned,
Maurice Ravel had already launched a more extensive concerto for two hands.
This work is presently finished, and the composer was willing to lift the veil of
secrecy with which he carefully surrounded this work, which demanded his
undivided attention for many months.

Next January 15, at Salle Pleyel, in a festival of his works, M. Maurice Ravel
will himself perform the première of his concerto, assisted by the Lamoureux
Orchestra. The concerto will then be taken on a world tour, with the composer
performing it himself everywhere.

—My only wish, M. Maurice Ravel said, was to write a genuine concerto,
that is, a brilliant work, clearly highlighting the soloist's virtuosity, without
seeking to show profundity. As a model, I took two musicians who, in my
opinion, best illustrated this type of composition: Mozart and Saint-Saëns.
This is why the concerto, which I originally thought of entitling *Divertissement*,
contains the three customary parts: the initial Allegro, a compact classical
structure, is followed by an Adagio, in which I wanted to render particular
homage to "scholasticism," and in which I attempted to *write* as well as I could;
to conclude, a lively movement in Rondo form, likewise conceived in accor-

dance with the most immutable traditions. In order not to needlessly weigh down the orchestral texture, I called for a reduced orchestra: the usual strings are joined only by one flute, piccolo, oboe, English horn, two bassoons, two horns, one trumpet, and one trombone.[2]

As one can see, M. Maurice Ravel is not among those who jealously guard secrets about their works which have not yet been revealed to the public. He also speaks about works which he has already written, and, incidentally, about those of his colleagues, with a frankness which reveals the critical sense of his judgment, which is sharp and incisive like his gaze.

—The true personality for a composer, he said on this subject, is not to seek to have one which is immediately recognizable and stylized in unchanging formulas. That is the weak side of Richard Strauss, who is otherwise a musician of genius, whereas the example of a Stravinsky, constantly seeking to renew himself and ceaselessly exploring extremely varied domains, seems infinitely preferable to me. A composer must be able to "isolate himself" completely from his previous work, and completely "forget" a work once it is finished. I confess that sometimes it gives me keen pleasure to listen to my String Quartet, *Shéhérazade,* or *Daphnis et Chloé,* while forgetting that I wrote them.

As we asked him if, despite everything, he didn't retain a particular predilection for some of his works, M. Maurice Ravel promptly replied that he had a particular affection for the *Chansons madécasses* and the *Boléro,* "the work which he realized fully and which permitted him to attain completely the goal that he set for himself." Similarly, the Sonata for Violin and Piano satisfies him entirely.

Does this deliberate state of mind actually reflect a lack of sensibility? If the style evolves, the man remains the same, guarding intact, in the depth of his being, all the treasures of his sensibility.

Suddenly pensive, his gaze lost in a sort of vision, M. Maurice Ravel said very simply that his dearest wish would be to be able to die gently lulled in the tender and voluptuous embrace of Claude Debussy's *Prelude to the Afternoon of a Faun,* this "unique miracle in all of music." Nothing could have been more moving in its simplicity and sincerity than this homage rendered by the undisputed leader of contemporary French music, to the one who, before him, had the honor to be its most glorious representative.

NOTES

1. *Excelsior,* October 30, 1931.
2. Ravel (or the interviewer) omitted the two clarinets, and the percussion section, consisting of tympani, harp, and seven other instruments. Furthermore, in keeping with classical tradition, the string section is limited to 32 players.

26

An Afternoon with Maurice Ravel[1]

Paris, January [1932]

The tiny pied-à-terre of Maurice Ravel, the great composer, who by the way is a strikingly small man, white-haired and wrinkly, yet unusually youthful and agile, in no way resembles an ordinary bachelor's apartment. In these two tiny rooms, one is struck at first glance by a bust of the master of the house done by Leyritz, the highly gifted Viennese sculptor,[2] who also designed all of the interior décor with Ravel and for him. The bust is overly stylized and yet incredibly true to life: no photographer could reproduce Ravel's very personal and distinctive face so strikingly and spiritually. Maurice Ravel is clearly an admirer of Austrian art. In a small glass display case under the bust, next to the unusual American kaleidoscope, the exotic bird from Madagascar, the shells from Arizona, the wooden fish- and duck-shaped tobacco boxes from Novgorod, there also stands an entire row of the familiar, vivid figurines from the Wiener Werkstätte.[3] In other respects, too, everything is curious about this tasteful interior. A small red round table represents the bar, around which are tall red leather bar stools, and behind which built-in book shelves conceal a well-stocked liquor cabinet. The bed, however, is an ordinary built-in sleeping-car berth, or better still the cabin bed of a luxury liner.

"A bit like Dekobra," I observed, as we sat down on the curious but comfortable steel armchairs, constructed from authentic airplane parts. "Dekobra went further," Ravel replied, his wonderful voice filling the room as clearly as a bell: "his barroom is a genuine bar, and his sleeper couldn't be more natural. I'm not completely in agreement with him. One can indeed visit an elegant bar on occasion, or travel on a stylish ocean liner, but who would want to spend his entire life in a bar or on an ocean liner? Where is the variety? The intellect obtains its nourishment only from variety."

Race and Music

"I love Vienna. Not only as a musician because it is a city of music, but simply because it is Vienna: unrivaled in its individuality, charming, gemütlich; aristocratic besides, and always itself. Like us Frenchmen, you Austrians also don't constitute a race. Something much better, though: a cultural community crystallized out of many different races. It is really odd that people still talk about races at all! Where do races still exist? *We French are far more Teutonic than the Germans, who are a mixture of the Slavic and Celtic races,* and certainly more than the Viennese, who developed out of six or seven different races into a unified people. A common climate, government, and way of life brought about the spiritual unity of France and Austria; that's how the individuality of nations originates in any case, and that's how it becomes pronounced through radically different periods of development, until finally, alas, the nations no longer understand each other at all.

"Of course, my thoroughly objective and nonliterary music is necessarily lyric to some extent. But this lyricism is that of a Frenchman, and worlds removed from German lyricism. I could say with some exaggeration: the lyricism of the French is reserved to the point of dryness, whereas the German is often expansive to the point of exhibitionism. The Frenchman never opens up without constraint. Like the Austrian, he is communicative, but never wears his heart upon his sleeve. He never lets a stranger approach him too closely, he doesn't want to be understood at any cost, and he never bites off more than he can chew. Perhaps that makes him insular and shortsighted. Still, surely he is always clear and precise, like the clear landscape of 'la douce France,' with its perpetually clear blue sky.

"My music is unequivocally French. Anything except Wagnerian. And just as little like that of Richard Strauss or the modern Viennese. That's why I hope it may please the Viennese, since it's so different from their own! Frenchmen, in turn, enjoy Viennese music. I personally feel particularly close to *Mozart*. My admirers exaggerate when they compare me with him. Beethoven strikes me as a classical Roman, Mozart as a classical Hellene. I myself feel closer to the open, sunny Hellenes.

"*The intellectual life of the Americans* is German—even though it is based on Anglo-Saxon foundations. Nevertheless, Americans have their peculiarities. Thus, I was greeted by a host of newspaper reporters, critics, and authors as a 'champion of *Jewish* music.' *Not one of my ancestors was in fact Jewish.* I was even more surprised over the origin of this curious assumption. 'Because your name is Maurice, like all Jews.' —'Of course,' I replied, 'like Saint Maurice, the crusader, for example.' 'No,' was the answer, 'we are in fact thinking of the German Moritzes.' —'You mean Moritz, the Saxon duke, right?', I couldn't help observing. Hardly anyone would believe not only that my father's name happened to be Joseph, but my mother's Mary! It never occurred to anyone that Joseph and Mary, unlike Maurice, are in fact Jewish names!

"As concert audiences go, however, the French, in my opinion, are the most interesting. Until the World War, my dear countrymen did not care for music, nor were they interested in it. But since then, they are obviously becoming more musical from day to day. I believe we must thank the radio for that. The frugal French bourgeois never went to concerts, and consequently never heard good music: but now it is available within his own four walls. In this way, he has been able to get to know music, gradually understanding it, and has grown to like it so much, that at last he buys tickets for hard cash, attends concerts, and has become an enthusiastic music lover.

"You, in Vienna, didn't need the radio for that."

NOTES

1. *Neue Freie Presse*, February 3, 1932. The interview is signed "C. B. L."

2. Léon Leyritz was in fact born in France and studied in Paris.

3. Literally, "Viennese workshops." These crafts studios, founded in 1903, specialized in decorative art.

27

Factory Gives Composer Inspiration[1]

Musical Dream of the Future
When Typewriters May Be in an Orchestra
M. Ravel's Theory
Factory Gave Him Idea for His Bolero

M. Maurice Ravel, the French composer, who has come to England to conduct the first performance in this country of his new pianoforte concerto tomorrow, confessed today that he admired jazz. He said:

"Each movement of my new symphony[2] has some jazz in it. I frankly admit that I am an admirer of jazz, and I think it is bound to influence modern music. It is not just a passing phase, but has come to stay. It is thrilling and inspiring, and I spend many hours listening to it in night clubs and over the wireless."

M. Ravel said he thought that the mechanics and machinery of the age would also leave their imprint on music of the present day. He added: "I gained much of my inspiration from machinery.

"I love going over factories and seeing vast machinery at work. It is awe-inspiring and great. It was a factory which inspired my *Boléro.* I would like it always to be played with a vast factory in the background.

"Do I think that at some future date we shall see on a concert platform rows of typewriters, lathes and saws in place of the usual instruments? It is not improbable; it has already been tried in one of the Russian ballets, where a typewriter being tapped was a legitimate instrument of the orchestra.[3]

"But, if it does come about, I do not think it can truly be called art. I do think it is art to make violins, horns, trombones, and all the other instruments of the orchestra sound like machinery. If machinery were put on the concert platform instead of musical instruments, however, it would conversely only be art if that machinery were made to sound like music. At present I do not see how this could be done."

Another Idea

Then M. Ravel discussed another idea. That was that in these days of cacophony it might be quite an original idea for the orchestra to start, say, in

C major, and then, through a series of discords the instruments should divide, some going up a semitone at every three or four bars, while others went down in the same way, eventually ending in perfect harmony in C major two octaves apart. He said:

"It is just an idea but it might be rather fun working it out and certainly a novel way of resolving harmony from discord."

M. Ravel said that for the first time in his life he had been engaged in writing two works at the same time—the concerto to be heard to-morrow and a piano concerto for the left hand only, especially written for Paul Wittgenstein, the one-handed pianist. This had been played by him in Vienna and Berlin, and it may be heard later in London.

M. Ravel leaves immediately after the concert to-morrow for Poland, where he is conducting some of his works. It is a disappointment to him not to be playing his own concerto, but he has been working day and night on these concertos. The strain has been so great that his doctors would not allow it, as also they would not allow it when it was produced at Paris recently.

NOTES

1. Unsigned interview in the *Evening Standard*, February 24, 1932 (in English).

2. That is, the Piano Concerto in G. It was first performed in London at Queen's Hall on February 25, 1932, with Ravel conducting the Royal Philharmonic Orchestra and Marguerite Long as soloist. Malcolm Sargent conducted the remainder of the program, which began with Mozart's Overture to *Idomeneo*, followed by Haydn's Symphony No. 94 and the Piano Concerto. After the intermission, the Concerto for Oboe and Orchestra by Eugene Goossens was performed (with Leon Goossens as soloist), and the program concluded with Manuel de Falla's Suite from *El Amor brujo.*

3. Referring to the Ballet Russe production of Satie's *Parade,* which was introduced at the Théâtre du Châtelet on May 18, 1917, with scenario by Jean Cocteau, choreography by Leonid Massine, décor and costumes by Pablo Picasso, and Ernest Ansermet conducting. In addition to the American-made typewriters in the orchestra, other unusual sonorities included sirens, pistol shots, and a lottery wheel. At a rehearsal of *Parade,* Ravel criticized its orchestration, telling Jean Cocteau that he did not understand the technique of a piece "which was not bathed in any sonorous fluid"—a revealing insight into Ravel's conception of sound.

28 : : :

Ten Opinions of Mr. Ravel[1]

On Compositions and Composers

*He Recognizes the Influence of the Classical Masters and Modern Jazz
on His New Piano Concerto
A Beautiful Piece by Jacques Beers*

The Concertgebouw is large, and clad in semi-darkness on the morning of a rehearsal it resembles a labyrinth. Maurice Ravel is present somewhere in this labyrinth, and it is not very easy to reach that specific spot. But we finally succeed, finding him in a corner of the empty, endlessly empty auditorium—the famous emptiness about which music critics always talk—an emptiness, mind you, while Mengelberg is conducting Franck's *Symphonic Variations* on stage with piano soloist and full orchestra.

Ravel sits there, small, thin, unobtrusive, a real Frenchman, looking sophisticated in his dress and manner, appearing even smaller and more unobtrusive than he really is because of the semi-dark space which surrounds him.

No, he is not interested in an interview. "They interviewed me here once before," he remarked, "and repeated the exact opposite of what I said about at least 21 things. They had me saying the most horrible things about Strauss. Thanks a lot!"

Instead of praising the dear Maestro, the interviewer had to begin with an apology for himself and for the honor of his profession. Was Beethoven always interpreted correctly? Then please let there be forgiveness for a poor interpretation of Maurice Ravel.

He appeared to soften. A genuine Frenchman does not like embarrassing situations, and the true nature of a composer is peaceful, except for the creator of "La Marseillaise." Our conversation continued, and from a distance we were accompanied as in a sort of modern drama, or a Bachian Quodlibet, by the serious yet joyous music of Franck, which every now and then caused Ravel to exclaim: "How wonderful that sounds! Isn't that charming?"

Admiration for Saint-Saëns

—Do you like Franck that much?

"Not everything. But some parts are beautifully orchestrated. Only Saint-Saëns orchestrated even better in his customary manner: mostly superb."

—This is an unexpected preference. Are there any younger French composers whom you esteem so highly?

"Certainly. Despite all of his shortcomings, I consider Milhaud one of the most important people we have. Ibert[2] is also very good, and has written some beautiful works. Among the very young there are a few of whom I have very high expectations, for instance Delannoy and Rosenthal, who has studied with me."

—What about neoclassicism?

"It need not be wrong. Stravinsky is sometimes very good in this new style, for instance in his *Symphony of Psalms.* But I do not appreciate his piano concerto, in which the orchestral accompaniment is so harmonically oriented. The piano does not blend well with the orchestra, and the work ultimately becomes an experiment. I prefer to say what I do like, because I think that makes more sense. Outside of France, Falla is excellent, in my opinion, and I consider Hindemith one of the most important German composers. I even appreciate the Viennese school, although I do think that they indulge too much in abstractions. In my opinion, art should be balanced between intellect and emotion, and although Berg has written some beautiful works, I think the music of the Viennese school is often too intellectual."

—What about the Italians?

"At the moment they are all writing fascist music, although it puzzles me how music can be fascist or Bolshevik. Maybe they are writing Rossini-like music, but they shouldn't do that, because nobody needs bad Rossini. Good Rossini was created by the master himself, so we don't need any more of that either. Don't forget Bartók and Kodály, whom I consider extremely important, as well as Harsányi,[3] and one of the more recent works by Obouhov."[4]

European Tour

—What about your work during the past few years? Have you written anything since you finished the piano concerto which is being performed here?

"No, the piano concerto has just been finished. As a matter of fact, I worked on it for three years, day and night, during which time I hardly got six hours of sleep each night. That is why I am making this concert tour now, in order to get some rest. It has turned out to be quite a trip. The concerto was first performed in Paris twice, then in Brussels, Liège and Antwerp, afterwards in Vienna, then

Bucharest. It was 5 degrees below zero in Bucharest, but the reception of the piece was considerably warmer than the temperature outside. The concerto was also performed by the London Philharmonic Orchestra, then in Warsaw, Prague, Lvov, and Berlin, and it is now finally here in the Netherlands, where it will be heard in five cities: Amsterdam, Haarlem, The Hague, Rotterdam and Arnhem."

—Do we find as much jazz influence in the piano concerto as we did in the violin sonata?

"What is being written today without the influence of jazz? It is not the only influence, however: in the concerto one also finds bass accompaniments from the time of Bach,[5] and a melody that recalls Mozart, the Mozart of the Clarinet Quintet,[6] which by the way is the most beautiful piece he wrote. What I wanted to do in the violin sonata was to accentuate the contrast between the percussive piano accompaniment and the weaker violin melody. In the concerto, I have also tried to realize this, but in a somewhat different way."[7]

Successful Piano Concertos

"I set out with the old notion that a concerto should be a divertissement. Brahms' principle about a symphonic concerto was wrong, and the critic who said that he had written a 'concerto against the piano' was right. Mozart's piano concertos and Mendelssohn's Violin Concerto are absolutely perfect. I also know a concerto written by a young Dutchman which I think is beautiful. It is a jazz concerto by Jacques Beers. Do you know it? He wrote this work for piano, saxophone, and a female voice with orchestra. It really should be performed once."[8]

And so our conversation continued. We went from one musical topic to another, and it proved impossible to change the subject and talk about another field.

The impression one gets from meeting Maurice Ravel for the first time is that the composer shows through every expression, every gesture, and every thought. That is also the impression one could have gotten a long time ago by listening to his many beautiful, unprofound but lovely compositions. His music is charming like he is, and an interview with him brings out clear and precise formulations, like the ones we find in his work.

NOTES

1. Unsigned interview in *De Telegraaf,* April 6, 1932.
2. Jacques Ibert (1890–1962) achieved international recognition with his orchestral

suite *Escales* (*Ports of Call,* 1919). In the postwar years he met Ravel at the Godebski salon, and was occasionally a guest at Le Belvédère.

3. Tibor Harsányi (1898–1954), the gifted Hungarian composer, studied with Kodály, and was later a leading member of the Ecole de Paris, a group of expatriates living in Paris. He received some artistic counsel from Ravel, as did other members of the group, Alexandre Tansman and the Romanian-born Marcel Mihalovici.

4. See letter no. 162, note 1 (the name is mistakenly written as "Nabokof").

5. Referring to the rhythmic ostinato in the left hand in the second movement.

6. Ravel told Marguerite Long that he composed the slow movement of the concerto "two measures at a time," with the assistance of Mozart's Clarinet Quintet. Furthermore, like Mozart's Piano Concerto in C Minor, this spacious movement features two soloists, the piano, and the woodwind family.

7. This element of contrast between soloist and orchestra appears in the first movement of the concerto: Ravel first introduces a cadenza for the harp, followed by a cadenza for the woodwinds playing harplike passages, and only then presents the traditional cadenza for the soloist.

8. Beers (1902–1947) was a composer, pianist, and organist. Following his studies in Amsterdam, he settled in Paris (1928–39) where he took composition lessons with Jean Huré and Nadia Boulanger. His concerto, which is dedicated to Marcelle Gerar, is a relatively traditional three movement work in C major. The soprano part is a vocalization. Mme Gerar introduced the concerto with Janine Weill, piano, Jules Viard, saxophone, and Roger Désormière conducting the Orchestre Symphonique de Paris at Salle Pleyel on February 19, 1933.

29 : : :

Maurice Ravel Between Two Trains[1]

BY NINO FRANK

Maurice Ravel, the sedentary, peaceful, and secluded inhabitant of Le Belvédère at Montfort l'Amaury, has just transformed himself into an indefatigable traveler: the success of his Concerto has taken him to the four corners of Europe with his interpreter Mme Marguerite Long, and it was only by chance that I was able to meet him in Paris, between two trains. Those who expect to meet the legendary Ravel, abrupt and distant, find instead a tiny man, elegant and smiling, his eyes sparkling with mirth and perspicacity, who speaks in a rather deep voice. Photographs have popularized the chiseled lines of his face, with its silvery hair and black eyebrows, a face that seems designed by a geometer, portraying strong determination; in reality, his face radiates an inexpressible affectionate bonhomie, an extraordinary youthfulness, and a brilliant intelligence, which humanize these features. Slim and small like a Spaniard, Ravel expresses himself without any petulance, with a mixture of modesty and timidity which is disconcerting. . . .

—I was so indisposed, in the country, that the doctors had to order me to stop all work for six months. Think of the long months of labor devoted to this Concerto . . . I overdid it. Thus, these trips are now a vacation for me. I'm hopping all over Europe: Austria, Czechoslovakia, Poland and Germany, Holland (where Mengelberg lent us the Concertgebouw Orchestra), England. . . . We were fortunate to receive a marvelous welcome everywhere, and great success. I am completely enchanted by these continual trips, by sudden encounters with worlds different from my own. . . . Moreover, I rather like conducting, and the rehearsals and all of the preparation keep my mind away from the temptation to work.

"And now, what is my opinion of this Concerto? A rather good one . . . I think that I found what I was looking for. Or rather, not entirely—let's not exaggerate: you never realize exactly what you are looking for. Fortunately, by the way . . . If some day, I think that I have succeeded, I'll be finished. In any case, this Concerto strikes me as one of the works in which I was able to shape the content and form that I sought, in which I was best able to assert the dominance of my will. . . . But am I perhaps partial with regard to this newborn? Of everything I have composed until now, the work which satisfies me the most is probably my *Chansons madécasses*. Let me add that only once did I completely succeed in realizing my ideas: in the *Boléro*; but it is an overly facile genre. . . . For the most part, you see, I have still not succeeded in finding what I want: but I still have time ahead of me. . . ."

—. . .

—You know that if I spend all of my time laboring at Montfort (and I can only work there: it's impossible in Paris), I'm not among those who compose quickly. I mistrust facility. I place a somewhat scientific stubbornness on constructing with solidity, seeking the purest material, and consolidating it well. My Concerto cost me two years of labor. . . . Yes, I was often tempted by symphonic form: and for a long time, some decades, I had undertaken one, struggling with it, for it is a wonderful form; I would let it go, take it up again . . . then, one day, I threw it aside. But all of that doesn't disappear, and perhaps I'll return to it. . . .[2] At the moment, I am preoccupied with the theater: for months I have been thinking of a *Joan of Arc*, based on Joseph Delteil's book, whose contents and structure have delighted me. I myself indicated to Delteil which episodes will be found in the libretto. . . . But nothing yet exists on paper; all of my work until now has been mental: I like to know clearly where I'm going before settling down to work.

"The challenge of the theater has always fascinated me: I have already made some attempts, but still haven't found the form that I'm looking for. Don't you find it incredible that progress stopped at—who knows?—at Meyerbeer, and that this type of spectacle has not evolved even one iota since? Wagner's theater is absurd; something else must be devised. But, you see, the youngest generation can hardly resist returning to the framework of Gounod and company. Perhaps the solution lies in a mixture of song and dance, based on a rapid, dramatic plot . . .[3]

"My favorite composer? Do I have one? . . . In any case, I believe that Mozart remains the most perfect of all. No doubt, he was the father of academic music, but you cannot blame him for what it became. He was music incarnate. I admire Beethoven, but Mozart's music transports you to another world. Mozart's great lesson for us today is that he is helping us to *liberate ourselves from music*, to listen only to ourselves and to our eternal heritage, to forget what immediately preceded us: this accounts for the present return to pure forms, this neoclassicism—call it what you will—which delights me, in a certain sense. Moreover, our epoch pleases me: this wonderful uneasiness, and sincere research in all directions—aren't these the signs of a fertile period? You speak to me of my influence, but it strikes me as nonexistent![4] And that's very good . . . You want some names? Well now! there is Milhaud, who nevertheless is somewhat of a genius; and Poulenc, who writes so little.[5] Among the youngest, who knows? a Delannoy, who has a fine dramatic sense. . . . The Germans? They're starting to become too intellectual; but Hindemith remains a true musician, probably too elaborate. There are young people with great talent everywhere: for instance, in Czechoslovakia (I can't cite any names: they're too difficult), I heard some excellent things."

Before leaving, I asked Maurice Ravel about the recording of his works: it is known that the composer of the *Histoires naturelles*, the Trio, and "Alborada del gracioso" is, of all French composers, the one whom our large firms prefer—very appropriately, by the way.

—Yes, I do like the phonograph, in any case better than the radio. . . . Of the various recordings of my works, the one which pleases me the most is the *Boléro*, issued by Polydor, which I conducted myself. As for all the versions of *La Valse*, the one conducted by Albert Wolff is the most successful, but it's a fact that not one of them was able to avoid the problems at the beginning: I will decide one day or another to make some modifications in the music, since the microphone partially distorts some of the sounds, and I myself will conduct the new version.[6] Note also that Polydor will soon release the *Chansons madécasses*, and that I will record the Concerto with Marguerite Long and the Straram Orchestra for Columbia. . ."

NOTES

1. *Candide*, May 5, 1932.

2. A one-page sketch of a trio is all that appears to have survived from this symphony (autograph in the private collection of Mme Alexandre Taverne).

3. This is essentially what occurs in *L'Enfant et les sortilèges*.

4. An overly modest statement. In an article written in 1921, Roland-Manuel commented upon Ravel's marked influence on the younger generation in Austria, England, France, Hungary, Italy, and Spain. The composer's imprint is naturally closest in spirit to the French school and may be seen in the work of Maurice Delage, Jacques Ibert, Louis Durey, Francis Poulenc, Germaine Tailleferre, and in the generation of French composers whose formative development took place in the 1930s. At this writing, however, Ravel's achievement appears to be self-contained rather than seminal.

5. Another example of Ravelian irony.

6. This project was never carried out.

30 : : :

M. Maurice Ravel Is Going to Write a "Joan of Arc"[1]

The Composer Talks about His Projects and His Conception of the National Heroine

BY GABRIEL REUILLARD

Le Belvédère, at Montfort l'Amaury, deserves its name! It indeed affords a beautiful view, perched like an eagle's nest on the side of a hill. It dominates the horizon. To the left, a landscape of the Île-de-France: the village with brown roofs and the soaring slate belfry. To the right, meadows with dales, surrounded by little woods. In the distance, the white speck of a château, half hidden by trees.

A gentle peace, conducive for meditation, hovers over all of this.

"The very extended view is encompassed by the line of hills on the horizon," M. Maurice Ravel says to me while leading me on to his balcony. Thought doesn't fly or steal away. It escapes, but comes back. It's as if the landscape "returned" it.

I am in the "retreat" of one of today's greatest and most justifiably celebrated musicians. There are small rooms with beautiful lacquered furniture, rare objets d'art, precious bibelots, Chinese vases, Japanese prints, and books which are beautifully bound in fine gold.

—You are working on a *Joan of Arc*, it is said. I have come to ask you to share with us your conception of our national heroine.

"I am not yet working on this piece. I am thinking about it, and have been dreaming about it for a long time. Certainly, this project is becoming increasingly close to my heart, but I am working it out slowly, caressing it gently. . .

"First, I have to write a ballet for next March, *Morgiane*; Ida Rubinstein will give the first performance. It's the story from the *Thousand and One Nights*, Ali Baba . . . But will I have the strength to realize this project? I feel weak. An attack of nervous depression. . . I am paying for the effort expended in completing my two piano concertos. For three years, almost without going out,

I worked without respite. Fatigue accumulated. Vallery-Radot, the grandson of Pasteur,[2] who is treating me, has forbidden me to undertake any new work.

"I also want to begin *Le Chapeau chinois* [The Chinese Hat] by Franc-Nohain,[3] with an operetta-like orchestra.

"My *Joan of Arc* will come after that. It is Delteil's book which inspired me. The book! Is that the precise word? Rather, the lyrical epopee."

—Is it the lyricism which attracted the composer?

"Of course! It's also the face, once again alive, of this touching child, cleansed from the legends which rendered her distant, almost foreign. It is not a statue more or less sanctified that we must adore, but a typical French girl, 'a great peasant girl of France, molded by the soil, common sense, and by God,' as Delteil says."

—There is however the distant epoch, and the archaism of the décor and language. . .

"That doesn't matter. It's of no importance. Delteil's achievement is that he linked the intervening centuries between Joan and us in order to make her almost a contemporary, a being of flesh and blood whom we see acting, whom we hear laughing, moaning, and crying, as if she were one of us.[4]

" 'I have brought her to me,' Delteil writes in his twenty-line preface, 'across the archeological desert. . . .' And he continues: 'The obsolete ideas of History and the desiccation of Time have neither stripped her fresh color nor her genuine smile. No, she is not a legend or a mummy. Who cares one iota about documentation or local color! My only intention is to portray a daughter of France. . . .'

"She is not even a daughter of France," M. Maurice Ravel continued, "she is the daughter of France, she is France, she is the permanent soul of France. It's not a Joan of Arc for high school or Sunday school that I dream of creating, but rather a hymn of love which extols France, which shows it to be eternal through this young girl who incarnates our race. And again, like Delteil, I am tempted to dedicate this hymn 'to the simple souls, the true believers, the children, the virgins, the angels. . . .' "

—And how do you plan to realize it?

"I envision the 'cuts' adopted by Delteil rather clearly: short scenes in rapid succession, like episodes in a film. First the combat of the children—Delteil calls it the *Flower War*—which immediately reveals Joan's personality: 'of violent temperament, naturally authoritative and brusque gestures, a harsh voice, bold gait, a fiery look, she enjoyed considerable prestige among the boys and girls of her own age! Strong and confident, she did not fail to inculcate her authority with punches. . .'

"That is Joan of Arc as a child. She grows up and develops. Now she is a young girl, which she will remain to the end of her brief life. Beginning with the chapter of the Visions ('The Companions of Heaven' in the romanticized biography), she has her definitive form."

—Do you therefore envision a few performers for Joan: one for Joan as a child, and another for Joan as a young girl?

"Yes, two at least. . . . Probably, because all of this, I repeat, is still in the planning stage. . ."

—But how would your music interpret this quality of permanence, of eternity, and link the various epochs together, as you hope to do in this work?

"Recall in the chapter of the Rite ('Go, go, go!' in Delteil's book). The author writes: 'The Reims cathedral is aglow from its illuminated columns and burning incense. The throng cries: Noël! The trumpets blare forth. The Armagnac[5] music plays *La Marseillaise*. . .' How that Armagnac Marseillaise, with the people shouting Noël, cuts through time and space, and speaks directly to us! The Noël conjures up an ancient epoch, the Armagnac music gives local color, and *La Marseillaise* is contemporary—everything is there! I'm also thinking of introducing a Marseillaise in the scene of the Rite, but a transformed Marseillaise, of course, an interpretation of *La Marseillaise* in my own way, making it a sort of triumphant hymn to the glory of its soil and of its race. This idea isn't new: Berlioz used it when he incorporated 'la Retraite' in *The Damnation of Faust.*"[6]

We go down to the garden while chatting. A bit disturbed by my presence, the composer's siamese cats, three animals with beautiful fur, escort us cautiously. Before us, basking in radiant sunshine, the landscape seems to crystallize as though in a definitive form: what it was yesterday, it will be tomorrow, a village of France, for now and for all time.

In the distance, a bell chimes. Could it be the bell of Domremy? . . .[7]

NOTES

1. *Excelsior*, September 24, 1933.

2. The celebrated chemist and microbiologist Louis Pasteur.

3. This project remained in the planning stage.

4. Based on conversations with Ravel, Hélène Jourdan-Morhange outlined the musical tableaus as follows: "Joan with her Sheep—The Court—Meeting with the King—the Siege of Orléans—the Taking of Orléans—the Trial before the French Priests and the English Officials (sarcastic music, he said), finally the Stake—Joan's Death—and . . . The Entry into Heaven." Ravel thought of his work as an "opera-oratorio," or a "grand opera," like those of Meyerbeer. During the siege of Orléans, he planned to have *Tipperary* coming from the English side, and the *Marseillaise* and *Madelon* (a song written in 1914 which became popular during the war) from the French side. This, Mme Jourdan-Morhange wrote, satisfied the composer's "penchant for

mystification," with its "anachronisms à la George Bernard Shaw, whose *Saint Joan* had enchanted Ravel. (Incidentally, I had the impression that Shaw's spirit gradually supplanted that of Delteil.)" See *Ravel et nous*, pp. 235–37, and plate 23, a drawing by Luc-Albert Moreau of the costumes for *Joan of Arc*.

5. The historic region of southwestern France, now in the department of Gers. During the Hundred Years' War, the Treaty of Calais (1360) awarded Armagnac to the English, but it was eventually united to the French crown (1607).

6. Referring to the Soldiers' Chorus, which appears in the finale of part 2, and in a very different setting in part 4 (scene 15). Furthermore, Berlioz orchestrated and expanded upon the Rakoczy march, which Ravel was analogously planning to do with *La Marseillaise*.

7. Joan of Arc's birthplace.

Appendixes

Appendix A : : :

Recollections of Ravel by Louis Durey
and Martial Singher

The following letters are of exceptional interest, and I wish to thank the late Louis Durey and also Mr. Martial Singher for their kind permission to print them here.

Louis Durey[1] to Arbie Orenstein

Valfère   December 14, 1972
St. Tropez 83990
Dear Sir,

I apologize for this late reply to your kind letter of November 29, and trust that you will excuse me.

However, the subject of your letter greatly interested me, because of the imperishable recollections which I preserve of my meetings with Maurice Ravel, and the immense admiration which I have always had and preserved for the most "optimistic" of French composers, all of whose works, with dazzling clarity, bear witness to the joie de vivre and the joy of accomplishing the unique task which was his to realize.

I met Ravel in the following circumstances:

In 1918, during the absence of Jacques Copeau,[2] Mme Jane Bathori had assumed the management of the Vieux-Colombier theater in order to present concerts there, and it was there, among other places, that most of the works of my comrades, the group *Les Six*, were first presented to the public.[3] During one of these programs, a piece I had written for piano four hands, "Carillons," was performed by Marcelle Meyer and Georges Auric.[4] Following the concert, when a number of friends were conversing with Jane Bathori in the foyer of the theater, I was surprised to see Ravel approaching, accompanied by Roland-Manuel; he asked to be introduced to me, as he was interested in my work which he had just heard.

After that, I often had the good fortune to see him again at friends' gatherings. He even intervened spontaneously to introduce me to the publisher Jacques Durand, who agreed to print my earliest works. I thus had the opportunity to receive some precious advice from him, which is contained in the letter he wrote to me from Mégève on January 28, 1919, the text of which is reproduced in the book by Frédéric Robert: *Louis Durey, l'aîné des Six* (Editions Français Réunis).[5]

Ravel was an extremely unpretentious man, affable and friendly. Very receptive to innovations (wasn't he struck by Schoenberg's *Pierrot lunaire?*), he took an interest in the early works of the young musicians that we were at the time, and faithfully attended the concerts in which our music was presented to the public.

For all that, our great composer did not disdain lighter spectacles, and I recall very well an evening which I spent with Ravel, Honegger, and Jean Marnold, the music critic of the austere *Mercure de France* . . . at the Casino de Paris, for a spectacular review starring the flamboyant Gaby Deslys!

I also had the opportunity to visit him at his home in Montfort l'Amaury, so curiously crowded with bibelots, one more out-of-date and unusual than the next, but which truly harmonize so well with the *Histoires naturelles, L'Enfant et les sortilèges,* and the sidesplitting *L'Heure espagnole,* which bear witness to a vivacity of spirit and a humor which were his alone.

I have been pleased to evoke for you these few recollections of an extraordinary epoch, and, dear Sir, I trust you will accept my best wishes.

Louis Durey

1. See letter no. 152, note 1.
2. The noted actor, writer, and theater director (1879–1949).
3. Although the Vieux-Colombier theater is no longer open to the public, its interior has been preserved intact as a historical site, and it is still used for rehearsals.
4. The recital on January 15, 1918, also included works by Tailleferre, Honegger, Auric, Roland-Manuel, and Poulenc, with commentary by René Chalupt (the program is reproduced in Linda Laurent, "Jane Bathori et le Théâtre du Vieux-Colombier").
5. Published in Paris, 1968.

Martial Singher[1] to Arbie Orenstein

Music Academy of the West   September 3, 1965
1070 The Fairway
Santa Barbara, California
Dear Mr. Orenstein,

The summer session of the Academy is just over, and I finally find the necessary time for answering your letter of August 2nd and not too late, I hope, for finding you still in New York. Here are the few and not too important informations that I can give you on the *Don Quichotte* songs. I have to rely on my memory only, and I have never been good at remembering dates . . . I have no documentation with me here.

Ravel gave me the manuscript of the songs after a lunch in the house of a common friend Mr. Lacombe, professor of mathematics, some time in the late spring of 1933. To a young singer with only three operatic seasons to his credit, and very little concert experience, it was a staggering and unbelievable event. Previous commitments, and a summer vacation in my home town of Biarritz delayed any action on the songs until the fall. I surrendered the manuscript to Durand publishers, more precisely to Mr. Garban who seemed to be in charge of its publication, and whom I saw later doing the correcting of the proofs. Very soon (November?) I was called upon to record the songs for "La Voix de son Maître," and the songs were performed directly with orchestra, before being published or performed with the piano arrangement, for that recording. Ravel was present at the recording session, and made several remarks about wrong notes, tempi, and dynamics, both for the voice and the instruments. (One notation which does not appear in the published songs is a ritardando, in the "Chanson romanesque" on the three eighth notes on the words "d̲e̲s̲s̲o̲u̲s̲ l̲e̲" (blâme) and again on the words "v̲o̲u̲s̲ b̲é̲n̲i̲s̲"(sant). The song was then called "Chanson romantique," and it is only at the proofs correction that the name was rightly modified. I never asked myself whether anybody but Ravel had written the orchestration, and I always believed—without proof—that the songs had been written directly for the orchestra.

The songs were given in public audition for the first time at the Concerts Colonne, under Paul Paray in early December (the date will be easy to find in the programs of that institution) with an enormous success.[2] I was able to bring Ravel on stage and he received an ovation. I had to sing the cycle six or seven times with orchestra in Paris alone that winter, and Ravel was present at several of the performances. Paul Paray commented to me that he felt the songs to be important, for, if Ravel had written such beautiful and melodic vocal lines, some other composers might dare to go back to melody too. I leave to you to judge whether he was right or simply optimistic . . .

At the time of the recording, it was decided that the short and delightful song "Ronsard à son âme" would be used as the fourth side of the records. A very light orchestration of winds and vibraphone was then composed: it is a fact that Ravel did not actually write the notes on paper, for his illness, still unseen to the uninformed eye, had already deprived him of his capacity to write. But I believe, without proof again, that he dictated to Mr. Garban, and he did make small changes of instrumentation at the recording session. Before the songs were printed, Ravel was gracious enough to ask me whether I would be pleased if he dedicated them to me. Actually blushing, I answered that I had not served him well enough or long enough for deserving such an honor. He laughed lightly and said "In this case, would you care to choose one of the three songs as being your favorite?" I chose the "Chanson épique," and he decided to dedicate it to me. But he was already unable to write the dedication with his own hand, and I saw my name in print on the song when it was published. He commentated later that "of course, I had chosen the right one!"

The metronomic figures were accepted by Ravel in my presence at the reading of the proofs, and I have always followed them through hundreds of performances of the songs over three continents. The first and the third songs are generally performed t̲o̲o̲ f̲a̲s̲t̲ in our days, a fact that I always stress for my students.

Would it be interesting to you to know that, to the best of my knowledge, I have been the first m̲a̲l̲e̲ singer to perform the three *Chansons madécasses* as well as "Asie" from *Shéhérazade*, at an all Ravel recital that I gave jointly with the pianist Gisèle Kuhn in the spring (late spring?) of 1938 at the Salle Gaveau (programs could probably be found).[3] I had remarked to Ravel that the texts of those songs were certainly meant for a man. He confirmed (this must have happened about 1935) that he had had in mind a male voice when writing them, but that only women singers, with strong musical backgrounds had been interested by them. By the time I felt strong enough to sing them, Ravel was dead, and I have always regretted to have failed giving him the joy to hear them sung as he had originally planned. I have recorded later the *Chansons madécasses* for "Concert Hall," but I am afraid that the records are by now about impossible to find. As to "Asie," he had allowed me to change to A♭ the climactic B♭ on the word "haine," without changing the chord under that note. He also stressed that, in the last lines of the song, in order to avoid embarrassment to the lady who sang the first performance (Jeanne Hatto?), he had a word erased from the original plate, the word "pipe" and had it replaced by the more convenient word "tasse."[4] He showed me that, in the printed copy, the word "tasse" is slightly out of line and of a slightly fatter print than the other words.

I suddenly remember that the then young man who played the piano from the manuscript of Ravel at Mr. Lacombe's was Passani,[5] who made later a name for himself in the world of music. Ravel must have been unable to play the piano at the time.

Following our work on the Don Quichotte songs, Maurice Ravel came for dinner to my house several times, and although he was often silent, he gave every proof to be in excellent mental health and in most friendly disposition.

I thank you, dear Mr. Orenstein, for having given me this opportunity to remember some proud moments of my musical life, and to feel anew my respect and affection for Ravel. Please forgive the hasty looks and writing of my letter. I shall arrive in Philadelphia the same day you leave for Paris: if I can be of service at a later time, do not hesitate to call on me. The best of luck in your work. Say "hello" to Paris for me.

Very truly yours,
Martial Singher

1. Following an active concert and operatic career in Europe, Mr. Singher (b. 1904) settled in the United States, where he performed at the Metropolitan Opera (1943–1959) and taught at the Curtis Institute of Music and the Music Academy of the West. This letter was written in English.

2. The concert took place on December 1, 1934, at the Châtelet theater. The program, which included works by Franck, Mozart, and Borodin, featured Franck's Symphony and several operatic arias sung by Mr. Singher; the second half of the program consisted of *Ma Mère l'Oye*, *Don Quichotte à Dulcinée*, and *La Valse*.

3. The recital took place on May 11, 1939. Mr. Singher also performed the *Don Quichotte* songs, the *Epigrammes de Clément Marot*, and several other songs. Among the works performed by Mlle Kuhn were the Sonatine, *Jeux d'eau*, and the *Valses nobles et sentimentales*.

4. Thus, Tristan Klingsor's verse "Like Sindbad, occasionally placing my old Arabic pipe between my lips," was altered to "Like Sindbad, occasionally raising my old Arabic cup to my lips" (Klingsor agreed to these modifications in the poem).

5. Emile Passani; see letter no. 341, note 2.

Appendix B : : :

Ballet Arguments by Ravel

Ravel's ballet arguments for Ma Mère l'Oye, Adélaïde, ou le langage des fleurs, *and* La Valse *are printed in the* Catalogue de l'oeuvre de Maurice Ravel *(Paris: Fondation Maurice Ravel, 1954, pp. 13–19). Although similar to the printed versions, the initial holographs of* Ma Mère l'Oye *and* Adélaïde *are considerably more detailed. They are in the Bibliothèque de L'Opéra:* Ma Mère l'Oye, *Ravel Autograph Letter no. 1;* Adélaïde, *Ravel Autograph Letter no. 14. The holograph of* La Valse *has not been recovered.*

Ma Mère l'Oye[1]
(Mother Goose)

PRELUDE.

SCENE I. *"Dance of the Spinning Wheel"*
An enchanted garden. An old woman is seated at her spinning wheel. Princess Florine enters, jumping rope. She stumbles, falling against the spinning wheel, and is pricked by its spindle. The old woman calls for help. The young ladies- and gentlemen-in-waiting rush in. They try in vain to revive the Princess. Then they recall the curse of the fairies. Two ladies-in-waiting prepare the Princess for her long sleep.

SCENE 2. *"Pavane of the Sleeping Beauty"*
Florine falls asleep. The old woman now stands erect, throws off her filthy cape and appears in the sumptuous clothing and charming features of the Good Fairy.
Two little Negroes appear. The fairy entrusts them with guarding Florine and granting her pleasant dreams.

SCENE 3. *"Conversations of Beauty and the Beast"*
Beauty enters. Taking her mirror, she powders herself. The Beast enters. Beauty notices him and remains petrified. With horror, she rejects the declarations of the Beast, who falls at her feet, sobbing. Reassured, Beauty makes fun of him coquettishly. The Beast falls down faint with despair. Touched by his great love, Beauty raises him up again and accords him her hand.
But before her is a prince more handsome than Eros, who thanks her for having ended his enchantment.

SCENE 4. *"Tom Thumb"*
A forest, at nightfall. The woodcutter's seven children enter. Tom Thumb crumbles a piece of bread. He looks about but cannot find any houses. The children cry. Tom Thumb reassures them by showing them the bread which he has strewn along their path.

They lie down and fall asleep. Birds pass and eat all of the bread. Upon awakening, the children no longer find any crumbs, and they depart sadly.

SCENE 5. *"Laideronnette, Empress of the Pagodas"*

A tent draped in Chinese style. Male and female pagoda attendants enter. Dance. Laideronnette appears in the Chinese style of Boucher. A green serpent crawls amorously at her side.

Pas de deux, then general dance.

SCENE 6. *"The Enchanted Garden"*

Dawn. Birds are singing.

Prince Charming enters, led by a cupid. He notices the sleeping Princess. She awakens at the same time that day is breaking.

All of the performers in the ballet group themselves around the Prince and the Princess, who are united by Cupid.

The Good Fairy appears and blesses the couple.

APOTHEOSIS.

1. Based on the suite for piano 4 hands. First performed at the Théâtre des Arts, Paris, January 29, 1912; Jacques Rouché, director; Gabriel Grovlez, conductor; décor and costumes, Jacques Drésa; choreography, Jeanne Hugard. Ravel added the Prelude, Dance of the Spinning Wheel, and several interludes for the ballet version.

Adélaïde, ou le langage des fleurs[1]
(Adélaïde, or the language of flowers)

Paris, about 1820, at the home of the courtesan Adélaïde. A salon furnished in the style of the period. At the rear of the stage, a window looks out onto a garden. On each side, vases full of flowers are placed on small round tables.

I. A soirée at Adélaïde's home. Couples are dancing. Others, seated or walking, are conversing tenderly. Adélaïde comes and goes among her guests, inhaling the fragrance of a tuberose (voluptuousness).

II. Lorédan enters, sullen and melancholy. He offers Adélaïde a buttercup. An exchange of flowers expresses Adélaïde's coquettishness and Lorédan's love.

III. She picks the buttercup to pieces and sees that Lorédan's love is sincere. The daisy discloses to Lorédan that he is not loved. Adélaïde wishes to renew the test. This time the reply is favorable.

IV. The two lovers dance while revealing their affection. But Adélaïde sees the Duke enter and stops, confused.

V. The Duke gives her a bouquet of sunflowers (vain wealth), then a jewel case containing a diamond necklace, with which she adorns herself.

VI. Lorédan's despair. Ardent pursuit. Adélaïde repulses him coquettishly.

VII. The Duke begs Adélaïde to grant him this last waltz. She refuses, and proceeds to fetch Lorédan, who has remained aside in a tragic pose. He hesitates at first, and is then won over by the tender persistence of the courtesan.

VIII. The guests retire. The Duke hopes that he will be detained. Adélaïde offers him an acacia branch (platonic love). The Duke leaves, indicating his displeasure.

Lorédan advances, sad unto death. Adélaïde offers him a corn poppy (forgetfulness). He refuses and runs out making gestures of eternal farewell.

Adélaïde goes to the rear window and opens it widely. She voluptuously inhales the scent of the tuberose.

Scaling the balcony, Lorédan appears, wild-eyed, his hair disheveled. He rushes toward Adélaïde, falls at her feet, and takes out a pistol which he places next to his temple.

Smiling, she draws a red rose from her bosom and falls into Lorédan's arms.

1. Based on the *Valses nobles et sentimentales* for piano, this ballet contains eight numbers: seven waltzes and an epilogue. First performed by the troupe of Natasha Trouhanova at the Théâtre du Châtelet, Paris, April 22, 1912, with Maurice Ravel conducting the Lamoureux Orchestra; décor and costumes, Jacques Drésa; choreography, Ivan Clustine.

La Valse[1]
(The Waltz)
Choreographic Poem for Orchestra

Through whirling clouds, waltzing couples may be faintly distinguished. The clouds gradually scatter: one sees[2] an immense hall filled with a swirling throng.

The stage is gradually illuminated. The light of the chandeliers reaches its peak at the *fortissimo.*[3]

An imperial court, about 1855.

1. First orchestral performance: Camille Chevillard conducting the Lamoureux Orchestra, Paris, December 12, 1920. First performance in Paris as a ballet at the Opéra, May 23, 1929, troupe of Ida Rubinstein; Gustave Cloez, conductor; décor, Alexandre Benois; choreography, Bronislava Nijinska.

2. At rehearsal no. 9, Durand orchestral score.

3. At rehearsal no. 17, Durand orchestral score.

Appendix C : : :

An Edition of Mendelssohn's Piano Works

Ravel's edition of Mendelssohn's complete piano music is part of a huge collection entitled "Edition classique A. Durand & Fils," which now contains some 700 volumes, among them Fauré's edition of Schumann's piano works, Saint-Saëns' edition of Rameau's music, and Debussy's edition of Chopin's complete works. Ravel's Mendelssohn edition included the concerti and was published by Durand in nine volumes (1915–18); only one volume, the Songs Without Words *(1915), contains any commentary.*[1]

Songs Without Words

PREFACE

For this new publication of the *Songs Without Words,* I have referred principally to the first Breitkopf edition, one of the most carefully prepared, which has served as a model for most of the editions in recent years.

There is, however, a version which contains some very marked differences from the early editions: the one by Stephen Heller (published by Brandus). The modifications which one discovers in this version, at times significant, often felicitous, are all the more interesting to point out as they are presented by a sensitive artist who was a sincere admirer of Mendelssohn. Their very importance, in certain passages, precludes the possibility that Heller composed them himself. Rather, we should either assume that a manuscript was written after the first edition, or that these corrections were indicated directly by Mendelssohn.[2]

The two versions may be compared by means of the following list.

No. 8, page 26 [op. 30 no. 2, m. 88]

No flat before the *d.* This is perhaps only an omission, but this *major seventh,* moreover correctly prepared and resolved, gives the chord a distinctive character.

No. 9, page 27 [op. 30 no. 3, m. 8]

In my opinion, the anticipatory encounter of the major third and the suppression of the passing tone which forms a seventh are less scholastic and more delicately charming.

No. 10, page 29 [op. 30 no. 4, m. 60]

These additional six measures [the first six in the example] are indisputably a better preparation for the reprise, which is a bit hasty in the early version.

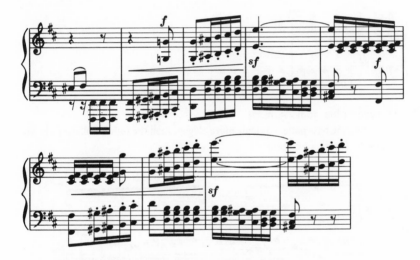

No. 10, page 32 [op. 30 no. 4, m. 119]

This modification, which avoids the redundant and hackneyed return of the principal theme, is most felicitous. The same holds true for the lengthy suspended resolution of the ninth chord.

No. 11, page 33 [op. 30 no. 5, m. 7]

This undulating bass pattern is truly more elegant than the rather dull formula which appears in the Breitkopf edition.

No. 11, page 35 [op. 30 no. 5, m. 36]

Here, on the other hand, I would prefer the early version.

No. 16, page 51 [op. 38 no. 4, m. 25]

No. 20, page 67 [op. 53 no. 2, m. 36]

No. 43, page 145 [op. 102 no. 1, m. 34]

In the Alphonse Leduc edition (*4 Songs Without Words*, opus posthumous), the piece corresponding to no. 43 in this collection contains a rather characteristic harmony.

Undoubtedly an editor considered this anticipatory resolution too bold; yet, it is found in the works of Mendelssohn's predecessors.

A *4th Barcarolle* [op. 102 no. 7] is included here among the *Songs Without Words*. (It has this title in the above mentioned posthumous collection.) This piece is published separately in all other editions.

I omitted the frequently childish titles which Heller took pleasure in bestowing upon these *Songs Without Words* ("Lost Illusions," "The Wanderer," "Meditation," "The Shepherd's Complaint"). I retained those which appear in the first editions, which were undoubtedly suggested by Mendelssohn.

No. 36 [op. 67 no. 6] is generally entitled *Serenade*, but some prefer to call this light and lively piece a *Lullaby*.

I have invariably substituted a pianistic *slur* in place of the orchestral *slur*, which is improperly used in piano writing by the majority of classical composers, and which can give rise to ambiguity. Thus, regarding this indication which is used in bowing:

No. 6, page 19 [op. 19 no. 6, m. 7]

the overly conscientious student will surely perform this:

whereas, from all evidence, the composer desired this interpretation.

(+ and + are connected by means of the pedal).

1. The references added in brackets will enable the reader to compare his score with the variant readings suggested by Ravel. Most of the *Songs Without Words* were first published simultaneously in French, German, and English editions. A recent critical discussion of the various sources and their discrepancies is found in the Henle edition, edited by Rudolf Elvers.

2. It is "more likely that Mendelssohn made some last-minute changes for the German edition which were not reflected in the French or English editions" (comment by Professor R. Larry Todd in a letter to the author dated May 2, 1986. I wish to thank Professor Todd for his kind assistance).

Appendix D : : :

Ravel Analyzes His Own Music

René Lenormand's Etude sur l'harmonie moderne *was published in Paris in 1913.[1] Lenormand (1846–1932), himself a composer and pianist, analyzed selected passages in the works of some 40 colleagues, most of them contemporary Frenchmen, and in his preface he thanked those composers who were kind enough to offer their assistance. In a letter to Lenormand dated September 9, 1912, Vincent d'Indy praised his undertaking and wrote:*

> *Harmony, a musical element very subject to changes in vogue, is consequently extremely transitory; to cite but two cases, the* diminished 7th chord, *an expression of terror and suspense in the 18th century, and the retardation of the fifth in the dominant 7th chord, discovered by Gounod, and which gave rise to so many controversies, are both relegated to the scrap heap. No composer would dare use them any longer. In about a decade the same thing will occur to the harmonies of* Pelléas *and* L'Heure espagnole; *that is why I find it useful to arrange a catalogue of these harmonies while they are still current, in order that they shouldn't be completely forgotten in time, and that a book explains their present significance.[2]*

Lenormand's work includes some twenty analyses of Ravel's music; on the basis of an unpublished manuscript,[3] it turns out that many of these analyses are entirely by Ravel himself. Moreover, Ravel's manuscript seems to be incomplete, and it is probable that other comments about his music are also his own. The analyses given here, however, are limited to those found in the manuscript.[4] With a keen, almost detached intellect, Ravel discusses complex chords with pedal points, chromatic alterations, or unresolved appoggiaturas, and in the example from Valses nobles et sentimentales, *he indicates an awareness of a larger structural prolongation (see plate 16).*

Ravel's Analyses

Sur l'herbe

(a) The 9th against the root in the upper parts. The root takes on the role of an inner pedal point.

Although the preceding explanation is better, one may also consider the *G* as forming a pedal point.

L'Heure espagnole

[Autorisation Durand & Cie, Editeurs-propriétaires, Paris]

(a) Pedal point on F♯.

(b) Chords of the minor 9th with altered 5th, proceeding by semitones.

(c) An inner pedal point on F♮, regularly struck and held over an integral note, thus forming a double pedal point on F♯ and F♮.

(d) The composer considers the notation of the bird songs as a picturesque, extra-musical effect. This is particularly true of the first passage (Le petit coq), whose notation is only approximate. This sonority, which may recall that of percussion instruments, is produced by the reed of the contrabassoon separated from the instrument.

Valses nobles et sentimentales

With regard to unresolved appoggiaturas, here is a passage which may interest you. It is taken from a suite of waltzes which were performed some time ago at the S.M.I., and which should be published shortly by Durand, entitled *Valses nobles et sentimentales*.

[Autorisation Durand & Cie, Editeurs-propriétaires, Paris]

This fragment is based upon a single chord:

which was already used by Beethoven, without preparation, at the beginning of a sonata [opus 31 no. 3]:

Here now is the passage with the appoggiaturas resolved; actually, the resolution does not occur until measure [A], when the chord changes.

The *E* [(a) and (b)] does not change the chord. It is a passing tone in both cases.

Miroirs ("Oiseaux tristes")

(e) The second version of (e) is the correct one. In fact, B♯ would be more correct than C♮. The resolution on the A♯ becomes quite natural, despite the A♮ in the lower part, whose ornamental role is obvious.

Les Grands Vents venus d'outremer

(a) An unresolved appoggiatura. Interesting as an ending, this passage calls for a careful examination on other grounds.

For greater clarity, here is the harmonic progression with its passing tones and appoggiaturas omitted (in D♯ minor for simplicity).

An unresolved appoggiatura ascending and descending from the D♯.

Miroirs ("Alborada del gracioso")

pedal point

The passage is transposed into D♯ for simplicity. The chord (a) is simply an inversion of the 9th.

1. A copy of the book, with a personal dedication to Ravel, is in the Music Division of the Bibliothèque Nationale. Lenormand's work was translated into English by Herbert Antcliffe, *Harmony in France to 1914* (London: Joseph Williams, 1915). Combined with Mosco Carner's *Contemporary Harmony*, the translation was reprinted by Da Capo Press under the title *A Study of Twentieth-Century Harmony* (New York, 1976).

2. Autograph in the Bibliothèque de l'Opéra.

3. Ravel's autograph, consisting of two pages, is in the Bibliothèque de l'Opéra—Rés. 1093 (2).

4. The following comments will clarify the relationship between Lenormand's book (=Len.) and Ravel's manuscript.

Sur l'herbe (Len., p. 40): The first paragraph does not appear in Ravel's manuscript, but the second sums up the composer's written opinion.

L'Heure espagnole (Len., p. 41): Only paragraph (d) appears in the manuscript.

Valses nobles et sentimentales (Len., pp. 63–65): The commentary, adapted by Lenormand, is quoted from Ravel's manuscript.

Miroirs ("Oiseaux tristes," Len., p. 65): The explanation is quoted from the manuscript. (Lenormand's statement differs slightly.)

Les Grands Vents venus d'outremer (Len., p. 85): Paragraph (a) is Lenormand's comment, and he quotes the remaining passages from the manuscript.

Miroirs ("Alborada del gracioso," Len., pp. 110–111): The comments are quoted from Ravel's manuscript. (Lenormand's statement differs slightly.)

Appendix E : : :

A Recording Contract with the Aeolian Company

(autograph in the private collection of Mme Alexandre Taverne)

AN AGREEMENT made the 15th day of MAY 1920 BETWEEN THE AEOLIAN COMPANY LIMITED, a Company having its registered office at the Aeolian Hall 131/7 New Bond Street in the County of London hereinafter called "the Company" of the one part, and Monsieur RAVEL of 7 Avenue Léonie, Saint-Cloud (Seine et Oise) hereinafter called "the Artist" of the other part.

WHEREAS the Company is concerned in the Manufacture and sale of (inter alia) a player piano called the "DUO-ART" Pianola embodying contrivances for the exact reproduction of musical expression by individual performers and has offered to engage the services of the Artist as an expert Professional Pianist upon the terms hereinafter specified NOW IT IS AGREED between the parties hereto as follows:—

1. The Company engages the Artist and the Artist hereby agrees during the period of TWO YEARS from the date hereof to make records for the Duo-Art Pianola by playing on the recording piano devised for the purpose musical works to be selected by the Company, none of which shall have been previously played by the Artist for the purpose of making player piano records. Ten at least of such records shall be played and corrected during the said term, the particular times for the making and correcting of such records to be mutually arranged between the parties and the Artist shall make and also correct the said records in London.

2. The Company shall pay to the Artist the sum of FIFTY Pounds Sterling per record, upon the satisfactory completion by him of the playing and correcting of the said record.

3. The Company shall have the right or option to call upon the Artist to play additional records during the said term and agrees to pay the said Artist the sum of FIFTY Pounds Sterling for each additional record thus played and corrected.

4. Should any record made as aforesaid fail to meet the mutual approval of the parties hereto, the selected work shall be played over again by the Artist or, if desired by the Company, another piece selected by the Company shall be substituted therefor and played as aforesaid by the Artist.

5. During the term of this Contract and any extension thereof, the Artist agrees to play musical compositions for the purpose of making records for mechanically operated pianos exclusively for the Company and the Artist hereby further agrees that he will not within the like period as aforesaid either alone or in concert with any other person or persons make or knowingly permit any recordings of his playing for such mechanically operated pianos for or by any person or concern other than the Company. It is further agreed that for the purpose of enabling the Company and the Artist to renew this Contract upon such terms as may hereafter

be agreed between them the Artist shall before entering into a contract or arrangement of a like character with any person firm or company give to the Company not less than fourteen (14) days previous notice in writing of his intention so to do together with a statement of the terms of the proposed contract.

6. Any selection or other musical piece or pieces which the Artist may perform under the terms of this contract shall not, except with the written consent of the Company, be repeated by the Artist so as to permit of similar records or reproductions being made or sold by any person or concern, it being intended and agreed for the purpose of the Copyright Act 1911 that the Company shall be sole owners of every original roll from which records of musical works rendered by the Artist under this contract may be derived and in particular shall have the right to permit the use of such original record or roll by any person firm or corporation with whom or which the Company may for the time being be affiliated or associated in business for the purpose of manufacturing and selling records in any part of the world and under any trade mark or trade name whatever.

7. The Company shall not be bound to include in its catalogue for the time being or offer for sale all or any records of musical works rendered by the Artist and may delete the same from such catalogue at any time.

8. In the event of any breach of the terms of this Contract being made by the Artist the Company shall have the right to terminate the same forthwith as and from which time all payments hereunder shall cease and determine without prejudice to any other remedy of the Company against the Artist.

9. The Artist agrees during his engagement under this contract not to give any endorsement recommendation or advertisement of any player pianos or mechanically operated pianos other than that of the Company.

10. The Artist undertakes at the expense of the Company to execute all documents and perform all acts and things which may be necessary to assist the Company to restrain the infringement of the Company's copyright in rolls or records manufactured under this contract or the passing off of any roll record or other contrivance as and for a record made under and by virtue of this contract.

11. The Artist shall commence recording on the 30th of November 1920 if requested so to do by the Company.

12. The Parties hereto have entered into this contract on the basis of English law and it is hereby agreed that all questions arising out of this contract shall be construed according to English law.

IN WITNESS whereof the parties have executed this agreement the day and year first above written.

Witness:—
    lu & approuvé [read & approved]
      Maurice Ravel
        St.-Cloud 15 Mai 1920
    For and on behalf of
      The Aeolian Co
      Alfred C. Mead
        May 15, 1920

Appendix F : : :

Historical Interpretations (1911–1988)

BY JEAN TOUZELET

1. Acknowledgments; 2. Introduction; 3. Ravel's activities on behalf of recorded music; 4. The nature of the recordings: rollography, discography, filmography, videography; 5. Sources; 6. Abbreviations; 7. Ravel's own interpretations: as pianist, as orchestral conductor, as conductor of chamber ensembles, as supervisor of recordings; 8. Eighty-seven interpreters and their recordings; 9. An important reissue of historical recordings; 10. Ravel's influence on jazz, popular music, and film.

1. Acknowledgments

I thank all the organizations, particularly the Bibliothèque Nationale and the Phonothèque Nationale, which, during the research into and preparation of my first discography, permitted me to discover many important elements found in the present work. I am also grateful to the individuals who kindly assisted me, in particular Jean-Michel Nectoux and Arbie Orenstein.

2. Introduction

Maurice Ravel's unique situation with regard to the history of recorded sound has two aspects: in the first place, he was the first great composer to have virtually all of his major works recorded during his lifetime; this aspect, which is mainly quantitative in importance, was treated in Arbie Orenstein's *Ravel: Man and Musician,* where appendix B lists recordings devoted to Ravel's works from the beginning until shortly after the composer's death. Second, his works were recorded not only during his lifetime, by himself and by many of his friends or colleagues, but also, mainly by colleagues, after his death and up to the present time. In other words these recordings, over 75 years, span virtually the entire history of recorded sound as well as almost all of the technical procedures successively employed from the beginning of the century until 1988, from piano rolls and acoustical recordings to digital records and compact discs; this second aspect, of qualitative and historical interest, is the object of the present study.

Any select discography, which generally points out the best available performances, can be controversial; the choices are subjective, varying widely from one critic to another, and the continual appearance of new recordings calls for a constant reevaluation. This study, on the contrary, dealing with the history of recording, has two characteristics which eliminate these difficulties: on the one hand, the unique, irreplaceable, and often exceptional quality of the performance under consideration, be it by Ravel himself or by professional interpreters, friends, or colleagues working closely with the composer. On the other hand, the practically definitive and immutable character of the study: some 50 years after the composer's death it seems unlikely that the very few friends or colleagues of Ravel still alive will make further recordings.

Excessive importance should not be attached to the fact that Ravel was acquainted with many of the interpreters of his works; but in view of the proliferation of versions, a connecting thread which ties the composer to his interpreter in a historical context permits the selection of recordings which have, for the most part, a certain quality of authenticity. Moreover, some of these recordings are listed in contemporary guides to recorded classical music, happily confirming the notion that some of these versions are exemplary, if not authoritative, for all time and in all places.

In 1988, a new digital filtering system was perfected, which allows older recordings to be reproduced with astonishing technical quality: surface noises, clicks, scratches, etc. have been eliminated. This process of restoration will no doubt be applied to the most important historical documents in this catalogue. Philips has introduced this system, and has produced two "No Noise" reissues of Ravel's works with the composer performing.

3. Ravel's Activities on Behalf of Recorded Music

Maurice Ravel's interest in recorded music was manifested not only by the personal role he played in the recording of his works, but also by his active participation in several committees or juries. In 1928, Ravel agreed to join the "French Committee for the Diffusion of Musical Studies through the Duo-Art." The "Musical Studies" were illustrated and descriptive player piano rolls ("Audiographic Music"), "annotated with a pedagogical purpose," by well-known musicians such as Nadia Boulanger, Maurice Emmanuel, Paul Le Flem, Roger-Ducasse, Louis Aubert, etc. Besides Ravel, the Duo-Art committee included Charles-Marie Widor, Henri Rabaud, Gabriel Pierné, Alfred Bruneau, André Messager, Isidor Philipp, Paul Paray, Philippe Gaubert, and Henri Busser. (This information appears on the rolls in question, which are in the private collection of Jean Touzelet.)

> In November, 1929, at the request of the President of Thomson, the doyen of French companies which manufacture electrical products, Ravel agreed to form a Music Committee with Gabriel Pierné and Reynaldo Hahn, a genuine committee of experts which today (1952) consists of Messieurs Arthur Honegger, Jacques Ibert, and Francis Poulenc. The committee's purpose was to follow the work of engineers closely, and to assist them with their criticism and suggestions. This brought about close cooperation between the engineers and the artists, whose role is to compose or interpret music. . . . Curious about everything, and passionately

attentive to the exploration of sonorous phenomena, Ravel welcomed and followed the progress of recorded music with great interest. The kindness and simplicity of his manner immediately won him the respect of the phonograph engineers and technicians, who were astonished by the infallible sureness of his ear, and who received extremely precious advice from him."

(Jean Dunoyer, *Guide français du disque, 1946–1952*, Paris, 1952, p. 861. Ravel had a Thomson phonograph installed at Montfort l'Amaury in 1931; see letter no. 329. See appendix G for his personal record collection.)

In 1931, Ravel agreed to be a member of the "Grand Prix du Disque" jury, which met for the first time in Paris. Ravel participated as a member of the jury each year, except 1934, when he "was absent from Paris and excused himself." In 1936, Ravel's name no longer appears on the list of jury members. (Issues of April, May, and June, 1931–36, *L'Edition musicale vivante* and *Revue des machines parlantes*.) A photograph which appeared in 1933 showed a group of people around a phonograph for the home, with the following legend: "Some members of the Grand Prix du Disque jury; Messieurs Maurice Ravel, Louis Lumière, Gustave Charpentier, Emile Vuillermoz, and Mme Colette." (*Miroir du monde*, no. 162, April 8, 1933, p. 58.)

4. The Nature of the Recordings

ROLLOGRAPHY

A piano roll is a roll of perforated paper reproducing the perforations of an original roll (matrix), made between 1911 and 1933 (with regard to Ravel), during a performance on an ordinary piano, but one equipped with a special recording device. These rolls, placed on an appropriate reading mechanism inserted in an ordinary piano, restore the original interpretation of the pianist (the keys are activated inside the piano by a complex pneumatic system). There are two types of these rolls.

The player piano roll is the more sophisticated, the expressive nuances being automatic. If the mechanism is correctly regulated—and the piano properly tuned—a precise reproduction of the original performance is obtained without any intervention. Most of the great composers and eminent pianists at the beginning of the century recorded on such rolls, and praised them.

The ordinary piano roll, with manual nuances, reproduces the artist's performance but without the nuances or the soft pedal. The nuances chosen by the original interpreter are graphically indicated from "ppp" to "fff" on the roll as it gradually unrolls, and must be realized by a person operating the handles placed on the exterior of the piano.

Developed at the beginning of this century, these pianos, called "mechanical," achieved great success from 1905 to 1928. All of the important piano manufacturers, including Steinway, agreed to incorporate reading mechanisms for piano rolls in all of their models, from uprights to concert grands. These instruments, nevertheless, became obsolete about 1930, owing to several unfavorable circumstances: the making of records and their sound reproduction by a new electrical procedure, the beginning of public radio, the appearance of sound pictures, and, finally, the great world-wide economic crisis, all of which sounded the death knell for this amazing and fascinating invention.

DISCOGRAPHY

When a recording is listed without further specification, it is a record. Details of speed, diameter etc. are given as follows:

80 rpm – 78 rpm – 45 rpm – 33 rpm: the speed of a record's rotation is expressed in revolutions per minute (33 rpm unless otherwise stated), except for compact discs (500 to 200 rpm, from the inside to the outside), which are designated by their diameter, 12 cm. Some records recorded acoustically at the beginning of the century, before the appearance of electrical recordings (about 1925), will be specified as 78 or 80 rpm "acoustic."

30 cm. – 25 cm. – 17 cm. – 12 cm. (compact disc): the diameter of a record is 30 centimeters (12 inches) unless otherwise stated.

DA – AD etc.: for certain disks which utilize techniques new in the 1980s, the following specifications appear; DA: digital recording, analogue mastering (on 30 cm. microgroove records using conventional reproducing equipment); and AD: analogue recording, digital mastering (on 12 cm. compact discs with laser-optical scanning). Several cases of AD are pointed out in which the reproduction D (of A) is longer than A, when normally the duration of D should be the same as A. The difference may be (1) insignificant: for example, about 10 seconds more or less for a total duration of one or several works of about one hour. This is a normal tolerance, or at least an admissible one, which may be disregarded; or (2) rather significant: for example, an additional minute for a total duration of one or several works of about one hour. Generally, in these cases, the difference would most likely be due to the restoration on the compact disc of "repeats," which were cut in order to remain within the limited time available on a long-playing record. AAD: analogue recording, analogue mixing and/or editing, digital mastering; ADD: analogue mastering, digital mixing and/or editing, digital mastering.

Mono – Stereo: (1) up to and including 1954 no indication is given, as all recordings are monaural; (2) from 1955 to 1965 it is specified whether the recording is monaural or stereophonic; and (3) from 1965 to 1988 no indication is given, as all recordings are stereo (except for reissues of old recordings, originally monaural, in which case the record is specified as mono).

"No Noise" indicates a recording produced with this digital filtering system (see p. 527).

In order not to overburden the discography, certain recordings which were reissued one or more times, occasionally with different couplings and with different references in various countries, and which may be reissued again, will not be listed systematically, either for all these diverse references, past and present, or for the issue and reissue of the same version. On the other hand, when an interpreter, alone, or with the same orchestra, the same artists or accompanists, recorded the same work several times,

subsequent versions are indicated, making it possible to distinguish the different recordings.

In order to acquire a particular recording, it is essential to furnish its provenance and
basic characteristics, which should suffice for a serious record dealer; these facts may
even be more helpful than a precise numerical reference, which may no longer appear in
the catalogue, and which may cause him to overlook a reissue which is perhaps available
under a different reference.

FILMOGRAPHY, VIDEOGRAPHY

Rare sound films have been produced of performances of Ravel's works given by the
composer himself and by interpreters who knew him (Ernest Ansermet, Jacques Février,
Lily Laskine, Jean Martinon, Vlado Perlemuter, and Paul Wittgenstein). They include
complete or partial performances of a work; one of them, the Ansermet film, contains an
orchestral rehearsal which precedes a public performance of *La Valse.*

It should be mentioned that three of these documents (Wittgenstein and Ravel,
excerpts of Février and Martinon) appear in the most important film ever undertaken on
the life and works of Maurice Ravel, realized by RTB (Belgian Radio and Television)
from 1973 to 1975 by Alain Denis and Paul Danblon. This film, entitled *Maurice Ravel,
l'homme et les sortilèges,* includes interviews with twenty-six people who knew Ravel
(interpreters listed in this study, four of whom gave premières of his works, friends,
colleagues), many of whom are no longer living. This exceptional document, lasting 4
hours and 30 minutes, was broadcast by RTB on the occasion of the centenary of
Ravel's birth, in three programs of 90 minutes each, on October 17, 24, and 31,
1975.

Another outstanding television documentary, *Ravel* (1 hour and 43 minutes, 1987),
was directed by Niv Fichman and Larry Weinstein for Rhombus Media, Toronto. Im-
portant places in Ravel's career are shown, interspersed with performances by Charles
Dutoit conducting the Montreal Symphony (*La Valse*), pianist Alicia de Larrocha (the G
Major Concerto), and others, interviews with colleagues of Ravel, among them Gaby
Casadesus and Manuel Rosenthal, and rare black and white footage of the composer.
This documentary has been shown throughout Europe, Asia, and North America.

5. Sources

Private collection of Jean Touzelet: piano rolls, records, and video cassettes (containing
virtually all of the recordings cited), catalogues, literature, documents and various
manuscripts concerning Ravel, some of which are unpublished or practically unknown. This private collection of piano rolls, records, and video cassettes has been
willed to the Phonothèque Nationale.

Bibliothèque Nationale and Phonothèque Nationale, Paris

F. F. Clough and G. J. Cuming, *World's Encyclopedia of Recorded Music,* London, 1950,
1951, 1952, 1956

R. D. Darrell, ed., *The Gramophone Shop Encyclopedia of Recorded Music*, New York, 1936, 1942, 1948

Diapason, Paris, 1956–87
L'Edition musicale vivante, Paris, 1928–34
Musique et instruments, Paris, 1910–29
Revue des machines parlantes, Paris, 1929–37
Revue disques, Paris, 1948–62
Revue Pleyel, Paris, 1923–27
The Musical Courier, New York, 1919–25
The Musical Digest, New York, 1925–30
Schwann Record & Tape Guide, Boston, 1949–88
The Gramophone, London, 1923–87
The Musical Times, London, 1921–39
Bielefelder, Germany, 1983–86
Die Musik, Berlin, 1927–39

6. Abbreviations

AD	analogue recording, digital mastering	Ger	Germany
arr.	arranged	HMV	His Master's Voice
DA	digital recording, analogue mastering	iss.	issued
		rec.	recorded
		rpm	revolutions per minute
Fr	France	US	United States
GB	Great Britain	VSM	La Voix de son Maître

7. Ravel's Own Interpretations

Maurice Ravel himself participated in recording some of his works in various capacities, (a) as a pianist, (b) as a conductor of an orchestra or (c) a chamber ensemble, or (d) by personally supervising recordings realized in his presence by other interpreters.

In this section, an attempt has been made to clarify in an objective and exhaustive manner the delicate question of Ravel's actual degree of participation in some of these recordings.

RAVEL AS PIANIST

It appears that, as a pianist, Ravel recorded only player piano rolls, although he was on occasion incorrectly named as the accompanist in three of his songs sung by Madeleine Grey (see pp. 537 and 541).

The first series of two recordings for player piano (rec. Autumn 1913, Paris), was realized for the German firm Welte, the first to have invented a player piano with automatic expressive nuances:

Sonatine (1st and 2d movements only)
1914   Player piano roll, Welte-Mignon (Ger) 2187

Valses nobles et sentimentales
1914   Player piano roll, Welte-Mignon (Ger) 2188

In an interview given in January 1958, shortly before his death, Edwin Welte, the former director of the Welte firm, specified that recordings were normally realized in Germany, in either Freiburg or Leipzig, but that "for some 'lions' like Debussy and Ravel," he had technicians and equipment sent to Paris (*High Fidelity*—US, June 1958). No commentary on these recordings has come down to us, to my knowledge, except for a letter from Debussy to Edwin Welte, written in Paris on November 1, 1913: "It is impossible to achieve greater perfection than the reproduction given by Welte instruments. What I have heard leaves me astonished." (This letter appears in facsimile in the official register of the Welte firm.)

Taking these circumstances into account, together with the fact that the most difficult movement of the Sonatine was not recorded when the maximum duration of a roll easily permitted it, there is no reason to doubt that Ravel indeed made these recordings.

These two rolls have been reproduced on records:

Valses nobles et sentimentales
1950   Columbia (US) ML4291 (Great Masters of the Keyboard, vol. 1), reproduced
          in Germany in 1948 under the supervision of Edwin Welte
1971   Superscope (US) KBI9—Klavier (US) KBI41072S (Great Composers Play
          their own Works), reproduced in the US

Sonatine (1st and 2nd movements) – *Valses nobles et sentimentales*
1964   Mono Telefunken (Ger) HT34, (US) TEL34, (GB) GMA79; reproduced in
          Germany in 1957 under the supervision of Edwin Welte
1964   Stereo Welte (US) 663 (The Welte Legacy of Piano Treasures), reproduced
          in the US

These realizations on records are fine, particularly the latter, but now technically obsolete and very difficult to find. It would be desirable to issue a new recording utilizing modern techniques.

: : :

On May 15, 1920, in Saint-Cloud, Ravel signed two copies of a contract with the English firm Aeolian, (subsidiary of the American firm Aeolian–Duo-Art) one in French, the other in English. He was engaged exclusively as a pianist to make at least ten recordings of his works for the Duo-Art player piano, to be realized and corrected in London. The Aeolian company agreed to pay Ravel £50 for each recording, and the records were made in London on June 30, 1922 (see appendix E).

In fact it appears that only five recordings were made, which were issued over a period of six years. It is possible that five others were rejected, either by Ravel or by the Aeolian Company, or were not issued. In the latter case they must be considered lost, for it is unlikely that they can be recovered after a period of more than sixty years. Indeed for many years, an English collector has attempted to find and purchase all of the English Duo-Art matrixes which were never issued. He now possesses over 100 of these unissued Duo-Art rolls, and he has informed me that there is no Ravel among them. Reginald Reynolds, the English technician who realized all the Duo-Art recordings in London for the Aeolian Company, photographed and filmed eighteen celebrated composers or pianists at their recording sessions. I have been assured by Roger Buckley of the Player Piano Group that, unfortunately, Ravel is not among them (reply from London, June 5, 1979).

Several of Ravel's letters confirm that he had appealed to a better pianist than himself to perform the most difficult pieces. In two letters to Calvocoressi he wrote: "You can reassure Mr. Mead . . . I'm presently working on 5 piano pieces . . . am busy finding a better pianist than myself for the 5 others, and will have everything ready for the month of June" (letter dated March 24, 1922, no. 191); and "Didn't you remember that Casadesus has asked that it be towards the end of June? I'm therefore planning our arrival for the 29th . . . The records can be made on the 30th" (letter dated June 9, 1922). These letters establish that it was Robert Casadesus, in preference to Richard Viñes, who accompanied Ravel to London and assisted him on June 30, 1922, probably interpreting the "Toccata" and "Le Gibet" in his place and under his supervision.

Robert Casadesus subsequently confided this to several people (testimony of Jean-Michel Nectoux), and Madame Gaby Casadesus, the pianist's wife, on hearing the five Ravel Duo-Art rolls on the author's piano in 1981, recognized her husband's performance in the "Toccata" and "Le Gibet"; she indicated that Ravel's hands were too small for certain chords in these pieces. She remained undecided about "La Vallée des cloches," but recognized Ravel's performance in the *Pavane pour une Infante défunte* and "Oiseaux tristes." Ravel frequently performed these last three pieces in public but a program listing his performance of the "Toccata" and "Le Gibet" has yet to be traced.

The commercial rolls of all five pieces are, however, autographed and presented as reproducing Ravel's own interpretation. The English edition bears the following statement: "This roll is a correct reproduction of my performance," and is followed by Ravel's printed signature. The American edition states: "This Music Roll is my interpretation. It was recorded by me for the Duo-Art and I hereby authorize its use with that instrument" and is signed "M.R.":

"Oiseaux tristes" (*Miroirs*)

1922 Player piano roll, Duo-Art (GB, Fr) 082; Duo-Art Audiographic (roll annotated with an explanatory introduction by Paul Le Flem) (GB) D929, (Fr) DF477; ordinary piano roll, Pianola (GB) D930

Pavane pour une Infante défunte

1922 Player piano roll, Duo-Art (GB, Fr) 084; Duo-Art Audiographic (roll annotated with an explanatory introduction by Maurice Emmanuel) (GB) D283, (Fr) DF283; ordinary piano roll, Pianola (GB) D284

"Toccata" (*Le Tombeau de Couperin*)
1922   Player piano roll, Duo-Art (GB, Fr) 086; Duo-Art Audiographic (roll
       annotated with an explanatory introduction by Maurice Emmanuel) (GB)
       D213, (Fr) DF213; ordinary piano roll, Pianola (GB) D214

"Le Gibet" (*Gaspard de la nuit*)
1925   Player piano roll, Duo-Art (GB, Fr) 0219; Duo-Art Audiographic (roll
       annotated with an explanatory introduction by Percy A. Scholes) (GB)
       D921; ordinary piano roll, Pianola (GB) D922

"La Vallée des cloches" (*Miroirs*)
1928   Player piano roll, Duo-Art (US) 72750

These five rolls have been reproduced on records twice, utilizing a special Duo-Art
piano; one, an analogue recording in 1965, the other digital, in 1984. A third, partial
recording was also made in 1965.

"Oiseaux tristes" – *Pavane pour une Infante défunte* – "Toccata" – "Le Gibet" – "La
Vallée des cloches"
1967   Everest, Archives of piano music (US) X912 (1983), Everest (US) 3403
       (1976), Vogue Contrepoint (Fr) CMC20186 (1968), Ember (GB) GCV39
       (1975), Eurodisk (Ger) 27487XAK (1976) (1983)—rec. 1965
1985   DA: Klavier Digital Audiophile (US) KD137—rec. 1984

Pavane pour une Infante défunte – "La Vallée des cloches"
       Turnabout-Vox (US) TV4256 (1969)—rec. 1965

On these recordings, the "Toccata" is not the exact reproduction of Ravel's performance, or rather Casadesus' performance approved of by the composer. Indeed, this
piece is abnormally long (4′45 in the 1965 recording, and 4′26 in the 1984 recording).
But the original roll has a printed tempo of 100, and played this way on my Steinway
Duo-Art piano, the "Toccata" lasts 3′45, the usual duration, which incidentally corresponds exactly with the duration of the piece as performed by Robert Casadesus in the
recorded set of Ravel's complete piano works (see p. 551).

All of the pieces in the new 1984 version are of shorter duration than those in the
1965 version (24′49 as opposed to 25′55).

RAVEL AS ORCHESTRAL CONDUCTOR

Boléro (15′50)
       Orchestre de l'Association des Concerts Lamoureux
1930   78 rpm, Polydor (Fr) 566030/1, Polydor-Grammophon (Ger) 66947/8,
       Polydor (Hungary) 66947/8, Decca (GB) CA8015/6, Brunswick (US)
       90039/40, Vox (US) 12012/3, set 167, Fonit (Italy) 96047/8—rec. Jan.
       1930, Paris; iss. March
       33 rpm, 25 cm., Polydor (Fr) 540008 (1955)
       33 rpm, 30 cm., Turnabout-Vox (US) TV4256 (1969)

33 rpm, 17 cm., Philips (Fr) in the set "Grande Anthologie Ravel" 8 records, 6747178 (1975) (1983).

1986 Claremont (GB) 785018 (Digitally remastered electronic stereo)—iss. Sept.

All of these records mention on their label: "under the direction of M. Ravel." One contemporaneous account, published the same month as the recording, confirms Ravel's direction in detail. In *L'Edition musicale vivante* (Jan., 1930, p. 15), edited by Emile Vuillermoz, the "monthly review of recorded music," signed by "Evariste," relates how the recording of the *Boléro* came about:

The Lamoureux Orchestra was assembled . . . on stage, the watchful eye of Albert Wolff . . . the orchestra plays, stops, Wolff rushes to the recording booth . . . Maurice Ravel is there, conscientious and precise, listening: "Not enough in the trumpets, too much celesta"; Wolff returns to the podium and gives the order. The horns are moved, a space is cleared in front of the oboes, and they begin again. After each attempt, the composer returns from the recording booth . . . he shakes his head, approving or disapproving. . . . After a number of attempts, the exact expression is achieved. Wolff gives his baton to Ravel. It is the composer indeed who is going to preside over the recording of this disk. Ravel gives the downbeat. With rigid gestures, his wrist traces the three beats which, in a mechanical way, govern this melody in C. . . . Everything goes well. Wolff indicates his keen satisfaction with a silent gesture. The instrumentalists hold their breath impatiently, waiting for the little green light bulb, which calls for silence, to be turned off. But Ravel, pleased with the results obtained, throws his baton on the score with relief, making a loud noise. A cry of horror emanates from the booth. They begin from the beginning. The performance is once again excellent. After the last chord, Ravel looks at the green eyeball, and waits for the eyelid to close before putting down his scepter with infinite care. They attack the next side. . . .

The *Menuet antique* was also recorded in the course of the same session, conducted by Albert Wolff.

: : :

Concerto for Piano and Orchestra in G
Marguerite Long, piano, Symphonic Orchestra
1932 78 rpm, Columbia (Fr) LFX257/9, LFX8114/6, (GB) LX194/6, (US) 68064/6D, set 176, (Australia) LOX271/3, (Italy) GQX10676/8, Odéon (Ger) 09413/5, 50239/41—rec. April 1932, Paris; iss. June
33 rpm, Columbia (Fr) COLC319 (1966), Seraphin (US) set 1C6043, Angel (Japan) GR2171 (1966) (1983), World Records (GB) SH209 (1975). VSM (Fr) 2C05116349M (1980) (Fr–GB 1983)

The label on these disks indicates "under the direction of M. Ravel." For this recording two authorized witnesses have been found who agree that it was Pedro de Freitas-Branco who actually conducted in Ravel's place, with the composer's active participation so that the recorded performance would fully conform to his views. On the other hand, these two witnesses disagree about the conductor of the *Pavane,* which was recorded at the same session. It is not difficult, however, to resolve the contradiction.

In her book, *Marguerite Long: Une Vie fascinante* (Paris: Julliard, 1969, p. 131), the pianist Janine Weill, a pupil and close friend of the interpreter of Ravel's concerto writes:

> Marguerite Long recalled a delightful incident at the recording sessions of the concerto in 1932. It had been decided that Ravel would conduct, but in the studio, Pedro de Freitas-Branco substituted for him, and only the *Pavane pour une Infante défunte* was conducted by the composer. Ravel was in the recording booth. He was pitiless, Marguerite Long said, and she added: "by two or three o'clock in the morning I was exhausted. Finally, it was done . . . When Ravel came out of the booth, ordering: we have to begin again! I could have killed him; nevertheless, I obeyed."

In an interview with J.-M. Nectoux (Jan. 24, 1982, preserved on tape in the archives of the Phonothèque Nationale), Jean Bérard, then artistic director of Columbia records in France, recalled:

> We recorded Ravel's G Major Concerto with Marguerite Long. Freitas-Branco actually conducted, as Ravel conducted poorly. The orchestra was composed of the best Parisian soloists. Ravel was present. The concerto took up five sides of three 78 rpm records. We decided to fill the remaining sixth side with the *Pavane.* Freitas-Branco asked Ravel, "Maître, would you indicate the tempo?" Ravel took the beginning so slowly, I estimated that the performance would last 6 to 7 minutes, when the maximum time possible on a 12-inch side was 4 minutes and 30 seconds. I took Ravel aside and suggested that we go to have a drink, to which he readily agreed. I took him to a bistro near the recording studio on rue Albert. When we returned, Freitas-Branco had already completed the record. A wax proof was replayed, which Ravel approved of, saying "it's perfect." It was 4 minutes and 32 seconds, which was just right.

Thus, there is no ambiguity: Freitas-Branco conducted the Concerto and the *Pavane,* with Ravel's active supervision and his final approbation.

: : :

Concerto for Piano and Orchestra in D, "For the Left Hand"
Paul Wittgenstein, piano; l'Orchestre Symphonique de Paris, music director, Pierre Monteux, conductor, Maurice Ravel

This sound film was realized by the cameramen of "Pathé-Journal" News and consisted of excerpts of a public performance (the première in France) on January 17, 1933. This took place in Salle Pleyel, Paris, with the Austrian pianist Paul Wittgenstein, who had commissioned the work (with exclusivity for 6 years), and to whom the

Concerto is dedicated (see pp. 593–595). This film was included in the "Pathé-Journal" News, which was shown in Pathé theaters throughout France in the last ten days of January 1933.

The spectacular star of this film is unquestionably the one-armed pianist, filmed with his empty right sleeve tucked into the pocket of his jacket; Ravel is at a disadvantage because, owing to the limited flexibility of the cameras, his face and body are hidden by the open top of the concert grand. But the essential point has been preserved, and it is possible to observe the conductor's gestures, which are perfectly visible. Throughout the film, Ravel's hands and arms can be seen keeping time, baton in the right hand, the left hand when necessary turning the pages of the score placed on a stand. The composer, thus, did not conduct from memory.

RAVEL AS CONDUCTOR OF CHAMBER ENSEMBLES

Introduction et Allegro
Miss Gwendolen Mason, harp; Robert Murcie, flute; Haydn P. Draper, clarinet; and
    string quartet (Charles Woodhouse, Mr. Dinsey, violins; Ernest Tomlinson, viola;
    Mr. James, cello)
1924   80 rpm acoustic, Columbia (GB) L1518/9, (US) 67091/2D (4 sides)—rec.
            1923, London. The label on the disk indicates: "Ravel Septet (*Introduction
            et Allegro*) conducted by the composer."

Chansons madécasses
Madeleine Grey, mezzo-soprano, accompanied by piano, flute, and cello
1932   78 rpm, 25 cm., Polydor (Fr) 561076/7, Brunswick (US) 85032/3, Vox (US)
            16035/6 set 186 (4 sides)—rec. Sept. 1932, Paris; iss. Nov.
        33 rpm, 25 cm., Polydor (Fr) 540008 (1955)
        33 rpm, 30 cm., Columbia (Fr) FCX50038 (1964), Angel (US) COLC152
            (1965), Turnabout-Vox (US) TV4256 (1969), World Records (GB) SH196
            (1974) (1983)
        ADD: 12 cm. (compact disc), Philips (Fr, Ger) 420778-2 (remastered
            according to the No Noise procedure (1988)

The labels on the original disks indicate "under the direction of M. Maurice Ravel." The names of the instrumentalists do not appear on the labels or in record catalogues. Questioned about this in 1973, Madeleine Grey told me that she didn't remember very well, but thought that "the flutist must have been René Leroy, soloist of the Conservatoire" (the orchestra). Two photographs of the recording session, which appeared in the Polydor monthly supplement of November 1932, show that Ravel was conducting, and not at the piano, as some reissues indicate (Turnabout).

Ravel wrote the following dedication to M.G. on a photo of himself: "For Madeleine Grey, the perfect interpreter of the *Madécasses* . . . among others, Maurice Ravel." (Document furnished and publication authorized by M.G. in Roger Nichols', *Ravel*, London, Dent, 1977. See Ravel's letter to M.G. on p. 315.)

RAVEL AS SUPERVISOR OF RECORDINGS

String Quartet

Galimir Quartet of Vienna (Felix Galimir, 1st violin and his three sisters, Adrienne, Renée, and Marguerite Galimir. Only the initials of the first names appear on the disks; the full names and the relationship of the participants are taken from an interview with Felix Galimir in the *New York Times,* Jan. 11, 1981).

1934   78 rpm, Polydor (Fr) 516578/80, (Ger) 27329/31, Decca (GB) LY6105/7, Brunswick (US) 90411/3 (6 sides—no reissues on 33 rpm). The label on the disks indicates "under the direction of Maurice Ravel"—rec. 1934, Paris; iss. Nov.

In his book of recollections, *On cherche jeune homme aimant la musique* ("Seeking young man who loves music," Paris: Calman-Lévy, 1978, p. 19), Jacques Canetti writes:

The Galimir Quartet also came to Paris. They were friends whom I had known in Vienna. I proposed to Polydor that they record Ravel's Quartet. Ravel agreed to come to supervise the sessions. One afternoon sufficed. In the recording booth, opposite me, he didn't utter a word. Then he said gently: "It's really very good: who wrote it?" His housekeeper said to me on the telephone: "Take a taxi, Monsieur Canetti, and bring him back immediately, he'll feel better."

At my request, Felix Galimir was interviewed in New York in December 1983, by Arbie Orenstein. He stated the following:

I met Ravel in Vienna in 1934. When we recorded his Quartet for Polydor, Ravel and Jacques Canetti were present. Ravel did not conduct, but stayed in the recording booth acting as a sort of "judge." He said "Yes, it's good," or he disapproved. We relistened to the wax proofs with him, and started over several times. Ravel occasionally made some comments, and indeed supervised the recording.

Without entering into a polemic, we may simply state that several of Ravel's interpreters have related that despite the progression of his illness, much of his "musical" lucidity was preserved intact (see Martial Singher's letter in appendix A). Madeleine Grey (in *La Revue musicale,* Dec., 1938, p. 178) recalled:

Ravel came to my home a few months before his death so that I might sing *Don Quichotte à Dulcinée* for him, accompanied by Francis Poulenc. When I had finished, I asked for his advice. He seemed preoccupied, and one might have thought he was hardly aware of what he had just heard. Then, he made a very precise observation, correcting a minuscule rhythmic liberty which Poulenc and I had allowed ourselves. He had noticed this slight alteration in his music.

: : :

String Quartet

The International String Quartet (André Mangeot, Boris Pecker, Frank Howard, Herbert Withers)

1927   80 rpm, National Gramophonic Society (GB) NGS78/81 (7 sides)—rec. June
       1927, London; iss. Sept.

The labels on these records indicate "interpretation of the composer," and printed
below is the signature of Maurice Ravel. André Mangeot, the founding violinist of the
I.S.Q. was an old friend of Ravel (he appears in the composer's address book; there is
correspondence dating from 1913).

In an article entitled "The Ravel String Quartet," which appeared in the English
journal *The Gramophone* (Sept., 1927, pp. 138–39), Mangeot recalled that he and his
colleagues had recorded the Ravel Quartet twice, but the results were not completely
satisfactory:

> Luckily for me Ravel himself came to London just then. . . . He consented to hear
> the records that we had made, and he heard them in a little cubicle at the Aeolian
> Hall, which was soon thick with cigarette smoke. I had the score with me, and as the
> records were played he marked it wherever there was an effect or a tempo that he
> wanted altered. It was very interesting. He is most precise—he knows exactly what
> he wants—how, in his mind, that quartet, every bar of it, ought to sound. So, armed
> with such final authority, we had another recording at the studio, and my colleagues
> and I rehearsed hard for it over those little details.

Several days later, Mangeot visited Ravel at Le Belvédère and played the new recorded
version for him:

> He was much pleased with the records, which we listened to from the terrace. . . .
> The old cook gave us a very simple and perfect dinner (Ravel is a firm bachelor),
> and we left him at 10:30 after a delightful visit, and afterwards he wrote the
> charming letter of appreciation which authorises us to call our records of the
> Quartet an "interpretation of the composer." Not only do I regard this as one of the
> finest compliments ever paid to our quartet, but, as Ravel said to me, "It will
> constitute a real document for posterity to consult, and through gramophone
> records composers can now say definitely how they meant their works to be
> performed.

Ravel's letter of appreciation, reproduced in facsimile in Mangeot's article, reads as
follows:

Le Belvédère   July 18, 1927
Montfort l'Amaury (S. & O.)
    I have just heard the disks of my Quartet recorded by the International String
Quartet. I am completely satisfied, as much with the sonority as with the tempi and
the nuances.
    Maurice Ravel

This recording was realized by a small, independent, and short-lived English company.
Despite the article in *The Gramophone,* the recording had a limited and local diffusion
(no foreign edition, nor any reissue on 33 rpm). Yet it appears to be "the composer's

interpretation" which is most authentic, supervised by Ravel, then in full command of his faculties, and presented by him as "a document to consult."

: : :

Boléro (15′30)
Grand Orchestre Symphonique, Piero Coppola, conductor
1930   78 rpm, Gramophone (Fr) w1067/8, Victor (US) 13659/60 set M793,
       13661/2 set DM793, Electrola (Ger) EJ551/2 (4 sides)—rec. Jan. 1930,
       Paris

In his book of memoirs, *Dix-Sept ans de musique à Paris 1922–1939* (Lausanne: F. Rouge, 1944, pp. 105–08), Piero Coppola, conductor and artistic director of the Gramophone Company, wrote:

> I asked for the authorization to record the *Boléro* from Durand (the publisher), then from Ravel; the composer replied that he had been engaged to conduct this work himself with the Lamoureux Orchestra, but he could give me satisfaction by being present at my recording session. Maurice Ravel, who honored me with his esteem and friendship, did not have confidence in me for the *Boléro.* He was afraid that my Mediterranean temperament would overtake me, and that I would rush the tempo. I assembled my orchestra in Salle Pleyel, and Ravel took a seat behind me. Everything went well until the final part, where, in spite of myself, I increased the tempo by a fraction. Ravel jumped up, came over and pulled at my jacket: "not so fast," he exclaimed, and we had to begin again. We finally managed to satisfy him and the recording was completed. He signed the autograph book of the company (Gramophone), which bears the date of the recording, and which specifies "first recording of the *Boléro.*" He then wrote a dedication on my personal score, with touching and charming simplicity, which gives me fond memories of this great Maître and friend. The next day, he conducted his *Boléro* for a competing firm, whose disks and ours were enthusiastically received by record lovers.

Once again, this may be considered an authentic "version of the composer," almost in the same way as Ravel's own recording of the *Boléro.* Coppola also observed:

> Maurice Ravel never hid the fact that he desired, indeed demanded that the interpreters of his *Boléro* conform *strictly* to his wish, which was to perform the *Boléro* in the tempo indicated in the printed score, without varying this tempo one iota until the end. He believed that the "crescendo" would come about by itself, thanks to the orchestration, and the effect that he desired above all was precisely this almost hallucinatory insistence of an immutable tempo. . . . The *Boléro* is *the easiest piece to conduct* because one beats in three from beginning to end, like an automaton. . . . That the *Boléro* is extremely easy to conduct was demonstrated by the fact that even Ravel, who was not at ease on the podium, conducted his work with no difficulty, obtaining the same success as if it had been conducted by a master of the baton.

It must be pointed out that Ravel's own score of the *Boléro*, formerly at his home in Montfort l'Amaury and now in the Music Division of the Bibliothèque Nationale, contains one annotation: the printed tempo indication, $\sqrt{ } = 76$, is crossed out by the composer and replaced by $\sqrt{ } = 66$. (The latter tempo indication is observed by Ravel in his recording of the *Boléro* with the Lamoureux Orchestra.) Later printings of the *Boléro*, however, suggest $\sqrt{ } = 72$.

Four recordings of the *Boléro* made in 1930 by Ravel himself and three celebrated conductors have lengths as follows: Ravel (15'50), Coppola under Ravel's supervision (15'40), Mengelberg (14'35), and Koussevitzky (13'20). It seems therefore that the proper length of the *Boléro* is about 15'30 to 16 minutes. Precise timings of the *Boléro* performances are given in this appendix. The slowest performance is conducted by Pedro de Freitas-Branco (18'25) and the quickest by Paul Paray (13'00).

A final curiosity: consultation of the monthly Schwann catalogue, the "World's First and Most Consulted Guide," reveals that the composition in any category which has the largest number of different recorded versions is Ravel's *Boléro*, with more than 40 available recordings. (The *Boléro* is followed closely by Beethoven's "Moonlight" Sonata.)

: : :

Menuet antique
Lamoureux Orchestra, Albert Wolff, conductor
1930   78 rpm, Polydor (Fr) 566032, (Ger) 66972, Brunswick (US) 90099 (2 sides). This recording was made at the same session (January 1930, Paris) as *Boléro*

Pavane pour une Infante défunte
Symphonic Orchestra, P. de Freitas-Branco, conductor; horn solo: M. J. Devemy (written on the label of the record)
1932   This record is the sixth side of the G Major Piano Concerto—rec. April 1932, Paris; iss. June

Trois chants hébraïques ("Kaddisch"; "L'Enigme éternelle"; "Chanson hébraïque") Madeleine Grey, mezzo-soprano, with piano accompaniment
1932   78 rpm, 25 cm., Polydor (Fr) 561075, (Ger) 62706, Decca (GB) P05066, Brunswick (US) 85022, Vox (US) 16034 set 186 (2 sides). The recording was made in Ravel's presence and under his supervision on the same day and during the same session as the *Chansons madécasses*—rec. Sept. 1932; iss. Nov.
1983   33 rpm, 30 cm., Columbia (Fr) FCX50038, Angel (US) COLC152, World Records (GB) SH196

Although M.R. frequently accompanied M.G. at the piano, in this case it is likely that the accompaniment was provided by the unnamed pianist in the *Chansons madécasses*. The original issue and the French reissues of this record, as well as contemporaneous catalogues, only mention "with piano accompaniment." This should be noted because certain foreign issues of this record (particularly the British on 78 and 33 rpm) erroneously mention: "with piano accompaniment by Maurice Ravel."

Don Quichotte à Dulcinée – Ronsard à son âme
Martial Singher, baritone, orchestra conducted by Piero Coppola
1935   78 rpm, 25 cm., Gramophone (Fr) DA4865/6, Victor (US) 4404/5—rec.
        Nov. 20, 1934, Paris (see Martial Singher's letter in appendix A)

Piero Coppola wrote that Ravel, for his part, "made an effort to be present at the session during which Martial Singher of the Opéra, accompanied by my orchestra, recorded the three *Don Quichotte* songs and *Ronsard à son âme,* with a very simple orchestral version which he [Ravel] had carried out for this occasion and which sounds marvelously." (*Dix-Sept ans de musique à Paris,* p. 188.) Arbie Orenstein (*Ravel: Man and Musician,* p. 107) writes: "Incapable of notating the score, Ravel had dictated the transcription [of *Ronsard à son âme*] to Manuel Rosenthal and Lucien Garban."

   This recording was made ten days before the première of *Don Quichotte a Dulcinée,* which took place on December 1, 1934, with Martial Singher and the Colonne Orchestra conducted by Paul Paray. *Ronsard à son âme* was introduced on February 17, 1935, with Martial Singher and the Pasdeloup Orchestra conducted by Piero Coppola, as part of a Ravel festival organized by Coppola.

8. Eighty-Seven Interpreters and Their Recordings

The following list of interpreters of Ravel's music is presented alphabetically. Each name (subsequently designated by initials) is followed by dates and on the next line by the area in which the musician performed: as conductor, player, or singer. The nature of Ravel's relationship with the performer in question, in so far as it can be established with certainty, is then given as follows:

Address book: an interpreter's name appears in Ravel's address book, written in his hand; name, address, perhaps telephone number, or other details.
Correspondence: there was an exchange of letters with Ravel.
Photograph(s): an interpreter appears in one photograph or more with Ravel.
Friendly and artistic relationship: implies a relationship with Ravel in the course of many meetings.
Artistic encounter: there was at least one artistic encounter with Ravel.

(The author would be grateful to have any important omissions or discoveries regarding documentation or information pointed out to him.)

   In each list of recordings the left margin shows the date of issue. Further information, if it is known, about where and when the recording was made and issued follows the details of the nature of the recording, the company of issue, and the designated number. If a recording is listed as available in a recent catalogue, its references are followed by the year in which the catalogue appeared.

LARRY (LAWRENCE) ADLER (b. 1914)
harmonica

Artistic encounter.

In 1935 I played Ravel's *Bolero* at the Alhambra in Paris. The musical critics veered between "formidable!" (that's good) and "sacrilège!" (that's bad) in judging my interpretation. A friend of mine, Jacques Lyon, who ran and still runs the Sinfonia record shop in the Champs Elysées, called me and said that "Le Maître" (Ravel) had asked him to bring me to his home to play the *Bolero* for him. I was honored and scared but I accepted. However, I could not see myself standing in a drawing room just playing the *Bolero* without any orchestra to help me. I decided to bring along my record, which I had made in 1934 in London. In those days I did not read music and had learned—or rather, as it turned out, mis-learned the *Bolero* by memory. We reached Montfort l'Amaury in the evening, found the house of "Le Maître", and within a minute of entering, the great man had snatched the record from me and put it on the turntable. . . . In the ensuing conversation I was quite convinced he loathed the whole thing, as he was sharply critical of the cuts I had made and the tempo I had used. I was so ill at ease that I did something I have never done before or since—I asked him if he would autograph the record for me. . . . To my amazement he said he had understood that the record was a present to him. In any case, he went on, he had palsy; he had not written a note of music for five years. I apologized, of course, and left the record with him. Three days later Jacques Lyon phoned me; "Le Maître" was at the shop and wanted to see me at once. . . . I found Ravel, heavily bundled in a greatcoat though it was a warm day, who told me that he had sat alone in a dark room for over an hour, had finally steadied his hand sufficiently to sign his name just once, and had brought this signature in to Paris for me!

Several years later I learned through his American publishers, Elkan-Vogel in Philadelphia, that he had given instructions that I had complete right to play the *Bolero* as I wished, in whatever medium, without the usual extremely expensive *droit d'auteur*.

(From the liner notes by Larry Adler for the record "Larry Adler in Concert.")

Boléro (arr. Roger Branga)
Orchestral accompaniment
1934   78 rpm, 25 cm., Columbia (GB) DB 1516, (US) 35515, set C 18, Regal-
Zonophone (GB) MR 1939, (Australia) G22413—rec. and iss. 1934,
London

Boléro (arr. Roger Branga)
"Larry Adler in Concert"
Pro-Arte Orchestra, Eric Robinson, conductor
1958   Mono: Pye (GB) CCL30125, Hamilton (US) 149—iss. London
Stereo: 25 cm., Pye (GB) CSCT71,000; 30 cm., Hamilton (US) 12149

ERNEST ANSERMET (1883–1969)
conductor

Address book—Correspondence—Photographs—Friendly and artistic relationship.

E.A. conducted the first performance of Chabrier's *Menuet pompeux* (orchestrated by Ravel) for the Ballet Russe on July 18, 1919, in London. He was supposed to conduct the première of the *Boléro:*

> Ida Rubinstein asked me to conduct the performances in which she was going to present the *Boléro.* I was at her home when Ravel came one day to play this work on the piano, which he had composed for her. Unfortunately, I could not conduct the première because of deplorable union disputes, and I had to be replaced at the last minute by Straram. . . . I met Ravel before World War I in Clarens, where he had come to work with Stravinsky. We had many conversations there. And I often saw him after the war, either in Paris with the Ballet Russe, or in Geneva, where he often came to see his uncle. One day, in Geneva, he asked me to try out certain passages of *La Valse* with the Orchestre de la Suisse Romande, before giving in his score to be printed. I was thus able to follow Ravel's creative activity closely from 1913 until the end, and we often discussed his aesthetic views, his taste, and the style and tempi of his works. (Ansermet-Piguet, *Entretiens sur la musique,* Neuchâtel, La Baconnière, 1963, pp. 34–35.)

In 1921, E.A. conducted the Geneva première of *La Valse.* Ravel was present and wrote to him in October: "Your understanding of *La Valse* is perfect. I could never get that rhythmic suppleness in Paris." E.A. has recorded the largest number of Ravel's orchestral works—20 out of 25. Many works were even recorded twice and some three times, such as *Shéhérazade, Tableaux d'une exposition,* and *La Valse,* without taking into account, for *La Valse,* the exceptional film of a rehearsal followed by a performance. The Ravel–Ansermet discography already has a record number of some 200 issues and reissues of these 20 orchestral works!

Almost all of the recordings made by E.A. and the Orchestre de la Suisse Romande were done for the English firm Decca, at Victoria Hall in Geneva (François Hudry, *Ernest Ansermet,* Lausanne, L'Aire, 1983, p. 162).

"Alborada del gracioso" (*Miroirs*)
Orchestre de la Suisse Romande. Recorded in the studio of Radio Geneva
  (mentioned on the label of the disks)
1947   78 rpm, Decca (GB) K1609, London (US) T5233, (Argentina) 346010
    33 rpm, 25 cm., Decca (GB, Fr, Ger) LW5031, LX3072, London (US) LS503,
    LD9031

La Valse
Orchestre de la Société des Concerts du Conservatoire. Recorded at Kingsway Hall
  in London (mentioned on the record label)
1947   78 rpm, Decca (GB) K1867/8, (Italy) 40086/7, London (US) T5114/5 set
    LA93
    33 rpm, London (US) LL22

Tableaux d'une exposition (Mussorgsky-Ravel)
London Philharmonic Orchestra
1948   78 rpm, Decca (GB) K1735/9, (US) set ED90

Shéhérazade
Suzanne Danco, soprano; Orchestre de la Société des Concerts du Conservatoire
1948   78 rpm, Decca (GB) K1966/7, (Fr) GAG1966/7, (US) set 100
        33 rpm, London (US) 23196.

Ma Mère l'Oye
Orchestre de la Suisse Romande
1950   78 rpm, Decca (GB) KX28459/61
        33 rpm, Decca (GB, Fr, Ger) LXT2632, London (US) LL388, Richmond (US)
        19007

Concerto for Piano and Orchestra in D, "For the Left Hand"
Jacqueline Blancard, piano; Orchestre de la Suisse Romande
1950   78 rpm, Decca (GB) K28202/3
        33 rpm, Decca (GB) LXT2565, London (US) LL76

Rapsodie espagnole
Orchestre de la Suisse Romande
1951   Decca (GB, Fr, Ger, Spain) LXT2637, London (US) LL530, Richmond (US)
        19044

Concerto for Piano and Orchestra in G – Concerto for Piano and Orchestra in D,
   "For the Left Hand" (2nd version)
Jacqueline Blancard, piano; Orchestre de la Suisse Romande
1953   Decca (GB, Ger, Spain) LXT2816, London (US) LL797, CM9068

Pavane pour une Infante défunte
Orchestre de la Suisse Romande
1953   25 cm., Decca (GB, Fr, Ger) LW5033, (Ger) D102, (US) LD9039
        30 cm., Decca (GB, Fr, Ger, Spain) LXT2760, (GB) ACL37, London (US)
        LL696, Richmond (US) 19097

Daphnis et Chloé (complete ballet)
Orchestre de la Suisse Romande; Motet Choir of Geneva, Jacques Horneffer,
   director
1953   Decca (GB, Fr, Ger) LXT2775, ACL53, London (US) LL693, Richmond (US)
        19094, Everest (US) SDBR3278

Le Tombeau de Couperin
Orchestre de la Suisse Romande
1953   25 cm., Decca (GB, Fr) LW5130
        30 cm., Decca (GB, Fr, Ger) LXT2821, ACL260, London (US) LL795

Valses nobles et sentimentales
Orchestre de la Suisse Romande

1953   Coupled with *Le Tombeau de Couperin* (above) only on the 30 cm. disks, with the same references

Don Quichotte à Dulcinée
Pierre Mollet, baritone; Orchestre de la Suisse Romande
1953   Association Ernest Ansermet (Switzerland) AEA30-775

L'Heure espagnole
Suzanne Danco, soprano; Paul Derenne, tenor; Michel Hamel, tenor; Heinz Reyffuss, baritone; André Vessières, bass; Orchestre de la Suisse Romande
1953   Decca (GB, Fr, Ger, Spain) LXT2828, ECS786, 220083, London (US) LL796, X5090, A4102, 23249, Decca (GB, Fr) 593016 (1983)

La Valse (2nd version)
Orchestre de la Société des Concerts du Conservatoire
1954   33 rpm, 25 cm., Decca (Fr) BR3002
       33 rpm, 30 cm., Decca (GB, Fr, Ger, Spain) LXT2896, LXT5004, ACL48, London (US) LL956, LL1156, CM9119, Richmond (US) 19073, Everest (US) 3283
       45 rpm, 17 cm., Decca (Fr) CEP565

Tableaux d'une exposition (Mussorgsky-Ravel)
Orchestre de la Suisse Romande
1954   Decca (GB, Fr, Ger, Spain) LXT2896, ACL48, London (US) LL956, Richmond (US) 19073

Boléro (16′00)
Orchestre de la Société des Concerts du Conservatoire
1955   Mono: 25 cm., Decca (Fr) BR3002, (Ger) D102; 30 cm., Decca (GB, Fr) LXT5004, (GB) ECS529 (1983), London (US) LL1156, CM9119, Everest (US) 3283, Decca (Ger) 648155, 642568 (1983)

L'Enfant et les sortilèges
Orchestre de la Suisse Romande; Motet Choir of Geneva, Jacques Horneffer, director; Flore Wend, mezzo-soprano; Marie-Lise de Montmollin, mezzo-soprano; Lucien Lovano, bass; Geneviève Touraine, soprano; Juliette Bise, alto; Gisèle Bobillier, soprano; Suzanne Danco, soprano; Pierre Mollet, baritone; Hugues Cuenod, tenor; Adrienne Migliette, coloratura soprano
1955   Mono: Decca (GB, Fr) LXT5019, London (US) LL1180, 4105, Richmond (US) 23086
       Stereo: Decca (GB, Fr) SLX2212, Richmond (US) 33086, AOD (Fr) SDD168, Decca (Fr) 593016 (1983), AOD (GB) SDD168 (1983)

Shéhérazade – Deux Mélodies hébraïques – Trois Poèmes de Stéphane Mallarmé
Suzanne Danco, soprano; Orchestre de la Suisse Romande
1955   Mono: Decca (GB, Fr) LXT5031, GOS602/3, ECS810, London (US) LL1196, 5361, STS15155/6

La Valse
"Ansermet Discusses and Conducts *La Valse*"
Orchestre de la Suisse Romande
1958   Black and white video film (duration 21'46) recorded in 1957 in Studio 1,
          Radio Geneva (now Studio Ernest Ansermet) by Suisse Romande
          Television; Jean-Jacques Lagrange, director. First broadcast Jan. 31, 1958

Before conducting *La Valse*, E.A. introduces and comments on the interpretation for
about 10 minutes in French and German. In light of the high praise given by M.R. to
E.A. for his understanding of *La Valse*, this film constitutes a historic document of great
importance. It is preserved (in 1988) at Suisse Romande TV, 20 Quai Ernest Ansermet,
Geneva, Switzerland.

Rapsodie espagnole (2nd version)
Orchestre de la Suisse Romande
1958   Mono: Decca (GB) LXT5424, London (US) 9228—rec. Nov. 1957
          Stereo: Decca (GB) SXL2061, (GB, Fr) AODSDD214, (GB) VIV34, SPA230
          (1983), London (US) 6024, STS15109 (1983), Decca (Ger) 642773 (1983)

Ma Mère l'Oye (2nd version)
Orchestre de la Suisse Romande
1958   Mono: Decca (GB) LXT5426, London (US) 9230
          Stereo: Decca (GB) SXL2062, (Fr) SDD376, 116374, London (US) 6023,
          STS15488 (1983)

Danse (Debussy-Ravel)
Orchestre de la Suisse Romande
1959   Mono: Decca (GB) LXT5454
          Stereo: (GB) SXL2027, SDD375, SPA131, (Fr) SP4231, STS15022, London
          (US) 6043

Tzigane
Ruggiero Ricci, violin; Orchestre de la Suisse Romande
1960   Mono: Decca (GB, Fr) LXT5527, London (US) 9016
          Stereo: Decca (GB, Fr) SXL2155, ECS670, (Fr) 220045, London (US) 6134

Tableaux d'une exposition (Mussorgsky-Ravel; 2nd version)
Orchestre de la Suisse Romande
1960   Mono: Decca (GB) LXT5665, London (US) 9246
          Stereo: Decca (GB) SXL2195, SPA229 (1983), (Fr) 117229, London (US)
          6177, STS15475 (1983), Decca (Ger) 641776, 648155 (1983)
          In the final chords, E.A. added a spectacular 32-foot organ stop.
1985   AD: 12 cm. (compact disc), Decca (GB) 414139-2

Pavane pour une Infante défunte (2nd version)
Orchestre de la Suisse Romande
1961   Mono: London (US) 9293
          Stereo: Decca (GB) SXL2287, SPA230 (1983), London (US) 6225

"Alborada del gracioso" (2nd version) – *Daphnis et Chloé*, Suite No. 2 – *Le Tombeau de Couperin* (2nd version) – *Valses nobles et sentimentales* (2nd version)
Orchestre de la Suisse Romande
1961   Mono: Decca (GB) LXT5633, London (US) 9279—rec. Nov. 1960
       Stereo: Decca (GB, Fr) 2273, London (US) 6210, STS15092

Boléro (14′10) – *La Valse*
Orchestre de la Suisse Romande
1963   Mono: London (US) 9367—rec. April 1963
       Stereo: Decca (GB, Fr) SXL6065, JB36 (1983), (Fr) 70301, 592063 (1983),
          London (US) 6367 (1983)
       Stereo: Decca (GB) SPA230 (a British re-edition of these last two disks with a
          different coupling, available in 1983: *Daphnis*, 2nd suite, *La Valse*, the
          Pavane, "Alborada," and the *Rapsodie espagnole*)

La Valse
A rehearsal followed by a performance
Hamburg Symphony Orchestra of the Norddeutscher Rundfunk (North German
   Radio)
1963   Black and white film recorded in May 1963, in Hamburg. Broadcast on
       German television on November 10, 1963, in honor of E.A.'s 80th birthday
       (F. Hudry, *Ernest Ansermet*, p. 132)
       Replying to a request for additional information, the Hamburg
       Norddeutscher Rundfunk sent a telegram dated September 13, 1983: "film
       destroyed." Copies of the program may have been made.

Shéhérazade
Régine Crespin, soprano; Orchestre de la Suisse Romande
1963   Mono: Decca (GB, Fr) LXT6081, London (US) 5821
       Stereo: Decca (GB, Fr) SXL6081, London (US) 0525821 (1983), Decca (Fr)
          7023, 592038 (1983), (GB) JB15 (1983), (Ger) JB15 (1983)
1987   ADD: 12 cm. (compact disc) Philips (Ger, GB, Fr) 417813-2

Daphnis et Chloé (complete ballet; 2nd version)
Orchestre de la Suisse Romande; chorus of the Romande Radio, Lausanne, André
   Charlet, director
1965   Mono: Decca (GB, Fr) LXT6204, London (US) CM9456
       Stereo: Decca (GB, Fr) SXL6204, London (US) CS6456
1984   AD: 12 cm. (compact disc), Decca (GB) 414046-2

Boléro – "Alborada del gracioso" – *Rapsodie espagnole* – *Valses nobles et sentimentales* –
La Valse
Orchestre de la Suisse Romande (reissue of the later preceding versions, 1957 to
   1963)

ANDRÉ ASSELIN (b. 1895)
violin

Address book—Photographs—Friendly and artistic relationship.

A score of the Sonata for Violin and Cello bears the following dedication from Ravel to A.A.: "in remembrance of the beautiful performance on October 15, 1926." A.A. performed Ravel's Sonata for Violin and Piano with the composer on several occasions: at the home of Jacques Durand (from the manuscript, in 1927); in two all-Ravel programs given at the American Conservatory at Fontainebleau on July 7, 1927, and July 3, 1930.

Ravel praised Paul Kochansky's violin transcription of the *Pavane pour une Infante défunte,* and persuaded A.A. to record it. His violin was a Gagliano (information provided by A.A.).

Pavane pour une Infante défunte
A.A.; Lucien Petitjean, piano
1930   78 rpm, Gramophone (Fr) L804—rec. 1930

JANE BATHORI (Jeanne-Marie Berthier; 1877–1970)
mezzo-soprano

Address book—Correspondence—Photographs—Friendly and artistic relationship.

J.B. introduced many songs by M.R.: *Histoires naturelles* (the first of which is dedicated to her) with M.R. at the piano, January 12, 1907; *Noël des jouets,* with M.R.; *Sur l'herbe,* with M.R.; *Trois Poèmes de Stéphane Mallarmé*; *Chansons madécasses*; *Rêves,* with M.R., March 19, 1927.

She recalled meeting M.R. during the winter of 1898–99:

He was then a student of Gabriel Fauré, and he was introduced to me by a mutual friend. . . . It is correct to say that in the *Histoires naturelles,* Ravel had completely broken with what is customarily called "melody." The voice was subservient to the prosody, which embraced the text to such an extent that the mute *e's* were no longer heard. This procedure, which Ravel also used in *L'Heure espagnole,* disconcerted quite a few singers, but made them acquire a more supple and more animated diction. (*La Revue musicale,* December 1938, pp. 179–80.)

Histoires naturelles ("Le Paon," "Le Grillon," "Le Martin-Pêcheur")
J.B., accompanying herself on the piano
1929   78 rpm, Columbia (Fr, GB) D 15179—rec. and iss. 1929, Paris
          33 rpm, Columbia-Voix illustres (Fr) FCX50030 (1963), Angel (Japan) GR2141
          (1966) (1983)

JACQUELINE BLANCARD
piano

Artistic encounter.

J.B. performed *Ma Mère l'Oye* with M.R.; a score of the four-hand work contains the following dedication: "in remembrance of our fine performance. M.R., Geneva, February 28, 1929." (Facsimile in the Orchestre de la Suisse Romande Documentation Bulletin, no. 19, March–April–May 1941.)

Concerto for Piano and Orchestra in D, "For the Left Hand"
Orchestre Philharmonique de Paris, Charles Münch, conductor
1938 78 rpm, Polydor (Fr) 566192/3, (Ger) 67192/3, Decca (GB) x204/5, Fonit
(Italy) 91077/8, 96045/6, Vox (US) set 168—rec. and iss. 1938, Paris

Concerto for Piano and Orchestra in D, "For the Left Hand"
1950 See Ernest Ansermet, above

Concerto for Piano and Orchestra in D, "For the Left Hand" – Concerto for Piano
and Orchestra in G
1953 See Ernest Ansermet, above

THE CALVET STRING QUARTET (1919–1940)
Joseph Calvet, Daniel Guilevitch, violins; Léon Pascal, viola; Paul Mas, cello

Address book (Joseph Calvet, 1897–1984)—Artistic encounter.

String Quartet
1937 78 rpm, Gramophone (Fr) DB5025/8—rec. Dec. 24, 1936 and Feb. 4, 1937;
iss. Paris
(Beginning of the third movement redone; Pathé Archives, Chatou, France)

Introduction et Allegro
Lily Laskine, harp; Marcel Moyse, flute; Ulysse Delécluse, clarinet; Calvet String
Quartet
1938 78 rpm, 25 cm., Gramophone (Fr) K8168/9, Victor (US) 4509/10—rec. May
1938, Paris
33 rpm, 30 cm., VSM, les gravures illustres (Fr) C061-11305M (1971)

ROBERT CASADESUS (1899–1972)
GABY CASADESUS (b. 1901)
piano

Address book—Correspondence—Photographs—Friendly and artistic relationship.

Both pianists were coached by M.R. In 1922, M.R. heard R.C. play *Gaspard de la nuit* and congratulated him on his interpretation, particularly the way he played "Le Gibet," in a slow tempo, evoking the nostalgia that he desired, while still underlining the harmony, more like a composer than a pianist. R.C. accompanied M.R. to London in order to record piano rolls, and substituted for him in the very difficult pieces. Preparing for an all-Ravel recital in Salle Pleyel on June 11, 1924, R.C. met with the composer frequently and received his counsel. R.C. often performed in M.R.'s presence or with him in France and abroad, frequently playing *Ma Mère l'Oye* with the composer. (Interview with Mme G.C. in November 1981 and extracts of her recollections printed in the liner notes of the complete piano works of M.R. by R.C., 1951–52, CBS 77346, cited below.)

Jeux d'eau (R.C.)
1928   78 rpm, 25 cm., Columbia (Fr) D 13054, (US) 1864D, 2080M—rec. and iss.
            1928, Paris

Sonatine – "Menuet" (*Le Tombeau de Couperin*) (R.C.)
1940   78 rpm, 25 cm., Columbia (US) 17215/6D, MX 17238/9D, set 179,
            (Argentina) 292546/7

Valses nobles et sentimentales (R.C.)
1941   78 rpm, 25 cm., Columbia (US) 17270/1D, MX 17280/1D, set 194, (Canada)
            10082/3, (Argentina) 292577/8

Menuet sur le nom d'Haydn – *Prélude* (G.C.)
1946   78 rpm, 25 cm., Vox (US) 16006, set 163

Jeux d'eau – "Prélude" (*Le Tombeau de Couperin*) (G.C.)
1947   78 rpm, Polydor (Fr) 566250, Vox (US) set 610

"Oiseaux tristes" (*Miroirs*) – *Pavane pour une Infante défunte* (G.C.)
1947   78 rpm, Polydor (Fr) 566251, Vox (US) set 610

Berceuse sur le nom de Gabriel Fauré
Zino Francescatti, violin, and R.C.
1947   78 rpm, Columbia (US) 72046D, set 280, (Fr) MX280

Concerto for Piano and Orchestra in D, "For the Left Hand"
R.C. with the Philadelphia Orchestra, Eugene Ormandy, conductor
1947   78 rpm, 30 cm., Columbia (US) 12663/4D, set 288, (GB) LX 1088/9, (Fr)
            MX288 (album of 2 records), (Italy) GQX11461/2—iss. US
            33 rpm, 25 cm., Columbia (US-GB) 1023, (Fr) 1032
            33 rpm, 30 cm., Columbia (US) ML4075, Philips (Fr, Holland) 03506
            45 rpm, 17 cm., Philips (Fr, Holland) AE409046

Pavane pour une Infante défunte – "A la manière de Chabrier" – "A la manière de
    Borodine" – Sonatine – *Miroirs* – *Ma Mère l'Oye*§ – "Habanera"§ – *Jeux d'eau* –
    Gaspard de la nuit – *Menuet antique* – *Le Tombeau de Couperin* – *Valses nobles et
    sentimentales* – *Prélude* – *Menuet sur le nom d'Haydn* (R.C., §R.C. and G.C.)
1952   3 records: Columbia (US) ML4518/20, Philips (GB) ABL 3012, 3046, and

3062, (Fr) A01112/4L, Odyssey (US) 32360003 (1983); CBS (Fr, Ger) 77346 (1983)—rec. Dec. 4, 1951, US

Concerto for Piano and Orchestra in D, "For the Left Hand" (2nd version)
R.C. with the Philadelphia Orchestra, Eugene Ormandy, conductor
1961   Mono: Columbia (US) ML5674—rec. 1960, US
       Stereo: Columbia (US) MS6274 (1982), CBS (GB) SBRG72008, (Fr) 76552

Sonatine – "Alborada del gracioso" (*Miroirs*)
Recital given by R.C. at the Concertgebouw
1978   Mono: CBS (Holland) AC4 (Association R.C.)—rec. Feb. 11, 1964,
       Amsterdam

GUSTAVE CLOEZ
conductor

Artistic encounter.

G.C. conducted the first choreographic interpretation of *La Valse* in Paris, presented by the troupe of Ida Rubinstein at the Opéra on May 23, 1929.

"La Flûte enchantée," "L'Indifférent" (*Shéhérazade*)
Suzanne Cesbron-Viseur, soprano; Orchestre de L'Opéra-Comique
1929   78 rpm, 25 cm., Odéon (Fr) 188630, Decca (US) 20537

PIERO COPPOLA (1888–1971)
conductor, piano

Address book—Correspondence—Friendly and artistic relationship.

P.C. was artistic director of the Compagnie Française du Gramophone (1923–1934). In his book of memoirs, *Dix-Sept ans de musique à Paris 1922–1939,* he wrote:

Enthusiastic about M.R.'s music since my Conservatoire days, I finally had the opportunity to conduct one of his works in 1923, and chose "Alborada del gracioso," which had just been printed. I keenly desired to understand the composer's wishes thoroughly. To this end, I wrote to him asking for an interview. One morning I was called to the telephone. It was Ravel, who proposed that he come to see me. He came and without ceremony invited me to join him for a glass of beer at a café on rue Châteaudun, where, around a table, we studied all of the delightful details of the sumptuous orchestral garb with which he had clothed "Alborada del gracioso." This first interview was to be followed by a second. Indeed, M.R. invited me to lunch at his home in Montfort l'Amaury. We discussed music, art, and everything, until late in the afternoon; I returned to Paris, happy, full of admiration and friendship for this great musician, and our relationship remained this way until his death. The concert took place on the evening of May 23, 1923, at the Champs-

Elysées theater. "Alborada" had been the object of my most meticulous care; at the end of the concert, M.R., who was present, congratulated me, and assured me that I had interpreted it well.

Pavane pour une Infante défunte – "Five o'clock" from *L'Enfant et les sortilèges,* arr. Roger Branga
L'Orchestre Symphonique du Gramophone
1928   78 rpm, Gramophone (Fr) w871, (GB) D1564, Victor (US) (Chile) 9306 (on the Victor (US) disk only, the label reads: "Dream of a Naughty Boy, Fox Trot Continental Symphony Orchestra")—rec. 1928

"Alborada del gracioso"
L'Orchestre Symphonique du Gramophone
1928   78 rpm, Gramophone (Fr) w955, (GB) D1594, Victor (US) 9702—rec. and iss. 1928, Paris

Shéhérazade
Marcelle Gerar, soprano, with orchestra
1929   78 rpm, 30 cm., Gramophone (Fr) w993 ("Asie")—rec. Nov. 1928, Paris
        78 rpm, 25 cm., Gramophone (Fr) P790 ("La Flûte enchantée," "L'Indifférent")

Rapsodie espagnole
Grand Orchestre Symphonique
1929   78 rpm, Gramophone (Fr) W1029/30, Victor (US) 9700/1—rec. 1929

Boléro
1930   (See "Ravel as supervisor of recordings," p. 540)

Menuet antique
Grand Orchestre Symphonique
1930   78 rpm, Gramophone (Fr) W1074, Victor (US) 11133—rec. and iss. 1930, Paris

"Oh! La Pitoyable Aventure" (*L'Heure espagnole*)
Fanny Heldy, soprano; Louis Morturier, bass; Pierre Favereaux, tenor; orchestra
1931   78 rpm, Gramophone (Fr, GB) DB1512—rec. Feb. 18, 1930, Paris
        33 rpm, VSM (Fr) FALP627, C06112847 (1974)

Introduction et Allegro
"Denise Herbrecht, harp, with string quartet, flute and clarinet under the direction of M. Piero Coppola"
1931   78 rpm, Gramophone (Fr) L903/4—rec. and iss. 1931, Paris

Histoires naturelles – Sur l'herbe (2nd side, K6397)
Elsa Ruhlmann, soprano; P.C., piano
1931   78 rpm, 25 cm., Gramophone (Fr) K6396/7 ("Le Grillon," "Le Martin-Pêcheur," "La Pintade")—rec. and iss. 1931, Paris
        78 rpm, 30 cm., Gramophone (Fr) L907 ("Le Paon," "Le Cygne")

Le Tombeau de Couperin

L'Orchestre de la Société des Concerts du Conservatoire

1931   78 rpm, Gramophone (Fr) W1163/64, (GB) D2073/4, Victor 11150/1 and
12320/1—rec. and iss. 1931, Paris

In his book of memoirs (p. 140) P.C. wrote: "We obtained our first Prix
Candide (Grand Prix du Disque in 1932) with *Le Tombeau de Couperin*, also
thanks to the astonishing virtuosity of that oboe 'ace' M. Bleuzet." This
soloist is not, however, mentioned on the record labels.

Danse (Debussy-Ravel)

L'Orchestre de la Société des Concerts du Conservatoire

1932   78 rpm, Gramophone (Fr) DB4860 (4th side of *Suite de ballet* by Grétry,
DB4859/60)—rec. and iss. 1932, Paris

Ma Mère l'Oye

L'Orchestre de la Société des Concerts du Conservatoire

1933   78 rpm, Gramophone (Fr-GB) DB4898/9, Victor (US) 13482/3, set M693—
rec. and iss. 1933, Paris

Daphnis et Chloé (Suite No. 1)

L'Orchestre de la Société des Concerts du Conservatoire

1934   78 rpm, Gramophone (Fr-GB) DB4930, Victor (US) 11882—rec. and iss.
1934, Paris

Valses nobles et sentimentales

L'Orchestre de la Société des Concerts du Conservatoire

1934   78 rpm, Gramophone (Fr-GB) DB4935/6, Victor (US) 11727/8—rec. and
iss. 1934, Paris

Don Quichotte à Dulcinée – Ronsard à son âme

1935   (See "Ravel as supervisor of recordings," p. 542)

ALFRED CORTOT (1877–1962)
piano

Address book—Correspondence—Photographs—Friendly and artistic relationship.

In their early teens, A.C. and M.R. were classmates at the Conservatoire. "In
Ciboure, M.R. had undertaken to compose a work for me entitled 'Basque Rhapsody,'
which would become his dazzling G Major Concerto. It turned out that I was not to be
the official dedicatee of the Concerto." (A.C., quoted by B. Gavoty, *Alfred Cortot*, Paris,
Buchet-Chastel, 1977, p. 126.)

Jeux d'eau

1921   78 rpm, acoustical; total width of grooves, 92 mm.; length 4'30; Victor (US)
one side, 74569, Gramophone (GB, Calcutta, India) one side, 05657, two
sides (GB) DB643—take (version) 2, rec. Jan. 27, 1920; iss. Feb. 1921

1923   78 rpm, acoustical; total width of grooves, 87 mm.; length 4′15; two sides:
       Victor (US) 6065, Gramophone (GB, Fr, Holland) DB643, take 5, rec.
       March 1, 1923

Take 1 (rec. January 27, 1920), and takes 3 and 4 (rec. February 27, 1923) were not issued. All recordings were made in a church at 114 North 5th Street, Camden, New Jersey. All labels, including those on records issued in France, state: "The Fountain (jeux d'eau)." It is worth noting that takes 2 and 5 are found under the same number DB643.

"Ondine" (*Gaspard de la nuit*)
       Takes 1 and 2, 78 rpm, electrical, Victor (US) matrix number 32140 (rec.
       April 6, 1925, Camden, N.J.) were not issued.

Sonatine – *Jeux d'eau*
1932   78 rpm, Gramophone (Fr, GB, Ger, Italy) DB1533/4, Victor (US) 7728/9
       (Japan A/D392/3)—rec. May 1931, Paris
       33 rpm, HMV (GB) HQM1182 (1969), Seraphim (US) 60143, (*Jeux d'eau*
       only): RCA Victor (US) LM2824 (1965)

Concerto for Piano and Orchestra in D, "For the Left Hand"
Orchestre de la Société des Concerts du Conservatoire, Charles Münch, conductor
1940   78 rpm, Gramophone (Fr, GB) DB3885/6, Victor (US) 15749/50 set M629—
       rec. May 12, 1939, Paris
       33 rpm, VSM (Fr) COLH98 (Fr, GB) 2C05143370 (1983), Angel (Japan)
       GR2112 (1966) (1983)

WALTER DAMROSCH (1862–1950)
conductor, piano

Address book (address in New York)—Photographs—Artistic encounter.

W.D. met M.R. in Paris in 1919 (see letter no. 157, note 5), during the composer's North American tour in 1928, and during a Ravel festival held at Fontainebleau in 1930.

Ma Mère l'Oye ("Laideronnette, Impératrice des pagodes," "Les Entretiens de la
      Belle et de la Bête")
W.D. and Polly Damrosch (daughter of W.D.), piano 4 hands.
1927   Automatic piano roll, Duo-Art (US) 7189—iss. Nov. 1927, US
       Reissued as a disk, Klavier (US) 102 (1971), KS132 (1978) (1983), length,
       6′19
1985   DA new issue: Klavier Digital Audiophile (US) KD137, length, 5′57—rec.
       1984

Ma Mère l'Oye
New York Symphony Orchestra
1928   78 rpm, Columbia (US) 67343/5D, set M74, (GB, Fr) 9516/8, (Australia)
       02905/7, (Ger) CS1063/5—rec. 1927, New York; iss. Feb. 1928

JEANNE-MARIE DARRÉ (b. 1905)
piano

Address book—Artistic encounter.

In 1929, J.-M.D. performed the Trio (with H. Arnitz, violin, and Gérard Hekking, cello), "Ondine" (*Gaspard de la nuit*), and the "Toccata" (*Le Tombeau de Couperin*) in an all-Ravel program in London's Aeolian Hall. M.R. also participated in the recital. She recalled the following: "When I played the 'Toccata' for him, I asked for his advice. He replied, 'play it as rapidly as possible, on condition that every note is heard distinctly.' He revealed 'Ondine' to me in an extraordinary way, and the memory of that lesson has remained with me throughout my career." (Excerpt of a letter dated August 5, 1981, J.-M.D. to Arbie Orenstein.)

"Ondine" (*Gaspard de la nuit*) – "Toccata" (*Le Tombeau de Couperin*)
1981   Art et Musique (Fr) MA 103/8007.

LUCETTE DESCAVES (b. 1906)
piano

Address book—Artistic encounter.

Jeux d'eau
1946   78 rpm, 30 cm., Gramophone (Fr) DB5192

"Alborada del gracioso" (*Miroirs*)
1946   78 rpm, 30 cm., Gramophone (Fr) DB5115

"Prélude"–"Rigaudon" (*Le Tombeau de Couperin*)
1946   78 rpm, 25 cm., Decca (GB) DAF 121

Le Tombeau de Couperin
1953   33 rpm, 25 cm., Decca (Fr) DFA 133031

Trio
L.D.; Jean Pasquier, violin; Etienne Pasquier, cello
1955   33 rpm, 30 cm., Mono Erato (Fr) DP43-1

ROGER DÉSORMIÈRE (1898–1963)
conductor

Friendly and artistic relationship.

He conducted the première of M.R.'s "Fanfare" for *L'Eventail de Jeanne* in Paris on June 16, 1927. R.D. owned an orchestral holograph of *La Valse* which is now in the Bibliothèque Nationale. Replacing Pierre Monteux, he conducted the Orchestre Symphonique de Paris in an all-Ravel program at Salle Pleyel on January 17, 1933, which also featured M.R. conducting the Parisian debut of his Piano Concerto for the Left Hand with Paul Wittgenstein as soloist.

Boléro (14′53)
Czech Philharmonic Orchestra
1950   78 rpm, 30 cm., Ultraphon (Czechoslovakia) H25522/3
1952   33 rpm, 25 cm., Supraphon (Czechoslovakia, Fr) LPM31
1959   45 rpm, 17 cm., Supraphon (Fr) M30020
1962   33 rpm, 30 cm., Parliament (US) Mono PLP 114, rechanneled for stereo
         PLPS 114
1979   33 rpm, 30 cm., Supraphon-Eurodisc (Fr, Ger) 300104B (in album 913296)

MAURICE DUMESNIL (1886–1974)
piano

Friendly and artistic relationship.

In January 1911 and December 1913 he concertized with M.R. in England.

Pavane pour une Infante défunte
1925   Ordinary piano roll (88 notes and 65 notes), Pleyela (Fr), Aeolian (Fr), and
         Odéola (Fr) AP5269—rec. 1925

GEORGES ENESCO (1881–1955)
conductor

Address book—Friendly and artistic relationship.

A child prodigy, G.E. arrived in Paris in 1893 and continued his studies at the Conservatoire. He was a classmate of M.R. in the composition course of Gabriel Fauré. On May 30, 1927, he performed the première of M.R.'s Violin Sonata with the composer at the piano. G.E.'s young violin pupil Yehudi Menuhin would later recall the following incident, which took place during a lesson:

> Maurice Ravel suddenly burst into our midst, the ink still drying on a piano-and-violin sonata which he had brought along. It seemed his publishers, Durand, wished to hear it immediately. . . . Then, with Ravel at the piano, [he] sight-read the complex work, pausing now and again for elucidation. Ravel would have let matters rest there, but Enesco suggested they have one more run-through, whereupon he laid the manuscript to one side and played the entire work from memory. (Yehudi Menuhin, *Unfinished Journey,* New York, Knopf, 1977, p. 70.)

Pavane pour une Infante défunte
Symphony Orchestra
1949   78 rpm, Silvertone (US) 47
1951   33 rpm, Mercury (US) MG 10021, Classic (Fr) C6010

HENRIETTE FAURE (1904–1985)
piano

Correspondence—Photographs—Friendly and artistic relationship.

H.F. was born on March 23, 1904, and not in 1906, as commonly stated. A copy of her birth certificate was kindly furnished by the town hall of Avignon.

A photograph of M.R. at the piano bears the following dedication: "to my charming and perfect interpreter, Henriette Faure, Maurice Ravel November 10, 1922." This photograph, together with several facsimiles of M.R.'s letters to H.F., is found in the book *Mon maître Maurice Ravel*, Paris, ATP, 1978, written by Henriette Faure.

The pianist relates how at the age of 17 (actually 19) she had the idea and the audacity to write to M.R. about a projected 2½-hour recital at the Champs-Elysées theater, which would be devoted to his complete piano works. The composer's reply was favorable, and he met H.F. at her parents' home in early November 1922. A cup of tea in hand, he asked H.F. to go to the piano.

> I began by playing the *Valses nobles et sentimentales* for him. Ravel, who was seated, got up, stood next to the piano, and proceeded to torment me in such a way that I haven't forgotten it for half a century, continually stopping me, criticizing the minutest details—a phrase, a rest, a pedal, an inflection . . . and beyond all of that, like a clock at the rear of a corridor, his inexorable 1-2-3, 1-2-3. It was exhausting, having to integrate fantasy with strictness, and giving a dreamlike or elegant passage the maximum of rhythm and precision. This torture lasted almost two and a half hours. Good! he said at the end, if you would like me to coach you on the other pieces, could you come to my home? (*Mon maître Maurice Ravel*, p. 20.)

Thus, H.F. went to Montfort l'Amaury for an entire day several times a week, having lunch with M.R., and studying the complete piano works with the composer. Her recital, apparently the first devoted entirely to M.R.'s complete piano music, took place on January 12, 1923 (not January 18 as often stated; see *Le Guide du concert* of January 1923) at the Champs-Elysées theater, before a large and distinguished audience. At the conclusion of the recital, M.R. was the first to come backstage and warmly congratulate the young artist. In her book, H.F. devotes a chapter of 65 pages to "the piano music of Ravel and the instruction I received from him about it." By 1959, H.F. had already given 380 recitals, broadcasts, concerts, and lectures, in which she had performed M.R.'s works. (Liner notes from the Pathé record cited below.)

Miroirs
1948   78 rpm, 25 cm., Decca (Fr) AF209/10 and AF2/8/9 (8 sides)

Jeux d'eau – Prélude
1949   78 rpm, 25 cm., Decca (Fr) AF220

Gaspard de la nuit – Jeux d'eau – Prélude
1955   Mono: 33 rpm, 25 cm., Decca (Fr) FS123639

Miroirs – Le Tombeau de Couperin
1959   Mono: Pathé (Fr) DTX292

JACQUES FÉVRIER (1900–1979)
piano

Address book—Photographs—Friendly and artistic relationship.

Son of the composer Henri Février, who was a comrade of M.R. during their student days at the Conservatoire, J.F. had met M.R. as a child. Dissatisfied with the freedoms taken in his Piano Concerto for the Left Hand by pianist Paul Wittgenstein (see below), who commissioned the Concerto and to whom it is dedicated, Ravel, in 1937, chose J.F. to be the first French pianist to perform this work in France (March 19, 1937, with the Orchestre Philharmonique de Paris conducted by Charles Münch), and the United States (November 1937, with the Boston Symphony Orchestra conducted by Serge Koussevitzky). J.F. had previously studied the Concerto in detail with the composer.

Concerto for Piano and Orchestra in D, "For the Left Hand" (5 sides) –
   "Noctuelles" (*Miroirs*), piano (6th side)
J.F.; Orchestre de la Société des Concerts du Conservatoire, Charles Münch,
   conductor
1943   78 rpm, Columbia (Fr) LFX631/3, LFX8102/4

Concerto for Piano and Orchestra in D, "For the Left Hand"
Orchestre National de la Radio Diffusion Française, Georges Tzipine, conductor
1958   Mono: Columbia (Fr) FCX680, PM30299

Miroirs – Menuet sur le nom d'Haydn – A la manière de . . . Borodine, Chabrier –
   Gaspard de la nuit – Sonatine *– Pavane pour une Infante défunte – Le Tombeau de*
   Couperin – Valses nobles et sentimentales – Menuet antique – Prélude – Jeux d'eau –
   Ma Mère l'Oye – Frontispice – Sites auriculaires
J.F., with Gabriel Tacchino for the 4-hand pieces, and Jean-Claude Ambrosini for
   the 5th hand in *Frontispice*
1971   Adès (Fr) 7041/4, ADE4 (1983) (set of 4 records)
1987   AD: 12 cm. (3 compact discs), Adès (Fr) no. 14, 105-106-107, reissue of the
      complete works issued in 1971—iss. Aug. 7

Concerto for Piano and Orchestra in D, "For the Left Hand"
Orchestre National de l'O.R.T.F. (Office de Radio Télévision Française), Serge
   Baudo, conductor
1971   Color film—approx. iss. date

PIERRE FOURNIER (1906–1986)
cello

Artistic encounter.

On November 10, 1924, at Salle des Agriculteurs, Robert Krettly and P.F. performed Ravel's Sonata for Violin and Cello in the composer's presence. In the same recital,

M.R. accompanied Jane Bathori in three of his songs. P.F.'s cellos are a Goffriler and a Miremont (Alain Pâris, *Dictionnaire des interprètes,* Paris, Robert Laffont, 1982).

Pièce en forme de Habanera
P.F.; Ernest Lush, piano
1952   78 rpm, 25 cm., Gramophone (GB, Fr) DA20005

Pièce en forme de Habanera
P.F.; Gerald Moore, piano
1959   Mono: Columbia (GB) 33 CX1644

"Kaddisch" (*Deux mélodies hébraïques*)
P.F.; Gerald Moore, piano
1959   Mono: Columbia (GB) 33 CX1644

ZINO FRANCESCATTI (b. 1905)
violin

Address book—Friendly and artistic relationship.

In 1926, Z.F. performed with M.R. in a concert tour of England and Scotland. He often collaborated with Robert Casadesus in performing M.R.'s works, and he composed a *Berceuse sur le nom de Ravel.* His violin is the Hart Stradivarius, made in 1727 (Alain Pâris, *Dictionnaire des interprètes,* Paris, Robert Laffont, 1982).

Tzigane
Z.F.; Maurice Faure, piano
1932   78 rpm, Columbia (Fr) LFX191, (GB) LX258, (US) 68102D, (Argentina)
            264967, (Japan) W270

Berceuse sur le nom de Gabriel Fauré
Z.F.; Robert Casadesus, piano
1947   78 rpm, Columbia (US) 72044D, set X280

Tzigane
Z.F.; Arthur Balsam, piano
1950   78 rpm, Columbia (US) 72771 D

Sonata for Violin and Piano – *Tzigane* – *Berceuse sur le nom de Gabriel Fauré* – *Pièce en forme de Habanera* – "Kaddisch" (transcription by Lucien Garban)
Z.F.; Arthur Balsam, piano
1954   Columbia (US) ML5058, Philips (Fr) L01261L, Sony (Japan) SOCU57 (only
            the Sonata)

Tzigane
New York Philharmonic, Leonard Bernstein, conductor
1963   Mono: Columbia (US) ML6017
            Stereo: Columbia (US) MS6017 (1983), CBS (Fr) S75247

JACQUES FRAY (1906–1963)
piano

Address book—Artistic encounter.

Boléro
J.F. and Mario Braggiotti, two pianos
1934   78 rpm, 25 cm., Victor (US) 24563, Gramophone (GB) в8264

PEDRO DE FREITAS-BRANCO (1896–1963)
conductor

Friendly and artistic relationship.

He was invited by M.R. to conduct several of his works at a Ravel festival on January 14, 1932 at Salle Pleyel.

1932   *Pavane pour une Infante défunte* (6th side of the 78 rpm version of the Piano Concerto in G; see p. 535)

The five orchestral works cited below were recorded by P.D.F.-B. and the Orchestre du Théâtre des Champs-Elysées, Paris, and have been issued with different couplings in France and abroad.

Boléro (18'25) – *La Valse*
1954   25 cm., Ducretet-Thomson (Fr) LA 1054—rec. 1953

"Alborada del gracioso" – *Pavane pour une Infante défunte* (Lucien Thévet, horn solo) – *Valses nobles et sentimentales*
    25 cm., Ducretet-Thomson (Fr, GB) LA 1055

"Alborada del gracioso" – *Pavane pour une Infante défunte* – *La Valse*
    25 cm., London (GB) EL93008

Boléro – *La Valse* – *Valses nobles et sentimentales* – "Alborada del gracioso" – *Pavane pour une Infante défunte*
    30 cm., Westminster (US) WL5297
    30 cm., Ducretet-Thomson (Italy) LTC6

"Alborada del gracioso" – *Boléro* – *Pavane pour une Infante défunte*
    25 cm., Ducretet-Thomson (Fr) 255CO68

La Valse – *Valses nobles et sentimentales*
    25 cm., Ducretet-Thomson (Fr) 255CO81

WILHELM FURTWÄNGLER (1886–1954)
conductor

Address book (address in Berlin)—Artistic encounter.

On March 21, 1932, in Berlin, W.F. and M.R. shared the podium of the Berlin Philharmonic Orchestra, with the composer conducting Marguerite Long in the G

Major Piano Concerto. In 1938, W.F. introduced the Concerto for the Left Hand in Berlin, with Alfred Cortot as soloist.

Valses nobles et sentimentales
Rehearsal followed by a performance
Berlin Philharmonic Orchestra
Private archive—rec. April 15 and 16, 1953, Hamburg; not issued

Rapsodie espagnole
Recorded during a concert
Symphony Orchestra of the R.A.I. of Turin
1971   Educational Media (US) BWS708—rec. March 3, 1952, Turin

Rapsodie espagnole
Recorded during a concert
Vienna Philharmonic Orchestra
1981   Fonit-Cetra (Italy) FE15—rec. Oct. 22, 1951, Stuttgart
1988   ADD: 12 cm. (compact disc) Fonit-Cetra (Italy) CDE1044 (reissue of the
          1981 recording)

Daphnis et Chloé (Suite No. 2)
Berlin Philharmonic Orchestra
1985   Melodiya (Russia) 459490008—rec. March 20 and 22, 1944

FELIX GALIMIR (b. 1910)
violin

Artistic encounter.

String Quartet
1934   (See "Ravel as supervisor of recordings," p. 538, Galimir Quartet)

String Quartet
Galimir Quartet (Felix Galimir, violin; Hiroko Yajima, violin; John Graham, viola;
   Timothy Eddy, cello)
1982   DA: Vanguard Audiophile (US) VA25009—rec. and iss. 1982, New York

RUDOLPH GANZ (1877–1972)
piano

Correspondence.

   The dedicatee of "Scarbo" (*Gaspard de la nuit*), R.G. was the second interpreter to have recorded a work by Ravel.

Pavane pour une Infante défunte
1913   Semiautomatic piano roll, 73 notes, Hupfeld-Phonola-Solodant (Ger) 14748

The year of the recording (1912) is embossed on this roll, and, affixed with a seal, the precise date of its issue (January 15, 1913). There is also a portrait of the interpreter and a reproduction of his signature.

Boléro
1933   Automatic piano roll, Duo-Art (US) 74728—iss. Oct. 1933

PHILIPPE GAUBERT (1879–1941)
conductor

Photographs—Friendly and artistic relationship.

As a flutist, P.G. participated in the première of the *Introduction et Allegro* in Paris on June 22, 1907. In the same capacity, he performed the *Chansons madécasses* with Madeleine Grey, M. Barouk, cello, and M.R., piano, at a Ravel Festival in Biarritz on August 24, 1930.

La Valse
Orchestre de la Société des Concerts du Conservatoire
1927   78 rpm, Columbia (Fr, GB, Spain) 12502/3, (GB) L2245/6, (US) 67384/5D, (Italy) GQX 11076/7

"Menuet" (*Le Tombeau de Couperin*)
Orchestre de la Société des Concerts du Conservatoire
1930   78 rpm, Columbia (Fr, GB) D 15208, (US) 67367D (12th side of César Franck's Symphony in D minor: D 15203/8), (US) set CM 121—iss. Jan. 1930

Daphnis et Chloé (Suite No. 2)
Orchestre des Concerts Straram
1930   78 rpm, Columbia (Fr) LFX41/2, (GB) LX 105/6, (US) 67827/8D set X32, MX70426/7D, (Ger) LWX253/4, (Australia) LOX81/2

MARCELLE GERAR (Regereau; 1891–1970)
lyric soprano

Address book—Correspondence—Photographs—Friendly and artistic relationship.

In 1923, M.R. invited M.G. to Le Belvédère, "showed her his home, offered her tea, and, as she wished to sing for him, he accompanied her in *Shéhérazade*, assuring her that she faithfully respected the interpretation he desired. . . . Shortly after, . . . he dedicated *Ronsard à son âme* to her and asked her to perform the première in London in April [1924]." (Statement of M.G. in Chalupt and Gerar, *Ravel au miroir de ses lettres*, p. 202.)

Shéhérazade
Orchestra, Piero Coppola, conductor
1929   78 rpm, 30 cm., Gramophone (Fr) W993 ("Asie")—rec. Nov. 1928, Paris

78 rpm, 25 cm., Gramophone (Fr) P790 ("La Flûte enchantée," "L'Indifférent")

HENRI GIL-MARCHEX (1894–1970)
piano

Address book—Correspondence—Photographs—Friendly and artistic relationship.

With violinist Jelly d'Aranyi, he introduced *Tzigane* in London on April 26, 1924, in the presence of the composer. In 1925–26, during a concert tour of 75 recitals, he gave the first performances of Ravel's piano works in Russia and in Japan, where he was the first foreign artist to have the honor of being presented before Her Majesty the Empress. (*Japan Advertiser,* Tokyo, December 23, 1925.)

"Five o'clock fox-trot" (Fantasy on *L'Enfant et les sortilèges,* transcription by H.G.-M.)
1928   Ordinary piano roll, Pleyela, Aeolian, Odéola (Fr) E 10370 (same recording issued on three different labels)—rec. Nov. 11, iss. Dec. 1928

"Oiseaux tristes" (*Miroirs*)
1930   Ordinary piano roll, Pleyela (Fr) E 16078—rec. Dec. 26, 1929
It is probable that the four other pieces of *Miroirs* were recorded at the same time (Pleyela E 16077-79-80-81). However, this is not certain, and only no. 16078 has been seen by the author who owns it. This was the end of an era for the mechanical piano in France; there are no more catalogues nor supplements.
The precise dates which are indicated appear on the piano rolls (at the end).

VLADIMIR GOLSCHMANN (1893–1972)
conductor

Address book—Photographs—Friendly and artistic relationship.

In 1919, he founded the Concerts Golschmann, which stressed avant-garde works, and in 1931 he became the conductor of the Saint Louis Symphony Orchestra, a position he held for almost three decades (see letter no. 275, note 3).

Le Tombeau de Couperin
The Concert Arts Orchestra
1953   Capitol (US) CTL7055, (Fr) P8244
       45 rpm, 17 cm., Capitol (Fr) FAP8251

Boléro (14' 17) – *Pavane pour une Infante défunte* – "Alborada del gracioso" – *Ma Mère l'Oye*
Orchestre des Concerts Lamoureux
1957   Mono: Philips-Réalité (Fr) C4, Fontana (Fr) 6549001

La Valse – Valses nobles et sentimentales
Saint Louis Symphony Orchestra
1957   Mono: Columbia (US) ML5155, Philips (GB) ABL3154, (Fr) L01313L

Tableaux d'une exposition (Mussorgsky-Ravel)
Vienna State Opera Orchestra
1960   Mono: Vanguard (US) SRV 117
  Stereo: Vanguard (US) SRV 117SD, S210 (1983), Classic (Fr) 991075

MARCEL GRANDJANY (1891–1975)
harp

Artistic encounter.

He performed the *Introduction et Allegro* under Ravel's baton (liner notes from the Seraphim record cited below).

Introduction et Allegro
M.G. and the RCA Victor String and Chamber orchestras, Sylvan Levin, conductor
1946   78 rpm, RCA Victor (US) M 118919/20, DM 118922/3, set M/DM1021

"Menuet" (*Le Tombeau de Couperin*, transcription for the harp by M.G.)
1957   Mono: Capitol (US) "For the Harp" P8401

Introduction et Allegro
M.G., harp; Arthur Gleghorn, flute; Hugo Raimondi, clarinet; The Hollywood
 String Quartet (Felix Slatkin, Paul Shure, Paul Robyn, Eleanor Aller)
1962   Mono: Capitol (US) L9217
  Stereo: Capitol (US) SL9217, Seraphim (US) S60142 (1983)

MADELEINE GREY (1896–1979)
mezzo-soprano

Address book—Correspondence—Photographs—Friendly and artistic relationship.

She introduced the *Deux Mélodies hébraïques* with Rhené-Baton conducting the Pasdeloup Orchestra on April 17, 1920. M.R. accompanied her at the piano in the course of many concert tours in France and abroad, notably in Spain in November 1928.

Chansons madécasses
1932   See "Ravel as conductor of chamber ensembles," p. 537

Trois Chants hébraïques
1932   See "Ravel as supervisor of recordings," p. 541

CLARA HASKIL (1895–1960)
piano

Address book (address in Switzerland)—Artistic encounter.

Sonatine
1951   25 cm., Philips (Fr) A00143
  30 cm., Fontana (Holland) 695090KL, Philips (Fr) 6599444, (Fr, Ger)
  6747055 (1983)

JASCHA HEIFETZ (1899–1987)
violin

Address book (address in New York)—Correspondence—Artistic encounter.

J.H. and M.R. met in New York in January 1928. His violins were the famous Guarnerius del Gesù (1742) which belonged to Pablo de Sarasate, and a Stradivarius of 1731 (Alain Pâris, *Dictionnaire des interprètes,* Paris, Robert Laffont, 1982).

Tzigane
J.H.; Arpad Sandor, piano
1934   78 rpm, Victor (US) 8411, (Japan) ND275
33 rpm, RCA (Ger) RL00943FK (1983)

Pièce en forme de Habanera
J.H.; Milton Kaye, piano
1945   78 rpm, 25 cm., Brunswick (GB) BO3617, Decca (US) A385
33 rpm, Brunswick (GB) AXL2017, Decca (US) DL5214, DL9780, CID (Fr)
US243046, Odéon (Argentina) LTC8503

Valses nobles et sentimentales (No. 6 and No. 7; transcription by J.H.)
J.H.; Emmanuel Bay, piano
1946   78 rpm, 25 cm., RCA Victor (US) M101294, set M1126, HMV (GB) DA1915

"Menuet" (Sonatine; transcription by Léon Roques)
J.H.; Emmanuel Bay, piano
1947   78 rpm, Victor (US) 120765
33 rpm, RCA Victor (US) LM2382 (1960)

Trio
J.H.; Arthur Rubinstein, piano; Gregor Piatigorsky, cello
1950   78 rpm, HMV (GB) 9620/2, Victor (US) set AM1486
33 rpm, RCA Victor (US) LM1119 (1983), HMV (GB) ALP1009, VSM (Fr)
FALPIII

Tzigane
J.H.; Los Angeles Philharmonic Orchestra, Alfred Wallenstein, conductor
1954   Victor (US) LM1382, LM2836, RCA (Fr) 630245, 630815A

Valses nobles et sentimentales (No. 6 and No. 7; transcription by J.H.)
J.H.; Brooks Smith, piano
1965   Mono: Victor (US) LM2856, RCA Victor (Fr) 635051
Stereo: Victor (US) LSC2856, RCA Victor (Fr) 645051

Tzigane
J.H.; Brooks Smith, piano
1975   Columbia (US) M233444 (1983), CBS (GB) 76420, (Fr) 79202—rec. Oct.
23, 1972, Dorothy Chandler Pavilion, Los Angeles

FANNY HELDY (1888–1973)
lyric soprano

Artistic encounter.

Following her performance as Concepcion in *L'Heure espagnole,* M.R. made a flattering comment: "The female subconscious is completely revealed in the very conscious interpretation of Fanny Heldy" (cited by Bernard Gavoty in the liner notes of record FALP627—see below).

"Oh! La pitoyable aventure" (*L'Heure espagnole*)
1931 See Piero Coppola, above

FRANZ-JOSEPH HIRT (b. 1899)
piano

Address book (with address in Switzerland and note: Professor at the Bern Conservatory)—Correspondence—Artistic encounter.

In Geneva, on November 20, 1926, F.-J.H. organized a Ravel festival in which the composer participated (see letter no. 273, note 2).

"La Vallée des cloches" (*Miroirs*)
1928 78 rpm, 25 cm., Gramophone (Ger, GB) EG815

Sonatine
1932 78 rpm, 25 cm., Gramophone (Ger) EG1762/3, (GB) B4127/8

MIECZYSLAW HORSZOWSKI (b. 1892)
piano

Artistic encounter.

M.H. participated with the composer in a Ravel recital in Milan, Italy on November 1, 1922. "He gave a perfect interpretation of *Gaspard de la nuit* before Ravel" (*La Revue musicale,* January 1, 1923, p. 265).

Sonatine
1923 Ordinary piano roll, Pleyela, Aeolian, Odéola (Fr) AP8156/8

DÉSIRÉ-EMILE INGHELBRECHT (1880–1965)
conductor

Address book—Correspondence—Friendly and artistic relationship.

A friend of M.R. during his student days, D.-E.I. conducted the première of the *Trois Poèmes de Stéphane Mallarmé* with Jane Bathori on January 14, 1914, and the ballet version of *Le Tombeau de Couperin* with Rolf de Maré's Swedish Ballet on November 8, 1920. (See M.R.'s letter of appreciation, no. 77.)

Ma Mère l'Oye
Orchestre Pasdeloup
1929   78 rpm, Pathé-Art (Fr) x5485/7

Daphnis et Chloé (complete ballet)
Choeur et Maîtrise de la Radio et Télévision Française, Orchestre du Théâtre des Champs-Elysées
1954   Ducretet-Thomson (Fr) 320C015, (GB) DTL93048, Pathé-Marconi (Fr) 2C06112148 (1973)

"Une Barque sur l'océan" (*Miroirs*) – *Ma Mère l'Oye* – *Rapsodie espagnole*
Orchestre du Théâtre des Champs-Elysées
1955   Mono: Ducretet-Thomson (Fr) 320C088
        Excerpts of these 33 rpm, 30 cm. records were issued by Ducretet-Thomson in 1958: 255C069 and 255C099 (both 25 cm.).

NINA KOSHETZ (1894–1965)
mezzo-soprano

Photographs—Artistic encounter.

In April 1928, aboard the liner "Paris," sailing from New York to Le Havre, N.K. performed Ravel's songs accompanied by the composer, who was returning from his American tour. This fact is confirmed by a photograph and poster of their joint recital.

"Kaddisch" (*Deux Mélodies hébraïques*)
N.K. with orchestral accompaniment
1928   78 rpm, Gramophone (GB, Fr) DB1205

SERGE KOUSSEVITZKY (1874–1951)
conductor

Address book—Correspondence—Friendly and artistic relationship.

On friendly terms with Ravel, S.K. suggested that he orchestrate Mussorgsky's brilliant piano piece *Pictures at an Exhibition*, and then commissioned the transcription. He introduced the work on October 19, 1922, as part of the Koussevitzky Concerts given at the Paris Opéra. Music director of the Boston Symphony Orchestra from 1924 to 1949, S.K. welcomed M.R. to Boston in January 1928 and conducted a concert devoted to his works.

Daphnis et Chloé (Suite No. 2)
Boston Symphony Orchestra
1929   78 rpm, Victor (US) 7143/4, Gramophone (GB) D1826/7, (Fr) W1084/5

Boléro (13′20)
Boston Symphony Orchestra
1930   78 rpm, Victor (US) 7251/2, set M352, DM18434/5, Gramophone (GB,
          Australia) D 1859/60, (Italy) AW175/6, (Japan) ND360/1 set JAS96
          33 rpm, RCA-Camden (US) CAL 161

Ma Mère l'Oye
Boston Symphony Orchestra
1930   78 rpm, Victor (US) 7370/1
          33 rpm, RCA-Camden (US) CAL 161

Tableaux d'une exposition (Mussorgsky-Ravel)
Boston Symphony Orchestra
1930   78 rpm, Victor (US) 7372/5, 17204/7, set M 102, Gramophone (GB, Fr)
          DB 1890/3, set M 180—first rec. of this work; rec. Oct. 28, 1930
          33 rpm, RCA-Camden (US) CAL 111 (1953), RCA-Victrola (GB) VICS 1514
          (rechanneled for stereo) (1953) (1970), RCA (Fr) 731025 (1971)
          Although out of print, this disk is listed in the *Diapason* record guide (1987)
          as a definitive interpretation.

"Sarabande" (Debussy-Ravel)
Boston Symphony Orchestra
1930   78 rpm, Victor (US) 7375, 17204, set M 102, Gramophone (GB, Fr) DB1893,
          set M 180

La Valse – Danse (Debussy-Ravel)
Boston Symphony Orchestra
1931   78 rpm, Victor (US) 7413/4, Gramophone (GB, Italy) DB1541/2

Daphnis et Chloé (Suite No. 2; 2nd version)
Boston Symphony Orchestra
1946   78 rpm, Victor (US) 118747/8, set SPI, 119496/7, set 1108, HMV (GB)
          DB6239/40

Pavane pour une Infante défunte
Boston Symphony Orchestra
1947   78 rpm, Victor (US) 119729, HMV (GB) 6699

Rapsodie espagnole
Boston Symphony Orchestra
1948   78 rpm, Victor (US) 120163/4, set 1200
          33 rpm, RCA-Camden (US) CAL376 (1957)

Boléro (13′22; 2nd version)
Boston Symphony Orchestra
1948   78 rpm, Victor (US) 120324/5, set 1220, HMV (GB) DB9601/2—rec.
          Tanglewood, Lenox, Mass.

        33 rpm, RCA-Victor (US) LM 1012, HMV (GB) ALP 1003, VIC 1021, (Fr)
        QALP 10020
        45 rpm, 17 cm., RCA-Victor (US) WDM 1220

Ma Mère l'Oye (2d version)
Boston Symphony Orchestra
1948   78 rpm, 120631/2, set 1268
        33 rpm, RCA-Victor (US) LM 1012, HMV (GB) ALP 1003, VIC 1021, (Fr)
        QALP 10020
        45 rpm, 17 cm., RCA-Victor (US) WDM 1268

Daphnis et Chloé (Suite No. 2; 3d version)
Boston Symphony Orchestra
1975   33 rpm, SID (US) 711—private recording, rec. 1948

ROBERT KRETTLY (b. 1891)
violin

Artistic encounter.

  See Pierre Fournier, above.

String Quartet
Krettly Quartet (R.K., R. Costard, F. Broos, A. Navarra)
1929   78 rpm, Gramophone (Fr) W975/7, Victor (US) 9799/801

JEANE KRIEGER
soprano

Address book—Correspondence—Friendly and artistic relationship.

  J.K., "widow of the baritone Arthur Endrèze, said that Ravel was consulted about the recording [of *L'Heure espagnole*] and specially asked for her to be engaged to sing the role of Concepcion. Ravel knew that she was not a professional opera singer—she was a répétiteur and an outstanding teacher and assistant to many eminent composers—but he wanted a first-rate musician with rather an acidulated, Spanish-sounding voice." (Patrick Saul, book review of Orenstein, *Ravel: Man and Musician*, in *Journal of the British Institute of Recorded Sound*, London, April 1976, p. 543.)

L'Heure espagnole (complete opera)
1929   See Georges Truc, below; J.K. as Concepcion

LILY LASKINE (1893–1988)
harp

Photograph (L.L. at the harp, M.R. next to her)—Friendly and artistic relationship.

  On several occasions, she performed the *Introduction et Allegro* with M.R. conducting, notably at a Ravel Festival given in Paris at Salle Gaveau on June 1, 1926.

Introduction et Allegro
1938   See Calvet String Quartet, above

Introduction et Allegro
L.L.; Jean-Pierre Rampal, flute; Ulysse Delécluse, clarinet; Le Quatuor Pascal de la Radiodiffusion française (Jacques Dumont, Maurice Crut, Léon Pascal, Robert Salles)
1956   Mono: Columbia (Fr) FCX707—iss. Paris

Introduction et Allegro
L.L.; Alain Marion, flute; Jacques Lancelot, clarinet; the Via Nova String Quartet (Jean Moullère, Alain Moglia, Claude Naveau, Roland Pidoux)
1975   Erato (Fr) STU70798—rec. 1974, Paris

Introduction et Allegro
L.L.; Michel Debost, flute; Claude Desurmont, clarinet; string quartet (Christian Crenne, Odile Graef, Tasso Adamopoulos, Paul Bonfil)
1980   CIP-Video color film (Fr) broadcast on FR3 (channel 3 on French television) in 1980 and 1983; Georges Bessonnet, director—rec. 1979, Paris

YVONNE LEFÉBURE (1898–1986)
piano

Friendly and artistic relationship.

As a very young student in Alfred Cortot's class, Y.L. played *Jeux d'eau* before Cortot and Ravel.

I began with a somewhat non-legato touch, even though the music calls for legato, in order to achieve crystalline sonorities. M.R. exclaimed "that's it." He later said with regard to my interpretation of *Jeux d'eau*—half serious, half jokingly—"transmit the tradition." Following Marguerite Long, I was the second interpreter of the G Major Piano Concerto, which Cortot conducted in Ravel's presence. I performed this concerto 85 times throughout the world, 15 times with Paul Paray. I had dinner with M.R. shortly before his death; his address was attached to the inside of his jacket. (Interview with Y.L. in October 1974, and Ravel program broadcast on Belgian television, 1975.)

Sonata for Violin and Piano
Jeanne Gautier, violin; Y.L.
1950   78 rpm, Chant du Monde (Fr) GA5056/7
1955   2nd version, Mono: 33 rpm, 17 cm., Chant du Monde (Fr) LDYA8115

Le Tombeau de Couperin – Jeux d'eau – Valses nobles et sentimentales – Ma Mère l'Oye
Y.L.; with Gersende de Sabran in *Ma Mère l'Oye*
1975   FY (Fr) 018 (distribution by RCA)
1986   AD: 12 cm. (compact disc), FYCD018—reissue of the above.

Jeux d'eau – Piano Concerto in G (excerpts)
1975 Color film on Ravel produced by Belgian Radio and Television (see
     filmography, p. 530)

Y.L. performs the same excerpt from *Jeux d'eau* twice, the first time in the way that
Ravel disapproved of, then in the way that made him exclaim "that's it," and comments
on this interpretation. She also performs the opening of the slow movement of the Piano
Concerto in G Major and then makes some comments about it.

Piano Concerto in G
Y.L.; Orchestre Philharmonique de l'O.R.T.F., Paul Paray, conductor
1988 AD: 12 cm. (compact disc) SOCD (Fr)55—rec. 1970

PAUL LE FLEM (1881–1984)
conductor

Friendly and artistic relationship.

He was introduced to M.R. about 1905, and the young composers would often meet
at concerts of contemporary music. (Interview with Arbie Orenstein in Paris on July 30,
1981, shortly after Paul Le Flem's 100th birthday.)

"Nicolette" (*Trois Chansons pour choeur mixte sans accompagnement*)
Les Chanteurs de Saint-Gervais, P.L.F., conductor
1930 78 rpm, 25 cm., Gramophone (Fr) P823

PAULE DE LESTANG
soprano, harpsichord, (piano)

Address book—Correspondence—Friendly and artistic relationship.

She introduced the Sonatine in Lyon on March 10, 1906.

"D'Anne jouant de l'espinette" (*Epigrammes de Clément Marot*)
1928 78 rpm, 25 cm., Gramophone (Fr) K5338—rec. Jan. 1927; iss. April, 1928
     Written on the record label is: "Performed and sung by Madame de
     Lestang—harpsichord and voice." All of the subsequent recordings of this
     work until now generally contain piano accompaniment, rarely orchestral
     (orchestration by Maurice Delage), and only one uses the harpsichord:
     Jean-Christophe Benoit, VSM (Fr) CVB2175—iss. 1968.

MARGUERITE LONG (1874–1966)
piano

Address book—Correspondence—Photographs—Friendly and artistic relationship.

M.L. introduced *Le Tombeau de Couperin* in Paris on April 11, 1919, and the Piano
Concerto in G Major (which is dedicated to her) on January 14, 1932, at Salle Pleyel,

with M.R. conducting the Lamoureux Orchestra. In 1932, she performed the Concerto under Ravel's baton in some twenty European cities during a three-month concert tour. The composer inscribed a photograph of himself to her as follows: "for M.L. 'record-woman' of the Concerto, [signed] M.R."

Concerto for Piano and Orchestra in G
M.L.; Symphonic Orchestra
See "Ravel as orchestral conductor," p. 535

Concerto for Piano and Orchestra in G
M.L.; Orchestre de la Société des Concerts du Conservatoire, Georges Tzipine, conductor
1952   Columbia (Fr) FCX 169, FCXPM30354 (1966), Angel (Japan) GRZ 132 (1966) (1983)—rec. 1952, Théâtre des Champs-Elysées

ANDRÉ MANGEOT (1883–1970)
violin

Address book—Correspondence—Friendly and artistic relationship.

String Quartet
The International String Quartet
1927   See "Ravel as supervisor of recordings," p. 538–39

MAURICE MARÉCHAL (1892–1964)
cello

Address book—Friendly and artistic relationship.

With violinist Hélène Jourdan-Morhange, he introduced the Sonata for Violin and Cello in Paris on April 6, 1922. One holograph of this work contains the following dedication: "for M.M., in remembrance of the beautiful first performance on April 6, 1922, his grateful [signed] M.R." (Hélène Jourdan-Morhange was the dedicatee of the Sonata for Violin and Piano, but was unable to introduce it as the onset of motor cramps forced her to abandon her career. Thus she never recorded any work by Ravel.)

Pièce en forme de Habanera
M.M.; Maurice Faure, piano
1929   78 rpm, 25 cm., Columbia (Fr) D 13101, (US) 2446D—rec. 1929

JEAN MARTINON (1910–1976)
conductor

Artistic encounter.

J.M. recalled M.R. as follows:

I had the good fortune to meet him and talk with him. I heard him conduct his own works; I played violin several times under his direction, in such works as *Boléro, Pavane pour une Infante défunte, Le Tombeau de Couperin*, and the Concerto in G. He was an affable person, and in contrast to the rather sensual character of his music, he demonstrated a neo-classic temperament in his conducting. His interpretations were curiously rigorous. (J.M., liner notes from the records RCA (Fr) 644532 and (GB) VICS 1619.)

Le Tombeau de Couperin
London Philharmonic Orchestra (recorded in Kingsway Hall, London)
1947   78 rpm, Decca (GB) AK 1838/9, London (US) set LA 193

Daphnis et Chloé (Suite No. 2)
Chicago Symphony Orchestra, Donald Peck, flute solo
1965   Mono: RCA-Victrola (US) LM2806
            Stereo: RCA-Victrola (US) LSC2806, Camden-Quintessence (US) PMC7017
            (1977), RCA-Victrola (Fr) 645061 A, (GB) GL42701 (1983)

"Alborada del gracioso" – *Ma Mère l'Oye* – *Rapsodie espagnole*
Chicago Symphony Orchestra
1968   RCA-Victrola (US) LSC3093, (GB) VICS 1619 (1971), (Fr) 644532 (1972)

Boléro (13'40)
Chicago Symphony Orchestra
1971   RCA (US) LSC5002, Camden-Quintessence (US) PMC7017 (1977)—iss.
            Aug. 1971

La Valse
Symphonic Orchestra of the RTB (Belgian Radio and Television)
Color video film—rec. early 1970s, studios of RTB, Brussels
The original of the complete version realized by Alain Denis was destroyed and is no longer in the archives of the RTB. Copies may exist elsewhere. Excerpts of *La Valse* appear in the color film on Ravel by the RTB (see filmography, p. 530).

Ravel: The Orchestral Works
Boléro (14'46; Marcel Galiègue, trombone solo) – *Rapsodie espagnole* – *La Valse* – *Daphnis et Chloé* (complete ballet) – *Valses nobles et sentimentales* – *Ma Mère l'Oye* – *Le Tombeau de Couperin* – *Pavane pour une Infante défunte* – *Shéhérazade* (Fairy Tale Overture) – *Menuet antique* – "Une Barque sur l'océan" – "Alborada del gracioso" (André Sennedat, bassoon solo) – Concerto en ré pour la main gauche – Concerto en sol (Jean-Claude Malgoire, English horn solo) – *Tzigane*
Orchestre de Paris, with Aldo Ciccolini, piano, and Itzhak Perlman, violin
1975   VSM (Fr) 2C 165-02583/7 (10 sides)—rec. 1975
Since its appearance as a boxed set in 1975, this most extensive collection of the complete orchestral works has enjoyed numerous reissues with various couplings in different countries (notably Ger, Fr, GB, US), with single disks available in 1983.

WILLEM MENGELBERG (1871–1951)
conductor

Artistic encounter.

In October 1922, he participated with Ravel in a festival of French music which took place in Amsterdam. W.M. and M.R. met again in Haarlem in April 1932, when they both conducted the Concertgebouw Orchestra.

Boléro (14'35)
Concertgebouw Orchestra of Amsterdam
1930   78 rpm, Columbia (GB) LX48/9, (Fr) LFX90/1, (Australia) LOX60/1, (US)
       67890/1D, set X22, (Italy) GQX 10639/40—rec. 1930

Daphnis et Chloé (Suite No. 2)
Concertgebouw Orchestra of Amsterdam
1977   Educational Media (US) RR506—rec. Oct. 6, 1938

LIVINE MERTENS (1901–1968)
mezzo-soprano

Artistic encounter.

In March 1931, she sang Ravel's *Deux Mélodies hébraïques* in Brussels under the baton of the composer. (Discussed in the Belgian journal *L'Eventail*, March 15, 1931.)

L'Enfant et les sortilèges (Duet of the Teapot and the Chinese Cup; The Arithmetic)
L.M.; Henri Marcotty, tenor
1931   78 rpm, 25 cm., Columbia (Fr) LF96

MARCELLE MEYER (1897–1958)
piano

Artistic encounter.

She was a pupil of Ricardo Viñes (Ravel's close friend, who introduced six of his most important piano works between 1898 and 1909). In 1920, in the company of Diaghilev, Stravinsky, and Massine, Francis Poulenc heard the first two-piano rendition of *La Valse*, played by M.M. and M.R. at the home of Misia Sert. (F. Poulenc, *Moi et mes amis*, Paris, La Palatine, 1963, pp. 178–79.)

"Alborada del gracioso"
1930   78 rpm, 25 cm., Columbia (Fr) LF11—rec. 1930

Valses nobles et sentimentales – "Alborada del gracioso," "La Vallée des cloches," "Oiseaux tristes"
1949   78 rpm, Les Discophiles Français (Fr) Album 25 (4 records, nos. 108/111)—
       iss. March, 1949

Ravel's Works for Piano Solo

Valses nobles et sentimentales – Sonatine — *Pavane pour une Infante défunte* – *Le
    Tombeau de Couperin* – *Menuet sur le nom d'Haydn* – *Menuet antique* – *Gaspard de la
    nuit* – *Jeux d'eau* – *Miroirs*

1954   Les Discophiles Français (Fr) DF 100/1, Alpha (Belgium) DB 102/3
         33 rpm, 17 cm., Les Discophiles Français (Fr) EX 17029 (*Jeux d'eau* –
         Sonatine)
         33 rpm, 17 cm., Les Discophiles Français (Fr) EX 17035 ("Alborada del
         gracioso" – *Pavane pour une Infante défunte*)

PIERRE MONTEUX (1875–1964)
conductor

Correspondence—Friendly and artistic relationship.

P.M. conducted the première of the Ballet Russe production of *Daphnis et Chloé* at the
Théâtre du Châtelet on June 8, 1912, and also introduced the orchestral version of the
Valses nobles et sentimentales in Paris on February 15, 1914. In February 1931, M.R. led
the Orchestre Symphonique de Paris in *Le Tombeau de Couperin* and *Boléro*, sharing the
all-Ravel program with P.M.

La Valse – "Petit Poucet" (*Ma Mère l'Oye*)
Orchestre Symphonique de Paris
1931   78 rpm, Gramophone (Fr) W 1107/8—rec. 1931

La Valse
San Francisco Symphony Orchestra
1942   78 rpm, RCA-Victor (US) 18160/1 set M820, Gramophone (GB) 5964/5,
         (Australia) ED316/7
         33 rpm, RCA-Camden (US) CAL282
         45 rpm, 17 cm., RCA-Camden (US) CAE 130

Rapsodie espagnole
The New York Philharmonic Symphony Orchestra
Recorded in New York's Carnegie Hall (November 12, 1944) under the auspices of
    the American War Ministry, and originally intended to be broadcast only to the
    armed services. The records were to have been destroyed after the war.
1944   78 rpm, V. Disc (US) Army 447/8, Navy 227/8

Valses nobles et sentimentales
San Francisco Symphony Orchestra
1947   78 rpm, RCA-Victor (US) 119681/2 set M 1143, HMV (GB) DB6676/7
         33 rpm, RCA-Camden (US) CAL 156
         45 rpm, 17 cm., RCA-Camden (US) CAE216

Daphnis et Chloé (Suite No. 1)
San Francisco Symphony Orchestra; San Francisco Municipal Choir
1947   78 rpm, RCA-Victor (US) 119683/4 set M1143
        33 rpm, RCA-Camden (US) CAL156

"Sarabande" (Debussy-Ravel)
San Francisco Symphony Orchestra
1947   78 rpm, RCA-Victor (US) 119684 set M1143
        33 rpm, RCA-Camden (US) CAL385, (GB) CDN1005 (1957)

"Alborada del gracioso"
San Francisco Symphony Orchestra
1950   78 rpm, RCA-Victor (US) 121107

Daphnis et Chloé (complete ballet)
London Symphony Orchestra; Chorus of the Royal Opera House, Covent Garden,
    Douglas Robinson, choral director
1959   Mono: Decca (GB, Fr) LXT5536, London (US) CM9028
        Stereo: Decca (GB, Fr) SXL2164, SDD170, (GB) JB69 (1983), (Fr) 592027
            (1983), London (US) CS6147, STS15090 (1983)

Pavane pour une Infante défunte – Rapsodie espagnole
London Symphony Orchestra
1962   Mono: Decca (GB, Fr) LXT5677, London (US) CM9317
        Stereo: Decca (GB, Fr) SXL2312, SDD425, (Fr) 592033 (1983), London (US)
            CS6248, STS15356 (1983)

Boléro (1965, 15'14; 1987, 15'20) – *Ma Mère l'Oye* (complete ballet) – *La Valse*
London Symphony Orchestra
1965   Mono: Philips (GB, Fr) L02380LY, (US) 500059
        Stereo: Philips (GB, Fr) 835258LY, (GB) 6527038 (1983), (Fr) 6500226
            (1983), (US) 900059, 6570092 (1983), (Ger) 6768339 (1983)
1987   ADD: 12 cm. (compact disc) Philips (GB, Fr) 420869-2—rec. Feb. 1964,
        London

MARCEL MOYSE (1889–1984)
flute

Friendly and artistic relationship.

M.M. performed the *Introduction et Allegro* on several occasions under the direction of
M.R.

Introduction et Allegro
1938   See Calvet String Quartet, above

CHARLES MÜNCH (1891–1968)
conductor

Artistic encounter.

He conducted the Orchestre Philharmonique de Paris in a Ravel Festival at Salle Pleyel on March 19, 1937, in the composer's presence. The concert included the Concerto for the Left Hand with Jacques Février as soloist.

Concerto for Piano and Orchestra in D, "For the Left Hand"
Jacqueline Blancard, piano; Orchestre Philharmonique de Paris
1938   See Jacqueline Blancard, above

Concerto for Piano and Orchestra in D, "For the Left Hand"
Alfred Cortot, piano; Orchestre de la Société des Concerts du Conservatoire
1940   See Alfred Cortot, above

Concerto for Piano and Orchestra in D, "For the Left Hand"
Jacques Février, piano; Orchestre de la Société des Concerts du Conservatoire
1943   See Jacques Février, above

La Valse – Pavane pour une Infante défunte
Orchestre de la Société des Concerts du Conservatoire
1943   78 rpm, VSM (Fr) W 1557/8

Boléro (16′44)
Orchestre de la Société des Concerts du Conservatoire
The record label states: "Recorded in the Assembly Hall, Walthams Row."
1947   78 rpm, Decca (GB) K 1637/8
          33 rpm, London (US) LL22-LL466, Richmond (US) 19001, Decca (GB, Fr)
          LXT2677

Daphnis et Chloé ("Nocturne," "Danse guerrière," "Lever du jour," "Pantomime,"
    "Danse générale")
Orchestre de la Société des Concerts du Conservatoire
1949   78 rpm, Decca (Fr) GAG 1584/6, (GB) K 1584/6, (US) set EDA29, London
          (US) set LA225

Concerto for Piano and Orchestra in G
Nicole Henriot-Schweitzer, piano; Orchestre de la Société des Concerts du
    Conservatoire
1950   Decca (GB) LXT2565, London (US) LL76

La Valse
Boston Symphony Orchestra
1951   78 rpm, Victor (US) 121207
          33 rpm, 25 cm., RCA-Victor (US) LRM7016, (Fr) A630217
          45 rpm, 17 cm., Victor (US) 491213

Rapsodie espagnole
Boston Symphony Orchestra
1952   25 cm., RCA-Victor (US) LRM7016
       RCA-Victor (US) LM 1700, (Fr) ALP 1245

Pavane pour une Infante défunte
Boston Symphony Orchestra
1953   25 cm., RCA-Victor (US) LRM7016
       RCA-Victor (US) LM 1741, (Fr) 630315, (Italy) A 12R0110

Daphnis et Chloé (complete ballet)
Boston Symphony Orchestra; Chorus of the New England Conservatory and Alumni,
   Robert Shaw, conductor, assisted by Lorna Cooke de Varon
1955   Mono: RCA-Victor (US) LM 1893, (Fr) 630294
       Stereo: RCA-Victor (US) LSC 1893, (Fr) 640659, (GB) VICS 1297, (Ger)
           2641181 AG (1983)

Daphnis et Chloé (Suite nos. 1 and 2)
Boston Symphony Orchestra; Chorus of the New England Conservatory and Alumni
1967   Mono: RCA-Victrola (US) 1271, Stereo VICS 1271—rec. Jan. 1955

Rapsodie espagnole (2nd version) – *Le Valse* (2nd version) – *Boléro* (13'42; 2nd version)
Boston Symphony Orchestra
1956   Mono: RCA-Victor (US) LM 1984, (Fr) 630370, (US, GB) VIC 1041, 1323
       Stereo: RCA-Victor (US) LSC 1984, (GB, Fr) SB2019, (US, GB) VICS 1041,
           1323

Concerto for Piano and Orchestra in G
Nicole Henriot-Schweitzer, piano; Boston Symphony Orchestra
1959   Mono: RCA-Victor (US) LM2271, (Fr) 630512, (US) VIC 1071
       Stereo: RCA-Victor (US) LSC2271, VICS 1071

Ma Mère l'Oye
Boston Symphony Orchestra
1959   Mono: RCA-Victor (US) LM2292, VIC 1060, (Fr) 630487
       Stereo: RCA-Victor (US) LSC2292, VICS 1060, (Fr) 640541

Daphnis et Chloé (complete ballet; 2nd version)
Boston Symphony Orchestra; Chorus of the New England Conservatory, Lorna
   Cooke de Varon, conductor
1961   Mono: RCA-Victor (US) LM2568, (Fr) 630610
       Stereo: RCA-Victor (US) LSC2568, AGL 11270 (1983)

Boléro (15'02; 3rd version) – *Pavane pour une Infante défunte* (2nd version) – *La Valse*
   (3rd version)
Boston Symphony Orchestra
1962   Mono: RCA-Victor (US) LM2664
       Stereo: RCA-Victor (US) LSC2664, AGL 13653 (1983), (GB) SB6556, (Fr)
           GL43711 (1983), (Ger) 2641187AG (1983)

Valses nobles et sentimentales
Philadelphia Orchestra
1963   Mono: Columbia (US) ML5925, Stereo MS6523, (Fr) S72153

Boléro (16′55; 4th version) – *Rapsodie espagnole* – *Daphnis et Chloé* (Suite No. 2) –
   Pavane pour une Infante défunte (Roger Abraham, horn solo) – Concerto for Piano
   and Orchestra in G
Orchestre de Paris; Nicole Henriot-Schweitzer, piano
1969   VSM (Fr) CVB2281/2, C16552511/4, Angel (US) S36584/5, (GB)
      ASD2497/8—rec. Sept. 1968
1985   AD: 12 cm. (compact disc), Pathé-Marconi (Fr) 1102392 (contains 4 of the
      preceding 5 works, not the Concerto; *Boléro* 17′03)

PAUL PARAY (1886–1979)
conductor

Address book—Correspondence—Friendly and artistic relationship.

He introduced Ravel's transcriptions of Debussy's "Sarabande" and *Danse* with the
Lamoureux Orchestra at Salle Gaveau on March 18, 1923. In 1933, M.R. asked P.P. to
replace him for a performance of the Piano Concerto for the Left Hand in Monte Carlo,
with Paul Wittgenstein as soloist. The composer was present, however, at the performance. Hélène Jourdan-Morhange recalled the following incident at a concert which
she attended with Ravel:

> Paray conducted *La Valse* in a dazzling and lilting manner which assured its
> complete success. Ravel said to me: "that's not it at all, but it's magnificent." And
> following Ravelian tradition he said to Paray: "I didn't hear the clarinet very
> well"—naturally without telling him how captivated he had been by his spirited
> rendition. Naive Ravel! How many artists, including Toscanini, might he have
> offended, without even being aware of it. (H. Jourdan-Morhange, *Mes amis musi-
> ciens*, Paris, Les Editeurs Français, 1955, pp. 38–39.)

Paul Paray was the music director of the Detroit Symphony Orchestra from 1952 to
1963. With two exceptions (the piano concerti and one version of *La Valse*), all of his
other recordings devoted exclusively to Ravel (9 works) were realized at that time with
the Detroit Symphony. But their multiple and disordered couplings in the United States
and France, among them and particularly with works of Debussy, Roussel, Chabrier,
Barraud, Ibert, Fauré, Franck, Rimsky-Korsakov, and Dukas, on 25 and 30 cm., in
mono and stereo, make any normal listing incoherent and incomprehensible. It will
therefore suffice to indicate first, the works recorded in mono, which are few in number,
then, the complete substratum of recordings in mono and stereo in their stereo versions
(1983), either complete (France and Holland) or partial (other countries).

Mono recordings (1954–55):
Boléro (13′00), Mercury (US) MG50020, (Fr) MLP7509

La Valse, Mercury (US) MG50029, (Fr) MLP7521
Rapsodie espagnole, Mercury (US) MG50056
Detroit Symphony Orchestra

Mono and stereo recordings (1956–62):
Boléro (13′16; 2nd version) – *La Valse* (2nd version) – *Rapsodie espagnole* (2nd version)
– *Le Tombeau de Couperin* – *Ma Mère l'Oye* – *Valses nobles et sentimentales* – *Daphnis
et Chloé* (Suite No. 2) – "Alborada del gracioso" – *Pavane pour une Infante défunte*
Detroit Symphony Orchestra
1983   2 records, Philips (Fr) 6768230; 3 records, Mercury (Holland) 75033, 75066,
        75100
1983   1 record, Mercury (US) 75033 (*Boléro, La Valse, Rapsodie espagnole*, "Alborada
        del gracioso," *Pavane pour une Infante défunte*)

Concerto for Piano and Orchestra in G
Monique Haas, piano; Orchestre National de l'O.R.T.F.
1965   DGG (Ger, Fr) 138988, 135107, (GB) 2548109 (1983), (US) 2535312
        (1983), (Ger) 2535483 (1983)

Concerto for Piano and Orchestra in D, "For the Left Hand"
Monique Haas, piano; Orchestre National de l'O.R.T.F.
1965   DGG (Ger, Fr) 138988, (US) 2535312 (1983)

La Valse
Orchestre de l'Opéra de Monte-Carlo
1970   Guilde (Fr) SMS2663, Festival (Fr) FC440 (1983)

EMILE PASSANI (b. 1905)
piano

Address book—Artistic encounter.

Concerto for Piano and Orchestra in G – *A la manière de . . . Borodine, Chabrier*
Orchestre de l'Association des Concerts Colonne, Jean Fournet, conductor
1949   78 rpm, Pathé (Fr) PDT 155/7, 8034/6—rec. Théâtre des Champs-Elysées

Sonatine – *Valses nobles et sentimentales*
1952   25 cm., Pathé (Fr) DT 1010

VLADO PERLEMUTER (b. 1904)
piano

Address book—Friendly and artistic relationship.

V.P. studied all of Ravel's works for the piano with the composer. For six months,
several times a week, V.P. took the train to Montfort l'Amaury in order to meet with

M.R. The Maître spoke about everything which should be done, but above all what should be avoided. One may assert that V.P. is one of the possessors of Ravelian thought.

(Hélène Jourdan-Morhange, in collaboration with V.P., *Ravel d'après Ravel,* Lausanne, Cervin, 1953, p. 8.) In this book, which has been re-edited several times (one edition is in Japanese), both authors examine and discuss Ravel's piano works, "with examples of what should be done and also what should be avoided." V.P. performed M.R.'s complete piano works in Paris in 1929.

Pavane pour une Infante défunte – Valses nobles et sentimentales — *Miroirs – Gaspard de la nuit – Menuet antique –* Sonatine *– Prélude – Le Tombeau de Couperin – Menuet sur le nom d'Haydn – Jeux d'eau –* Concerto for Piano and Orchestra in G – Concerto for Piano and Orchestra in D, "For the Left Hand"
V.P., piano; Orchestre des Concerts Colonne, Jascha Horenstein, conductor
1956   3 record set, Mono Vox (US, Fr) set DL153, (US) SVBX5410 (rechanneled for stereo)—rec. in France
        Single records which are excerpts of the above set:
        Pathé Vox (Fr) VP370 (*Miroirs – Gaspard de la nuit*)
        Vox (GB) STGBY610 (1968) (Both Piano Concerti *– Pavane pour une Infante défunte – Menuet antique*)

Sonatine
1975   Denon (Japan) OX7012N—rec. 1972, Tokyo

Menuet antique – Pavane pour une Infante défunte – Jeux d'eau – Gaspard de la nuit
1979   Nimbus (GB) 2101—rec. 1977

Miroirs – Sonatine *– Menuet sur le nom d'Haydn*
1979   Nimbus (GB) 2102—rec. 1977

Valses nobles et sentimentales – Prélude – "A la manière de . . . Borodine, Chabrier" *– Le Tombeau de Couperin*
1979   Nimbus (GB) 2103—rec. 1977
1984   AD: 12 cm. (compact discs):
        Vol. I: Nimbus (GB) NIM5005 (length, 59'20)—iss. Jan.

Miroirs – Jeux d'eau – Pavane pour une Infante défunte – Gaspard de la nuit
1984   Vol. II: Nimbus (GB) NIM5011 (length, 64'12)—iss. Sept.

Sonatine *– Valses nobles et sentimentales – Le Tombeau de Couperin –* "A la manière de . . . Borodine, Chabrier" *– Menuet antique – Menuet sur le nom d'Haydn*
These two compact discs were transferred from the digital recordings issued in 1979. Without exception, all of the pieces in the 1984 version are longer than those of 1979 (total length of the compact discs: 123'32, of the records: 121'00).

Ma Mère l'Oye
with David Gourdon, a pupil of V.P.
1984   Color video film (Fr) broadcast on FR3 (channel 3 on French television). The

program, entitled "Prélude à la nuit," was hosted by Charles Imbert and directed by Alain Jamy—rec. 1984

GABRIEL PIERNÉ (1863–1937)
conductor

Address book—Correspondence—Photographs—Friendly and artistic relationship.

As conductor of the Colonne Orchestra, he introduced "Une Barque sur l'océan" (February 3, 1907), the Suite No. 1 of *Daphnis et Chloé* (April 2, 1911), and with violinist Jelly d'Aranyi, the orchestral version of *Tzigane* (November 30, 1924).

Ma Mère l'Oye ("Petit Poucet," "Laideronnette, Impératrice des pagodes," "Le Jardin féerique")
Orchestre de l'Association des Concerts Colonne
1929 78 rpm, Odéon (Fr) 123546/7, Parlophone (GB) 20066/7, Decca (US) 25319/20

Pavane pour une Infante défunte
Orchestre de l'Association des Concerts Colonne
1929 78 rpm, Odéon (Fr) 123617, (Spain) 173186, Columbia (US) G67785D

Rapsodie espagnole
Orchestre de l'Association des Concerts Colonne
1931 78 rpm, Odéon (Fr) 123770/1, (Ger) 07882/3, (Argentina) 177218/9, Decca (US) 25321/2

FRANCIS POULENC (1899–1963)
piano

Address book—Correspondence—Friendly and artistic relationship (see letter no. 158, note 2).

Sainte – Sur l'herbe
F.P.; Pierre Bernac, baritone
1936 78 rpm, 25 cm., Gramophone (Fr) DA4891
33 rpm, VSM (Fr) OVD50036

Don Quichotte à Dulcinée
F.P.; Pierre Bernac, baritone
1947 78 rpm, 25 cm., Gramophone (GB, Fr) DA1869

Histoires naturelles – Chansons hébraïques (*Deux Mélodies hébraïques;* "Chanson hébraïque")
F.P.; Pierre Bernac, baritone
1951 78 rpm, Columbia (US) set MM958—rec. March 2, 1950
33 rpm, Columbia (US) ML4333, (Fr) FCX141, (GB) CX1119, Odyssey (US) 32260009 (1983)

Shéhérazade ("La Flûte enchantée," "L'Indifférent") – *Noël des jouets*
F.P.; Denise Duval, soprano
1985   Mono: Clio (Fr) CL 10001—rec. May 16, 1958, Bordeaux

MANUEL ROSENTHAL (b. 1904)
conductor

Address book—Correspondence—Friendly and artistic relationship.

He began to study with Ravel in 1926, and remained one of his closest associates until the composer's death. He recalled the lessons as follows:

> I would go to his house in Montfort l'Amaury outside of Paris and spend the day talking. We would have lunch together, walk in the woods near his house, and he would go to the piano and show me things. "I cannot tell you how to compose," he would say, pointing to a certain section, "but if this is what you intended, there are better solutions." Then he would find a similar situation in the music of Mozart and show me how he had solved the same problem. . . . He could also be cruel. I once brought Ravel a two-voice fugue of which I was particularly proud. . . . He told me that later in life I could do what I wanted in a fugue but that what I had done was too free given the rules of this exercise. He took my fugue and tore it up. I became very angry and left the house in tears and went toward the train back to Paris. Then Ravel's figure appeared out of the rain, and he asked me why I had left his home without saying goodbye. It made me feel very good again.

(Bernard Holland, "Remembering Creators of the French Tradition," *New York Times*, Sunday, November 24, 1985, section II, p. 25.)

Danse – "Sarabande" (Debussy-Ravel)
Orchestre du Théâtre National de l'Opéra de Paris
1959   Mono: Vega (Fr) C30A294/5
1984   Stereo: Adès (Fr) 70097—iss. Nov. 1984

Ravel: The Complete Works for Orchestra
Orchestre du Théâtre National de l'Opéra de Paris
1959   Vol. 1 *Daphnis et Chloé* (complete ballet)
        Choeurs de la Radiodiffusion Télévision Française; René Alix, choral director
        Mono Vega (Fr) C30A 196, Westminster (US) 18753
        Vol. 2 *Boléro* (15'16) – *Pavane pour une Infante défunte* (Lucien Thévet, horn solo) – *Ma Mère l'Oye*
        Mono Vega (Fr) C30A 197
        Vol. 3 *Rapsodie espagnole* – "Alborada del gracioso" – *Valses nobles et sentimentales*
        Mono Vega (Fr) C30A 198
        Vol. 4 *Le Tombeau de Couperin* – *La Valse* – *Menuet antique*
        Mono Vega (Fr) C30A 199

These recordings of 10 orchestral works were reissued in stereo by Decca
(Fr) 130013/4 (2 albums of 2 records), then in a new stereo pressing
(1984) by Adès (Fr) COF7093 (boxed set of 4 records).

Daphnis et Chloé (complete ballet; reissue of the 1959 recording)
1985   AD: 12 cm. (compact disc), Adès (Fr) 14074-2—iss. Aug. 1985

"Alborada del gracioso" – *Rapsodie espagnole* – *Ma Mère L'Oye* – *La Valse* (reissue of
the 1959 recording)

Tzigane
Arthur Grumiaux, violin; Orchestre des Concerts Lamoureux
1966   Philips (Fr) 802708LY (1983), (US) 900195, (GB) 3587 (1983), (Ger)
           6570026 (1983)
1986   AAD: 12 cm. (compact disc) Adès (Fr) 14092-2

Boléro (15' 16) – *Pavane pour une Infante défunte* – *Valses nobles et sentimentales* – *Menuet*
antique – *Le Tombeau de Couperin* (reissue of the 1959 recording)
1986   AAD: 12 cm. (compact disc) Adès (Fr) 14093-2

ARTHUR RUBINSTEIN (1886–1982)
piano

Photographs—Friendly and artistic relationship.

"Ravel was a great friend of mine since the astonishing year 1904. During his lifetime
we met quite often in Saint-Jean-de-Luz, Biarritz and also in Paris. We played sometimes 4 hands and he showed me some new creation of his that he had just finished."
(Excerpt of a letter dated June 27, 1975, A.R. to Arbie Orenstein.)

"Forlane" (*Le Tombeau de Couperin*)
1935   78 rpm, Gramophone (GB, Fr) DB2450—rec. Feb. 23, 1934
           33 rpm, Electrola (Ger) IC 15103244/5M

Trio
A.R.; Jascha Heifetz, violin; Gregor Piatigorsky, cello
1950   See Jascha Heifetz, above

Valses nobles et sentimentales – "La Vallée des cloches" (*Miroirs*)
1964   Mono: Victor (US) LM2751, RCA-Victor (GB) RB6603, (Fr) 635024
           Stereo: Victor (US, Italy) LSC2751, RCA-Victor (GB) SB6855, (Fr) 645024

ELSA RUHLMANN
soprano

Address book—Artistic encounter.

The daughter of François Ruhlmann, who conducted the première of *L'Heure es-*
pagnole, she owned a score of the opera with a dedication signed by the composer.

Histoires naturelles – Sur l'herbe
E.R.; Piero Coppola, piano
1931   See Piero Coppola, above

VICTOR DE SABATA (1892–1967)
conductor

Friendly and artistic relationship.

On March 21, 1925, he conducted the first performance of *L'Enfant et les sortilèges* at the Monte Carlo Opera (see letter no. 249).

Boléro (13'15) – *La Valse* – *Ma Mère L'Oye*
New York Philharmonic Orchestra; recorded during a concert
1988   AD: 12 cm. (compact disc) Nuova Era (Italy) 2219—rec. March 1950, New York

CARLOS SALZEDO (1885–1961)
(harp), piano

Artistic encounter.

On January 15, 1928, in New York's Aeolian Hall, C.S. was the harp soloist in a performance of the *Introduction et Allegro* conducted by M.R.

Introduction et Allegro
C.S., piano; accompaniment only
1925   Automatic piano roll, Duo-Art (US, GB) 11838

GUSTAVE SAMAZEUILH (1877–1967)
piano

Address book—Correspondence—Friendly and artistic relationship.

A lifelong friend of Ravel, G.S., who was also a composer, frequently summered with M.R. in the Basque country, and in one recital devoted to their works they performed *Ma Mère l'Oye* together. (Gustave Samazeuilh, "Maurice Ravel en Pays Basque," *La Revue musicale*, December 1938, p. 202.)

Daphnis et Chloé (Suite No. 2: "Lever du jour," "Pantomime," "Danse générale"; piano transcription by G.S.)
1928   Ordinary piano roll, Pleyela, Aeolian, and Odéola (Fr) TR10367/9

CHARLES SCHARRES
piano

Address book (address in Brussels)—Artistic encounter.

"Forlane" – "Menuet" (*Le Tombeau de Couperin*)
1922   78 rpm, acoustical Gramophone (Fr) L297

E. ROBERT SCHMITZ (1889–1949)
piano

Address book (address in New York)—Correspondence—Friendly and artistic relationship.

In 1917, on leave from the front, he performed the Trio with Hélène Jourdan-Morhange and cellist Félix Delgrange. M.R., who was present at the recital, came over to congratulate the performers, and thus began a warm friendship. (Hélène Jourdan-Morhange, *Ravel et nous*, pp. 17–18.) In 1919, E.R.S. settled in the United States, and he was largely responsible for Ravel's North American tour in 1928.

Jeux d'eau
1919   Automatic piano roll, Duo-Art (US) 6199—iss. Oct. 1919; reproduced on
        record, Klavier (US) KS 117 (1970) (length: 4'20)
1985   DA: New issue, Klavier Digital Audiophile (US) KD 137 (length: 4'18)—rec.
        1984

The last recording is probably unavailable, as the Klavier Piano Roll company (US) went out of business on August 16, 1986.

Pavane pour une Infante défunte
1926   Automatic piano roll, Ampico (US) 65473H—iss. Jan. 1926

Jeux d'eau (2nd version)
1928   Automatic piano roll, Ampico (US) 69383H—iss. Dec. 1928

Pavane pour une Infante défunte (2nd version)
1947   78 rpm, Victor (US) 120066

LUCIEN SCHWARTZ
violin

Address book—Artistic encounter.

Tzigane
L.S.; Lucien Petitjean, piano
1929   78 rpm, Gramophone (Fr) W 1033

DOLORES DE SILVERA (Mme Berty Maurel)
mezzo-soprano

Address book (Mme Berty Maurel is written in parenthesis after Dolores de Silvera and before the address)—Artistic encounter.

"Kaddisch" (*Deux Mélodies hébraïques*)
D.D.S.; Maurice Faure, piano
1931   78 rpm, Columbia (Fr) RFX 14

MARTIAL SINGHER (1904–1990)
baritone

Friendly and artistic relationship.

M.S. is the dedicatee of the "Chanson épique," one of the three songs of *Don Quichotte à Dulcinée*, which he introduced in Paris on December 1, 1934, with Paul Paray conducting the Colonne Orchestra. He also introduced the orchestral version of *Ronsard à son âme* on February 17, 1935, with Piero Coppola conducting the Pasdeloup Orchestra. M.R. was present at both concerts.

Don Quichotte à Dulcinée – *Ronsard à son âme*
1935   See "Ravel as supervisor of recordings," p. 542

Chants populaires ("Chanson espagnole," "Chanson française," "Chanson italienne," "Chanson hébraïque") – "Nicolette"
M.S.; R. Gonzalez, piano
1948   78 rpm, 25 cm., Odéon (Fr) 195147/8

Don Quichotte à Dulcinée
M.S.; The Columbia Broadcasting Symphony Orchestra, Maurice Abravanel, conductor
1949   78 rpm, 25 cm., Columbia (US) 17579/81 D
         33 rpm, Columbia (US) ML4152

Histoires naturelles – *Deux Epigrammes de Clément Marot* – *Chansons madécasses* – *Chants populaires*
M.S.; Paul Ulanowsky, piano; Samuel Baron, flute; Daniel Soyer, cello
1952   Concert Hall (US) CHS 1124, Classic (Fr) CLP6260, Guide Internationale du Disque (Fr) MMS3007

Chants populaires – "Nicolette"
M.S.; Dorothy Angwin, piano
1977   1750 Arch Records (US) 1766

VICTOR STAUB
piano

Artistic encounter.

V.S. was a professor of piano at the Conservatoire when this recording was made.

"Rigaudon" (*Le Tombeau de Couperin*)
1928   78 rpm, 25 cm., Odéon (Fr) 166045

WALTHER STRARAM (Marrast; 1876–1933)
conductor

Friendly and artistic relationship.

He introduced the *Boléro* with Ida Rubinstein's troupe at the Paris Opéra on November 22, 1928.

"Alborada del gracioso"
Orchestre des Concerts Straram
1931   78 rpm, Columbia (Fr) LFX185, (US) 68077D, (Japan) JW56

CHARLES STRONY
conductor

Address book (address in Lyon).

C.S. was the founder and music director of the Trigentuor Instrumental Lyonnais. On April 25, 1932, during a Ravel Festival at Salle Rameau in Lyon, he shared the podium with M.R., who conducted the Piano Concerto in G with Marguerite Long as soloist.

"Laideronnette, Impératrice des pagodes," "Les Entretiens de la Belle et de la Bête"
(*Ma Mère l'Oye*)
Le Trigentuor Lyonnais
1929   78 rpm, Gramophone (Fr) L750

JOSEPH SZIGETI (1892–1973)
violin

Artistic encounter.

He performed the Sonata for Violin and Piano with M.R. in New York on January 15, 1928 (see letter no. 290, note 2). His violin was a Guarnerius (Alain Pâris, *Dictionnaire des interprètes*, Paris, Robert Laffont, 1982).

Pièce en forme de Habanera
J.S.; Nikita Magaloff, piano
1937   78 rpm, Columbia (GB) LX575, (US) 68922D, (Australia) LOX323

Sonata for Violin and Piano
J.S.; Carlo Bussotti, piano
1955   Mono: Columbia (US) ML5178

JACQUES THIBAUD (1880–1953)
violin

Photographs—Friendly and artistic relationship.

He performed the Sonata for Violin and Piano with M.R. at a Ravel Festival in Biarritz on August 24, 1930. His violin, a Stradivarius made in 1709, was destroyed in the airplane crash which took his life (Alain Pâris, *Dictionnaire des interprètes*, Paris, Robert Laffont, 1982).

Pièce en forme de habanera
J.T.; Tasso Janopoulo, piano
1945   78 rpm, 25 cm., VSM DA4999—rec. May 28, 1944

DIMITRI TIOMKIN (1898–1979)
piano

Friendly and artistic relationship.

A Russian emigré, D.T. began his career as a concert pianist, specializing in contemporary music, particularly Ravel's, which he admired. His piano recitals received critical acclaim in New York, Berlin, and Paris. In 1926, he asked Manuel Rosenthal to introduce him to Ravel, and they rented a car in order to visit the composer in Montfort l'Amaury. (Interview with Manuel Rosenthal in October 1983.) D.T. recalled the following:

> I knew Maurice Ravel very well; he was my favorite composer, and I often met him in Montfort, Paris, and then in the United States during his tour in 1928, which was organized by a mutual friend, the pianist E. Robert Schmitz. I was very proud to have performed an all-Ravel piano recital in New York in 1928, and to have played the first performance of *La Valse* in the United States. At that time, I actually made a private recording of the "Menuet" from the Sonatine and "Oiseaux tristes" for the president of a player piano company. I have not recorded any other works by Ravel.

(Interview with D.T. in February 1975.) With the arrival of sound movies, in the course of some forty years, he became one of Hollywood's most celebrated film composers (*Rio Bravo, High Noon,* etc.).

"Menuet" (Sonatine) – "Oiseaux tristes" (*Miroirs*)
Automatic piano roll, Ampico (US)—Private recording, rec. 1928, neither iss. nor cataloging
1973   Issued on an automatic piano roll and distributed in 1973 by Klavier piano rolls, (US) Ampico N 12

ARTURO TOSCANINI (1867–1957)
conductor

Correspondence—Friendly and artistic relationship.

"It was Toscanini who launched the career of the *Boléro*" (Alexandre Tansman, Ravel film, RTB, 1975). Following its American première on November 14, 1929, with A.T. conducting the New York Philharmonic Symphony, the *Boléro* "made Ravel almost an American national hero, and caused such wild excitement and enthusiasm as had never been seen in American concert halls" (liner notes of Koussevitzky's 1930—first American—recording of *Boléro*, RCA-Victor set M352). In an article entitled "Toscanini causes furor with Boléro," Olin Downes wrote in the *New York Times* on November 15, 1929: "*Boléro* brought shouts and cheers from the audience and delayed the performance by prolonged applause. . . . The craft, the virtuosity are really thrilling."

Many contradictory versions of the Toscanini–Ravel "affaire" have been offered—all by eyewitnesses. Piero Coppola, a close friend of both men, explained as follows:

> Toscanini thought it proper to conduct the *Boléro* in a faster tempo than the composer conceived of it, and, furthermore, he accelerated the tempo toward the

end in order to obtain an effect of Iberian dynamism, which he believed to be justified by the nature of the work. It is known that Ravel openly expressed his disapproval at the concert, and that afterwards he had a friendly discussion with the conductor, who was incidentally an admirer of the Maître. After that, the two great artists were linked by reciprocal esteem. (P. Coppola, *Dix-Sept ans de musique à Paris*, p. 105.)

In late 1956, A.T. told pianist Mario Delli Ponti of his great admiration for Ravel's orchestration of Mussorgsky's *Pictures at an Exhibition*, and observed that "the two great treatises on instrumentation were the one written by Berlioz and Ravel's orchestration of *Pictures*." (Harvey Sachs, *Toscanini*, London: Weidenfeld and Nicolson, 1978, p. 316.)

Daphnis et Chloé (Suite No. 2)
N.B.C. Symphony Orchestra
1950   78 rpm, Victor (US) set DM 1374—rec. Nov. 21, 1949, Carnegie Hall, New York
          33 rpm, RCA (US) LM 1043, HMV (GB) ALP 1070, (Fr) FALP 160, QALP 10046, RCA (Italy) A 12R0150

Tableaux d'une exposition (Mussorgsky-Ravel)
N.B.C. Symphony Orchestra
1954   RCA (US) LM 1838, HMV (GB) ALP 1218, (Fr) A630249, RCA (Italy) A 12R0125, (US) LSC3278 (1952) (rechanneled for stereo)—rec. Jan. 26, 1953, Carnegie Hall
          Coupling of these two recordings (*Daphnis* and *Pictures*) on one record: RCA-Victrola (US) VIC 1273 (1983), (Fr) 730078, (GB) AT 10710 (1972), (Ger) 2641012AG (1983)
1985   AD: 12 cm. (compact disc), mono: RCA (Japan) RCCD-1009

Boléro (13'25)
N.B.C. Symphony Orchestra
1980   BWS (US) 526—rec. Jan. 21, 1939

La Valse
Orchestra not mentioned on the record
1980   ATRA-BWS (US) 3001 (from a taped performance given in Italy; issued under the auspices of the Arturo Toscanini Recording Association, Milan, Italy)—rec. 1943

GEORGES TRUC (b. 1893)
conductor

Address book—Artistic encounter.

L'Heure espagnole (complete opera)
Jeane Krieger, soprano; Louis Arnoult, tenor; J. Aubert, baritone; Raoul Gilles, tenor; Hector Dufranne, bass; orchestra conducted by G.T.

1929   78 rpm, Columbia (Fr, GB) D15149/55 (a 7-record album), (US)
        68838/44D (set OP14)

MADELEINE DE VALMALÈTE (b. 1899)
piano

Artistic encounter.

She was introduced to M.R. by a mutual friend, the composer Pierre-Octave Ferroud (1900–1936).

Jeux d'eau
1928   Polydor (Fr, Ger) 95176

Le Tombeau de Couperin
1933   25 cm., Polydor (Fr) 522754/5, Decca (GB) P05088/9, Brunswick (US)
        B85027/8
        30 cm., Polydor (Fr) 516577, Decca (GB) LY6079, Brunswick (US) B85027/8

ALFRED WALLENSTEIN (1898–1983)
conductor

Artistic encounter.

Tzigane
Jascha Heifetz, violin; Los Angeles Philharmonic Orchestra, A.W., conductor
1954   See Jascha Heifetz, above

Boléro (13'43)
Virtuoso Symphony of London
1959   Stereo-Audio Fidelity (US) FCS 50005

Pictures at an Exhibition (Mussorgsky-Ravel)
Virtuoso Symphony of London
1959   Stereo-Audio Fidelity (US) FCS 50004

BEVERIDGE WEBSTER (b. 1908)
piano

Friendly and artistic relationship.

With violinist Samuel Dushkin, he introduced the version of *Tzigane* for piano with luthéal (see letter no. 244, note 2) in Paris on October 15, 1924. The young American pianist came to France in 1921. At age 14, he received a Premier Prix from the American Conservatory at Fontainebleau, as well as a warm reception from the Parisian public. B.W. was the first American to obtain a Premier Prix from the Conservatoire, and between 1926 and 1932 he studied all of Ravel's piano works with the composer. He performed all-Ravel recitals in France and abroad, and occasionally performed with M.R. (liner notes from the recording cited below). Since 1946, he has been on the Piano Faculty of the Juilliard School in New York.

Gaspard de la nuit – Jeux d'eau – Le Tombeau de Couperin
1964   Mono, Dover (US) 5213, Stereo, Dover (US) 7000, 7213

SUZIE WELTY
piano

Address book—Correspondence—Friendly and artistic relationship.

She performed *Ma Mère l'Oye* with M.R. at Salle Pleyel on May 15, 1928.

Jeux d'eau
1925   Ordinary piano roll, Pleyela, Aeolian, Odéola (Fr) E8746
       Automatic piano roll, Auto-Pleyela (Fr) AP8746

CUTHBERT WHITEMORE
conductor

Address book (address in London)—Artistic encounter.

Ma Mère l'Oye ("Pavane de la Belle au bois dormant," "Petit Poucet,"
   "Laideronnette, Impératrice des pagodes," "Le Jardin féerique")
The Aeolian Orchestra
1923   78 rpm, acoustical, Vocalion (GB) JO 4019 and DO 2121, JO 4022 and DO 2123

It may be noted that in April 1923, Ravel conducted a concert in London which included *Ma Mère l'Oye*.

"Menuet," "Rigaudon" (*Le Tombeau de Couperin*)
The Aeolian Orchestra
1923   78 rpm, acoustical, Vocalion (GB) JO 4044 and DO 2139

PAUL WITTGENSTEIN (1887–1961)
piano

· Correspondence—Photographs—Artistic relationship.

Having commissioned the Piano Concerto for the Left Hand, P.W. had exclusive performance rights for a period of six years (1931 to 1936). See Jacques Février, above.
   First performances of the Concerto by P.W. were as follows: world première, Vienna, January 5, 1932, Grosser Musikvereinssaal, Vienna Symphony Orchestra, Robert Heger, conductor; London, 1932, BBC Symphony Orchestra, "Promenade Concerts,"

Sir Henry J. Wood, conductor; Paris, January 17, 1933, Salle Pleyel, Orchestre Symphonique de Paris, Maurice Ravel, conductor; Monte Carlo, April 12, 1933, Orchestre National de l'Opéra de Monte-Carlo, Paul Paray, conductor, performed in the composer's presence; Boston and New York, November 10 and 17, 1934, Boston Symphony Orchestra, Serge Koussevitzky, conductor.

On January 30, 1932, Ravel and Marguerite Long traveled by train from Paris to Vienna, where they would perform the G Major Piano Concerto. P.W. organized an elegant dinner in their honor, followed by a musicale, in which he performed the Concerto for the Left Hand, accompanied by a second piano, so that Ravel could finally hear his work. Marguerite Long remembered the evening as follows:

> During the performance, I followed the score of the Concerto which I did not yet know, and I could read our host's enterprising faults on Ravel's face, which became increasingly somber. As soon as the performance was over, I attempted a "diversionary tactic" with ambassador Clauzel, in order to avoid an incident. Alas, Ravel walked slowly toward Wittgenstein and said to him: "But that's not it at all!" He defended himself: "I am a veteran pianist and it doesn't sound well." That was exactly the wrong thing to say. "I am a veteran orchestrator and it sounds well!", was the reply. One can imagine the embarrassment! I remember that our friend was in such a state of nervous tension that he sent back the embassy automobile and we returned by foot, counting on this walk in the bitter cold to calm his nerves. (M. Long, *Au piano avec Maurice Ravel*, pp. 87–88.)

In a letter to P.W. written on March 7, 1932, Ravel spoke of "infringement," and asked for a formal commitment to play his work henceforth strictly as written. In his reply dated March 17, 1932, P.W. refused to comply, and their points of view appeared to be irreconcilable. He wrote:

> As for a formal commitment to play your work henceforth strictly as it is written, that is completely out of the question. No self-respecting artist could accept such a condition. All pianists make modifications, large or small, in each concerto we play. Such a formal commitment would be intolerable: I could be held accountable for every imprecise sixteenth note and every quarter rest which I omitted or added. . . .
> You write indignantly and ironically that I want to be "put in the spotlight." But, dear Maître, you have explained it perfectly: that is precisely the special reason I asked you to write a concerto! Indeed, I wish to be put in the spotlight. What other objective could I have had? I therefore have the right to request the necessary modifications for this objective to be attained. . . . As I wrote to you, I only insist upon several of the modifications which I proposed to you, not all of them: I have in no way changed the essence of your work. I have only changed the instrumentation. In the meanwhile, I have refused to play in Paris, as I cannot accept impossible conditions.

(Unpublished letter, in a private collection.) Differences were apparently worked out, at least with regard to the orchestration, as composer and pianist finally agreed to present the Parisian première of the Concerto on January 17, 1933.

P.W.'s interpretation of the Concerto is not recommended as a model—a unique exception to our general premise—as the pianist takes liberties with the score, often giving the impression of playing his own arrangement of the work.

Concerto for Piano and Orchestra in D, "For the Left Hand" (excerpts)
Paul Wittgenstein, piano; Orchestre Symphonique de Paris, Maurice Ravel,
   conductor
Cinema film, 35 mm. black and white; direction and production, Pathé-Journal
News—rec. January 17, 1933, Salle Pleyel, Paris

The original is preserved at the Archives du Film, Bois d'Arcy, France. Two 2-minute excerpts exist in:—

Video film *L'Homme et sa musique: Maurice Ravel*; producers, Pierre Volzlinski and Jacques Trébouta; director, Claude Santelli. Broadcast on French television, channel 2, on April 18, 1971; the film, one hour and ten minutes long, is preserved at the Institut National de l'Audiovisuel, Archives Audiovisuelles, 40 rue Jean-Jaurès, Bagnolet, France.

Cinema and video film (color, and black and white) *Maurice Ravel, l'homme et les sortilèges* (see p. 530). The film is preserved at the RTB, Institut des Emissions Françaises, Service de la Télévision, Cité de la Radio-Télévision, 52 Boulevard Auguste Reyers, Brussels, Belgium.

Concerto for Piano and Orchestra in D, "For the Left Hand"
Paul Wittgenstein, piano; Metropolitan Opera Orchestra of New York, Max Rudolf,
   conductor
1958   Mono: Period (US) 742, Orion (US) ORS7028 (rechanneled for stereo),
        (1970) (1983), Ars Nova (Italy) VST6041 (rechanneled for stereo) (1974),
        MXT (Ger) AN6041 (rechanneled for stereo) (1983)—iss. April 1958

ALBERT WOLFF (1884–1970)
conductor

Friendly and artistic relationship.

He introduced the *Menuet pompeux* (Chabrier-Ravel) in the concert hall with the Pasdeloup Orchestra on March 21, 1936. See also "Ravel as orchestral conductor", p. 535.

Pavane pour une Infante défunte
Berlin Philharmonic Orchestra
1928   78 rpm, Polydor (Ger) 66726, (Fr) 516649, Decca (GB) CA8230, Brunswick
        (US) 90149

Menuet antique
Orchestre Lamoureux
1930   78 rpm, Polydor (Fr) 566032, (Ger) 66972, Brunswick (US) 90099.
        Recorded under the supervision of the composer

La Valse
Orchestre Lamoureux
1931   78 rpm, Polydor (Fr) 566068/9, (Ger) 67016/7, Brunswick (US) 90186/7
This version is listed as having had the approval of the composer. See
L'Edition musicale vivante, no. 39, May, 1931, p. 17.

Ma Mère l'Oye
Orchestre Lamoureux
1933   78 rpm, Polydor (Fr) 566161/2, Brunswick (US) 90342/3

Rapsodie espagnole
Orchestre Lamoureux
1933   78 rpm, Polydor (Fr) 566166/7, (Ger) 67052/3, Decca (GB) CA8174/5,
Brunswick (US) 90340/1, Fonit (Italy) 96067/8

Boléro (15'10) – "Alborada del gracioso"
Orchestre de la Société des Concerts du Conservatoire
1959   Mono: London (US) 9256
Stereo: Decca (Fr, GB) SXL2105, London (US) 6077

Boléro (same recording as above)
Mono: 45 rpm, 17 cm., Decca (Fr) CEP634
Stereo: 45 rpm, 17 cm., Decca (Fr) SEC5044

SIR HENRY J. WOOD (1869–1944)
(conductor), piano

Artistic encounter.

He introduced the orchestral version of the *Pavane pour une Infante défunte* at the Gentlemen's Concerts in Manchester, on February 27, 1911. (Henry J. Wood, *My Life of Music*, London, Victor Gollancz, 1938, pp. 322 and 469.)

This performance predated the French première, which Alfredo Casella conducted in Paris at the Concerts Hasselmans on December 25, 1911. Following the first performance, H.J.W. also conducted the *Pavane* several times during the summer "Promenade Concerts" in London.

On February 1, 1908, and February 17, 1909, also in London, he conducted rehearsals of the *Prelude to the Afternoon of a Faun* (and *La Mer* and the *Nocturnes*) under Debussy's supervision, and was present at the two performances which Debussy conducted (*My Life of Music*, pp. 297–98). He also attended the London rehearsals of *Ma Mère l'Oye*, in which M.R. conducted his orchestra (pp. 129–30). H.J.W. orchestrated Mussorgsky's *Pictures at an Exhibition* and conducted the première in 1915; following the publication of Ravel's version, he withdrew his own from circulation (pp. 388–89).

Prélude à l'Après-midi d'un faune (Debussy-Ravel; for piano 4 hands, transcribed and published in 1910)
H.J.W. (roll signed by the performer)

1911 Metronomic piano roll, 88 notes, Themodist-Métrostyle: Aeolian, Pianola
(GB) TL35001—rec. 1911

This roll presents some interesting peculiarities: First, the direct metronomic transcription, following the score, mechanically eliminates, in principle, any possibility of altering the work. Second, several years before making this recording, H.J.W. worked on this piece (for orchestra) with Debussy himself, and it is likely that his interpretive indications reflect those of the composer. And finally, his performance was the only recording of this transcription until 1983. There are, however, several recordings of other transcriptions (for 2 pianos by Debussy, for piano solo by E. Robert Schmitz, Leonard Borwick, and George Copeland).

"Themodist-Métrostyle" in the recording details above implies that the piano roll's matrix was perforated by hand, following the indications in the score (without the intervention of a pianist). Metronomic rolls perform a piece in such a way that if one doesn't touch the handle for the Tempo, measures in the same meter unfold in equal units of time, as if the work were performed with a metronome. The performer modifies the speed of the roll as he wishes by means of the Tempo handle, and other handles are used to obtain the nuances. H.J.W. originally introduced all of the variations in tempo and the nuances, according to his conception of the piece, which were concretized on the commercial rolls by a sinuous red line (tempo) and by indications (nuances). These may be followed today by manipulating the handles ad hoc, in order to reproduce the performance of H.J.W. as he realized it in 1911.

Maurice Ravel discovered music upon listening to the *Prelude to the Afternoon of a Faun,* and on several occasions he declared that he would wish to die while listening to this "unique miracle in all of music" (see p. 486). Since this list of interpreters has followed a strict alphabetical order, it is quite extraordinary to conclude with a recording whose characteristics are unique: the only version by Ravel of this "unique miracle in all of music"; a unique recording procedure (the only one of a work by Ravel in this rare category); a unique interpreter (the only recording of Ravel or Debussy by this interpreter, who knew both composers); the first recording (and unique in 1911) of a composition by Maurice Ravel.

At this juncture, some fifty years after Ravel's death, his music continues to be interpreted and recorded widely. Among today's performers are musicians who have studied with Ravel's colleagues, and through them we may observe the ongoing tradition of Historical Interpretations.

9. An Important Reissue of Historical Recordings

In 1987, Pathé-Marconi reissued the following historical recordings on a three-record set:

LP2912163 (side A)
1. String Quartet: The Calvet String Quartet (Joseph Calvet and Daniel Guilevitch, violins; Léon Pascal, viola; Paul Mas, cello)

2. *Tzigane:* Zino Francescatti, violin; Maurice Faure, piano
3. *Pièce en forme de Habanera:* Maurice Maréchal, cello; Maurice Faure, piano

LP2912163 (side B)

1. *Introduction et Allegro:* Gwendolen Mason, harp; Robert Murcie, flute; Haydn P. Draper, clarinet; and string quartet (Charles Woodhouse and Mr. Dinsey, violins; Ernest Tomlinson, viola; Mr. James, cello); conducted by Maurice Ravel
2. *Jeux d'eau:* Alfred Cortot, piano
3. Sonatine: Alfred Cortot, piano
4. "Alborada del gracioso" (*Miroirs*): Marcelle Meyer, piano
5. "Noctuelles" (*Miroirs*): Jacques Février, piano
6. "Toccata" (*Le Tombeau de Couperin*): Maurice Ravel, piano (in fact, Robert Casadesus; see "Ravel as pianist," p. 533

LP2912173 (side A)

1. *La Valse:* Orchestre Symphonique de Paris, Pierre Monteux, conductor
2. *Boléro:* Grand Orchestre Symphonique, Piero Coppola, conductor
3. "Le Jardin féerique" (*Ma Mère l'Oye*): Orchestre de l'Association des Concerts Colonne, Gabriel Pierné, conductor
4. "Danse guerrière" (*Daphnis et Chloé*): Orchestre de la Société des Concerts du Conservatoire, Piero Coppola, conductor
5. "Alborada del gracioso" (*Miroirs*): Orchestre des Concerts Straram, Walther Straram, conductor

LP2912173 (side B)

1. Concerto for Piano and Orchestra in D, "For the Left Hand": Jacques Février, piano; Orchestre de la Société des Concerts du Conservatoire, Charles Münch, conductor
2. *Pavane pour une Infante défunte:* Orchestre de la Société des Concerts du Conservatoire, Charles Münch, conductor
3. *Daphnis et Chloé* (Suite No. 2): Orchestre des Concerts Straram, Philippe Gaubert, conductor

LP2912183 (side A)

1. *Histoires naturelles* ("Le Paon," "Le Grillon," "Le Martin-Pêcheur"): Jane Bathori, mezzo-soprano, accompanying herself on the piano
2. *Sainte:* Pierre Bernac, baritone; Francis Poulenc, piano
3. *Sur l'herbe:* Pierre Bernac, baritone; Francis Poulenc, piano
4. *Mélodies populaires grecques* ("Quel galant," "Là-bas, vers l'église," "Tout gai!"): Pierre Bernac, baritone; Jean Doyen, piano (these artists did not receive counsel from Ravel, and this recording is therefore not listed in the catalogue)
5. *Epigrammes de Clément Marot* ("D'Anne jouant de l'espinette," "D'Anne qui me jecta de la neige"): Maggie Teyte, soprano; Gerald Moore, piano (not listed in catalogue)

6. "Chanson espagnole": Charles Panzéra, baritone; Madeleine Panzéra, piano (not listed in catalogue)
7. *Trois Chants hébraïques* ("Kaddisch," "L'Enigme éternelle"; "Chanson hébraïque"): Madeleine Grey, mezzo-soprano; with piano accompaniment
8. *Chansons madécasses:* Madeleine Grey, mezzo-soprano; accompanied by piano, flute, and cello; conducted by Maurice Ravel

LP2912183 (side B)
1. *Shéhérazade:* Marcelle Gerar, soprano; orchestra conducted by Piero Coppola
2. "Kaddisch": Nina Koshetz, mezzo-soprano; with orchestral accompaniment
3. *Don Quichotte à Dulcinée:* Martial Singher, baritone; orchestra conducted by Piero Coppola
4. *Ronsard à son âme:* Martial Singher, baritone; orchestra conducted by Piero Coppola
5. "Oh! La pitoyable aventure!" (*L'Heure espagnole*): Fanny Heldy, soprano; Louis Morturier, bass; Pierre Favereaux, tenor; orchestra conducted by Piero Coppola

10. Ravel's Influence on Jazz, Popular Music, and Film

Toward the end of his life, Maurice Ravel evinced keen interest in two current musical developments, jazz and popular music. In recent years, the tables have been turned: jazz and popular artists (composers and performers) have been influenced by Ravel's art, and have also arranged his music, for example *The Lamp is Low* (*Pavane pour une Infante défunte*) and *Boléro.* The extensive number of these recordings suggests that Ravel is at the forefront of classical composers whose works have been adapted by jazz and popular musicians, among them Bix Beiderbecke, Tommy Dorsey, Duke Ellington, Earl Garner, the Hi-Los, Harry James, Quincy Jones, Stan Kenton, Michel Legrand, Glen Miller, George Shearing (who has recorded three different arrangements of *The Lamp is Low*), and Sarah Vaughan.

Furthermore, Ravel's name appears in a list of fourteen classical composers whose music has been performed most frequently in films (François Porcile, *Présence de la musique à l'écran*, Paris, Editions du Cerf, 1969, pp. 27–35). Other composers include Bach, Beethoven, Brahms, Mozart, Rossini, Satie (the only other French composer listed), Schubert, Vivaldi, and Wagner. The specific works of Ravel which are cited are the *Boléro*, Piano Concerto in G, *Daphnis et Chloé*, *Ma Mère l'Oye*, *Pavane pour une Infante défunte*, and *La Valse*. In particular, the *Boléro* has been periodically rediscovered and reinterpreted; comment has already been made on its unprecedented American reception (p. 590) and its extraordinary number of recorded versions (p. 541).

1934—Film (US) *Bolero*, directed by Wesley Ruggles, starring George Raft (who dances to the *Boléro*) and Carol Lombard.
1941—Film (Fr) *Boléro*, directed by Jean Boyer, starring Arletty, Jacques Dumesnil, and André Luguet; music by Georges Van Parys. A comedy about an architect who takes a

disliking to the *Boléro* (heard in its entirety), which is played continually on his neighbor's phonograph.

1950—Film (Japan) *Rashomon*, directed by Akira Kurosawa. The (Western) music for this classic Japanese film was composed by Takashi Matsuyama. In one extended scene, Ravel's *Boléro* is imitated: the same C Major tonality, harmony, and *Boléro* rhythm in the drum accompany a pseudo-*Boléro* melody.

1972—Video (US) *The Bolero*, directed by Allan Miller and William Fertik, with Zubin Mehta conducting the Los Angeles Philharmonic (total length of the film, 26 minutes). This film contains a rehearsal of the *Boléro*, with comments by the conductor and members of the orchestra, and concludes with a performance of the work (14'53).

1981—Film (Fr) *Les Uns et les autres*, directed by Claude Lelouche, which contains a complete performance of the *Boléro* (with chorus added), arranged and conducted by Michel Legrand (16'20).

1984—Film and video (Canada) of the World Championship in artistic ice dancing, held in Ottawa. The first prize was awarded to an English couple, Jane Torville and Christopher Dean, who skated to the *Boléro*. Retransmitted live by satellite and later rebroadcast by National Television Networks, the *Boléro* was thus heard by hundreds of millions of television viewers around the world.

Appendix G : : :

Ravel's Personal Record Collection

COMPILED BY BRUNO SÉBALD

The following catalogue, drawn up by Bruno Sébald, record librarian at the Conservatoire, 14 rue de Madrid, Paris, constitutes the inventory of the Ravel legacy, on deposit at the Conservatoire since 1975. These recordings were previously at the composer's home in Montfort l'Amaury. Some complementary information has been added to this catalogue in order to provide a clearer picture of Maurice Ravel's personal record collection.

It appears that several records of works by Ravel are missing, which were certainly sent to him by the recording companies. (Before the transfer of these records, during a visit to Le Belvédère, I had noted, for example, Shéhérazade, *sung by Marcelle Gerar, and the* Rapsodie espagnole, *conducted by Piero Coppola.)*

It would seem that Ravel was interested in many forms of musical expression, as his record collection contains a wide variety of genres. Classical music predominates, naturally, with a strong emphasis on French composers: Berlioz, Bruneau, Caplet, Chausson, Debussy, Dukas, Duparc, Fauré, Franck, Hahn, Ibert, d'Indy, Lalo, Lekeu, Lully, Massenet, Messager, Milhaud, Pierné, Poulenc, Reyer, Roussel, Saint-Saëns, Schmitt, Tournemire, Widor. There are few foreign composers, particularly nothing of Beethoven.

Popular music, notably the chanson, follows immediately in order of importance, well before the theater and folk music. This is not surprising. Indeed, in an interview (see p. 536), Jean Bérard relates that he invited Ravel and Marguerite Long to lunch shortly after the recording of the G Major Piano Concerto in 1932, and played a new chanson for Ravel, Couchés dans le foin,[1] *which had just been recorded by the Pills and Tabet duo (voice and piano). He recalled that Ravel found the song "delightful" and "very amusing," and M. Bérard cited the opinion of their mutual friend Dominique Sordet (a music critic who, with Ravel, was a member of the Grand Prix du Disque jury): "A chanson can contain all of the forms of musical expression."*

In the years 1932 to 1933, the chanson began evolving from general mediocrity towards increasingly sophisticated quality in both lyrics and musical invention. An analysis of the list of popular music in Ravel's record collection reveals a surprisingly prophetic choice: the only chanson recordings later than 1933 are the very first by Jean Tranchant,[2] the precursor of the new chanson. One of his followers, Pierre Dudan,[3] recently wrote the following homage in a pamphlet devoted to the popular chanson in France during the past fifty years: "Jean Tranchant, in my opinion, is the true creator of today's chanson, of the great chanson performed by its author."[4]

—Jean Touzelet

ABBREVIATIONS

acc.	accompaniment	MHS	Music Hall Singer
accor	accordion	op.	opus
act.	actor	Orch	Orchestra
acts.	actress	org	organ
arr.	arranged by	pf	piano
Bar	baritone	S	soprano
cimb	cimbalom	sax	saxophone(s)
cl	clarinet	SFB	Small Folk Band
cond	conductor	str qt	string quartet
CS	cabaret singer	T	tenor
exc.	excerpts	tpt	trumpet
gui	guitar	v	voice
hn	horn	Vau.	Vaudeville
mand	mandolin	vc	violoncello
Mez	mezzo-soprano	vn	violin
MHE	Music Hall Entertainer		

The Recordings

ORCHESTRAL AND INSTRUMENTAL MUSIC

Composer	Title	Interpreter	Reference
Albéniz, Isaac	Triana	J. Dupont (pf)	Pathé x98177
Berlioz, Hector	L'Enfance du Christ (Le Repos de la Sainte Famille)	F. Ruhlmann (cond) J. Planel (T)	Pathé x93102
⎡ Caplet, André	Epiphanie, Danse, Petits Nègres	M. Maréchal (vc) R. Casadesus (pf)	Columbia LFX86
⎣ Debussy, Claude	Sonata		
Chausson, Ernest	Concerto in D Major, op. 21	A. Cortot (pf) J. Thibaud (vn) str qt	Gramophone DB1649
⎡ Davidoff, Charles	La Source	M. Marcelli-Herson (vc)	Gramophone L827
⎣ Lalo, Edouard	Arlequin	L. Petitjean (pf)	
⎡ Debussy, Claude	Bruyères	C. Guilbert (pf)	Pathé x9982
⎣ Fauré, Gabriel	6th Barcarolle		
Dukas, Paul	Villanelle	J. Devemy (hn) G. Andolfi (pf)	Pathé x98067
Franck, César	Cantabile	C. Tournemire (org)	Polydor 561047

Composer	*Title*	*Interpreter*	*Reference*
⌈Franck, César	Chorale in A Minor	C. Tournemire (org)	Polydor 566057/8
⌊Tournemire, Charles	Cantilène et improvisation		
Franck, César	Symphony in D Minor	A. Wolff (cond) Lamoureux Orch	Polydor 566093/4/6
Ibert, Jacques	Donogoo (incidental music, play by Jules Romains)	J. Doyen (pf) J. Ibert (cond)	Artiphone Z2008 Artiphone F1017
Indy, Vincent d'	Le Camp de Wallenstein	V. d'Indy (cond)	Pathé x8806/7
Indy, Vincent d'	Symphony on a French Mountain Air	J. M. Darré (pf) A. Wolff (cond) Lamoureux Orch	Polydor 566130/1/2
⌈Kreisler, Fritz	Liebesfreud No. 1	Viard (sax)	Pathé x9976
⌊Dvořák, Antonín	Humoresque (2 sax, pf)	Martin (sax) G. Andolfi (pf)	
⌈Kreisler, Fritz	Rondino on a Theme of Beethoven	M. Quivoga (vn) Mme Quivoga (pf)	Pathé x98001
⌊Lehár, Franz	Serenade		
⌈Kreisler, Fritz	Schön Rosmarin	C. Vladesco (cimb)	Pathé PA67
Durand, Auguste	Première Valse	E. Lazar (pf)	
⌈Kreisler, Fritz	Schön Rosmarin	Y. Curti (vn)	Pathé x98113
⌊Piot, Julien	Pensées fugitives	G. Andolfi (pf)	
Lalo, Edouard	Symphonie espagnole	H. Merckel (vn) P. Coppola (cond) Pasdeloup Orch	Gramophone 923/4/5/6
Lekeu, Guillaume	Sonata in G	Koch (vn) Van Lancker (pf)	Polydor 516549/ 50/51/52
Lully, Jean-Baptiste	Alceste (scène funèbre)	R. Désormière (cond)	Ultraphone EP429
Lully, Jean-Baptiste	Alceste (overture)	R. Désormière (cond)	Ultraphone EP430
Lully, Jean-Baptiste	Cadmus et Hermione (arr. H. Prunières)	R. Désormière (cond) soloists and choir	Ultraphone EP428
Milhaud, Darius	La Création du monde	D. Milhaud (cond)	Columbia LFX251/2

Composer	*Title*	*Interpreter*	*Reference*
Mompou, Federico	Jeune fille au jardin; La rue, le guitariste	M. Tagliafero (pf)	Gramophone P855
⌈Mossolov, Alexandre	Fonderie d'acier	J. Ehrlich (cond) Orch de Paris	Pathé x96300
⌊Meytus, Julius	Dienprostroï		
Moszkowski, Moritz	Spanish Dances (op. 65)	D. Herbrecht (vn) L. Petitjean (pf)	Gramophone L828
Mozart, W. A.	The Magic Flute (overture)	H. Rabaud (cond)	Pathé x5526
Mussorgsky, Modeste	Night on the Bare Mountain	A. Wolff (cond) Lamoureux Orch	Polydor 566006
⌈Lacome d'Estalenx, Paul	Rigaudon (cl & pf)	L. Cahuzac (cl) (pf not listed)	Odéon 165921
⌊Pierné, Gabriel	Canzonetta (cl & pf)		
Pierné, Gabriel	Ramuntcho	G. Pierné (cond) Colonne Orch	Odéon 123574
Poulenc, Francis	2 Novelettes, Caprice	F. Poulenc (pf)	Columbia LFX266
Ravel, Maurice	Boléro	P. Coppola (cond) Grand Orch Symphonique	VSM w1067/8
⌈Ravel, Maurice	Boléro	H. Kemp (cond)	Brunswick 6629
⌊Lecuona, Ernesto	Jungle Drums (canto karabali)	G. Lombardo (cond)	
Ravel, Maurice	Chansons madécasses	M. Grey (Mez) M. Ravel (cond)	Polydor 561076/7
Ravel, Maurice	3 Chants hébraïques	M. Grey (Mez)	Polydor 561075
Ravel, Maurice	Concerto in G Major Pavane . . .	M. Long (pf) P. de Freitas-Branco (cond)	Columbia LFX257/8/9
Ravel, Maurice	Daphnis et Chloé (Suite No. 2)	P. Gaubert (cond) Straram Orch	Columbia LFX41/2
Ravel, Maurice	L'Heure espagnole	J. Krieger (S) G. Truc (cond)	Columbia D15149/55
Ravel, Maurice	Le Tombeau de Couperin	P. Coppola (cond) Conservatoire Orch	Gramophone w1163/4
Roussel, Albert	Symphony No. 3	A. Wolff (cond) Lamoureux Orch	Polydor 566126/7/8

Composer	Title	Interpreter	Reference
Saint-Saëns, Camille	Septet	Faure (pf) Foveau (tpt), etc.	Columbia D11001/2
Saint-Saëns, Camille	Symphony No. 3	P. Coppola (cond) A. Cellier (org)	Gramophone W1095
Schmitt, Florent	Reflets d'Allemagne	F. Schmitt (cond)	Pathé X96093
Schmitt, Florent	Ronde burlesque	G. Poulet (cond)	Parlophone 59096
Shostakovich, Dmitri	L'Age d'or (exc.)	J. Ehrlich (cond) Orch de Paris	Pathé X96301
Strauss, Richard	Till Eulenspiegels lustige Streiche	R. Strauss (cond) Berlin Opera Orch	Polydor 66887
Stravinsky, Igor	L'Histoire du soldat	I. Stravinsky (cond) Foveau (tpt) Godeau (cl), etc.	Columbia LFX263
Widor, Charles-Marie	Toccata from the 5th Symphony	C.-M. Widor (org)	Gramophone DB4856
Tournemire, Charles	Fantasy No. 3	C. Tournemire (org)	Polydor 566061
Tournemire, Charles	Improvisation on Te Deum	C. Tournemire (org)	Polydor 561050
Tournemire, Charles	Paraphrase-Carillon	C. Tournemire (org)	Polydor 566118
Weber, Carl Maria von	Euryanthe (overture)	H. Rabaud (cond)	Pathé X5525

SONGS, EXCERPTS OF OPERAS AND OPERETTAS

Alix/Darcourt/ Ardot/Lupin	Mon amant (exc.)	G. Bredy (v) Ville (v) V. Alix (cond)	Parlophone 85325
Benatzy, Ralph/ Stolz	L'Auberge du cheval blanc	M. Loria (v) Reda-Claire (v) V. Alix (cond)	Parlophone 85515
Berlioz, Hector	La Damnation de Faust (exc.)	C. Panzéra (Bar) P. Coppola (cond)	Gramophone L889
Beydts, Louis	Moineau	L. Arnoult (v) A. Bernard (cond)	Ultraphone EP204
Caplet, André	Oraison, salutation	C. Croiza (Mez) M. Kahn (harp) Pascal str qt	Lumen 30008

Composer	*Title*	*Interpreter*	*Reference*
⌈Chopin, Frédéric	Tristesse (Etude op. 10 no. 3)	voices and pf	Columbia 4423
⌊Russian folk song	Song of the Black Hussars	S. Kogan (cond) Vau. Theater Orch	
⌈Debussy, Claude	Pelléas et Mélisande (Act 1 scene 2)	G. Cernay (Mez) G. Cloez (cond)	Odéon 123590
⌊Fauré, Gabriel	Pénélope (dance)		
Duparc, Henri	Soupir Chanson triste	C. Panzéra (Bar) Mme Panzéra (pf)	Gramophone DA4808
Fauré, Gabriel	Après un rêve	N. Vallin (S) G. Andolfi (pf)	Pathé X93081
Hahn, Reynaldo	Brummell (exc.)	L. Baroux (act.) R. Hahn (cond)	Odéon 338316
⌈Lalo, Edouard	Le Roi d'Ys (exc.)	J. Planel (T)	Pathé X90036
⌊Massenet, Jules	Manon (exc.)	F. Ruhlmann (cond)	
⌈Massenet, Jules	Sapho (exc.)	G. Thill (T)	Columbia LFX38
⌊Bruneau, Alfred	L'Attaque du moulin	E. Bigot (cond) A. Bruneau (cond)	
⌈Messager, André	Véronique (exc.)	Charpini &	Pathé X2230
⌊Szulc, J.	Divin mensonge	Brancato (Vau. duo, v & pf)	
Mozart, W. A.	Litanies, K. 243 (exc.)	Y. Tinayre (T) A. Ceilier (org)	Lumen 32016
Proch, Heinrich	Theme and Variations	L. Ben Sedira (S) M. Frigara (cond)	Parlophone 29525
⌈Reyer, Ernest	Sigurd (exc.)	C. Cambon (Bass)	Polydor 522381
⌊Saint-Saëns, Camille	Samson et Dalila (exc.)	F. Weiss (cond)	
⌈Leroux, Xavier	Le Nil	N. Vallin (S)	Odéon 123664
⌊Rimsky-Korsakov, N.	Chanson hindoue	M. Barthalay (vn) Mme d'Aleman (pf)	
⌈Rossini, Gioacchino	Guillaume Tell (exc.)	A. Endrèze (Bar) F. Rulhmann	Pathé X90060
⌊Saint-Saëns, Camille	Samson et Dalila (exc.)	(cond)	
⌈Rossini, Gioacchino	Guillaume Tell (exc.)	C. Cambon (Bass) F. Weiss (cond)	Polydor 522406
⌊Verdi, Giuseppe	Rigoletto (exc.)		

Composer	*Title*	*Interpreter*	*Reference*
Schumann, Robert	Frauenliebe und Leben	N. Vallin (S) G. Andolfi (pf)	Pathé X3464/70
Schütz, Heinrich	Sinfonia sacra (VIII)	Y. Tinayre (T) A. Cellier (org)	Lumen 32015
Verdi, Giuseppe	Otello (Willow Song)	G. Martinelli (S) A. Wolff (cond)	Polydor 561064
Wagner, Richard	Siegfried (exc.)	Kirchhoff (T) von Hoesslin (cond)	Pathé X7204
⌈ Wagner, Richard ⌊ Berlioz, Hector	Tannhäuser (exc.) La Damnation de Faust (exc.)	A. Endrèze (Bar) F. Ruhlmann (cond)	Pathé X90073

THEATER

Beaumarchais, Pierre	Le Barbier de Séville	Berr Dehelly	Odéon 166401
Cocteau, Jean	La Voix humaine	B. Bovy	Columbia DFX40/41
⌈ Dumas, Alexandre ⌊ Hugo, Victor	Le Demi-monde La Tristesse d'Olympio	Le Bargy	Odéon 171106
Fonson, F./ Wicheler	Le Mariage de Mlle Beulemans	Legrand	Pathé X93090
Molière, Jean-Baptiste	L'Ecole des femmes; Les Femmes savantes	L. Bernard	Pathé X3441
Musset, Alfred de	Une Soirée perdue	J. Marchat	Odéon 238054
Pagnol, Marcel	Topaze (exc.)	Provost Lefaur	Pathé X92006
Ponchon, Raoul	La Muse au cabaret	L. Bernard	Pathé X93012
Racine, Jean	Andromaque Bérénice	J. Bartet Jeane Sully	Gramophone DB4829

POPULAR MUSIC

Alongi, F.	Trapos viejos Acordate	R. Barrios (v) F. Alongi (pf)	Gramophone K6013
Anonymous	Tiger rag Tyrolian song	Kentucky singers	Pathé X94428

Composer	*Title*	*Interpreter*	*Reference*
Aurelli/Keyne/ Leneko	Rien	Heritza (MHS) G. Aubanel	Polydor 522357
Larmanjat, J./ Carco, F.	Le Doux caboulot	(cond)	
⌈ Bach/Laverne, Henry	Les Gaités de la radio	Bach (MHE) Laverne (MHE)	Odéon 238188
⌊ Gangloff/Carré	Les Gendarmes à pied		
⌈ Benech/Dumont	Tout en causant	Bertrande (v)	Parlophone 85478
⌊ Ackermans	Déchire	with orch acc.	
Bontemps, François	Le Cirque Bilboquet	Bilboquet (MHE)	Columbia DFX64
Chepfer, George	Le Cousin de Molsheim	G. Chepfer (MHS)	Odéon 250261
⌈ Erwin, Ralph	Garde moi ton amour	Guy Berry (MHS)	Parlophone 85256
⌊ Jurmann	Tu n'es pas la première	with orch acc.	
Fyscher, Ñilson	Te souviens-tu? Seul, toi seule	Heritza (MHS) G. Aubanel (cond)	Polydor 522399
Heymann/ Zimmer	A qui vais-je donner mon coeur?	Jules Berry (act., MHS) Wal-Berg Orch	Polydor 522392
⌈ Hollander/Boyer, Jean	Qui j'aime	Florelle (acts.) J. Lenoir Orch	Polydor 522173
⌊ Lenoir/Diamant-Berger	Escales		
⌈ Lenoir, J./Carco, F.	Il pleut dehors	Mme Caro-Martel (MHS)	Polydor 522417
⌊ Claret, G./Rayle, P.	Si petite	Wal-Berg Trio	
⌈ Lenoir, Jean	Ne dis pas toujours	Heritza (MHS) G. Aubanel	Polydor 522444
⌊ Monnot, M./ Hely, Marc	Viens dans mes bras	(cond)	
⌈ Lenoir, J./Olivier, A.	Rest encore . . . ce soir	Germaine Lix (MHS)	Polydor 522152
⌊ Sab, André/ Herbey, René	Ne coupez pas, Mlle	J. Lenoir Orch	
⌈ Mariel, R./ François, C.	Au fond de tes yeux	Heritza (MHS) with orch acc.	Polydor 522326
⌊ Wal-Berg/Mai, E.	Vivre sans toi		

Composer	Title	Interpreter	Reference
[Martini	Plaisir d'amour	Davson (MHS)	Parlophone 80909
∟ Fyscher, Nilson	Folie	Destrey (v and pf)	
Noël-Noël	La Soupe à toto, souvenirs	Noël-Noël (CS) with pf acc.	Odéon 166447
Scotto (Vincent)	Berce moi, tu m'fais rire	Cora Madou (MHS) with pf and gui acc.	Gramophone K6637
Simons	La Voyante Témoignage	Dariel (MHE) Simons (MHE)	Pathé X94110
Tranchant, Jean	La Chanson du large Ici l'on pêche	Jean Tranchant with orch acc.	Pathé PA96
[Tranchant, Jean	Le Piano mécanique	M. Ditrix (MHS) with pf acc.	Pathé X94416
∟ Mireille	Le Petit chemin		
Wal-Berg/ Francois, C.	Je veux t'aimer Viens	Heritza (MHS) with orch acc.	Polydor 522325
Xanrof, Léon	Bébé qui chante	S. Feyrou (MHS) Guttinguer (cond)	Lumen 33016
[Yvain, Maurice	Pourquoâ	Paul Colline (CS)	Pathé X94086
∟ Delaunay, Jean	Donogoo	with pf acc.	

FOLKLORE

Egyptian folk song	Min husni tabaaki[5] (mawal)[6]	Effendi Farid	Polyphon V4231415 Polyphon 4264213
Egyptian popular song	Ya Masr abki ala faqr al-zain[7]	Effendi Asfour	Polyphon V4351718
Egyptian popular song	Eeh illi gara fil-mandara?[8]	Sitt Ratiba	Polyphon V4402213
Kouguell, Arkadie	Prélude oriental Danse kurde	A. Kouguell (pf)	Pathé X98057
[Lancel	Cantatille	Vanni-Marcoux	Gramophone
∟ Weckerlin, J. B.	Chanson normande	(Bass) P. Coppola (pf)	DA4804
Romanian folk song, Cantec de nunta	La Barbieritul mirelui[9]	Ionita Badita's SFB	HMV AM2752

HISTORICAL RECORDINGS

Composer	Title	Interpreter	Reference
Boncour, Paul	Discours aux anciens combattants (A speech to veterans)		Polydor 516544
Le Procès de Louis XVI (The Trial of Louis XVI)	Interrogatoire/ Plaidoirie (Prosecution/ Defense)	M. Jacquelin G. Colin, de Sèze	Hébertot EY4004
Saint Thérèse de Lisieux	Extraits de ses écrits (Excerpts of her writings)	M. Renaud	Polydor no. 1 (noncommercial record)

MISCELLANEOUS RECORDINGS

Composer	Title	Interpreter	Reference
Hirschmann, Henri	Roselinde	J. Dennery (pf)	Parlophone 28544
⌈ Lope, S.	Gallito (Flamenco paso doble)	Sacha Petrov (cond)	Pathé X96163
⌊ Rosas, Juventino	Sur les vagues (waltz)		
Mayerl, Billy	Jasmine, Hollyhock (syncopated impressions)	C. Guilbert[10] (pf)	Pathé X98041
Mayerl, Billy	Marigold, Robots (syncopated impressions)	C. Guilbert (pf)	Pathé X98042
⌈ Silvestri, Joseph	Célèbre sérénade d'autrefois	M. Scivittaro (mand) with pf acc.	Pathé X98196
⌊ Arienzo, V.	2ème caprice de concert		
⌈ Varney, Jean	Sérénade du pavé	E. Buffet (v)	Gramophone
⌊ Buxeuil, René de	La Voix de maman	M. Chaumette (pf) J. Lacroix (accor)	K6889

1. Lyrics by Jean Franc-Nohain (son of the librettist of *L'Heure espagnole*), and music by Mireille. This song won the Grand Prix du Disque, which was awarded on April 3, 1933, by a jury consisting of celebrities in the artistic world, including Ravel (see p. 528). The song was a huge success in France, England, and even in the United States, where the American version, *Lying in the Hay*, was recorded by the Andrews Sisters.

2. The lyricist-composer-performer Jean Tranchant (1904–1972) made his first recording in

1934 (Pathé PA96). In an interview with the artist, Georges Hilleret observed: "A veritable one-man orchestra, Jean Tranchant invented the one-man show. In 1935, he rented Salle Pleyel for his famous song revue. Emile Vuillermoz, the celebrated critic, and Maurice Ravel himself, continually spoke highly of him." (*Télé-Sept-Jours,* 595, September 1971, 95.)

3. The lyricist-composer-performer Pierre Dudan (1916–1984) composed film music and wrote over 1,700 chansons.

4. Pierre Dudan, *Vive le Show-Biz* (Nice: Editions Alain Lefeuvre, 1980), p. 37.

5. "Because of your beautiful nature."

6. A type of rhyming poem set to music.

7. "Oh Egypt, I am crying at the loss of the beautiful one."

8. "What happened in the parlor?"

9. "The shaving of the groom"; a wedding song from the Arges region of Romania.

10. Known as a classical pianist, Carmen Guilbert recorded one work by Ravel in 1935: "Alborada del gracioso," 78 rpm, 30 cm., Pathé (Fr) PAT23.

Appendix H : : :

Sources of the Letters

SOURCES (letter no.: source)

1: p.c. Mme Alexandre Taverne; 2: p.c. B. de Saint-Marceaux; 3: p.c. Mme Marc Julia; 4: *F: Pn*/a.l./M.R., no. 135; 5: *F: Pn*/a.l./M.R., vol. XI (294–95); 6: *F: Pn*/a.l./ M.R., no. 136; 7: p.c. Mme G. Dallan; 8: p.c. Pierre Courteault; 9: *US:NYpm;* 10: FDT.

11: FDT; 12: p.c. Pierre Courteault; 13: a.p.c.; 14: *F: Pn*/a.l./M.R., no. 172; 15: n.t.; 16: *F: Pn*/a.l./M.R., no. 1; 17: p.c.a.; 18: p.c. Claude Roland-Manuel; 19: p.c. Claude Roland-Manuel; 20: p.c. Claude Roland-Manuel.

21: p.c.a.; 22: *US:NYpm*/Koch; 23: p.c. B. de Saint-Marceaux; 24: *US:NYpm*/ Koch; 25: p.c. Jean Godebski; 26: Dur.; 27: p.c. Dr. A. Hauriou; 28: n.t.; 29: p.c. Eric Van Lauwe; 30: *F: Pn*/a.l./M.R., no. 2.

31: a.p.c.; **32:** p.c. Claude Roland-Manuel; **33:** *US:NYpm*/Koch; **34:** p.c. Pierre Courteault; **35:** p.c.a.; **36:** p.c. Jean Godebski; **37:** Dur.; **38:** a.p.c.; **39:** Archives Laloy; **40:** a.p.c.

41: a.p.c.; **42:** p.c. Jean Godebski; **43:** p.c. Pierre Courteault; **44:** *F: Pn*/a.l./M.R., no. 4; **45:** *US:NYpm*/Koch; **46:** *US:NYpm*/Koch; **47:** *GB: Lbm;* **48:** p.c. Jean Godebski; **49:** *US:NYpm*/Koch; **50:** p.c. Jean Godebski.

51: *US:NYpm*/Koch; **52:** *US:Wc;* **53:** *US:NYpm*/Koch; **54:** *US:Wc;* **55:** *US:NYpm*/ Koch; **56:** p.c. Jean Touzelet; **57:** p.c. Jean Godebski; **58:** *F: Pn*/a.l./M.R., no. 9; **59:** p.c. Yves Koechlin; **60:** *US:NYpm*/Koch.

61: *GB: Lbm;* **62:** *GB: Lbm;* **63:** p.c. Claude Ecorcheville; **64:** p.c. B. de Saint-Marceaux; **65:** p.c. Claude Ecorcheville; **66:** *US: Wc;* **67:** Archives of Editions Alphonse Leduc; **68:** *F: Pn*/a.l./Marie Ravel, no. 2; **69:** *US: AUS/hr;* **70:** n.t.

71: *F: Pn*/Fonds Fauré-Frémiet; **72:** *US: AUS/hr;* **73:** *US:NYpm*/Koch; **74:** *F: Pn*/a.l./M.R., no. 95; **75:** *F: Pn*/a.l./M.R., no. 14; **76:** p.c. Mme A. Clément-Pierné; **77:** *F: Pn*/a.l./M.R., no. 160; **78:** *US:NYpm*/Koch; **79:** *USSR: Mcm;* **80:** *US:NYpm.*

81: *F: Pn*/a.l./Satie., no. 21; **82:** *US:NYpm*/Koch; **83:** p.c. Jean Touzelet; **84:** n.t.; **85:** p.c. Pierre Courteault; **86:** *US:NYpm*/Koch; **87:** a.p.c.; **88:** p.c. Jean Godebski; **89:** *F: Pn*/a.l./M.R., no. 90; **90:** p.c. Nicolas Touzelet.

91: p.c. Nicolas Touzelet; **92:** n.t.; **93:** *GB: Lbm;* **94:** p.c. Jean Touzelet; **95:** *GB: Lbm;* **96:** *F: Pn*/a.l./M.R., no. 162; **97:** PSF; **98:** p.c. Mme G. Dallan; **99:** a.p.c.; **100:** p.c.a.

101: p.c.a.; **102:** p.c.a.; **103:** a.p.c.; **104:** p.c. Claude Roland-Manuel; **105:** PSF; **106:** *F: Pn*/a.l./M.R., no. 233; **107:** p.c. Claude Roland-Manuel; **108:** PSF; **109:** *US:NYpm;* **110:** a.p.c.

111: a.p.c.; **112:** *US:NYpm*/Koch; **113:** *GB: Lbm;* **114:** n.t.; **115:** p.c. Mme G. Dallan; **116:** a.p.c.; **117:** p.c. Eric Van Lauwe; **118:** *F: Pn*/a.l./M.R., no. 167; **119:** *US:NYpm*/Koch; **120:** *F: Pn*/a.l./Edouard Ravel, no. 23.

121: p.c. Eric Van Lauwe; **122:** p.c. Eric Van Lauwe; **123:** *F: Pn*/a.l./Manuel de Falla, no. 17; **124:** p.c. Señora Maria Isabel de Falla; **125:** PSF; **126:** *F: Pn*/a.l./Igor Stravinsky, no. 17; **127:** *GB: Lbm;* **128:** *F: Pn*/a.l./Edouard Ravel, no. 48; **129:** *F: Pn*/a.l./Famille Ravel, no. 3; **130:** *F: Pn*/a.l./M.R., no. 198.

131: *F: Pn*/a.l./M.R., no. 201; **132:** *F: Pn*/a.l./M.R., no. 43; **133:** *F: Pn*/Fonds Jane Bathori; **134:** p.c. Mme G. Dallan; **135:** p.c. Mme G. Dallan; **136:** *F: Pn*/a.l./M.R., no. 50; **137:** *GB: Lbm;* **138:** *F: Pn*/a.l./M.R., no. 51; **139:** *F: Pn*/a.l./M.R., no. 53; **140:** *F: Pn*/a.l./M.R., no. 17.

141: p.c. Claude Roland-Manuel; **142:** p.c. Mme G. Dallan; **143:** *US:NYpm*/Koch; **144:** p.c. Claude Roland-Manuel; **145:** p.c. Yves Koechlin; **146:** p.c. Claude Roland-Manuel; **147:** a.p.c.; **148:** *US:NYpm*/Koch; **149:** *US:NYpm*/Koch; **150:** a.p.c.

151: p.c. B. de Saint-Marceaux; **152:** n.t.; **153:** a.p.c.; **154:** a.p.c.; **155:** p.c. Mme

Alexandre Taverne; **156:** a.p.c.; **157:** *US:NYpm*/Koch; **158:** *US:NYpm*/Koch; **159:** *GB: Lbm;* **160:** p.c. Señora Maria Isabel de Falla.

161: *F: Pn*/a.l./M.R., no. 167; **162:** *F: Pn*/a.l./M.R., no. 114; **163:** *US:NYpm/* Koch; **164:** *US:NYpm*/Koch; **165:** p.c. Mme G. Dallan; **166:** p.c. Claude Roland-Manuel; **167:** p.c.a.; **168:** *F: Pn*/a.l./M.R., no. 71; **169:** *US:NYpm*/Koch; **170:** p.c. Mme G. Dallan.

171: *F: Pn*/a.l./M.R., no. 178; **172:** p.c. Claude Roland-Manuel; **173:** *US: AUS/hr;* **174:** p.c. Mme Adrienne Fontainas; **175:** *F: Pn*/a.l./M.R., no. 119; **176:** *F: Po*/a.l./ M.R., no. 5; **177:** p.c. Yves Koechlin; **178:** *US:NYpm;* **179:** a.p.c.; **180:** *CH: Gpu.*

181: p.c. Pierre Courteault; **182:** *CH: Gpu;* **183:** *F: Pn*/a.l./M.R., no. 143; **184:** a.p.c.; **185:** *US:NYpm*/Koch; **186:** *F: Pn*/a.l./M.R., no. 88; **187:** *US:NYpm*/Koch; **188:** *F: Pn*/a.l./M.R., no. 98; **189:** p.c. Eric Van Lauwe; **190:** Dur.

191: *F: Pn*/a.l./M.R., no. 99; **192:** p.c. Mrs. Monique Leduc; **193:** HPF; **194:** *US:NYpm*/Koch; **195:** *USSR: Mcm;* **196:** *US: Wc;* **197:** a.p.c.; **198:** p.c.a.; **199:** *US:NYpm*/Koch; **200:** p.c. Anne-Sophie Touzelet.

201: p.c. Claude Roland-Manuel; **202:** p.c.a.; **203:** p.c. Mme Robert Casadesus; **204:** *F: Pn*/a.l./Jean Cocteau, no. 5; **205:** a.p.c.; **206:** p.c. Frank Emmanuel; **207:** *F: Pn/* a.l./Gabriel Fauré, no. 105; **208:** *F: Pn*/a.l./Henry Prunières, no. 25; **209:** *F: Pn*/a.l./ Richard Strauss, no. 14; **210:** p.c. Jean Françaix.

211: *US:NYpm*/Koch; **212:** p.c.a.; **213:** a.p.c.; **214:** p.c. Yves Koechlin; **215:** *F: Pn*/a.l./M.R., no. 101; **216:** a.p.c.; **217:** n.t.; **218:** a.p.c.; **219:** p.c. Jean Touzelet; **220:** *F: Pn*/a.l./Rudolph Mayer, no. 1.

221: *US:NYpm*/Koch; **222:** p.c. Señora Maria Isabel de Falla; **223:** PSF; **224:** p.c. Mme Alexandre Taverne; **225:** p.c. Mme Piero Coppola; **226:** Dur.; **227:** p.c.a.; **228:** p.c. Jean Touzelet; **229:** p.c. Señora Maria Isabel de Falla; **230:** p.c. Mme Robert Casadesus.

231: p.c.a.; **232:** *US:NYpm*/Koch; **233:** p.c. Jean Godebski; **234:** *F: Pn*/a.l./M.R., no. 150; **235:** a.p.c.; **236:** p.c. Claude Roland-Manuel; **237:** *US:NYpm*/Koch; **238:** p.c. Mme G. Dallan; **239:** a.p.c.; **240:** p.c. Señora Maria Isabel de Falla.

241: p.c. Mme Robert Casadesus; **242:** p.c.a.; **243:** *F: Pn*/a.l./M.R., no. 86; **244:** *US: Wc;* **245:** p.c. Yves Koechlin; **246:** p.c.a.; **247:** p.c.a.; **248:** p.c. B. de Saint-Marceaux; **249:** Dur.; **250:** a.p.c.

251: *F: Pn*/a.l./M.R., no. 152; **252:** p.c. Mme G. Dallan; **253:** a.p.c.; **254:** *F: Pn*/a.l./M.R., no. 103; **255:** p.c.a.; **256:** p.c.a.; **257:** n.t.; **258:** p.c. Alexandre Tansman; **259:** *US: Wc;* **260:** *F: Pn*/a.l./M.R., no. 193.

261: p.c.a.; **262:** *F: Pn*/a.l./M.R., no. 174; **263:** p.c. Claude Roland-Manuel; **264:** a.p.c.; **265:** p.c. Mme Robert Casadesus; **266:** *US:NYpm*/CAH; **267:** a.p.c.; **268:** *US:NYpm*/Koch; **269:** n.t.; **270:** *F: Pn*/a.l./Alexander Steinert, no. 1.

271: New York Public Library, Lincoln Center; 272: p.c. Robert Stallman; 273: p.c. Mme Marcelle Perrin; 274: p.c. Mrs. Monique Leduc; 275: *US:NYpm*/Koch; 276: *F: Pn*/a.l./Darius Milhaud, no. 5; 277: p.c.a.; 278: *F: Pn*/a.l./Paul Morand, no. 1; 279: a.p.c.; 280: a.p.c.

281: *CH: Gpu;* 282: *US:NYpm*/CAH; 283: n.t.; 284: *US: Wc;* 285: HPF; 286: *US:NYpm*/Koch; 287: p.c.a.; 288: a.p.c.; 289: p.c. Claude Roland-Manuel; 290: p.c. Mme Alexandre Taverne.

291: p.c. Mme Alexandre Taverne; 292: p.c. Jean Touzelet; 293: p.c. Jean Touzelet; 294: p.c. Mme Alexandre Taverne; 295: p.c. Eric Van Lauwe; 296: p.c. Mme Alexandre Taverne; 297: *F: Pn*/Fonds Nadia Boulanger; 298: p.c. Eric Van Lauwe; 299: p.c. Jean Godebski; 300: p.c. Vicente Moya Francés.

301: p.c. Mme Robert Casadesus; 302: *F: Pn*/a.l./Jacques Durand, no. 20; 303: p.c. Claude Roland-Manuel; 304: p.c.a.; 305: p.c. Jean Touzelet; 306: p.c. Mme Alexandre Taverne; 307: p.c.a.; 308: *US: Wc;* 309: p.c. Pierre Courteault; 310: *F: Pn*/a.l./M.R., no. 104.

311: p.c. Jean Godebski; 312: *F: Pn*/a.l./M.R., no. 154; 313: *US: Wc;* 314: p.c. Mme Piero Coppola; 315: *F: Pn*/a.l./Jean Wiéner, no. 1; 316: *US:NYpm*/Koch; 317: *US: AUS/hr;* 318: Arturo Toscanini Collection, New York; 319: *US:AUS/hr;* 320: p.c. Jean Touzelet.

321: *US:NYpm*/Koch; 322: *US: Wc;* 323: *US:NYpm*/CAH; 324: p.c. Jean Touzelet; 325: a.p.c.; 326: a.p.c.; 327: p.c. Señora Maria Isabel de Falla; 328: p.c. Mme Marcelle Perrin; 329: a.p.c.; 330: p.c. David Diamond.

331: *F: Pn*/a.l./M.R., no. 179; 332: National Archives, Paris, Series F 21; 333: a.p.c.; 334: a.p.c.; 335: p.c. Pierre Courteault; 336: p.c. Mme G. Dallan; 337: a.p.c.; 338: p.c. Claude Roland-Manuel; 339: a.p.c.; 340: *F: Pn*/a.l./M.R., no. 184.

341: p.c. Jean Touzelet; 342: n.t.; 343: n.t.; 344: *CH: Gpu;* 345: *F: Pn*/a.l./M.R., no. 185; 346: *F: Po*/a.l./Edouard Ravel, no. 2.

Appendix I : : :

Autograph Letters of Ravel in Public Institutions

Some 600 autograph letters of Ravel are now permanently housed in public institutions in Europe and the United States.

BELGIUM

Brussels
Bibliothèque du Conservatoire: 1 letter to Mme L.-C. Battaille (1912).

FRANCE

Paris
Bibliothèque de l'Opéra: 13 letters to Jacques Rouché (1912–32).
Music Division of the Bibliothèque Nationale: 235 letters
    58 to Jean Marnold (1905–18)
    29 to Georgette Marnold (1919–25)
    26 to Mme Joseph Ravel (1916)
    25 to Nicolas Obouhov (1919–27)
    12 to Michel D. Calvocoressi (c. 1906–29)
    9 to Florent Schmitt (1900–21)
    7 to Jacques Rouché (1910–30)
    6 to Maurice and Nelly Delage (1905–27)
    6 to Edouard Ravel (1914–16)
    5 to Lucien Garban (1924–25)
  and 99 letters on microfilm
    57 to Roland-Manuel and Mme Fernand Dreyfus (1912–28)
    30 to Lucien Garban (1901–34)
    12 to Maurice Delage (1905–14).
Manuscript Division of the Bibliothèque Nationale: 50 letters
    43 to Georgette Marnold (1918–28)
    7 to Jean Marnold (1908–18).
National Archives: 1 letter to Anatole de Monzie (1933).

GREAT BRITAIN

London
British Museum (Library): 16 letters to Mr. and Mrs. Ralph Vaughan Williams
  (1908–19).

Oxford
  Taylorian Institute: 2 letters to Sigrid Harding (1923–27).

SWITZERLAND

Basel
  Paul Sacher Foundation: 15 letters
14 to Igor Stravinsky (1913–23)
  1 to Jacques Rouché (1915).
Geneva
  Bibliothèque Publique et Universitaire: 5 letters
    4 to Ernest Ansermet (1921–37).

UNION OF SOVIET SOCIALIST REPUBLICS

Moscow
  Glinka Museum of Musical Culture: 2 letters to Marie Olénine d'Alheim
    (1910–22).

UNITED STATES OF AMERICA

New York
  New York Public Library at Lincoln Center: 4 letters
      3 to Alexander L. Steinert (1926–30)
      1 to Mme Eva Gautier (1923).
Pierpont Morgan Library: 190 letters
122 to the Godebski family (1905–30): Ida, 88; Cipa, 32; Misia, 2
      17 to Mme Louise Alvar (1922–31)
      11 to Georges Jean-Aubry (1907–27)
      11 to Jean Jobert (1922–28)
      7 to D.-E. Inghelbrecht (1906–15)
      4 to Edwin Evans (1914)
      1 to Alfred Cortot (1921)
      1 to Serge Diaghilev (1917)
      1 to Tristan Klingsor (1922).
Texas
  Humanities Research Center, University of Texas at Austin: 16 letters
      7 to Emile Vuillermoz (1907–22).
  Southern Methodist University, Dallas: 1 letter to Gavriel Paitchadze (1929).
Washington, D.C.
  Library of Congress: 47 letters
      34 to Theodor Szántó (1908–27)
      5 to Serge Koussevitzky (1922–31)
      3 to Elizabeth S. Coolidge (1925–27)
      1 to Rudolph Ganz (1908).

Selected Bibliography

(see also the Selected Bibliography in
Ravel: Man and Musician*)*

Alajouanine, Théophile. "Aphasia and Artistic Realization." *Brain* (September 1948), 71(3): 229–41.

Berkeley, Lennox. "Maurice Ravel." *ADAM* (1978), 41(404–6): 13–17.

Cahiers Maurice Ravel. No. 1, 1985; no. 2, 1986.

Calvocoressi, Michel D. *Musicians Gallery: Music and Ballet in Paris and London.* London: Faber & Faber, 1933.

—— "Ravel's Letters to Calvocoressi." *Musical Quarterly* (January 1941), 27: 1–19.

Carley, Lionel. *Delius, the Paris Years.* London: Triad Press, 1975.

Catalogue de l'oeuvre de Maurice Ravel. Paris: Fondation Maurice Ravel, 1954.

Chalupt, René and Marcelle Gerar. *Ravel au miroir de ses lettres.* Paris: Robert Laffont, 1956.

Durand, Jacques. *Quelques souvenirs d'un éditeur de musique.* Paris: Durand, 1924.

Falla, Manuel de. "Notes sur Ravel." Trans. Roland-Manuel. *La Revue musicale* (March 1939), 20(1): 81–86.

Faure, Henriette. *Mon maître Maurice Ravel.* Paris: Les Editions ATP, 1978.

Gubisch, Nina. "Le Journal inédit de Ricardo Viñes." *Revue internationale de musique française* (June 1980), 1(2): 154–248.

Harris, Donald. "Ravel Visits the *Verein:* Alban Berg's Report." *Journal of the Arnold Schoenberg Institute* (March 1979), 3(1): 75–82.

Jourdan-Morhange, Hélène. *Ravel et nous.* Geneva: Editions du Milieu du Monde, 1945.

Lalo, Pierre. "Quelques ouvrages nouveaux de M. Ravel et le Debussysme: L'Art Debussyste et l'art de M. Debussy." *Le Temps,* March 19, 1907.

—— "Encore le Debussysme: Une Lettre de M. Ravel." *Le Temps,* April 9, 1907.

Laloy, Louis. *La Musique retrouvée.* Paris: Plon, 1928.

—— "Le Mois: Concerts, Société Nationale: Histoires naturelles, de Jules Renard, par Maurice Ravel." *Mercure musical et bulletin français de la S.I.M.* (February 15, 1907), 3: 155–57.

Laurent, Linda. "Jane Bathori et le Théâtre du Vieux-Colombier, 1917–1919." *Revue de musicologie* (1984), 70(2): 229–57.

Lesure, François. " 'L'Affaire' Debussy-Ravel: Lettres inédites." In Anna Amalie Abert and Wilhelm Pfannkuch, eds., *Festschrift Friedrich Blume*, pp. 231–34. Kassel: Bärenreiter, 1963.

Lesure, François and Jean-Michel Nectoux. *Maurice Ravel, 1875–1975.* Paris:

619

S.A.C.E.M., 1975. [A selection of contemporary writings and iconography honoring the centenary of Ravel's birth.]

—— *Maurice Ravel.* Paris: Bibliothèque Nationale, 1975. [A catalogue of the Ravel exhibition (367 items) held at the Bibliothèque Nationale in 1975.]

Long, Marguerite. *Au piano avec Maurice Ravel.* Paris: Julliard, 1971 (Eng. trans., 1973).

Marnat, Marcel. *Maurice Ravel.* Paris: Fayard, 1986.

Marnold, Jean. "Le Scandale du Prix de Rome." *Le Mercure musical,* 1 (June 15, 1905), 155–58, and (July 1, 1905), 178–80.

Milhaud, Darius. "Hommage à Maurice Ravel." *Le Soir,* December 29, 1937.

Musical. "Ravel." Special issue, no. 4 (June 1987).

Narbaitz, Pierre. *Maurice Ravel.* Côte Basque, 1975.

Nectoux, Jean-Michel. "Ravel/Fauré et les débuts de la Société Musicale Indépendante." *Revue de musicologie* (1975), 61(2): 295–318.

—— "Maurice Ravel et sa bibliothèque musicale." *Fontes artis musicae* (1977), 24: 199–206.

—— "Fauré, Henry Prunières et la Revue musicale." *Etudes Fauréennes,* no. 17 (1980), 17–24.

Nichols, Roger. *Ravel.* London: Dent, 1977.

Orenstein, Arbie. *Ravel: Man and Musician.* New York: Columbia University Press, 1975. (Ger. trans. by Dietrich Klose, Stuttgart: Reclam, 1978.)

—— "L'Enfant et les sortilèges: Correspondance inédite de Ravel et Colette." *Revue de musicologie* (1966), 52(2): 215–20.

—— "Maurice Ravel's Creative Process." *Musical Quarterly* (October 1967), 53: 467–81.

—— "Some Unpublished Music and Letters by Maurice Ravel." *Music Forum* (1973), 3: 291–334.

—— "L'Oeuvre de Maurice Ravel pendant la première guerre mondiale." *TAM* [French Army magazine] (March 28, 1975), 284: 62–65.

—— "Ravel's Letters to Charles Koechlin." *ADAM* (1978), 41(404–6): 20–25.

—— "Ravel and Falla: An Unpublished Correspondence, 1914–1933." In E. Strainchamps, M. R. Maniates, and C. Hatch, eds., *Music and Civilization: Essays in Honor of Paul Henry Lang,* pp. 335–49. New York: W. W. Norton, 1984.

—— "La Correspondance de Maurice Ravel aux Casadesus." *Cahiers Maurice Ravel* (1985), 1: 113–42.

Prunières, Henry. "Trois Silhouettes de musiciens: César Franck, Saint-Saëns, Maurice Ravel." *La Revue musicale* (October 1, 1926), 7: 225–40.

Ravel, Maurice. "Contemporary Music." *Rice Institute Pamphlet* (April 1928), 15: 131–45.

Revue Musicale, La. "Maurice Ravel." April 1925, and December 1938 [2 special issues].

Roland-Manuel. *Ravel.* Paris: Gallimard, 1948.

—— "Maurice Ravel." *La Revue musicale* (1921), 2: 1–21.

—— "Réflexions sur Ravel." *La Grande Revue* (April 1938), 42: 40–44.

—— "Maurice Ravel à travers sa correspondance." *La Revue musicale* (January–February 1939), 20(188): 1–7.

—— "Lettres de Maurice Ravel et documents inédits." *Revue de musicologie*, 38 (July 1956), 49–53.

Rorem, Ned. "Historic Houses: Maurice Ravel at Le Belvédère." *Architectural Digest* (September 1986), 43(9): 182–88 and 212.

Stuckenschmidt, H. H. *Maurice Ravel*. Frankfurt am Main: Suhrkamp Verlag, 1966 (Eng. trans., 1968).

Szmolyan, Walter. "Maurice Ravel in Wien." *Österreichische Musikzeitschrift* (March 1975), 30(3): 89–103.

Vaughan Williams, Ursula. *R.V.W.: A Biography of Ralph Vaughan Williams*. London: Oxford University Press, 1964.

Vuillermoz, Emile, et al. *Maurice Ravel par quelques-uns de ses familiers*. Paris: Editions du Tambourinaire, 1939.

Zuckerkandl-Szeps, B. "Souvenirs sur Maurice Ravel." *Revue d'Alger* (1945), 2(6): 47–53.

Articles by Maurice Ravel
(all reprinted in full in Part III of this book)

Laloy, Louis. "Wagner et les musiciens d'aujourd'hui: Opinions de MM. Florent Schmitt et Maurice Ravel—Conclusions." *La Grande Revue* (May 10, 1909), 13(9): 160–64.

"Les Polonaises, les nocturnes, les impromptus, la Barcarolle—Impressions." *Le Courrier musical* (January 1, 1910), pp. 31–32.

"Sous la musique que faut-il mettre? De beaux vers, de mauvais, des vers libres, de la prose?" *Musica* (March 1911), 10(102): 59–60.

"Concert(s) Lamoureux." *Revue musicale de la S.I.M.* (February 15, 1912), 8(2): 62–63.

"Concerts Lamoureux." *Revue musicale de la S.I.M.* (March 1912), 8(3): 50–52.

"Les 'Tableaux symphoniques' de M. Fanelli." *Revue musicale de la S.I.M.* (April 1912), 8(4): 55–56.

"*La Sorcière* à l'Opéra-Comique." *Comœdia illustré* (January 5, 1913), 5(7): 320–23.

"Fervaal: . . . Poème et musique de Vincent d'Indy." *Comœdia illustré* (January 20, 1913), 5(8): 361–64.

"Au Théâtre des Arts." *Comœdia illustré* (February 5, 1913), 5(9): 417–20.

"A propos des *Images* de Claude Debussy." *Les Cahiers d'aujourd'hui* (February 1913), pp. 135–38.

"*Boris Godounoff*." *Comœdia illustré* (June 5, 1913), 5(17): n.p.

"A L'Opéra-Comique: *Francesca da Rimini* et *La Vida breve*." *Comœdia illustré* (January 20, 1914), 6(8): 390–91.

"*Parsifal*: . . . Version française d'Alfred Ernst." *Comœdia illustré* (January 20, 1914), 6(8): 400–03.

"Les Nouveaux Spectacles de la saison russe: *Le Rossignol*." *Comœdia illustré* (June 5, 1914), 6(17): 811–14.

"Les Mélodies de Gabriel Fauré." *La Revue musicale,* 3 (October 1922), 3: 22–27.
"Sur l'inspiration." *The Chesterian* (January–February 1928), 9(68): 115.
"Take Jazz Seriously!" *Musical Digest* (March 1928), 13(3): 49 and 51.
"Mes souvenirs d'enfant paresseux." *La Petite Gironde,* July 12, 1931, 1.
"Concerto pour la main gauche." *Le Journal,* January 14, 1933.
"Finding Tunes in Factories." *New Britain,* August 9, 1933, 367.
"Les Aspirations de moins de 25 ans." *Excelsior,* November 28, 1933.
"Nijinsky, maître de ballets." [Undated holograph. See plate 15.]

Interviews with Maurice Ravel

(all printed in full in Part IV of this book)

"Maurice Ravel's Opinion of Modern French Music." *The Musical Leader* (March 16, 1911), 21(11): 7.
Bizet, R. *"L'Heure espagnole." L'Intransigeant,* May 17, 1911.
—— *"Ma Mère l'Oye." L'Intransigeant,* January 28, 1912.
Fèvre, Georges Le." 'Le Lynx': Maurice Ravel aux champs." *Bonsoir,* October 8, 1920.
"Wiener Eindrucke eines französischen Künstlers." *Neue freie Presse,* October 29, 1920. [Viennese Impressions of a French Artist. In German.]
"Ravel and Modern Music." *The Morning Post,* July 10, 1922.
"Het Fransche muziekfeest." *De Telegraaf,* September 30, 1922. [The French Music Festival. In Dutch.]
"M. Ravel in London." *The Morning Post,* April 18, 1923.
"Famous French Composer in London." *The Star,* October 16, 1923.
Révész, André. "El gran musico Mauricio Ravel habla de su arte." *ABC de Madrid,* May 1, 1924. [The great musician Maurice Ravel talks about his art. In Spanish.]
"Avant-Première: A l'Opéra de Monte-Carlo: *L'Enfant et les sortilèges." Le Gaulois,* March 20, 1925.
"Maurice Ravels ankomst." *Berlingske Tidende,* January 30, 1926. [Maurice Ravel's Arrival. In Danish.]
"Skadinaviskt inflytande på fransk komposition." *Svenska Dagbladet,* February 9, 1926. [Scandinavian Influence on French Composition. In Swedish.]
Roland-Manuel. "Maurice Ravel et la jeune musique française." *Les Nouvelles littéraires,* April 2, 1927.
Downes, Olin. "Maurice Ravel, Man and Musician." *New York Times,* August 7, 1927.
"Ravel Says Poe Aided Him in Composition." *New York Times,* January 6, 1928.
Downes, Olin. "Mr. Ravel Returns." *New York Times,* February 26, 1928.
Calvocoressi, M. D. "Maurice Ravel on Berlioz." *Daily Telegraph,* January 12, 1929.
"Probleme der modernen Musik." *Der Bund,* April 19, 1929. [Problems of Modern Music. In German.]
André, José. "Maurice Ravel y su 'Bolero'." *La Nación,* March 15, 1930. [Maurice Ravel and His Bolero. In Spanish.]

"Entretien avec Ravel." *La Revue musicale* (March 1931), 12: 193–94.

"Op Bezoek bij Maurice Ravel." *De Telegraaf,* March 31, 1931. [A Visit with Maurice Ravel. In Dutch.]

Calvocoressi, M. D. "M. Ravel Discusses His Own Work." *Daily Telegraph,* July 11, 1931.

Bruyr, José. "Un Entretien avec . . . Maurice Ravel." *Le Guide du concert* (October 16, 1931), 18(3): 39–41.

Leroi, Pierre. "Quelques confidences du grand compositeur Maurice Ravel." *Excelsior,* October 30, 1931.

"Ein Nachmittag bei Maurice Ravel." *Neue freie Presse,* February 3, 1932. [An Afternoon with Maurice Ravel. In German.]

"Factory Gives Composer Inspiration." *Evening Standard,* February 24, 1932.

"Tien opinies van M. Ravel." *De Telegraaf,* April 6, 1932. [Ten Opinions of Mr. Ravel. In Dutch.]

Frank, Nino. "Maurice Ravel entre deux trains." *Candide,* May 5, 1932.

Reuillard, Gabriel. "M. Maurice Ravel va écrire une 'Jeanne d'Arc'." *Excelsior,* September 24, 1933.

Additional Interviews

(Some appear in this book, in part; none add anything substantial to those cited above)

Arnoux, André. "Avant-Premières: Opéra de Monte-Carlo: *L'Enfant et les sortilèges.*" *Le Figaro,* March 20, 1925.

Bernier, René. "Un Entretien avec Maurice Ravel." *Voix,* April 1, 1931.

Del Brezo, Juan. "Musica y musicos; Una charla con Mauricio Ravel." *La Voz,* May 6, 1924. [Music and musicians; A talk with Maurice Ravel. In Spanish.]

Devaise, Georges. "Raveliana." *Gringoire,* January 14, 1938.

Jean-Aubry, Georges. "A Visit to Ravel." *Christian Science Monitor,* September 17, 1927.

Méry, Jules. "Opéra de Monte-Carlo: Avant-Première: *L'Enfant et les sortilèges.*" *Le Petit Monégasque,* March 21, 1925.

Montabré, Maurice. "Entretien avec Maurice Ravel." *L'Intransigeant,* January 28, 1923.

Saint-Prix, Pierre de. "Ce qu'est l'oeuvre nouvelle de M. Maurice Ravel: 'L'Enfant et les sortilèges'." *Excelsior,* July 10, 1925.

Tenroc, Charles. "Les Avant-Premières: 'Thérèse' et 'L'Heure espagnole' à l'Opéra-Comique." *Comœdia,* May 11, 1911.

Unsigned or Initialed Interviews

"Een Onderhoud met Maurice Ravel." *De Telegraaf,* March 9, 1926. [An Interview with Maurice Ravel. In Dutch.]

"Ravel Says He Began Classic Revival as Reaction to Debussy." *New York Herald Tribune,* January 6, 1928.

"Retour d'Amérique: Le Beau voyage de Maurice Ravel." *L'Intransigeant*, April 29, 1928.

"Ravel en de nieuwe school." *De Telegraaf,* May 29, 1928. [Ravel and the New School. In Dutch.]

"Gespräch mit Maurice Ravel." *Neue freie Presse*, February 1, 1932. [A Conversation with Maurice Ravel. In German.]

Articles and Interviews of Questionable Authenticity

Goudeket, Willy. "La Confession de Ravel." *Presse du Sud-Ouest*, July 8–9, 1933. [This "interview" is highly suspect and probably never took place.]

Chambrillac, René. "Survie de Ravel." *Page musicale*, February 4, 1938. [Ravel's Immortality; ostensibly an interview given to René Chambrillac, this is largely a plagiarism of the article by Willy Goudeket.]

Ravel, Maurice. "What I Think of Modern Music" (as told to David Ewen). *The Etude*, September 1933, 571. [The authenticity of this interview was challenged by Ravel's close friend Maurice Dumesnil, the French pianist and author. In a letter dated November 16, 1933, James Francis Cooke, the president of Theodore Presser Co., publishers of *The Etude*, wrote to him as follows:

> David Ewen has been a very voluminous writer in America and I am shocked to think that he did not convey Mr. Ravel's opinions accurately, providing he did really meet him . . . I am very indignant and very angry over this whole matter and I trust that you will not hesitate to indicate to Mr. Ravel that such an occurrence is entirely opposite to anything The Etude has previously permitted. Our reputation has been founded upon scholarship and conscientious accuracy. I shall hesitate ever to publish anything by Mr. Ewen again because I feel we have been duped in this matter.

[Autograph letter in the private collection of Jean Touzelet.]

Another interview with David Ewen, "Maurice Ravel on Jewish Music" [*B'nai Brith Magazine* (January 1936), 50(4): 111], also appears highly suspect. Ravel's failing health would have precluded such an interview, which should be considered a fabrication.

Index